AF449240

POETIC AUTONOMY IN ANCIENT ROME

Poetic Autonomy in Ancient Rome

LUKE ROMAN

OXFORD

UNIVERSITY PRESS

OXFORD
UNIVERSITY PRESS

Great Clarendon Street, Oxford, OX2 6DP,
United Kingdom

Oxford University Press is a department of the University of Oxford.
It furthers the University's objective of excellence in research, scholarship,
and education by publishing worldwide. Oxford is a registered trade mark of
Oxford University Press in the UK and in certain other countries

Published in the United States of America by Oxford University Press
198 Madison Avenue, New York, NY 10016, United States of America

British Library Cataloguing in Publication Data
Data available

Library of Congress Control Number: 2013947225

ISBN 978–0–19–967563–0

As printed and bound by
CPI Group (UK) Ltd, Croydon, CR0 4YY

for Monica

Acknowledgements

This book derives from a dissertation advised by Martin Bloomer many years ago. The final product owes a great deal to his initial encouragement and kind support and to the stimulating atmosphere of the Stanford Classics Department. Denis Feeney, as reader of the dissertation, exerted a formative influence, and has contributed much to the development of my ideas and progress of my career since its completion. My work has been greatly advanced by exchange of thoughts on Martial and Latin poetry generally with Stephen Hinds. The penultimate draft was scrutinized and improved with generous care and acute insight by Aaron Kachuk. Peter Smith of the Department of Greek and Roman Studies at the University of Victoria showed great kindness in reading the entire typescript and offering valuable comments. I offer sincere thanks to the anonymous readers for Oxford University Press, who made this a much better book than it was, and to Hilary O'Shea and Taryn Das Neves for their help, patience, and guidance. John Henderson wrote a penetrating critique of an earlier version of this book: whether or not the current version would meet his approval, it truly has benefited from his comments. I am grateful to *The Journal of Roman Studies* for allowing me to reprint a somewhat altered version of 'The Representation of Literary Materiality in Martial's *Epigrams*' (2001) as part of Chapter 4. I have derived great benefit from the friendly erudition of my colleagues at the Department of Classics at Memorial University, the Intercollegiate Center for Classical Studies in Rome (2007–8), and the Department of Greek and Roman Studies at the University of Victoria. I am especially grateful to Walter Englert, Cedric Littlewood, Alex Meyer, and Greg Rowe for encouraging words and ideas. For any errors, of course, I bear sole responsibility.

Contents

Introduction

Autonomy ancient and modern

> Although I am separated from home . . . and fatherland, and though every-
> thing that can be taken from me has been taken, yet my literary talent still
> accompanies me, I still have recourse to my talent: Caesar could not have any
> jurisdiction over this.[1]

These words were written by P. Ovidius Naso, relegated by imperial decree in AD 8 to the shores of the Black Sea. He observes that, although the emperor, in sending him to the margins of the empire, asserted power over his body's location in space, he could not fully control his body of work, which is not confined and delimited in the same way as the author himself. How did a poet writing in the early years of the first century AD come to represent his poetry as being beyond the control of the emperor—as being, for all intents and purposes, 'autonomous'? We tend to think of aesthetic autonomy as a distinctly modern concept,[2] and yet this passage and others suggest that there is at least some basis for identifying autonomist ideas in the literature of ancient Rome. This book is premised on the conviction that 'autonomy' does not belong exclusively to modern aesthetic thought, but that different formulations of autonomy have informed literary and artistic production throughout Western history. Specifically, I will argue that autonomy is a recurrent, organizing concept in Roman poetry of the late republic and early empire.

---

[1] Ovid *Tristia* 3.7.45–8:

> en ego, cum caream patria vobisque domoque,
> raptaque sint, adimi quae potuere mihi,
> ingenio tamen ipse meo comitorque fruorque:
> Caesar in hoc potuit iuris habere nihil.

Unless otherwise indicated, translations are my own. In many cases throughout this book, I have indicated where I follow a particular text, reading or emendation. In cases where no such indication is made, the default texts of the main authors and works studied (Catullus, Horace, Virgil, Propertius, Tibullus, Ovid, Persius, Martial, Statius, Juvenal) are the *OCT* editions of Mynors (1958), Garrod and Wickham (1901), Mynors (1969), Barber (1960), Postgate (1905), Kenney (1994), Owen (1915), Clausen (1959), Lindsay (1929), Courtney (1990).

[2] For a rare defence of the applicability of the concept of autonomy to ancient Roman poetry, see Zetzel (1982) and (1992). The argument offered here by Ovid for poetic autonomy is, of course, a limited one, representing only one element in a broader array of autonomist arguments employed by Roman writers (see below).

TERMS AND DEFINITIONS

Autonomy is a powerful idea. In aesthetics, the basic meaning of 'autonomy' can be summarized as the idea that art or literature constitutes an independent sphere of activity that defines its own rules and adheres to its own criteria of value. Autonomy is defined as 'self-rule' or 'self-government', and encapsulates 'the thought that aesthetic experience, or art, or both, possess a life of their own apart from other human affairs'.[3] An autonomist view of art or literature does not point to any single, discrete phenomenon, but rather a connected nexus of ideas and practices. This interconnectedness does not mean that 'autonomy' is too diffuse a concept to be useful, but rather that an autonomist view of art or literature can encompass 'aesthetic judgments, the mental faculties responsible for aesthetic experience, artworks, formal qualities and meanings inherent in artworks, the actions and purposes of artists, the development of styles, genres, or media in art history, and the practices or institutions that sustain artistic activity in society'.[4]

The issue of autonomy in ancient literature, however, has been clouded, and at times simply avoided, because of the predominance of autonomy in *modern* aesthetic thought and practice.[5] Autonomy is not only an important theme within modern aesthetics, but a foundational condition of modern aesthetics, insofar as the dedicated, specialized study and theorization of aesthetics as its own branch of knowledge are themselves premised on an autonomist impulse. In other words, establishing 'aesthetics' as a distinct realm of knowledge is inherently an autonomizing tendency: it concerns the very separateness of the category of Art. Autonomy has come to define the core parameters of modern aesthetic experience, even, to some extent, in popular culture; it can be seen embodied in the institution of the museum, the concept of the artwork, the figure of the artist or the writer, the formation of academic disciplines, and in various sub-categories of cultural production such as the avant-garde. One outcome of the inextricability of autonomy within the modern experience of literature and art is the perception that aesthetic autonomy is a uniquely and exclusively modern concept. The application of the term autonomy to ancient cultural activity has thus been judged anachronistic.[6] I will argue that this judgement is hasty and one-sided. Ancient

---

[3] Haskins (1998), 170.   [4] Haskins (1998), 170.

[5] For some problems with applying the concept of autonomy to pre-modern or early-modern literary and artistic practices, see Bürger (1998), 175.

[6] Note, for example, the sceptical position of Fitzgerald (1989), 90–1 n.18—a comment which is unusual and valuable for its explicit consideration of the question of aesthetic autonomy in relation to Roman poetry. Roller (2001), 18, observes: 'in response to certain midcentury modes of literary criticism that see literature as a highly autonomous realm following its own rules, analyzable on its own terms, and substantially insulated from (or at least transcending) the everyday preoccupations of the producer and the world in which he or she lived, some scholars have sought to bring the social engagement of literary texts into sharper focus . . . [They] are interested in the "politics" of literature'. This approach Roller approves as justified, but then distinguishes a narrower understanding of 'politics' from a more sophisticated one. Habinek (1998), more or less along the same lines, views 'Latin literature as instrumental to the maintenance of aristocratic cultural hegemony and Roman political dominance' (5). This approach contrasts with that of 'Gildersleeve and other second-generation Romantics who avoided the historical reality of Rome in order to actuate their own fantasies of the apolitical innocence of literature and literary studies' (14). The focus of Barchiesi (1997) is on

autonomy is indeed distinct from modern aesthetic autonomy, but it does not follow that questions of aesthetic autonomy are irrelevant to ancient society, and in particular, literature.

Before examining more closely the ancient Roman material that will constitute the main focus of this study, it will be useful briefly to consider the history of the concept of aesthetic autonomy, and some of the consequences of contemporary (mis)interpretations of this concept for current critical approaches to literature.

AUTONOMY: A BRIEF HISTORY

Some of the more salient instances of autonomist or proto-autonomist ideas in the ancient world concern poetry. Poetry, for the ancient Greeks, involved a distinctive combination of words and music that differentiated poetic utterance from other uses of language. The poet himself enjoyed an unusual connection with the gods, which, in turn, marked him out as a special kind of person.[7] We are very far, in this case, from a modern conception of autonomy, especially autonomy in its formulation as 'art for art's sake': the poet's role and song, as numerous recent studies have appreciated,[8] were embedded in the civic and religious culture of ancient Greek communities. Yet the distinctive cultural contribution of the poet, the special status of his utterance, and the singularity of his language were acknowledged from a very early period, and, in later philosophical discussion, became the basis for more overt claims for certain aspects of autonomy.

Andrew Ford has investigated instances where Greek authors 'ascribe to verbal composition a special value and truth that art alone can confer'.[9] In doing so, he is looking back to the Greek literary and philosophical tradition in order to elicit 'the prototype for the notion of literature'.[10] At the further end of this development, Ford observes the emergence of literary criticism and poetics, as exemplified by the concept of 'a system of genres defined in their reciprocal formal relations'.[11] Starting in the fifth century, and continuing in the fourth, philosophers, language experts, and intellectuals began to pay attention to the special qualities of language and especially literary language. The sophists emphasized the value of literary craftsmanship and the dispersal of the text over space and time in ways that look forward to Hellenistic and Roman poetics. In tension with conceptions of poetry emphasizing literary craftsmanship, however, was the Platonic conception of poetry as mimesis. Plato's ideas about both poetry and mimesis are more complex

---

deconstructing or problematizing the politics/poetry divide through close readings of Augustan poetry (e.g. 7–8, 43–5). Of course, a similar approach could be persuasively applied to literature of the modern era, where autonomist ideas *are* well established. In other words, the fact that there exists in poetic practice no unproblematic, stable boundary between aesthetics and politics hardly rules out the existence of autonomist models of literary activity and autonomist rhetoric.

[7] Haskins (1998), 170, includes some remarks on the figure of the poet in ancient Greece.

[8] To cite only a few examples: Dougherty and Kurke (1998); Nagy (1979), (1990), (1996); Goldhill (1991); Ford (1992) and (2002).

[9] Ford (2002), 230.   [10] Ford (2002), 249.   [11] Ford (2002), 251.

than is usually acknowledged,[12] and his view of mimesis is not as purely negative as is often assumed. Nevertheless poetry, and in particular tragedy,[13] in the Platonic conception, produced a mimesis of reality that was inevitably inadequate and incapable of higher truth. The seductive power of poetry therefore made it all the more pernicious, since it had the capacity to mislead people and undermine their ability to seek truth in a more appropriately philosophical manner. It is for this reason that Plato famously banished poetry from his ideal city in the *Republic*. Plato holds poetry liable to moral criteria, and judges it in terms of its mimetic capacity, or rather its incapacity, to draw the listener towards comprehension of a higher reality.

Aristotle, in his subsequent work on the question in his *Poetics*, is generally viewed as rejecting the Platonic subordination of poetry to morality and reconceiving poetry and the study of poetry in autonomist terms. On this common view, he examines the formal features, structures, qualities, and functions proper to poetry itself rather than judging its success or failure according to its capacity to represent truth as understood from the vantage-point of moral philosophy. Stephen Halliwell, however, has argued that this common view of Aristotle and his understanding of poetry and poetic mimesis is too simple. Instead, he ascribes 'to Aristotle a "dual-aspect" model of mimesis that enables him to take account of both the artifactuality and the representational content of mimetic works, and thus to hold these two aspects in a creative tension that makes the *Poetics* neither formalist nor moralist in its essential outlook'.[14] Even in this case, however, the criteria for judging poetry are no longer predominantly moral, and Aristotle emphasizes his aim of awarding poetry the distinctive treatment it is due as a *tekhnē*. As Ford has observed, Aristotle's *Poetics* enabled the appreciation of poetry as 'a special kind of discourse (*logos*) with its own values and ends'.[15]

In subsequent centuries, the legacy of Aristotle and classical poetic theory continues to be explored and developed by writers throughout the Hellenistic period. The fragmentary works of the Epicurean philosopher Philodemus (ca. 110–40/35 BC) afford a glimpse of his highly sophisticated philosophical investigation into poetics, including his ideas regarding 'the autonomy of art'.[16] Philodemus appears to represent only the tip of the iceberg. A significant portion of the surviving papyri consists in Philodemus' commentary on and critique of other Hellenistic poetic theorists. The arguments of these theorists ranged from a formalist prioritization of verbal arrangement to Platonic arguments demanding both utility and pleasure from the work of poetry. Philodemus' summaries of these theorists offer a tantalizing picture of an ongoing debate over literary aesthetics

---

[12] See Halliwell (2002), 37–147. A recurrent element in Halliwell's work is his critique of the influence of modern, Kantian ideas of aesthetic autonomy on perceptions of Plato and Aristotle and their views on poetry and the arts. On the default modern view, Plato comes to stand for instrumentalism and Aristotle for autonomism. See also Halliwell (1986), 4ff., and (1984), 49ff.

[13] Halliwell (2002), 26.   [14] Halliwell (2002), 28. Compare Ford (2002), 269–70.

[15] Ford (2002), 229; note also 270, 'Poetics is established as a field of expertise and an independent academic discipline'.

[16] On Philodemus, see the essay collection of Armstrong (2004), and Obbink (1995); the monograph of Gigante (1995), and editions of his poetry and *On Poems*: respectively Sider (1997) and Janko (2000), (2010).

that seems strikingly 'modern'. For example, the formalist Crates of Mallos, in Asmis' view, 'belies the oft-repeated claim that there was no science of aesthetics until the eighteenth century'.[17] Crates 'attempted to found a science of literary judgment that was distinct from both grammar and philosophy', insisting that the judgement of poetry required 'recognition of principles of good sound together with an awareness of the meaning of the sounds'.[18] Philodemus resists the euphonists' reduction of poetic excellence to sound and verbal arrangement, and even allows that we may judge the moral benefit or harm of a poem. At the same time, he insists that 'poems, insofar as they are poems, do not provide benefit', and thus, in a complicated way, argues for the 'emancipation of poetry from morality'.[19]

However we interpret Philodemus' surviving arguments and critical summaries, the very fact of poetry's more overtly specialized theorization beginning in the fourth century BC and continuing throughout the Hellenistic period bespeaks at least some limited tendency of the autonomization of poetics as a distinct branch of knowledge. The emergence of treatises on poetry and poetics heralds a recognition of poetry's status as a specialized sphere, a distinct form of language and expression, with its own rules, ends, and intrinsic features. These treatises, moreover, in many instances appear to argue for formalist, non-utilitarian criteria of poetic value and success. It must be stressed that the significance of this development is not limited to the Greek world. Philodemus lived in the Bay of Naples, advertised Piso as a patron, and was connected with major figures in Roman poetry in the Augustan period. Philodemus addresses central Augustan literary figures: Virgil, Varius Rufus, Quintilius Varus, and Plotius Tucca.[20] Philodemus' ideas about poetry and his erudite immersion in Hellenistic literary theory were therefore fully available for the contemplation and potential assimilation of this crucial generation of Roman poets. It can therefore no longer be claimed that Roman poets did not have access to the concept of literary autonomy. In fact, they almost certainly were acquainted with the very latest autonomist (and instrumentalist) theories through the teachings of an expert in the field.

The development of specifically *Roman* concepts of poetic autonomy is the subject of this study, and so will not be discussed at length at this point. It suffices to point out at this stage that many Roman writers were well-acquainted with Greek literary theory, if not, as in the case of Philodemus, with Greek literary theorists. A mere handing down of Greek ideas, however, does not account for the Roman poets' interest in poetic autonomy, but rather, as I will argue below, specific aspects of Roman society play an important role. In subsequent phases of Western culture, efforts to define literary space and value often refer back to Roman texts both because defining literature and literariness was an abiding preoccupation for Roman writers, and because the basic categories of ancient literary, rhetorical, and philosophical thought were largely transmitted through the medium of the Latin language. It would exceed the scope of the present study

---

[17] Asmis (1995), 152.   [18] Asmis (1995), 152.

[19] Asmis (1995), 148. According to Halliwell (2011), 304–26, there is an unresolved tension in Philodemus' arguments. He appears to wish to propound an autonomist theory of poetry yet cannot relinquish the possibility that poetry can be 'beneficial'.

[20] Armstrong (2004), 2–3. It is also clear that he moved in the same circles as Horace.

to trace fully the history of autonomist moments in Western culture from the ancient world to early modern Europe, but it is worth pointing out that scholars of modern aesthetics such as Peter Bürger identify proto-elements of the autonomist paradigm in the Renaissance concept of art and the artist and other phenomena of early modern European literary and artistic culture.[21]

The watershed period in terms of aesthetic autonomy in the modern world is the eighteenth century, especially in Germany.[22] Aesthetics first becomes an explicitly articulated philosophical topic in Alexander Gottlieb Baumgarten's *Aesthetics*, published in 1750. Baumgarten's treatise invents the term aesthetics along with the corresponding philosophical category—an indication that art is beginning to be recognized as a segregated realm of activity and experience. The question of autonomy itself is taken up subsequently by other writers such as Karl Philip Moritz.[23] While Moritz, Baumgarten, and others make important first steps in the project of aesthetic philosophy, the philosophical work with the most profound consequences for the development of subsequent ideas about the autonomy of art is Immanuel Kant's Third Critique, *The Critique of Judgment*. While Kant nominally concerns himself only with the act of judging objects of beauty, his comments on the nature of beautiful objects, including artworks, and his arguments about the judgement of taste, have broader consequences for the understanding of art and literature.[24] For Kant, as similarly for Moritz, the work of true art or poetry[25] is not designed to accomplish some external end, but rather is 'purposive for itself'. Kant's treatise is a major contribution to 'the eighteenth century's larger development of a new concept and model of an autonomous and "distinterested" realm of experience that came by many to be described as "aesthetic"'.[26]

In German philosophy of the eighteenth century, we begin to see both the formation of aesthetics as a topic and more systematic justifications for the idea of art's autonomy. Autonomy subsequently becomes the reigning aesthetic paradigm in the West through the nineteenth and twentieth centuries. The aesthetics of genius, already important in Kant's conception of artistic creation, deeply informs Romantic poetry of the nineteenth century. Poetry is emancipated simultaneously from the formal dictates of rulebook propriety and from the banality of utilitarian interests. Towards the end of the century, the doctrine of 'art for art's sake' emerges as perhaps the most overtly recognizable version of autonomist aesthetics, but also the most vulnerable to disparaging caricature. To this day, 'art for art's sake' is routinely equated with autonomy, which is then condemned

---

[21] e.g. Bürger (1984), 41.

[22] On the origins of the idea of aesthetic autonomy, see Woodmansee (1984); Hess (1999).

[23] See especially Woodmansee (1984).

[24] On Kant and the concept of autonomy, see Haskins (1989) and (1990).

[25] Consider the following as an example of Kant's thoughts on poetry: 'I must admit that a beautiful poem has always given me a pure gratification, while the reading of the best discourse, whether of a Roman orator or of a modern parliamentary speaker or of a preacher, has always been mingled with an unpleasant feeling of disapprobation of a treacherous art which means to move men in important matters like machines to a judgment that must lose all weight for them on quiet reflection' (*Critique of Judgment* § 53 n.13, tr. Bernard). This passage anticipates Croce's conception of 'lyric' poetry, and is relevant to aspects of the current practice of literary criticism in the field of Latin literature.

[26] Halliwell (2002), 9.

pars pro toto.[27] It must be stressed, however, that 'art for art's sake' represents only one reflex of a more diverse set of autonomist tendencies in the field of modern aesthetics.[28]

The twentieth century hardly represents a period of wholesale acceptance of the doctrine of autonomy; indeed, there are signal instances of resistance and criticism. Yet autonomy continues to define the core concepts and institutions of art, literature, and music. To name only two major twentieth century developments, the institution of the museum and the academic institutionalization of literary and artistic criticism demonstrate the deeply embedded status of autonomist ideas about art. Even in instances where autonomist doctrine begins to meet serious and sustained criticism, the status of aesthetic autonomy as the predominant motif in modern artistic activity ensures that oppositional critique remains defined by and locked in dialogue with the traditions of autonomist thought.

The philosophers and theorists of the Frankfurt school, in particular, represent a major phase in the reception and reworking of autonomist ideas and practices. The distinctive viewpoint of writers of the Frankfurt school such as Theodor Adorno, Jürgen Habermas, and Walter Benjamin derives from their simultaneous immersion in the traditions of German aesthetic philosophy and the techniques and perspective of Marxist dialectic. For Adorno,[29] whose monumental *Aesthetic Theory*[30] attempts to come to grips with the status of art in advanced capitalist societies, 'autonomy' is a social phenomenon susceptible to being analysed in dialectical terms. He specifically connects works of autonomous art with aspects of modern capitalist society such as the fetishization of consumer objects and bourgeois artistic taste. At the same time, Adorno is unwilling to dispense with autonomy, since, for him, autonomy remains the precondition for truth in art. By its very self-segregation, by its refusal to participate in the mechanisms of economic production, autonomist art remains capable of providing insights into society that would be otherwise unavailable.

I call special attention to Adorno's thinking on autonomy because he represents a subtlety of approach, and a connection with the deeper currents of the philosophical tradition, which have been lost in subsequent critical methodologies. Particularly important is Adorno's recognition that the detachment from society enacted by autonomist art is itself a socially significant phenomenon, and must be analysed as such. In his essay 'On Lyric Poetry and Society', he explores how lyric poetry's 'virginal' separateness is informed by the very burdens it endeavours to escape: 'the more heavily the [social] situation weighs upon it, the more firmly the

---

[27] Habermas (1997), 46–7, provides a summary of the big picture: 'One can trace a line of progressive autonomization in the development of modern art. It was the Renaissance which first saw the emergence of a specific domain categorized exclusively in terms of the beautiful. Then, in the course of the eighteenth century, literature, the plastic arts, and music were institutionalized as a specific domain of activity distinct from ecclesiastical and court life. Finally, around the middle of the nineteenth century, there also arises an aestheticist conception of art which obliged artists to produce their work with the conscious outlook of l'art pour l'art. The autonomy of the aesthetic was thereby explicitly constituted as a project'.

[28] Haskins (1990), *passim.*

[29] On Adorno and the autonomy of art, see, for example, Zuidervaart (1990), Harding (1992), Martin (2000), Roberts (2000), Osborne (1989).

[30] Adorno (1997).

work resists it by refusing to submit to anything heteronomous and constituting itself solely in accordance with its own laws'.[31] Some modern approaches assume that any acknowledgement of autonomy means naively ascribing to art a sublime uselessness and remoteness from reality. Adorno shows, however, that art's autonomy is, in some sense, the inverse image of the social phenomena from which it seeks to detach itself.

The critical approaches and theories that populate academic journals of the past fifty years ultimately derive from and are premised on the aesthetic ideas that arise out of the writings of Kant, Marx, Schiller, Hegel, and their later exegetes and inheritors. Typically, however, they play out only one relatively superficial reflex within the broader tradition of philosophical aesthetics. On the question of autonomy, in particular, there has been an alternation of critical trends either favouring or opposing aesthetic autonomy. Indeed, such bias is evident even in cases where autonomy is not consciously introduced as an explicit topic. The New Criticism, which can be seen as part of a 'growing trend in the twentieth century towards understanding the literary text as an organically unified and self-sufficient linguistic object from whose aesthetic interpretation all direct reference to the external world or the author's intentions are properly excluded', is a case in point.[32] A great advantage of the New Criticism was that it insisted on a highly disciplined attention to 'the poem itself' (indeed, poetry was not accidentally the key object of criticism for New Critics), which was understood to be a kind of delicate fabric of connotations and formal effects where each element was intricately bound up in the totality of its meaning. A major disadvantage of the New Criticism was that it failed to come to grips with and consciously analyse its own foundational investment in the concept of autonomy.

Subsequent critical methodologies and hermeneutic fads have been remorseless in castigating the New Criticism's reliance on a doctrine of literary self-sufficiency, although these approaches, in their own way, have fallen prey to the same one-sidedness, predictably playing out the old autonomy vs instrumentality debate whose basic terms were inherited from eighteenth-century German philosophy. Deconstruction can be counted among theoretical approaches that reject the New Critical notion of the organic unity and integrity of the poem, yet Derrida's famous dictum—*il n'y pas de hors-texte*—reiterates the autonomy of the literary work at the level of human semiosis itself.[33]

More recently, the various strands of historicist criticism gathered together under the umbrella term New Historicism reject the idea of the autonomous text as the founding gesture of their methodology. Yet there are problems with this blanket rejection. First of all, the insistence of historicist criticism on the heteronomous status of the work of art awards the denial of autonomy the status of framing critical trope.[34] In this sense, the entire historicist turn in recent criticism

---

³¹ Adorno (1991), 39–40; cited and discussed by Lowrie (2009), 248, in the context of Roman poetry.
³² Haskins (1998), 173.   ³³ Haskins (1998), 173.
³⁴ A similar suggestion in Hinds (2001), 239: 'is it possible that a "cultural poetics" actually depends for its methodological *frisson* upon the transgressive breaking of an aesthetic spell, and hence is parasitic upon the very aestheticism which it seeks to demystify?'

plays out a modern debate over art's autonomy conceived in absolute terms: is art autonomous or not?[35] Rather than exorcising autonomy's hold over modern hermeneutics, New Historicist readings may actually work to perpetuate it: insisting on 'the social' at the expense of the aesthetic keeps the old autonomist distinction in play. A further limitation arising from this problem is the fact that historicist approaches, predisposed as they are to emphasize the literary work's *lack* of self-sufficiency, its immersion in contemporary discourses, tend to be ill-equipped to examine instances of autonomist rhetoric. As Adorno long ago appreciated, the gestures and institutions of autonomy betray a social significance that demands interpretation.

Our contemporary investment in autonomy can be measured by the extent to which our critical methodologies continue to reiterate the question of autonomy vs instrumentality. In this sense, whether we advance an autonomist or instru-mentalist position, we are all still Kantians, insisting on the distinction between pure and impure, interested and disinterested, purpose-driven and sublimely purposeless.[36] New Historicism no less than the New Criticism insists that we make such a choice: literature must either be free or subordinate, self-governing or heteronomous, and that choice will inform how we interpret and define it. Examining the autonomist rhetoric at work in pre-modern works, as in the case of Roman poetry, may help us attain a broader perspective on this impasse. The imperative to take either one position or the other on this issue *is* distinctly modern, and historicist critical stances not infrequently fall into this trap at the very moment they are championing the heteronomy or instrumentality of art as a feature of the pre-modern past. Recognizing autonomist strategies in other periods where the distinctive modern polemic is not at work can be a helpful first step towards progressing beyond the autonomy/instrumentality dualism that confines much contemporary debate.

The tendency to oscillate between shallow, polemical alternatives is at the heart of recent misconceptions of the autonomy of art. If the autonomy of art can only be absolute, then the idea is bound to be rejected as indulgent fantasy or a cloak for hidden ideological designs. The latter notion has come into ascendancy in recent critiques of autonomist thought: for if we believe that all art is inherently political, then an autonomist position must be concealing the artist's or writer's actual, regressive politics beneath the pretext of aesthetic neutrality. The aesthetic itself, relying on the transcendent notion of beauty, is interpreted as a sinister device for suppressing the forms of social subordination on which the elitist categories of Western high culture are premised. Correspondingly, it is often hastily assumed that in order to pursue a more progressive post-colonialist, feminist, or class-based critical agenda, the mystifying concepts of beauty and aesthetic autonomy must be rejected from the outset.

There are some signs that beauty, the aesthetic, and even autonomy are undergoing a modest revival, and that these words are no longer taboo items in

---

[35] Haskins (2000) describes the divide between autonomist and instrumentalist conceptions of art, arguing that this apparently irresolvable debate represents one reflex of a specifically modern tendency of thought.

[36] See Haskins (2000), 11–15.

the critical lexicon.[37] This project, however, remains inchoate and fragmentary, and the field of Latin poetry has been largely untouched by it. Crucial to this nascent project, in my opinion, is appreciation of the fact that autonomy need not be narrowly identified with the credo of 'art for art's sake'. If we assume that the aesthetic inherently involves suppression of the ideological, then we are providing *de facto* affirmation of high-Romantic ideas of the purity and transcendence of the aesthetic. The postmodern rejection of aesthetic autonomy thus advances a paradoxically retrograde outcome: instead of examining how aesthetics and politics, autonomist and instrumentalist impulses, are intertwined in sometimes revealing ways, we end up confirming their separation, and perpetuating more extreme formulations of the autonomy of art. Thinkers of the Frankfurt school such as Adorno and Habermas were already suggesting promising paths towards overcoming this dilemma earlier in the twentieth century. They recognized that the segregated realm of the aesthetic might yet provide a space for reflection on social structures and roles, for rethinking ingrained patterns of social behaviour. Even today, defenders of the value of literature have recourse to its separate status in articulating its social uses. Literature's autonomy and social instrumentality are not necessarily mutually exclusive.

Even if we do not happen to share the optimism of some contemporary defenders of literature's broader social value, it is fairly evident that the case against aesthetic autonomy has been hastily and shoddily constructed in deference to intellectual fads. G. Jusdanis, in his essay 'Two Cheers for Aesthetic Autonomy', criticizes the notion that autonomy is a politically unconscionable cloak for a host of repressive ideologies. He insists on a distinction between the ideal of absolute autonomy (obviously unrealizable), and the real and important institutional autonomy established through decades of hard work by artists, writers, and critics.[38] Do we really want art to be reducible to its political message? Would we find it gratifying if there were no institutionally autonomist spaces for the appreciation and study of works of art, no museums or departments of art history? Is this even a politically desirable outcome? Whereas it is arguable whether the concept of the autonomy of art has substantially contributed to maintaining systems of postcolonial domination, recognition of the distinct status of works of literary art surely did play a role in striking down the publication ban of James Joyce's *Ulysses*. Finally, radical professors who reject the idea of an institutionally separate space for art are generally happy to remain safely ensconced within the structurally and conceptually analogous cocoon of intellectual autonomy afforded by academic tenure.

C. Haskins has forwarded comparable arguments from the ground of aesthetic philosophy. He notes that there is an important distinction to be maintained between viewing the autonomy of art in terms of purpose and in terms of

---

[37] For example, Scarry (2006), Eco (2004); for a revival of aesthetics in the context of the interpretation of Latin Poetry, Martindale (2005). There is perhaps already a more robust revival of interest in aesthetics among Hellenists: Tanner (2006); Porter (2010); Halliwell (2011); Ford (2002).

[38] Jusdanis (2005), 23: 'If we consider the aesthetic an oppressive category, how can we fight measures to terminate funding for the arts in elementary schools? If we believe art has no special value, what arguments can we muster against politicians who attack galleries for displaying controversial works?'.

function. This distinction is comparable to Jusdanis' distinction between institutional and ideal autonomy:[39] a writer or artist may have the purpose of establishing art's radical separateness from the rest of human affairs, yet, viewed in terms of function, the project of aesthetic autonomy may nonetheless produce concrete social outcomes, both positive and negative. Haskins further distinguishes between a strict autonomist position and what he calls 'instrumental autonomy'.[40] Apparently a contradiction in terms, 'instrumental autonomy' is in fact a helpful designation that is consistent with the views of major theorists of autonomy such as Kant, Adorno, and Habermas. On this view, it is possible to advance autonomy in institutional and practical terms in order to bring about concrete social benefits such as the freedom of the artist, the elevation and refinement of human culture, and the safeguarding of a space of social critique and reflection.[41]

The more radical versions of autonomist aesthetics are indeed unique to modern society. The concept of the radically autotelic artwork or text is a development of the modern world, and should not be mapped unthinkingly onto past societies. It is possible, however, to identify instances in past societies where writers and artists have sought to differentiate the particular value of literature or art from the broad range of use-oriented objects and practices. Other societies than ours have seen the emergence of specialized cultural roles and spheres of expertise and envisaged concrete benefits accruing from the autonomization of literary or artistic endeavour.

An example from ancient Rome illustrates this point. Horace, in his 'Epistle to Augustus', addresses a ruler eager to be immortalized in verse, yet insists that praise, in order to be effective *as praise*, must adhere first and foremost to the stringent standards of literary art.[42] By an apparent paradox, poetry must be single-mindedly and ferociously devoted to its own literary aims in order to fulfil broader purposes in the world. Conversely, the shallow, purpose-driven work will fail in its purpose. This line of argument coheres well with Haskin's concept of 'instrumental autonomy'. The underlying idea is that art can be a more effective force in the world if it is organized in an integral manner, if it rigorously respects its own principles and values, and if its practitioners partake of the focus bred of intense specialization. This idea is not new or unique to modernity. If we are able to move beyond the narrow specificity of modern autonomist thought as defined by 'art for art's sake', we will be capable of appreciating important early articulations of autonomism in the literary culture of the ancient world.

AESTHETIC AUTONOMY AND CLASSICAL CULTURE

There is an important difference between seeking confirmation, in ancient literature, of one's own prescriptive preference for aesthetic autonomy, and recognizing

---

[39] Jusdanis (2005), 28. [40] Haskins (1989), 43ff.
[41] Jusdanis (2005), 38: 'the capacity of intellectuals to evaluate reigning social, cultural, and political norms was ensured by the sovereign enclave originally declared for art'.
[42] *Epist.* 2.1, especially 229–70.

and studying elements of autonomist rhetoric, i.e. examining autonomy as a social and cultural phenomenon. F. S. Halliwell has acutely observed: 'proponents of aesthetic autonomy' misrecognize a crucial dimension of ancient art and literature, insofar as they are 'dismissive of the strong ancient tendency to connect both art and beauty to more general accounts of human needs and values', a tendency which 'marks out a vital alternative to doctrines of aesthetic self-sufficiency'.[43] It is important to recognize the distinctness of ancient aesthetic thought, to resist the impulse to make it conform with a modern, post-Kantian sensibility. Yet Halliwell also notes that, while 'it would be wrong to pretend that ancient thinkers had discovered all the concerns of modern aestheticians', it is 'equally mistaken to suppose that there is a chasm between the two'.

The present study, while informed by the broader concerns of modern aesthetics, investigates poetic autonomy as it arises within the context of ancient Roman literary culture. An initial adjustment of perspective and focus is required: we will be concerned mostly with poetic and literary autonomy as distinct from the modern paradigm of *aesthetic* autonomy. The ancient concept of the aesthetic does not necessarily coincide with the modern one.[44] Paul Oskar Kristeller has further argued in a classic study that the ancient world does not produce anything like the 'irreducible nucleus of the modern system of the arts'[45] (painting, sculpture, architecture, music, and poetry) located within a broader aesthetic domain and 'clearly separated by common characteristics from the crafts'.[46] He further states that 'the ancient writers and thinkers ... were neither able nor eager to detach the aesthetic quality of ... works of art from their intellectual, moral, religious and practical function or content, or to use such an aesthetic quality as a standard for grouping the fine arts together or for making them the subject of a comprehensive philosophical interpretation'.[47] It is possible that Kristeller overstates his case. As Halliwell has argued, the ancient idea of the 'mimetic arts' as developed in Plato and Aristotle, while hardly identical to the modern category of 'Fine Arts', affords some substantial points of similarity to modern conceptions of the arts.[48] The ancient concept of the mimetic arts, however, does not fully correspond to the modern category of the aesthetic, in which the idea of 'fine art' is combined with theories of beauty and perception. Even if some of Kristeller's statements are misleading, the project of distinguishing ancient and modern conceptions of art and aesthetics is surely a valid one.

Consideration of the broader category of the aesthetic in modern and ancient thought thus affords interesting points of comparison and intersection, although the differences are often as striking as the similarities. This study, while remaining alert to larger issues in the history of aesthetics, will focus on Roman poetry. In the case of poetry, there are indeed signs that 'the aesthetic quality' of the work was often isolated in emphatic ways, even if it could never be *fully* detached from its

---

[43] Halliwell (2003), 30.   [44] Halliwell (2003), 30; note also Fitzgerald (1995) 1–2, 44.

[45] Kristeller (1951), 497.

[46] Kristeller (1951), 498. Kant *Critique of Judgment* § 51 divides the arts into the arts of speech (rhetoric and poetry), formative arts (painting, architecture, sculpture), and the art of the play of sensations (music, the art of colour).

[47] Kristeller (1951), 506.   [48] Halliwell (2002), 7–9.

intellectual, moral, religious, and practical functions, and that there is a drive on the part of Roman poets to separate their literary products both from humbler forms of craftsmanship and from utility-driven endeavour generally. This autonomist impulse in Roman poetry need not be explained by resorting to an anachronistic, wholesale application of modern aesthetic autonomy to ancient literary culture. My argument concerns *poetic* autonomy, and the social conditions in ancient Rome conducive to the development of autonomist rhetoric in Roman poetry.

Greek ideas of literary craft, the internal requirements of genre, and the relation between literary and ethical qualities form an important background to Roman constructs of autonomy. Greek poetry, moreover, could claim an ancient and continuous tradition going back to Homer and Hesiod, and so might be seen as enjoying a limited form of *de facto* autonomy conferred by a deeply established role and sphere of operations: the Greek poet enjoyed a social honour that was distinctly his own. Again, to recognize this specialized role is hardly to deny the intricate embeddedness of Greek poetry in the civic, religious, and cultural life of the Greek city-states. The point is not that Greek poetry was somehow radically independent of the social context in which it was produced, but rather that, in institutional terms and in terms of accepted social categories, Greek poets enjoyed the prestige of an established place within the broad framework of cultural practices.

At the same time, Greek poetry does not usually manifest the *explicit* insistence on demarcated realms of endeavour and axiological self-differentiation that we see in the overtly autonomist rhetoric of the Roman poets. Certainly Greek lyric poets such as Archilochus and Sappho define their own values and preferences in ways that also work to give shape to their individual profiles as poets. Pindar conveys pride in his endeavour and the distinctive value of poetry, while balancing encomiastic aims with insistence on poetic integrity. Yet, as D. C. Feeney has noted, poetry enjoyed an established place in the Greek *mousikē*, an accepted role in cultural education and Greek life, by contrast with the relative isolation of Roman poets.[49] Accordingly, Roman poets needed to craft a social role and *honos* for themselves, to define, within an often adversarial environment, the value of an activity at odds with the traditional emphases of public life. At issue are poetry's standing and function within society. Was poetry merely ancillary to an eminent Roman's more important activities in the political sphere, or did poetry possess its own intrinsic value and social prestige? Could poetry occupy a position of self-validating primacy comparable to the self-validating primacy of political affairs? In a society marked by a strong focus on moral exemplarity, an ideological insistence on the public utility of cultural practices, and recurrent rhetorical topoi expressing distrust of imported, aesthetic activities, a more sharp-edged and aggressive effort was required to define an independent space for poetic value and poetic prestige.

Political power, military predominance, and immense wealth of the aristocratic classes, and later, the imperial family, tended to draw all other cultural practices and practitioners into their orbit, and considerations of public utility threatened to

---

[49] Feeney (2002) 187.

subsume or constrain literary endeavour. Poets, if they did not wish to see themselves defined as mere clients of the powerful and their occupation as an ancillary diversion, needed to sharply differentiate the specific value of their literary endeavour. This project of self-definition and self-positioning began in earnest in the latter half of the first century BC. The reasons for this shift are complex, but the main points can be briefly summarized. The intensifying momentum of Hellenization in the second and first centuries BC had succeeded in making literary pursuits a major interest of the upper classes. Members of the political elite not only were patrons of writers, but also began to foster and advertise their own literary accomplishments. At the same time, the increasing disintegration and instability of republican government engendered a new cynicism regarding public life, and opened up new opportunities for those who might wish to experiment with aligning themselves with non-traditional pursuits and axiological priorities. Poetry was part of a broader phenomenon. Public building, villa ownership and art objects, the cultivation of learned leisure activities, and other forms of activity that B. Krostenko classifies as 'social performance', increasingly became important means of building up cultural capital in a highly competitive environment.[50]

The latter half of the first century BC thus sees the convergence of two tendencies with culturally transformative results: the weakening of the axiological primacy of public life, and the increasing adoption of aesthetic pursuits among the Roman elite. It is important, of course, to avoid the totalizing tendencies of some of the more hackneyed narratives of cultural change which we inherit from the ancient world, especially in cases where those narratives were ironically meant or deployed for localized rhetorical effect in the first place. Horace, for example, in his 'Epistle to Augustus', traces a path from serious, practical and traditionally 'Roman' pursuits to a fad for trivial, Hellenizing diversion and a mania for poetry.[51] While such narratives of sudden, total cultural change, if interpreted literally, are clearly problematic, it is equally true that scholars, in their haste to show their imperviousness to the allure of a simplifying narrative, all too often lose sight of elements of truth concealed within the cliché. In the current instance, it is not a question of the wholesale transformation of society, but rather of the emergence of new cultural possibilities, which had their own limitations and complications, and which were realized in different ways by different individuals. For example, while we hardly see a wholesale abandonment of the public career by Roman aristocrats, members of the provincial elite (*domi nobiles*),[52] who had less to lose and more to gain, did in several instances turn to writing as a means of creating a reputation for themselves.

One way in which these new cultural possibilities were pursued, both in literature and in the broader cultural scene, was through new strategies of self-representation. In the closing decades of the first century BC, there is an

---

[50] On the traditional avoidance of a public association with intellectual activity, Zanker (1995), 199–200; on the rise of aestheticism, and its paradoxical advantages, Krostenko (2001), 31 and *passim*; on the Roman attitude toward Greek culture, Horsfall (1993), 59–60, 63–4; Gruen (1990) and (1992), esp. 52–83, 223–71.

[51] Sall. *Cat.* 10–13; Hor. *Epist.* 2.1.103–17.   [52] Wiseman (1987); McCarthy (1998).

appreciable increase in the frequency of poetic works in first-person genres: polymetric *nugae*, epigram, satire, lyric, elegy, the literary epistle.[53] Repositioning poetry vis-à-vis public life means crafting poetic *personae* that embody and enact these shifts. The Romans, for whom the exemplary deeds and practices of celebrated men both motivated individual conduct and justified fields of endeavour, define the nature of poetic activity through representations of the poet's character. Such an enterprise is inevitably self-interested. Roman poets are engaged in what Pierre Bourdieu, writing of nineteenth-century France, has called 'the conquest of autonomy', the 'invention of a new social personality' that confers legitimacy and prestige on its inventors.[54]

The Roman elite especially valued pursuits that were not seen as being subordinate or ancillary. The lowest pursuits belong to those whose labour was devoted to the entertainment, pleasure, or quotidian utility of others (slaves, actors, musicians, prostitutes, gladiators). By contrast, a pursuit that was self-validating and primary belonged at the top level of the pyramid of occupations. If literature was to become more than a restorative diversion of intermittent *otium*, or encomiastic medium subordinated to commemoration of the deeds of political participants, then its status as autonomously valid, first-order occupation needed to be established. Cicero, whose life alternated between action and writing, political activity and literary pursuits, devoted substantial thought to the question of literature's role in society.[55] In an extended discussion of the active life and the life of retirement (*Offic.* 1.69–92), Cicero describes different types of retirement:

> Multi autem et sunt et fuerunt qui eam quam dico tranquillitatem expetentes a negotiis publicis se removerint ad otiumque perfugerint, in his et nobilissimi philosophi longeque principes et quidam homines severi et graves nec populi nec principum mores ferre potuerunt, vixeruntque non nulli in agris delectati re sua familiari. His idem propositum fuit quod regibus, ut ne qua re egerent, ne cui parerent, libertate uterentur, cuius proprium est sic vivere ut velis. Quare cum hoc commune sit potentiae cupidorum cum his quos dixi otiosis... (1.69–70)

> There have been many, and there still are, who have sought that kind of tranquillity by abandoning public business and fleeing to a life of leisure. These include the noblest and foremost philosophers, and also certain strict and serious men who could not endure the behavior of the populace or its leaders. Some of these have spent their lives on their estates finding their delight in their family wealth. Their aim was the aim of kings: that needing nothing, and obeying no one, they might enjoy liberty, the mark of which is to live just as one pleases. That aim, then, is common both to those who desire power and to such men of leisure.[56]

---

[53] It is necessary to recognize two previous studies that have attempted large-scale treatment of the emergence of first-person poetry in Rome: W. R. Johnson (1983) and Miller (1994). In both instances, however, the focus is on the category of 'lyric' somewhat broadly defined, rather than first-person poetry per se.

[54] Bourdieu (1993), 111.

[55] A few studies are particularly relevant to the present concern with the place of the writer in Rome and Cicero's attitude toward literary leisure: Boes (1990); Narducci (1997) and (1989); Griffin and Barnes (1989); Habinek (1994). On literature and nationalism, Fantham (1996), 34–40.

[56] Translation of Atkins and Griffin (1991).

Whereas nothing in this discussion reverses the priority of public affairs over private *otium* (leisure),[57] the crisis of late republican politics generates the realization that other, quieter modes of living may claim a new validity, that an altered political climate might make for a certain 'mobility of values'.[58] Different styles of living an elite life—and not exclusively the political career—are now valued and justifiable. Yet even as new life-paths become possible, certain core concepts of self as determined by social class remain constant. Cicero perceives that creating one's own world (literary or otherwise), and ruling the world, belong to a comparable impulse. Both kings and writers, politicians and men of retirement, wish for the same thing: to live as they like (*sic vivere, ut velis*), to be self-sufficient (*ne qua re egerent*), to obey no one (*ne cui parerent*), to enjoy freedom (*libertate uterentur*, 1.70).[59] Both writers and members of the political class, in other words, value autonomy.[60]

In fact, these two modes of autonomy—political autonomy and autonomy of leisured withdrawal—were often combined in various ways and to varying degrees. For members of the Roman political class, it was important both to enjoy autonomy and agency in public life, and to be able to retreat to a 'space of one's own' as embodied in a country estate infused with aesthetic sophistication and removed from the pressing demands of public life. The autonomy afforded by *secessus* ('withdrawal') was essential even for figures at the pinnacle of the Roman hierarchy of status and power: the so-called Teatro Marittimo at Hadrian's Villa at Tivoli, represented by the plan on the cover of this book, appears to have been a private retreat for the emperor himself. Designed on a pattern of concentric circles, Hadrian's 'island villa' is a private apartment or sheltered sanctum that includes its own bathing suite and latrine, is centred on an inner courtyard and fountain, and is surrounded by a moat, which, in turn, is ringed by a covered passageway supported by Ionic columns. With its play of light and shade, its curvilinear design, and its alternation of concave and convex, water and solidity,

---

[57] On Roman *otium*, see André (1966); Connors (2000); Toner (1995); Balsdon (1960) and (1969); Laidlaw (1968).

[58] Labate and Narducci (1981). Note also Narducci (1989), 550ff., who argues that Cicero develops 'una nuova concezione dell'attività culturale, che, per quanto spesso si sforzi di indicarne e rinsaldarne il legame con l'impegno al servizio dello Stato, lascia anche emergere con prepotenza le ragioni autonome delle diverse discipline, la loro volontà emanciparsi dalla sudditanza al primato della politica, il loro radicamento in un ceto intellettuale talora non più direttamente coinvolto nella gestione del potere' (552). On the emergence of 'autonomous' intellectual disciplines of knowledge, see Wallace-Hadrill (1997), 12–15, who draws on Frier (1985); compare Moatti (1997), 109–24. Note also the discussion of 'structural differentiation' and the emergence of specialized domains of expertise in the late republic in Hopkins (1978), 37, 89ff., 96. Narducci (1989), 561–4, includes the 'emancipation of poetry' among the new cultural tendencies emerging in the late republic; on the esotericism of the new poetry, 562.

[59] On the phenomenon of elite withdrawal, Hopkins (1983), 120ff., 149–75; Griffin (1976).

[60] Sailor (2008), especially 6–50, offers an illuminating analysis of Tacitus' historical writings in terms of autonomy, the writer's authority, and concepts of elite prestige. In general, there is an underappreciated link between Tacitus' understanding of his cultural role as historian and the social position of Augustan poets: both needed to craft a rhetoric, or social performance, of autonomy in order to ground a sense of their authenticity within the context of imperial society. One thinks in particular of the *Dialogus* and Tacitus' interest in Augustan poetry, the nature of the poet's role, and poetic autonomy (see Chapter 4, below).

the Teatro Marittimo is a 'tiny architectural jewel'[61] whose very form perfectly embodies the ideal of aesthetically exquisite withdrawal so highly valued by the Roman elite.

Roman writers assimilated and adapted these social concepts, representing themselves and their poetry not only in terms of leisured withdrawal but also in terms of autonomous agency, self-determination, and power. Horace, the master architect of lyric (*exegi monumentum*, *Carm.* 3.30.1), is 'powerful' and 'foremost' (*potens/princeps*, 12–13) in his poetic field. Propertius makes himself out to be a triumphing general of elegy (3.1.8–12). The lover, who can claim no great prestige on the basis of wealth or noble ancestry, 'reigns' within his elegiac world through the power of his *ingenium* (Propertius 2.34.55–8). Virgil claims primacy (*Georgics* 3.10) and a poetic triumph alongside Octavian (17–18). His 'temple' will honour the ruler, but the poet's own prestige and power are hardly occluded,[62] and the close juxtaposition of poet and *princeps* at the opening of Book 3 (*mihi Caesar . . . illi victor ego*, *Georgics* 3.16–17)[63] is carefully balanced by their division into separate realms at the close of Book 4 (559–66). From these and other such statements a pattern emerges: the poet abdicates forms of prestige and power outside his domain; within the sphere of his poetry, he is powerful, and ultimately, immortal. These claims of power and self-determination are made simultaneously in the aesthetic and the sociological registers: Callimachean *leptotes* (stylistic refinement) and socio-political *libertas* ('freedom', 'autonomy') are inextricable elements within an integrated self-representational system.

In order to satisfy the deeply ingrained criteria of worth among the Roman elite, poetry needed to measure itself against the standards of *libertas* and self-determination cherished by political participants. The challenge was to position poetry simultaneously as distinct from politics, and yet comparable with politics as first-order occupation. The recurrent oppositions that we see in Roman poetry between *amor* and *arma*, poetry and forum, form part of this continual dialect of resemblance and differentiation. Even though Roman poets from the time of Catullus reject the politician's career, the very concept of the poet's vocation resembles the *cursus honorum*. Poetry, like the pursuit of political office, involves hopes for lasting renown, and, in some cases, a pattern of ascending ambition.[64] The practice of self-commemoration through monumental works is also held in common by poets and members of the Roman political class: both literary

---

[61] Sear (1992), 176, who also supplies the more helpfully descriptive name 'island villa'. Others have responded to the sense of autonomy conveyed by the design of the Teatro Marittimo, e.g. Charles W. Moore (1960), 25: 'the image of an island, with all the sense of withdrawal and independence that an island implies . . . an inviolate place, a perfect circle surrounded by water'. The residences of other emperors suggest that this is not an isolated instance: Augustus liked to retreat to a private study at the top of his house which he called 'Syracuse' and *technyphion* ('little workshop'; Suet. *Aug.* 72.2); and, according to Claridge (1998), 140, the lower court of Domitian's palace was a 'world of its own' that could be reached only via a single staircase.

[62] It is perhaps significant that the monument in honour of Octavian is motivated, if we take Virgil at his word, not in the first instance by the ruler's deeds in and of themselves, but by the exhaustion of Hellenistic mythological subject matter: Octavian thus becomes the poet's novel *materia*.

[63] Thomas (1988), ad loc.

[64] See the discussion of Roman 'literary careers' in Farrell (2002); note also Hardie and Moore (2010).

works and public commemorative structures were termed *monumenta*. Poets, moreover, appropriate key terms from political and military life (*officium, nomen, laus, princeps, triumphus, militia*), in each instance adapting a word notionally foreign to their own sphere of operations to emphasize the distinctness of *literary* values. Thus *militia* becomes the lover's campaign (*militia amoris*); the poet celebrates a 'triumph' for *literary* victories. Such appropriation sets up an interesting paradox: poets come to rely on and introduce into the heart of their poetic discourse the organizing concepts of public life. Do such tactics of 'transvaluation' establish their autonomy, or underline their continuing dependence and subordination?

There is no absolute or 'objective' answer to the question. Autonomy is established in rhetorical terms, through constant efforts of persuasion on the part of individual poets as they position and reposition themselves before their readers. It is for this reason that I attempt to distinguish between the terms 'autonomist' and 'autonomous' in my usage throughout this book. In most instances, the question is not whether a given poet somehow achieves autonomy (as if that could be determined on some neutral grounds), but to what extent that poet represents himself in autonomist terms. Autonomy is a key, orienting ideas around which poets in late republican through early imperial Rome organized their rhetoric of self-definition. Tracing the different ways in which this self-representational game plays out in different texts and different authors is one of the main purposes of this book. This approach is based, in turn, on the recognition that autonomy, in Roman terms, lacks the theoretical tightness and severity of its modern philosophical articulations.

The two opening odes of Horace's lyric collection provide an example of the tensions and enlivening irregularity of the autonomist project at Rome. Horace spends most of *Odes* 1.1 enumerating the various occupations that absorb the populace at large: athletic competition, farming, commerce, hunting, war, hedonistic repose. Finally, at the culmination of the ode's great priamel-structure, he turns towards his own poetic occupation:

> me doctarum hederae praemia frontium
> dis miscent superis, me gelidum nemus
> nympharumque leues cum Satyris chori
> secernunt populo, si neque tibias
> Euterpe cohibet nec Polyhymnia
> Lesboum refugit tendere barbiton.
> quodsi me lyricis uatibus inseres,
> sublimi feriam sidera uertice.   (*Carm.* 1.1.29–36)

Me ivy garlands, the reward of learned foreheads, set among the gods above, me the chill grove and light-footed choruses of Nymphs and Satyrs cut off from the populace, if neither Euterpe holds back the pipes nor Polyhymnia refuses to offer the Lesbian lyre. But if you include me in the canon of lyric poets, I shall strike the stars with my exalted head.

Horace, in one of the most powerful and influential expressions of poetic autonomy in the Roman tradition, locates himself in a secluded *nemus* (grove), cut off from the populace in a poetry-world inhabited by the Muses and adorned with such essential poetic furniture as the ivy and lyre. This self-portrait involves a subtle balancing of forces in tension: Horace occupies a private space publicly advertised; retiring yet self-consciously vainglorious, he withdraws to the lyric *angulus*,[65] where his vatic status depends, however, on his patron Maecenas' judgement. His autonomy is hardly total or absolute. It is restrained by ties of friendship and deference, and Horace makes sure to take the edge off his highly Greek self-portrait as unworldly, Muse-inspired bard with the closing touch of humorous exaggeration: 'I will bump up against the stars with my inflated head'.

There is nonetheless a serious side to the lyric poet's claims; indeed, one of Horace's signature rhetorical strategies is to disarm his reader's scepticism by framing with humorous self-deprecation a self-representational scenario he wishes to be taken seriously. All this is a far cry from modern autonomism. Horatian autonomy, far from manifesting theoretical rigour and austerity, is comprised of an intricate combination of bold rhetorical gestures and socially astute tactics of accommodation of his friends' and readers' viewpoints. Nor does the story end there. The next poem in the collection manifests a strikingly different focus. Here Horace reflects on the civil violence of the recent past, the anger of the gods against the Romans, and the need for a divine figure to 'expiate' communal transgressions. The lyric poet now projects a strongly civic voice, focuses on the city rather than the remote rural *nemus*, and, after identifying the *princeps* as divine saviour in the form of the god Mercury, ends with an oblique salute to 'Caesar' (*te duce, Caesar, Carm.* 1.2.52). *Odes* 1.1–2 can thus be interpreted as playing out tensions in Horace's role as lyric *vates*. The movement from secluded literariness to imperial encomium is traced not least by the trajectory from Maecenas, the sponsor and protector of Horace's literary leisure and the first word of *Odes* 1.1, to Caesar Augustus, the most powerful man in the Roman world and the last word of 1.2. Horace's autonomist self-portrait is suspended mid-way between the two weighty *nomina* with their different yet related connotations.

It is the wrong question, then, to ask whether or not Horace *is* autonomous as lyric poet. The more pertinent question is how he organizes his autonomist poetic discourse. Even a less severe line of questioning—whether or not Roman literary practices suggest a degree of institutional autonomization—is difficult to answer with any certainty. The sociological claims of this study are necessarily limited and modest. In studying ancient literature in its social dimension, we do not have the rich cache of evidence that, for example, Pierre Bourdieu can access in his study of cultural attitudes and practices in modern France.[66] Therefore, while it is interesting to ask to what extent and in what ways literature might or might not have achieved institutional autonomy in ancient Rome, in practice we are often at the mercy of highly self-interested textual representations of literary culture. As Greg Woolf has recently argued, Roman writers such as Pliny the Younger, for their own tactical reasons, depict a Roman social world in which literary *studia*

---

[65] On the concept of the *angulus* ('corner'), defined as 'la qualità di uno stare separato', see Ferri (1993), 22ff.; in general on Horatian groves and spaces of retreat, Troxler-Keller (1964).

[66] Bourdieu (1984); the closest we have to a sociological study of Roman poetry is White (1993); note also White (1978) and (1982). A sociological approach to the economic status of poets and of Virgil's Roman readership has been attempted recently by Thibodeau (2011), 245–56.

constitute a thriving, highly prestigious realm of activity of nearly equal import-ance to public life.[67] We may be cautious about taking this picture of social reality literally, but that does not preclude examining its rhetorical and self-representa-tional significance. Equally, however, we should resist the faddish temptation to reduce textual images of literary activity to *mere* representation, a textual game with no relation to reality. This study will assume that Roman literary works, while they are hardly transparent windows onto Roman society, inevitably bear traces of and themselves constitute meaningful interventions in the social world in which they were produced.

A central aim of this study is to cease subjecting ancient literature to the modern instrumentality/autonomy dichotomy, and to investigate instead what Roman poets had to say about autonomy. Roman poets engaged in autonomist strategies of self-representation that are worth studying on their own terms within the context of Roman culture and society. An advantage of this approach is that it affords a new perspective from which to re-evaluate important aspects of Roman poetry and modern scholarly responses. Many well-established themes in Latin literary scholarship are at some level issues of autonomy. To take only a few examples, the relation of poets and patrons,[68] the question of Augustan and anti-Augustan content,[69] and the opposition between Callimachean aesthetics and panegyric are scholarly topoi persistently organized around autonomist di-lemmas. The problem is that much of this scholarly inquiry has proceeded neither with explicit awareness of the modern autonomist discourses by which these controversies are informed, nor with close examination of the ancient Roman autonomist rhetoric that links these diverse phenomena. Scholars of Roman poetry have long struggled with questions of aesthetics and history, poetry and propaganda, loyal and dissident poetic attitudes, but have not systematically examined the Roman rhetoric of autonomy that structures these familiar debates.

This study focuses on poetry in self-representational genres: satire, elegy, lyric, epigram, occasional poetry. Autonomist rhetoric, however, belongs to a larger reorientation of literary values and pursuits that also encompasses prose literature. Catullus' comments on the corrupted *res publica* can be read alongside Nepos' *Life of Atticus*, Sallust's prefaces, and Cicero's philosophical works written under Caesar's dictatorship. Anyone who has read the praises of literary *otium* in imperial poets such Horace and Statius will find illuminating parallels in the *Letters* of Pliny the Younger.[70] I will introduce such comparisons and parallels throughout this study, yet the focus will remain on works of poetry for reasons of scope and manageability of topic. A secondary reason for this focus is the fact that poetry claims for itself a notionally sequestered space at the margin of society (*secessus*), whereas prose authors tend to maintain a connection with the social rituals of daily Roman reality (letters), and with the notion of providing concrete

---

[67] Woolf (2003).

[68] On patronage, both patronage of poets and more broadly in Roman society, see White (1978) and (1993); the essays in Gold (1982); Saller (1982); the essays in Wallace-Hadrill (1989); Konstan (1995).

[69] A vast topic, but note in particular the landmark discussion in Kennedy (1993); for an alternate view, Davis (1999).

[70] On Pliny and imperial literary culture, Roller (1998), Riggsby (1998), Guillemin (1929); compare Myers (2000).

moral benefit (philosophy, history[71]). Poetry was already seen as being situated at one degree of remove from everyday social transactions, and thus affords an especially salient version of autonomist self-presentation.

I have chosen to examine the tradition of *first-person* poetry[72] in particular because of the way in which first-person poets delineate their literary occupation and sphere of activity. The image of the writer has consequences for the perception of his activity and product; hence in first-person works the metaliterary dimension is unusually salient. The main works of first-person poetry, ranging from Lucilius to Juvenal, were written in the late republic through the early empire, the same period that sees an intensification of autonomist rhetoric. These two phenomena—the turn towards poetry in first-person genres and the rise of autonomism in Roman poetry—are closely related. As I will discuss in the book's opening chapter, the effort to define a form of activity distinct from public life coheres with a set of individualizing and self-differentiating gestures.[73] Poets, in order to distance themselves from traditionalist criteria of worthwhile activity, engage in antinomian styles of self-definition best articulated within a first-person framework: 'others value wealth and power . . . *I* have created an immortal work of poetry'. The fact that the period in which first-person poets such as Catullus began to craft such statements in verse corresponds to the decline of the republican system of government is worth contemplating. The opportunity to champion poetry's autonomous validity as occupation arises at a moment when Roman public life's unacknowledged superiority to all other modes of life was, if not overturned, at least newly vulnerable to scepticism.

This is not to say that the interest in autonomy was invented out of whole cloth in the late republican period. Autonomy was arguably already a concern among earlier writers, and some recent studies of early Roman poetry have specifically highlighted the question of autonomy. Yet while early Roman poets such as Ennius had a broad interest in maintaining their independence and the dignity of their social position,[74] autonomist rhetoric, for the reasons outlined above, achieved its newly explicit and aggressive articulation in the late republican period. Similar questions arise in relation to genres such as epic which are not predominantly self-representational. To suggest that autonomy is not relevant to epic would be to dismiss as irrelevant most of the central scholarly debates surrounding Virgil, Lucan, and Statius in recent decades.[75] The question of how these texts engage with imperial ideology is a crucial facet of their interpretation,

---

[71] Fantham (1996), 184, notes the 'orientation of the senatorial class toward oratory, history, biography—literary genres used in public life or in recording public careers'.

[72] A good overview is McCarthy (2010), who also notes some of the problems with the category itself (435).

[73] But note also the 'publicity potential of the minor genres': White (1993), 22; Myers (2000), 106. Self-differentiation and autonomist rhetoric goes hand in hand with the celebration of patrons and public figures: see especially Chapter 3 below.

[74] Gruen (1996), 119.

[75] It would be tedious to cite all the works examining questions of Roman epic and ideology, but simply to note a few: on the ending of Virgil's *Aeneid*, see, for example, Galinsky (1988) and (1994) and Putnam (1990); on Lucan, John Henderson (1987), Masters (1992), Leigh (1997), Bartsch (1997); on Statius, McNelis (2007), John Henderson (1991). On epic and imperial ideology generally, Feeney (1991), Philip Hardie (1993), and Quint (1993). On politics in Roman poetry more generally, see Ahl (1984a).

and this study, I hope, will contribute a new perspective from which to re-examine such concerns. Focusing on first-person poetry, however, has the advantage of facilitating the examination of shifts in the representation of the poet and his mode of activity across different authors, genre, and periods. Through the carefully crafted *personae* of first-person poets, questions of autonomy and heteronomy, independence and subordination, are posed with special clarity and intensity. Remaining focused on this set of genres will afford greater comparative insight and precision as we attempt to trace changes in autonomist rhetoric and the definition of poetic space.

This last point elicits a further question: are shifts in poetic self-representation available to interpretation in the way that I am suggesting? Some might argue that *genre* is the determining force behind differences in poetic self-definition, not shifting constructions of poetic autonomy. Indeed, much scholarship on Roman poetry has been devoted to demonstrating the power of genre to control features of poetic discourse.[76] While this emphasis on genre has been of fundamental importance in furthering our understanding of Roman poetry and ancient literature generally, the centrality of genre is sometimes in danger of being exaggerated to the point of significantly underestimating the mutual determination of genre and content. Genre does have a determining power over the kinds of things the poet says, but the poet also selects and constructs his genre as a suitable receptacle for what he wants to say in the first place. In the context of a specifically metaliterary reading of first-person poetry, this approach would stress that the power of genre to determine the representation of literary activity enjoys no inherent priority over the poet's power to adapt his genre to suit the image of literary activity he wishes to project. We cannot simply appeal to the notional priority of genre to explain away distinctive metaliterary tendencies: these tendencies are fully available to interpretation as the consequence of specific authorial choices. I propose to examine the social/ideological dimension in the very formation of genres, how genres are shaped in accordance with historically conditioned needs and interests.

Another major nexus of interpretive issues concerns the poetic representation of literary personality.[77] The articulation of personal autonomy through antinomian social gestures is an especially salient aspect of Roman autonomist rhetoric. Starting with Catullus, Roman self-representational poets claim to follow axiologically marginal life-paths that diverge from traditional morality and publicly approved values. This project of axiological self-differentiation takes diverse forms such as the risqué *otium* and sophisticated *urbanitas* of Catullus, the rural autarky and lyric symposia of Horace, and the totalizing love-realm of Propertius.

---

[76] There would be little point in recording here the vast bibliography on genre in the field of Latin literature. Landmark discussions of genre include: Conte (1986) and (1994a); Hinds (1987a) and (1992); Cairns (1974a); Zetzel (1983); Labate (1990).

[77] The question of *persona* has been an important one in Latin literary studies. For a summary of the issues, acute analysis, and some relevant bibliography, see McCarthy (2010), who calls for 'a layered and sensitive appreciation of the ways that the act of publishing poetry constitutes an act of communication that is neither simply coextensive with the acts of communication represented in the poetry nor rigidly dissevered from those represented acts' (446). Thus while the speaker of a Latin poem cannot be equated with the biographical author, neither is there a clean, simple division between author and persona, real-world efficacy and poetic text.

In each case, the poet's ostensibly natural inclination coincides with a sequestering or radically self-enclosing life-realm that serves as vivid embodiment of the poet's autonomy. The same poets, however, frequently call attention to disjunctions between author and poetic persona, authorial presence and circulating text. Catullus, for example, famously announces that there is a difference between sexually provocative *versiculi* and the morally sound 'poet himself' (c.16, further discussion in Chapter 1, below). This strategy forms the basis of a distinct model of autonomy: the autonomy of the poetic work as premised on the division between ethics and aesthetics. Roman poets thus simultaneously flaunt their antinomian ethical tendencies in order to elicit notions of personal autonomy *and* claim poetic autonomy on the basis of the text's independence of authorial *vita* and *mores*. This dual strategy is not wholly coherent, and points towards tensions inherent to the project of autonomist self-representation.

It should be evident by now that it is not a question of a single, theoretically coherent concept of poetic autonomy, but rather an array of autonomist paradigms that are often closely interrelated and complementary, if not always logically consistent. One paradigm of autonomy might be termed the autonomy of aesthetic[78] value. This model is characterized by an emphasis on aesthetic criteria of poetic value, and a division between ethics and aesthetics. Poetry's detachment from the world at large is reinforced by its apparent uselessness and adherence to its own intrinsic ends. A second model of poetic autonomy might be termed axiological autonomy or personal autonomy. On this model, the poet makes claims of autonomy based on antinomian social gestures and a stance of ethical autarky;[79] he makes it clear that his values are not shared by the vast majority of humankind, that he occupies 'his own world'. A third type of autonomy might be called political or ideological autonomy. In this instance, the poet endeavours to maintain his independence from powerful men and dominant public ideas. It is unlikely, of course, that we will find a 'pure' articulation of any one of these ideas in Roman poetry. Roman poets, in crafting their autonomist positions, often shift subtly and insensibly from one autonomist strategy to another. This study will call attention to different models of autonomy employed in Roman poetic texts,

---

[78] I use the term loosely. As I argued above, there is no exact ancient correlate for the modern term 'aesthetic'. I employ the term here to refer to aspects of Roman verse relating to craftsmanship and intrinsic literary quality as distinct from social or moral benefit.

[79] I follow the general tendency of modern scholars and lexical tools in interpreting the Greek term *autarkeia* as 'self-sufficiency' and *autonomia* as 'self-government, self-rule' and hence, broadly, 'independence'. Thus when I refer to 'autarky', I am usually thinking of the ethical ideas of self-sufficiency common in Hellenistic philosophy and Roman poetry: being 'content with little', and so forth. My primary focus, however, is not lexicographical, and the word 'autonomy' is here employed with the elasticity of its English usage. This very elasticity makes 'autonomy' a more heuristically useful key-term than 'autarky' for this study, since it encompasses the various interconnected rhetorical themes I have identified as central to Roman poetic self-representation (aesthetic autotelicity, antinomian marginality, ideological independence, etc.). 'Autarky' refers to the smaller subset of this thematic nexus that concerns ethical self-sufficiency. (Self-sufficiency, of course, can contribute to, or metonymically represent, broader modes of independence and autonomy.) On the political meaning of the term *autonomia*, as distinct from *autarkeia*, see for example Hansen (1995), especially p. 37. In general, *autonomia* was not used in a literary sense, although Himerius does employ the term *autonomia poiētikē* in a context which refers to poetic license as opposed to the rules of *tekhnē* (*Orat.* 1.1).

examining how those different models are both in tension with and in complementary relation to each other.

Before offering a more detailed outline of this study's content, I wish to emphasize a few methodological points about literary criticism and literary history in a post-modern climate, which will serve to orient this study for the reader. First, it is important to be clear about one possible pitfall. Precisely because 'autonomy' is such a contentious issue in modern aesthetic and literary debates, there is a danger that my arguments in this study will be seen as an attempt to vindicate the autonomy of Roman poetry, i.e. Roman poetry's *actual* detachment from the workings of Roman society. Such a divorce of cultural product and the culture in which it was produced would be impossible, but recognizing this impossibility does not entail that we should therefore neglect to examine rhetorical constructions of autonomy, what I have called 'autonomist' arguments and positions. There is a difference, in short, between autonomy and 'autonomy'—a difference I attempt to respect throughout this study.

Nor should we fail to recognize, however, that powerful rhetorical constructs can exert a determinate effect on social behaviour and practices. One recent critical trend has been a kind of automatic scepticism regarding any large-scale claims about cultural change or literary historical shifts. Doctrinaire postmodernist criticism manifests a hasty compulsion to 'deconstruct differences' and 'destabilize dichotomies'. There is no reason to insist that all intentions are irrecoverable phantoms, all meanings indeterminate and polysemic, all boundaries blurred and self-deconstructing. This knee-jerk impulse causes postmodern criticism to be congealed with the kind of unvarying rigidity which ought to be the very opposite of its intention.[80] The miniaturist claims of positivist classical philology, moreover, merge more comfortably than might have been expected with a postmodern scepticism regarding any larger conceptual claims or literary historical arguments. Both tendencies join forces to circumscribe all claims to the local effects of lexical nuance or the malleable 'polysemism' of the infinitely deconstructable trope. The outcome, however, is that the large-scale *idées fixes* of literary history remain in place, unrevised, presumably in order to serve as convenient fodder for deconstructive critique. Is it possible to revive the lost art of generalization? In this spirit, I wish to offer the present study as an attempt to tackle some of the large questions of Roman literary and cultural history, without, I hope, falling victim to unexamined clichés or generalities unsubstantiated by the rigour of close reading.

I am aware that an interest in the emergence of autonomist rhetoric in Roman poetry may be seen as infringing on the dangerous territory of certain received narratives of Roman cultural history: the emerging cultural impact of the equestrian class, the weariness with civil conflict, the emergence, starting with Catullus and continuing under Augustus, of a generation of literary men devoted to the values of *otium*.[81] We can extend this narrative further back and join it to the

---

[80] Compare Habinek (1998), 4: 'a postmodern suspicion of generalities'.

[81] The thesis developed in Foucault (1986) is taken up by Skinner (1993); arguing against the notion of a turn inwards in this period, however, is Riggsby (1998) on Pliny; see also Edwards (2002), 32. Absorption in literary activity need not be seen as a retreat from politics and power: Hinds (2001), 224, remarks that 'immanent literary history has its own power-plays'. Roller (1998), 267, 300, argues that,

intensified cultivation of elite culture practices, categorized as *luxuria* in Roman texts,[82] following the Carthaginian Wars and the conquest of the great Hellenistic kingdoms in the second century BC. The problem is that, if we simply accept such narratives, we risk reifying the rhetorical practices endemic to Roman literary texts as a determinate sociological phenomenon, when the reality was probably more complex. Were Horace, Propertius, and Tibullus truly apolitical 'poet-priests', carrying out the arcane rites of Callimachean aesthetics at a remove from the Roman populace? On the other hand, it would be misleading simply to ignore core patterns and motifs of Roman poetic self-representation.

In the present study, I intend neither to mistake iterated rhetorical topoi for sociological truth, nor to dismiss such narratives as mere rhetoric—as if a set of densely interconnected ideas, recurrently and powerfully expressed across a range of texts in response to specific challenges in the contemporary cultural and political climate, were simply a superficial rhetorical game, a textual construct to be unmasked as such. The question of autonomy, I would suggest, benefits from a more nuanced approach that neither reduces autonomy to a textual trope nor claims to offer a lucid, objective narrative of the autonomization of literary practices. Autonomist rhetoric is built upon the evasion of a determinate position, the creation of a 'free' realm of play, irony, and political indeterminacy, yet, as I hope to show, politics and political opinions are not thereby wholly excluded, and the construct of autonomy itself can be read as having been created for determinate purposes, under specific historical conditions, and with concrete outcomes.

The opening chapter, 'First-Person Poetry and the Autonomist Turn: Lucilius, Catullus, and Cicero's *Consulatus suus*', will consider three instances of self-representational poetry in the late republican period, exploring the relation between poetic self-representation and traditional criteria of worthwhile activity. Gaius Lucilius is a foundational figure both for the satiric genre and for self-representational poetry. Lucilius, who was well born and well connected, could have pursued a political career. His choice to devote his time to literary matters is therefore a significant one, especially in the context of the escalating violence of the Gracchan period. Yet Lucilius does not systematically counterbalance poetry against politics; nor does he retreat into his own axiologically differentiated sphere of aesthetic refinement and counter-traditional morals. He does, however, establish his satiric poetry as a space in which he can articulate his own attitude towards contemporary cultural and political developments. Amidst the welter of rhetoric and posturing, Lucilius crafts a sceptical, humane, self-aware, sane literary voice. While *poetic* autonomy is not a primary impulse in Lucilian satire, his use of first-person verse as medium of satiric *libertas* constitutes an important example for later poets.

while recitation may be semi-private and removed from the forum, it is still informed by its own sort of 'politics' in the wider sense of the term. On literary space and time under the early Empire, see Connors (2000); Myers (2000), 120ff., is excellent on the shift in meaning *otium* undergoes in the early imperial period; note also Corti (1991). Recitation and declamation are often viewed as instances of the new forms of and focus on literary activity that emerge in the imperial period: Bonner (1949), 39–40; Dupont (1997); Bloomer (1997).

[82] On such moralizing narratives, see in particular Edwards (2002).

Catullus belongs to a generation more terminally disillusioned about politics. Yet while he rejects a political career in favour of poetry and a life of aesthetic pursuits, he does not fully renounce the impulse to address political figures and intervene in political culture. Catullus represents a key phase in the development whereby first-person Roman poets first display *libertas* in their capacity to comment on political events and figures (Lucilius), and later end up defining their *libertas* by their distance and exclusion from the public realm (Augustan lyric and elegy). Despite his political interests, however, Catullus has no illusions about achieving a seamless synthesis of the political and the literary. Catullus isolates the intrinsic aesthetic qualities of poetry at the expense of traditional content and conventional notions of moral benefit, and sharply refuses to allow that social heft or political prestige can have any influence over, or be translated into, literary worth. He playfully assumes diverse literary *personae*, even as he casts doubt on his verses' capacity to represent their author's life and morals. Catullus does not commit to a stable model of literature's social role, but instead premises his autonomist strategy at least in part on the elusiveness of his self-representational gestures.

Cicero's *Consulatus suus* pursues a markedly different self-representational project in the epic genre. His third-person poetic narration of his deeds during his own consulship harnesses the communal ideology of epic to the promotion of his personal glory. Cicero, no less than Lucilius and Catullus, represents the splintering of the putative communal project of epic praise into individual acts of self-fashioning, yet he still struggles to accommodate the aims of individual self-promotion with the ideal of heroic action on behalf of the whole Roman community. Cicero's solution to the problem of, on the one hand, epic's traditional corporatist ideology, and, on the other, the need for individual self-promotion in an age of antagonistic politics and conflicting factions, was to identify his personal accomplishments with the salvation of Rome. He avoids any appearance of an open break with traditional axiological priorities, and so poetry and other learned pursuits remain explicitly subordinate to the interests of the state and public life. Catullus, by contrast, endeavours to persuade his readers in a series of meta-self-representational poems (c.4, c.10, c.11) that he will *not* harness his poetry to self-promotional utility. Catullus at once fashions poetic *personae* and calls attention to their manufacture, frustrating any straightforward attempt to link literary self-representation with a stable set of shared values. Catullus' autonomist self-representational tendencies present a sharp contrast to Cicero's continual attempts to integrate literary pursuits with service to the *res publica*.

Chapter 2, 'Autarky, Withdrawal, Confinement: The autonomist niche in early Augustan poetry', examines poetic works written in the closing years of the republic and the immediate post-Actium period. I argue that in these transitional years the Lucilian and Catullan model of invective *libertas* makes way for a very different conception of *libertas* grounded in the security of high-level patronage and the *otium* afforded by social stability. Horace *Satires* 1, Virgil's *Eclogues*, Propertius *Elegies* 1, and Tibullus *Elegies* 1 fashion slender realms of autonomy in which the poet pursues a life of autarkic seclusion, rural tranquility, and/or amorous absorption. In all but one of these works, the poet's slender poetic domain is embodied in an elegant *libellus* of ten poems, and the poet's autonomist 'niche' relies on the support of a grand patron figure (Maecenas, Octavian, Messalla). The poets of this period strive to create a world apart from the chaos that surrounds them, even as they recognize that their own powers to do so are limited and that any autonomy they achieve may be short-lived and dependent on the whim of those in power.

Horace, in *Satires* 1, at once follows and distances himself from the Lucilian model, redefining satire as a genre of verbal restraint and autarkic contentment. For the satirist, however, maintaining a condition of autarky is not easy: he is constantly assaulted by the rumours, in-fighting, and social posturing of urban life. He claims to be contented, self-sufficient, and happily removed from the fray, yet his own friendship with the influential Maecenas renders these claims dubious in the eyes of contemporaries. Virgil's *Eclogues*, while not a work of first-person poetry per se, merits some consideration within this chapter because of its intensely metaliterary mode of mimesis. The poet's bucolic landscape is peopled by poet-shepherds who discuss their song and the conditions in which their song is produced. Virgil, like Horace, struggles to maintain a slender domain of tranquility, a refuge from the turbulence that threatens to overwhelm him. In a certain sense, pastoral poetry *is* that space of autonomy—but it remains a fragile one. Propertius' first book of elegy also describes itself as a kind of refuge, a delimited world where love dominates and from which politics and warfare are excluded. The first-person speaker claims to be trapped in a condition of *servitium* which is ostensibly the opposite of autonomy. Yet by a counter-intuitive twist, this continuous state of servitude shores up the autonomy of Propertius' elegiac realm by reinforcing its boundaries and excluding non-amorous discourse and concerns. Behind the claims of helpless servitude, one may discern the carefully designed strategies of Propertius' autonomist poetics. Finally, I will examine how Propertius' contemporary and fellow love-poet, Tibullus, combines Propertian elegiac *servitium* with rural autarky reminiscent of Virgil and Horace. Tibullus, often dismissed as marginal, is in fact a centrally Augustan figure: he explores the complementarities and contradictions of these two major paradigms of Augustan literary self-sufficiency.

In Chapter 3, 'The Expansion of Autonomy: Augustan poetry (ca. 25 BC–AD 17)', I examine how in the middle and later Augustan period autonomist rhetoric shifts to accommodate a more public status and importance for literary activity and a less sequestered position for the poet. Horace's *Odes* and *Epistles*, Propertius Books 2–4, and Ovid's love and exile poetry diversely reflect the need to renegotiate poetic autonomy in changing conditions. The victory of the faction of Octavian and Maecenas means that poets connected with them now enjoy a greater public profile, while the explicit cultural interests of the new regime, as embodied in the Temple of Palatine Apollo, award poetry a newly prominent place in the city. The autonomist 'niche' of early Augustan poetry is rapidly becoming obsolete, yet autonomist rhetoric remains central to poets' efforts to negotiate their status and maintain an image of integrity in this ideologically fraught setting. Much previous criticism, in attempting to decide whether a given Augustan text should be judged 'pro-Augustan' or 'anti-Augustan', propagandistic or autonomous, has missed the central point: the poets' approach is designed to render decisive answers to such questions impossible. My argument, however, is distinct from the common claim that it is wrong to label texts anti- or pro-Augustan

because of their intrinsic 'indeterminacy'. The Augustan poets' politically 'indeterminate' stance must rather be understood as a deliberate feature of autonomist
rhetoric.

Propertius *Elegies* 2–4 illustrate aspects of the transition from the early Augustan autonomist 'niche' to the more explicitly public negotiation of poetic
autonomy in the middle and later Augustan period. Propertius progressively
abandons his opening fiction of amatory utility, and moves towards defining his
elegy as a monumental work visible in the public realm. In these later books,
Propertius less frequently employs the fiction of *servitium* to limit the lover's
scope of vision, and more frequently works to position love elegy as an overtly
literary discourse in relation to other poetic genres, the emperor's military and
political prestige, and aspects of public morality. Horace does not present himself
as an overtly 'oppositional' figure, as Propertius in some respects arguably does;
hence he is less invested in the avoidance of panegyric. Nonetheless he works hard
in his *Odes* to frame, qualify, and delimit the nature of the praise he offers, while
solidifying his autonomist rhetoric. The autarkic realm of the Sabine farm, in
particular, functions as a figure for the autonomy of poetic space.

In the case of both poets, the project of autonomist rhetoric should not
necessarily be understood as simply vindicating poetic *libertas* in the face of
ideological pressures, or if they do seek 'freedom' of a certain kind, it is a reduced
and contracted *libertas*. While Propertius espouses a more overtly counter-cultural style, and Horace has seemed to many scholars to be more accommodating
to the interests of the Augustan regime, both writers work within the ideological
framework of *otium* underwritten by the *pax Augusta*. The autonomist poetic
strategies of the Augustan poets can be read equally as establishing claims of
poetic integrity and as contributing to an 'ideology of the aesthetic' that keeps
literature contained within its own domain. The invective ferocity of Catullus and
Lucilius has no place in the new cultural order; the role of Maecenas' poets, at least
in part, is to redraw the boundaries of poetic discourse in order to reinforce this
exclusion.[83] At the same time, the notionally apolitical, aesthetic integrity of their
poetry confers on instances of praise and affirmation of Augustan values all the
greater persuasive force.

Horace's *Epistles* continue to be concerned with the question of how a public
poet can maintain (the appearance of) autonomy, yet with some striking
changes of emphasis. The *Epistles* pose a question that will resonate throughout
the subsequent early imperial period: on what basis can autonomist rhetoric
subsist without the sequestered space of ludic seclusion? In the later decades of
Augustus' reign, Ovid pushes autonomist rhetoric to a new degree of confrontational intensity. His *Amores* and *Ars amatoria* assume the autonomous validity
of poetic/amorous activity with a cool, ironic insouciance, while expanding the
field of love beyond its earlier Callimachean exclusiveness to include the urban
crowd and mass spectacle. There is no longer any question of a secluded poetic
realm or the poet's autarky. Questions of autonomy are displaced onto the more
expansive dynamics of Augustan ideology, urban seduction games, and the
sophisticated *mores* of the contemporary City. His exile poetry, however,

---

[83] On this project of 'segregation', see in particular Ruffle (2003).

represents perhaps the most extreme and testing scenario for poetic autonomy. The poet, relegated to the edge of the civilized world by the emperor, must explore what it means to continue writing poetry in a condition of apparent heteronomy.

Chapter 4, 'Materialities of Use and Subordination: The challenge of the autonomist legacy', examines how the idea of poetic *heteronomy* comes into its own as a major organizing concept in works of the early imperial period. Persius, Statius, Martial, and Juvenal are all self-conscious heirs to the Augustan self-representational tradition, which includes autonomy among its core themes. Autonomy is now part of the 'DNA structure' of first-person poetry, and yet, for various reasons, autonomist rhetoric cannot be simply reproduced on the Augustan model. For one thing, the Augustan themselves saturated the literary field with their autonomist self-portraiture. Direct replication of the Horatian lyric poet in his rural *secessus,* or the elegiac lover enslaved to his narrow frame of concerns, would risk appearing excessively derivative. Second, and more important, is the fact that the social and cultural conditions for writing poetry are no longer the same. The immense celebrity achieved by the most successful Augustan poets has given the lie to the idea of the reclusive, autarkic poet-figure. At the same time, Ovid's example and the less tolerant cultural climate of the early imperial period have severely compromised the idea of poetry as a 'safe' space of tranquility and freedom.

The old *cliché* of the poet sequestered in his *nemus* persists, yet is now hedged around by irony, equivocation, and, in some cases, ferocious satiric denunciation. Nevertheless the new rhetoric of heteronomy keeps autonomist rhetoric in play by systematically inverting it. If Martial and Statius place stress on the ephemeral, occasion-bound, and use-directed nature of their poetry, they cannot help evoking, and maintaining contact with, the concept of the poetic work as transcendent, immortal, and detached from quotidian uses. Persius depicts the banalization of poetry, the nauseating fatuity of its conversion into social capital, and yet the pessimism of this critique is accompanied by a fierce effort to prevent his own satiric verse from being corrupted by the preening mellifluousness of the age. Finally, for Juvenal, the city of Rome works to destroy any possibility of poetic autonomy. Urban life demands a constant servility on the part of everyone except the rich, and poetry is as desperately self-promoting and materialist as any other occupation. This very idea, however, depends on the (inverted, tarnished) ideal of autonomy for its formation, and the satirist's later work explores more overtly the possibility of reviving, in sometimes ironic, fragmentary, and qualified fashion, the inherited motifs of autonomist rhetoric.

Autonomy, then, was not an achieved state for Roman poets, a condition they simply embraced and could then take for granted on an unchanging theoretical basis. There was continual effort, through an ingenious and always-changing gambit of rhetorical strategies, to promote poetry's status as first-order occupation, to advertise its prestige as comparable with that of public life, to secure patronal support even while maintaining an image of autarkic self-sufficiency, to define poetic value and literary 'utility' in opposition to conventional valuations of worthwhile activity. In the early imperial period, these strategies shift again to produce a series of brilliant heteronomist inversions of autonomist rhetoric—a testimony, however darkly pessimistic, to the continuing importance of the autonomist paradigm. Despite its importance, autonomy could never fully be taken for granted, but rather followed the jagged, irregular line of the continually shifting tactics of Roman poets. In the modern world, autonomy has achieved the status of a default doctrine, but in the ancient world the institutional and theoretical apparatus underpinning such stability was not in place. It is thus all the more illuminating and absorbing to attempt to trace the path of this powerful yet profoundly unstable idea in a period when its very validity was in question.

1

First-Person Poetry and the Autonomist Turn

Lucilius, Catullus, and Cicero's
Consulatus suus

INTRODUCTION

Writing a verse-epistle in elegiac couplets from Verona to a friend in Rome, Catullus begs indulgence for not having sent him any poems. His excuse affords an unusual glimpse into the everyday working conditions of the *doctus poeta*:

> nam, quod scriptorum non magna est copia apud me,
>   hoc fit, quod Romae vivimus: illa domus,
> illa mihi sedes, illic mea carpitur aetas;
>   huc una ex multis capsula me sequitur.   (c. 68.33–6)

As for the fact that I do not have a great abundance of writers with me, that is because I live at Rome: that is my home, that is my dwelling-place, there my life is led; only one little book-box out of many follows me here.

Catullus needs a great supply of books to write poetry properly (*magna . . . copia*), and his main collection of books resides, not at Verona or in his villa, but at Rome, where the poet's life is.[1] Life, books, and writing are fused in one location, one *sedes*, for Catullus. By implicit association, the poet's life becomes defined by the central tasks of reading and writing: in Verona, where only one book-box (*capsula*) follows him, his life is incomplete.

This scenario is deceptively familiar to us as modern readers: the writer, ensconced in his book-filled study, is wholly absorbed in his occupation and the toils of his literary trade. In the modern, autonomist paradigm, writing does not subserve any greater purpose than the aesthetic perfection of its task, and is presumed to be a worthwhile end unto itself. While it would be going too far to

---

[1] See Fordyce (1961), ad loc. This interpretation works best if *scriptorum* is the genitive plural of *scriptor*, but others see it as the genitive plural of *scripta*, i.e. Catullus' own: Thomson (1997), ad loc.

ascribe to Catullus so radically disembedded a conception of literary activity,[2] less arguable are his serious devotion to poetic craft, his project of severing literary value from conventional notions of worthwhile subject matter, and the self-reflexive tendency of his poetry. Poetry, for Catullus, is an absorbing and worthy occupation on its own terms, not an ancillary supplement to some other more important sphere of achievement.[3] Again, for us moderns, steeped in the doctrine of aesthetic autonomy, the idea seems reasonable enough, but in republican Rome, Catullus' case was unusual, if not provocative.[4] Poetry was classed among non-essential cultural pursuits associated with the Greeks. The Romans traditionally distrusted such pursuits, and made a point of adopting them only in instances where they served the aims of the Roman state and the ruling elite.[5]

These constraining conditions inform the dominant stereotypes of the poet's social role: the client poet, who pens the praises of eminent individuals and noble families; the professional poet, who writes patriotic epic or drama for public performance at *ludi scaenici;* and, in a later development, the aristocratic dilettante, who composes verses during periods of *otium* at his villa. These dominant poetic types do not always respond to the full complexity of individual cases, but remain heuristically useful insofar as they provide a rough sketch of existing *idées fixes* regarding the poetic role in middle to late republican Rome. Catullus at once responds to and plays at the edges of these paradigms. For example, his metapoetic lexicon often evokes the ludic dilettantism of aristocratic leisure: his poems are *nugae* ('trifles'), *facetiae* ('witticisms'), *ioci* ('jests'), *versiculi* ('light verse'). But elsewhere he makes it clear that he despises the wealthy amateur who writes poetry to gratify himself, and in general, his poetic practice cannot be sequestered within a sophisticated, Hellenizing niche. Neither, however, can he be classified as a 'professional' or 'client' poet.[6] Catullus often seems to be working both with and against contemporary Roman paradigms of the poet's role and poetry's social

---

[2] Fitzgerald (1995), 55, especially wishes to 'bring into focus aspects of poetry and the aesthetic relation that have been obscured by modern emphasis on textuality, figurativeness, and even expressivity of poetic discourse'.

[3] Zetzel (1982), 92: 'where earlier poets if they were well-to-do, Lutatius Catulus for example, could not have regarded their literary endeavors as anything more than a relaxation from public life, the neoterics seem to regard poetry as a way of life itself, a social code with its own exclusively literary hierarchy of values and relationships'.

[4] Again, the term is Fitzgerald's (*Catullan Provocations*, 1995). He was referring mostly to other types of provocation, but in broad terms his model applies here as well: 'the Catullus I have described is one who provokes us to think about what kind of a practice poetry is, about its continuities with the situations of everyday speech, and about why we read it' (237). I would add that Catullus' simulation of everyday speech-situations may also work to call attention to *discontinuity*, the distance between poetic 'speech' and quotidian communication.

[5] 'On the writing of poetry ... the Roman aristocrat, though he might turn a verse with ease, or fill a volume, set no especial value. But it was now becoming evident that poetry, besides and above mere invective, could be made an instrument of government by conveying a political message, unobtrusive, but perhaps no less effective, than the spoken or written word of Roman statesmen' (Syme (1939), 251).

[6] Catullus appears to be closely connected with prominent men in Roman society who would normally be interpreted as fulfilling the role of patron for him: Cornelius Nepos, Gaius Memmius, Licinius Calvus, and even Julius Caesar. He is careful, however, not to give even the appearance of praising anyone's deeds, least of all being anyone's client: Zetzel (1982), 92. See Wiseman (1982), 39, and Stroup (2010), 13. The latter is rightly sceptical of the idea of Catullus as 'the first and last villa-owning Republican who willingly assumed the position of the *cliens*' (13).

value. There is no already established category that corresponds to his ambitions and interests.

A further layer of complexity derives from the elusively playful approach to autobiography in Catullus' first-person poetic mode, and the question of the alignment of ethics and aesthetics. The citation at the opening of this chapter provides only one instance of the ways in which the poet from Verona offers his readers compelling fragments of a writer's life amid his artfully informal literary 'trifles'. The portrait of Catullus that emerges especially from his polymetric poems is that of a clever, transgressive devotee of risqué *otium*, who flouts traditional Roman seriousness in favour of the sophisticated milieu of love-affairs, poetry, and urbanity. He derides dusty *Annales* and immerses himself instead in a world of elegant toys and playthings. This self-portrait, as I will argue, comprises an important facet of Catullus' autonomist rhetoric. The image of a life lived independently of traditionalist values is employed to suggest the writer's autonomy. At the same time, if one scratches beneath the surface of this rhetorical pose, it becomes apparent that axiological autonomy is not simply equivalent to poetic autonomy. The values of sophisticated *otium* and urbanity were shared by Catullus with members of the Roman political class, and do not in themselves constitute a radical basis for the autonomy of poetry as practice or as mimetic sphere. Catullus himself, moreover, problematized the link between biographical author and poetic work (c. 16, on which, see below). Catullus thus combines and moves between two different autonomist strategies: he at once evokes vivid images of a life infused with autonomist values (*otium*, *urbanitas*, rejection of politics and *mos maiorum*), and asserts the autonomy of the poetic work as premised on a division between aesthetics and ethics. These two strategies may appear to be logically exclusive of each other, but in Catullus' poetic practice, are employed in subtle combination and alternation.

Strategies of poetic self-representation such as Catullus' are framed in relation to (perceived) social and political conditions. In the late republican period at Rome, political discord and the dysfunctional status of the *res publica* are inevitably dominant themes. Here too we need to beware of absorbing a seductively compelling origins-story: high-principled provincials such as Catullus were disillusioned with the communal project of politics, and driven to the refuge of first-person poetry and aesthetics. Missing in this account is an awareness of the tactical aspect of Catullus' self-representational rhetoric, how he at once responds to and takes advantage of the political discord of the late republic in order to fashion his autonomist position. One casualty of late republican political discord was a weakening of the traditional ethical priorities premised on the primacy of the *res publica* and public life. At the same time, the heightened attention to individualized self-promotion within the intensified competitive environment of late republican politics afforded a model for comparably individualist acts of *literary* self-commemoration. Now that a shared core of traditionalist values no longer even notionally bound literary activity to the communal ends of the Roman state, the writer was less constrained to adopt a utilitarian and corporatist model of literary production. An ambitious writer was thus all the better enabled to employ images of the shipwrecked *res publica* in order to establish and frame his first-person voice. Factional discord provided both model and justification for literary self-fashioning.

In order to better understand the fraught and often violent context in which the first-person rhetoric of poetic autonomy takes shape, I will begin by examining extant fragments of the late second-century BC satirist Lucilius. Lucilius, arguably the first major Roman poet to create a sustained, first-person literary *persona* in Latin verse, wrote in the Gracchan period, which saw the beginning of a series of intra-elite conflicts that would end with the establishment of the principate. It is significant that, in such circumstances, Lucilius does not turn away from politics to a private realm of aesthetic refinement, but uses his satiric pulpit to set different voices and discourses in dialogue with each other. Lucilius persuasively represents himself as an independent voice, an example of authenticity and *libertas* in a world of faddish imitators, shabby poetasters, and pretentious scoundrels. He does not fence off a separate domain for poetry, so much as seek to chart a path of commonsense integrity amid the chaotic chatter of the age.[7]

I will go on to examine the poetry of Catullus, with particular but not exclusive focus on his vividly self-representational polymetrics (c. 1–c. 60).[8] Catullus continues the Lucilian tradition of *libertas*, but in a more overtly disillusioned mood and with frequent intimations of the impotence of poetic speech. Catullus' turn away from politics to the private sphere of love, friendship, and poetry distinguishes his first-person voice from Lucilius', and forms the basis for the autonomist *personae* of imperial poetry. At the same time, he initiates a tradition of playful manipulation of text and reality, *persona* and author. Even as his verses vividly evoke a life of urbane *otium*, he intermittently casts doubt on the poetic text's status as faithful reflection of the poet's extra-textual ethics.[9] This strategy of simultaneously evoking and undercutting poetic *personae* contributes to an autonomist strategy of evasion. More conspicuous than the tendency to identify himself with a specific value-set of the Roman elite (e.g. *urbanitas*) is Catullus' project of avoiding compromising alignment with any single prestige-garnering discourse.

---

[7] For a synthetic discussion, see Gruen (1992), 272–318.

[8] The distinctive literary and stylistic qualities of the polymetrics have been examined by many scholars: for example, Ross (1969); Svennung (1945); Solodow (1989). Skinner (1981) provides a detailed argument for a polymetric *libellus* (1–51). But note a recent challenge of the category in Jocelyn (1999). Although I am sympathetic to the idea that our collection retains at least significant traces of an original Catullan ordering, my argument does not require either a distinct polymetric mode, or a polymetric *libellus*; my focus is on self-representational and poetological poems, and the polymetrics offer some of the most important, although hardly the only, instances.

[9] The traditional application of the persona-theory to Catullus is represented by Nappa (2001). Other work on Catullus from the last two decades or so does not tend to accept a stable division between Catullus the author and Catullus the persona: e.g. Fitzgerald (1995); Wray (2001). In general, recent work on poetic self-representation in Latin poetry problematizes the persona–author divide and lifts the ban on terms such as 'autobiography'; see, for example, Gowers (2003), and the overview in McCarthy (2010). My present use of the term *persona* is similarly not meant to evoke a monolithic division of realms—fictive on one side, and real or biographical on the other. As Cicero knew, people, including Roman authors, have recourse to different 'masks' in the course of negotiating diverse scenarios of daily life, and while the type of mask employed in a literary text may indeed be different in certain ways from other sorts of masks and avail itself of certain distinctive forms of fictionality, the literary author's use of a *persona* ultimately cannot be separated from his intentions, reputation, actions, and interests in the world any more than can his quotidian use of *personae* in social interactions.

I will begin by examining Catullus' metaliterary poems in an effort to unpack his recurrent rhetorical strategy of distinguishing intrinsic poetic value (craft, inspiration, labour) from extrinsic factors (conventionally valued subject matter, resplendent deeds), and his poetic play with concepts of time. In these ludic reflections on literary aesthetics, Catullus often aggressively argues for ideas of literary value, yet ultimately evades being linked with a stable cultural domain or explicit set of aesthetic principles. I will then go on to explore the interaction of poetry, politics, and self-representation, the ways in which Catullus interrogates the techniques and ethics of self-representation. Here too we note an evasive tendency in Catullan self-representational rhetoric. He represents scenes of travel and transit, but avoids settled life-conditions and stable axiological identifications. Autonomist rhetoric for Catullus displays a dynamic aspect; he plays between various models of poetic identity without committing to any single existing paradigm. This strategy speaks to the fact that existing models of the poet's role were heteronomist in overall tendency. In the project of defining his poetry's non-ancillary status, Catullus was seeking to articulate largely unprecedented concepts of literary value.

Finally, I will compare Catullus' approach to poetic self-representation with the very different set of self-representational, ethical, and literary assumptions in Cicero's *Consulatus suus*. Cicero and Catullus represent, respectively, integration-ist and autonomist approaches to literature: for Cicero, there is a persistent impulse to accommodate literary activity to a traditional, unified Roman value system; Catullus tends to expose the breakdown of coherent systems of value, and to use that breakdown as the background to his autonomist project. Here it might be objected that Cicero writes in a wholly different genre from the polymetric Catullus, but this difference is at the core of my argument. In order to understand the emergence of the first-person poetic tradition at Rome, we need to understand the ideological and aesthetic consequences inherent in the very choice and formation of genres.

LUCILIUS: SATIRE AND THE SELF-REPRESENTATIONAL TRADITION

Well-born, well-connected, and wealthy, Lucilius might have pursued a political career had he chosen to do so. The quality of his work, comparable to that of the professional poets,[10] suggests that he spent a great deal of time writing, although to what extent he embraced anything like a writer's vocation remains an open question. Most accounts of self-representational poetry in Rome underrate Lucilius' significance, and begin effectively with Catullus. His influence has been underestimated not least because modern scholars, following Horace, place him in a lower category of literary achievement. Lucilius' facetious, prolix style is presumed inept compared with Catullus' erudite Callimacheanism. Yet Lucilius

---

[10] Farrell (2002), 41: 'the first member of the patron class whose contribution to Latin literature stands comparison with that of any professional'.

resembles Catullus in several important respects: he writes in a self-representational genre, narrates humorous incidents of everyday life, employs a broad lexical and tonal range, and demonstrates invective *libertas* in attacking the grand figures of his times. Nor is it accidental that Horace, casting about in the 30s for a form of self-representational verse adequate to his interests and ambitions, turned to the genre Lucilius pioneered. If Horace made a point of disparaging Lucilius' technical faults, he clearly admired his project of literary autobiography.[11] Lucilius, from this perspective, is a foundational figure not only for satire, but for Roman self-representational poetry.[12] He provides a notable, early example of a writer of the Italian equestrian class using the medium of verse to promote an image of himself and his life.[13]

Verse, however, is not necessarily 'poetry' in the grand sense, and a tensional attitude towards poetry itself is a key part of Lucilius' literary position. Lucilius is the inventor of the satiric tradition of informal speech (*sermo*) later explicitly defined by its distance from poetry proper.[14] Surviving instances of metaliterary vocabulary applied by the satirist to his own work do not include words derived from the Greek term *poiēsis*. Rather Lucilius employs the lexicon of ludic informality: *schedium* ('improvisation'), *sermo* ('talk, conversation'), *ludus* ('play').[15] Lucilius appears to have been highly critical of the respected *poetae* of his age, Pacuvius and Accius, and writes more as a chatty social commentator than as a figure inspired by Muses or Camenae. Modern readers tend to be sceptical of claims of non-poetic status when the writer enunciates such claims in verse while otherwise displaying an acute awareness of poetic traditions. The question appears to have been less straightforward in ancient Rome, where poetry was at least notionally defined by an established set of *Greek* genres.[16] Lucilius' insistence on an informal, speech-based genre (*sermo*) without Greek precedent at the very least renders his poetic identity controversial.

Lucilius may even have designedly chosen a genre that did not stamp him indelibly as a poet because of the associations of poetry in Rome with humble

---

[11] Hor. *Sat.* 2.1.30–4, 71–4.

[12] This is the emphasis of K. Haß (2007), a study of Lucilius and 'der Beginn der Persönlichkeitsdichtung in Rom': 20–5 and *passim*.

[13] He is known to have been closely connected with Scipio Aemilianus, and in older scholarship, considered one of the members of the 'Scipionic circle'. More recent work denies both the existence of a formally established circle, and even a consistent political alignment of Lucilian satire with Scipio's policies and enmities: see Zetzel (1972), and Gruen (1992), 273 and *passim*.

[14] There is a long history of debate over the existence of pre-Lucilian satire, chiefly in the case of Ennius, whose fragments passed down under the title of 'satires' may or may not have been originally designated as such: see Knoche (1975), 16; Hooley (2007), 172, n. 4; Coffey (1976), 28; Horsfall (1981); Hendrickson (1911), 129ff.; Ingersoll (1912); Wheeler (1912). Lucilius himself may not have called his work *satura*. Yet the name in the end may matter less than the specifically Roman concept of informal, sub- or counter-poetic writing variously designated *satura*, *sermo*, *lusus*.

[15] *Ludo ac sermonibus nostris* (1039 Marx); *sermonibus* (1015, 1016 Marx). The term *poemata* (1013 Marx) apparently is put in the mouth of Lucilius' poetic adversary with whom he conducts some kind of literary debate in Book XXX. Likewise, when he uses terms such as *poesis* and *poema* (338–47 Marx), he speaks as a philosopher or critic employing technical vocabulary, not as a practitioner. See also Goldberg (2005), 26.

[16] Hor. *Sat.* 1.4.39–63; Persius *prologue*. The largely non-mythological content of the *Bellum civile* and absence of divine machinery led some ancient readers of Lucan to deny him the status of poet, whereas others championed him precisely as a great poet (Martial *Epigrams* (*Spect.*) 14.194).

social status, professional expertise, and *clientela*.[17] Lucilius displays an aristocratic disdain for technical expertise and excessive erudition, explicitly demanding a middle-brow readership, neither too ignorant nor too erudite.[18] The entire Lucilian literary stance is opposed to a technical degree of specialization, which might seem too Greek. He displays a gentleman's broad range of knowledge; he is a competent dabbler in various fields, an amusing mimic of the learned idiolects circulating throughout an increasingly Hellenized Rome, but refuses to be confined to any one domain. In some sense, this position at the margins of poetry, which later Horace and Persius will adopt in differing circumstances and for different reasons, enhances his personal autonomy as satiric writer. He is not circumscribed by poetic traditions, the poet's social status, and poetic group-identity as embodied, for example, in the *collegium poetarum* ('poets' guild').[19] Lucilius, however, represents a unique case. If he insists strongly on his own independent path as writer, it is equally clear that other writers of inferior social status could not follow that same path. His satiric *libertas* does not belong to a broader set of poetic possibilities available for others to imitate and build upon; he is *sui generis*.

Coherent with Lucilius' designedly amateurist self-definitional tendency is the absence of any discernible 'cult' of craft—an absence that has had a negative impact on his subsequent literary reputation. No doubt Lucilian verse was perfectly respectable, not to mention well crafted, given the standards of his time.[20] But too much care over such matters would have been counter to Lucilius' programmatic disdain for excessive refinement and his critique of learned pretensions generally. Lucilius never gives the impression that literary artifice and aesthetic perfection might be seen as ends in themselves. The surviving fragments are peppered with satirical references to the fetishization of trendy, Hellenizing *objets d'art*, aesthetic pretensions, and newfangled oratorical practices that privilege dazzling artisanal effects over straightforward communication. Some of the better-known fragments of Lucilius show Q. Mucius Scaevola, brought up on charges of extortion in 119 or 118 BC, disparaging his adversary Albucius' oratorical pretensions.

> 'quam lepide lexis compostae ut tesserulae omnes
> arte pavimento atque emblemate vermiculato.'
>
> 'Crassum habeo generum, ne rhetoricoterus tu seis'.   (84–6 Marx)

'How ingeniously his *bons mots* are arranged, artfully like all the little *tesserae* in a paved floor or a mosaic inlaid with wriggly patterns.'

'I have Crassus as a son-in-law lest you are too much inclined to play the *rhetor*.'

---

[17] Konstan (2005), 349, observes that 'the Roman aristocracy of the [middle republican] period disdained to write poetry, at least in the popular forms of drama, epic, and commissioned lyrics', citing as further support Cicero's statement that poets were 'recognized late' in Rome (*Tusc.* 1.1.3.). This does not mean that aristocratic patrons failed to respect poets, or to treat them in an amicable way with a loose assumption of 'easy comradeship' (Konstan, 348, on Ennius and the Scipios).

[18] 592–6 Marx.

[19] Note his apparent feud with Accius (or a literary adversary variously identified), with sarcastic reference to his position in the collegium: *cui sua committunt mortali claustra Camenae* (1028 Marx); so Krenkel (1970), ad loc. (fr. 1068). On the *collegium poetarum*, see Horsfall (1976).

[20] Horace declares that Lucilius, if he had lived in contemporary Rome, would have adopted current standards and taken exquisite pains over his verse: *Sat.* 1.10.67–71.

The trendy vocabulary of 'social performance'[21] (*lepide*) and Greek terminology (*lexis, rhetoricoterus*) signal Mucius' parodic dismissal of Albucius in his adversary's own language. Can we assume Lucilius shared his disdain of such artfully fashioned phrases? While the satirist's version of the trial likely offered astute commentary on both parties rather than a condemnation of one side,[22] he is still far from endorsing Albucius' Hellenizing artificiality. Lucilius, moreover, surely appreciated Scaevola's sharp reminder that at Rome social and familial connections matter more than a rhetorician's posturing. As the practical joke Scaevola played on Albucius in Athens shows,[23] there was nothing wrong with having specialized Greek knowledge per se; it was being publicly 'outed' as a self-indulgent enthusiast of such knowledge that was humiliating and left one vulnerable to others' disdain. Lucilius' position as satirist, his capacity to mimic others' faddish modes of speech within the distancing frame of satire, enabled him to derive a rich vein literary material from the culture wars of the second century BC without necessarily committing himself to one faction or the other.

In some cases, however, his opinions are clear enough. The following fragment might serve, *unum pro multis*, to demonstrate Lucilius' feelings about the ornate, hyper-literary vocabulary of contemporary tragic poetry.

> lascivire pecus Neri rostrique repandum.   (Warmington 235=212 Marx)
> Nereus' flock frolics with turned-up snouts.

Poetry's distance from everyday speech is here ridiculed, and in general, Lucilius is critical of what might be termed the autonomization of poetic style. Lucilius does not subscribe to the isolation of the intrinsic, aesthetic dimension of literary craft or an insistence on a specialized conception of poetic expertise. Indeed, Lucilius' off-the-cuff remarks tend in the opposite direction. He displays a healthy scepticism towards, or, at the very least, an amused, ironic sufferance of, the pretensions of specialized vocabularies and autotelic literary display. This does not mean, of course, that he is averse to showing off his sometimes considerable skill, but much of his skill resides in the very simulation of off-handedness that disavows properly literary ambitions. Anticipating and influencing Horace, Lucilius develops a formidable facility in balancing the literary formality of the hexameter line with the uneven rhythms of colloquial *sermo*.

> num censes calliplocamon callisphyron ullam
> non licitum esse uterum atque etiam inguina tangere mammis,
> conpernem aut varam fuisse Amphitryonis acoetin
> Alcmenam atque alias, Helenam ipsam denique—nolo
> dicere; tute vide atque disyllabon elige quodvis—
> κούρην eupatereiam aliquam rem insignem habuisse,
> verrucam, naevum, punctum, dentem eminulum unum?   (540–6 Marx)

---

[21] The term used by Krostenko (2001).

[22] Gruen (1992), 274 states, in general terms, that 'Lucilius stood apart'; he could 'enjoy a combination of internal connections and external detachment' (280). See also Gruen's discussion of Lucilius' attitude towards Hellenism and 'Hellenic affectations' (307).

[23] 88–94 Marx.

Surely you don't think it's forbidden for any 'lovely-tressed', 'beautiful-ankled' heroine to have breasts touching her stomach or even her groin, for Alcmena, 'consort of Amphitryon', to have been knock-kneed or varicose-veined, and others—Helen herself, in fine... (I'm reluctant to say—you look to it and choose whatever disyllabic word you want)... for a *jeune fille de bonne famille* to have some distinguishing mark—a wart, a mole, a mark, a little tooth that sticks out?

Ornamental Greek adjectives (*calliplocamon, callisphyron, eupatereiam*) are skilfully integrated into the long sentence that punctures their artificiality. This ostensibly meandering question—which includes a nicely witty parenthetical *praeteritio* of possible disyllabic words to describe Helen (e.g. *scortum, moecham*)—is in fact a *tour de force* demonstrating Lucilius' ability to sustain intricate syntax over several lines without losing force or point. The fragment ends brilliantly with an asyndetic crescendo of realistically singular physical marks: *verrucam, naevum, punctum, dentem eminulum unum* ('a wart, a mole, a mark, a little tooth that sticks out?'). The last word, *unum*, aptly embodies the veristic singularity of satire that puts the lie to epic's top-heavy apparatus of generic praise-terminology. Satire's spare aesthetic brusquely refuses literary polish and prettiness while tacitly developing sophisticated literary artifice of another kind.[24]

Despite Lucilius' underappreciated literary skill, the core impetus of his literary criticism opposes the cult of esoteric poetic style and aestheticizing distance from everyday speech. Lucilian *sermo*, rather than pointing to the intrinsic separateness of poetic language, is a mode of vigorous engagement with the Roman world and its leading figures. The prime scenario of Lucilian satire is not sequestration, but public engagement, invective rancour, disagreement. Such conflict can be seen as a catalysing ingredient in the development of the first-person voice in Roman poetry. Lucilius at once joins the fray and stands outside it, excoriating his contemporaries' extremity in *their* voices in order to define his own. Still, there is a limit to satiric mimicry beyond which he will not go. The following fragments specifically treat the question of a limit to the 'mutations' of the Lucilian persona.

> at libertinus, tricorius, Syrus ipse, at mastigias,
> quicum versipellis fio et quicum conmuto omnia.   (669–70 Marx)
>
> publicanus vero ut Asiae fiam, ut scripturarius,
> pro Lucilio, id ego nolo, et uno hoc non muto omnia.   (671–2 Marx)

...but a freedman, a rascally whipping boy three times over,[25] Syrus himself, with whom I change my skin and with whom I exchange everything... But to become a tax-farmer in Asia, a collector of tax on pasturage, instead of Lucilius—that I do not wish, and won't take the whole world in exchange for this one thing.

---

[24] See discussion of Morgan (2005), 176–7, who notes the deliberate juxtaposition of flowing Homeric hexameters and Lucilius' own rough-edged use of the metre, and hails the second line of the fragment as a 'splendid piece of metrical vandalism' (177).

[25] For *tricorius*, compare Plautus *Poen.* 138: *heri in tergo meo / tris facile corios contrivisti bubulos.* The reader for Oxford University Press makes the intriguing suggestion that 669–70 may refer obliquely to the Saturnalia. Certainly the combination of an impertinent servile figure and the exchange of roles would support this link, and it would have the added benefit of affording a Lucilian background to the figure of Davus in Horace *Sat.* 2.7.

Lucilius, apparently faced with some kind of trickster figure of low social status, is in danger of 'changing his skin' and 'exchanging everything'. A limit to such 'exchange' eventually emerges, however, and the contentious issue of *publicani* ('state contractors/tax-farmers') in the province of Asia in particular serves to articulate that limit for Lucilius. He would not accept the 'world' (*omnia*) in exchange for paying such a price. The capacity to say 'no' (*id ego nolo*), to insist on one limit, one strict and immoveable criterion of what it means to be 'Lucilius', is at the core of the satirist's first-person identity, and recalls the 'one little protruding tooth' that, from satire's perspective, defines what is real and the authentic as distinguished from the generic and false. In this case, however, the 'one' limit-case that grounds Lucilian identity could not exist without the useful foil of the Asian *publicanus*. Conflict and contention ground the satirist's identity.

Lucilius' social world is one in which one can hear the constant chatter of disagreement, of behind-the-scenes gossip and backstabbing among the Roman elite. Satire is truly a long distance from Ennian epic and its narration of worthy deeds. The difference in genres, once again, is not arbitrary or a simple matter of preference. Rather, the invention of a genre that is the polar opposite of epic is a literary act itself worth contemplating. Is it possible to be an Ennius in Lucilius' Rome? It might have been difficult to rise to Ennian heights of song on behalf of the communal endeavours of the Roman people and ruling class[26] at a time when the ruling class was divided against itself, to proclaim the unity of aristocratic and patriotic interests in the face of an emerging, wealth-infused aristocratic culture that further distanced the elite from ordinary Romans. The Gracchan period commences a phase in Roman history when even the idealizing pretence of such community becomes increasingly difficult to sustain. Hence the emergence of a genre that thrives on conflict and disagreement, the articulation of one's own point of view amid a chaotic welter of opinions. We should not necessarily see Lucilius' turn towards first-person poetry in negative terms, as the *loss* of the communal voice of Ennian epic, but rather as the experimental exploitation of a new literary opportunity made possible by the prominence of the adversarial dimension in Roman public life.

Attempting to define one's own point of view in an admittedly adversarial environment is distinct, however, from disillusioned rejection of public life and the *mos maiorum* altogether. In one famous passage, Lucilius criticizes the activities of the forum, the deceptions, manipulations of language, and in-fighting among politicians.[27]

> nunc vero a mani ad noctem, festo atque profesto
> totus item pariterque die populusque patresque
> iactare indu foro se omnes, decedere nusquam,
> uni se atque eidem studio omnes dedere et arti,
> verba dare ut caute possint, pugnare dolose,
> blanditia certare, 'bonum' simulare 'virum' se,
> insidias facere, ut si hostes sint omnibus omnes.   (1228–34 Marx)

---

[26] For Goldberg (1995), the epic 'sweep of the *Annals* subordinated individual achievement to the greater cause of Roman *gloria*' (124).

[27] For Gruen (1992), 272, the more turbulent aspects of the late second century BC made the cultural pretensions of the elite seem less merited and more foolish, thus giving rise to the possibility of satire.

But, as it is, from morning to night, on holiday and working-day, the entire populace along with the senators all alike make a spectacle of themselves in the forum; they do not go away; all devote themselves to one and the same pursuit, the same art: the capacity to cheat with circumspection, to fight with cunning, to vie in flattery, to represent themselves as 'good men', to lay traps—as if everyone were everyone else's enemy.

Lucilius' description implies a certain world-weariness and cynicism regarding political motives and strategies. Indeed, for the satirist the forum is a site of continual, relentless disagreement. Everyone, Roman people and senators, appears to be devoted to 'one and the same' thing, but that 'thing' turns out to be the art of deception, simulation, and specifically, deceptive self-representation (*bonum simulare virum se*). Yet even as they make nice in words, they lay traps, 'as if everyone were everyone's enemy'. Still, even in this rather cynical description, we do not find the sense of terminal disillusionment that marks the Catullan attitude towards politics. Lucilius' tone is at once bemused and robustly satirical, but does not go as far as to proclaim the demise of the *res publica* and his own irrevocable rejection of politics. He objects to the contemporary tenor, but not the basic viability, of public life.

In another equally famous passage, the speaker provides a definition of *virtus* ('manliness, virtue').

> virtus, Albine, est, pretium persolvere verum
> quis in versamur, quis vivimus rebus, potesse,
> virtus est, homini scire id quod quaeque habeat res,
> virtus, scire, homini rectum, utile quid sit, honestum,
> quae bona, quae mala item, quid inutile, turpe, inhonestum,
> virtus quaerendae finem re scire modumque,
> virtus divitiis pretium persolvere posse,
> virtus id dare quod re ipsa debetur honori,
> hostem esse atque inimicum hominum morumque malorum,
> contra defensorem hominum morumque bonorum,
> hos magni facere, his bene velle, his vivere amicum,
> commoda praeterea patriai prima putare,
> deinde parentum, tertia iam postremaque nostra.   (1326–38 Marx)

Virtue, Albinus, means being able to pay in full the true price in the dealings in which we are involved, in the affairs of our life; virtue means knowing what each matter may hold for a man; virtue means knowing what is right, what is expedient, what is honourable for a man, what things are good, and likewise what things are bad, what is inexpedient, disgraceful, and dishonourable; virtue means knowing the limit and proper measure in seeking wealth; virtue means being able to pay the price in full with one's store of wealth; virtue means awarding to honour what it actually merits; it means being an enemy and an opponent of bad men and bad ways, and conversely, being the defender of good men and good ways; it means placing a great value on such men, showing good will towards them, living as their friend; moreover, it means considering the interests of our country first, then the interests of our parents, and third and last, our own.

He prioritizes the importance of duty to the *patria*, followed by duty to one's parents, and lastly, one's self.[28] The axiological terms used here (*utile, inutile, honestum, inhonestum, malus, bonus*) are conventional items in the lexicon of

---

[28] Raschke (1987), a study of Lucilius' moral outlook, classifies him as broadly traditional in his value-set.

Roman morality. Lucilius' satiric world is the world of the Roman aristocracy broadly defined, its foibles and sophistications. He does not flee to a leisure-world infused with the poet's antinomian values. Insisting on one's own independence of thought in an age of overriding passions and mob violence is not the same as devising a sequestered axiological realm apart from the *mos maiorum*. Lucilian satire, far from embracing an overtly counter-traditional lifestyle, exemplifies the virtues of diplomatic intelligence, astute criticism, and commonsense judgement within the familiar arena of public life. Lucilius wrote when powerful orators such as the Gracchi were employing formidable eloquence to work on the emotions of their fellow Romans. Lucilius' is a conversational eloquence that is *not* likely to stir up anyone's passions. Lucilian satire, if it stirs up anything, excites scepticism of extremity and the awe-inspiring theatre of political display.[29]

CATULLUS: METALITERARY TRIFLES

We notice a new theme in the self-representational repertoire as we turn from Lucilius to Catullus: the rejection of public life and the world of the forum in favour of an existence of sophisticated leisure. By the middle of the first century BC, disillusionment with politics among the Roman elite has become intense and pervasive, and there is the sense, both in Catullus' poetry and elsewhere—Cicero's letters for example, or Sallust's historical writings—that the *res publica* is a broken system, and that 'everything' (*omnia*) has been lost.[30] Even before Catullus' time, the patterns of dysfunctional government had established themselves as habitual and endemic: the disruptive power of tribunes, the emergence of rival military strongmen, the erosion of the system of power-sharing and limited tenure of political office, *popularis* and optimate political strategies alternating in mutual obstruction. This sense of hopelessness in the public sphere afforded potential opportunities to writers. Though public life maintained its prestige, there was now plausible justification for an attitude of deep disillusionment, for rejection of the traditional masculine career.[31] Catullus differs from Lucilius in that his poetry works to articulate an axiologically distinct sphere of endeavour: a realm of

---

[29] For Stroup (2010), 10, Lucilius 'stands as our first example of a member of the political class who chose the life of the poet over that of the politician, and, standing coolly outside the world of the forum, criticized it actively'.

[30] Catullus c. 29.24. What Syme (1939) says of Rome under the triumvirs applies reasonably well to Catullus: 'The revulsion from politics, marked enough in the generation that had survived the wars of Marius and Sulla, now gained depth, strength, and justification' (264).

[31] See Skinner (1993); on 'the poetics of manhood' in Catullus, Wray (2001). Nappa (2001) argues that Catullus constructs a fictive literary persona through which he engages in critique of Roman society and in particular makes 'virility . . . an object for scrutiny' (42). While I will argue that Catullus does, in many cases, explore the failures and contradictions of traditional Roman values and concepts of virility, he does so, on my reading, as part of a broader set of autonomist strategies aimed at vindicating the distinctive value of poetry and poetic activity. His engagement with traditional moral categories, on this account, is strategic and informed by his particular self-representational interests; it is not a disembedded intellectual project of social critique.

provocative nugatory poetry, disreputable love affairs, *homines venustiores*, games, toys, trivialities, and aesthetic pleasures pursued to excess. At the same time, Catullus does not allow himself to be totally absorbed by a leisure-domain removed from political concerns: he turns away from public life, yet continues to write, sometimes scathingly, about the major figures of the age.[32] Catullus represents a key phase in the development whereby first-person Roman poets first display *libertas* in their capacity to comment on political events and figures (Lucilius), and later end up defining their *libertas* by their distance and exclusion from the public realm (Augustan lyric and elegy).[33]

Catullan self-representational rhetoric thus works to establish poetry 'on its own ground' by evoking a milieu of urbane *otium* to which its author notionally belongs, yet this project remain ambivalent and tensional. Furthermore, the milieu of sophisticated leisure is not in itself sufficient to establish his poetry's independent, enduring, and exclusive value. To define poetry as something rare, difficult, and worthy of its own specialized attention involves severing core aspects of its identity from the very milieu with which it is initially linked. Poetry's value is not simply reducible to the values of elite Roman *otium*. Catullus is thus involved in a subtle balancing act. He works to align his poetic activity with a determinate set of values and area of life-praxis (*urbanitas*, *otium*, *amores*, *lusus*, etc.), yet he also calls attention to points of disjunction and tension within this alignment. An elegant and witty person will not necessarily write elegant verse; morally provocative poetry might be written by a morally scrupulous author; a good person may transgress against aesthetic laws. Catullus, in his project of defining poetry's distinctive value, allows his readers to take very little for granted. In the case of Lucilius, literary style and language cohere with an approved set of elite ethical paradigms. Catullus establishes his poetry's autonomy at least in part by refusing to allow it to be identified easily with any single social domain or ethical position.

Much scholarly attention has been paid to discovering aesthetic (almost always 'Callimachean') principles seamlessly embedded in concrete scenarios of Catullan self-representation. Less attention has been paid to the dynamics of Catullan rhetoric, the disjunctive strategies whereby he seeks to narrow and define the qualities of aesthetically rigorous poetry and the nature of the expert poet. These strategies display two main tendencies. First, intrinsic factors of the poetic art—skill, *doctrina*, labour, inspiration—tend to be valued at the expense of extrinsic

---

[32] See, for example, Stroup (2010), 3: 'Catullus, a man who seems to hold himself aloof from the work of the forum—even as he is obviously well versed and deeply engaged with its activities, as befits his social status...'

[33] Buchheit (1976), 177: 'Zum ersten Mal in Rom wird der literarische Bereich ernsthaft als Lebensform deklariert'. Catullus' double-edged strategy of vindicating the value of the ostensibly trivial (*ioci*, *nugae*, etc.) produces diverging emphases in modern scholarship, depending on whether one chooses to emphasize the bold act of vindication or the self-deprecating vocabulary of triviality. With the statement of Quinn (1973), 216, that Catullus did not occupy the position of full-time writer in the Augustan manner ('We are still a long way away from Horace's life-long commitment... to a career as man of letters, from the dedicated craftsmanship of Virgil, or from the life of acknowledged *desidia* of the poet-lover Propertius') one may compare the remarks of Ross (1975): Catullus represents the first instance of a 'full-time poet of independent means' at Rome (5), and Augustan poetry is 'a natural growth in the soil prepared by Catullus' (2).

ones—morally 'worthy' subject matter, utility to the state and powerful men.[34] In making this observation, I am aware of the essentializing tendency of the distinction between extrinsic and intrinsic, utilitarian and aesthetic, and am not endorsing it, so much as tracing its workings in Catullus' autonomist rhetoric. Defining what is intrinsic and extrinsic to poetry is itself a subtle representational game, and one which Catullus plays very effectively. Second, Catullus seeks to establish that poetry is taken as seriously as political activity, and attracts a comparable degree of emotion and effort. A pervasive tension continues to mark this project, however. In order to achieve autonomy, poetic activity must be defined as essentially *different* from politics, but at the same time, *equal* to politics as an important and fully absorbing field of endeavour. Thus Catullus, even as he (at least partially and nominally) rejects politics, constructs his poetic activity as comparable with politics insofar as it too is a worthy pursuit in its own right.[35] A key aspect of Catullus' argument on behalf of poetry involves the manipulation of Roman concepts of time and memory. He rejects traditional notions of what is worthy of commemoration, supplanting Roman history with fleeting games of love and leisure, yet he also at times makes his readers aware of his dissatisfaction with the model of poetry as ephemeral diversion of *otium*. Catullus plays with and subverts expected alignments of the ephemeral and the ludic, commemoration and public worth.

In the metaliterary poems examined in the following pages, Catullus insists on the primacy of aesthetic quality over traditionalist criteria of worth and demonstrates how seriously he takes poetry, even as he deliberately aligns his writing with the jocular informality of light verse (*versiculi*). Here resides another site of tension between ethics and aesthetics: a highly polished and aesthetically 'serious' poem might be written on a trivial topic or take the ostensible form of a light jest. This tension is heightened by Catullus' frequent employment of materially concrete images of writing and texts in the poems considered below. He refers to poetry and the act of poetry composition not in materially indeterminate or figurative terms, but concretely by means of terms such as *libellus, charta, membrana, papyrus, pumex, umbilici, palimpsestus,* and *tabellae*. By gesturing towards or, in some cases, apostrophizing the material text as an object necessarily independent of himself and his voice, Catullus reinforces the division between author and poetic work, ethics and aesthetics.[36] Perhaps paradoxically, this same rhetorical gesture, which in Russian formalist criticism is termed 'baring of the device', invests the poet's first-person voice with a greater impression of vividness. 'Honest' disclosure of the text's mediation allows the poet's speech to appear

---

[34] Compare Zetzel (1982), 101: 'What was apparently in Alexandria an emphasis on the proper style of poetry was extended to include subject as well, and the dismal situation of Roman politics in the mid first century easily lent itself to such inclusion. Because they had neither the financial need nor the poetic belief nor the moral desire to write of kings (or consuls) and battles, their poetry developed into that set of countercredos which we refer to under the general rubric of neotericism'.

[35] In making this observation, I am indebted to J. Farrell's (2002) analysis of the concept of the literary career in ancient Rome, and the formation of careerist conceptions of literary activity on the model of the political career pursued by members of the 'patron class'. The present discussion will show how many of the same phenomena as those which Farrell cites can be productively viewed in terms of the question of poetic autonomy as well as poetic careerism.

[36] See, for example, Nappa (2001), 147.

unmediated and real. Even as Catullus defines the text as independent physical object, he reasserts personal agency and presence, seemingly collapsing the barrier of textual mediation.[37]

This tension between authorial voice and material text informs the first poem of our collection. In c. 1, Catullus offers up a freshly polished book (*libellus*) to his friend and fellow writer Cornelius Nepos. The deft incorporation of aesthetic concepts into this dedicatory poem offers powerful testimony to Catullus' poetic expertise. Ostensibly, however, the *doctus poeta* remains self-denigrating and humble.

> cui dono lepidum novum libellum
> arida modo pumice expolitum?
> Corneli, tibi: namque tu solebas
> meas esse aliquid putare nugas
> iam tum, cum ausus es unus Italorum
> omne aevum tribus explicare cartis
> doctis, Iuppiter, et laboriosis.
> quare habe tibi quidquid hoc libelli
> qualecumque; quod, o patrona virgo,
> plus uno maneat perenne saeclo.

To whom do I give my spruce new book, recently polished with dry pumice? To you, Cornelius: for you were accustomed to consider my trifles something even then, when you alone of the Italians dared to unroll the whole of history in three rolls—learned ones, by Jupiter, and full of toil. So take this book, whatever it is, of whatever quality; and may it endure, o patron muse,[38] for more than one generation.

Catullus writes trifles (*nugae*), but the book containing his trifles is the object of the poet's considerable aesthetic attention. The description of the book as polished (*expolitum*) by dry pumice affords an image of literary materiality emblematic of the literary polish conferred by the poet's intensive labour. All this remains implicit, however, and carefully balanced by denigratory qualifications: *nugas . . . quidquid hoc libelli / qualecumque* ('trifles . . . this book, whatever it is, of whatever quality').[39] As many have noted, the scope of the poet's desiderated literary

---

[37] The fullest treatment of this phenomenon is Selden (1992), esp. 485–9: 'no amount of understanding of the poet's craftsmanship will entirely undo the rhetorical production of his persona, just as, however forceful, this impression lacks the power to efface the knowledge of its own linguistic means' (489). As Selden points out, this structural impasse explains why the critical tradition on Catullus remains 'perennially bifurcated' (489).

[38] Fordyce (1961), ad loc., prefers Bergk's emendation, observing that '*virgo* is curiously unexplicit' and wondering, 'who is the Muse for a *libellus* of *nugae*?' Yet this 'somewhat inconsequent appeal to an indeterminate muse' is not necessarily ill-suited to Catullus' designedly offhand style in this poem; compare Elder (1967), 148. Fordyce prefers the compliment to Nepos as *patronus*, but this is even more problematic, as the persuasive arguments of Wiseman (1982), 39–40, show. Aside from the strangeness of calling him *patronus* rather than *amicus* (a problem that vanishes in the case of the evidently metaphorical description of the relation between mortal and divinity as *clientela*, as supported by examples in Fordyce), the 'displacement of the patron' by Muse or love-object fits better with the pattern of Callimachean poetic strategies in first century bc Rome; on which, see Zetzel (1982). On the language of *amicitia* and inapplicability of the term *patronus* in such contexts, White (1978).

[39] On the series of aesthetic contrasts implicit in c. 1, see especially Elder (1967); Batstone (1998).

afterlife is fairly humble, at least compared with later declarations of poetic immortality: *plus uno . . . saeclo* ('for more than one generation'). The question of Catullan self-denigration is a complicated one, but it is worth remarking, if only briefly, that such cautious phrasing tends to support rather than undermine the implicit representation of Catullus as poetry-expert. Only a dilettante would assume instant and unproblematic poetic success. In this introductory poem, carefully poised between seriousness and play, informality and 'polish', vivid authorial voice and mediating textuality, Catullus fashions the beguiling image of a serious writer who does not take himself too seriously.

Catullus, however, is not content with describing his own book's qualities in isolation; an important aspect of his self-definition resides in implicit comparison with the writings of the book's dedicatee Cornelius Nepos. Most scholars place greater emphasis on contrast than comparison, assuming that Catullus could only favourably contrast his elegant, small-scale productions with un-Callimachean tomes of chronology. But we need to be careful about projecting onto Catullus the systematic distinctions of the Augustan age.[40] Nepos, like Catullus, is a native of Cisalpine Gaul who has made an original and daring contribution to Roman literature (*ausus es unus Italorum . . .*), a masterpiece of concision and *doctrina* (*doctis . . . laboriosis*). Catullus all the more plausibly claims Nepos' authority for the literary importance (*aliquid*) of his comparably erudite, laboriously crafted trifles (*nugae*). Especially prominent in this negotiation of the value of Catullus' book is a concern with the passage of time. The book is freshly pumiced (*modo*, 2), a freshness that, however, will be meaningfully altered for the reader of posterity (*plus uno . . . saeclo*). Nepos himself plays a role in a longer history: he used to consider (*solebas . . . putare*) the trifles of Catullus to be of some worth already then (*iam tum, cum . . .*) when he dared to unroll (*explicare*) the whole of time (*omne aevum*) in a mere three volumes, i.e. when he wrote his *Chronica* (3–7). The word 'unroll' (*explicare*) is a Latin term for reading (unrolling a book-scroll). We are naturally alert to this meaning after reading the detailed description of Catullus' slender, pumiced book. If Nepos' work unrolls the entirety of human time (*omne aevum . . . explicare*), Catullus' reader may be wondering what kind of a history will unfold as he scrolls through the *libellus*.

What follows is not a history of the world, but a series of micro-histories that play out in the sphere of private life.[41] The poems that follow in our collection narrate the history, or perhaps the tragedy, of Catullus' love-affair relation with Lesbia from playful beginnings to bitter disintegration (c. 1–c. 11). So convincing is the 'chronology' produced by these poems that some scholars have attempted to construct a real-life chronology of the affair between Catullus and Lesbia.[42] While this excessively literal approach is now long (and rightly) out of fashion, the literary production of a sense of chronology remains an important feature of Catullus' poetry, and invites interpretation. The chronology Catullus teasingly evokes hardly

---

[40] See above all Wiseman (1979), 141ff., and on c. 1, 167–75.

[41] The contrast, or comparison, between Catullus' book and Nepos' has been a scholarly topic for a long time: see, for example, Wheeler (1934), 20ff.

[42] Most famously, Schwabe (1862); for discussion, see Ancona and Hallett (2007) 500 n. 18; Skinner (2003) xix–xx; Wiseman (1985), 215.

approximates, of course, a lucid timeline, but rather a series of moments that require the reader's complicity in being constructed and re-constructed. Unravelling Catullus' life-history will thus be rather different from unrolling the three volumes of Nepos' *Chronica*.[43] The poet's attention to and manipulation of time and timelines cannot be equated with a straightforward attempt to iron out ambiguities (*explicare*, *OLD* 3) or create a linear sequence; instead, his collection of poems consists of a series of loosely linked occasional poems that invite us to read backward and forward among the diverse fragments of his book/world.[44]

Catullus replaces the history of the world with a fragmented, elliptical history of his private, intensely literary life. His elegant vignettes of urbane sociability represent small, conventionally forgettable episodes in everyday life—a dinner party, a joke, a personal provocation. One potential outcome of this strategy is isolation of the autonomous value of his poetry *qua* poetry. Nugatory episodes and jottings cannot rely on the justification of officially memorable subject matter, as in the case of the deeds of great men or signal exploits in Roman history. The image of Catullus' freshly polished and physically separate *libellus*, moreover, reminds us of the gap between the author's life and the poetry book's mimetically constructed 'life in letters'. The poet's life, however vividly evoked, is also a product of consummate literary craft.

Particularly salient in Catullus' re-focusing of literary priorities is the emphasis on commemoration of the ephemeral. The very next poem after c. 1 concerns Lesbia's pet bird, or 'sparrow' (*passer*), which appears to provide the book's informal title.[45] As A. S. Gratwick has argued, the short life-span (*saeculum*) of the sparrow (reported dead in c. 3) contributes an important dimension to its meaning. If indeed Catullus' collection, informally titled *Passer* ('The Sparrow'), will endure for more than one life-span (*saeculum*), the collection's eponymous bird emphatically does not.[46] The bird is a mere pet/love-object/plaything: *deliciae*. Yet trivial subject matter, at an implicit level, works to heighten our admiration for the poet's craft: it can only be the writer's labour and talent (we are encouraged to conclude) that endow the various toys, playthings, and ephemera represented in his poetry book with a longer than natural life-span. A living creature dies once and for all (*nobis cum semel occidit brevis lux . . .*, c. 5.5), but the readers of Catullus' *libellus* can peruse the life and death of the *passer*, and of Catullus' affair with Lesbia, repeatedly as they unroll its contents.

Catullus' polished *libellus* will thus preserve its nugatory contents beyond his own lifetime, and will endow them with sufficient literary substance (*aliquid*) to justify comparison with Nepos' learned work of historical chronology. Without an expert poet's laborious attentions, however, the poetic *libellus* may simply *be*

---

[43] See Quinn (1972), 9–20, and Wiseman (1987), 266, on the possibility that the 'three volumes' of Nepos are themselves matched with three putative volumes of Catullus, roughly corresponding to polymetrics, *carmina maiora*, and elegiac poems.

[44] Compare Miller (1994), 53ff.

[45] Martial *Spect.* 4.14—a poem which engendered a contentious debate, regarding the possible obscenity of Catullus' *passer*, beginning in the Renaissance and continuing into the present day; for a partisan summary, see Hooper (1985).

[46] Gratwick (1991). On some of the difficulties involved in imagining a collection entitled *Passer*, see Farrell (2009), 167 n. 7.

ephemeral. Poem 14 presents precisely such a book, whose contents are ascribed to 'the worst poets'.

> Ni te plus oculis meis amarem,
> iucundissime Calve, munere isto
> odissem te odio Vatiniano:
> nam quid feci ego quidve sum locutus,
> cur me tot male perderes poetis?
> isti di mala multa dent clienti,
> qui tantum tibi misit impiorum.
> quod si, ut suspicor, hoc novum ac repertum
> munus dat tibi Sulla litterator,
> non est mi male, sed bene ac beate,
> quod non dispereunt tui labores.
> di magni, horribilem et sacrum libellum!
> quem tu scilicet ad tuum Catullum
> misti, continuo ut die periret,
> Saturnalibus, optimo dierum!
> non non hoc tibi, false, sic abibit.
> nam, si luxerit, ad librariorum
> curram scrinia, Caesios, Aquinos,
> Suffenum, omnia colligam venena,
> ac te his suppliciis remunerabor.
> vos hinc interea valete abite
> illuc, unde malum pedem attulistis,
> saecli incommoda, pessimi poetae.

Did I not love you more than my own eyes, most delightful Calvus, I would hate you for that gift of yours with the hatred Vatinius bears you: for what have I done or what have I said that you should destroy me utterly with so many poets? May the gods give much unhappiness to that client of yours who sent you such a heap of sacrilegious poets. But if, as I suspect, Sulla the schoolmaster gives you this book—new and recherché—as a gift, I am not dismayed, but pleased and delighted that your labors have not been wasted. Great gods, horrific and accursed book! No doubt you sent it to your friend Catullus so that he would die instantly, on the Saturnalia, best of days! No indeed, you will not get away with it, deceiver. For at first light I will run to the booksellers' stalls, gather together Caesiuses, Aquinuses, and Suffenus—all the poisons—and pay you back with these punishments. You in the meanwhile, off with you, fly hence to the place whence you brought your infelicitous foot, nuisance of the age, abysmal poets.

This poem about a bad *libellus* recalls the putatively good *libellus* of c. 1.[47] While c. 1 offered up the figure of a playful author-figure of exacting

---

[47] In both poems, the book moves as an object of exchange between friends and fellow-writers, first Catullus and Nepos, then Catullus and Calvus. In c. 1 (*cui dono?*), and perhaps especially in c. 14, the notion of the book as gift is conspicuous (*munere isto*, 14.2; *munus*, 9; *remunerabor*, 20). Catullus is metaphorically a client of the Muse in c. 1 (*patrona virgo*); in c. 14, the worthless book comes into Calvus' hands as a gift from a more prosaic kind of client. Whereas Catullus intimates that his own book may last more than one generation (*saeclum*) in c. 1, in c. 14 he describes the incompetent poets as *incommoda saecli*, burdens on their own age, rather than poets who will provide a legacy for future ages. Finally, Catullus sarcastically presents this time-bound poetry in terms reminiscent of his own little book: 'new and exquisite' (*novum ac repertum*). The parallel is argued persuasively by Hubbard (1983); of course, there are other possible explanations for the correspondences between c. 1 and c. 14 than Hubbard's intriguing thesis that c. 1–14 form a *libellus* unto themselves.

standards but appealing lack of pretentiousness, c. 14 additionally works to win over the reader's sympathy by creating a sense of complicity, of being 'in on' the joke shared by Catullus and Calvus. The joke, in this instance, is a clever manipulation of the customs of Saturnalian gift-exchange that places the criticized work in the role of entertaining but worthless gift. Like the ephemeral joke-books (*libelli*) circulated on the Saturnalia,[48] the 'poisonous' *libellus* of the bad poets will not outlive the highly specific occasion on which it provided temporary merriment (*Saturnalibus, optimo dierum*, 'on the Saturnalia, best of days'). Catullus' *libellus*, not poisonous but elegant/witty (*lepidus*), is situated in a context of exchange, but at the same time pulled away from its immediate recipient's hands towards *future* generations.[49] The image of the physical book, which in c. 1 was suggestive of the poetic text's autonomy, here points in a different direction: this throwaway Saturnalian *libellus* is a finite physical object, ephemeral like other similarly expendable gift-items.

Much hinges, once again, on the question of time: will poetry succeed in salvaging itself and its contents from the ephemeral fabric of everyday life? The question is not merely a rhetorical one: Roman poetry's immortality could not be taken for granted in the middle of the first century BC. Still, if Catullus' prayer to the *patrona virgo* ('patron muse') of c. 1 is successful, poetry will save these fleeting life-fragments by *making* them memorable. The bad *libellus*—Catullus' complicit reader is drawn to conclude—lacks such resources and will perish. Poem 36 presents a comparable instance of jocular, aesthetic scapegoating, yet here the sacrificial function of bad poetry is even more explicit: Catullus will throw Volusius' *Annales* to the flames reserved for his own poetry.

> Annales Volusi, cacata carta,
> votum solvite pro mea puella.
> nam sanctae Veneri Cupidinique
> vovit, si sibi restitutus essem
> desissemque truces vibrare iambos,
> electissima pessimi poetae
> scripta tardipedi deo daturam
> infelicibus ustulanda lignis.
> et hoc pessima se puella vidit
> iocose lepide vovere divis.
> nunc o caeruleo creata ponto,
> quae sanctum Idalium Uriosque apertos
> quaeque Ancona Cnidumque harundinosam
> colis quaeque Amathunta quaeque Golgos
> quaeque Durrachium Hadriae tabernam,
> acceptum face redditumque votum,
> si non illepidum neque invenustum est.
> at vos interea venite in ignem,
> pleni ruris et inficetiarum
> annales Volusi, cacata carta.

---

[48] See Citroni (1989).

[49] This double gesture offers the book to the protection of both the mortal friend and the immortal muse. An illuminating discussion of the dual status of the *libellus* as 'both a delightful physical object and a polished work of art that is not confined to any one of its instantiations' may be found in Fitzgerald (1995), 39–40.

Annals of Volusius, shit-covered paper, discharge a vow on my girl's behalf. For she vowed to holy Venus and Cupid that, if I were restored to her, and ceased to hurl harsh iambics, she would give the choicest writings of the worst poet to the lame-footed god to be burnt on unlucky logs. And the worst of girls perceived this vow to the gods was a witty joke. Now then, o thou born of the dark-blue sea, who inhabit holy Idalium and open Urii, Ancona and reedy Cnidus, Amathus and Golgi and Durrachium, inn of the Adriatic, enter this vow as received and duly paid, if it is neither charmless nor inelegant. Meanwhile you go into the fire, full of rusticity and dullness, *Annals* of Volusius, shit-covered paper.[50]

As in c. 14, Catullus responds to a mock-hostile performance of wit (. . . *vidit / iocose lepide vovere* . . . 'she perceived this vow was a witty joke') with his own counter-performance in poetic form.[51] The girl, presumably Lesbia, has demanded, as a price of reconciliation, that the 'choicest writings of the worst poet' (i.e. Catullus' iambic verses about her) be burned. To this mock-vow, Catullus responds with a mock-prayer of fulfilment, deliberately misunderstanding the terms of Lesbia's original vow: the worst poet is surely not himself, but Volusius. The joke pivots around two meanings of the term *pessimus*, worst in moral terms, and worst in poetic terms. Volusius, like the *pessimi poetae* condemned by Catullus in c. 14, is *pessimus* in an aesthetic sense. Once again, the poet playfully manipulates evaluative terms and categories: the moral and the aesthetic do not necessarily correspond, and may even be pitted against each other. The actual, substantive content of 'good' and 'bad' matter less than their strategic disjunction in Catullus' elusive literary critical performance.

The cover afforded by nugatory playfulness enables a strategic vagueness in literary critical content and criteria. The slightness of Catullus' shorter compositions also affords a sharp temporal contrast. This vicious attack on Volusius' *cacata carta* is worlds away from Catullus' compliment to Nepos, yet it remains significant that both literary foils—the respected and the despised—feature time prominently in their titles, a symmetry that should alert us to Catullus' project of restructuring literary time. Like Callimachus, who unrolls his *Aetia* 'little by little, like a child' (fr. 1.5–6), Catullus prefers small, temporally discrete narrative units. Catullus immortalizes in verse, not a continuous fabric of worthy Roman *exempla* across the ages, but the insubstantial tissue of wit woven between himself and his *puella* in a passing moment. The traditional correspondence of literary heft, temporal scope, and posthumous endurance undergoes alteration at the nugatory poet's hands. Weighty poetic tomes of Roman history are burned; ephemeral *nugae* endure, and wittily record the bonfire.

---

[50] But perhaps Nappa (2001) is correct in that stating *caco* does not represent *concaco* here, and that Catullus means to evoke Volusius 'actually excreting the pages' (136).

[51] This apparently trifling and elusive poem has been variously appreciated: there is discussion in Citroni (1995), 170–3, of how the poem parodies solemn, public language in order to create a sense of complicity within the exclusive circle of friends; it is interpreted as a demonstration of poetic power by Wray (2001) 77; and discussed within the context of literary criticism by Buchheit (1975). Østerud (1978), 139, sums up the various options: 'it has proved impossible for the critics to agree whether the poem is literary criticism in verse leveled at a fellow poet, a parody of a hymn to Venus, or just a playful comment on some incident in the relationship between Catullus and his mistress'.

In an annalistic poem, the political/military year structures poetic content. Just as the *Annales* synthesize political time and poetic form, so they fold literary into social value. The rhetorical effort of vindicating autonomously *poetic* value involves a restructuring of temporal and axiological priorities.

> Zmyrna mei Cinnae nonam post denique messem
>   quam coepta est nonamque edita post hiemem,
> milia cum interea quingenta Hortensius uno
>
> .   .   .   .
>
> Zmyrna cavas Satrachi penitus mittetur ad undas,
>   Zmyrnam cana diu saecula pervolvent.
> at Volusi annales Paduam morientur ad ipsam
>   et laxas scombris saepe dabunt tunicas.
> parva mei mihi sint cordi monimenta [sodalis],
>   at populus tumido gaudeat Antimacho.   (c. 95)

My friend Cinna's *Smyrna*, at last published nine harvests and nine winters after it was begun, while Hortensius, in the meanwhile [has produced] five hundred thousand [verses] in one [year] . . . *Smyrna* will be carried as far as the deep waters of Satrachus; the centuries will grow gray in turning the pages of *Smyrna*. But the *Annals* of Volusius will die by the river Padua itself, and will often provide loose-fitting coats for mackerel. Be the small-scale memorials of my [comrade] dear to my heart—let the crowd rejoice in their bloated Antimachus.

Insofar as the meaning of this challenging and lacunose epigram can be reconstructed, Catullus appears to contrast his friend Cinna's poetic masterpiece with the work of three different poets, focusing on different aspects of literary achievement in each instance: duration of compositional period; duration and extent of literary fame; exclusivity of readership. The most pointed contrasts concern time. Volusius' *Annales* commemorates the vast chrono-logical sweep of Roman history, yet will achieve a life-span of only a few years before succumbing to an early death (*morientur*). The 'life cycle' of the *Smyrna* transcends ordinary limits, beginning with its laborious, nine-year gestation period: *post denique messem / quam coepta est nonamque edita post hiemem* . . . ('at last published nine harvests and nine winters after it was begun', 1–2). Throughout Catullus' poetry, life-span (*saeculum*) functions as metaphor for the duration of literary works.[52] Here he employs the figure to describe the inversely proportional relation between the rapidity of the poet's labour and the duration of his work's posthumous survival, between extent of years narrated and extent of literary afterlife. Volusius covers historical epochs; Cinna focuses on a single mythic birth. The *Smyrna*, however, will last centuries (*saecula*), Volusius' *Annales* . . . mere years.[53]

---

[52] Hallett (1988) argues that Catullan metaphors for composition trace a path from literary/erotic 'play' (*lusus*) through childbirth to the production of offspring (*fetus Musarum*). The vocabulary of 'play' is more common in the polymetrics, whereas the *carmina maiora* tend to see poetry more in turns of product and achievement.

[53] On time as the central focus of c. 95, Noonan (1986), 303–4: 'the unexpressed concept of a poem's lifetime is . . . the matrix of the other ideas in the poem'. Thus, whereas *nonam post denique messem* suggests 'gestation and birth . . . . Volusius' *Annales* will "die"' (304 n. 13). I adopt the conjecture *sodalis* in line 9 and view the poem as a unity, but scholars are divided: see Thompson (1997), ad loc.

A similarly inverse proportion describes the relation between expansiveness of narrative scope and breadth of literary circulation. Volusius' versified chronicle of the grandeur that was Rome will perish by the banks of a local river, failing to overcome its parochial origins, whereas Cinna's *Smyrna* will circulate as far as the exotic river featured in its own narrative.[54] At the same time, Catullus draws attention to a discrepancy in moral texture and purpose. Volusius' *Annales* are informed by the historical tradition of the preservation and transmission of morally useful *exempla*. Cinna's *Smyrna*, by contrast, concerns one of the least edifying myths of classical mythology, the story of how Smyrna (or Myrrha) conceived Adonis by committing incest with her father. Catullus has chosen to juxtapose a morally dubious patch of mythology and signal exploits of Roman history. Yet it is Volusius' publicly edifying *Annales* that end up being reduced to a more ignominious utility. Catullus envisages two rather different uses for the pages of Cinna's and Volusius' works. While the passing centuries will 'unroll' Cinna's integral work (*cana diu saecula pervolvent*), Volusius' poem will be dispersed amidst multiple (*saepe*) use-occasions, the individual pieces of its *cacata carta* detached from the larger opus to serve as fish-wrapping.

In the epigram's closing couplet, Cinna's mythological poem is described by a term that can refer generally to works of literature, but is especially appropriate for a commemorative, historical work: *monimenta* ('memorial'). Catullus audaciously manipulates concepts of space, time, and memorial in articulating his novel construction of literary value and cultural importance. He especially undermines any taken-for-granted link between what is accepted as 'good' in moral terms, and what is 'good' in poetic terms. The application of the positive, value-laden term *monumentum* to ostensibly amoral, risqué subject matter flaunts the disjunction between aesthetic value and traditional ethical probity. It is not only traditionalists, however, that fail to fulfil Catullus' criteria of literary importance. In c. 22, Catullus provides a long description of the inept Suffenus rejoicing in and admiring his own prowess as a poet even when occupied in the very act of writing.[55] Suffenus is perfectly adequate as a social performer (*venustus et dicax et urbanus*, 'charming, witty, and urbane', 2)[56] in the elegant modern style. As poet, however, he is a hopeless rustic.

> haec cum legas tu, bellus ille et urbanus
> Suffenus unus caprimulgus aut fossor
> rursus videtur: tantum abhorret ac mutat.
> hoc quid putemus esse? qui modo scurra
> aut siquid hac re scitius videbatur,
> idem infaceto est infacetior rure,
> simul poemata attigit: neque idem umquam
> aeque est beatus ac poema cum scribit:
> tam gaudet in se tamque se ipse miratur.　　(c. 22.9–17)

---

[54] On this elegant reference, and the Callimachean connotations of rivers in c. 95, Clausen (1964), 188–90. Noonan argues that the river Satrachus, in Cinna's *Smyrna* and again in Catullus' poem, evokes a ritual re-enactment of the immersion and covering of Adonis; the fate of the Annals of Volusius is thus a conscious 'perversion of the Adonis-ritual' (302).

[55] Close commentary on this poem's references to writing materials can be found in Gamberale (1982).

[56] Use of this language in c. 22, the vocabulary of 'social performance', is discussed in Krostenko (2001), 268–70; on the 'distinction between the character of one's writing and the character of the writer', see the analysis of Nappa (2001), 138–42.

When you read these [verses of his], that fine, urbane Suffenus now seems a mere goat-milker or ditch-digger: so different and changed is he. What are we to think of this? The same man, who just now seemed to be a dinner-party wit, or something even more clever than that, is duller than the dull countryside the moment he touches poetry. And at the same time, he is never so happy as when he is writing poetry: so much does he rejoice in himself and admire himself.

Catullus sharply insists that elegant manners and good intentions are not enough to make someone a poet. But what is required? As in c. 14, the qualities of failed as opposed to good poetry are not explicitly described: what matters, at least in part, is the distinction between ethics and aesthetics that Catullus generates, and the persuasive power of his disarmingly jocular style. We feel we 'know' the poetaster Suffenus, despite the vague evocation of his qualities as writer, and we also 'know' the essential aesthetic qualities his poetry lacks.

Catullus himself, we recall, appreciates an elegantly made book, but remains wary, even in the case of his own pumiced *libellus*, of making grand claims for nugatory writing: *quicquid hoc libelli, / qualecumque* ('this little book, whatever it is, of whatever quality', 8–9).[57] This very hesitation, however, is strategic: it is designed to suggest an appreciation of the stern requirements of poetic craft, and the justified doubts of the true poet as to whether or not his work has attained the requisite degree of polish. Suffenus' enthusiastic, amateur writing-project, by contrast, is uncontrolled and evidently un-Callimachean, but supplied with top-of-the-line materials: '[he has composed a great number of verses], and not, as is usually done, written them down on recycled scrap paper: royal sheets, new rolls, new bosses, red ties for the wrapper—all ruled with lead and smoothed with pumice' (*nec sic ut fit in palimpseston / relata: cartae regiae, novi libri, / novi umbilici, lora rubra membranae, / derecta plumbo et pumice omnia aequata,* 4–8). Catullus only allows his poems to be presented to Nepos in a polished book *after* they have undergone the process of revision and achieved final literary form, and even then with some trepidation. Suffenus, who blithely equates aesthetic polish with pumiced writing materials, is the inverse image of the Catullan polymetric author: he valorizes the external appearance of completion, and takes his status as literary author pompously for granted. Whereas the materiality of the physical book in c. 1 favours the impression of the aesthetic polish and textual autonomy of the Catullan *libellus*, here the reference to physical writing materials, while confirming the division between writer and work, inverts the consequences. Suffenus' urbane manners are obliterated the moment he 'touches' poetry (*simul poemata attigit*).

Suffenus, unlike Cinna, is unable to appreciate the necessity of a long poetic gestation period, and does not seem to recognize the category of the rough draft. It is no wonder that Suffenus' name appears among the 'worst poets' that make up the *libellus* Calvus sent Catullus as a practical joke on the Saturnalia. Even good poets, of whom Catullus approves, however, might need to be reminded of the

---

[57] Nappa (2001), 139–41, draws a comparison between c. 22 and c. 1.

importance of applying oneself to the labour of properly finishing, i.e. of applying the proper degree of literary finish to, the poetic work. Concerns with literary completion pervade c. 35,[58] in which Catullus directs his papyrus to invite his friend Caecilius to visit him in Verona.

> Poetae tenero, meo sodali,
> velim Caecilio, papyre, dicas
> Veronam veniat, Novi relinquens
> Comi moenia Lariumque litus.
> nam quasdam volo cogitationes
> amici accipiat sui meique.
> quare, si sapiet, viam vorabit,
> quamvis candida milies puella
> euntem revocet, manusque collo
> ambas iniciens roget morari.
> quae nunc, si mihi vera nuntiantur,
> illum deperit impotente amore.
> nam quo tempore legit incohatam
> Dindymi dominam, ex eo misellae
> ignes interiorem edunt medullam.
> ignosco tibi, Sapphica puella
> musa doctior; est enim venuste
> Magna Caecilio incohata Mater.

Papyrus, please convey to Caecilius, a tender poet and my close friend, that he is to leave the walls of Novum Comum and the shore of Lake Larius, and come to Verona; for I want him to hear certain thoughts of a friend of his and mine. So, if he is wise, he will devour the road, even though a pretty girl should call him back a thousand times from going, and throwing both hands on his neck, ask him to linger. She, if the report I hear is true, now perishes with uncontrolled love for him. For ever since the time she read his unfinished *Magna Mater*, flames have been eating away the poor girl's inmost marrow. I don't blame you, girl more learned than the Sapphic muse—Caecilius' *Magna Mater* is charmingly begun.

Caecilius is working on a longer poem in the erudite, Alexandrian style of the Catullan *carmina maiora* or Cinna's *Smyrna*—the kind of poem that ideally takes years to complete. It is not clear whether Caecilius considers his poem to be finished, but Catullus certainly does not: he twice observes that Caecilius' *Magna Mater* is not completed, but merely 'begun' (*incohatam*, 13; *incohata*, 18). Catullus' poem and the 'thoughts' he intends to offer Caecilius remain fairly elusive, yet the repeated designation *incohata* suggest that the completion or aesthetic 'finish' of Caecilius' poem is at stake. Catullus, as often in his polymetric *nugae*, offers us a tantalizing life-fragment that toys with the impression of unfinishedness and

---

[58] As always, uncertainty limits our ability to advance interpretations of Catullus based on positioning within the collection, but the juxtaposition of c. 35 and c. 36 is certainly suggestive. Despite the appearance of two separate, occasion-bound communications, it is possible to view Catullus' critical attitude more synthetically as envisaging two types of poetic production: one historical epic, the other neoteric epyllion; one a blatant failure, the other a promising effort. On connections between the two poems, Skinner (1981), 31; Solodow (1989), 316. Both are tellingly addressed to physical objects, writing materials good and bad—on the one hand, the copious, excremental *carta* of Volusius, and on the other, Catullus' brief, elegant papyrus.

informality[59]—all the more strikingly in this instance, where completion is the stated theme.

Yet the more closely we examine Catullus' letter, the more keenly we become aware how he has painstakingly constructed the fiction of inchoate communication. Poem 35 constitutes, in short, a highly polished literary papyrus, however humble its sub-literary pretensions. The intricate *mise-en-abyme* created by Catullus' apostrophe of his own papyrus, which in turn relays and embeds the very voice apostrophizing it, intensifies the sophisticated metapoetic play and literary self-reflexivity. The contrast is instructive. Caecilius' grand-sounding *Magna Mater* gets high praise from his adoring *docta puella*, and may even have been sent to Catullus as a completed manuscript, but does not (yet) meet the requirements of the *doctus poeta*, whose understatedly elegant and intricately metapoetic epistle is itself meant as a demonstration of the difference between advertising literary refinement and achieving it.[60] There is a gender dynamic at work here as well.[61] The male poet/friend condescendingly pardons the girl's passionate response (*ignosco tibi*), while pointedly appending his own judgement: however attractive (*venustus*), the poem is only a beginning.[62]

Catullus uses this concrete scenario of pre-publication commentary and criticism to show us, yet again, just how elusive the criteria of excellent poetry are. Poetry is not necessarily good, he insists, because someone feels good about himself while writing it, or writes it on expensive paper, or because his well-read girlfriend swooned in appreciation upon first reading it. Just because a book is sold in a bookshop on the poetry shelf does not mean that it merits the name. A man who gives splendid dinner parties does not have the right to have his inferior book praised (c. 44). Even the appearance of official, literary status as conferred by an established tradition (*Annales*), or an impressive-sounding title and appropriately erudite subject matter (*Magna Mater*), can be deceiving. Conversely, generically indeterminate, versified squibs such as Catullus offers up in his polymetric corpus

---

[59] Solodow (1989), contrasting the polymetric c. 35 with the very different c. 95, notes: 'Catullus embeds his literary criticism in events that he represents as occurring in daily life' (317); note also Buchheit (1959), (1976). Part of the sense of 'unfinishedness' derives from the elliptical omission of certain details: the *cogitationes*, the *amicus* (either, with Ellis ad loc., self-referentially, or some third figure). The mysterious remarks might have to do with Caesar and the contentious new name, Novum Comum. Caesar was charged with *ambitio* in his scheme of enfranchisement (Suet. *Iul.* 28, Appian *B Civ* ii.26); but see Fredricksmeyer (1985), 213–14.

[60] On this poem, see Fredricksmeyer (1985); Copley (1953); Heine (1975); Fisher (1971); Citroni (1995) 148ff.; Solodow (1989). The precept of the poem's self-sufficiency was laid down by Copley (1953), and developed by Fredrickmeyer (1985), who states that Catullus' 'own poem, far from *incohatum*, is a finished little masterpiece' (221).

[61] On gender and 'doctitude', see Habinek (1998).

[62] Kutzko (2006) offers a different reading: *Sapphica musa* is a learned allusion to Lesbia (his 'source of inspiration' or *musa*). The Catullan persona, in a typical, self-denigrating gesture, is found to be complaining about Caecilius' poem, but envying the fact that he has an adoring girlfriend. Poem 36, in fact, shows Lesbia wishing to consign Catullus' poetry to the flames—a sharp contrast indeed. For Hansen (2007), the central question of the poem is Caecilius' (poetic) response, and the choice between love poetry for his *puella* in the style of Catullan *nugae*, and a longer, erudite poem on the Magna Mater. Hansen notes that it is not appropriate for a poem on the Magna Mater to be written *venuste* (218)—perhaps a sign that Caecilius should be drawing, instead, on the inspiration provided by his *puella*. That is, Caecilius does not know his own mind: no wonder he cannot finish his *Magna Mater*; his very style reveals erotic preoccupations.

might turn out to have greater claims to literary polish than self-proclaimed works of literature. There is no automatic route to authentic literary quality, no template; but this is probably a good thing. Catullan scholarship has traditionally represented his devotion to aesthetic quality as inherent in the 'neoteric creed' of Callimachean *labor/ponos* ('toil'). But rather than reifying Catullus' interest in poetic craft as an inert feature of fashionable dogma, we need to appreciate the strategic aspect of his insistence on literary quality. By complicating and problematizing the criteria of poetic achievement, and by severing specifically *literary* excellence from other qualities broadly accepted as positive in Roman society, the expert poet retains his aura of exclusivity and stakes his claim of autonomy.

In crucial ways, however, this project remains marked by internal tensions. The language of self-denigration and trifling leisure (*ioci, nugae, facetiae*) employed by Catullus, while effectively confounding his potential critics through anticipation of their criticism, leaves scholars in a difficult position as they strive to characterize the ambitions and structural contours of his poetic activity.[63] Will his poetry be immortal or ephemeral? Does poetry enjoy permanent, intrinsic validity as cultural pursuit, or does it take place only on fortuitous occasions of indulgent play? In c. 50, Catullus represents what appears to be precisely such a precarious occasion of ludic diversion. He and his friend Calvus, having agreed to be aesthetes (*delicatos*),[64] compose playful verses.

> Hesterno, Licini, die otiosi
> multum lusimus in meis tabellis,
> ut convenerat esse delicatos:
> scribens versiculos uterque nostrum
> ludebat numero modo hoc modo illoc,
> reddens mutua per iocum atque vinum.
> atque illinc abii tuo lepore
> incensus, Licini, facetiisque,
> ut nec me miserum cibus iuvaret
> nec somnus tegeret quiete ocellos,
> sed toto indomitus furore lecto
> versarer, cupiens videre lucem,
> ut tecum loquerer simulque ut essem.
> at defessa labore membra postquam
> semimortua lectulo iacebant,
> hoc, iucunde, tibi poema feci,
> ex quo perspiceres meum dolorem.
> nunc audax cave sis, precesque nostras,
> oramus, cave despuas, ocelle,
> ne poenas Nemesis reposcat a te.
> est vemens dea: laedere hanc caveto.

Yesterday at leisure, Licinius, we played around a great deal on my writing tablets, since we had determined to indulge ourselves. Each of us took turns writing verses and playing now in one meter, now in another, answering back and forth amidst joking and wine. I went

---

[63] The question informs Farrell (2009), who stresses the ephemerality of the poetic enterprise in Catullus.

[64] Fordyce (1961), ad loc., provides a useful discussion of the word's connotations; see also Buchheit (1976), 166–8; Fitzgerald (1995), 35–6.

away from this so enflamed by your charm and wit, Licinius, that neither did food do me any good in my wretched state nor did sleep cover my eyes with quiet, but uncontrolled in my fury I tossed and turned all over the bed, longing to see the light, so that I might talk with you and be with you. But when my limbs were exhausted with exertion and lay half-dead on the bed, I made this poem for you, charming friend, so that you could discern from it my pain. Beware now of being haughty and despising my entreaties, beware, precious, I beseech you, lest Nemesis claim retribution from you. She is a powerful goddess: beware of offending her.

Catullus represents poetic activity as a mode of complicity, presence, spontaneity, play, and eroticism between two people, not as the production of a classic text intended for a general audience.[65] Yet the perspective from which the poem speaks is that of nostalgia, the consciousness of lost presence: 'I made this poem for you, delightful friend, so that you could discern from it my pain' (*hoc, iucunde, tibi poema feci, / ex quo perspiceres meum dolorem*). F. Dupont suggests that, whereas Calvus presumably returns to his forensic business (indeed, in c. 52 we see him engaged in precisely this), Catullus remains trapped within the mentality of *otium*,[66] replaying their improvisation over and over in his mind.[67] The two poets' original agreement (*convenerat*) consisted in a limited 'pact' of indulgent aestheticism coextensive with an occasion of sympotic pleasures (*per iocum atque vinum*). Catullus intimates something further: not satisfied with the ephemeral occasion of improvisatory play, he desires to replay that moment, to extend the occasion beyond its natural limits. Potentially more shocking than the provocative aestheticism described in the opening lines is Catullus' pose as an infatuated lover who cannot remain content with a

---

[65] Perhaps for this very reason c. 50 has become an icon of neoteric poetics in modern scholarship. See especially Buchheit (1976) on the programmatic status of c. 50. The position of c. 50, as well as c. 14 (another poem involving Calvus), within the collection is seen as important by some scholars: c. 14 in one account ends the *libellus* (Hubbard 1983) and in other accounts, marks a point of transition within the *libellus*; for it is followed by a fragment that appears to introduce the Furius and Aurelius cycle to its *lectores*: Skinner (1981), 44. Poem 50 has likewise been identified as a poem that ends the collection (Clausen 1976, 40) or is at least paired with c. 51 that ends the collection (Skinner 1981, 80ff.). (On book-arrangement in Catullus more generally, Skinner (1981) and (2003); Wiseman (1969); Most (1981); Block (1984); Jocelyn (1999), Van Sickle (1981), among many others.) However this may be, it is significant that these particular poems play out central concerns with text and occasion, immortal and ephemeral production. For the links between c. 14 and c. 50, both addressed to Calvus: Nemeth (1974–5). On c. 50–51 as a possible end-point recalling themes from the beginning of the *libellus*, Van Sickle (1981), 70.

[66] Buchheit (1976), 164–5, sees a deliberate contrast with Ciceronian *otium*, insofar as Cicero is the addressee of the preceding poem in the collection (c. 49). Much of the scholarship on c. 50 has focused on the question of *otium*: e.g. Segal (1970); Pucci (1961).

[67] Dupont (1999), 117. Courtney (1993), 201, observes that Calvus 'had a very active career as politician and orator'. But, as Hollis points out (2007, 58), there is no evidence he ever held political office, while the extant poetic fragments and *testimonia* suggest that, as poet, Calvus was placed in roughly the same category as Catullus, and that his poetic works encompassed a strikingly comparable range and displayed similarity of subject matter and style: see Hollis (2007) 49–86, especially 58–9. Hence I would not draw so strong a contrast as Dupont between the status of Calvus (a 'notable') and Catullus (surely not 'a professional, an entertainer . . . a jester . . . a troubadour'). Nor can I agree with Dupont's puzzling conclusion that such a poem is merely an inert signifier or remnant, the *libellus* itself nothing more than a 'museum piece' (126–7). Dupont's important study of 'the invention of literature' is limited at times by an insistence on the primary status of orality.

single, discrete encounter,[68] uncontrolled in his *furor*, consumed by insatiable desire for Calvus and poetry.[69]

The tone of amorous desperation continues into the poem that follows in the collection.[70] If the longing for repetition and iterated presence drives c. 50, the damaging potential in the repeat leisure-play requested by c. 50 emerges clearly in the closing strophe of 51.

> otium, Catulle, tibi molestum est:
> otio exsultas nimiumque gestis:
> otium et reges prius et beatas
>   perdidit urbes.   (c. 51.13–16)

Leisure, Catullus, is your bane; in leisure you exult and revel too much; in the past leisure has destroyed both kings and flourishing cities.

Whereas c. 50 narrates a fleeting occasion of *otium* experienced as pleasurable, c. 51 warns against long-term *otium* destructive on historical and personal levels. In both cases, the poet comes up against barriers to the pursuit of his literary project as he undergoes a painful recognition of the limits of *otium*.[71] The pleasurable leisure of *lusus* is fleeting, whereas a long-term absorption in leisure undermines virility and cities.

Does Catullus truly view the life of literary leisure as destructive, or is this comment merely the arch joke of an ultra-sophisticated *littérateur* who would never really doubt the value of his leisured existence? Throughout this section, we have examined poems in which Catullus advertises (albeit *sotto voce*) his Calli-machean erudition and compositional rigour, yet these (again, implicit) claims of literary seriousness, devotion, and expertise are embedded in jocular *nugae* that disavow their own status as literature. Given the duality of Catullus' stance, scholars have understandably come down on both sides of the question. But instead of trying to decide the matter in favour of Catullus' 'real' beliefs, and reducing the opposite side of the dialectic to mere pretense, we need to appreciate the dynamics of the rhetorical game he is playing.

Catullus' movement between the opposing poles of careerist devotion and casual dilettantism plays a part in a broader set of strategies that at once intimate

---

[68] Note Finnamore (1984), 17: 'Catullus' *excessive* desire for Calvus' companionship' (italics added). Catullus adds *identidem*, not present in Sappho, also present in Catullus' other poem in Sapphics (c. 11): *identidem omnium / ilia rumpens* (19–20); see Van Sickle (1981), 71; Putnam (1974), 20.

[69] Compare the highly similar 'agreement' between Caesar and Mamurra in c. 57: these two also 'agree' (*convenit*; compare *convenerat*) with each other 'beautifully', paired, like Catullus and Calvus, in literary indulgence: *uno in lecticulo erudituli ambo* (7); *pulcre convenit improbis cinaedis* (1). The negative side of the same coin?

[70] On *amor and otium* in c. 50 and c. 51: Segal (1970); Finnamore (1984). David Wray has revived an old interpretation of the two poems that would make them even more concretely paired: the *poema* which Catullus composed in order to make his *dolor* visible to Calvus is precisely c. 51, for which c. 50 serves as accompanying cover-letter: Wray (2001), 88–109.

[71] The best interpretations of c. 50–51 stress Catullan ambivalence: thus for Segal (1970), 30, *otium* is 'not necessarily repudiated', but nor is '*otium* . . . an easy possession'. In Skinner (1981), 82, c. 51 is the poet's ironic *sphragis*, a declaration of adherence to the life of literary *otium* he overtly disavows. Finnamore (1984), 14, observes that physical suffering is present in both poems, as is the phrase *me miserum* (c. 50.9 and c. 51.5–6).

his poetry's alignment with rigorous standards of aesthetic excellence, and disavow excessive literary seriousness through a jocular tone and elusively playful authorial persona. Catullus avoids telling us what he is, avoids defining the cultural space within which his poetic activity falls. Instead, in his polymetrics, he offers up a series of typically brief, ludic textual performances that play at the edges of a poetic identity without ever fully sketching it out. He avoids being pinned down to the unserious 'games' of the aristocratic dilettante, and, equally, to the client poet's lacklustre professionalism. There is no stable, established set of cultural concepts for what Catullus is attempting to do; conversely, poetic roles that *are* well-established belong to a heteronomous conception of literary activity. This is one reason why Catullus, in his project of poetic autonomy, constructs an elusive stance, shifting between different paradigms of literary identity which he playfully evokes without allowing himself to yield wholly to their constraints.

POETRY AND PUBLIC LIFE

Even the aspect of Catullus' poetic persona that has seemed to many relatively salient and straightforward—the rejection of politics in favour of *otium*—becomes more difficult to characterize the more closely it is examined. Catullus' poetry, at least on one level, commemorates a different kind of life—not the life of the distinguished politician or commander, but the life of an elegant city-dweller, who, although well connected and well off, does not choose to pursue a political career. Far from commemorating public achievements, Catullus ridicules poetry of the annalistic cast, and laments the corruption of contemporary political culture. Catullus writes about his own and his friends' experiences on provincial tours of duty, but 'mainly to express his boredom and exasperation with that life in comparison with one of cultivated leisure'.[72] While Catullus never explicitly states that he rejected (or even considered) a political career in favour of literary *otium*, his poetry's celebration of leisure-time activity and disparagement of politics together have suggested to many of his readers and interpreters a choice of poetry over public life.[73]

Not all scholars, however, are equally convinced by the thesis of Catullus' rejection of politics. For some, Catullus' bitter poems of political invective demonstrate the poet's unabated interest in politics: by expressing indignation and outrage, he intervenes in contemporary disputes and political episodes,

---

[72] Farrell (2002), 42. There is a good overview of the topic of Catullan social and political invective, including a close reading of some of the poems discussed below, in Tatum (2007), who stresses Catullus' manipulation of the traditions of Roman invective, but also the instability of his persona.

[73] Konstan (2007) sees a darkening in Catullus' attitude towards politics in the years following his trip to Bithynia in 57. But the perspective of Braund (1996) may also help explain why he savagely attacks Mamurra's plundering of the empire yet complains himself of receiving too little plunder in Bithynia: Catullus, in c. 10, is actually obliquely praising Memmius for exerting tight control over his *cohors*, preventing them from plundering their province. On this reading, the attitude on display in c. 10 would not be at odds with his criticism of Mamurra, but consistent with it.

and affects the reputation of major political players.[74] Then again, Catullus speaks of public life as someone not *in* it. Catullus' political poems would appear to fall more on the side of despair over a crisis without remedy than the productive and engaged outrage of a committed political participant. It is worth considering a few of these poems in order to assess their tone and rhetorical stance.

> Quid est, Catulle? quid moraris emori?
> sella in curuli struma Nonius sedet,
> per consulatum peierat Vatinius:
> quid est, Catulle? quid moraris emori?   (c. 52)

What is it, Catullus? Why do you put off dying? Nonius the wart sits in the curule chair; Vatinius swears falsely on his consulship. What is it, Catullus? Why do you put off dying?

This annalistic snapshot—Nonius currently occupying the *sella curulis* and Vatinius greedily hovering over his pre-ordained consulship—tells us all we need to know about the jettisoning of constitutional procedure in favour of Pompey and Caesar's favourites. Not only the present, but the future, is botched irreparably. The stark factual tone of the poem, with its present indicative verbs, unadorned syntax, and end-stopped lines, suggest that the perversion of political normality is a *fait accompli*: why not die immediately?

In his most ambitious political poem, Catullus laments that Caesar and Pompey, by allowing the voracious and unscrupulous Mamurra to flourish, have undermined the core principles of the *res publica* beyond the possibility of repair.

> cinaede Romule, haec videbis et feres?
> es impudicus et vorax et aleo.
> eone nomine, imperator unice,
> fuisti in ultima occidentis insula,
> ut ista vestra diffututa mentula
> ducenties comesset aut trecenties?
> quid est alid sinistra liberalitas?
> parum expatravit an parum elluatus est?
> paterna prima lancinata sunt bona,
> secunda praeda Pontica, inde tertia
> Hibera, quam scit amnis aurifer Tagus:
> nunc Galliae timetur et Britanniae.
> quid hunc malum fovetis? aut quid hic potest
> nisi uncta devorare patrimonia?
> eone nomine † urbis opulentissime †
> socer generque, perdidistis omnia?   (c. 29.9–24)

Romulus the queer, will you look upon these things and endure them? You are a slut, a glutton, and a gambler. O One-And-Only-Commander, did you go to the furthest island of the Western World for this purpose—so that fucked-out prick of yours could devour

---

[74] For example, Syndikus (1986) has argued that his political opinions, insofar as they can be gleaned from the extant corpus, cohere approximately with the traditionalist republican establishment, who deplored the erosion of senatorial authority, the plundering of the provinces, and the enrichment of Caesar's and Pompey's favourites. Note also Konstan (2007), Tatum (2007), 338–44.

200,000 or 300,000? What is this but perverse generosity? Has he gobbled up too little, feasted too little? First his father's estate was ripped to shreds, then the spoils of the Black Sea, and third, that of Spain, which the gold-bearing river Tagus knows—and now there is fear for Gaul and Britain. Why do you encourage this bane? What is he capable of doing besides gobbling down greasy inheritances? Was it for the sake of this, o father-in-law and son-in-law, that you destroyed everything?

Mamurra[75] has made a *cinaedus* ('queer') of Romulus, an alias apparently referring to Caesar,[76] but not accidentally suggesting that Romulus' city has been perverted by Mamurra's spectacular greed. Mamurra's fluid invasion of all goods private and public smoothly makes a transition from paternal wealth (*paterna . . . bona*) to the spoils of the Roman empire. In view of the unlimited greed of Caesar's chief of engineers and the apparently limitless indulgence of his betters, it is not surprising that the entire political fabric (*omnia*) has been destroyed.

The closest Catullus came to participating in any phase of a public career was the Bithynian expedition of 54 BC. In two poems on the topic, Catullus describes his brutal exploitation at the hands of his praetor Memmius in terms of the sexual act of *irrumatio* (oral rape):

> . . . praesertim quibus esset irrumator
> praetor, nec faceret pili cohortem.   (c. 10.12–13)
>
> . . . . especially for those who had a mouth-fucker of
> a praetor, who didn't give a damn for his staff.
>
> O Memmi, bene me ac diu supinum
> tota ista trabe lentus irrumasti.
> sed, quantum video, pari fuistis
> casu: nam nihilo minore verpa
> farti estis. pete nobiles amicos!   (c. 28.9–14)

O Memmius, long and well, in leisurely fashion, did you ream me, supine, with the entirety of that shaft of yours. But, as far as I can see, you [two] were in a similar situation: with no less a prick were you stuffed. 'Make friends in high places!'

As David Braund has aptly observed, sexual control, in this graphic metaphor, signifies the social control of Memmius over Catullus and other members of the *cohors* ('staff'). The experience of being at the mercy of a brutally exploitative superior inspires a pessimistic assessment of the traditional life-path that normally begins with cultivation of friendships among the political elite. Catullus accordingly mimics, with magnificent sarcasm, the Polonius-like exhortation that Roman parents bestowed on their aspiring sons: *pete nobiles amicos* ('seek out noble friends'). There is no point in pursuing the traditional life-path—you only end up being used and discarded by your 'noble friends'. Catullus' complaint of passive victimization in Memmius' cohort resonates with a broader pattern of passive identifications throughout his oeuvre.[77] In the mythical register, his most

---

[75] For Catullan treatment of Mamurra, see Deuling (1999).

[76] Scholars have worked to identify the various figures and addressees of the poem: see, for example, Scott (1971).

[77] He is trampled by Lesbia's promiscuous libido, victimized by thieves and other ruthless individuals; close friends turn out to be unscrupulous betrayers: see Skinner (1993); Konstan (1977).

memorable first-person surrogates are passive, female, or feminized.[78] Compromised or lost virility is a particularly frequent theme in Catullan self-representation: after waking to the realization that he has castrated himself, the mythic figure Attis laments the loss of his virile identity and the institutions that supported and defined it.[79] In the case of elite Roman men, those institutions included above all a functioning *res publica* within which to pursue a political career. Marilyn Skinner has accordingly read Catullus' interest in feminized personae against the background of 'elite despair over real decreases in personal autonomy and diminished capacity for meaningful public action during the agonized final years of the Roman Republic'.[80]

It is fair to ask to what extent Catullus really experienced despair: there is no evidence that in his case a genuine desire to pursue a political career was frustrated by the 'diminished capacity for meaningful public action'. As an *eques municipalis*, he probably did not feel entitled to political office or the *libertas* of a high-level participant. Yet despair over lost political autonomy, whether or not authentically felt, creates a rhetorical opportunity. The topos of an unsalvageable *res publica* is employed by political participants who turn to literature as a refuge from a frustrated political career. Cicero's friend, Pomponius Atticus, who belonged to a respectable equestrian family, retired into literary *otium* in the 80s BC because he did not think the conditions of political life would allow him to pursue a political career in accordance with his *dignitas*.[81] Cicero himself, under Caesar's dictatorship, diverted his immense rhetorical energies to the composition of philosophical dialogues and treatises: here, at least, in his philosophical writings, he could give speeches, deliver harangues, and exercise the free right of expression that was denied him in the forum itself.[82] Sallust, like Cicero a *novus homo* ('new man') and member of the municipal nobility, retreated from a failed political career to the dignity of historical writing. It is not accidental that Sallust's central concern is the fracturing of *virtus* ('manly excellence') in a morally degenerate society.[83] The firm hold that the traditional ethos of political participation had on elite aspirations was weakened by the spectacle of the civil wars. Civil conflict simultaneously provided the writer with a rich vein of literary material, and justified his choice of occupation.

When the traditional forms of the active life threatened to undermine the dignity and self-determination of its devotees, new styles of virile identity became more likely to succeed. The critique of *virtus*, in other words, is not so much objective social commentary as a self-interested origins-story of the writer's

---

[78] Compare c. 64, where the abandoned Ariadne laments Theseus' ruthlessly exploitative behaviour, and her marginalized position is contrasted with the hero's unflagging forward trajectory: see Fredrick (1999) on 'haptic poetics'.

[79] C. 63.60: *abero foro, palaestra, stadio et gyminasiis?*

[80] Skinner (1993), 117, and Tatum (1997), 482–3.

[81] Nepos *Atticus* 2: *Itaque interfecto Sulpicio, posteaquam vidit Cinnano tumultu civitatem esse perturbatam neque sibi dari facultatem pro dignitate vivendi, quin alterutram partem offenderet, dissociatis animis civium, cum alii Sullanis, alii Cinnanis faverent partibus, idoneum tempus ratus studiis obsequendi suis, Athenas se contulit.*

[82] Cic. *Div.* 2.2.7: *In libris enim sententiam dicebamus, contionabamur, philosophiam nobis pro rei publicae procuratione substitutam putabamus.*

[83] On Sallustian morality, see Earl (1961), Sklenar (1998).

occupation. In Catullus' case, exasperation with the traditional life-path is an implicit *aetion* of literary activity: instead of taking part in a provincial expedition, he writes with bitterly sarcastic sympathy to friends still suffering the abuses of the system (c. 28; c. 47). Still, there remain important differences between Catullus and others of his contemporaries who espoused the safe harbour of literary *studia*. The historian Sallust and the orator Cicero at least overtly conceded and sometimes insisted on the underlying priority of politics and consequent secondary status of literature. Even Atticus, who might appear to be the furthest removed from Roman politics, produced literary works that reflect a prioritizing of the political sphere. He composed a *Liber Annalis*, and wrote selected histories of noble families.[84] Atticus clearly viewed Italy as an unstable place and Roman politics as unacceptably dangerous, yet enthusiastically carried out his civic duties in the Athenian polis, where he enjoyed the status of a notable public figure.[85] Atticus' choice to avoid Italy and Roman politics was not a radical rejection of public life, but a specific response to the conditions in Rome in the mid first century BC. Atticus maintained contacts with major players on different sides of the factional conflicts, and it is to his keen interest in the Roman political scene that we owe Cicero's epistolary updates and thus much of our knowledge of the history of the period. Cicero, who knew Atticus well, describes him succinctly as 'political by nature'.[86]

Many of those who, like Atticus, live a life of permanent withdrawal still define their leisure and leisure-time activity in terms that do not radically undermine the traditional priorities of *otium* and *negotium*. Cicero, in his discussion of withdrawal and the active life in *De Officiis* (cited above, introduction), confirms the respectability of Atticus' lifestyle.

> There have been many, and there still are, who have sought that kind of tranquility by abandoning public business and fleeing to a life of leisure. These include the noblest and foremost philosophers, and also certain strict and serious men who could not endure the behaviour of the populace or its leaders. Some of these have spent their lives on their estates finding their delight in their family wealth.[87]   (*Off.* 1.69)

The *otiosi* ('men of leisure') whom Cicero approves are of high moral character, and withdraw to their private estates precisely because they care too much about the *res publica* to participate in a corrupted one. The pattern of Atticus' life was perhaps novel, and distinctively suited to the political conditions of his times, but he does not intend to challenge the primacy of public life. Others adopted a position that was more contentious.

---

[84] Millar (1988), 50–5, offers an illuminating discussion of how Atticus' interests in antiquarianism and genealogy, combined with his tactic of political neutrality, anticipate and contribute to the 'Roman revolution' that produced the Augustan principate.

[85] Nep. *Att.*, 2.

[86] Cic. Att. 4.6.1: *nam tu quidem, etsi es natura politikos, tamen nullam habes propriam servitutem, communi † fueris non ne †...* ('For you, though you are political by nature, are not subject to any peculiar servitude, you *** in common with the rest', text and translation Shackleton Bailey (1999)). Atticus has a strong political instinct, but does not adhere to any particular faction or show loyalty to any one grand man.

[87] Tr. Atkins (Atkins and Griffin 1991).

> When, however, those without a reason claim to despise the commands and magis-
> tracies which most men admire, I do not think that should be counted as
> praiseworthy—indeed no, but rather as a vice. It is a difficult thing not to approve
> their view insofar as they disdain glory and think it worthless. But they appear to be
> afraid of hard work and trouble, and also, or so it seems, the humiliation and disrepute
> which results from failure or defeat.　　(*Off.* 1.71, tr. Atkins (Atkins and Griffin 1991))

It is debatable whether Catullus 'disdains glory', although his bitter comments on
the Memmius episode suggest some aversion to humiliation and failure. Ultimately, Catullus' life will not fit into a niche in Cicero's philosophical system.
Catullus neither retreats to his villa in order to live out his life in quiet, respectable
otium, nor does he devote himself to a publicly edifying form of literature.[88]
Catullan poetry challenges the primacy of political life while refusing to remain
wholly sequestered in the niche of dilettantish *lusus* ('play').[89]

Part of Catullus' project of self-differentiation as poet involves distancing
himself from and inverting conventionally accepted categories of value: wealth,
moral probity, virile mastery of social inferiors and women. Yet as often in the
representation of antinomian types, the abnegation of a concern for status is
only apparent. Catullus begins with self-denigration, yet by the end vindicates
the life of poetry as a new paradigm of elite status, perhaps all the more authentic
and credible for its negative articulation. Catullus is not really poor, as he
suggests in c. 10 and c. 13, and his Bithynian narrative, while overtly self-
castigating, subtly discloses his prestigious connections, and his insider's perspective on the workings of imperial administration.[90] The social humiliation he
suffers at the hands of Memmius is inflicted by him in turn on Furius and
Aurelius. The complex literary self-portrait that results, however, does not add
up either to a fully engaged public figure, or to the coherent ethical model of a *vir
urbanus* wholly withdrawn from public life and the axiological criteria of elite
Roman manhood.[91]

---

[88] Cicero makes a particular exception for inherently worthy *artes* 'associated with the investigation
of what is true' (astronomy, geometry, dialectic, civil law; *Off.* 1.19).

[89] On *lusus* and *ludus*, see Wagenvoort (1956). Catullus does of course employ this vocabulary and
partially identify his poetry-composition as a ludic activity, yet his appropriation of other terms to
indicate the seriousness of his poetic endeavour—*officium*, *munus*, the vocabulary of *amicitia* and
political alliance—as well as his evident intensity of devotion to literary matters, render a full correspondence between Catullan poetry and the category of *lusus* impossible. See further below.

[90] See Hinds (2001); Fitzgerald (1995), 174–5.

[91] The complex assessment of Labate (1990) is worth citing here: in Augustan elegy, 'l'amore finisce
per costruire un mondo assiologico autosufficiente, un'ideologia che si oppone all'ideologia della
civitas, e si mostra alternativa proprio nel momento in cui ne mutua alcuni valori fondamentali
(*fides, pietas, virtus*, ecc.) per trasportarli nel proprio spazio e trascodificarli (*da questo punto di vista
è giusto dire che Catullo aveva posto le premesse più importanti dell'elegia latina*)' (italics added, 946–7).
By contrast, 'nella scelta letteraria di Catullo...trova invece espressione una profonda conflittualità
culturale e ideologica: i valori nuovi si misurano con valori largamente accreditati nella società, perché
radicati nella struttura stessa del potere e della vita civile'; Catullus' poetry does not produce
'un modello di *vir urbanus* che...possa presentarsi con la coerenza di una proposta alternativa
autosufficiente' (932). Note also Nappa (2001), 84: 'Catullus, the persona, represents the man who
intellectually comprehends the validity of his actions and arguments, but who can never quite liberate
himself from the anxiety which accompanies a break with societal approval'.

Attempts have been made, of course, to characterize Catullus' cultural stance. Scholars have traditionally identified Catullus' antinomian position with the *urbanitas*-paradigm and its corresponding vocabulary: *bellus* ('lovely'), *venustus* ('attractive'), *facetus* ('witty'), *lepidus* ('charming'). As B. Krostenko has demonstrated, the *urbanitas*-vocabulary emerged as a means of adjudicating a new subset of aristocratic prestige-acquisition, the sophisticated 'social performances' that increasingly supplemented the public achievements of Roman elites.[92] Whereas traditional approbative vocabulary designated qualities of manly excellence and military and political achievement—*bonus, strenuus, fortis, nobilis*—the trendy new vocabulary of *urbanitas* shifted the focus to broadly aesthetic qualities of personal wit, charm, and elegance. Yet for all that the *urbanitas*-vocabulary, especially in the polymetric poems, succeeds in evoking a sophisticated milieu and articulating a non-traditional value-set, *urbanitas* per se does not exhaustively describe Catullus' poetic world and its values.[93] Catullus unambiguously states, in his poem on Suffenus (c. 22), that urbane social manners do not suffice for the creation of poetry worthy of the name. Catullus' use of the language of *urbanitas* in his polymetrics creates space for non-political forms of prestige, yet without collapsing poetry into a mere recapitulation of cultivated elite leisure practices.

The language of urbanity and refinement is not the only vocabulary Catullus transposes and redefines. In the epigrams (c. 69–116), Catullus describes the breakdown of his relation with Lesbia in what scholars have termed the 'language of aristocratic obligation': *officium* ('duty'), *benefecta* ('favours'), *fides* ('reliability'), *pietas* ('dutifulness'), *gratia* ('favour, gratitude'), *foedus* ('pact'), *amicitia* ('friendship').[94] The tragedy of Lesbia's betrayal is narrated in the same moral language as the tragedy of the *res publica* and the corruption of Roman morality. One outcome of Catullus' 'transcodification of values' is to confer moral depth on an area of experience ordinarily classified as mere *nugae*. Catullus' appropriation of a politically freighted moral vocabulary prevents his love/poetry from being reduced to the category of trifling diversion, yet at the same time, emphasizes all the more his distance from the public arena by conspicuously transferring the terminology of aristocratic friendship-obligation to his private love-affair. Charles Platter lucidly characterizes the polemical aim behind such lexical appropriation in his study of *officium* ('duty, service, obligation') in Catullus and love elegy:

> The concept of the citizen-lover is exploited by erotic elegy as part of the poets' self-conscious effort to reposition poetry to rival politics as the true *officium* of a Roman. The result, even when the attempt is facetious, is both to destabilize political discourse by connecting it with the *levia* of poetic speech and to make an implicit claim for the privileged status of poetry as opposed to politics. For poetry to adopt and incorporate the language of the hegemonic discourse of politics is to argue implicitly for its superiority as the more inclusive and hence more powerful form of speech.[95]

---

[92] Krostenko (2001); Ross (1969), 104–12.

[93] Krostenko (2001), 233–90, is emphatic in pointing out that the language of social performance, which was already a prestige-conferring vocabulary employed by the political elite before Catullus, is not simply accepted uncritically by him as the expression of his own ideals.

[94] Ross (1969), 80–95. [95] Platter (1995), 216.

Taken together, these two well-known instances of lexical appropriation are suggestive of Catullus' critical and disjunctive approach to autonomist rhetoric. He assimilates and reworks value-laden vocabulary-sets while refusing to allow them to be merged with his literary position. By this ongoing effort of self-differentiation, Catullus resists the absorption of his poetic discourse within any single reputation-building discourse of the political elite.

SCRIBAM IPSE DE ME: POETRY AND SELF-REPRESENTATION

Whereas Catullus works hard to keep his literary identity in tension with inherited value-systems, other writers and thinkers of the period seek to integrate literary culture with more traditional conceptions of moral utility. The status of poetry, in the eyes of many Romans, remains circumscribed by the hierarchy of *otium* and *negotium* and the primacy of political aims. In traditional terms, action on behalf of the *res publica* is the sole truly worthy elite occupation; other pursuits of less manifest public utility are justifiable only during temporary periods of holiday or retreat. The centrality of warfare and political office in the Roman ideology of aristocratic status remains relatively unshaken despite the increasing Hellenization of elite leisure practices beginning in the second century BC. As late as 49 BC., when he was sidelined under Caesar's dictatorship, Cicero could write: 'all the praise that belongs to virtue lies in action'.[96] However pessimistic his estimate of the viability of the *res publica*, Cicero remains overtly committed to politics as the prime field of activity for the Roman man. This underlying commitment to the active life determines his conception of poetry, whose chief value, on his view, consists in the commemoration of deeds and glorification of the Roman state. Cicero wrote some early poetry in the esoteric Alexandrian style, but his explicit statements about poetry in the *Pro Archia*, scattered remarks in letters (e.g. his disdain of the *neoteroi*),[97] the judgements implicit in his patterns of citation (above all Ennius),[98] and finally, the evidence of his most substantial poetic work, the *Consulatus suus*, suggest a strong emphasis on poetry's public utility and moral exemplarity.

The emergence of an autonomist model of poetic activity challenges both the nature of poetry's moral exemplarity and its subordinate status within the traditional hierarchy of occupations and aims. Catullus' and Cicero's contemporary, the Greek poet and philosopher Philodemus of Gadara, who was at the centre of a group of Epicureans at Piso's villa at Herculaneum, argues for the independence of

---

[96] *Off.* 1.19 (tr. Atkins (Atkins and Griffin 1991)): *virtutis enim laus omnis in actione consistit.*

[97] *Att.* 7.2.1; *Orat.* 161; *Tusc.* 3.45. See Crowther (1970); Clausen (1986); more recently, Knox (2011), who makes a central distinction: 'Cicero was always a Hellenistic poet, never a Callimachean' (193).

[98] Roller (1998), 289, nicely characterizes Cicero's selective incorporation of Ennius, 'an Ennius who will serve as a textual repository of correct, community-oriented aristocratic values and patterns of action'.

poetic excellence from the criterion of moral utility.[99] In concrete terms, he claims that it is possible to represent bad characters in a good poem, and even that a bad person can write good poems. His position is not a rigid or simplistic one. On his view, poetry can have moral utility, and can be studied for its ethical dimension, but a poem's qualities *per se* do not reside in its moral utility: 'poems, insofar as they are poems, do not provide benefit'. This argument may be the closest we will come to finding an explicit *theoretical* vindication of poetic autonomy. Philodemus' own epigrammatic poetry, largely written on erotic and convivial topics, broadly coheres with his theoretical views.[100] Cicero, as it happens, had occasion to comment on Philodemus' style of poetry. Cicero, in the *In Pisonem*, undermines the defendant's character by alluding to Piso's luxurious pursuits as evidenced by Philodemus' poems.

> poema porro facit ita festivum, ita concinnum, ita elegans, ut nihil fieri possit argutius. In quo reprehendat eum licet si qui volet, modo leviter, non ut improbum, non ut audacem, non ut impurum, sed ut Graeculum, ut adsentatorem, ut poetam... Rogatus invitatus coactus ita multa ad istum de ipso quoque scripsit ut omnis hominis libidines, omnia stupra, omnia cenarum conviviorumque genera, adulteria denique eius delicatissimis versibus expresserit; in quibus, si qui velit, possit istius tamquam in speculo vitam intueri.   (Pis. 70)

> He is the author of a poem, moreover, so delightful, so skillfully put together, so elegant, that there could be nothing more clever. One might criticize him for this, if one should wish, but gently, treating him not as a wicked, reckless, and defiled person, but merely as a Greekling, a flatterer, a poet... Begged, invited, and compelled, he addressed so many compositions to the defendant, and about him wrote so many things that he has represented in the most exquisitely refined verses all the man's lusts, immoral sex acts, various sorts of dinners and parties, and, in sum, all his adulteries. In these verses, anyone who wishes may view the defendant's life as in a mirror.

Cicero wishes to demonstrate that he is effortlessly superior in the very pursuits in which Piso affects to be *au courant*. Philodemus is perfectly respectable as an Epicurean philosopher, but his pupil Piso stopped listening after he heard what sounded to his ears like a straightforward exhortation to pleasure (69). The Greek writer's poetic sophistication is similarly reduced to the level of his patron's baseness. Employing the trendy 'language of social performance',[101] Cicero suggests that, while Philodemus may well be a polished and witty writer (*perpolitus... festivum... concinnum... elegans... argutius... delicatissimis versibus*), his poetry's content is determined by his patron's manifold debauchery (*libidines... stupra... adulteria*). Cicero, at once recognizing and subverting Philodemus' autonomist

---

[99] Discussed also in introduction above. For discussion of Philodemus' views on poetics, see Grube (1965) 193ff., and two edited collections, Armstrong (2004) emphasizing his connection with the Augustans, and Obbink (1995), focusing on his poetics; on Philodemus as philosopher in Italy more generally, see Gigante (1995). Sider (1997) offers an edition of Philodemus' epigrams that illuminates the relation between his poetry and his poetic theory, and Janko (2000) an edition of *On Poems*.

[100] Grube (1965), 195, perhaps exaggerates: 'He repeatedly protests... against requiring a moral and educational purpose from a poet, and his own poetry obviously had none'.

[101] Cicero's treatment of Philodemus is discussed by Krostenko (2001) at 157ff.

doctrine, converts his poetry into an unflattering mirror (*speculum*), not of the poet's, but of his patron Piso's life.[102]

Outside the boundaries of Piso's villa, poetry's independence of moral criteria can be reinterpreted adversarially as a sophisticated excuse for dissipation and *luxuria*. Catullus, whose shorter poems in many ways resemble Philodemus', undergoes a comparable risk. What might appear to the *homines venustiores* of his literary coterie as elegant, witty, and sophisticated, to others constitutes evidence of corrupt morals and compromised virility. Catullus' traditionalist readers Furius and Aurelius assume, like Cicero, that poetry is a mirror of life, and conclude on the basis of his love poems to Lesbia (c. 5, c. 7) that he is an effeminate man.

> Pedicabo ego vos et irrumabo,
> Aureli pathice et cinaede Furi,
> qui me ex versiculis meis putastis,
> quod sunt molliculi, parum pudicum.
> nam castum esse decet pium poetam
> ipsum, versiculos nihil necesse est.   (c. 16.1–6)

I'll fuck you in the ass and in the mouth, Aurelius the pathic and Furius the queer, who, because my occasional verses are effeminate, deemed me immoral. For it befits the poet of moral integrity to be pure himself; it is not at all necessary for his verses to be so.

Catullus insists that there is a difference between the poet's personal morality (*pium poetam / ipsum*), and the decorum that governs light verse (*versiculi*). The poet himself preserves a moral integrity that his witty poetry necessarily lacks. Yet in his notionally effeminate verses (*molliculi*), the poet abruptly turns the tables by making a hyper-masculine threat of penetrative assault: 'I will fuck you in the ass and in the mouth' (*pedicabo ego vos et irrumabo*).[103] Catullus is no denizen of Epicurus' garden: his poetic activity is set within the context of fierce contestations of virile primacy among his urban peers. It is not enough for him to make theoretical claims for his poetry's aesthetic autonomy; he must vigorously defend himself against those who would trample the distinction between poetic and personal morality. Some will appreciate the poet's sophisticated literary stance,[104]

---

[102] Grube (1965) 195–6, discusses Philodemus' scepticism of the importance of mimesis to poetry, or 'any direct relation between poetry and reality'. This is not to say, however, that Philodemus is a strict formalist or 'euphonist'.

[103] The most extensive and intricate treatment is Selden (1992); see also Nappa (2001), 45ff. Note the suggestive remarks of Roller (1998), 284, on Pliny's reading of the poem, and the older, still illuminating reading of Macleod (1973) alongside the qualifications of Fitzgerald (1995), 31–2. Traditionally critics have taken the distinction between the 'pious poet himself' (*pium poetam / ipsum*, 5–6) and the poet's playful verses (*versiculos*, 6) to signify a fundamental distinction between art and life. Richlin (1992), 12–13, 145–7 and Fitzgerald (1995), 34, 249 n. 1, usefully challenge this received idea which goes too far both in domesticating Catullus' poetics of virile obscenity and in establishing a reassuring temenos around the aesthetic. Yet Catullus' emphatic contrast between the poet's personal character, and the literary decorum of *versiculi*, sharply marked by word-order and line-break (*poetam / ipsum, versiculos*), can be retained without resorting to the monolithic art/life division rejected by Fitzgerald and Richlin.

[104] This conflict in c. 16 follows a broader pattern whereby Catullus never describes himself as a poet *tout court*, but only introduces the term under the pretext of a highly contested description or debate. Compare c. 49, discussed below; c. 36, discussed above, and c. 35, also discussed above, in which the *tener poeta* Caecilius is too distracted by a love-affair to apply himself to poetry.

but to those who do not understand it, or pretend they do not, Catullus responds in terms they cannot fail to comprehend: *pedicabo ego vos et irrumabo.*

Poets who write with exquisite artifice about morally questionable behaviour are not the only ones who need to defend themselves against adversarial interpretations. Immediately after the forensic exegesis of Philodemus' immoral poetry in Cicero's *In Pisonem* comes a defence of the orator's self-representational poem, the *Consulatus suus.* Appropriately enough, he must defend it against an overly intrusive biographical reading. Piso criticized Cicero's infamous line: *cedant arma togae, concedat laurea laudi* ('let arms yield to the toga, the laurel give way before [civic] glory'). In Piso's eyes, the line implies that Cicero, as consul, surpassed the laurels of Pompey. Cicero, in return, offers Piso a lesson on how to read poetry, placing his adversary in the role of thick-headed pupil.

> 'Tuae dicis' inquit 'togae summum imperatorem esse cessurum.' Quid nunc te, asine, litteras doceam? Non opus est verbis, sed fustibus. Non dixi hanc togam qua sum amictus, nec arma scutum aut gladium unius imperatoris, sed quia pacis est insigne et oti toga, contra autem arma tumultus atque belli, poetarum more locutus hoc intellegi volui, bellum ac tumultum paci atque otio concessurum. Quaere ex familiari tuo, Graeco illo poeta: probabit genus ipsum et agnoscet neque te nihil sapere mirabitur.   (*Pis.* 73–4)

> 'You claim', you say, 'that the highest commander is to yield to *your* toga'. What—am I to give you a literature lesson now, idiot? Cudgels are needed, not words. I did not refer to this toga, which I am wearing, nor the arms, the shield, or the sword of a particular commander. But because the toga is indicative of peace and stability, whereas arms are indicative of instability and war, speaking in the manner of poets, I wanted it to be understood that war and instability would yield to peace and stability. Ask your friend about it—that Greek poet: he will approve and acknowledge this type of figure; nor will he be surprised at your lack of sense.

Philodemus has failed to instill in Piso the basic principles of poetic interpretation. Piso, whose Greek friend simply functions, willingly or not, as an 'authorizer of lust' (*auctorem libidinis*, 69), evidently needs a less pliable (*facilis*) and charming (*venustus*) teacher in order to absorb the lesson properly. Cicero will thus beat it into him (*fustibus*). Cicero is at pains to demonstrate that Piso, who dared to interpret his poem, is not really in his league as student of philosophy or poetry.

Cicero's rough treatment of Piso and Philodemus demonstrates the challenges faced by an autonomist poetic stance. The Greek philosopher's distinction between ethics and aesthetics is not likely to be appreciated in Rome's unforgiving public arena. Cicero himself, however, is not safe from criticism, as his angry response to Piso's comment demonstrates. He too must invoke the limits of biographical interpretation, and like Catullus, aggressively confronts his (mis)reader with violent threats. This very public drama of poetic interpretation affords a glimpse into a watershed phase in the history of poetic activity in Roman society, a moment when the conditions of reception are still highly unstable. Is poetry beholden to moral criteria? Or does poetry occupy its own sequestered realm, detached from public utility and ordinary moral norms?[105]

---

[105] In the subsequent generation of poets, under Augustus, there would be no Cicero to excoriate Horace, Tibullus, and Propertius for their immoral poetry about *libidines* and *convivia* and their

Genre is crucial for any attempt to articulate an answer to these questions. Cicero on the one hand, and Catullus and Philodemus on the other, represent opposite ends of the spectrum. Cicero's epic poem on his own consulship, the *Consulatus suus*, employs a third-person narration to represent its author's achievements in the traditional arena of public life. The epic genre sets individual heroic achievement within the framework of the shared interests of the entire Roman community. Catullus and Philodemus, on the other hand, write in first-person genres that are slender in scope, non-public in subject matter, and that represent figures who are withdrawn from or at odds with public life. Both poets occupy a position physically or axiologically at the margins: Philodemus writes as an Epicurean philosopher in the Bay of Naples, while Catullus poses as an antinomian poet in Rome. Both choose to embody their literary projects in slender, first-person poetic forms, and, in Catullus' case, novel poetic modes such as epyllion that are explicitly distanced from traditional epic.

A major factor underlying these disputes is the erosion of traditional authority and the primacy of the epic genre as expression of the shared moral and political values of the Roman community. The best example of such authority is Ennius' *Annales*, which merged the aristocratic code of honour and the pursuit of *gloria* with the interests of the Roman people. Goldberg's analysis is particularly helpful in describing the underlying ideological profile of Ennian epic: by creating a narrative structure that both '[fulfilled] aristocratic desires for personal honor' and at the same time 'subordinated individual achievement to the greater cause of Roman *gloria*', Ennius 'introduced the first open partnership between aristocratic and poetic interests'.[106] Ennius' articulation of aristocratic values was widely accepted as authoritative because his broad vision of aristocratic *virtus* in service of the Roman state transcended individual and factional interests. By the mid first century BC., however, the Ennian integration of patriotic interests and the aristocratic pursuit of glory were no longer clearly feasible, as individual political participants and factions pursued their own ends often in violent conflict with their adversaries and to the detriment of the *res publica*. The proliferation of works in first-person poetic genres starting with Lucilius and Catullus can be interpreted as one response to the splintering of the (presumptive) ideological unity on which epic was based. This funnelling of literary energies into private spaces and individualist ideological niches would culminate in the otiose warriors of love elegy who claim to be 'triumphant' in their slender poetic/erotic domains.[107]

Some remained committed, however, to the corporatist ideals of the epic genre and Roman public life. Cicero, who long harboured hopes that a 'consensus of good men [of means]' (*consensus bonorum*) would remedy the ills of the *res publica*, was deeply sympathetic to Ennius' political vision, as his frequent, appreciative citations show. He longed for a return to a state of affairs in which the Roman people would be unified under the direction of a wise, benevolent ruling class, rather than torn apart by the ambitions of conflicting dynasts. In the

---

flattery of Augustus, Maecenas, and Messalla. Horace situates Maecenas in erotically charged sympotic scenes in his poetry, confident that no one's extra-textual *gravitas* will be damaged.

[106] Goldberg (1995), 123.   [107] Galinsky (1969).

end, however, Cicero could not avoid being absorbed into factional politics, and in representing himself and his position, frequently had to vindicate his own courses of action against the charges of his adversaries. Cicero's solution to the problem of, on the one hand, epic's traditional corporatist ideology, and, on the other, the need for *individual* self-promotion in an age of conflicting factions, was to identify his personal accomplishments with the salvation of the *res publica*. Cicero's epic poem thus attempts with some awkwardness to harness the Roman epic ideal of heroic action in the service of the community to the vehicle of his personal praises. Cicero, unable to escape the individualist tendencies of the age, uses the communal ideological framework of epic to promote a self-interested account of recent history.

Catullus' self-representational project does not rely on the increasingly discredited ideals of Roman public life, but instead thrives amid the wreckage of communal values. Carving out one's own, autonomous space as antinomian poet becomes more comprehensible when the framework of communal values has come into question. This autonomist turn is even more readily comprehensible when considered in the light of Cicero's ultimately unsuccessful project of poetic self-praise, which neither satisfies rigorous criteria of literary value, nor convincingly integrates self-promotion with patriotic devotion to the *res publica*. Instead of forcing an inevitably unsatisfying harmony out of discordant interests and fractured value-systems, Catullus embraces the splintering of communal ideals, and makes ideological discord into a central preoccupation of his poetry. It will be helpful to consider at greater length what is at stake in the choice between the autonomist poetics of a first-person genre, and traditionalist self-praise within an epic framework.[108] In the following pages, I will consider the respective approaches of Cicero and Catullus to poetic self-representation in greater depth. In comparing Cicero and Catullus, we need not suppose that Catullus is specifically defining himself against Cicero, although he may do so in certain cases.[109] The two poets work out distinct responses to a shared sociopolitical climate: the different options they represent can be understood as participating in broader debates over the function of poetry in late republican society.

The pinnacle of Cicero's career was his consulship and suppression of the conspiracy of Catiline in 63 BC. Scholars are divided on the question of the seriousness of the conspiracy, and to what extent Cicero fabricated or exaggerated the threat, but Cicero apparently considered himself a saviour of Rome. The city, he would later write, underwent a rebirth when he was consul. Cicero dearly wished to benefit from the glory of this achievement, and sought writers, both poets and an historian, to compose an account of the episode. After exhausting

---

[108] Catullus and Cicero are seen as representing different facets of a shared cultural environment in Krostenko (2001), and more recently, Stroup (2010). Stroup's comments (3ff.) on the different approaches of Catullus and Cicero to what she dubs the late republican 'society of the text' are especially relevant to the present discussion. She writes, for example, of 'Catullus' apparent *a principio* rejection of political and forensic activity in favor of the world of the text' (23)—an interesting updating of the New Criticism idea of the 'world of the poem' (applied to Catullus among others). She summarizes: 'we have in Catullus not a man who did not care about the Republic, we have a man who did use his texts to try to change the Republic, because he chose to locate the cultural work of his texts in the textual world alone' (23).

[109] Davis (2002) argues that Catullus does take a position against Ciceronian features of style.

other possibilities, he decided to compose a commemorative poem about the events of his own consulship in verse—not a panegyrical work, he assures Atticus, but a historical one.[110] Later, he would attempt to continue this project by narrating the subsequent story of his exile and return in the *De temporibus meis*, of which no fragments survive. Cicero's *Consulatus suus*, whose circulation is well attested and which survives in substantial fragments, in its basic aims and orientation likely resembled the poem Archias wrote commemorating the deeds of the Luculli, or Cicero's own poem in praise of Marius, a fellow *novus homo* from Arpinum.[111] The underlying justification of poetry in all three instances is the perpetuation of political and military *gloria*.

Unlike Marius, however, Cicero was obliged to write his own history. In a letter to the historian L. Lucceius attempting to persuade him to include a narrative inset on his consulship within his *History of the Social and Civil Wars*, Cicero reveals that he is aware of the key disadvantages of self-commemoration.

> Quod si a te non impetro, hoc est, si quae te res impedierit (neque enim fas esse arbitror quicquam me rogantem abs te non impetrare), cogar fortasse facere, quod nonnulli saepe reprehendunt—scribam ipse de me—multorum tamen exemplo et clarorum virorum. Sed, quod te non fugit, haec sunt in hoc genere vitia: et verecundius ipsi de sese scribant necesse est, si quid est laudandum, et praetereant, si quid reprehendendum est. Accedit etiam ut minor sit fides, minor auctoritas, multi denique reprehendant et dicant verecundiores esse praecones ludorum gymnicorum, qui, cum ceteris coronas imposuerint victoribus eorumque nomina magna voce pronuntiarint, cum ipsi ante ludorum missionem corona donentur, alium praeconem adhibeant, ne sua voce se ipsi victores esse praedicent.   (*Fam.* 5.12.8)

> But if I do not obtain this favour from you, i.e., if something prevents you (for I do not consider it possible that I should ask you for a favour and not get it), I shall be forced perhaps to do what a fair number often criticize—I shall write about myself—though this is supported by the precedent of many illustrious men. But, as you are well aware, there are flaws in this kind of approach, as follows: it is necessary for those writing about themselves to do so rather modestly, if there is anything to be praised, and they must pass over it, if there is anything to be criticized. There is also the fact that the writer's authority diminishes as his reliability diminishes. Many, in short, find fault, and say that the heralds at athletic games are more modest, who, when they crown other victors, announce their names in a loud voice, but when they themselves, before the end of the games, are presented with a crown, summon another herald so as not to pronounce themselves victors in their own voice.

Cicero anticipates that the project may constrain his choices as writer, and provoke criticism in some readers. It is worth remarking, however, that Cicero's worries about the project of poetic self-praise are practical, not fundamental. The comparison of the herald (*praeco*), who calls upon another herald to announce his own victory, effectively undermines the notion of true humility. The herald *wants* his victory proclaimed, but conforms to the etiquette of *verecundia* (modesty) precisely in order to have his victory pronounced in an unabashedly loud voice by someone else. Cicero is concerned with creating a work that attracts the least disparagement (*reprehensio*), and that has the most reliability (*fides*) and authority

---

[110] *Att.* 1.19.10.   [111] A substantial fragment is cited at *Div.* 1.106.

(*auctoritas*) in commemorating his deeds. He does not register any scruples regarding the use of poetry as a medium of political self-glorification. Cicero is adhering to the aristocratic norm in his commitment to maximizing his own fame, and claims the 'example of many illustrious men' in producing a memoir of his own deeds.

In many ways, however, the *Consulatus suus* is a unique and even innovative project. As so often, the *novus homo* from Arpinum dons the mantle of traditionalist patriotism even as he redefines and extends the horizons of cultural possibility. In choosing to write about his own accomplishments, Cicero disrupts the traditional division of labour: he absorbs the roles of both poet and patron, *scriptor* and *laudandus*.[112] He is not simply writing a memoir (*commentarii*), but an epic poem of which he himself is the hero. As a poet who represents his own life rather than a patron's deeds, Cicero anticipates, obliquely and counter-intuitively, both Augustus' *Res gestae* and the first-person genres of the Augustan age.[113] He potentially generates prestige both from the representation of his deeds, and from the accomplished style of the poem that represents him. Calliope and Urania address Cicero at some length in the poem, and the goddess Minerva, with whom the poet/statesman especially identifies himself, is represented as having educated him in the *artes*.[114] Cicero uses the poetic medium to make his literary image conform with his ideal of the strenuous public figure endowed with literary culture and *humanitas*. His narrative goes beyond the recording of *virtus* in the political sphere to include the poet/hero's education and erudition.

The anomalous status of the *Consulatus suus* within the epic tradition is signalled by the fact that the epic hero is the addressee of lengthy speeches from the Muses. Normally, an epic hero engages in dialogue with his special patron gods or goddesses, whereas the poet calls upon the Muse briefly but significantly for inspiration and mnemonic aid. Cicero, who is both poet and hero at once, is significantly exhorted to heroic action by the Muses who also sponsor his poetic endeavour. The longest extant fragment is the speech of Urania (*Div.* 1.7).[115] After discussing omens and predictions that took place during Cicero's consulship, Urania concludes with an allusion to Cicero's early education and literary pursuits.

> haec adeo penitus cura videre sagaci,
> otia qui studiis laeti tenuere decoris,
> inque Academia umbrifera nitidoque Lyceo
> fuderunt claras fecundi pectoris artis.
> e quibus ereptum primo iam a flore iuventae
> te patria in media virtutum mole locavit.
> tum tamen anxiferas curas requiete relaxans,
> quod patria[e] vacat, id studiis nobisque sacrasti.
> (fr. 10.71–8 Courtney = Büchner fr. 6, *Div.* 1.17–22).

---

[112] I owe this point to an anonymous reader for Oxford University Press.

[113] The *Consulatus suus* exerted an underestimated influence on the Augustans, at the very least as a negative example: see especially Lowrie (2002).

[114] Quintilian *Inst.* 11.1.24; *Invective Against Cicero* 7.

[115] As Courtney notes, it is perhaps unsurprising that the single longest citation of Roman poetry in ancient literature is a self-citation by Cicero: Courtney (1993), 162.

Such [duties] were deeply understood with wise contemplation by those who gladly spent their leisure hours in noble studies, and who, in the shady Academy and the gleaming Lyceum, poured forth the brilliant theories of their prolific minds. Your fatherland tore you away from these studies in the first flower of your youth, and set you in the midst of the weighty toils of public life. Nonetheless, soothing your anxious cares with tranquil pursuits, whatever time the fatherland leaves free, you have devoted to literary studies and to us.

Ciceronian self-representation is doubly at stake in this instance, since the passage is quoted in a philosophical dialogue between Cicero and his brother Quintus. It is Cicero's brother who quotes the lines, thus reproducing in prose the indirect mode of self-representation exemplified by the cited passage itself. Just as Cicero has Urania describe to him his own involvement in literary *studia* and public life, so he has Quintus remind him of his own poetry and deeds (. . . . *qui et gesseris ea quae gessisti, et ea, quae pronuntiavi, accuratissime scripseris,*' . . . given that you did those things which you did, and you very scrupulously composed those things which I have quoted', *Div.* 1.22). The passage is well-designed to advertise Cicero's achievements in poetry, philosophy, and politics all at once. Urania, however, still leaves no doubt as to the hierarchy of importance within which literary activity falls: *quod patria[e] vacat, id studiis nobisque sacrasti* ('whatever time the father-land leaves free, you have devoted to literary studies and to us'). There are limits to indulgence in literary pursuits: when the *patria* calls, the qualified man must give up the games of youth to exercise his *virtus* in the public arena. The Muse herself insists on the subordination of literary to political activity.

In another Ciceronian self-citation, the *Consulatus suus* once again stresses the priority of public life. In a letter to Atticus, in which he debates whether or not he should resist Caesar's agrarian bill, Cicero closes with a rousing citation of a passage from the third book. Cicero's muse Calliope in this instance exhorts him to win glory by acting on behalf of the *res publica* (*Att.* 2.3.4).

> interea cursus, quos prima a parte iuventae
> quosque adeo consul virtute animoque petisti,
> hos retine atque auge famam laudesque bonorum.
> (fr. 11 Courtney = Büchner fr. 6)

In the meanwhile, maintain those paths which you have pursued from the first period of youth and still follow as consul according to your valour and spirit, and increase your fame and the praises of good men.

The Muse's words, both within the context of the poem and within the context of the letter to Atticus, function as an exhortation to active *virtus* and the pursuit of glory (*auge famam laudesque bonorum*). The rest of the speech appears to have followed a similar bent. As he writes to Atticus, the book contained 'many aristocratic sentiments' (*eo libro in quo multa sunt scripta* ἀριστοκρατικῶς).[116] Cicero's citation of his own poem does not inspire further poetic labours, but a fresh commitment to a risky course of public action which, as he concedes,[117] may actually end up wrecking his peace of mind and *otium*.

---

[116] *Att.* 2.3.4, tr. Shackleton Bailey (1999).
[117] *Att.* 2.3.4: he will forego *reditus in gratiam cum inimicis, pax cum multitudine, senectutis otium*.

Especially noteworthy in these passages is the dense interweaving of literary and political prestige. Even as Cicero announces the primacy of public life, his poetic erudition is simultaneously on display. Yet the fact that poetry must insert itself amidst other more pressing commitments in a crowded life means that it will not be treated as a fully absorbing sphere of accomplishment in itself. Cicero did not spend an inordinate amount of time crafting and perfecting his *Consulatus suus*: he completed its three books in a single year.[118] Getting the history of his consulship into circulation quickly was a priority; for, as Cicero states quite explicitly in the letter to Lucceius, he wanted to enjoy the *gloria* accruing to his deeds as soon as possible. Cicero certainly wrote skilfully and competently, but he does not display an overriding concern for poetic quality as an end in and of itself.

The bulk of Cicero's self-representational writings, in poetry, speeches, and memoirs, was produced from the late 60s through the mid to late 50s BC. In roughly the same period, Catullus, in his mid to late twenties, was creating a very different kind of literary self-portrait. Catullus immortalizes in his *libellus* an antinomian figure, who cannot be evaluated according to the traditional criteria of the aristocratic reputation.[119] He expends impressive literary labour and erudition on trifling life-fragments (*nugae*) that have little public value, and are even disreputable by traditional moral criteria. Catullus' autonomist poetic project thus engages in a re-evaluation of the traditional criteria by which a Roman man is judged by his peers. At the same time, he devotes considerable attention to the processes of self-representation itself—its media and techniques, the means by which a persona is manufactured out of language.[120] This scrutiny of the workings of persona-construction has the outcome of making his reader aware of the rift between author and textually represented personality. Catullus therefore once again pursues a dual approach to autonomist self-representation. He both undermines the premise of traditional self-promotional utility by laying claim to qualities and behaviour conventionally seen as disreputable, and calls into doubt the referentiality of poetic self-portraiture altogether. To put it simply, he paints a vivid picture of a failed *vir* and makes us doubt whether we can believe any such picture.

An important component of this project is Catullus' critique of what I will term an optimizing self-representational mode: i.e. a mode of self-representation that defines the poet/writer/speaker as possessing the best possible qualities. Catullus applies special scrutiny to self-representational narratives of foreign travel, their pretensions and pitfalls. In c. 4, the self-promoting narrative of a yacht (*phaselus*), whose trajectory appears to map closely onto Catullus' Bithynian journey, is

---

[118] On the poem's rapidity of composition, see Courtney (1993), 149; on versification and word-placement, 150–1.

[119] On negative aspects of Catullus' persona and 'failure', see Nappa (2001), 93 and *passim*. For Nappa, however, these negative aspects of the Catullan persona in the end subserve a 'sophisticated and sustained critique of traditional Roman morality' (18). In the present argument, negative-slanting self-representation does not support disinterested critique of the flaws in Roman society, but an autonomist strategy. By distancing himself, or his persona, from traditionally approved qualities, Catullus problematises the self-promotional utility of his poetry.

[120] See, once again, Selden (1992), *passim*.

framed within a fictive dedicatory inscription.[121] Two features are especially salient: the insistent marking of indirect discourse, and the yacht's exaggeration of its own accomplishments and virtues.

> Phaselus ille quem videtis, hospites,
> ait fuisse navium celerrimus,
> neque ullius natantis impetum trabis
> nequisse praeterire, sive palmulis
> opus foret volare sive linteo.
> et hoc negat minacis Hadriatici
> negare litus insulasve Cycladas
> Rhodumque nobilem horridamque Thracia
> Propontida trucemve Ponticum sinum,
> ubi iste post phaselus antea fuit
> comata silva: nam Cytorio in iugo
> loquente saepe sibulum edidit coma.   (c. 4.1–12)

The yacht that you see, strangers, claims that it was the swiftest of ships, and that it was not incapable of surpassing the speed of any floating bark, whether there was need to travel by oars or sail. The ship further states that these claims are not denied by the shore of the menacing Adriatic, the islands of the Cyclades, famous Rhodes, Propontis shivering with the wind from Thrace, and the savage gulf of Pontus, where earlier it was a leafy forest (afterwards a yacht): for on the ridge of Cytorus it often sent forth a whispering sound from its talkative leaves.

Catullus, in c. 4, attempts an unusually complex framing of poetic speech: the poem represents a dedicatory inscription addressed to passersby (*hospites*), which reports, in turn, the speech of the loquacious yacht. The distancing-effect of the numerous markers of indirect discourse (*ait fuisse . . . negat . . . negare*) encourages us to view the yacht's claims with some scepticism, and even to adopt a condescending attitude towards the yacht's naive self-promotion.[122] The yacht's claims are humorously pompous: calling to witness the exotic locations on its route, the yacht claims, in posh Greek syntax,[123] to have been 'the speediest of ships' (*navium celerrimus*), and to have surpassed all other 'floating timber' (*natantis . . . trabis*). The yacht further claims to have braved all manner of storms, and to have done so without the aid of vows to the gods made on its behalf (18–24).

The yacht is patently constructing a self-promotional narrative,[124] humorous in its extravagance, but for Romans of the period, not totally implausible as an instance of boastful one-upmanship. Without going further afield, one might think of Ciceronian self-representation and the *Consulatus suus*: the yacht shares Cicero's penchant for self-praise, which it indulges in a notably fulsome manner. Gregson Davis provides detailed support for this suspicion, arguing that Catullus'

---

[121] Cat. c. 4 in some ways presents itself as a puzzle, and has thus been 'solved' in various ways according to shifts in scholarly approach: e.g. the New Criticism in the case of Copley (1958), and, in a different way, allowing for more emotional expressivity, Putnam (1962); Hornsby (1963) offers an appreciation of its literary artistry; for Griffith (1983), the boat is a model boat made out of boxwood, for Davis (2002) a vehicle for commentary on literary style, and for Fitzgerald (1995), 104–10, it is freighted with concerns about social class and condescension. Most recently, c. 4 has been read in terms of the anxiety of dependence of Roman authors on the books and scholars of the Greek East: Young (2011). In the text cited here, note that I read *Thracia* in line 8 and *novissime* in line 24.

[122] Fitzgerald (1995), 108.   [123] Fordyce (1961), ad loc.

[124] On the poem's urbane wordplay, Fitzgerald (1995), 109.

main target in c. 4 is the Asianist oratorical style, of which Cicero was seen as a prime exponent.[125] The richly ornate syntax and the proliferation of superlatives (*celerrimus…cognitissima…novissime*) provide only the more obvious examples. Beyond stylistic parody, Catullus draws attention to the pompous superfluity of the yacht's speech in proportion to the actual poverty of its achievement. The yacht has merely completed a single journey safely, yet boasts of its heroic seafaring in quasi-epic terms. This humorous discrepancy would seem to fit Cicero's case quite well. He eagerly embraced the opportunity to celebrate his consulship as the rebirth of Rome itself, though others ascribed considerably less importance to his intervention.[126] Again, Catullus is not necessarily referring to Ciceronian self-representation, so much as subjecting to parodic critique an excessively self-promoting self-representational mode. Catullus and Cicero represent different reflexes of a cultural climate that was saturated in self-representational narratives, monuments, and images.[127]

Beyond deflating the pretensions of a self-promoting rhetoric, the yacht's discourse provides an occasion for Catullus to reflect on his position as self-representational poet. The itinerary described in c. 4 roughly corresponds to Catullus' return-journey from Bithynia to his villa on the Lago di Garda (.... *novissime hunc ad usque limpidum lacum*, 24). The yacht's current tranquil retirement, on this line of interpretation, would correspond to Catullus' condition of *otium* as poet:[128] *nunc recondita / senet quiete seque dedicat tibi, / gemelle Castor et gemelle Castoris* ('now [the yacht] grows old in the tranquillity of retirement, and dedicates itself to you, twin Castor and Castor's twin', 25–7). Of course, Catullus hardly writes in the persona of an old man, as the opening lines of the poem that immediately follows c. 4 in our collection reinforce: *vivamus, mea Lesbia, atque amemus, / rumoresque senum severiorum / omnes unius aestimemus assis* ('Let us live, my Lesbia, and let us love, and reckon the worth of all the rumours of crabbed old men at one penny', c. 5.1–3). On the other hand, the anomaly of a boat that retreats into instantaneous retirement after its maiden voyage may be an implicit comment on the anomalous status of the polymetric 'Catullus', who, after a single tour of duty abroad, has apparently devoted himself to poetry and *otium*. The yacht's speech—indeed the yacht itself—are not obscurely associated with the medium of poetry itself. The theme of sea travel generally has a metapoetic resonance in ancient poetry, and the speech of this particular *phaselus* is cited in a pure iambic trimeter. Even more striking is Catullus' careful tracing of the boat's origin as wooden *materia* ('wood'/'subject matter') that already in its primeval state

---

[125] The poem's string of vacuous superlatives and ornate syntax parody the style Catullus would have seen as the antithesis to his friend Calvus' spare, Atticist oratory: Davis (2002).

[126] In any case, as Goldberg (1995), 152, aptly notes, Cicero's accomplishments as consul did not stand up well to the test of time: 'the laurels so proudly worn in the glory days of 63 did not look equally fine by the 50s "harsher light"'.

[127] See in particular Selden (1992), 489–99. Another major self-representational mode of the period, of course, is represented by the third-person *commentarii* of Julius Caesar; on their considerable literary and rhetorical artifice, see Batstone and Damon (2006), *passim*. Caesar, like Cicero in the *Consulatus suus* and elsewhere, and like Catullus (humorously) in c. 4, is interested in various strategies of deflecting first-person narration.

[128] Fredrick (1999), 50, reads 'the retirement of the *phaselus*' as 'a metaphor for poetics in the face of cultural transformation'.

emitted sibilant speech. The boat, like 'Catullus', goes from making a voyage to making poems out of the experience of having been on a voyage.[129] The boat's distinctive path from a life of action to loquacious, self-representing retirement, from achievement to textual inscription, encapsulates issues surrounding the pursuit of poetry at the expense of a traditional career-path.

Yet despite some resemblance to the Catullan persona, the speaking *phaselus* does not offer, and is not meant to offer, a satisfactory model of representational poetry. The yacht's chief fault lies in the attempt to make too much of itself in words. Catullus emphatically divorces self-representational poetry from established laudatory paradigms, and thus demands to be evaluated on a radically different basis. He goes out of his way to create poetry that could not be interpreted as subserving his public image in the way that Cicero's poetry so clearly did. We must assume that at some level Catullus' poetry projects an image that the author approves, and considers potentially attractive to fellow *urbani*, but it is decidedly at odds with the boastful superlatives of the *phaselus*. Catullus likes to represent figures (including his own *ego*) who are exquisite wrecks.

Talking about journeys, and the Bithynian expedition in particular, is one way for Catullus to articulate the position of writer, and to examine different attitudes towards and constructions of the life of action.[130] In c. 10, Catullus explicitly treats the topic directly and at length. While several scholars have noted the ironic effects of Catullus' anecdotal framing of his own speech, the broader structural resemblance of c. 10 to the yacht's reported discourse in c. 4 has not been sufficiently appreciated. Poem 10, like c. 4, constitutes an instance of reported self-representational speech. Yet here it is 'Catullus' himself, not the yacht, who reflects on a Bithynian journey, and whose efforts at self-promotion are subjected to scrutiny.

> Varus me meus ad suos amores
> visum duxerat e foro otiosum,
> scortillum, ut mihi tum repente visum est,
> non sane illepidum neque invenustum.
> huc ut venimus, incidere nobis
> sermones varii, in quibus, quid esset
> iam Bithynia, quo modo se haberet,
> et quonam mihi profuisset aere.
> respondi id quod erat, nihil neque ipsis
> nec praetoribus esse nec cohorti,
> cur quisquam caput unctius referret,
> praesertim quibus esset irrumator
> praetor, nec faceret pili cohortem.
> 'at certe tamen,' inquiunt 'quod illic
> natum dicitur esse, comparasti
> ad lecticam homines.' ego, ut puellae
> unum me facerem beatiorem,
> 'non' inquam 'mihi tam fuit maligne,
> ut, provincia quod mala incidisset,

---

[129] See Fredrick (1999), 66–70.

[130] The same might be said of the Augustan poets, who produce their own highly metaliterary versions of the *propemptikon* and its variations: for example, Horace *Odes* 1.3, 1.22; Propertius 1.6, Tibullus 1.3.

> non possem octo homines parare rectos.'
> at mi nullus erat nec hic neque illic,
> fractum qui veteris pedem grabati
> in collo sibi collocare posset.
> hic illa, ut decuit cinaediorem,
> 'quaeso', inquit 'mihi, mi Catulle, paulum
> istos commoda: nam volo ad Serapim
> deferri.' 'mane,' inquii puellae,
> 'istud quod modo dixeram me habere,
> fugit me ratio: meus sodalis—
> Cinna est Gaius,—is sibi paravit.
> verum, utrum illius an mei, quid ad me?
> utor tam bene quam mihi pararim.
> sed tu insulsa male et molesta vivis,
> per quam non licet esse neglegentem.'

Varus led me, when I was at leisure, out of the forum to see his girlfriend, a little wench, as it struck me at first glance, not at all lacking in charm and looks. When we got there, various topics of conversation came up, among which the question of how Bithynia was at present, how its affairs were going, and whether I had made any money. I responded with the truth: there was no way either for the natives, or the praetors, or the staff, to make themselves any richer than before, especially for those who had a fucker of a praetor who didn't give a damn for his cohort. 'Well at any rate', they say, 'you must have obtained what is said to be the native product—litter-bearers'. I said, in order to make myself seem particularly successful to the girl, 'Things did not go so badly for me—bad as the province was that fell to my lot—that I could not get eight sturdy men'. Now, I did not have a single one, neither here nor there, who could hoist onto his back the broken leg of an old cot. Thereupon she—the little whore that she was—said, 'I beg you, my dear Catullus, lend them to me for a little: for I want to be taken to the temple of Serapis'. 'Hold it', I said to the girl, 'what I just said now about me having them—I wasn't thinking: my friend—Gaius Cinna, I mean—he bought them for himself. But what is it to me whether they are his or mine? I use them as freely as if I had bought them myself. But you are tasteless and a hindrance, who do not let a man be off his guard for a moment.'

The poet leaves the public space of the forum, and enters a private dwelling where he engages in urbane conversation with a strikingly stylish 'little whore' (*non sane illepidum neque invenustum*).[131] Amongst *urbani* who presumably share his counter-conventional sensibility, Catullus is able to speak frankly about a failed public venture, specifically his own failure to make money in the cohort of Memmius in Bithynia. When asked how he made out, Catullus is at first unflinchingly honest—'I told it as it was' (*respondi id quod erat*).

Catullus' candid answer to the question about money at first suggests that he is able to assume a degree of nonchalance (*neglegentia*) about a competition that, if his poems of political invective are any indication, can vouchsafe victory only to a few immensely rich and powerful men and their parasitical supporters. The atmosphere of sophisticated complicity seems to promise an opportunity to

---

[131] As Segal (1970), 27, observes: 'it may be more than accident or anecdotal realism that Varus leads the *otiosum Catullum* of 10 *e foro*'. He further remarks: the '*otiosus* [man of leisure] not only leads a life which has its centre far from the forum and is discrepant with its occupations; he also devotes his energies to analysing, savouring, recording these "unforensic" experiences' (27).

make social capital out of failure, to impress others with an irreverent, uncensored narrative of his exploitation as member of Memmius' staff. Provocatively avowing the status of victim, as W. Fitzgerald's subtle exegesis of c. 10 and c. 11 demonstrates, displays a novel form of confidence, defining the person who can do this successfully as urbane.[132] But this attitude can only succeed in the end if the person professing it really *is* indifferent to wealth, or in any case, can sustain the claim under intense scrutiny. Varus' girlfriend uncovers Catullus' ruse, and forces an awkward recantation. In a brilliant twist, the question of Catullus' worth in material terms is transposed onto the scene of idleness where he might have hoped to find refuge. Urbane conversation (*sermones varii*) supplants the public speech of the forum; male *negotium* is displaced by sociability centred around an elegant, sexually attractive woman. The very attractiveness of the woman, however, inspires in Catullus a desire to make himself appear 'especially well-off' (*unum . . . beatiorem*), plunging him back into the anxieties over wealth and status he affected to transcend.

At first, Catullus appears to take an approach to self-representation directly opposed to that of the *phaselus*: asked how much he profited, he answers simply, 'nothing' (*nihil*). As Catullus is exposed to further pressures, however, this 'nothing' is compromisingly expanded into 'well, not quite nothing, exactly'. Catullus' series of awkwardly negated negations begins to resemble the boat's magnification of its far-flung exploits: *non . . . mihi tam fuit maligne . . . ut . . . non possem . . . parare* ('things did not go so badly for me that I couldn't get . . .'; compare c. 4.6–7, *negat . . . negare*). But whereas the inscriptional speaker of c. 4 laces his report of the yacht's speech with the subtle hint of condescending irony, the poetic speaker of c. 10 directly refutes the lie of the 'Catullus' within the anecdote: *at mi nullus erat nec hic neque illic, / fractum qui veteris pedem grabati / in collo sibi collocare posset* ('But I had neither here nor there anyone who could hoist onto his back the broken foot of an old cot', 21–3). Here, however, a more subtle ploy emerges. The authorial Catullus at once distracts the reader by disclosing his dishonesty and moral weakness within the anecdote, and at the same time, tacitly regains the reader's admiration and trust through a show of honesty at the level of poetic text. Through this rhetorical ploy, he comes off as someone with an appealing capacity for self-criticism, and who is capable of precisely the cool indifference to conventional criteria of social worth the anecdote appears to disavow. There is an effortlessness in Catullus' easy anecdotal style that is belied by the strenuous effort of self-differentiation apparent on closer examination. We are made to understand that he is *not* an uncritical self-promoter in the manner of the grandiloquent *phaselus*.

In the process of renegotiating the terms of his self-description, Catullus promotes a form of self-representational poetry advertised as distinct from the

---

[132] The discussion of the 'ruse of the victim' in Fitzgerald (1995), 169–79, is of critical importance, as is the fundamental discussion in Skinner (1989). Skinner shows how c. 10, previously read merely as a humorous anecdote demonstrating, if anything, the disarming charm of *urbanitas*, is in fact all about power, domination, exclusion and the mapping of these concerns onto sex, gender roles, and sociability. Note also Nappa (2001), 87–93, on Catullus' apparently negative self-portrait in this poem. On Catullus' exposure of an imperialist mentality (and the limits of such exposure), see Hinds (2001), 231–6. Both Skinner (1989) and Pedrick (1986) call attention both to the unreliable speaker's manipulation of his audience and to their possible resistance to manipulation; see Skinner (2001) for more detailed speculation as to Catullus' audience(s) and occasion of performance.

yacht's self-aggrandizing narrative of its deeds. The poem that follows in our collection further develops the theme of foreign travel and the poet's counter-traditional life. Catullus, who reflected bitterly on his lack of profit from the Bithynian journey in c. 10, at the opening of c. 11 envisages a renewed expedition to the boundaries of Roman territory, accompanied by Furius and Aurelius.[133]

> Furi et Aureli, comites Catulli,
> sive in extremos penetrabit Indos,
> litus ut longe resonante Eoa
>   tunditur unda,
> sive in Hyrcanos Arabesque molles,
> seu Sagas sagittiferosve Parthos,
> sive quae septemgeminus colorat
>   aequora Nilus,
> sive trans altas gradietur Alpes,
> Caesaris visens monimenta magni,
> Gallicum Rhenum horribile aequor ulti-
>   mosque Britannos,
> omnia haec, quaecumque feret voluntas
> caelitum, temptare simul parati,
> pauca nuntiate meae puellae
> non bona dicta.　(c. 11.1–16)

Furius and Aurelius, comrades of Catullus, whether he will penetrate into furthest India, where the shoreline is pounded by the far-resounding Eoan wave, or whether he will travel to the Hyrcani and effeminate Arabs, or to the Sacae or arrow-bearing Parthians or to the plains tinged with color by the seven-mouthed Nile, or whether he will traverse the high Alps, going to see the memorials of great Caesar, the Gallic Rhine—a rough body of water—and Britain at the end of the world; you who are prepared to risk all these adventures with me, whatever the will of the gods brings, deliver this short nasty message to my girlfriend.

Furius and Aurelius are apparently ready and willing to follow Catullus anywhere and undergo any number of dangerous tasks.[134] Just as the poem's long opening sentence comes to an end, however, Catullus overturns its meaning and rejects the conventional scenario of virile exploits in foreign lands. The masculine duo, who are the objects of Catullus' pederastic wit in c. 16, come in for equally humiliating treatment here. These would-be *comites* will be converted into the bearers of a sordid lover's note.

Especially noteworthy is the swift, brutal conversion of one scenario into a radically different one mid-poem. This conversion dramatizes the poet's re-focusing of attention from public, imperial concerns to the private domain of his erotic obsession. Poem 10 moved from the forum into *otium*, from Bithynia to the Roman demimonde. Poem 11 now maps a similar trajectory from far-away

---

[133] The challenging twists and turns of c. 11 have inspired many scholars to make sense of its 'unity', to achieve a comprehensive understanding of its structure and core concerns: for example, Putnam (1974); Fotiou (1975); Duclos (1976); Mulroy (1977); Heath (1989); Yardley (1981); Scott (1983); Sweet (1987); Forsythe (1991); Fredricksmeyer (1993).

[134] Nisbet and Hubbard (1978), 97, observe: 'to declare one's willingness to share arduous journeys was a conventional sign of devotion . . . formalized in the military oath'.

lands to urban gossip, public duty to private invective, *cohors* to *scortum*. It should be noted, however, that Catullus does not simply reject serious themes in favour of the light, erotic distractions of his leisure-world. The poet shifts focus from one domain to another, yet he appropriates the rejected domain's attributes in order to build up the importance and autonomous validity of his Lesbia-centred poetry. Catullus transfers imperial themes of conquest, possession, and dominance to the description of Lesbia's promiscuous sexual appetites (*penetrabit...tunditur... molles*, 2–5, 'will penetrate... is pounded... effeminate'; *tenet...rumpens*, 18, 20).

> cum suis vivat valeatque moechis,
> quos simul complexa tenet trecentos,
> nullum amans vere, sed identidem omnium
>   ilia rumpens;
> nec meum respectet, ut ante, amorem,
> qui illius culpa cecidit velut prati
> ultimi flos, praetereunte postquam
>   tactus aratro est.   (c. 10.17–24)

Let her live and flourish with her adulterous lovers, whom she holds in her embrace three-hundred at once, loving none truly, but repeatedly bursting all of their groins; nor let her look, as before, to my love, which, through her fault, has fallen like a flower at the edge of the field, touched by the plough as it passes by.

Following the contours of the Sapphic stanza, Catullus designedly reduces the poem's scope to the boundaries of his erotic interests. We move from *omnia* to *pauca*, from 'Britain at the edge of the world' (*ultimos Britannos*) to a 'flower at the edge of a field' (*prati / ultimi flos*), from the Roman empire to Lesbia's bed. The figure of the poet himself undergoes a comparable diminution of status. Whereas at first he is notionally the leader of an expedition and the subject of active verbs (*penetrabit... gradietur* 'will penetrate... will go'), by the end he is Lesbia's victim, metaphorically aligned with the feminine flower cut down by Lesbia's masculine plough.[135]

It is hard to imagine a sharper renunciation of the kind of foreign exploits advertised by the *phaselus* in c. 4. Rather than pursuing a virile itinerary, penetrating foreign lands, travelling among conquered Gauls and effeminate Easterners (*Arabesque molles*), Catullus will remain in Rome as a conspicuous example of *mollitia* ('softness/effeminacy'), rehearsing in his memory and poetry Lesbia's destructive domination of him. There are numerous ways, of course, in which Catullus' apparent renunciation of virile status actually redefines his virile status and serves his self-representational interests. Being the victim of a shameless, unscrupulous woman, as in c. 10, is not necessarily discreditable. The victim preserves a degree of moral integrity that the victimizer does not.[136] Catullus, moreover, is the creator of Lesbia's literary image, and thus, in poetic terms, he controls her as much, and perhaps more, than she dominates him.[137] Specifically, Catullus uses her to answer and defeat the devotees of a traditional career. Furius and Aurelius, we are to understand, cannot hope to stand up to the poetic force generated by the representation of Lesbia. Even if she is monstrously destructive,

---

[135] On this 'process of circumscription', see Janan (1994), 64.
[136] Again, Fitzgerald (1995), 169–79.
[137] Catullus thus provides the model of Propertius' 'written woman': Wyke (1987a).

her domination confers a paradoxical kind of autonomy on Catullus as poet.[138] Drawn by Lesbia's irresistible pull, he turns away from Caesar's *monumenta* in Gaul and the whole panorama of empire, and focuses on the reduced yet powerfully absorbing domain of erotic poetry.

Poems 4, 10, and 11 are about voyages, travel, and transit: they move from seafaring to retirement, from *forum* to *otium*, from imperial to erotic domination. These voyages, however, may end up leaving the reader with a sense of incompletion and 'unfinished business'. The focus, in each instance, falls on the voyage itself, the act of transition from one realm to another, and not on an achieved state or condition of being. It is difficult, moreover, to locate the still-point of autobiographical truth in Catullus' narrated voyages. This sequence of meta-self-representational poems draws explicit attention to the ways in which the writer constructs a literary self in relation to such key coordinates as 'the life of action' and the 'life of withdrawal', but without committing to a clearly outlined self-representational profile. In broad terms, Catullus projects an antinomian literary personality, often actively disavowing conventionally admired ethical traits, yet as we have seen, this disavowal at times appears unstable and even disingenuous. At the same time, he applies close attention to the linguistic medium of poetic self-representation itself, bringing into sometimes uncomfortable focus the techniques, syntax, media, and social dynamics of self-promotional rhetoric. Such emphasis on technique, medium, and device elicits the recognition that his own literary personality is a sophisticated construct.

The difference between Catullan and Ciceronian poetic self-representation merits some final comment. At first glance, Catullus' tactic of actively disavowing conventionally admired qualities presents a sharp contrast with Cicero's efforts at self-promotion as saviour of the state. Catullus' antinomian treatment of the concepts of action and *otium* and his refusal to harmonize the value of literature with the value of public duty could not be more different from Cicero's persistent tendency to prioritize service to the *res publica* over literary *studia* and harness the latter to the benefit of the former. Catullus' autonomist approach to self-representation is carefully designed to undermine (the appearance of) self-promotional utility in his poetry. His poetry's value, if it does not contribute to boosting the poet's reputation and virile status, must reside (we are encouraged to conclude) in some other quality, i.e. its aesthetic dimension.

At some level, of course, Catullus' and Cicero's self-representational motives were not so very different. Both sought ways to present themselves effectively before their elite peers in a highly competitive, adversarial cultural climate. Nevertheless their tactics diverged. Whereas Cicero generally seeks to integrate his literary interests with the interests of the Roman state and merge poetic self-representation with traditional conceptions of excellence and public duty, Catullus' autonomist poetic self-representation works to effect a series of fractures, disjunctions, and evasions. He avoids fully identifying himself either with the values of public life or with a stable model of otiose withdrawal, often focusing instead on the very dynamics of persona-construction. Rather than mapping a clear itinerary ('from crisis of the *res publica* to salvation under M. Tullius Cicero's leadership'), Catullus explores complicated transitions, violent, unstable shifts in

---

[138] See the discussion of similar dynamic in Propertius: McCarthy (1998).

focus, transformations that are afterwards regretted, movements from one sphere to another that remain incomplete. Catullus, who, by contrast with Cicero, is attempting to confer on poetry its own, distinctive value *not* subordinate to traditional schemes of value, has no recourse to an already established cultural space and axiological position. He defines his activity less in terms of a final destination than in terms of what he is rejecting and leaving behind.

THE WORST POET

The single poem that Catullus addresses to Cicero might seem like an ideal peg on which to hang any interpretation of the relation between the two writers. Poem 49, however, is infamous for the elusiveness and tantalizing paucity of its substantive remarks on the nature of their connection.

> Disertissime Romuli nepotum,
> quot sunt quotque fuere, Marce Tulli,
> quotque post aliis erunt in annis,
> gratias tibi maximas Catullus
> agit pessimus omnium poeta,
> tanto pessimus omnium poeta,
> quanto tu optimus omnium patronus.

Marcus Tullius, most eloquent of Romulus' descendants, as many as there are, as many as there have been, and as many as there shall be in later years, to you Catullus gives very great thanks, Catullus, who is the worst poet of all—as much the worst poet of all as you are the best advocate of all.

Scholars have drawn differing conclusions from this enigmatic speech-act.[139] My own view is most closely approximated by W. J. Tatum, who views c. 49 as an 'ironic *actio gratiarum*', in which Catullus, 'by presenting himself as a grateful, abject *cliens*, flouts the public image which Cicero had labored so assiduously to acquire and maintain'.[140] Catullus deliberately employs terms that were widely recognized as central to Cicero's own idealizing self-representation, and does so in a faintly pompous Ciceronian style. If our collection represents Catullus' original ordering, then, as Clausen points out, 'the contrast between 49 and 50 . . . would be pointed: Cicero, ornate and pompous (an effect contrived in seven hendecasyllables) and Calvus, witty and elegant'.[141] But neither

---

[139] Some insist that the poem is 'meant to be taken at face value, as a genuine expression of admiration and gratitude' (Fordyce (1961) ad loc.). Most discern irony or implicit criticism of Cicero, although even here the nature of the sneer varies widely on different estimates. Stylistic parody certainly appears possible, given that the poem's language recalls Cicero's predilection for syntactic parallelism and honorific superlatives. For some it is the indiscriminate nature of Cicero's advocacy that is being criticized, though in a letter to Caecina he applies the very term *omnium patronus* to himself without disparagement; for others, Catullus was necessarily disdainful of someone who denigrated the *neoteroi*; and for yet others, Catullus' close friendship with Calvus explains his subtle denigration of an orator who both defended Vatinius against Calvus' prosecution and exemplified the faults of an Asianist rhetorical style. See Laughton (1970); Fredricksmeyer (1973); Tatum (1988); Svavarsson (1999).

[140] Tatum (1988), 184.   [141] Clausen (1986), 160 n. 3.

the ordering nor the implicit contrast with Calvus can be taken for granted. Even in Tatum's estimate, 'the poem remains a puzzle'.[142]

If the underlying attitude remains elusive, however, the poem's overt gestures remain available for interpretation—and these gestures, I wish to point out, are highly relevant to the question of poetic self-representation. Poem 49 sharply differentiates the occupations of poet and addressee, and attaches to each of their respective vocations its own superlative adjective. Not only are they paired, they are correlated according to an inversely proportional relation. Catullus is the 'worst poet of all' (*pessimus omnium poeta*) to the precise degree that (*tanto... quanto*) Cicero is the 'best advocate of all' (*optimus omnium patronus*).[143] Some have detected a hint of competitiveness. Catullus' status rises only insofar as Cicero's falls. At an even more essential level, it is remarkable that Catullus enacts so explicit and severe a division of roles in the first place. Despite his later reputation as the quintessential bad poet, Cicero contributed substantially to the refinement of the Latin hexameter, and produced a translation of Aratus' *Phaenomena*. Catullus could hardly have failed to notice a major competitor. As one critic writes, 'before the rise of Lucretius and Catullus... Cicero was the poet of his age'.[144] In c. 49, however, Catullus refuses to allow Cicero to enter into the poetry competition. In Catullus' autonomist construction of poetic identity, the field of poetry does not admit any and all practitioners. Cicero, however unjustly, is excluded from that field, and confined within *his own* area of expertise: advocacy.

Catullus' divisive approach to this issue contrasts with Cicero's own tendencies. In his conception of the relation among the various branches of learned pursuits and their relation to the life of action, Cicero is profoundly inclusive and integrationist. Cicero promotes the idea of a certain 'kinship' among the various liberal arts,[145] and views literary *otium* and the pursuit of political *dignitas* as ideally compatible. The 'best sort' of men, described variously as *boni, honesti*, and *optimi,* are simultaneously men of wealth, ethical integrity, and culture. They recognize the benefits of civilization and the arts of a peaceful, stable society, among which may be counted literary pursuits (*studia*). The liberal arts contribute to *humanitas*, a term which, in Ciceronian usage, refers to civilization in general and sometimes specifically literary culture. The cultural heroes who inhabit Cicero's philosophical dialogues are explicitly represented as men of excellent character and the highest importance to the *res publica*, who also take an interest in matters of literary culture, and can dispute philosophical points at a high level of competence. They do not expend excessive time and energy on literary *studia* to the point of detracting from their public duties; they recognize and respect the hierarchy of importance governing *otium* and *negotium*. Cicero's model public figures and orators benefit from learned pursuits, some of which may even aid them in the public sphere, without losing sight of the paramount status of the *res publica*. Cicero concedes that the strikingly high level of disputation in his

---

[142] Tatum (1988), 179.

[143] Interpreted by some as cuttingly ambiguous: 'the best advocate of all', or the unscrupulous defender of one and all.

[144] R. Y. Tyrrell (1895), 15; cited by Spaeth (1931), 501. Note also the famous praise for his poetry in Plutarch's *Cicero* (2).

[145] *Pro Archia* 2.

philosophical dialogues is a commonplace fiction (*morem dialogorum*),[146] but it nonetheless represents his ideal of the harmonious integration of literary erudition and practical experience in the public realm.

Catullus defines himself and his activity as poet around a sharper-edged series of oppositions. Catullus does not mind being called *pessimus poeta* ('worst poet'), provided that *pessimus* indicates his playfully risqué poetic persona and not a lack of technical capacity (c. 36, c. 49). Suffenus, in the meanwhile, displays excellent personal qualities (*belllus, urbanus, facetus*), but fails utterly as a poet. Catullus himself admits to projecting a morally questionable persona in his effeminate verses (*molliculi*), but insists that their generically determined moral laxity does not extend to the 'the dutiful poet himself' (c. 16). This claim may appear to preserve the poet's moral integrity, but the opposition is unstable. Ultimately the poet's personal morality cannot be neatly sequestered from his verses. Catullus' division of literature and ethics is not rigid, but neither does he allow a facile union of the two.[147] The reader is left in an uncertain position, unable to decide whether the antinomian poetic persona represents the author's life or not. In c. 49, it is difficult to tell whether the evaluative terms *optimus* ('best') and *pessimus* ('worst') refer to technical proficiency, moral qualities, or both. Catullus' marked reticence on this question leaves open a range of contentious possibilities. The 'worst' poet, for example, may turn out to be morally rakish, but technically excellent. Whereas Cicero prefers to integrate public dignity and literary pursuits, Catullus creates a series of fractures. The Ciceronian ideal of the multi-faceted excellence of the publicly strenuous man of impressive erudition and broad literary culture may not exist in Catullus' world. In any case, we are not encouraged to take for granted the congruence of different spheres of achievement within a broader conception of 'excellence'.

The problem of how to negotiate different spheres of achievement forms part of a broader Catullan concern with self-representation, both his own and others'. Catullus was highly sensitive to the dangers of inflated self-description, and adept at turning approbative terms against those by whom they are especially coveted. Suffenus' social persona is urbane, but when you read his poetry, 'that suave [*bellus*] and urbane [*urbanus*] fellow . . . now resembles a mere goatherd or ditch-digger' (*bellus ille et urbanus . . . . unus caprimulgus aut fossor / rursus videtur*). The smug regulars of the *salax taberna* in c. 37, who apparently think very highly of themselves, are sarcastically presented as 'men of rank and fortune': *hanc boni beatique / omnes amatis* (14). Catullus singles out the fatuous vanity of Egnatius, 'made a gentleman (*bonum*) by his thick beard and teeth polished with Spanish piss' (19–20). Catullus' heightened awareness of the fatuity of self-approbation no doubt made him wary of the pitfalls of self-representation in his own poetry. In c. 22, after demolishing Suffenus' claims to poetic seriousness, Catullus has not yet fully come to an end of what he wants to say.

---

[146] *Fam.* 9.8.2.

[147] In this he follows Philodemus, who likewise made a subtle distinction: works of poetry could be read for their moral significance and utility, but their quality *as poems* cannot be judged according to a moral scheme.

> nimirum idem omnes fallimur, neque est quisquam
> quem non in aliqua re videre Suffenum
> possis. suus cuique attributus est error;
> sed non videmus manticae quod in tergo est.   (c. 22.18–21)

Doubtless we are all likewise deluded; nor is there anyone whom you could not see in some respect as a Suffenus. Everyone has been assigned his own failing—but we don't see the part of pack that is on our back.

We all have our own failing; indeed, it is something of which we are least likely to be aware, precisely because it is our own.

Cicero was hardly naive of the social uses of approbative terms, and could unveil their pretensions to great effect. He remained committed, however, to the core vocabulary of civic virtue, even when he was reinterpreting the meaning of words for his own ends. The word *optimus* is a well-known case in point. Cicero tended, although irregularly, to support the optimate side in factional politics, and in an extended passage, in the *Pro Sestio* of 56 BC., promoted a modified version of what it meant to be the 'best' sort of Roman.

> duo genera semper in hac civitate fuerunt eorum qui versari in re publica atque in ea se excellentius gerere studuerunt; quibus ex generibus alteri se popularis, alteri optimates et haberi et esse voluerunt. qui ea quae faciebant quaeque dicebant multitudini iucunda volebant esse, populares, qui autem ita se gerebant ut sua consilia *optimo cuique* probarent, optimates habebantur. quis ergo iste *optimus quisque*? numero, si quaeris, innumerabiles, neque enim aliter stare possemus; sunt principes consili publici, sunt qui eorum sectam sequuntur, sunt maximorum ordinum homines, quibus patet curia, sunt municipales rusticique Romani, sunt negoti gerentes, sunt etiam libertini *optimates*. numerus, ut dixi, huius generis late et varie diffusus est; sed genus universum, ut tollatur error, brevi circumscribi et definiri potest. omnes *optimates* sunt qui neque nocentes sunt nec natura improbi nec furiosi nec malis domesticis impediti. esto igitur ut ii sint, quam tu 'nationem' appellasti, qui et integri sunt et sani et bene de rebus domesticis constituti. Horum qui voluntati, commodis, opinionibus in gubernanda re publica serviunt, defensores *optimatium* ipsique *optimates* gravissimi et clarissimi cives numerantur et principes civitatis. quid est igitur propositum his rei publicae gubernatoribus quod intueri et quo cursum suum derigere debeant? id quod est praestantissimum maximeque optabile omnibus sanis et *bonis et beatis*, cum dignitate otium.   (*Sest.* 96–8)

In this city, there have always been two types of men who were devoted to participating in the republic and to conducting themselves with distinction in its affairs; of these two types, some have wished to be, and to be deemed, populists, and others, to belong to the class of best men. Those whose actions and words were intended to be pleasing to the crowd, were populists, whereas those who conducted themselves in such a way as to win approval for their plans from all the best citizens, were considered to belong to the class of best men. Who are 'all the best citizens'? Since you ask: in number, the best citizens are innumerable, for if they were not, we could not stand; they are the foremost men of the public council; they are those who follow their party; they are men of the highest orders to whom the senate house is open, they are Romans from the towns and the countryside, they are businessmen, and even freedman are the best citizens. The number, as I have said, of this class of men is widely and variously distributed; but the entire class, to avoid any error, can be briefly delimited and defined. All those belong to the class of best men who are neither guilty of crime nor depraved in their nature nor frenzied nor encumbered by their domestic difficulties. Let it be established, then, that these men, whom you have called the 'breed of the best', are those who are irreproachable, sound, and well set up in their domestic affairs. Those who, in governing the state, serve the will, the interests, and the opinions of these men, are counted as the champions of the best men, as the best men themselves, as the most venerable and illustrious citizens, and as the leading lights of the city. What, then, is the principal aim that these helmsmen of the state are bound to keep in view, and toward which they must guide their course? That which is most excellent, most desirable in the eyes of the sensible, the good, and the prosperous— social stability conjoined with political dignity.

Cicero dramatically redefines the term 'optimate'. Responding to the prosecution's comment on the 'breed of optimates' (*natio optimatium*), he strives to undermine its association with an entrenched aristocracy of birth, and even expands the category of optimates to include worthy freedmen. Cicero recalls the factional term optimate to the underlying concept of excellence. His prime criterion for excellence is a sense of patriotic duty and commitment to an orderly yet free society. The best citizens of all ranks (*optimus quisque*) want social stability (or 'leisure') combined with the pursuit of honours (*otium cum dignitate*).[148]

Cicero proceeds to deliver a sermon for the instruction of the youth, in which he fleshes out his conception of the best citizenry, and offers as *exempla* famous figures from Roman history, many of whom defended the republic at great personal danger. Prime among the examples of worthy Romans harassed by their unscrupulous enemies to the detriment of the *res publica* is Cicero himself. For Cicero, articulation of political ideals is inextricable from the continual project of self-representation. Even if he does not explicitly describe himself as *optimus*, the entire structure of the argument is designed to class him among Rome's best men who bravely defended the state against its enemies. There is no reason to think that Catullus, when he describes Cicero as *optimus patronus* ('best advocate') in c. 49, is necessarily referring to this or any other specific speech by the orator. The passage in the *Pro Sestio* nevertheless provides a good example of Cicero's civic and political ideals and the language he uses to promote them. Catullus does not overtly mock Cicero, but paints him with an 'optimistic' brush, leaving him exposed to the risks of his own conceit. Modern readers may be imposing anachronistic standards of modesty when they criticize Cicero's vanity, yet it is not only moderns, but many ancients as well, who find Ciceronian self-representation excessively fulsome and pompous.[149] Cicero's claim to represent the ideals of the 'best' citizens is temptingly easy to deflate. Catullus, no doubt for self-interested reasons of his own, prefers the path of ironic self-denigration: *pessimus omnium poeta*.

---

[148] The phrase has been variously interpreted: Boyance (1941); Wirszubski (1954); Furhmann (1960).

[149] On Ciceronian *iactatio*, see, for example, Quintilian *Inst. Orat.* 11.1.18–26; Quintilian's defense implies, of course, plentiful criticism from others.

CONCLUSION

As we have seen in this study of Catullan self-representation, the breakdown of the republican political system can be seen as providing an opportunity to justify a more serious devotion to literary studies. There is a difference, however, between viewing literature as a temporary or contingent refuge and embracing it as a new, potentially superior way of life. An explicit autonomist view will stress the inherent validity of poetry as activity rather than framing it as a second-best or substitute occupation for politics. Catullus pushes for a more explicit autonomist stance than his contemporary Cicero, and in that sense, he anticipates the rejection of public life and its attendant anxieties in Augustan poetry. Whereas Cicero harnesses poetic self-representation to his political interests, the promotion of his public reputation, and (he claims) the good of the *res publica*, Catullus' autonomist self-representational rhetoric manifests less obvious self-promotional utility, and does not subordinate itself to traditional ethical priorities. Even in this case, however, poetic autonomy can never be absolute or taken for granted, since political life continues to set the benchmark for elite prestige. The full-time *otiosus* is in the complicated position of needing to define himself both through and against politically informed conceptions of worthwhile activity.

The definition of poetry as a sphere of activity is connected, in complicated ways, with the ethical definition of the figure of the poet who inhabits and imposes his vision on that sphere. Catullus is an especially complicated case. On the one hand, he projects an antinomian literary personality that anticipates the Augustan love elegists and their self-definition in terms of *otium* and *inertia*. On the other hand, as we have seen, he practices an evasive self-representational rhetoric that leaves the reader unsure of his precise ethical stance. Catullus contributes a new sharpness and urgency to the tradition of manipulating textual personae and playing between the categories of life and poetry, aesthetics and morals. These strategies at once undercut the illusion of the textually produced *ego*, and point towards a different aspect of autonomy—not the autonomy of an antinomian axiological system (*otium, amor*, etc.), but the autonomy of the poetic text. This core tension will continue to inform Augustan poetry, even as the conceptual divisions between leisure and action, poetry and public life, *amor* and *arma*, become more highly regularized and explicitly developed.

Another aspect of Catullan literary autonomy did not live on in the Augustan period. Both Catullus and Cicero provide vivid and impressive examples of this kind of autonomy: political invective as an expression of *libertas*. Catullus, for all that he rejected public life and its corruption, could never fully withdraw himself from an interest in Roman politics. In one notable case, he professed his total indifference to Caesar's existence (c. 93). Yet professing indifference to Caesar in a poem is not truly indifference: true indifference would be manifested by saying nothing at all. In the following period, it was equally impossible to be indifferent to political developments, but increasingly inadvisable to comment heatedly on them. It is not coincidental that the Augustan poets 'choose' to turn away from the worries and burdens of public life when social conditions no longer tolerated robust poetic contribution to adversarial debate over politics and political figures. Syme's remarks are trenchant:

> Catullus ... could not have been domesticated, tamely to chant the regeneration of high society, the reiterated nuptials of Julia or the frugal virtues of upstarts enriched by the Civil Wars. His books would have been burned in the Forum, with the greatest concourse and applause of the Roman People.[150]

It might be objected that Syme's picture is overly dramatic: the path from Rome in the 50s to the Augustan principate is not simply a path from *libertas* to servile conformity. Still, it is striking that the elegists both define their literary personae much more explicitly in terms of *servitium*, and at the same time avoid frank and open criticism of those in power. Redefining elite *libertas* will be a central task of the principate, and so also of Roman poetry. This project of redefinition will form the topic of the next chapter.

---

[150] Syme (1939), 461.

2

Autarky, Withdrawal, Confinement

The autonomist niche in early Augustan
poetry (ca. 39 BC–25 BC)

INTRODUCTION

The poets of the early Augustan period[1] develop models of literary autonomy that reflect the emerging conditions of autocratic government. Whereas *libertas* in Lucilius and Catullus included the licence to attack public figures, the freedom of the early Augustan writers comes to reside in sheltered realms of literary absorption. Literary freedom develops into an inwardly oriented concept; self-regulation and self-sufficiency are emphasized at the expense of the capacity for aggression. An implicit assumption in this new paradigm of literary freedom is the interconnectedness of two distinct yet related meanings of the term *otium*: social stability (*otium*) provides the basis for the writer's peaceful existence of leisure (*otium*). The paramount value now placed on social order and cohesion is reflected in a historical shift in the meaning of *libertas*: 'even during the last generations of the Republic, *libertas* was more and more equated with material *securitas* of every sort, and the Principate became the main ideological guarantor of *libertas-securitas*'.[2] The changing meaning of *libertas* begins to be perceptible even before Actium, when the ideological and political conditions of possibility for authoritarian government are being formed. The set of texts composed and published on either side of Actium are therefore especially interesting. Their renegotiation of elite values both informs and is informed by the emerging ideology of the principate. In summary, the writers of the 30s and 20s BC do not subscribe to the traditional, aristocratic conception of *libertas* as political self-assertion. They seek to ground their poetic freedom in the protection afforded by

---

[1] Periodization is inevitably subjective and approximate; the divisions employed here are designed to be heuristic rather than to make claims about decisive historical/cultural shifts. Compare the helpful periodization of Farrell (2005), who divides the Augustan period into three phases: 44 BC–29 BC; 29 BC–2 BC; 2 BC–AD 14/17. My approximate dating scheme is meant to accommodate the earliest poetic collections of Virgil, Horace, Propertius, and Tibullus, which I see as having certain important features in common (see below).

[2] Summary by Oost (1976) of Stylow (1972). Ruffle (2003) offers an insightful examination of the redefinition of literary *libertas* and the ideological closure imposed on the literary field under Augustus. For further discussion, see, for example, Wyke (2007), 214, Galinsky (1996), 54–7.

high-level patronage and in the hopes for a new age of social-political stability
(*securitas/otium*).

The central challenge is to accommodate, on the one hand, the ideal of literary
libertas, and on the other, the need for social stability and security. Limiting the
scope and nature of freedom is one means of meeting this challenge. Poets of the
30s and early 20s BC occupy emphatically *limited* spaces of freedom. Limitation, in
this context, incorporates both an aesthetic and an ethical dimension. Callimachean 'slenderness' is accompanied by an ethos of humility, withdrawal, and
autarky. This last point applies, in different ways, to Horace *Satires* 1, Virgil's
Eclogues, Propertius Book 1, and Tibullus Book 1. In all but one of these works, the
poet's slender poetic domain is embodied in an elegant *libellus* of ten poems. The
early Augustan poets typically renounce claims of external power and agency in
order to assert control over their circumscribed literary worlds. In most contexts,
freedom and self-determination inevitably depend on power, the power to control
others and/or one's own circumstances. For Roman poets of this period, the
crucial sense of 'power' is not 'power over *the* world' so much as 'power over
my world'. Abdicating some kinds of power can confer others. The poet disavows
wealth, military glory, the power of the magistrate or general, in order to articulate
control over his own poetic domain.

Yet even as they appoint themselves rulers of their own poetic realms, the
Augustan poets need to position themselves in relation to their powerful patrons.
The problem is how to reconcile an autonomist model of poetic activity with the
social conditions of emerging empire. This tension becomes a defining feature of
poetry of the Augustan age. On the one hand, we have sequestered spaces of
aesthetic control, and on the other, the presence of larger-than-human figures:
Octavian/Augustus, Maecenas, Pollio, Messalla, Agrippa. Poetic autonomy and
patronage are not necessarily at odds with each other. In many instances, the
security of high-level patronage underpins the poet's freedom within his circumscribed domain. Conversely, the poet's freedom potentially serves the interests
of the patron, since any mention of him will be all the more effective
and persuasive coming from a poet who insists on high standards of integrity
and self-determination. Yet the tension between the poets' claims of personal
autonomy and their dependence on powerful patrons cannot be entirely resolved.
It thus becomes all the more important in rhetorical terms for the poet to design
his literary realm as integral and notionally uncompromised by the patron's
wealth, accomplishments, and power.

In the following pages, I will examine key themes in the poetic self-representation of Horace, Virgil, Propertius, and Tibullus. Horatian satire will provide an
appropriate starting-point. Freedom (*libertas*) and literary/ethical integrity are
among the defining concerns of Horace's first book of satires (*Sermones*, 'Conversations').[3] I will go on to explore concepts of freedom and refuge in Virgilian
pastoral, and the paradoxical interconnection of freedom and servility in Propertian elegy. Finally, and at somewhat greater length, I will examine the intricately
interwoven strands that make up the literary fabric of Tibullan elegy. Tibullus

---

[3] For discussion of *Satires* 1, see, for example, Zetzel (1980); Du Quesnay (1984); Anderson (1963);
Schlegel (2005); Oliensis (1998), 18–41.

represents both the potential for integrating different models of poetic autonomy and the contradictions of their co-presence.

HORACE'S *SATIRES*: REDEFINING *LIBERTAS*

Horace, in *Satires* 1.6, discloses the fact that he was born to a 'freedman father' (45–6). This ostensibly humble gesture also attests to Horace's astonishing social mobility. He rebukes himself with the admonition that he ought 'to stay within his own skin' (22), although his life presents a pattern of rising status and proliferating social connections—and this despite a major setback early on. In 43 BC, the year of Cicero's death, Horace joined Brutus' army and held the post of *tribunus militum*, usually reserved for *equites*, but had his hopes dashed and 'wings clipped' (*Epistles* 2.2.50) in 42 by the defeat of the tyrannicides at Philippi. Soon after, however, he obtained the post of *scriba quaestorius*, and was introduced to Maecenas by Virgil and Varius Rufus. This brought Horace into a new, if different, prominence as friend of one of the more influential and powerful men in the city. The first words of Horace's first book of *Satires*, find him in the enviable position of conversing with Maecenas:

> Qui fit, Maecenas, ut nemo, quam sibi sortem
> seu ratio dederit seu fors obiecerit, illa
> contentus vivat, laudet diversa sequentis?   (*Sat.* 1.1.1–3)

How is it, Maecenas, that no one lives content with his lot, whether it was granted to him by design or chance cast it in his path, but everyone praises those who follow pursuits different from their own?

The theme of the present discussion (*sermo*) is discontentment with one's own lot. Why does everyone wish to change and become something else? Yet the simple fact that Horace names Maecenas as his addressee implies that he has risen beyond the humble lot of a freedman's son.[4]

The tension that informs these lines extends throughout the entire first book of satires. Horatian self-representation articulates an ethos of contentment despite his evident rise in status. Everyone praises someone else's occupation, yet, if offered a chance by Jove himself to change places, they would refuse (*Sat.* 1.1–22). Horace, as it happens, *did* change his life, when he went from being *tribunus militum* in Brutus' army to a *scriba* and poet in Rome. The change, however, is not in the direction of more ambition, but less—or so Horace claims in his sixth satire.[5]

---

[4] Gowers (2003), 65, and Gowers (2012), ad loc., from whom I also take 'design' for *ratio*. Unfortunately, I was not able to consult Gowers' commentary on *Satires* 1 until shortly before the present book went into production: for this reason, Gowers' interpretations have been cited after the fact rather than more fully incorporated from the outset.

[5] On *Sat.* 1.6, see, for example, Rudd (1966), 36–53; Schlegel (2005), 51–8; Oliensis (1998), 30–6; Fraenkel (1957), 101–7; Armstrong (1986); and Williams (1995) and Schlegel (2000) on the question of Horace's 'freedman father'.

> nunc ad me redeo libertino patre natum,
> quem rodunt omnes libertino patre natum,
> nunc quia sim tibi, Maecenas, convictor; at olim,
> quod mihi pareret legio Romana tribuno.
> dissimile hoc illi est; quia non, ut forsit honorem
> iure mihi invideat quivis, ita te quoque amicum,
> praesertim cautum dignos adsumere, prava
> ambitione procul.   (*Sat.* 1.6.45–52)

Now to return to myself, born of a freedman father: everyone disparages my birth from a freedman father, in present circumstances because I am a close companion of yours, Maecenas, but previously because as military tribune I was in command of a Roman legion. The latter case is distinct from the former, because, although anyone might with reason grudge me that honour, he could not similarly grudge me my friendship with you, especially because you are careful to select only those who are worthy and who keep well away from crooked self-promotion.[6]

Earlier, Horace commanded a legion, not unlike Maecenas' illustrious ancestors (*magnis legionibus imperitarent*, 4); now, however, he is envied and admired as Maecenas' table-companion (*convictor*).[7] He has moved from a public position to a private friendship, yet, he is keen to remind us, enjoys equal or greater renown in his present condition as private citizen. Paradoxically, however, Horace's present dignity is not premised on his ambition; he stands aloof from ambition (*ambitione procul*, 52), and far removed from the vain judgements of the crowd (*a volgo longe longeque remotos*, 18).[8]

The emphasis on withdrawal is striking. The main context for understanding this emphasis is the increasingly autocratic Roman political climate. Julius Caesar became *dictator perpetuus* (dictator on a continuing basis) before being assassinated in 44 BC; Cicero was killed in 43 for his attacks on Antony, and in 42, the tyrannicides were defeated by the combined forces of Antony and Octavian. In the mid 30s when Horace's *Satires* were published, Antony and Octavian were (ostensibly) attempting to share control of the Roman world between them.[9] The question was not whether the republican constitution could survive the emergence of dynastic figures, but which dynast would achieve sole autocratic power. Cicero's example was a powerfully negative one for writers who might have wished to write about any aspect of public life, while the battle of Philippi did much to undermine the republican ideals of young men like Horace. The winner-take-all pattern of civil conflict had established itself with unmistakable clarity, and even some major political players might be excused for considering the risk of involvement excessive. Asinius Pollio, a major figure of the period, retired from politics after his triumph over the Parthini in 39 BC, and spent the rest of his life devoted to

---

[6] On *prava / ambitione*, see Gowers (2012), ad loc.

[7] It is crucial to what Lyne calls Horatian 'image-management' (1995), 14ff., that he represent Maecenas as selecting his friends strictly on the basis of worthy character. For another take on these issues in *Satires* 1, see Du Quesnay (1984).

[8] See Gowers (2012), 215: a new form of elitism, 'which includes judicious discrimination and scorn for the rat-race'.

[9] On some of the political background of literature of the period, see Jasper Griffin (1984); Du Quesnay (1984); Nisbet (1984).

literary pursuits. We should not be surprised if a freedman's son from Venusa, whose patrimony was reduced by his decision to support Brutus at Philippi, chose to distance himself from public conflicts and craft an image of autarkic withdrawal.[10]

Being a member of Maecenas' circle at once encourages and complicates the inclination to withdraw into a private existence of leisure. Maecenas himself made the conspicuous decision to remain an *eques* ('knight') and not to pursue political office. It is not hard to imagine Maecenas' circle cultivating a milieu of literary sophistication at a distance from the turmoil of the political arena. Some known members of the circle, including Virgil, Plotius Tucca, Varius Rufus, and probably Horace himself, were associated with the Epicureans philosophers Philodemus and Siro. Yet even denizens of Epicurus' garden could not fail to notice that Maecenas was connected with Octavian, and involved in high-level decision-making. When men on the street press Horace for news about the latest military developments, the implication is that Horace has inside information from his good friend Maecenas. He strongly denies it.[11]

> septimus octavo propior iam fugerit annus
> ex quo Maecenas me coepit habere suorum
> in numero, dumtaxat ad hoc, quem tollere raeda
> vellet iter faciens et cui concredere nugas
> hoc genus, 'hora quota est? Thraex est Gallina Syro par?'   (*Sat.* 2.6.40–44)

The seventh year, going on the eighth, will soon have passed, since the time Maecenas began to count me in the number of his friends, but only so far—as someone he might take in his carriage while making a trip, someone to whom he might entrust trifles of this sort: 'What time is it?' 'Is the Thracian Gallina ("Chicken") a match for Syrus?'

Maecenas includes Horace in his circle (*suorum/in numero*), a distinction that he clearly prizes. The honour, however, is inseparable from Maecenas' position in the world and his own connections. Maecenas' importance as a patron, and indirectly, Horace's importance as a writer, are premised on Maecenas' close association with Octavian. Yet Maecenas, as Horace would have us believe, allows their friendship to extend 'only so far' (*dumtaxat ad hoc*). In Horace's representation, Maecenas maintains a barrier between the administration of empire and their personal familiarity.

Satire 1.5, which describes the poet's journey to Brundisium in Maecenas' company, provides the best illustration of how Horace can be closely attached to Maecenas, and yet remain cloistered in his own private mental space.[12] The journey in question was an important diplomatic mission whose exact occasion is disputed.[13] Maecenas and M. Cocceius Nerva represented Octavian,

---

[10] On the ways in which Horace reframes and defines his satiric position in relation to Brutus and earlier, disavowed modes of invective *libertas* in *Sat.* 1.7, see Gowers (2012), 250–2, and on the transitional perspective and position of 1.8, 263–5.

[11] See again Lyne (1995), 18, on 'image-management'; note also Oliensis (1998), 34.

[12] Indeed, the satire's notional mode of 'diary entry' is designed to suggest the unvarnished truth of this representation: Oliensis (1998), 27.

[13] See Gowers (2012), 183, who leans toward the meeting between Antony and Octavian in Athens in 38 BC, although the satire might represent a fictionalized conflation of different events. 1.5, of course, is also in dialogue with Lucilius' satiric trip to Sicily, of which only fragments survive.

while Fonteius Capito represented Antony (27–33). Horace, however, frustrates any hopes on the part of his readers that he will provide an insider's perspective on the political aspects of the embassy, and pointedly ends his poem with the party's arrival in Brundisium: *Brundisium longae finis chartaeque viaeque est* ('Brundisium marks the end of a long piece of paper and a long voyage', 104). Horace demonstrates, without making any explicit statement, that he either does not know the details of his friend Maecenas' political dealings, or if he does, would never make the error of revealing them.[14] From his perspective, the embassy is simply a matter of 'bringing estranged friends back together' (*aversos . . . componere amicos*, 29). Indeed, friendship is one of the key (Epicurean) themes of the composition: we note especially Horace's joy in meeting Plotius Tucca, Varius Rufus, and Virgil (39–42) and later, the general sadness at Varius' departure (93).

For all that Horace appears to have little connection with the mission's diplomatic purpose, he does not lack sufficient objects for his poetic attention. A salient feature of Horace's literary travelogue is the minute focus on details of everyday life and their sometimes subtle moral implications.

> quattuor hinc rapimur viginti et milia raedis,
> mansuri oppidulo, quod versu dicere non est,
> signis perfacile est: venit vilissima rerum
> hic aqua; sed panis longe pulcherrimus, ultra
> callidus ut soleat umeris portare viator.
> nam Canusi lapidosus (aquae non ditior urna),
> qui locus a forti Diomede est conditus olim.
> flentibus hinc Varius discedit maestus amicis.
> Inde Rubos fessi pervenimus, utpote longum
> carpentes iter et factum corruptius imbri.
> postera tempestas melior, via peior ad usque
> Bari moenia piscosi. dein Gnatia lymphis
> iratis exstructa dedit risusque iocosque,
> dum flamma sine tura liquescere limine sacro
> persuadere cupit. credat Iudaeus Apella,
> non ego: namque deos didici securum agere aevum,
> nec, si quid miri faciat natura, deos id
> tristis ex alto caeli demittere tecto.
> Brundisium longae finis chartaeque viaeque est.   (*Sat.* 1.5.86–104)

From here we are rolled along twenty-four miles by carriage with the plan of staying in a little town whose name can't be said in verse, but can easily be shown by tokens: here water, the cheapest thing in the world, must be purchased, but the bread is by far the finest; so the shrewd traveller acquires the habit of carrying it further on his shoulders. For at Canusium, the place brave Diomedes founded long ago, the bread is hard as rock, but the place isn't a jug richer in water. At this point Varius departed sadly to the tears of his

---

[14] See Oliensis (1998), 27, on Horace's 'manifesto of discretion' in this satire, which (inevitably) becomes political in avowing a lack of interest in politics; note also Jasper Griffin (1984), 197–8; Freudenburg (2001), 52ff., for whom the point of the satire is the absurd, almost demeaning, limitation of Horatian vision, whereas for Schlegel (2005, 59–76), Horatian satire still has its 'satiric bite', although the political point is submerged within a kind of allegory (76). Gowers' reading of 1.5 (1993a) focuses on the implication of this poetic journey for the writing of satire and, as in Freudenburg, Horace's relation with Lucilius; note also Gowers (2012), 182–6.

friends. Thence we came to Rubi, exhausted, since we had travelled a long way and the trip was still more marred by the rain. Weather the next day was better, the road worse all the way to the walls of Barium, plentiful in fish. Then Gnatia, built when the water nymphs were angry, gave occasion for laughter and jest: she would have us believe that incense melts without flame on the temple threshold. Apella the Jew may believe it—I won't. For I have learned that the gods pass a carefree existence, and that, if nature does something amazing, it is not the gods in a gloomy mood sending down a portent from their lofty dwelling in the sky. Brundisium marks the end of a long trip and a long piece of paper.

Moral insight and critique are woven seamlessly into the fabric of Horace's satiric travelogue. The local official at Fundi represents the pitfalls of self-deluding ambition. Horace's 'idiotic' (*stultissimus*, 82) vigil in expectation of a girl is contrary to the Epicurean doctrine of sexual pleasure, and ends in a description of a wet dream reminiscent of a similar passage in Lucretius (*Sat.* 1.5.84–5; *DRN* 4.1030–6). The local miracle of incense burning without fire at Gnatia offers a closing example of superstition, and is followed by an explicitly Lucretian reference. In Horace's satiric *De rerum natura*, a sublime didactic style is eschewed in favour of casual *sermo*, the vast fabric of the cosmos replaced by the microcosmic details of quotidian necessity.[15] In one location (unnamable in hexameter verse), water must be purchased, but the bread is excellent, whereas at Canusium the bread is inferior and there is hardly any water at all. At Rubi, the journey is obstructed by rain; the next day, the weather improves, but the road deteriorates. In the journey of life, all one's needs are rarely fully satisfied, but one may nonetheless learn to accept this fact cheerfully, and discover the pleasures of alternation: lack in one area is balanced by abundance in another, and vice versa.

One implication of Horace's reduction of Lucretius' vast, sublime canvas is an aesthetic one: the very smallness and triviality of the episodes represented, as in the case of the Catullan polymetrics, highlight the autonomous aesthetic quality that makes poetry out of seemingly forgettable subject matter not accorded conventional social importance. At the same time, Horace's portrayal of the vicissitudes of travel also has an ethical lesson built into it: the world is imperfect, our pleasures and comforts are limited, and we must learn to accept those limits. The gods, as Lucretius intones, live a carefree life in a realm separate from ours. As the poem ends, we may well turn our mind back to those other gods, Maecenas and his fellow ambassadors, and the even greater men they represent. They too inhabit a different realm, and their dealings have little to do with the everyday existence of the humble satirist, who rigorously limits his gaze to objects in close proximity. It is perhaps not accidental that Horace draws attention to his ophthalmic condition in this particular satire: we cannot see beyond the myopic limits of the satirist's immediate surroundings.[16] An underlying concept in this rich mimesis of everyday life is the importance of limits: the importance of imposing limits on ambition and desire, of limiting our expectations in a life ruled by contingency; the limits of vision, and finally, the aesthetic limits of the poem itself. In art as in life, it is important to know when to impose an ending (*finis*).[17]

---

[15] On the assimilation and transformation of Lucretian teaching in Horatian *sermo*, see Ferri (1993), 33–58.

[16] See Freudenburg (2001), 52; Cucchiarelli (2001), 70; Gowers (2003), 68; Oliensis (1998), 27–8.

[17] Of course, actually enforcing and securing such limits may prove more difficult in practice than precept initially suggests: e.g. as Oliensis (1998), 28, notes, civil war is 'displaced' onto humorous forms

Horace often appears in transit from one location to another in the first book of *Satires*. Physical mobility is a worthy symbol of his movement within Roman society, and thus plays a part in the ethical tension between stasis and change that pervades the book. In 1.6, a satire largely concerned with Horace's connection with Maecenas and rising social prominence, images of travel are infused with ethical connotations. Specifically, political office-holders and aspirants are depicted as being burdened, fettered, obligated, weighed down by their duties and by their own putative grandeur as they travel through life. The pinnacle of any public career ought to be the triumph procession, in which the victorious general rides in a chariot, and enemy prisoners are displayed to the populace. In Horace's view, however, the pursuit of Glory is imprisoning, and her devotees are the true captives: *sed fulgente trahit constrictos Gloria curru / non minus ignotos generosis* ('But Glory drags, bound to her gleaming chariot, the nameless no less than the noble', 23–4). Paradoxically, having more expansive ambitions of glory means being more tightly circumscribed (*constrictos*), having less autonomy (*trahit ... Gloria*).[18] Later in the satire, when he describes how he presented himself to Maecenas for the first time, Horace stresses that he did not try to make himself out to be grander than he was, but told the simple truth: *non ego me claro natum patre, non ego circum / me Satureiano vectari rura caballo / sed quod eram narro* ('I told him—not that I was born of an illustrious father, not that I rode around my estates on a Tarentine nag—but simply what I was', 1.6.58–60). Horace does *not* possess a vast ancestral property that needs to be traversed on horseback. Toward the satire's end, Horace picks up the same strand of transit-imagery to contrast the burdens of official status with his own preference for travelling light.

> nam si natura iuberet
> a certis annis aevum remeare peractum
> atque alios legere ad fastum quoscumque parentis
> optaret sibi quisque, meis contentus honestos
> fascibus et sellis nollem mihi sumere, demens
> iudicio volgi, sanus fortasse tuo, quod
> nollem onus haud umquam solitus portare molestum.
> nam mihi continuo maior quaerenda foret res
> atque salutandi plures ducendus et unus
> et comes alter, uti ne solus rusve peregreve
> exirem, plures calones atque caballi
> pascendi, ducenda petorrita. nunc mihi curto
> ire licet mulo vel si libet usque Tarentum,
> mantica cui lumbos onere ulceret atque eques armos:
> obiciet nemo sordes mihi, quas tibi, Tilli,
> cum Tiburte via praetorem quinque sequuntur
> te pueri, lasanum portantes oenophorumque.
> hoc ego commodius quam tu, praeclare senator,
> milibus atque aliis vivo.   (*Sat.* 1.6.93–111)

of warfare, but not altogether removed; the aesthetic limitation and polish of Callimacheanism, moreover, are only problematically assigned to this satire; see Gowers (1993a).

[18] Compare Gowers (2012), 217, 227.

For if Nature commanded us to retrace the span of time already traversed, beginning from some fixed year, and to choose other parents, whichever ones each of us wanted for himself according to our sense of pride, I would be content with my own parents and would not wish to take parents ennobled by rods of office and curule chairs—and while I would be deemed mad in the judgement of the crowd, I would perhaps be deemed sensible in your judgement, for not wishing to bear a troublesome burden to which I have never been accustomed. For at once I would be obliged to seek more money, to exchange more social calls, and to take on one or two companions[19] so as not to depart alone to the countryside or abroad; more grooms and nags would need to be maintained, more four-wheeled carriages taken along. As things stand, I may, if I like, even go all the way to Tarentum on a gelded mule, so that his loins are made sore by the weight of the saddle-bags and his forequarters are chaffed by the rider. No one will charge me with meanness as they do you, Tillius, when, as praetor, you are accompanied on the road to Tibur by five slaves carrying a chamber pot and wine-jar. In this and a thousand other ways I live more comfortably than you, illustrious senator.

Horace imagines a journey back in time: *aevum remeare peractum*. But going back and changing one's parentage 'for the better' would only mean adding a new, unaccustomed burden. The very notion of the social status arising from political office (*honores/honestus*) is punningly linked with the burden (*onus*) of its obligations.[20] Horace, by contrast, is content/self-contained: *contentus*. The life of the senator is one of continual obligation, as expressed by a series of gerundives in artfully chiastic arrangement: *quaerenda . . . salutandi . . . pascendi . . . ducenda*.[21] Horace could go all the way to Tarentum, travelling light, with a single, imperfect mule; no one would criticize the poverty of his mode of transport. Satire, with its emphasis on realism, sordidity and imperfection, has a moral advantage: the satirist does not need to constantly keep up a façade for others, as the senator must. The latter is a slave to his possessions and his own standing (*dignitas*). Just to get to his villa at nearby Tibur, the praetor needs five slaves to carry his belongings—and *still* he gets criticized for lack of sufficient dignity.

Travelling light, moving through life with minimal apparatus (*commodius*), affords unexpected freedom. Horace follows his own course and his own whim, and because he makes no claims on public attention, no one impedes him or makes demands of him. Horace offers us a glimpse of what such freedom might look like in the justly famous passage outlining his 'Epicurean day'.[22]

> quacumque libido est,
> incedo solus; percontor quanti holus ac far;
> fallacem Circum vespertinumque pererro
> saepe Forum; adsisto divinis; inde domum me
> ad porri et ciceris refero laganique catinum.
> cena ministratur pueris tribus, et lapis albus
> pocula cum cyatho duo sustinet; adstat echinus
> vilis, cum patera gutus, Campana supellex.
> deinde eo dormitum, non sollicitus mihi quod cras

---

[19] So Gowers (2012), ad loc.   [20] Gowers (2012), ad loc.
[21] Compare Gowers (2012), ad loc.
[22] For discussion of this conventionalized day, and the hints of luxury behind Horace's claims of simplicity, see Armstrong (1986), 277ff.

> surgendum sit mane, obeundus Marsya, qui se
> voltum ferre negat Noviorum posse minoris.
> ad quartam iaceo; post hanc vagor; aut ego, lecto
> aut scripto quod me tacitum iuvet, unguor olivo,
> non quo fraudatis immundus Natta lucernis.
> ast ubi me fessum sol acrior ire lavatum
> admonuit, fugio Campum lusumque trigonem.
> pransus non avide, quantum interpellet inani
> ventre diem durare, domesticus otior. haec est
> vita solutorum misera ambitione gravique;
> his me consolor victurum suavius ac si
> quaestor avus pater atque meus patruusque fuisset.   (*Sat.* 1.6.111–31)

Wherever whim takes me, I stroll alone; I inquire about the price of greens and flour; in the evening, I often wander over the grounds of the cheating Circus and the Forum. I stand near the fortune-tellers; thence I take myself back home to a dish of leek, chick-pea, and fritters. My dinner is served by three slave boys, and a white stone supports two cups and a ladle; a cheap salt-cellar stands nearby, an oil-flask and saucer—Campanian ware. Then I go off to sleep, not worried at having to get up the next morning and appear before Marsyas, who says he cannot endure the face of Novius the Younger. I lie in bed up to the fourth hour; after this I go wandering about; or, after reading or writing something to please me in a quiet mood, I am anointed with oil, but not with the stuff filthy Natta uses, cheating the lamps. But when I am tired and a stronger sun has reminded me to go to the baths, I flee the Campus and the ball game. After dining in temperate fashion, just enough to prevent me from lasting the day on an empty stomach, I laze about at home. This is the life of those who are emancipated from the wretched weight of ambition. With these pursuits I console myself that I will live in a finer manner than if my grandfather had been a quaestor, and my father and uncle as well.

As in the journey to Brundisium, Horace appears to offer an account of the micro-texture of his daily existence, yet this portrait of his quotidian routine is clearly constructed with exquisite care. He claims to lead a simple (but not sordid) life, in accordance with Epicurean doctrine: simple fare, simple pleasures that satisfy his natural needs. He is able to slip into the urban fabric by being inconspicuous; no one expects him to be followed by a crowd of supporters. He can wander around the Circus and Forum at his leisure, consult fortune-tellers, purchase the ingredients for his unassuming dinner. Horace is emancipated by the simplicity of his needs. Excessive appetite is aligned with ambition, and ambition with obligation and hence loss of self-determination. Ambition is a heavy weight (*ambitione gravique*), and the grammar of obligation once again weighs down the political aspirant (*surgendum . . . obeundus*). Whereas the ambitious Novius Jr must go to the Forum and endure the dour gaze of Marsyas' statue, Horace can remain in bed. He finds freedom in the comforts of his daily life. The description of Horace's unambitious life culminates in the rare verb *otior* ('I am at leisure, I idle'), and the adjective *domesticus* ('at home').

Lexical markers of freedom and release frame the entire passage. Horace is initially shown walking about wherever he likes (*quacumque libido est*), and at the close, released (*solutorum*) from the weight of ambition.[23] Horace's

---

[23] Oliensis (1998), 35, notes Horace's 'autonomous leisure' in this passage. Note also the figure of Marysas, who, as Gowers (2012), 247, observes, might 'be considered a mascot of satirical *libertas*' (see

Epicurean freedom, however, is not the aggressive freedom of Lucilian invective *libertas*, and definitely not the republican politician's freedom to pursue *honores*.[24] Horace represents himself as achieving freedom in the autonomist niche of his everyday existence. His emancipation, perhaps paradoxically, consists in embracing passivity. He leaves politics to others, but follows his own inclinations amidst the many small choices and rituals of everyday life. A series of deponent, passive, impersonal, reflexive and intransitive verbs emphasizes the speaker's curiously insouciant wandering through the diverse scenes of his life: *incedo* ('I walk about')...*me refero* ('I take myself back')...*ministratur* ('I am served [dinner]')...*eo dormitum* ('I go to sleep')...*iaceo* ('I lie [in bed]')...*vagor* ('I wander...')...*unguor* ('I am anointed')...*me ire lavatum admonuit* ('I have been admonished to bathe')....*otior* ('I idle')...*me consolor* ('I console myself'). Horace's lexicon in this passage minimizes aggressive, externally oriented action. Much of what he does is reflexively self-contained (*me refero... me consolor*); in other cases, things are done for him as passive recipient (*ministratur, unguor*).[25]

Notably absent from this description of Horace' life is Maecenas, the satire's addressee and the man whose friendship motivated Horace's reflections on status and contentment in the first place. In Roman terms, being the close friend of someone meant 'living with' them. Horace elsewhere boasts of 'having lived with the great' (*cum magnis vixisse*, *Sat.* 2.1.76), and in 1.9, he must be counted among those who 'live' in Maecenas' *domus* (48–50). Here, however, he is careful to delineate the outlines of his Epicurean life (*me...victurum sauvius...*) independently of his grand friendship with Maecenas. He walks emphatically alone (*incedo solus*), not accompanying his powerful friend; and even more to the point, he dines alone. He evidently does not need to wake up early in order to greet his patron. In this passage articulating the core freedoms and values of the satirist's existence, Maecenas plays no explicit role. Horace is solitary, autarkic.

Maecenas is merely kept out of this particular scene, however—not removed from the broader picture of Horace's life. Maecenas, in fact, is the 'absent presence' that makes the scene of freedom possible. We know that Horace *does* spend time with Maecenas, and elsewhere is unambiguously shown doing so. At some level, the humility of Horace's Epicurean day is redeemed and valorized by the fact that Horace is Maecenas' friend. Horace can afford to advertise a life so humble and inconspicuous for the very reason that it is not really humble and inconspicuous. Horace lays great stress on his ease, his lack of extraordinary exertion to maintain his status. The less hard he tries, the more insouciant he appears, the more solid and undeniable his social standing as Maecenas' poet friend comes to seem. Maecenas' unique friendship thus underwrites and provides

---

also 218–19); or perhaps Horace is implicitly contrasting his Epicurean freedom with the public, civic *libertas* advertised in the Roman forum. Gowers (2012), 247, also notes that *non sollicitus* in line 119 Romanizes 'Epicurean *ataraxia*'.

[24] On Horace's conscious rewriting of Lucilian *libertas* to fit the triumviral period, see Du Quesnay (1984), 29–32.

[25] Compare Gowers (2012), 218, who emphasizes how Horace's choice of words and construction here seems to both allude to and fend off the lexicon of servile *clientela*.

the conditions of possibility for Horatian autonomy. He does not need to rely on external sources of prestige, because he already derives status from Maecenas' distinctively unburdensome friendship.

The ending of the satire is implicitly premised on its beginning. Horace's capacity to simply relax (*otior*) in life, as described in the satire's culminating passage, is premised on the powerful friend addressed in the opening lines.[26] As in 1.5, the satirist is simultaneously attached to Maecenas and absorbed in his own autonomous world of ethical meditation and Epicurean ease. Freedom, for Horace, does not mean being a fiercely independent agent in the Lucilian or Catullan sense; it means carving out his humble realm of freedom under the sheltering protection of Maecenas' patronage. In redefining satiric *libertas* for his own times and purposes, Horace stresses the ethical trait of contentment. The term *contentus* derives from the verb *contineo* ('I restrain, retain, enclose, limit'), and refers to an ethical capacity to remain confined within certain boundaries. Horace replaces the aristocratic autonomy of self-assertion with the autonomy of self-containment. This replacement involves a crucial redefinition of what it means to write satire.

It is well known that Horace merges ethical self-limitation with Callimachean aesthetics. Callimachus' Apollo, in his *Hymn to Apollo* (109–13), contrasts the vast muddy river with the narrow, pure stream. When Horace, in *Satires* 1.1, is discussing the merits of living 'within the boundaries of Nature' (*intra / naturae finis*, 49–50), he points to the advantages of a tiny, clear stream (*foncticulo*, 56) over a vast, dangerously raging, muddy river (*magno ... flumine*) for the person who simply wants a cup of water. At the end of the first satire, Horace links ethical and aesthetic restraint, etymologically associating the concept of contentment with the genre of satire (*satura*) itself.

> inde fit ut raro, qui se vixisse beatum
> dicat et exacto contentus tempore vita
> cedat uti conviva satur, reperire queamus.
> iam satis est. ne me Crispini scrinia lippi
> compilasse putes, verbum non amplius addam.   (*Sat.* 1.1.117–21)

And so it turns out that we are rarely able to find someone who says that he has led a happy life, and who, once his time is expended, departs from life content, like a sated dinner-party guest. Enough now. Lest you think I have pillaged the book-boxes of blear-eyed Crispinus, I shall not add another word.

Someone who has learned to adopt a properly satiric perspective will leave life with a sense of contentment, satisfied (*satur*) like a banqueter at the end of a feast. As if suddenly reminded that he too must impose literary limits on his *sermo*, Horace pulls himself up short: *iam satis est* ('that's enough'). To avoid becoming a windbag like Crispinus, he must rein in his speech (*verbum non amplius addam*).[27]

---

[26] A structure essentially reproduced in *Odes* 1.1: address to Maecenas at the beginning; the poet's secluded *nemus* at the end.

[27] On satire and satiety (*satis*), see, e.g. Freudenburg (2001), 15–16, 27ff., 44ff.; Knoche (1975), 13–14; Hooley (2007), 14, 34. On the reference to Lucretius and (it is argued) Virgil in *satur*, see Gowers (2012), ad loc.

In his book of *Sermones* ('Talks'), Horace carefully regulates the economy of speech and silence. At times he invites comparison with the pretentious babblers and diatribists, street sermonizers and witty, loquacious parasites, who played so conspicuous a role in Roman social life. Horace is aware that the moment he opens his mouth to lecture others on how to live he risks falling into one of these familiar roles. Indeed, though he claims that he will not add another word (*verbum non amplius*), he continues sermonizing through the following nine satires. Is satire a genre of limit/contentment, or is it, on another, related line of etymological thinking, a genre stuffed full with all manner of things? Is the imposition of a limit possible amidst the constant flow of talk in the endlessly discursive city?[28]

Horace's answer to the preceding question would probably be: 'yes'. While remaining alert to the expansive tendencies of his genre, Horace's slim *libellus* of ten poems places a paramount value on paucity of words. Self-limitation is not only possible; it is necessary for a satisfactory life. Indeed, one of the motivations for choosing satire as a genre in the first place may have been the opportunity to dramatize the paring down of aesthetically and ethically excessive modes of speech. Satire is the republican genre par excellence, the genre of free speech and unrestrained commentary on public figures. By writing a *new* kind of satire, Horace is able to chart how the times have changed both in standards of versification and in the possibilities for *libertas*. The chief exemplar of the genre is, of course, Lucilius. In Satire 1.4, Horace criticizes Lucilius for harsh versification, prolixity, and excessive haste in composition.[29] He was lazy, incapable of putting up with the 'labour of writing well' (*garrulus atque piger scribendi ferre laborem, / scribendi recte*, 12–13). In this context, Horace finally cashes in his metaphorical investment in Callimachean watery-imagery: he compares Lucilius to a vast, muddy river full of superfluous elements (*cum flueret lutulentus, erat quod tollere velles*, 11). Immediately after this comparison, Crispinus makes another appearance. He challenges Horace to a writing competition (13–21), which Horace refuses to take up. Naturally sparing in his speech, he is unable to match Crispinus' continual bellows-like verbal puffing.

Patterns of opposition recur in different semantic fields. On one side are bellows, fat udders (*distentius uber*, 1.1.110), and cheeks blowing hot air, and on the other, closed lips, the pruning, pairing and regulation of speech. The New Man, Novius, is an important Horatian foil-figure and prime example of someone who puffs himself beyond his natural rank. Not surprisingly, Novius' moral defects become evident chiefly through an insufficient show of verbal restraint: Novius has a voice that could drown out the horns and trumpets of three funerals (1.6.42–4). Horace himself, of course, represents precisely the kind of immense gains in status many Italians of relatively modest social origins made in this period; he resembles Novius more closely than he might be willing to admit, and thus must take care to differentiate himself all the more sharply. Horace is also trying to make his way in society, and, like the political aspirant, must answer

---

[28] On Horace's satiric engagement with Callimachean aesthetics, see Freudenburg (1993), 185ff.; Gowers (1993a); Scodel (1987); Zetzel (2002).

[29] On 1.4, see Freudenburg (1993), *passim*; Schlegel (2005), 38–51; Oliensis (1998), 18–26; on his engagement with Lucilius, Rudd (1966), 86–131.

to concerns about his origins. Horace's crucial scene of self-depiction, however, occurs in a highly private setting. Novius' senatorial braying tellingly contrasts with the verbally incapacitated Horace who finds himself, for the first time, in Maecenas' intimidating presence. Both partners in the exchange, in fact, display an exemplarity paucity of speech.[30]

> ut veni coram, singultim pauca locutus,
> infans namque pudor prohibebat plura profari,
> non ego me claro natum patre, non ego circum
> me Satureiano vectari rura caballo,
> sed quod eram narro. respondes, ut tuus est mos,
> pauca: abeo; et revocas nono post mense iubesque
> esse in amicorum numero.   (*Sat.* 1.6.56–62)

When I came into your presence, I choked out just a few words (for a childish/speechless bashfulness prevented me from saying more) and told you—not that I was the son of an illustrious father, not that I rode around my estates on a Tarentine nag—but simply what I was. You responded, as is your custom, with few words. I went away, and you called me back nine months later, and bade me join the number of your friends.

Horace manages only a few stuttering words, phonically mimicked in his narration: *ut veni coram, singultim pauca locutus, / infans namque pudor prohibebat plura profari* (56–7).[31] Maecenas responds with similar paucity, presumably for the rather different reason of his quiet authority (*respondes, ut tuus est mos, / pauca*, 60–1). In this description of their interaction (*sed quod eram . . . pauca*), there is only one word of more than two syllables; the brief, staccato syntactic rhythm, with the key word *pauca* ('few') dropped bluntly at the start of the following line, is nicely evocative of verbal restraint and honesty without rhetorical flourish. In the end, Maecenas rewards Horace's honest humility with his friendship. If we believe this narrative, Horace manages to become connected with the most powerful men in Rome by *not* being ambitious and (even more unbelievable) by *not* making a display of his considerable powers of speech.

The rich productiveness of the Horatian imagery-repertoire of sound and silence derives from its simultaneous application in aesthetic, ethical, and poetological domains. Excessively prolix writers are also excessive in their vanity of self-advertisement. Horace is especially skilled at linking the self-inflating hyper-production of bad writers with specific objects. The material imagery of the writer's book-boxes (*scrinia*) and cases (*capsae*) becomes a marker of a compromised aesthetic. Too large for a mere *libellus*, the works of Crispinus require a bulk container (*scrinia*, 1.1.120). The self-admiring Fannius (*beatus Fannius*) gratuitously offers up his scroll-cases (*capsae*), along with a portrait bust (*imagine*, 1.4.21–2). Cassius Etruscus outdoes all these: more tumultuous than a rushing river (*rapido ferventius amni*), he makes his funeral pyre out of his own books and book-cases (*capsis . . . librisque*, 1.10.61–4). In each instance, the material objects and venues involved in the reproduction of aristocratic reputation (the portrait-bust, the funeral), are compromisingly juxtaposed with the

---

[30] On this 'primal scene' of Horatian satiric self-representation, see Gowers (2012), 217–18.
[31] Armstrong (1986), 260; Gowers (2012), ad loc.

instruments of literary circulation (books, book-boxes, scroll-cases). Excessive production and circulation are associated with an ethical loss of control, a heteronomist orientation to the tastes of the crowds and the writer's own vanity. For Horace, the exacting labour of literary revision coheres with his contentment with few readers (*contentus paucis lectoribus*, 1.10.74). He eschews more uncontrolled venues of circulation (schools, theatres, poetic recitations).

In the autonomist niche of Horatian satire, slender, well-crafted poems are worth more than inflated bombast; self-containment trumps self-advertisement. On both points, Horace agrees with Catullus, for whom poetry is a specialized form of expertise, sharply distinguished from the traditional aims of aristocratic self-aggrandizement. Yet unlike Catullus, Horace renounces the use of poetry, in his *Satires* at least,[32] as a medium of invective attack. The central paradigm of invective *libertas* for a satirist is provided not by Catullus, but, naturally enough, by Lucilius. In Satire 1.4, Horace negotiates his satiric inheritance from Lucilius, and in the process, redefines the meaning of satiric *libertas*. Lucilius, he states at the outset, depends wholly (*omnis pendet*) on the poets of Old Comedy, Eupolis, Cratinus, and Aristophanes, who left their 'mark' on blameworthy individuals 'with great freedom' (*multa cum libertate notabant*, 5). Horace, unlike the prolix Lucilius, favours careful writing and paucity of speech (9–21). He does not recite, because people fear the poet's public censure of their conspicuous vices (25–38). The poet, on the popular perception, is a dangerous figure, distinguished from the rest of the herd by his aggression: *faenum habet in cornu: longe fuge*! ('he has hay on his horn: keep well away!', 34).

Horace offers a multi-layered response to the public perception of poetic aggression. Of course, he may well be exaggerating the intensity of the stigma. But whether or not the citizens of Rome routinely quake in fear at the mention of poets, Horace intends to demonstrate that they need not fear *him*. First, he argues that, as the author of a quotidian genre, he is not really a poet (38–62). Second, whether he writes poetry or mere verse—and he concedes that the point is at least arguable—he does not aim to reach a broad audience. He further insists that there is no true malice in his satiric writing—not the kind of verbal violence, in any case, perpetrated by a drunken party-guest who unlocks his heart at the bidding of Bacchus/Liber, liberator of speech. Such a man is lauded as genial, urbane, and frank (*hic tibi comis et urbanus liberque videtur*, 90). How is it that *Horace* comes to seem black-hearted? Despite the common prejudice against poets, true venom—*libertas* in its most destructive form—comes from elsewhere. Yet Horace, who rejects a defamatory model of *libertas*, concedes that he may speak 'somewhat freely' (*liberius*) as a satirist. He ascribes this impulse not to malice, but to his father's proto-satiric instruction.[33]

---

[32] Of course, Horace's roughly contemporary *Epodes* belong precisely to a tradition of iambic invective. Here, too, however, we can appreciate how Horace transforms the iambic genre and redirects its aggressive impulses toward carefully chosen, 'appropriate' targets.

[33] Schlegel (2005), 38–58, reads both Maecenas and Lucilius as satiric father-figures. Leach (1971) traces the connection with the Greek/Roman father of New Comedy.

> liberius si
> dixero quid, si forte iocosius, hoc mihi iuris
> cum venia dabis: insuevit pater optimus hoc me,
> ut fugerem exemplis vitiorum quaeque notando.   (*Sat.* 1.4.103–6)

If I say anything too freely, if perchance I speak too facetiously, you will be forgiving and grant me this degree of justification.[34] My excellent father instilled this [habit] in me by marking out the various instances of vice by example so that I would flee them.

Horace's father pointed out (*notando*) concrete examples of virtue and vice to his son.[35] Now, as an adult, Horace has internalized the habit of self-improving, ethical meditation: *neque enim, cum lectulus aut me / porticus excepit, desum mihi* ('for neither on a reading-couch nor in a portico, am I wanting to myself', 133–4). We have moved from the public venues of recitation and circulation (the book-stall, the Forum, the baths) to Horace' private couch and introspective strolling. Once again, as in the description of his 'Epicurean day' in 1.6, a wandering stroll around the city provides the concrete form for Horace's autarkically self-absorbed meditations.

Still, in placing such emphasis on the solitary meditations of the satirist/flâneur, Horace is going against the grain of his crowded, urban, confrontational, dialogic genre. This may be precisely the point: Horace's autonomy is all the more impressive and convincing if it can be sustained with people crowding all around him and adversaries constantly impinging on his thoughts. He is surrounded by the flotsam and jetsam of the city, yet remains absorbed in the flow of his internal monologue. But how is it that meditations so inwardly oriented, so emphatically *self*-regulating, come to be published in the *Liber Sermonum*? Horace has an answer.

> haec ego mecum
> compressis agito labris; ubi quid datur oti,
> illudo chartis. hoc est mediocribus illis
> ex vitiis unum.   (*Sat.* 1.4. 137–40)

These are the thoughts I turn over in my mind, with lips closed tight: when I'm granted a moment of leisure, I make a mockery of[36] pieces of paper. This is one of those mild peccadilloes aforementioned.

Horace does his best to minimize the impression of a publicizing impulse. In moments of leisure, he playfully wastes (*illudo*) writing paper, recording the thoughts he previously worked out silently (*compressis... labris*). The book of satires, in the present conceit, is a casual by-product of Horace's project of ethical self-regulation. In some cases, we even see the sermonizer *avoiding* conversation. The satire that opens with the public branding (*notabant*) of individuals in the Athenian theatre (Old Comedy), and later recalls the domestic theatre (or New Comedy) of Horace's father's moral teachings (*notando*), ends with Horace's 'lips shut tight' and autarkic writing-games.[37]

---

[34] So Gowers (2012), ad loc., following Brown (1993).

[35] As Oliensis (1998), 25, observes, the combination of *liberius* and *notando* recalls the satire's opening reference to the Greek comic poets (*libertate notabant*). *Libertas*, of course, is a central preoccupation of Horatian satire here and elsewhere: Freudenburg (2001), 4, 44–51; Freudenburg (1993), 86–92.

[36] i.e. he wastes paper by scribbling on it; so Gowers (2012), ad loc., following Brown (1993).

[37] Compare the similar observations in Gowers (2012), 151–2.

We may be sceptical of Horace's casual relegation of satiric writing and publication to the status of an afterthought, but the broader figural intent behind this fiction remains important. Expansiveness, dilution, and dispersal of voice are emblematic of the loss of aesthetic and ethical control. Conversely, Horace's 'shut lips' (*compressis labris*) are the sign of his literary/ethical integrity. He is 'content with few readers', and does not court popularity with the crowd. The book's opening tension between contentment and ambition, stasis and change, thus re-emerges in the tension between publication and private meditation. In objective terms, it is hard to see how Horace can reconcile the two extremes. On the other hand, the dialogic flexibility and humour that define his genre work to his advantage. As Horace states revealingly in *Satires* 1.10, laughter is effective at solving a knotty dilemma (14–15). The contradictions in Horace's self-portrait as autarkic satirist cannot be entirely resolved; nor are they fully dispelled by Horace's series of sleight-of-hand manoeuvres in this astonishing satire that starts with the Old Comedy, and gradually whittles down the satiric impulse to a private game on sheets of paper. Yet at the very point the reader might question this minimalist version of satiric activity, Horace quips:

> hoc est mediocribus illis
> ex vitiis unum; cui si concedere nolis,
> multa poetarum veniat manus, auxilio quae
> sit mihi (nam multo plures sumus), ac veluti te
> Iudaei cogemus in hanc concedere turbam.　　(*Sat.* 1.4.139–43)

This is one of those mild peccadilloes aforementioned: if you should refuse to make allowance for it, a great band of poets would come to back me up (for we are a significant majority) and, like the Jews, we will force you to join our crowd.

The jocular threat with which he closes neatly inverts all the points Horace has separately and cumulatively made throughout the course of the satire. Horace now evokes, not a solitary, self-regulating, and sub-poetic mode of writing, but a coercive, proselytizing, poetic group-identity, a 'band of poets' (*poetarum . . . manus*). Even worse, he and his poet friends form a *turba*—the byword for urban disorder and thoughtless judgement throughout the *Satires*.[38] He evokes, in short, the opposite of autonomy: poetry as a form of coercion.

Horace constantly shifts the grounds of discussion, and when all else fails, makes a disarming joke. The very mobility of satiric dialogue facilitates Horace's autonomist argument, while humour and evasion help prevent the argument's contradictions from being exposed. Throughout *Satires* 1, Horace frees himself from the potentially constraining implications of his own position, both as friend of Maecenas and as poet. Horace works hard to cleanse his satiric poetry of the taint of heteronomous uses at the precise moment when his poetic talent is bringing him into meteoric prominence. The favour Maecenas evidently conferred on literary doctitude made a poetic career especially suspect in the eyes of contemporaries: surely Horace was using his literary skill to impress Maecenas, and thereby make his way in life? This is precisely the opinion held by the most formidable and stubborn

---

[38] See Schlegel (2005), 47. On this closural 'sting in the tail', see Gowers (2012), 152, and on the reputation of Jews for proselytism, 182.

adversary in Horatian satire, the unnamed man, conventionally called the boor or pest, who buttonholes Horace as he passes by on the Via Sacra.[39]

> Ibam forte via Sacra, sicut meus est mos,
> nescio quid meditans nugarum, totus in illis.
> accurit quidam notus mihi nomine tantum,
> arreptaque manu, 'quid agis, dulcissime rerum?'   (*Sat.* 1.9.1–4)

I was walking, as it happened, along the Sacred Way, contemplating, as is my wont, some triviality or other, utterly absorbed in it. A certain man known to me only by name ran up, seized my hand, and said, 'How are you doing, my dearest fellow!'

Horace is engaged in the kind of meditative strolling though the city evoked at the end of 1.4 and identified as the originating practice of Horatian satire.[40] He is utterly absorbed (*totus in illis*) in his meditative 'trifles' (*nugae*)—a term that, at least since Catullus, potentially refers to trifling literary compositions. Perhaps Horace's *Musa Pedestris* is concretely at work, limning the outlines of a satiric meditation that will later find its way onto paper. The unnamed figure (whom Horace teasingly describes as someone known to him 'only by name') intrudes upon the satirist's meditative autarky, and forces him to acknowledge their exiguous social connection, physically seizing his hand (*arreptaque manu*). The man is uniquely designed to exasperate Horace, and in many ways, his character constitutes the inverse image of Horace's satiric persona: he is ambitious, self-aggrandizing, intrusive, and above all, garrulous. Much of the humour derives from the fact that the naturally restrained Horace cannot simply shake the man off by shouting abuse at him:

> 'O te, Bolane, cerebri
> felicem!' aiebam tacitus, cum quidlibet ille
> garriret, vicos, urbem laudaret.   (*Sat.* 1.9.11–13)

'O Bolanus, how you are fortunate in your temper!' I was saying to myself, as he prattled on about anything and everything, praising neighbourhoods, the city.

Horace rages inwardly, silent (*tacitus*),[41] while the man goes on talking. Horace facetiously reflects that his adversary's capacity to talk may well be the end of him, recalling a (supposed) prophecy that a chatterbox (*garrulus*) would bring about his demise (29–34).

The satire's parody of the epic duel intensifies the humour, while reminding us that this is a duel of words, the Revenge of the Interlocutor, if you will. The satiric interlocutor, who might otherwise appear to be a straw man, now takes on the flesh-and-blood form of an actual man who physically pursues Horace through the city. It quickly emerges that the nameless man wants an introduction to Maecenas, and that he considers such an introduction to be a means to making his way in the world. First, however, he must impress Horace with his skills.

---

[39] For discussion of *Satires* 1.9, see Anderson (1982), 84–102; Henderson (1993); Schlegel (2005), 108–26; Oliensis (1998), 36–9; Freudenburg (2001), 64–6.

[40] Compare Oliensis (1998), 37; Courtney (1994), 1.

[41] Freudenburg (2001), 64, observes the irony: if Horace were *less* Epicurean and more Lucilian, he would not have to suffer this intrusion on his Epicurean privacy.

incipit ille:
'si bene me novi non Viscum pluris amicum,
non Varium facies: nam quis me scribere pluris
aut citius possit versus? quis membra movere
mollius? invideat quod et Hermogenes ego canto'.   (*Sat.* 1.9.21–5)

He begins: 'If I know myself, you will not value Viscus more as a friend, not Varius: for who could write more verses or write them more quickly than I? Who could move their limbs more pliantly? And my singing is something that would make even Hermogenes envious.'

For the boor, writing is one among several forms of aesthetic performance that will gain a person admittance to Maecenas' circle. Especially troublesome is the impression of Horace's own role in Maecenas' circle this casual acquaintance appears to harbour. In the man's eyes, Horace has presumably used his various talents—poetic or otherwise—for social advancement, and now vies with others for Maecenas' favour.

'Maecenas quomodo tecum?'
hinc repetit. 'paucorum hominum et mentis bene sanae'.
'nemo dexterius fortuna est usus. haberes
magnum adiutorem, posset qui ferre secundas,
hunc hominem velles si tradere: dispeream, ni
summosses omnis'. 'non isto vivimus illic
quo tu rere modo; domus hac nec purior ulla est
nec magis his aliena malis; nil mi officit, inquam,
ditior hic aut est quia doctior; est locus uni
cuique suus.' 'magnum narras, vix credibile.' 'atqui
sic habet.'   (*Sat.* 1.9.43–53)

'How is it with you and Maecenas?' he starts up again from this point. 'He is a man of few friends and very sound judgement.'[42] 'No one has made use of his luck more expertly. You would have a great helper, who could play second fiddle to you, if you were willing to introduce yours truly: hang me if you wouldn't supplant all competition!' 'We do not live there in the manner that you think; there is no house more unsullied than this one or further removed from such flaws. It does me no harm, I tell you,[43] that someone is richer or more erudite; everyone has his own place.' 'Some story you are telling—impossible to believe!' 'And yet, so it is.'

The man finally succeeds in intruding so far upon Horace's autarkic ethos that he provokes a heated response.[44] After suggesting that Horace might like a 'helper' to 'clear away' the competition, the satirist replies emphatically: *non isto vivitur illic / quo tu rere modo . . . est locus uni / cuique suus* ('we don't live there in the way you think . . . each one has his own place'). This remark encapsulates Horace's satiric self-representation in his first book. Being a friend of Maecenas does not mean that he is in competition with others, fawning on his patron in order to rise higher in the world. He remains independent, self-contained/contented, securely established in his *own* space.

It is important to recognize that, in conventional terms, the boor actually advances a more plausible picture than Horace, whose representation of the purity of Maecenas' *domus* stretches the bounds of credulity (*vix credibile*, 52).

---

[42] I here adopt the distribution of speakers recommended by Courtney (1994), 5. *Paucorum*, on this reading, is pointed, but the irrepressible pest goes on talking without taking Horace's point.

[43] So Gowers (2012), ad loc., who is inclined to assign *inquam* to 'Horace' rather than the narrator.

[44] Or, as Oliensis (1998), 38, nicely puts it, a 'staged rupture'. The outburst is indeed 'rhetorically marked as "heartfelt"' (39).

It is Horace's account that requires special pleading. As readers, we may be tempted to shake our heads in dismay at the man's tasteless imposition on the unambitious satirist's contemplative stroll through the city, but that is largely because *Satires* 1.1–8 have already pre-conditioned us to perceive Horace in a certain way, as autarkically absorbed in his own ethical meditations—the least likely person to attempt to convert a friendship into social capital. By contrast, the image of the dependent poet, parasitically attached to his more powerful friend and ambitious of exploiting the attachment, *is* the Horace that many of his contemporary Romans were at least initially inclined to accept as the real one. Satire 1.9 dramatizes Horace's attempt to escape from a stereotype of the client poet which threatens to define him in a constraining and unwelcome manner— and for good reason: it comes uncomfortably close to how he was perceived, and for all we know, what he was. Horace is attempting to escape an aspect of his own public image, a shadow-self he denigrates but can never entirely disavow.[45]

In *Satires* 1, Horace is most typically seen in transit. He has no secure place of his own, and is vulnerable for that reason. People stop and detain him, point at him and discuss his fortunes, as he moves through the city. He claims to have 'his own place' (*locus . . . suus*), but that place is a notional location within Maecenas' *domus*. In some ways, Horace occupies the traditional position of a dependent, who accompanies his patron and forms part of his patron's household. As we have seen, however, Horace has ways of maintaining his autonomy even when attached to Maecenas: he occupies his own separate realm of experience and perception; he follows his own path ethically and aesthetically. Horace's independence is not expressed by a removed position in space, but by a difference in perspective and outlook. He finds freedom in continual movement.

The second book of satires, published after the Battle of Actium in 31 BC, no longer features many descriptions of the satirist in transit. As has been observed by various commentators, the satirist of the second book vacates the urban stage and occupies a dignified remove, looking on while others—a series of *doctores inepti*[46]—make fools of themselves with their extreme yet entertaining sermons and diatribes. He becomes part of the adjudicating audience,[47] and at the same time, lays claim to the stronghold (*arx*) of his Sabine estate.

> Hoc erat in votis: modus agri non ita magnus,
> hortus ubi et tecto vicinus iugis aquae fons
> et paulum silvae super his foret. auctius atque
> di melius fecere. bene est. nil amplius oro,
> Maia nate, nisi ut propria haec mihi munera faxis.
> si neque maiorem feci ratione mala rem
> nec sum facturus vitio culpave minorem,
> si veneror stultus nihil horum, 'o si angulus ille

---

[45] Gowers (2012), 282: 'recognizably H.'s doppelgänger'.   [46] Anderson (1982), 41ff.

[47] Oliensis (1997b). Of course, Horace's satiric self-definition as writer continues to be at stake in this second book as well, not least because he must now confront the fact that literary prowess has produced social prestige for him in ways that his previous satires denied: thus 'the dependence of social on literary success . . . is both aggressively advertised and defensively ruptured', as Horace at once rearticulates and playfully/strategically dismantles his literary and ethical ideals (Oliensis (1998), 42).

> proximus accedat qui nunc denormat agellum!
> o si urnam argenti fors quae mihi monstret, ut illi,
> thesauro invento qui mercennarius agrum
> illum ipsum mercatus aravit, dives amico
> Hercule!' si quod adest gratum iuvat, hac prece te oro:
> pingue pecus domino facias et cetera praeter
> ingenium, utque soles custos mihi maximus adsis.
> ergo ubi me in montis et in arcem ex urbe removi,
> quid prius illustrem saturis Musaque pedestri?   (*Sat.* 2.6.1–17)

This is what I prayed for: a portion of land not so very large, where there would be a garden, a spring of continually flowing water near the house, and above them, a little bit of forest. The gods gave me more and better than I wished for. I am satisfied. I do not pray for more, Maia's son, except that you make these gifts permanently mine. If I neither have made my wealth greater by immoral means, nor intend to diminish it by bad behaviour or negligence, and if I do not foolishly make any prayers of this sort: 'O if only that nearest corner of my neighbour's land could be added to my own—as things stand, it makes the shape of my property irregular! O if some stroke of luck would show me a pot of silver, as it did for the man who discovered a treasure and bought and ploughed the very same land that he had worked as a paid labourer, enriched by Hercules' good will!' If what I already have gratifies and pleases, this is the prayer I make to you: make fat the flocks for their master, and everything else except my literary talent, and, as is your wont, stand by me as my chief guardian! And so, once I have retreated from the city to this citadel in the hills, on what first should I confer fame with my Satires and pedestrian Muse?

The theme is once again contentment, having enough and more than enough for the satisfaction of one's humble desires: *nil amplius oro* ('I ask nothing more'). The modest country estate that forms the basis of Horatian contentment is significantly described in terms of a limit/boundary (<u>*modus agri non ita magnus*</u>). In Satire 1.6, Horace was content as he moved through the various scenes of his Epicurean day: 'contentment with little' was a mental condition that could be achieved anywhere, even in the midst of the crowded city. The limits he respected were the inherent limits of satisfaction in life. Now the site of contentment has changed. The limit of Horace's desires is embodied in his retreat in the Sabine hills. Horace's previous words in 1.9—*est locus uni / cuique suus* ('each has his own place')—take on a new resonance. Now Horace, in a newly concrete and material sense, possesses a place of his own.

Maecenas apparently gave Horace the property.[48] As Oliensis acutely observes, the 'son of Maia' (*Maia nate*) addressed and thanked at the opening of the hexameter, bears phonic resemblance to the name 'Maecenas', who, like the patron god Mercury, has a claim to being Horace's 'chief guardian' (*custos . . . maximus*). Horace avoids openly thanking Maecenas, but manages to thank him implicitly all the same. Horace has now retreated to a concrete locus of withdrawal, his stronghold outside the city, yet the withdrawal into autarkic independence is premised on his patron's generosity. What does it mean to be 'autonomous' in this context? In the first book, Horace struggled with the tension between contentment and social mobility, between the value-system of Epicurean

---

[48] Suetonius *Vita Horati*. Perhaps we should not take Horace at his word by using the term 'farm': Lyne (1995), 6–7, 9–11. On the oblique 'thank you' to Maecenas, see Oliensis (1998), 48.

withdrawal and the social prominence Maecenas and his friends enjoyed in Rome by virtue of their connection with the rising Octavian. Horace was in danger of appearing to be an entertaining parasite enriched by his powerful friend, and had to fight off this impression with all his rhetorical skill. In his newly rural situation, the rhetorical struggle continues, and the language and figures Horace employs to ward off the impression of heteronomous poetic activity, to establish the purity of his wishes and prayers, are revealing: he refers to 'work for hire' (*mercennarius*) and the increase of wealth (*maiorem . . . rem*) through questionable means. He must work to mediate between his commitment to an autonomist self-image, newly embodied in the Sabine farm, and the burden of obligation imposed by the gift of the estate, while demonstrating the continuing purity of his intentions toward his friend Maecenas. If you have a powerful god as a friend (*amico / Hercule*), how can you be sure of not abusing the connection for gain, of maintaining ethical integrity and autarky? Once again, Maecenas both enables Horace's autonomy and threatens it.

Nor are Horace's wishes completely fulfilled: city obligations prevent him from continuously enjoying his rural estate, and so the farm itself becomes the object of desire. Horace's self-representational momentum, however, has shifted: in establishing the site of rural withdrawal, Horace has made a decision that will shape his entire subsequent poetic oeuvre. From now on, poetic autonomy will be closely linked with rural refuge, the relentlessly signified absence of the city. In the Sabine hills, no one will be able to stop Horace to ask a favour, comment on his parentage, or expose his value-system of withdrawal to the gruelling test of a doggedly adversarial conversation. Octavian's, and thus Maecenas' and thus Horace's, side has won; and in the meantime, Horace's first book of satires has been published. Octavian has become *princeps*, and Horace is an author. This solidification of status is accompanied, in Horace's case, by a new detachment from the sometimes humiliating negotiations carried out on city streets. At the same time, in the metaliterary register, Horace offers a much more emphatic division between the aesthetic criteria governing well-written poetry and moral/ legal criteria. In the opening satire of Book 2, Horace suggest, with playful seriousness, that if he were accused of composing defamatory ('bad') verses (*mala . . . carmina*), he would successfully defend himself by pointing to the fact he has written *good* (*bona*) poetry and won the positive 'verdict' of Caesar's praise (*iudice . . . laudatus Caesare*, 2.1.82–4). Political power, with striking clarity, grounds a claim of literary autonomy.

Satire itself is coming to an end along with its *raison d'être*. Autonomy is no longer vindicated by the evasive twists and turns of Horatian dialogue and the urban wanderings of his *Musa Pedestris*, but is now articulated as a literary ideology and linked with a fixed location. Indeed, it is significant that Horace first names, and proposes to glorify (*quid prius illustrem . . . ?*), his satiric Muse at the precise moment when he has withdrawn from its customary arena of urban foot-travel. He no longer physically enacts satiric itineraries, but cites/frames/ celebrates Satire. Horace is now in the position of defining, defending, and articulating the ethical/aesthetic attributes of a specific place. This shift will have a major impact on his mature poetic production. The core self-representational tendencies of the *Odes* and the *Epistles* are grounded in the autarkic refuge of the Sabine farm. A physical villa in and of itself, of course, does not necessarily confer *poetic* autonomy. Horace's portrait of himself in autarkic seclusion on his farm has been a powerfully persuasive one, and substantial archaeological efforts have been devoted to its discovery,[49] yet from our present perspective, the reality of the farm is less important than the literary work it is made to perform. While there is no reason to doubt that Horace enjoyed the seclusion of the Sabine farm, it is equally important to appreciate his careful construction of this image of the autonomous author-figure in rural withdrawal. The sequestration of the farm is made to coincide with the sequestration of poetry itself and to align with core aspects of Horace's poetic text.

VIRGIL'S PASTORAL REFUGE

Virgil is not primarily a first-person poet, and thus does not bear direct comparison with the poets who are the main objects of this study. But Virgil does, in certain key instances, represent himself as poet, and even more frequently, explores the poet's role and social function through metapoetically resonant fictions: ecphrastic descriptions of works of art and monuments, narratives about poets and artificers, dramatizations of song-culture. Virgil's book of *Eclogues*—a series of mimetic dialogues among poet-shepherds—is especially rich in poetological reflection.[50] Like other poets of the 30s, Virgil works to reinvent Roman poetic identity, yet does so with constant reference to Greek models. Virgil's central Greek model, Theocritus, is good to think with in poetological terms: Theocritus is arguably the Greek poet who offers the most intricate fictive representation of the everyday conditions of poetic production. Theocritus' *Idylls* situates themselves in a space of rural tranquillity emphatically removed from the arena of heroic action. He focuses on the lives of humble inhabitants of the pastoral landscape, whose main source of prestige, competition, and entertainment is pastoral song. The pastoral genre thus provides an excellent pretext for representing diverse occasions of song-competition and performance.

The *Eclogues* are an intensely metapoetic work. One strong reason why Virgil chose to imitate Theocritean pastoral in the first place may have been the opportunities pastoral afforded for (re)defining the figure of the poet. Virgil is at the forefront of a new lexical dimension of the Roman's poet's identity, the increasingly common Augustan use of the term *vates* ('seer, bard') to describe a poet. The exact connotations of the term can vary, and modern scholarship has been at times incautious in equating the vatic model with a new enthusiasm for socially responsible poetry. In a broad sense, the term appears to confer a more solemn, sacred resonance on the poetic vocation. It may also provide a further layer of 'Romanness' to the poetic identity: *poeta* is a word originally derived from Greek, whereas *vates* aligns poetry with a native Latin concept and social role. Conventional literary history identifies the rise of the term *vates* with a break from

---

[49] See Frischer and Brown (2001), Frischer et al. (2006), and Chapter 3, n. 113 below.
[50] On the 'self-reflexiveness' of the *Eclogues*, see Alpers (1979), 221–2; on writing, orality, and textuality, Reed (2006), *passim.*

the neoteric past and the evolution toward a more serious, socially committed poetry.[51] Yet it is equally plausible to argue that Virgil and his contemporaries are building on the neoteric project of defining poetic activity in Roman terms. This project is ongoing, and the older term *poeta* remains in use. Like Horace, Virgil is attempting to find a place, both literally and metaphorically, for poetic activity in Roman society. One of Virgil's early uses of *vates* at once comments obliquely on the co-presence of the two terms, and brings to the fore the uncertainty of the project of Roman poetic identity: *et me fecere poetam / Pierides, sunt et mihi carmina, me quoque dicunt / vatem pastores; sed non ego credulus illis* ('Me, too, the Pierian Muses have made a *poeta*; I too have songs; me also the shepherds call a *vates*; but I do not believe them', 1.9.32–4).[52]

Contributing to the uncertainty surrounding the changing role of poetry in Roman society was the political turmoil of late 40s and early 30s BC. After the battle of Philippi, Octavian was assigned the thankless task of settling the veterans on Italian land, which, since there was no more state-owned land, had to be confiscated from existing owners. This policy created considerable disturbance in the Italian countryside, and in one instance, motivated a serious uprising. The revolt was quelled by Octavian's grim and bloody siege of Perugia in 40 BC. It is hard to imagine a countryside less evidently idyllic and further from the pastoral ideal than Italy during the period of the land confiscations, and yet it is precisely at this moment in history, and with explicit reference to this historical background,[53] that Virgil chooses to produce a book of ten pastoral poems in imitation of Theocritus. The concepts of refuge, quietude, simplicity, and autarky furnish core elements in the identity of the pastoral genre,[54] and yet the status of the Italian countryside as a tranquil refuge came into serious doubt in this period: the *rus* (countryside) was subject to the political exigencies of the *urbs* (city). The result is a constant, defining tension between internal and external, pastoral's idyllic *locus amoenus* and the powerful outside forces that constantly intrude upon it.

Virgil's disrupted countryside bears a peculiar resemblance to Horace's satiric city. In both settings, the writer struggles to maintain a slender domain of tranquillity, a refuge from the turbulence that surrounds him. In a certain sense, poetry *is* that space of autonomy. Only by maintaining his autonomist niche of meditative self-absorption can the satirist maintain his integrity amidst the pressures and insinuations of the triumviral city; and only through the tremendous literary effort of re-creating the fictions of Theocritean pastoral on Italy's devastated soil can Virgil succeed in imposing his unique vision of refuge and freedom. Poetry, on the Virgilian model, is fragile, tenuous (not just in the Callimachean sense), and, compared with the greater forces of the world, weak. Poetry is a

---

[51] See Newman (1967).

[52] Compare Theocritus 7.37–41; Verg. *Ecl.* 7.25–8; and the comments of Clausen (1994), ad loc.

[53] For more on this background, and Virgil's own possible involvement in these events, see Wilkinson (1966a). The possibility of teasing a coherent historical narrative out of Virgil's poetry is highly controversial, however: see Bowersock (1971), Tarrant (1978), Zetzel (1984), Mankin (1988), Farrell (1991).

[54] Numerous scholarly works address the question of the identity of the pastoral genre: for example, Rosenmeyer (1969); Gransden (1970); Halperin (1983); Patterson (1987); Alpers (1996).

'breakable' thing, or in Latin, *fragilis*, like the 'fragile reed' (*fragili . . . cicuta*, 5.85) offered as emblematic gift-object at the close of Eclogue 5.[55] At the same time, however, other Virgilian paradigms of poetry endow it with the power to control the poet's surroundings. Orpheus, an important cultural figure in both the *Eclogues* and the *Georgics*, exemplifies this primal power: his song was able to move rocks and trees. Yet even Orpheus' power, as the *Georgics'* closing epyllion demonstrates, is fatally limited. He failed to bring back his wife Eurydice from Hades—a failure that is emblematic of the poet-hero's inevitably losing struggle with mortality itself. We must also remember that Orpheus, even when successful and capable, is a mythic figure of the ancient past. Can the modern *vates* call upon comparable powers and capacities?

Moeris, the older, world-weary herdsman of Eclogue 9,[56] is not optimistic on this point. His youthful interlocutor, Lycidas, has heard a rumour that the master poet Menalcas saved properties from confiscation by the power of his song. Moeris' testimony presents a less encouraging picture.

> Audieras, et fama fuit; sed carmina tantum
> nostra valent, Lycida, tela inter martia, quantum
> Chaonias dicunt aquila veniente columbas.
> quod nisi me quacumque novas incidere lites
> ante sinistra cava monuisset ab ilice cornix,
> nec tuus hic Moeris, nec viveret ipse Menalcas.   (*Ecl.* 9.11–15)

You had heard, and so the rumour went: but amid the weapons of war, Lycidas, our songs alone are as effective as, they say, Chaonian doves when the eagle comes. If a raven on the left side had not first warned me from a hollow holm-oak to cut off, insofar as I could, this fresh quarrel, neither your Moeris here nor Menalcas himself would be alive.

Song is not as powerful as the weapons of war, and the singer, like Orpheus himself, turns out to be all too mortal. Following this dark revelation,[57] the two shepherd-singers continue to walk toward the city, exchanging citations from the repertoire of their absent master, Menalcas. The pair of shepherds do not present whole songs or works, as happens elsewhere in Virgil and Theocritus, but reproduce Menalcas' songs only in fragmentary patchwork as night falls on the road. They are moving from the *rus* toward the city, just as, in this penultimate eclogue, the pastoral itinerary itself is coming to an end. Pastoral song begins to seem like a distant memory, tenuously sustained by these two melancholy wayfarers.

The sense of the fragility and fragmentation of the pastoral realm is not purely a factor of the closural position of Eclogue 9, although this may add some poignancy. The imminence of pastoral closure is disquietingly present from the very beginning.[58] The first eclogue[59] tells the tale of two shepherds: one shepherd,

---

[55] Compare *Ecl.* 8.82 (*fragilis . . . laurus*), 8.40 (*fragilis . . . ramos*), and in an especially relevant context, *fracta cacumina* (9.9).

[56] A poem often read in conjunction with *Eclogue* 1, as Clausen (1994), 266, notes, and rarely appreciated for its own merits: but see Putnam (1970); Henderson (1998b); Perkell (2001).

[57] See the discussion of Putnam (1970), 302–4, who notes that 'although his *carmina* fail him, the poet-shepherd still retains one of the negative aspects of a *vates*, the ability to predict oncoming doom' (304).

[58] Theodorakopoulos (1997), 162: 'Eclogue 1 is the beginning of the end'.

[59] On Eclogue 1, see, for example, Putnam (1970), 20–81; Alpers (1979), 65–95; Du Quesnay (1981); Wright (1983); Clausen (1994), 29ff.; Hubbard (1995).

Meliboeus, must leave the Italian countryside to go into exile; the other, Tityrus, has been vouchsafed the right to remain on his land by an unnamed young man hailed by the admiring shepherd as a 'god' (*deus*). Tityrus's restored position within the pastoral landscape is tantamount to his continuing status as pastoral singer. Meliboeus, however, is moved to proclaim: *carmina nulla canam* ('I shall sing no songs'). Meliboeus' description of Tityrus emphasizes how, as pastoral singer, he remains protectively enfolded within the musically resonant landscape.

> Tityre, tu patulae recubans sub tegmine fagi
> silvestrem tenui musam meditaris avena:
> nos patriae finis et dulcia linquimus arva;
> nos patriam fugimus; tu, Tityre, lentus in umbra
> formosam resonare doces Amaryllida silvas.   (*Ecl.* 1.1–5)

Tityrus, you, reclining beneath the cover of a spreading beech, are composing the woodland muse on slender oat-pipe. I am departing from the boundaries of my fatherland and my beloved fields; I go into exile from my fatherland. You, Tityrus, at ease in the shade, are teaching the woods to echo with the name of beautiful Amaryllis.

Tityrus remains under the shelter (*tegmine*) of a beech tree, within the boundaries (*finis*) of his homeland, in the refuge of the shade (*umbra*). The pastoral realm is defined from the outset as a delimited space of refuge, where the herdsman's song resonates within the protective embrace of an idyllic and aesthetically sympathetic landscape. The exile's fate involves exposure, contagion, dispossession, homelessness, *dis*placement, and concomitantly, the absence of song. Poetry, on the Virgilian model, requires a sheltering, stable, integral space within which to flourish.

Poetry also requires a certain degree of freedom—free time, and the basic freedom from care needed to sustain the shepherd-singer's *otium*.[60] For Tityrus, however, freedom must also be understood in a very concrete and particular sense. A slave, he went to the city in order to purchase his freedom; now he is a freedman. The herdsman's newly won freedom rings out conspicuously in verse-initial position at the beginning of his long autobiographical speech:

> MELIBOEUS
> Et quae tanta fuit Romam tibi causa videndi?
> TITYRUS
> Libertas, quae sera tamen respexit inertem . . . .   (*Ecl.* 1.26–7)
>
> MELIBOEUS
> And what was this great need of yours for seeing Rome?
> TITYRUS
> Freedom, who, though late, looked upon me in my state of inaction . . .

Tityrus went to Rome in order to purchase his liberty. Yet somehow this trip to Rome also appears to have won Tityrus the right to remain on his land. Winterbottom summarizes the somewhat confusingly presented situation: '[Tityrus] has visited Rome to buy his freedom, and, receiving it in return for his *peculium*, has

---

[60] On pastoral *otium* and freedom, see Rosenmeyer (1969), 65–129.

also received something for which he did not pay—permission from the *iuvenis* to go on working his small farm'.[61]

Serious questions of interpretation nevertheless arise: is the godlike *iuvenis* (young man), as most commentators have supposed, the young Octavian, who obviously had some authority over the land confiscations?[62] If so, is there an implicit political significance attached to the highly prominent term *libertas*? Finally, to what extent can Tityrus' situation be aligned with Virgil's, who owned a farm in Mantua, and, owing to his connections both to Pollio and Octavian, also appears to have come out of the confiscations relatively unscathed? While these questions cannot be answered with any certainty, it is significant that, in the case of the two confusingly overlaid narrative trajectories (from *servitium* to *libertas*, from loss to restoration of property), freedom appears to be at stake. I would suggest, following Clausen,[63] that the confusion is largely deliberate: Virgil, through Tityrus' sometimes elliptical narration, manages to align the *servitium–libertas* trajectory with the narrative of loss and restoration. The outcome in both cases is emancipation. In the one case, Tityrus achieves a change in juridical status, and in the other, he enjoys the liberty to 'play what [he] wants on his rustic pipe'.[64] He enjoys *otia* ('conditions of leisure'), the freedom from immediate constraint, obligation, and threat necessary to enjoy his musical pursuits in tranquillity.

The autarkic freedom of Horace's urban satirist, which might appear to belong to a different world, actually shares some key features with the freedom of Virgil's ex-slave herdsman. First of all, both Tityrus and Horace's satiric speaker are humble figures who rise socially: Tityrus is a slave who becomes a freedman, Horace a freedman's son who becomes Maecenas' friend. A dynamic of emancipation also applies to each in less literal ways: Tityrus' *libertas*, as discussed above, has a broader symbolic aspect, and Horace follows up his father's juridical manumission with an ethical emancipation of his own. Finally, Tityrus' freedom in the first eclogue, like Horace's in *Satires* 1, is underwritten and endowed with stability by the generosity of a powerful patron. A god, as he vividly states, created the conditions for his leisure and security (*deus nobis haec otia fecit*, 1.6). Once again, we are a long way away from the *libertas* of a socially elevated poet on the Lucilian or Catullan model. Tityrus' freedom is a slave's hard-won emancipation; his humble realm of autonomy is bestowed on him by the godlike *iuvenis*. The old ex-slave of the first eclogue, of course, cannot simply be identified with the collection's author. Yet insofar as Tityrus' ability to remain in his pastoral world and continue creating pastoral song constitutes the introductory premise of Virgilian pastoral poetry, the construct of *libertas* articulated in Tityrus' first-person narration must also have broader implications for our conception of the nature of the pastoral refuge. In Virgil's world, the right to do as one pleases, the *libertas* of self-assertion, does not apply to the humble pastoral singers, whose limited freedoms, and whose very right to exist in the pastoral idyll, are dependent on their masters and patrons.

---

[61] Winterbottom (1976), 56.   [62] See again Wilkinson (1966a).
[63] Clausen (1994), 31.   [64] Alpers (1996), 25.

Virgil makes it painfully clear just how tenuous and fragile a refuge pastoral is. The land confiscations threaten pastoral tranquillity, and even the modest degree of security achieved by some fortunate herdsmen depends on the whim of those in power. Virgil's argument might at first appear to be counter-autonomist in its broader tendency: poetry has no sheltered precinct or refuge, no autonomist niche within which the writer may enjoy the freedom of his literary pursuits. And yet, in an important sense, the entire poetic *labor* of the *Eclogues* is directed toward *maintaining* pastoral's space of refuge and freedom, however slim and fragile its confines may appear to be. All the important projects of civilization, in the Virgilian world-view, involve *labor*, and poetry is no exception. Both Virgil's Callimachean creed and his vision of the human role in the cosmos demand continual hard work for the maintenance of order in the literary and the social realms. The refuge of the pastoral realm would be less convincing if it were *not* threatened, *not* contingent, *not* won by a combination of hard work, talent, and sheer luck.

Virgil, like Horace, is keenly aware of the potential weakness of any excessively idealizing construct of poetic autonomy. Given the turbulent political conditions in which they lived and wrote, would an autonomist poetics be credible, if it were not vindicated by continual effort and rhetorical labour, under constant duress? Virgil's pastoral vision is not escapist, but soberly cognizant of the dangers present at its edges. The Virgilian construct of the pastoral shelter derives an important dimension of its identity from the conditions that oppose it. What is a shelter, if it is not a shelter *from* something?[65] In Eclogue 1, Meliboeus' exilic condition, not to mention his considerable poetic eloquence, define the significance of Tityrus' idyllic refuge. Tityrus is not in nearly as good a position to appreciate the extent of his good fortune as the dispossessed Meliboeus, who lacks the liberty and ease that Tityrus so evidently enjoys. If Meliboeus did not provide a negative example, we would not be able to appreciate the precious value of Tityrus' humble realm of security. Pastoral autonomy depends for its meaning at least in part on the forces that threaten to disrupt it.

The boundaries of Virgil's pastoral realm derive a further degree of definition from the confrontation with non-pastoral genres and discourses. The final eclogue of the collection brings pastoral into dialogue with the emerging genre of love elegy, as represented by the poetry of Virgil's friend Cornelius Gallus.[66] Gallus, we learn, is deeply in love with Lycoris, who, however, has gone off to follow 'another [man] amid snows and rugged camps' (23). Like Theocritus' dying Daphnis, Gallus is approached by a series of pastoral figures and deities, who sympathize with him, and lament the destructive madness of his insatiable love (12–30). Gallus appears to be tempted by the shelter of the pastoral landscape, and even

---

[65] This tension recurs in accounts of Virgil's life: see the contrast drawn by Tarrant (1997), 169, between the reclusive image of Virgil that comes out of the ancient biographers, and his evident connection with powerful figures throughout his life. He goes on to argue that Virgil, in each of his major works, 'engages with contemporary political reality in a serious and sustained way', but makes an effort to prevent 'his poetry from becoming simply a vehicle of political comment' (173).

[66] A multitude of scholars have attempted to characterize the association between Gallus and Virgil, and to reconstruct Gallus' lost works on the basis of Virgil (e.g. Ross (1975)); on the tenth eclogue in particular, see Kidd (1964); Conte (1986), 100–29; Putnam (1970), 342–94; Alpers (1979), 223–40; Perkell (1996).

proclaims that he will become a pastoral poet (50–1). And yet, at the very moment when Gallus' fantasy departs from the future tense into present-tense *enargeia*, the possibility of pastoral refuge collapses into the unreality of subjunctive verbs.

> iam mihi per rupes videor lucosque sonantis
> ire; libet Partho torquere Cydonia cornu
> spicula—tamquam haec sit nostri medicina furoris,
> aut deus ille malis hominum mitescere discat.   (*Ecl.* 10.58–61)

Now, as it seems to me, I am passing over rocks and echoing groves; I enjoy shooting Cydonian arrows from Parthian bow . . . as if this could offer a cure for my frenzy, as if that god could learn to show mildness toward the sufferings of men!

The god who presides over love elegy, a cruel, unremitting *Amor*, will never allow Gallus to exit the confines of love poetry: love, according to the elegiac rule, is incurable. By contrast with the Theocritean Daphnis, who resists love at the cost of his own life, melting into the pastoral landscape rather than giving in to the invading god, Gallus is unable even to enter the pastoral realm, because love continues to dominate him. The hope of escape is an illusion, and therefore the elegist might as well concede defeat: *omnia vincit Amor, et nos cedamus Amori* ('Love conquers all; let us too yield to Love', 69).

Pastoral would appear to enjoy decisive advantages over Gallan love elegy. The lover, in this early version of the *servitium amoris*, is the prisoner of Love, unable to exert autonomous agency. The book which begins with the freedman Tityrus' idyllic *libertas* ends with the aristocratic Gallus' defeat at the hands of a proud, subjugating *Amor*. The irony could hardly be more explicit, and would appear to favour Virgil's humble domain of liberty and ease. Yet, as we shall have opportunity to observe in our subsequent consideration of Tibullus and Propertius, the elegists themselves employ the figure of *servitium* as part of an autonomist strategy of poetic self-representation that ultimately works to enhance the status of the elite poet rather than undermine it. Virgil understands this, and pays Gallus a considerable compliment in Eclogue 10. Not only does he engage in extensive imitation of Gallus' poetry; he demonstrates the power and autonomy of Gallus' literary genre. Virgil depicts *Amor* asserting absolute control over the elegist in a manner that Gallus himself would have approved. Gallan elegy, like Virgilian pastoral, constitutes an autonomous literary sphere that resists the incursions of alien genres and discourses. Gallus' inability to depart from love elegy shows just how tightly and effectively his generic domain has been constructed.

Neither space of notional autonomy, of course, is absolute. No matter how well constructed, no literary genre can be seamlessly divided from other genres and the outside world. Gallus, who appears to be on active military service,[67] does not reliably remain cloistered in his elegiac realm. And as we have argued throughout this section, Virgilian pastoral affords the poet a sheltered space of withdrawal that is at best temporary, at worst assailed and potentially subverted by outside forces. It is to Virgil's credit that he shows the fragile pastoral realm as persistently infringed upon by the shadows of un-pastoral figures and events. There is no permanent, unassailable space of refuge, but only a temporary shelter, a place to

---

[67] For interpretation of the difficult line 10.45, see Clausen (1994), ad loc.; Coleman (1977), ad loc.

rest on the green grass for the night—*fronde super viridi* (1.80)—before the long
journey into exile inevitably begins. The book of ten bucolic poems is itself a
temporary resting-spot, a locus of alluring beauty and repose that betrays awareness of its own contingency and short-lived duration. We cannot remain in the
rural idyll any more than Virgil could remain content with the pastoral genre.

There is not sufficient space here to discuss Virgil's later career in depth, but it
will be worthwhile at least briefly to glace at that later trajectory to appreciate how
his earlier concerns with autonomy continue to inform his work. In the *Georgics*,
Virgil further explores metaphors for poetic toil, the space of the Italian countryside, and the relation between political events, poetry, and the world of nature.
The first book opens with a striking panegyrical flourish, in which the poet
hesitates as to which divine role best suits Octavian (1.24–42). The opening of
the third returns to the panegyrical mode. Apparently anticipating his own
Aeneid, Virgil evokes a temple complex which he will 'build' in honour of
Octavian, yet in which his own role as monumental builder is to be stressed
alongside Octavian's as *honorandus* (3.10–39). Finally, at the close of Book 4, an
intricate neoteric epyllion on Orpheus, Eurydice, and Aristaeus (4.315–558)
precedes the poet's bold, Callimachean *sphragis*, in which he juxtaposes his own
Neapolitan literary *otium* with Caesar's role as warrior-princeps (559–66). Virgil's
final and most ambitious work, the *Aeneid*, has come to encapsulate the central
questions of poetry and ideology for the Augustan period in modern scholarship.
The forward drive of the teleological narrative—toward Rome's foundation and
empire, toward Augustus' principate—is in constant tension with a tendency to
contemplate and linger on the losses inextricably linked with this drive. Virgil's
Aeneid provides the blueprint for the genre that, in the early imperial period,
immanently reflects on dynamics of power, authority, freedom, ideology, and
historical teleology, and thus constitutes the conspicuous site of engagement
between poetry and empire, Roman writers and political reality.[68] We are left
with the paradoxical figure of a poet who is supremely retiring and yet also central
to the formation of imperial narrative ideology. This tensional juxtaposition of an
intense awareness of political reality alongside vivid evocations of withdrawal is
already present in Virgilian pastoral. The *Eclogues* establish the fabric of poetic
ideas—freedom and destiny, poetry and prophesy, the land of Italy as site of
conflict and as tranquil idyll—that will inform his later works.

Virgil's identification of the countryside as a place of quiet refuge, and thus as
the ideal site of poetic production, also exerted a powerful influence on his
contemporaries. Horace would later write: *scriptorum chorus omnis amat nemus
et fugit urbem* ('The whole chorus of writers loves the grove the shuns the city',
Epistles 2.2.77). As we have mentioned, Horace of the *Odes* and *Epistles* models the
autonomy of the poetic text on the metaphor of the writer's sequestered detachment in the counstryide. Freedom from the obligations of urban life figures poetic
autonomy. Not all poets equally fell under the spell of this powerful idea, however.
In the classic scenario of elegiac love, the lover-poet finds no true freedom, only
continual obsession and degradation, whether in Rome or elsewhere. Propertius,
following and developing Gallus' example, offers the most unrelenting model of

---

[68] See above, Introduction, n. 72.

elegiac love-servitude: he proclaims himself the continual slave (*servus*) of his mistress (*domina*) Cynthia.

PROPERTIUS BOOK 1: AUTONOMY AS CONFINEMENT

The poetry books examined so far in this chapter are coterminous with distinctive poetic 'worlds'. The poet's slender *libellus*, in each case, embodies the narrow, autarkic domain of his poetic world/genre. The early elegiac love poetry of Propertius conforms to this broader pattern of restrictive poetic worlds elegantly encompassed within slender books. Propertius' first book of poetry (ca. 29 BC), although it differs from the others in number of poems,[69] represents a similarly limited and confining perspective, and manifests a comparable rigour of internal structure. The ways in which 'Callimachean' aesthetic compression and density were imposed with deliberate artifice on Augustan texts has been amply appreciated, but it has been only intermittently observed how the literary personalities projected by works in first-person poetic genres were in many cases comparably crafted and designed to produce a sense of restriction and confinement. Such a tactic is strongly in evidence in early Propertian elegy, and constitutes a key feature of his autonomist rhetoric. The vivid images of the lover's life fashioned by Propertius are part of a broader discursive strategy.

From the outset, Propertius works to create the sense of narrowed boundaries and enclosure. In the first instance, the restrictive domain that enforces the boundaries of the poetic speaker's existence is not a physical space per se, but the narrowed axiological horizons of his relentless love-obsession. The opening lines of his first book narrate how he first came to be subjugated, and his life to be reconstituted, by his love for Cynthia.

> Cynthia prima suis miserum me cepit ocellis,
> contactum nullis ante cupidinibus.
> tum mihi constantis deiecit lumina fastus
> et caput impositis pressit Amor pedibus,
> donec me docuit castas odisse puellas
> improbus, et nullo vivere consilio.
> et mihi iam toto furor hic non deficit anno,
> cum tamen adversos cogor habere deos.   (1.1.1–8)

Cynthia was the first to capture with her eyes my pitiable self, previously uninfected by any desire. Then Love forced down my gaze of steady hauteur and trampled my head beneath his feet, until the heartless one taught me to have no use for chaste girls, and to live aimlessly. For a whole year now this madness has not left me, while I am yet forced to endure the gods' hostility.

Propertius' elegiac lover has not simply fallen in love with a particular girl and gone through various determinate stages of a relationship, but rather crossed a line beyond which the basic rules of existence are different. Being in love with Cynthia is not a yearning that finds its fulfilment in possession, but a madness

---

[69] 22 or 23, depending on the division or unity of 1.8a and 1.8b; see Manuwald (2006), 229.

(*furor*) that characterizes an entire stretch of time: it has lasted an entire year (*toto anno*), and will continue indefinitely.[70] Built into the lover's life is an element of irrationality (*nullo vivere consilio*), but it is a *systematic* irrationality;[71] his disdain for decent girls is generalized.[72]

Although Propertius' first book is known among scholars for avoiding explicit poetological reference, this opening scene of 'love at first sight' is rich in meta-poetic implication,[73] and commences his autonomist project. The Propertian lover, we are to understand, occupies his own segregated, self-enclosing field of experience. Immediately following the mythic scene of Propertius' instantaneous capture by Cynthia and Love comes the text's first overtly mythological *exemplum*:

> Milanion nullos fugiendo, Tulle, labores
>   saevitiam durae contudit Iasidos.
> nam modo Partheniis amens errabat in antris,
>   ibat et hirsutas ille videre feras;
> ille etiam Hylaei percussus vulnere rami
>   saucius Arcadiis rupibus ingemuit.
> ergo velocem potuit domuisse puellam:
>   tantum in amore preces et bene facta valent.
> in me tardus Amor non ullas cogitat artes,
>   nec meminit notas, ut prius, ire vias.   (1.1.9–18)

It was by shirking no trials, Tullus, that Milanion subdued the cruelty of the hard-hearted daughter of Iasus. For now he wandered deranged among the dells of Mount Parthenius, and now he would go to face shaggy wild beasts. He was also struck with the blow of Hylaeus' club, and, wounded, groaned in pain on the rocks of Arcadia. Therefore he was able to tame the swift girl; so much do entreaties and good deeds avail in love. In my case, sluggish Love devises no stratagems, and does not remember to tread well known paths as of old.

Once again Propertius constructs an amatory personality that is designed to merge conveniently with his literary aims and self-positioning. Here he confers further definition on his elegiac *ego* through comparison with a figure from myth. Milanion, like 'Propertius', suffers the cruelty (*saevitia*) of a hard mistress (*dura domina*),[74] and yet his story (in this version) ends on a remarkably un-elegiac note: his labours, simply, succeed; he masters the girl, and the efficacy of entreaties (*preces*) and good deeds (*bene facta*) is confirmed. Propertius' labours, by contrast, are programmatically endless

---

[70] Uninterrupted *furor* implies continual devotion to love poetry; for *furor* as a term referring to the poet's 'divine madness' or inspiration, see Buchheit (1976), 172.

[71] Conte (1994), 38 discusses the 'systematically pervasive' nature of the elegiac ideology of *servitium*, how elegy transforms the world's values in setting up its own (restricted) world. The continuous and systematic nature of the elegiac love-experience is also at stake in the well-known allusion to an epigram of Meleager (*Anth. Pal.* 12.101), who, in other epigrams, will turn to other matters and other loves; see the remarks of Fedeli (1986), 277–8, and discussion below.

[72] But the question of Cynthia's relation to the category of *castae puellae* is vexed and much debated: for an overview (and an eccentric solution), see Heyworth (2007a), 4–5.

[73] See, for example, Hinds (1987b), 11–12; Cairns (1974b); Ross (1975), 59–71; Batstone (1992); Lyne (1998a); Booth (2001); Keith (2008), 45–6, with bibliography (n. 2).

[74] This difficult mythological *exemplum* has been discussed by countless scholars; but note in particular Ross (1975), 61–5, Cairns (1974b), Allen (1950).

and strategically achieve nothing. Unlike the favours (*bene facta*) that oblige a return in relations of friendship among freeborn Romans, Propertius' continual, non-voluntary labour without recompense defines his status as slave of love.

Propertius, then, works hard to produce the impression of a lover so deeply absorbed and 'enslaved' by his object of desire that he cannot see outside the confines of his amatory experience. At the same time, however, this same first-person speaker draws a series of apt comparisons, defining his position in literary and mythological terms. As previously in the case of Catullus, there is a double strategy of simultaneously identifying the poetic speaker with a sequestered, autonomist sphere of life-experience (*otium, amor, pax*) and of intimating poten-tial rifts and points of tension between this self-representational construct and the author who creates it. Surely a lover whose viewpoint is so narrowly enslaved and externally determined would not have the mental liberty to situate himself in erudite, analogical terms. Another analogical figure is the addressee Tullus whose name is embedded in the Milanion exemplum.[75] His name, as we will learn as we read further into the book, comes to signal a debate over whether the lover or the administrator of empire has a truer claim to 'toils' (*labores*).[76] The lover gains definition in contrastive relation to both Tullus and Milanion:[77] the Pro-pertian speaker's 'labours', unlike Tullus', are amatory, but unlike Milanion's, perpetually fail.

This conspicuous failure, however, functions as a claim of literary originality. Propertius' slow-witted or late-arriving Love (*tardus Amor*) does not remember (*nec meminit*) to go by the well-known paths of old: that is, Propertius' (belated) poetic contribution is not a slave to the shared memory of the poetic tradition.[78] Propertius' novelty, then, consists in the permanence of his slavery, which, in literary terms, means submitting himself to the constraining force of Love (i.e. the topoi of love poetry) more thoroughly than anyone previously.[79] This reference to poetic memory (*meminit*) has a further layer. The opening depiction of Proper-tius' capture by Love cites the Greek epigrammatist Meleager, who, in *Anth. Pal.* 12.101,[80] relates how the boy Myiskos has wounded him with his eyes, though he was previously untouched by love. Meleager's *eromenos*, like Propertius' *Amor*, triumphs over his once arrogant lover.[81]

---

[75] Sharrock (2000), 268, notes the tension between myth and Roman friendship: 'When we read the words "Tullus", "Bassus", "Ponticus", "Gallus", we are meant to respond to them as signifiers of Roman men, real people of whom a life-story can be told.'

[76] *Et tibi non umquam nostros puer iste labores / afferat et lacrimis omnia nota meis* ('and may that boy never bring you toils such as mine, and all the misfortunes known to my tears', 1.6.23–4).

[77] Sharrock (2000), 269.   [78] Compare Heyworth (2007a), 8; Batstone (1992), 298.

[79] On originality in this elegy, see the discussion of Ross (1975), 61–5, who argues that a Gallan precedent lies behind the Milanion example. Compare Wyke (1987a), 55, on 2.12: 'a Propertian discourse ceaselessly concerned with love'.

[80] See Keith (2008), 46–7.

[81] The various facets of the allusion are nicely brought out in Höschele (2011), 20ff. In particular, she observes that the allusion to 'Meleager' adds a further layer of playful metapoetic commentary to the Milanion *exemplum*: 'the text invites its readers to recall Atalante's link with [Meleager], thus casting Propertius (= Milanion) implicitly in the role of Meleager's (the mythic figure's and the poet's) successor', 25.

Myiskos shot me, hitherto unwounded by Desire, below the breast with his eyes, and shouted these words: 'I have captured the arrogant one. Look, that impudence of sceptered wisdom he wore on his brow I now tread underfoot'. To him, barely gathering sufficient breath, I said: 'Dear boy, why are you amazed? Eros brought even Zeus himself down from Olympus'.

Immediately striking is the different tone affected by Propertius, who comes off as despairing where Meleager seems urbanely detached.[82] The closing conceit—'Eros brought Zeus himself down from Olympos'—is an ingeniously witty gesture of capitulation, but hardly the desolate utterance of one who has been permanently subjugated by love and consigned to a senseless mode of existence. Propertius, by contrast, represents the poetic speaker as wholly absorbed in love to the point of losing any sense of proportion. A second, related point concerns the more limited scope and occasion-specific focus of Meleager's erotic epigram. The poem represents an occasion of erotic intensity directed toward Myiskos, but in other epigrams, Meleager's speaker finds himself in love with a long list of other boys and women. Indeed, the constant turnover in lovers' names in Meleager's corpus suggests that Love (proverbially equipped with 'wings'[83]) is by nature changeable and shifts from one object to another.

It might be objected that epigram is a genre that inherently represents a greater variety of small-scale occasions rather than one continually elaborated fabric of experience. Yet this objection actually offers some support to the present argument. Propertius goes out of his way to allude to and thus also differentiate himself from epigrammatic eros.[84] If love in an epigrammatic treatment such as Meleager's tends to be episodic, temporally delimited, occasion-specific, and varied in object and tone, Propertius shows how a similar scene of capture leads, in his case, to a permanent and systematic subjection to a single girl (*una . . . puella*).[85] Meleager's epigram depicts the scene of capture—and that is all: his elegant, self-contained set-piece has accomplished its end within the compass of its lines. For Propertius, the scene of capture initiates a new stage in the poet's existence. He proceeds from capture as prisoner of war to continual existence as slave of love—a transition Meleager's snapshot of infatuation necessarily omits. Propertius uses the Meleagrian intertext to establish important properties of his continuous elegiac mode.[86]

---

[82] It is hard to imagine Propertius offering this cool response to his lover's taunts: 'why so amazed?' (*ti thambeis?*).

[83] We might compare Propertius 2.12, where the poet programmatically insists that, in his case, Love *lacks* wings, contrary to the usual iconography. But note Höschele (2011), 22, who points out that Myiscus is Meleager's most important *eromenos*.

[84] Keith (2008), 47, points out that *miserum*, a word not paralleled in Meleager's epigram, hints at the derivation of elegy from *eleos*. For the relation between Roman love elegy and epigram generally, see the essays in Keith (2011b).

[85] 1.11.29. That the love-object is a girl, rather than, as in Meleager, a boy, also seems to be a crucial part of the point. Propertian elegy adheres to a largely heterosexual paradigm, and elsewhere, Propertius contrasts the facile, pliable nature of boys with the more difficult and resistant temperament of *puellae* (2.4.17–22).

[86] For discussion of 1.1, including characterization of the differences between elegiac and epigrammatic love-poetry, see Hubbard (1974), 14–20.

Even as Propertius sets up a contrast with Meleager's epigrammatic eros, he turns his attention toward a Roman and specifically elegiac model. Assuming that the arguments of Ross and others are correct, Propertius not only cites Meleager in the opening lines, he also, in the subsequent passage, rings the changes on the Milanion exemplum of Cornelius Gallus.[87] Much of the rhetorical energy of Propertius' first book of elegies derives from the continual effort of differentiation from other modes of life and of poetry. In all cases, he stresses an interrelated set of qualities defining his elegiac condition: immobility, fidelity to one lover, incurability, relentlessness, slavery. Yet the manner in which the elegiac speaker comments on specific predecessors and comparanda, situating himself precisely and intricately in relation to them, belies to a certain extent the very concept of a figure wholly controlled by and subordinated to an overwhelming passion. Even as Propertius differentiates himself from others in emphasizing the totalizing absorption of his love-condition, he implies a very high degree of authorial awareness and discursive control. This duality of erudite, controlling author and hapless, enslaved persona hardly takes the form of a neat division, but involves a complex awareness of simultaneous layers of literary identity in tension with each other.

I wish to argue that one aim behind this complex self-representational rhetoric is to shore up the poet's autonomist position. On the one hand, the enslaved lover is confined to a sequestered field of experience, resistant to outside discourses and interests, and on the other hand, the elegiac author enjoys the freedom of discursive control over his textual realm. There is no clear line dividing author and persona, yet Propertius profits from this blurring of boundaries in order to simultaneously assert axiological autonomy (Love as totalizing sphere) and literary freedom (the power to generate and manipulate personae). This logically difficult but rhetorically effective combination produces the distinctively Augustan construct of autonomy *as* confinement. Catullus plays a similar game, simultaneously representing himself as leading a life of *otium, amor,* and *urbanitas,* and asserting his freedom to fashion and refashion poetic personae independently of moral norms and life-praxis. He at once defines his persona through antinomian moral and social postures, and insists on a division between ethics and aesthetics. Propertius, in distinction from Catullus, pushes further the idea of the equivalence between literary genre and literary persona, between lover and love poetry.[88] Whereas Catullus oscillates between different stances and modes,[89] Love is an all-pervasive atmosphere from which Propertius does not depart until the end of the third book (and perhaps not even then).[90] As Conte has argued, the

---

[87] Ross (1975), 59–71; Rosen and Farrell (1986); Pincus (2004); Heyworth (2007a) ad loc.

[88] On the equivalence between love and poetry, Commager (1974), 4ff.; note also Fedeli (1980), 191–2. Zetzel (1996), 82, is even stronger: 'to speak of a Roman elegy as being in some sense "about poetry" is automatically redundant . . . there is no distance at all from bed to verse'.

[89] On the oscillation and even fragmentation of the Catullan self, see Greene (1998), 1–17, which builds on Janan (1994).

[90] On the all-absorbing tendency of elegiac love, see Fedeli (1986), 277–8: the idea of love as totalizing life-choice derives at least in part from Virgil's Tenth Eclogue (282); by contrast, in Catullus, 'la coscienza del nesso inscindibile fra scelta di poesia e scelta di vita' has not yet been overtly theorized, as it will be in Propertius (288).

fact that the lover cannot find any cure prevents him from departing from the genre.[91]

By comparison with Catullus, Propertius goes further in the project of giving literary genre the *appearance* of being coterminous with poetic self. The argument might be made that Catullus did not write in the elegiac genre per se, and so any comparison is necessarily asymmetrical. This very asymmetry, however, is significant. It is not until the generation of Virgil, Gallus, and Propertius that the concept of genre as a regulated and totalizing domain comes into prominence.[92] As Virgil's portrait of the amorously enslaved Gallus in *Eclogues* 10 is meant to suggest, the boundary-lines of genre are becoming more visible and emphatic. A key outcome of this new tendency toward the streamlining and systematization of genre itself as an organizing principle in literary texts is that the world of the poetic work appears to be imbued with a higher degree of definition and boundedness; it is more susceptible to being presented in autonomist terms as its own independent, autarkic realm to the very degree that the internal regulating principles of genre are more rigorously totalizing.

This newly totalizing concept of genre cannot simply be accepted at face value; rather, it must be appreciated and examined as a crucial facet of early Augustan autonomist rhetoric. In the case of elegy, being enslaved to the same unchanging condition, trapped within an amorous state, subserves the poet's sequestration within his own carefully regulated literary realm. In a straightforward sense, being hopelessly and desperately in love is continually available as a pretext for refusing non-amorous poetic projects and life-paths. This argument, however, depends for its efficacy on the equivalence between the nature of the amatory persona and the nature of the literary work, which, as we have argued, is not seamless and unproblematic. The sense of the lover's haplessness remains at odds with the discursive mastery elsewhere on display. These simultaneous self-representational tendencies, while not logically coherent, are rhetorically effective. A seamless, autonomist sphere of literary genre corresponding to a highly regulated literary persona is combined with intimations of an extra-textual author who, rather than being 'enslaved' and 'confined' by his discursive system, is the creator and manipulator of that system.

A similar dynamic can be seen at work in the elegiac manipulation of gender roles. The elegist, in representing himself as dominated by a woman, at least partially deflects and distracts from the more sensitive topic of social subordination to other men.[93] Effectively, Propertius puts himself so fully under the control of his mistress as to set himself outside the ordinary arena of elite male competition for status and power. Yet because servitude to a woman is likely to be received as a sophisticated fiction manipulated by the male author, the stakes of submission to a mistress are not dangerously high. Propertius at once exempts himself from a traditional competition he is not likely to win, and strategically controls the terms and circumscribes the scope of his 'submission'. He profits

---

[91] Conte (1994a), 42ff.   [92] See in particular Zetzel (1983).
[93] See the discussion in Oliensis (1997a), 152ff. Modern scholars designate Tullus as Propertius' patron, but the poet displays only a modest degree of deference toward Tullus: see Heyworth (2010), 95ff.; note also Syme (1978), 179–82, on Propertius' social status and association with Tullus.

simultaneously from the enslavement of his persona and the privilege of his authorial position.

Loss of freedom, then, paradoxically represents a gain in autonomy,[94] both because the poet-lover's subjugation by Love shores up the boundaries of the elegiac realm, and because it displaces more compromising relations of social subordination. It is far from clear, however, that other lovers profit from a similar gain in autonomy. In elegies addressed to friends, Propertius further demonstrates the power and autonomy of Love, even as he points to his own privilege as elegiac author. He anticipates that they one day will fall in love and suffer a loss of self-determination,[95] but they will lack the elegist's capacity to frame (and perhaps assert control over) his experience in words. Thus 'Gallus' is represented as having a distinguished family (1.6.19–20; 1.5.23–4),[96] yet his proud self-determination will be undermined by the humiliating power of *Amor*.

> a, mea contemptus quotiens ad limina curres,
> cum tibi singultu fortia verba cadent,
> et tremulus maestis orietur fletibus horror,
> et timor informem ducet in ore notam,
> et quaecumque voles fugient tibi verba querenti,
> nec poteris, qui sis aut ubi, nosse miser!   (1.5.13–18)

Ah, how often you will run to my doorstep after suffering rejection, when your brave words will break down amidst sobbing, quaking and shuddering will arise with sorrowful tears, fear will put a disfiguring mark on your face, the words you seek as you complain will elude you, and in your distress you will not be able to know where or who you are!

Propertius imagines what will happen to Gallus if he should learn first-hand what harsh servitude (*grave servitium*, 19) to a girl really entails. In Propertius' self-vindicating fantasy, Gallus will undergo a total loss of self-control, run in indecorous panic, sob, and tremble; fear will contort his features. All are signs that his friend will have lost the composure of speech, countenance, and gait *de rigueur* in a Roman of high status. This catalogue of physical symptoms ends in Gallus' total confusion: 'you will not know where or who you are'.[97] Propertius, by contrast, is able to give a precise account of Gallus' love-condition, as demonstrated in the present elegy.

---

[94] In some sense, Propertius transposes onto his elegiac text aspects of Roman social life. The personal autonomy of elite Roman males may well have been experienced as confining and circumscribed, given that elite masculinity was a performance that had to be strictly and constantly maintained, and given that, in the Augustan period, the newly monarchical system of government posed challenges to the maintenance of the notion of elite autonomy as traditionally conceived. The elegiac lover's sphere of freedom/enslavement may be one means of exploring these issues of elite personal autonomy within a controlled framework. (I owe the kernel of these remarks to a suggestion by the anonymous reviewer for Oxford University Press.)

[95] Insightful discussion of *libertas... loqui* at 1.128 in McCarthy (1998), 176–7: 'the poetry itself is the author's assertion of his *libertas* (freedom), even though its content seems to be a chronicle of his *servitium* (servitude)' (176). On *libertas* and servility, compare Lyne (1979), 126.

[96] There have been many debates on the identity of Gallus: for recent discussions, see, for example, Nicholson (1998); Janan (2001), 33–52; and now Cairns (2006), 70–103, for whom 'Gallus' and the elegies of Cornelius Gallus constitute a major influence on Propertius.

[97] See Nicholson (1998), 152, for the thematic recurrence of words related to *nosco* in this elegy (*nobilitas, nomen*, etc.).

In the following lines, Propertius begins to elaborate the consequences of Gallus'
prospective condition.

> tum grave servitium nostrae cogere puellae
>   discere et exclusum quid sit abire domum;
> nec iam pallorem totiens mirabere nostrum,
>   aut cur sim toto corpore nullus ego.
> nec tibi nobilitas poterit succurrere amanti:
>   nescit Amor priscis cedere imaginibus.   (1.5.19–24)

Then you will be forced to learn of the harsh bondage of my girl and what it means to go
home when you are shut out of doors; nor at that time will you so often wonder at my
pallor, or why my whole body is shrunk to nothing. Your high birth will not be able to come
to your aid when you are a lover: Love scorns to yield to images of ancestors.

Propertius briefs Gallus on the basic tenets of elegiac love: servitude, the exclusion
of the lover, his physical wasting, the irrelevance of nobility, and in lines 27–8,
incurability. Particularly notable in this summary is the important work done by
the term *cogi* ('to be forced'). Gallus, having lost self-determination, will be forced
to learn what servitude to a girl means and what being shut out of doors means:
that is, he will be versed in the lexicon of *Amor*. In his new role as lover, the
nobility that previously defined him will mean nothing. The term 'yield' (*cedere*)
performs a function similar to that of *cogi* in affirming the priority of Love over all
other terms. Love, as the organizing term of elegy, does not yield to nobility, but
nobility (and the noble Gallus) must yield to Love.[98]
The very aspects of love that subjugate and overwhelm the Propertian elegiac
speaker are employed, in dialogues with rhetorical foil-figures, to establish the
superiority and autonomy of elegy. Love's harsh power is rhetorically useful both
from an internal perspective (articulating the autonomy of elegiac love as totalizing realm of experience), and externally (establishing elegy's primacy and power
in relation to other genres and spheres of activity). 1.7, paired thematically
with 1.5, plays out yet another scene of prospective capitulation, but this time
Propertius' autonomist rhetoric represents the determining force of elegiac *Amor*
explicitly in terms of literary genre. While the epic poet Ponticus writes about
Thebes, Propertius occupies himself with his typical concerns:

> nos, ut consuemus, nostros agitamus amores,
>   atque aliquid duram quaerimus in dominam;
> nec tantum ingenio quantum servire dolori
>   cogor et aetatis tempora dura queri.
> hic mihi conteritur vitae modus, haec mea fama est,
>   hinc cupio nomen carminis ire mei.   (1.7.5–10)

I, as is my wont, am occupied with my love poetry, and seek something to use against a
hard-hearted mistress. I am forced to serve not so much my talent as my pain, and to bewail
the hard times of my youth. In this way my life is spent; this is my glory; from this I wish the
renown of my song to arise.

---

[98] Compare Virgil: *et nos cedamus Amori* (*Ecl.* 10.69)—an instance of Gallan intertextuality applied
to the Gallus figure in Propertius' text.

Propertius' activity (simultaneously love and love poetry) is a customary pursuit (*ut consuemus*), described by the frequentative verb *agito*:[99] he is forced (*cogor*) to serve (*servire*) his own anguish, and to elegiacally lament his own sad condition. Such anguish and lament comprise a harsh, relentless mode of existence (*hic mihi conteritur vitae modus*, 'in my way my life is spent'), especially if the sense of attrition (or triteness) is present in *conteritur*. All this is put forward as the source of Propertius' renown as a poet. Ponticus' fame, in the meanwhile, derives from a very difference source—his rivalry with Homer (1.7.3). But the elegist later imagines what would happen if Love infected Ponticus with desire as previously Gallus: he would perform the quintessentially elegiac activity of lamenting (*flebis*), not, in the first instance, his amorous fate, but the fact that all his camps and squadrons 'lie unresponsive in perpetual neglect' (*in aeterno surda iacere situ*, 18). The grand movements of epic warfare will lapse into eternal stasis.[100] Such inertia, anathema for the epic poet, befits the lover. He cannot depart from his condition of amorous obsession with his mistress, but agitates endlessly within the same, narrow circuit.[101]

Once again Propertius stresses the status of elegiac love as an independent discursive domain that regulates and determines the identity of those who occupy it. At the same time he argues for the validity of elegy in literary terms against the grain of the conventional hierarchy of generic grandeur. Whereas the arrogant (*fastu*, 25) epic poet Ponticus will end up admiring Propertius as 'no mean poet' (*non humilem . . . poetam*, 21), Propertius, ostensibly humble in generic terms, will be hailed as a great poet (*magne poeta*, 24) after his death.[102] Here too Propertius shifts between the internal perspective of the enslaved lover forced to lament his sad fate, and the external viewpoint of the masterful author celebrated for his skill in representing the lover's servitude. What is viewed negatively by the lover as the overpowering and totalizing experience of love is recouped by the poetic author as the basis for the self-sufficiency of elegiac discourse.

Elegy is not missing anything, since the experience it represents through its words, although restricted in scope, is felt as large, absorbing, overwhelming, to the extent that it constitutes a world unto itself.[103] As Propertius himself declares in the opening poem of his second book, Cynthia as erotic object is sufficient to inspire whole 'Iliads' (2.1.14), and material enough for the 'greatest history' (*maxima . . . historia*, 2.1.16) can be derived from the intensely absorbing minutiae of Propertius' love-affair. The well-known motif of the *militia amoris* ('warfare of love') articulates the same set of concepts and effects a similar transvaluation of values. Love partakes of its own labours, triumphs, vigils, spoils, bravery, and battles, and promises its devotees a share of glory and renown. Love is sufficient as

---

[99] On iterativity and poetics, see Lowrie (1997), 49.

[100] For the various meanings of *iacere* in elegy, see Pichon (1902), 165, s.v. *iacere*.

[101] Propertius 3.3.21 provides an image of the space of elegy as a race-course within which the elegist must run.

[102] Solmsen (1970) and Fedeli (1985), ad loc., defend the transmitted ordering of lines. The couplet's position conforms with a pattern of transition from the immediate utility or effect of his poetry on Cynthia and contemporary *amici* to the image of a posthumous readership.

[103] See Conte (1994a), 42ff.

arena of exertion and accomplishment to fulfil the ambitions of an elite Roman male.[104]

Elegiac claims of self-sufficiency are directed at traditionally prestigious genres such as epic, and at the same time, at the traditionally prestigious occupation of public life. Propertius' engagement with the traditional categories of political and military prestige is arguably not as explicit in his first book of elegies as in later books. Scholars have noted the scarcity of political and historical reference in Book 1. It is not until Book 2 that Maecenas, Augustus, and Roman history begin to play a substantial role in his poetry. Yet this relative absence of overtly political content in Propertius' first book is compensated by the accrued significance of emblematic interactions and dialogue. Besides the overt reference to the siege of Perugia at 1.21–2 (discussed below), analysis of the arrangement of poems in Book 1[105] reveals a key role awarded to Propertius' differentiation of his elegiac vocation from the public career of its dedicatee Tullus. Tullus,[106] whom Propertius represents as a young man embarking on a public career of imperial administration, and whose uncle, L. Volcacius Tullus, was consul in 33 BC, is addressed in the first (1.1) and last (1.22) poems of the collection, and in two elegies at intermediate points in the collection (1.6, 1.14).[107]

The latter two poems addressed to Tullus explore the themes of the public career and of wealth respectively. In each instance, Love trumps a conventionally valued pursuit or resource. In 1.6, Propertius contrasts his own life of *nequitia* (worthlessness) with Tullus' participation in imperial government. Propertius begins the elegy by declaring that, while he would be willing to follow Tullus on voyages to the far corners of the empire, fear of his mistress' anger forces him to linger indefinitely (*sed me complexae remorantur verba puellae*, 5). He then pursues an extended comparison between the worthless lover and the noble Tullus.

> tu patrui meritas conare anteire secures,
>   et vetera oblitis iura refer sociis.
> nam tua non aetas umquam cessavit amori
>   semper et armatae cura fuit patriae;
> et tibi non umquam nostros puer iste labores
>   afferat et lacrimis omnia nota meis!
> me sine, quem semper voluit fortuna iacere,
>   huic animam extremam reddere nequitiae.

---

[104] Antonio La Penna (1977), 139ff., long ago remarked on the parallel interest in self-sufficiency that can be observed both in Horatian lyric and in elegiac love poetry. Whereas scholars have recognized the retiring, philosophical Horace as having a stake in maintaining an image of rural autarky, the needy, ostensibly unreflective lover has been viewed as possessing a very different cast of mind. La Penna's remark, however, brings out an important aspect of the elegiac fiction, the way in which the lover's absorption in love supports a paradoxical kind of autarky.

[105] For discussion of the structure of Propertius Book 1, see, for example Skutsch (1963), Courtney (1968), Otis (1965), King (1975), Petersmann (1980), Hutchinson (1984), Eckert (1985), Manuwald (2006).

[106] On Tullus, see Keith (2008), 2; Cairns (2006), 35–69.

[107] The 'man of action' Tullus thus effectively structures the collection, marking its division into four segments of five elegies each, assuming we bracket, as a coda, the three exceptional, non-amorous elegies occupying the book's closural sequence.

> multi longinquo periere in amore libenter,
>   in quorum numero me quoque terra tegat.
> non ego sum laudi, non natus idoneus armis:
>   hanc me militiam fata subire volunt.
> at tu, seu mollis qua tendit Ionia, seu qua
>   Lydia Pactoli tingit arata liquor,
> seu pedibus terras seu pontum remige carpes
>   ibis et accepti pars eris imperii:
> tum tibi si qua mei veniet non immemor hora,
>   vivere me duro sidere certus eris.   (1.6.19–36).

You must attempt to surpass the well-deserved axes of office of your uncle, and restore to forgetful allies long-standing laws. For your youth has never flagged to pursue love, and your concern has always been for your fatherland in arms. May that boy never impose on you the toils I endure, and all the misfortunes known to my tears! Permit me, whom Fortune has always wished to lay low, to devote my last breath to this worthless existence. Many have willingly perished in long-lasting love; in their number may the earth cover me also. I was not born suited to glory and warfare: this is the campaign fate wishes me to undergo. But you, whether you go where effeminate Ionia extends, or where the water of the Pactolus moistens the ploughlands of Lydia, whether you traverse the lands on foot or the sea with oar, you will go forth and become a part of welcome imperial rule.[108] Then, if any hour arrives that brings me to your mind, you will be certain that I am living under an unforgiving star.

Propertius, who is fated to be 'lie prostrate' (*iacere*), while carrying out the military service of love (*hanc . . . militiam*), ostensibly concedes the superior life-path to Tullus. Lexical nuance, however, works to qualify the virility of Tullus' endeavour. Whereas Tullus is imagined travelling to soft/effeminate (*mollis*) Ionia, Propertius will be living under a hard (*duro*) star. It is, after all, Propertius who, without recompense of glory (*laudi*, 29), will undergo hard labours (*labores*, 23), waging his 'war' to the death, while Tullus has an easy time sailing around the rich Eastern provinces and ruling territories that obligingly accept Roman rule (*accepti . . . imperii*, 34).

Propertius' autonomist rhetoric here emphasizes the permanence of commitment to the elegiac life-path and the values that inform it. He is 'fated' to live a life of love; Tullus can be 'certain' (*certus*) of Propertius' manner of living; 'fortune has always willed' that Propertius lie prostrate in love, as he will be doing until his very last breath (*animam extremam*). In 1.14, where Tullus is also addressee, Propertius applies equally strong contrastive rhetoric to the theme of wealth. Tullus is once again imagined in a condition of effeminizing luxury (*tu . . . abiectus Tiberina molliter unda . . .* 1.14.1), whereas Propertius knows that Love does not yield to wealth (*nescit Amor magnis cedere divitiis*, 8), and is capable of

---

[108] The emendations of Housman and Skutsch have been adopted in lines 26 and 33 respectively. For discussion of 1.6, see Keith (2008), 127–9. In Keith's acute reading, Propertius 'collapses distinctions between the elegiac life of love and his addressee's life of imperial service by drawing Tullus into the ambit of the elegiac lifestyle and depicting his own enjoyment of elegiac love in the material terms of military conquest' (129). An autonomist reading is not necessarily incompatible with this insight: Propertius defines at once the distinctiveness and complementarity of his own elegiac activity vis-à-vis Tullus' imperial service. This dialectic of similarity and difference, of differentiation and appropriation, is a recurrent aspect of autonomist rhetoric.

'breaking' the strength of heroes (*magnas heroum infingere vires*, 17). Even kings will 'yield' (*cessuros*) to Propertius' joys in love (13). Notable here is the elegist's anti-intuitive use of metaphors of hardness and malleability. Love, associated with soft, feminine indulgence and sensuality, displays a hard edge in discursive conflicts, whereas kings, wealth, and nobility are malleable in the face of Love's steely force. Once again Propertius sets the strong, unyielding (*nescit . . . cedere, cessuros*) power of love against a competing discourse or value, and finds the latter wanting.

Propertius builds up the power of Love as irresistible and unyielding in order to enforce the boundaries of his literary genre and to establish the autonomy of his elegiac realm. We can see how this strategy operates at a more general level by considering the elegies in Book 1 in typological terms. The first book consists of, on the one hand, elegies addressed to male *amici* who serve as object lessons in the core principles of Propertian poetics: the futility of resisting Love, the irresistible erotic force of Cynthia (1.5), the superiority of faithful devotion to a single girl (1.4, 13), the indispensable utility of elegy as a poetic mode for those who have fallen in love (1.7, 9).[109] Another set of elegies illustrates the workings of the affair itself: Cynthia to depart on a voyage (1.8a); Cynthia to remain in Rome (1.8b); Cynthia accused of infidelity (1.15); Propertius accused of infidelity (1.3); and so forth. The elegies concerned with Cynthia depict the elegist's vacillations of mood as he plays out the recurrent, systematic contradictions of his inescapably circular condition. We see the imprisoned lover shift between possession and lack, anger and tenderness, annihilating desolation and crowing exuberance, fear of separation and grateful reunion. Alternating these two types of elegy, Propertius manages to represent the internal dynamics of love that produce and maintain the lover's condition of immobile confinement, and to demarcate and defend the elegiac realm against competing discourses, life-paths, and axiological criteria. Together, they work to define the elegiac poet's autonomist domain both from within and from without: as elegiac lover, he is irrevocably sequestered within generic confines of Love's domain; as elegiac author, he is in full control of Love's powerful, irresistible discursive system, and is able to manipulate its tropes to defeat competing discourses and systems of prestige. He is at once confined and free, subjugated and masterful.

This typology, while helpful in heuristic terms, does not fully account for the complexities of individual poems, and certainly not for the distinctive qualities of the three closing poems, 1.20–22, which have been seen as constituting the book's coda.[110] In 1.20, addressed to 'Gallus', Propertius advises his friend 'in view of our unbroken affection' to keep a careful guard over his boy-love, who may otherwise be lost to Gallus as Hylas was to Hercules. The main portion of the elegy consists in an erudite narration of the Hylas *exemplum* enriched with allusions to Theocritean, Apollonian, and, presumably, Gallan and other neoteric treatments.[111] In structural terms, the elegy initiates a break in the book's

---

[109] On this series of elegies, see Keith (2008), 115–38; Stahl (1985), 48–98; Oliensis (1997a), 157f.

[110] There are numerous scholarly discussions of these difficult yet clearly crucial elegies: Du Quesnay (1992); Keith (2008), 7–8; Nicholson (1998); Janan (2001), 50–2; Stahl (1985), 99–129; Fedeli (1980), ad loc., Heyworth (2007a), ad loc., and now Heyworth (2010).

[111] For the rich metapoetic dimension of 1.20, see especially Petrain (2001).

hitherto continuous series of poems on the topic of heterosexual love and Cynthia (1.1–19). The following elegy, 1.21, also concerns a figure named Gallus, but effects an even more dramatic rupture with the foregoing tone and content. This Gallus, almost certainly distinct from the Gallus of the previous elegy, is a soldier killed in the Perusine war of 41 BC. In this elegy, he addresses a fellow soldier who happens to be passing by, and conveys the manner of his death.

> Tu, qui consortem properas evadere casum,
>   miles ab Etruscis saucius aggeribus,
> quid nostro gemitu turgentia lumina torques?
>   pars ego sum vestrae proxima militiae.
> sic te servato possint gaudere parentes,
>   haec soror acta tuis sentiat e lacrimis:
> Gallum per medios ereptum Caesaris enses
>   effugere ignotas non potuisse manus;
> et quaecumque super dispersa invenerit ossa
>   montibus Etruscis, haec sciat esse mea.

You, who hurry to avoid your comrade's fate, a wounded soldier from the Etruscan ramparts, why do you twist your bulging eyes away from my groaning? I am the member of your company closest to you. On this condition may your parents rejoice at your safety: let your sister learn of these events from your tears, that Gallus, snatched from amid Caesar's forces, could not escape unknown hands; and whatever bones she finds scattered over the Tuscan hills, let her know that they are mine.

Many details are difficult to interpret, and the solutions proposed by scholars are too many and complicated to sift through here. To cite only one key issue: it is not clear whether or not the dead man and the soldier he addresses are related by marriage, and correspondingly, whether *soror* refers to Gallus' sister, or the passing soldier's sister and Gallus' wife or bride.[112] Regardless of the precise interpretation, however, the shift in tone, from fictionalized *amor* in 1.1–19 and neoteric mythology in 1.20 to brutal death in one of the darkest episodes of the civil wars in 1.21, is startling, and is clearly meant to be. As Hutchinson observes, 'the change of feeling in 21 and 22 is heightened by the opposite change in the poem before', where the myth of Hylas 'puts love itself in a fantastic setting and alters its atmosphere'.[113]

The book's final elegy, 1.22, continues with this 'change of feeling' and makes further, yet more pointed, reference to the siege of Perugia.

> Qualis et unde genus, qui sint mihi, Tulle, Penates,
>   quaeris pro nostra semper amicitia.
> si Perusina tibi patriae sunt nota sepulcra,
>   Italiae duris funera temporibus,
> cum Romana suos egit discordia cives—
>   sic mihi praecipue, pulvis Etrusca, dolor,
> tu proiecta mei perpessa es membra propinqui,

---

[112] For a recent summary of the issue, see Heyworth (2007a), ad loc., who opposes the idea that the *soror* can be the sister of anyone but the speaker, and, accepting Scaliger's emendation, reads *haec soror Acca*. The text of 1.21 and 1.22 printed here follows that of Goold (1990).
[113] Hutchinson (1984), 104.

> tu nullo miseri contegis ossa solo—
> proxima suppositos contingens Umbria campos
> me genuit terris fertilis uberibus.

You are always asking, Tullus, in the name of our friendship, what is my status, where my family comes from, and what is my place of origin. If our fatherland's Perusine tombs are known to you, the graveyard of Italy in dark times, when Roman discord drove fellow citizens to violence (a source of pain for me in particular, O Etruscan dust, for you suffered my kinsman's bones to lie exposed, you cover the wretched man's bones with no soil)— neighbouring Umbria, which borders on Perugia's plains below, fertile in abundant fields, gave me birth.

The problems of interpretation are only multiplied with this sequel to the previous elegy's themes. Asked about his family and his background by his friend Tullus, Propertius replies that he comes from Umbria near Perugia, where many citizens died during civil war, including the poet's own kinsman. Many scholars have considered it natural to assume that the dead kinsman whose bones went unburied is the Gallus of 1.21, while others remain agnostic. Whatever solution one prefers, it is undeniable that Propertius' tone and frame of reference in 1.21–2 represent a marked shift from the rest of the book. The speaker is no longer (simply) Cynthia's obsessed lover, but an Umbrian poet, who has lost a relative in civil violence.

Tullus' inquiry thus occasions a break from the generically defined amatory speaker of Book 1. Propertius' response to his friend's question points to historical events outside the carefully demarcated world of elegiac *amor* that has hitherto largely constituted the book's content. Here, as elsewhere, poetic autonomy is not asserted naively in an unproblematic void, but attains its meaning in contrastive relation to the violent forces of history it seeks to keep at bay. Propertius' love-world knows itself to be a fictional refuge, and a fragile one. But this acknowledgement does not mean that elegy's fictions are taken any less seriously, nor that the poet's autonomist endeavour is half-hearted. Like Virgil in the *Eclogues*, Propertius both creates a delimited sphere of refuge from politics, history, and violent forces in the world at large, and shows us that those violent forces are never far away, and that their existence burdens and informs the space of refuge he has designed.

This tensional combination of sequestration and proximity find expression in the concept of separate yet contiguous territories that arises in both texts. Virgil's *Eclogues* begins with a juxtaposition of two herdsmen, one who is allowed go on occupying, and another who must leave, the pastoral refuge. The figure who represents the continuing viability of pastoral stands side by side with his shadow image, the herdsman Meliboeus, who has been sent into exile by the confiscations. In the book's penultimate poem, the theme of proximity once again comes to the fore. Moeris recalls a song of Menalcas aimed at sparing Mantua from the land confiscations: *Mantua vae miserae nimium vicina Cremonae* ('Alas Mantua, too close to wretched Cremona', 9.28). Propertius, too, awards special prominence to concepts of proximity and contiguity[114] in his book's final hexameter: *proxima suppositos contingens Umbria campos* ('neighbouring Umbria, which borders on

---

[114] Janan (2001), 51, observes the theme of borderlines and contiguity.

Perugia's plains below').[115] Violence, in both cases, cannot be wholly contained, and spills over into neighbouring territories. As Propertius' mention of his dead *propinquus* (another proximity-word) shows, those lucky enough to escape violence themselves still feel the effects. The speaking corpse of 1.21 identifies himself to the passing soldier as *pars . . . vestrae proxima militiae* ('the closest person to you among your comrades-in-arms', tr. Gould, 1.21.4). Violence and death are present, yet always contiguous, nearby. Propertius' Umbrian *patria* borders on Perugia, a place associated with horrific violence. Appropriately, the elegy commemorating this place and its grim history stands at the outer edge of the collection in the closing coda-sequence.

Thanks to the revelations of 1.21–2, we know more about the author of the book we have been reading, and can begin to appreciate new aspects of his literary fiction. Tullus asks where Propertius comes from, and his answer[116]—Perugia, Umbria, Italy, *Romana discordia*, funerals, the violence of civil war—incidentally provides a clue for understanding where his *poetry* comes from. In a straightforward sense, we can appreciate that someone who has seen the consequences of civil violence in his own family might prefer *otium*[117] and love's battles to actual war. *Elegies* 2.15 makes the point succinctly: if everyone devoted themselves to love instead of war, then the waters of Actium would not be strewn with men's bones (41–6). Mention of Actium may remind us of Mark Antony and his famous love affair with Cleopatra. Propertius makes it clear that he will confine his love affair to a more circumscribed domain: an erotic obsession defined by the *absence* of political or military ambitions. Unlike his fellow elegist Cornelius Gallus, who committed suicide in disgrace three years after the probable publication date of the *Monobiblos*,[118] Propertius refuses to combine the roles of soldier and love elegist. Like Horace, he at least overtly insists on the self-enclosure of his poetic domain and its segregation from political dangers.

Propertius' elegiac fiction, however, is not merely escapist. Propertius' pacifist domain of *amor* is infused with the dangerous currents of contemporary politics. Some recent interpretations of 1.21–2 have stressed their thematic responsion with the main body of Book 1, thereby drawing this apparent realist intrusion back into the fabric of the amatory fiction. I wish to argue for a related but inverse line of interpretation that emphasizes, not the thematic integration of 1.21–21 with the preceding love elegies, but the potential in 1.21–22 for altering the reader's perception of the foregoing book. The unpleasant reality of warfare, civil conflict, subjugation, and actual, as opposed to morbidly imagined, death can be mapped back onto the ostensibly diverting fiction of amorous *servitium* that makes up elegies 1–19. The book's coda, on this line of interpretation, invites

---

[115] Reading Postgate's conjecture for *supposito . . . campo*: see Heyworth (2007a), ad loc.

[116] Stahl (1985), 99–101, discusses the old question of Propertius' oddly evasive, apparent non-answer to Tullus' question.

[117] On elegiac values, lifestyle, and *otium*, Boucher (1965), 13–40, is still indispensable. He sets the emergent, alternative value-system of *otium* within the context of the crises of the late republic, and characterizes it as based on 'three rejections': 'trois refus, communs à l'idéal bucolique et à l'élégiaque,—argent, guerre, honneurs—, sont les manifestations directes de cette attitude' (18–19). See also the discussion of idleness in Keith (2008), 139–65, who explores 'the intersection of leisure and love with Roman imperialism' (141).

[118] See, e.g. Richardson (1977), 7–8.

re-reading of a fiction we thought we understood, infusing it with new and potentially discomfiting awareness of contemporary politics.

Propertius Book 1 begins with a scene of martial subjugation: an absolutist Love crushes Propertius beneath his feet. From this point on, he will be Love's and Cynthia's slave, displaying obeisance with sometimes outrageous flattery of his masters. It is well known, but bears recalling in this context, that 'slavery' is a frequently employed metaphor for the loss of political liberty under conditions of authoritarian rule in writers such as Cicero.[119] A book published in 29 BC in the wake of the battles of Actium and Alexandria and around the time of Octavian's magnificent triple triumph in Rome is unlikely to be wholly innocent of the political connotations of its own central metaphor, or to present its opening image of a ruthlessly subjugating *Amor* with no expectation of contemporary resonance.[120] It is neither possible nor desirable, of course, to sustain a systematic reading of erotic *servitium* as a political allegory. Attempting to draw parallels in the political realm for every one of Propertius' amatory gestures and predicaments would lead to absurdity.[121] But awareness of the political resonance of elegiac *servitium*—brought more vividly to mind through the overtly political references of 1.21–2—provides a new perspective from which to re-evaluate the core fictions of Propertian elegy.

This relation of tensional contiguity—a separate space that is nonetheless affected by what lies next to it—is one way of understanding the Propertian construct of literary autonomy. Propertius creates what appears to be a rigorously delimited realm of elegiac love, and then, in the closing poems of the collection, draws our attention to an origins-story (*unde . . . quaeris*, 'whence . . . you ask') very different from the scene of erotic capture and conquest in the book's opening lines. If we take this origins-story seriously, we can begin to appreciate how Propertian love elegy maintains constant awareness of the political realm against which it defines itself. The pastoral refuge, for Virgil, is imbued with an awareness of the violent forces that at once threaten its tranquillity and motivate its creation in the first place. A similar paradox lies at the core of elegiac autonomy. The elegist's antinomian embrace of *otium*, love, and *inertia* is both a flight from the political sphere, and a serious re-examination of its core dynamics. Propertian autonomy entails neither overt political resistance nor escapist retreat into an apolitical fantasy world; rather, the poet creates a literary world that replays on its own terms and within its own boundaries the characteristic obsessions and anxieties of Roman public life.

It is worth considering for a moment Propertius' relation to the self-representational attitude of his contemporary Horace. Both poets fashion vividly persuasive images of a restrictive 'niche' of life-experience that serves as figurative correlate for the autonomist literary domain of the poetic text. Yet Horace's freedom-seeking, rural autarkist is the inverse image of the servile, city-bound lover of Propertian elegy. Together, they afford some sense of the duality of the autonomist model and its implications for the writer's role in Augustan society. Tibullus is

---

[119] See Roller (2001), 213–32.
[120] Heyworth (2010) has recently offered a compelling and critically sophisticated 'anti-Augustan' reading of 1.21–2.
[121] But see the insightful remarks of Fear (2000).

interesting to consider in this context. He both draws influence from Virgil in his representation of the countryside as a place of security and contentment, and combines Propertian and Horatian elements in his construction of a first-person persona. Tibullus simultaneously occupies an enslaving love-realm and an autarkic country estate. From this perspective, Tibullus is not the marginal figure he is sometimes made out to be, but a centrally Augustan poet. He brings into dialogue the major styles of authorial self-representation in the period, absorbing into the structure of his literary persona the debate over different models of literary autonomy. The remainder of the chapter will be devoted to an examination of Tibullan constructs of poetic autonomy and the dissonance among them.

TIBULLUS BOOK 1: THE IRONIES OF SECURITY

Tibullus' first book of elegies, like Virgil's *Eclogues* and Horace *Satires* 1, consists in a slim volume of ten poems.[122] Like Horace, moreover, Tibullus confers a central poetic role on the rural estate as site of withdrawal, autarky, and contentment: he finds enough to satisfy him (*satis*) within the boundaries of his slender poetic/ethical domain. And like Horace, Tibullus remains 'content' (*contentus*) with his present circumstances, though he enjoyed greater landed wealth in the past; indeed, there is more than a hint of Epicureanism in his self-portrait as country gentleman.[123]

Virgil's *Eclogues* and *Georgics* nevertheless constitute the more prominent intertextual background for our understanding of Tibullan elegy. Tibullus, like Virgil, invests the Italian countryside with a rich mythology of song, and integrates poetic self-representation with the everyday rituals of country life.[124] Tibullan self-representation in the first book is especially reminiscent of the dilemma of the Virgilian Gallus in Eclogue 10: he is a prisoner of love who dreams of rural tranquillity, while contrasting both love and country life with the soldier's harsh existence. Yet Tibullus, rather than declaring the incompatibility of Love and rural tranquillity, as Virgil does, at least initially fuses the two in an integrated picture of rural/amatory *securitas*. Whereas Propertius accepts as foundational Virgil's insistence on Love's exclusivity, Tibullus re-opens the dialogue between the poetics of Love and the poetics of the countryside. As we shall see, however, Tibullus' integration of *amor* and *rura* is far from seamless. His approach to autonomist rhetoric is once vividly evocative, and playful, detached; he creates beguiling visions of self-sufficiency only to dismantle them later on.

---

[122] On the three collections of ten, see Leach (1978); note also Leach (1980), Ball (1983), 225–31, Bright (1978), 260ff., Littlewood (1970), Powell (1974), and Lee-Stecum (1998), 1–9.

[123] It is perhaps not accidental that Horace addresses a markedly Epicurean epistle to 'Albius' (generally assumed to be Tibullus), in which he commends the addressee on his wealth (*divitias*)—a knowing reference and worthy of Horace's sophisticated irony and hermeneutics. As an *eques* of considerable means, yet with a stated preference for the simple satisfactions of his farm's modest abundance, Tibullus would have appreciated the finesse of Horace's characterization: *et cui / gratia, fama, valetudo contingat abunde, / et mundus victus non deficiente crumina* (*Epistles* 1.4.9–11).

[124] Feeney (1998), 123, citing Ross (1986), observes that the reality of rural life as represented by Tibullus is 'very largely the real world as mediated through Virgil's *Georgics*'.

Propertius Book 1 began with Cupid's triumphant capture of the poet and consequent determination of his identity as lover. Tibullus begins more obliquely with what (he claims) he is *not*.[125]

> Divitias alius fulvo sibi congerat auro
>   et teneat culti iugera multa soli
> quem labor adsiduus vicino terreat hoste,
>   Martia cui somnos classica pulsa fugent:
> me mea paupertas vita traducat inerti
>   dum meus adsiduo luceat igne focus.   (1.1.1–6)

Let another man heap up riches of yellow gold, and let him possess many acres of cultivated soil, so that continual toil may keep him in a state of high alarm with the enemy nearby, and the sound of war trumpets drive away his sleep. May I be drawn by my poverty[126] through a life of inactivity, so long as my hearth blazes with continual fire.

'Riches' (*divitias*) is a provocative way to begin a corpus of elegies. While the next word (*alius*, 'another...') soon provides a corrective for the first worrying impression, and the poet's claim of a simple mode of existence (*me mea paupertas*) four lines below completes the correction, Tibullus has left enough of a hint to make us wonder in what sense his first book of elegies will concern wealth. The rhetorical 'other' is hardly marginalized, and not wholly distanced from the poetic speaker.[127] This subtle interplay of self and other is characteristically Tibullan, and effectively differentiates his dialogic approach to elegiac identity from the Propertian model of erotic domination.

The attributes of the speaking ego (*me mea paupertas ... meus ... focus*) emerge out of a series of oppositions: battlefield and hearth, motion and stasis, riches and poverty, fear and security. This technique of contrastive self-description, however, is at the same time a tactic of appropriation. The continual fire blazing (*adsiduo ... igne*) in the poet's hearth replaces, as many have observed, the continually dangerous toil (*labor adsiduus*) to which the *alius* is exposed on the battlefield.[128] While outdoor danger gives way to indoor security, the quality of continuousness survives the transition from harassed soldier to tranquil smallholder. Tibullan inertia is presented as a continuous way of life (*vita ... inerti*), an entire life-path

---

[125] Lyne (1998b) is fundamental on some of the points of comparison and difference between Propertius and Tibullus. The general pattern coheres with many of my observations here: Tibullus seems to go out of his way to distinguish himself from and even playfully dismantle Propertian erotic monomania and sublime *Angst*. He undermines the severity of Propertian oppositions (poverty/wealth, *militia/amor*, etc.) with a witty insouciance.

[126] *Paupertas*, of course, does not mean harsh poverty or indigence, but rather something like 'modest means' or 'simple living'. Occasionally, I translate *paupertas* as 'poverty' in cases where a more accurate periphrasis would be awkward.

[127] Commentators note the prevalence of the *alius–ego* contrast in Augustan poetry and ancient literature generally: Maltby (2002), ad loc., Ball (1983), 20. But see Putnam (1973), ad loc.: 'the singular rouses the suspicion that a special instance, *perhaps even himself*, is in the poet's mind' (italics added). Tibullus' own military service under Messalla makes a life of rustic/amorous tranquillity seem like a dream evoked in subjunctive verbs: on questions of 'reality', note in particular Kennedy (1993), 13–15.

[128] Lee-Stecum (1998), 30; Maltby (2002), ad loc.

of non-traditional activity (or inactivity). He matches the careerist intensity of the soldier's traditional life with the focused energy of poetic toil.[129]

Tibullus defines his elegiac self through a series of cross-crossing oppositions. The paradoxical toils of the poet's *vita iners*[130] ('life of inactivity') answer the soldier's *labor adsiduus* ('continual toil') by producing their own sort of riches—a book of poetry informally titled *Divitias* ('Wealth'). There is an implicit play here on the concept of cultivation, which encompasses both the farmer's attentiveness to the soil (*culti … soli*, 1.1.2) and the poet's to his work.[131] The toils of the inactive Tibullus still worry some commentators, and in particular the abrupt transition from the *vita iners* of line 5 to the agricultural toils to be performed by the poet himself (*ipse seram … 7ff.*) has seemed problematic. How can the speaker move so quickly from avowal of gentlemanly inactivity to agricultural labour degrading for an *eques*?[132] The answer lies in the very nature of poetic work—absorbing, intensive, yet utterly unprofitable in material terms. The poet's *labor iners* (indolent toil) creates its own paradoxical harvest—a slim, Callimachean crop of poetry that suffices for the poet (*parva seges satis est*, 1.1.43). We may laugh at the image of Tibullus as sweating farmhand, but this humour, in combination with the scarcity of indicative verbs in the passage, only serves to reinforce the literariness of his toils.

A continual strategy at work here involves the transfer of concepts such as labour, harvest, productivity, cultivation, and ownership to the literary terrain. The landed wealth that actually provides the material basis for the poet's financial independence is subtly displaced by Tibullus' agricultural metapoetics. On one level, Tibullus claims the autarkic existence of a rustic smallholder: he does not need more, since everything he wants resides within the boundaries of his modest (even reduced) estate. But on another level, Tibullus re-locates self-sufficiency within the literary domain itself, transcending the merely material basis of autarky in favour of the endlessly self-replenishing bounty of his poetic *fundus* (rural estate):[133] he needs nothing beyond the idyll of rural autonomy and security which he has fashioned out of elegiac verse. This form of autarky is the more absolute for being ultimately collapsible within the text itself, and the more enduring for not being limited to the finite material resources of an actual farm.

The precise content of Tibullus' poetic autarky, however, remains an open question. Farming and love provide material for parallel declarations of autarkic satiety. These two modes of autarky correspond structurally to the two halves of the elegy: farming (1–44) and love (45–74). The central passage that includes the transition from *rura* to *amor* is worth examining at greater length:[134]

---

[129] 'Given the probably literary implications of *labor adsiduus …* it would seem likely that the contrasting phrase *adsiduo … igne* should also carry some literary significance, possibly referring to T.'s constant attention to love poetry' (Maltby (2002), ad loc.).

[130] There may be etymological play on *iners* as meaning 'lacking *ars*', thus further underlining Tibullus' artful inertia.

[131] Compare, e.g. Fitzgerald (1996). Ovid displays his awareness of this theme by the epithet he confers on Tibullus: *culte Tibulle* (*Amores* 1.15.28, 3.9.68).

[132] Murgatroyd (1980), ad loc.; Maltby (2002), ad loc.

[133] Feeney (1998), 123: in 2.1, Tibullus figuratively 'circumscribes his own terrain of creativity'.

[134] I depart from Postgate (1905) in the choice of *igne* in line 48 rather than *imbre*, and in lines 25–8 cited further below, of *modo* rather than *mihi*. The relation between *amor*, *rura*, and *militia* has been variously analysed by Leach (1980), Gaisser (1983), Boyd (1984), and Lee-Stecum (1998), 27–71. For recent discussion (and Lacanian reading of same), see Miller (2004), 107ff.

> non ego divitias patrum fructusque requiro
>   quos tulit antiquo condita messis avo:
> parva seges satis est, satis est requiescere lecto
>   si licet et solito membra levare toro.
> quam iuvat immites ventos audire cubantem
>   et dominam tenero continuisse sinu
> aut gelidas hibernus aquas cum fuderit Auster
>   securum somnos igne iuvante sequi.
> hoc mihi contingat: sit dives iure furorem
>   qui maris et tristes ferre potest pluvias.
> o quantum est auri pereat potiusque smaragdi
>   quam fleat ob nostras ulla puella vias!
> te bellare decet terra, Messalla, marique
>   ut domus hostiles praeferat exuvias:
> me retinent vinctum formosae vincla puellae,
>   et sedeo duras ianitor ante fores.
> non ego laudari curo, mea Delia; tecum
>   dum modo sim, quaeso segnis inersque vocer.   (1.1.41–58)

I do not feel the loss of my forebears' wealth and the gains which the stored-up harvest brought to my ancestor of old. A small field's harvest is enough; it is enough, if I may lie in my bed and rest my limbs on the familiar couch. How pleasing it is to listen to the unrelenting winds as I lie, and to hold my mistress in tender embrace, or, when the wintry South Wind has poured out its chill waters, to pursue sleep, carefree, with the fire's help. May this fall to my lot; let him be rightly rich, who can endure the raging of the sea and the gloomy rains. O sooner may all the world's gold and emeralds perish than any girl weep because of my journeying! It befits *you*, Messalla, to wage war on land and sea, so that the front of your house may display enemy spoils. The bonds of a beautiful girl hold *me* fettered, and I sit as doorkeeper before her heartless doors. I do not care for glory, my Delia; so long as I am with you, I am happy to be called idle and inactive.

The passage is framed by two parallel constructions (*non ego divitias . . . requiro . . .* 41; *non ego laudari curo*, 57), which disavow, respectively, wealth in favour of the poet's modest farm, and military glory in favour of the poet's life of love with Delia. By the end of the passage, the life of rural smallholder has been insensibly mingled with the life of love: the *inertia* associated with the unambitious ease of the gentleman farmer in the opening lines (*vita . . . inerti*, 5) has been tacitly transformed into the lover's well-known *inertia* and *segnitia* (58). Whereas previously the acquisitiveness and far-flung toils of the soldier were contrasted with rural contentment, now they are contrasted with the sedentary, confining immobility of amatory obsession. In a preceding passage, rural ease (27–8) was opposed to military journeying (*longae . . . viae*, 26); now prospective journeys (*nostras . . . vias*) are anathema to lovers (51–2).

This analogical tendency uniting farmer and lover within a single elegiac subjectivity works to integrate two styles of autarky. Being 'content with little' on a modest farm keeps the poet within his sheltered space of self-sufficiency. He does not need to venture beyond the farm's boundaries in search of anything external or additional to what he already possesses and enjoys:

> Iam modo, iam possim contentus vivere parvo
>   nec semper longae deditus esse viae,
> sed Canis aestivos ortus vitare sub umbra
>   arboris ad rivos praetereuntis aequae.   (1.1.25–8)

If only now at last I might live content with little, and not be always devoted to long journeying, but instead avoid the rising of the Dog-Star in the summer beneath the shade of a tree by the streams of water flowing by.

This imagery is picked up again further on in lines 42–3, when the poet declares that he is satisfied (*satis est, satis est*) with his small harvest and with resting his limbs on his familiar couch (*solito . . . toro*, 43). Now, however, he has moved inside rather than outside, and whereas he initially hears water flowing by the river banks, now he hears winds howling outside the walls of his home (*immites ventos audire cubantem*), while embracing his mistress (*dominam tenero continuisse sinu*). Tibullus replays the opening lines' contrast between inside and outside, danger and security, but in an explicitly erotic setting. The sheltering space of the home and hearth (especially if we read *igne*, line 48) is further intensified by the image of the embrace 'hemming in'[135] the mistress in line 46. This image of snug confinement recurs at line 55, but with an inversion of roles: now the 'chains' of the beautiful girl confine Tibullus (*me retinent vinctum formosae vincla puellae*).[136]

This state of pleasurable confinement is defined contrastively in relation to his patron Messalla's world-wide travels and achievements. The poet insists that the erotic confinement in which he finds himself is what he desires: *non ego laudari curo . . . quaeso segnis inersque vocer* ('I am not keen to be praised . . . I seek to be called idle and inactive'). The external criteria of decorum, as expressed by an impersonal verb (*decet*), define Messalla's arena of achievement, whereas the poet's first-person verbs of preference and willingness (*curo, quaeso*) articulate his distinctive life-path. The contrastive rhetoric extends to Messalla's house: he travels the entire world (*terra . . . marique*) in order that his house may display (*praeferat*) enemy spoils (*hostiles . . . exuvias*). This brief notice resonates back into Tibullus' earlier description of the scene *inside* his house, with its concentric circles of inwardness and containment: walls, bed, lovers' embrace. Whereas his patron considers it fitting to display martial accomplishments on his house's outer façade, the lover cares only about the realm of pleasure and tranquillity contained within his four walls.

There is a philosophical aspect to Tibullus' depiction of his life of security and self-sufficiency. In contrasting the dangerous fury of the storm outside with his safety indoors, Tibullus is responding to the famous passage opening *De rerum natura* 2.[137] Tibullus, however, narrows the scope of vision, supplanting Lucretius' sublime seascape with the cosy boundaries of his bedroom. The elegist's modest estate furnishes the *sapientium templa* ('precincts of the wise') from which he

---

[135] Maltby (2002), ad loc., gives this gloss, and notes that *continuisse* is a 'witty use of a military technical term'. Note also that this notion of being confined/detained is also implicit in the term *contentus* (Maltby on line 25).

[136] Both Lee-Stecum (1998), 48, and Putnam (1973), 58, view Tibullus' position outside the door of his mistress as parallel to the spoils of war displayed outside Messalla's doors.

[137] *DRN* 2.1–13. This passage, like Tibullus 1.1, concerns the labor of 'someone else' (*alterius spectare laborem*, 2.2), and the position of tranquillity from which the detached spectator 'looks down' (*despicere*, line 9; compare Tibullus 1.1.78, *despiciam . . . despiciamque*) on others' toils, dangers, and continual struggle (*noctes atque dies niti praestante labore*, 2.12; compare Tibullus' *adsiduus labor*).

may 'look down' on others wandering in pursuit of wealth and honours.[138] An Epicurean interest in freedom from care (*ataraxia/securitas*)[139] manages to survive the passage to Tibullus' ostensibly un-Epicurean[140] scene of passionate love: *quam iuvat...securum somnos igne iuvante sequi* ('how delightful...to pursue carefree sleep with the aid of the fire', 45–8). The same term occurs with similar emphasis at the elegy's end in reference to the poet's modest accumulation of agricultural wealth:

> hic ego dux milesque bonus. vos, signa tubaeque,
>   ite procul; cupidis vulnera ferte viris,
> ferte et opes; ego composito securus acervo
>   dites despiciam despiciamque famem.   (1.1.75–8)

Here [i.e. in love], I am a commander and a good soldier; you, standards and trumpets, go far away; take wounds to greedy men, and bring them wealth too. I, free of anxiety with my gathered heap, shall look down on hunger as I look down on the rich.

The safety of the lover's existence is skilfully merged with the security of a modest rural estate. The poetic speaker claims to be a soldier only in non-violent love, unlike real soldiers exposed to actual dangers, and two lines below, he enjoys the security of his garnered heap of agricultural wealth. For both lover and farmer, safety is emphatically linked with self-sufficiency. The lover has all that he needs in his bed (*satis est, requiescere lecto / si licet*, 'it is enough, if I may lie in bed', 43–4), and the farmer is content with occupying the mid-point between wealth and poverty (*dites despiciam despiciamque famem*, 'I shall look down on hunger as I look down on the rich', 78). Because they are satisfied with what they already have in their own modest domain, both figures can enjoy the security of a quiet existence rather than braving the dangerous world outside.

But how far can we really go in reconciling the rural smallholder's agrarian autarky with the lover's autarkic inertia? Whereas the ideal of rural self-sufficiency is premised on the real productivity of the farm, the lover can be deemed self-sufficient only in a more paradoxical and challenging sense. He is self-sufficient insofar as he has appropriated, as poetic subject matter, a permanently unattainable object of desire that utterly absorbs him: he does not need anything more, because all his need is permanently focused on one object. The lover's paradoxical economy of need is not easily compatible with the picture of the disdainful, self-satisfied farmer of the final couplet.

The lover and the farmer are therefore 'safe' in two distinct ways, and they 'have enough' of two very different things. The elegy's closing comments on love's soldiery (*hic ego dux milesque bonus*, 'in this sphere [of love] I am a commander and a good soldier'), while ostensibly differentiating the lover's from the soldier's life, actually complicates the distinction. For not only has Tibullus appropriated

---

[138] The Tibullan lover is a long way from the Lucretian spectator of the storm: hearing (*audire*) replaces sight, and the outdoor spectator is transformed into the lover held within his mistress' embrace, capable of seeing nothing but her. In its Lucretian form, Epicurean vision penetrates the vast limits of the universe. Tibullus locates the pleasures of conscious safety within the confines of the lover's bedroom: see Ferri (1993) on the ways in which the grand didactic voice of the *DRN* was adapted to the smaller confines of first-person genres.

[139] On the etymology, Maltby (2002), ad loc.

[140] Again, Ferri (1993) on the paradoxical *dispiaceri* of the Epicurean Horace may also be relevant here.

the language of soldiering for himself, he has adapted the terminology of love to soldiers: *cupidis vulnera ferte viris* ('take wounds to greedy men').[141] In being affected by *cupido* (desire), the soldiers notionally resemble lovers. 'Wounds', of course, are appropriate for soldiers, but in juxtaposition to *cupidis* ('greedy/ desirous'), 'wounds' (*vulnera*) must also evoke the exceedingly common amatory cliché: wounds of love.[142] Tibullus' play on literal and metaphorical registers of language is worth appreciating: the *vulnera* metaphorically appropriated by lovers revert, with renewed literalness, to their original owners (soldiers), but with an erotic subtext that reactivates the metaphorical sense.

This complicated interweaving of literal and figurative meanings of *vulnus* ('wound') underlines the problematic synthesis of lover and farmer. Compared with the self-endangering soldier forever pursuing greater heaps of wealth, both lover and rural smallholder are notionally equivalent in their adherence to the security of a self-sufficient existence. The transgressive implications of *vulnus*, however, bring out the fault-lines in this cohesive picture. Tibullus consigns soldiers to the dangers of excessive desire, but in language recalling the dangerous desire to which he, as lover, remains especially vulnerable.[143] It is all well and good for him to wish wounds upon soldiers, but as readers of elegy we know that Cupid inflicts wounds on lovers too—a familiar narrative perhaps glanced at here (*cupidis vulnera*).[144] We can understand how the lover, who remains safely confined to the orbit of his mistress, does not undergo the dangers of *militia*, but the tranquillity implied by the term *securus* ('carefree') is less intuitively ascribed to the passionate lover. In ancient etymology, *securus* derives from *sine cura* ('without care')—a condition difficult to reconcile with the lover's constant anxiety regarding his object of desire (*cura*). If we look beneath the surface of Tibullus' skillfully engineered transitions, we discover tensions endemic to his project of integrating erotic and agrarian security.

The more closely we examine Tibullan self-representation, the more the contradictions multiply.[145] The figure who contrasts his life of easy tranquillity with

---

[141] On the dual sense of *cupidis*, see Lee (1982), ad loc.; Maltby (2002), ad loc.; Lee-Stecum (1998), 64–5.

[142] Pichon (1902) s.v. *vulnus/vulnera*, 302.

[143] Again, see the remarks of Lee-Stecum (1998), 64–5.

[144] Lewis and Short, *Latin Dictionary*, s.v. *Cupido*, II.A.2.

[145] See, in particular, Lee-Stecum (1998), 27–71, for an extended reading of Tibullus 1.1 in terms of the contradictory representation of his persona, and in terms of the 'slippage, or erosion of separation, between . . . various categories', such as *amor* and *militia*, the life of *otium* and the life of toil. As often in postmodern readings of classical texts, the subversion or erosion of categories appears to be a self-explanatory end in itself—because writers (always) subvert certainties, because language is polysemic, because the processes of reading condition meaning, etc. Miller (2004), 95–129, offers a similar reading in a Lacanian vein, emphasizing the 'polyphonic quality of Tibullan verse' (95) and the absence of a unified subject (citing also Johnson (1990), 108). But note also Cairns (1979), 229, who offers a less overtly postmodern version of the same sentiment: Tibullus, who was 'torn between and sometimes contriving to reconcile the twin poles of private life and public life, of leisure and active service of the state, of town and country, of duty and love, of war and farming. . . . [was] a man divided in himself'. But was Tibullus really so conflicted, so 'fractured' in his very self? Or has he designed these fractures as part of a broader literary strategy? See below for an interpretation of Tibullus' shifting poetic identity in terms of autonomist rhetoric.

the soldier's risky toils, and claims to be a soldier in love, later turns out to be an actual soldier in the *cohors* of Messalla. Tibullus, after all, did not so much *declare* himself a tranquil smallholder as *wish* for such an existence. Conspicuous intertextual markers align the speaker with figures who either are exiled from the rural idyll (Virgil's Meliboeus) or never manage to arrive there (Horace's money-lender).[146] The farmer is potentially compatible with the soldier, especially in Rome's traditionalist vision of the peasant-soldier imbued with virile fortitude. Yet this ethos hardly fits the *segnitia* of Tibullus' lover/farmer. And, as we noted above, lover and farmer are not equally likely to succeed in being tranquil, carefree, and conscientious in accumulating agricultural wealth: their respective interests and attitudes are contrasted in the traditions of ancient thought.[147] Tibullus' project of integrating the security of love and the security of rural withdrawal can never entirely succeed. Indeed, if his interest lies in exploring the tension between different models of autarkic *securitas*, it is far from clear that he wanted it to succeed. Tibullus shares his contemporaries' interest in poetic autonomy, but not their willingness to commit to one predominant paradigm of autonomist identity.

The ironies produced by the *miles-rusticus-amator* triangle are further explored in the following elegy, 1.2, where, according to the conventional scenario of the paraclausithyron,[148] the lover finds himself excluded from his mistress' door. Much of the learned controversy on the elegy has focused on the question of the consistency of the poem's notional setting. Does the lover remain outside the door the entire time, or is there a more free-ranging monologue?[149] The dramatic consistency of the elegy's setting, however, is less important than the shift in spatial imagery from 1.1 to 1.2: we move from inside to outside, from shelter to exposure. Whereas 1.1 focuses on the site of the speaker's rural *Lares*, 1.2 is at least initially spoken from the (presumably urban) threshold of *someone else's* door, the *coniunx* (spouse/partner) of Delia. An affective shift accompanies the change in setting: the calm equilibrium of the closing lines of 1.1 has been utterly lost. The opening lines of 1.2 appear to comment on this changed attitude: *adde merum vinoque novos compesce dolores* ('more wine—with wine suppress fresh agonies'). The agonies of the lover are indeed fresh or unaccustomed, since all we heard about in 1.1 were (anomalously for elegy) the pleasures and security of love.[150]

We have thus moved from country to city, from home and blazing hearth to cold vigil on another man's doorstep, from the farmer's self-sufficiency to the lover's excessive passion, from the farmer's secure possession of sufficient wealth to the lover's reckless consumption of unmixed wine (*merum*). In this revised picture, the city is a place of anxiety and even danger for the lover (*tota vagor*

---

[146] Compare Tibullus 1.1.19–20 (*vos quoque, felicis quondam, nunc pauperis agri / custodes*) and Virgil *Ecl.* 1.74 (*ite meae, felix quondam pecus, ite capellae*); and Tibullus 1.1.25 (*iam modo, iam possim*) with Horace *Epod.* 2.68 (*iam iam futurus rusticus*). For comments on both reminiscences, see Maltby (2002), ad loc.

[147] An obvious example is the character of Sostratos in Menander's *Dyskolos*.

[148] Copley (1956), 91–107.

[149] Lee-Stecum (1998), 72; Copley (1956), 91–107; Vretska (1955); Cairns (1979), 166–7; Murgatroyd (1980), 72; Maltby (2002), 153.

[150] On the newness of Tibullus' *dolores*, see Lee-Stecum (1998), 75; for an alternate reading (*novo* in place of *novos*), Henderson (1987).

anxius urbe, 'I wander in distress through the entire city', 25). Whereas the lover of 1.1 lay in his mistress' embrace protected from the wind and rain by the walls of his house, now he lies outside on the threshold exposed to the cold and rain. He attempts to divert the rage of the elements onto the offending door (*ianua difficilis domini te verberet imber*, 'door of an obdurate[151] master, may the rain beat on you', 1.2.7), but it is the lover himself who is now unprotected. He nonetheless attempts to reassert his underlying safety, not now in view of the tutelary *Lares* of his autarkic estate, but as a factor inherent in his protected status as lover.[152]

> en ego cum tenebris tota vagor anxius urbe
>
> . . . .
>
> nec sinit occurrat quisquam qui corpora ferro
>   vulneret aut rapta praemia veste petat.
> quisquis amore tenetur, eat tutusque sacerque
>   qualibet; insidias non timuisse decet.
> non mihi pigra nocent hibernae frigora noctis,
>   non mihi cum multa decidit imber aqua.
> non labor hic laedit, reseret modo Delia postes
>   et vocet ad digiti me taciturna sonum.   (1.2.25–32)

Look when I wander in distress[153] through the entire city in the dark . . . [Venus] does not allow anyone to attack who might wound my body with iron or make off with the prize of my stolen clothes. Whoever is possessed by love may pass safe and sacrosanct wherever he likes; he ought not fear an ambush. The numbing cold of a winter night does not harm me; I am unharmed when a rainstorm falls with a great soaking. My hardship in this case does no harm, if only Delia unlock the door and silently call me with the tap of her finger.

In declaring that the goddess Venus protects the lover from harm, Tibullus adapts a well-known type-scene from epic. But whereas the guardian deity saves the epic hero from being slain in battle and having his armour stripped as spoils, Venus saves the lover from being mugged on city streets and stripped of his clothing. Military vocabulary (*ferro vulneret, rapta praemia, insidias*) is not only a means of heightening the 'sense of danger',[154] but also of continuing to explore the paradoxical *vuln*erability of the lover's *securitas* intimated at the close of 1.1. The sleight-of-hand trick that reattributed wounds to the soldier yet without discarding their metaphorical register is here repeated with a twist. Now the lover, the expected victim of metaphorical *vulnera*, is indeed the potential recipient of wounds (*vulneret*), but literal ones—he risks being knifed by a robber.

We are given ample reason to doubt the core claims of the previous elegy, which assigned dangers, labours, and wounds to soldiers and security to the lover/farmer. Now the lover, returning home late at night on darkened streets,

---

[151] So Maltby (2002), ad loc., for *difficilis*.

[152] Maltby (2002), ad loc.: 'The lover is a sacred person, divinely protected from harm'; he compares Propertius 3.16.13–14, but also Tibullus 2.5.113–14 on the sanctity of poets (compare on Horace in Chapter 3, below). The underlying idea is coherent with the Tibullan theme of the autarkic *securitas* of the poet-lover.

[153] Putnam (1973), ad loc., observes that the phrase *vagor anxius* paradoxically combines ideas of expansive wandering and 'choking' restriction (*anxius-ango*)—a good encapsulation of Tibullus' lover who is at once liberated and confined, freed from *labores* and yet bound tightly to his mistress.

[154] Murgatroyd (1980), ad loc.

undergoes dangers of being physically wounded, is exposed to the harsh outdoor conditions a soldier would be expected to endure on campaign (29–30), and subjects himself to potentially harmful toil (*labor*, 31). Tibullus claims that he remains unharmed, yet makes his claim dependent (*modo...*) on Delia's compliance—which is hardly guaranteed, and not demonstrated in the present elegy.[155] It is worth pointing out the simple fact that in 1.1 Tibullus embraced Delia within the walls of his house, apparently unchallenged by any rival: *mea Delia* (57). Now Delia has a *coniunx*, and Tibullus enlists the aid of a witch to ensure her mutual affection and deceive his rival. The *pietas* amply on display in 1.1 is now in question (1.2.79–86), and the easy sleep of the lover/farmer that played so prominent role in 1.1 can no longer be taken for granted (77–8).

The crowning ironies are reserved for the elegy's closing passage, which responds with some precision to the closure of 1.1. The latter is an exhortation to enjoy love in the here and now, since a lover's words and ways will no longer be seemly when he is old (71–2): *nunc levis est tractanda venus, dum frangere postes / non pudet et rixas inseruisse iuvat* ('now is the time for taking part in light-hearted love, while it is not embarrassing to break down doorposts and it is pleasing to engage in lovers' quarrels'). In 1.2 a different rhetorical drive is manifested, not so much seductive as corrosive. As proof that Love will eventually bring even the haughtiest low, Tibullus declares that he witnessed a youthful mocker of love forced to stoop to disgraceful courtship-rituals in old age (1.2.89–96). This re-contextualization of *senilis amor* ('love in old age')[156] precisely inverts the previous elegy: rather than contrasting the decorum of youthful love with the disgrace of love in old age, the lover of 1.2 bears witness in awed tones to the power of love to degrade anyone at any age in any condition. We have moved some distance from the agrarian idyll of 1.1 that integrated love within its safe, carefree domain, and ended with a vision of contentment and moderate accumulation (*composito... acervo*). This distance becomes palpable in the final couplet of 1.2, where the lover complains of Venus burning her own harvest: *quid messes uris acerba tuas*? ('why do you mercilessly burn your own harvest?').

Tibullus thus dismantles the imagery of *securitas* built up in his opening elegy. The diverse motifs of inclement weather, sleep, toil, wounds, and finally, old age and harvest are systematically, pointedly, and in the closing passage, explicitly rewritten to suit a harsher environment and harsher vision of love. Tibullus claims to be safe and protected in this new environment, but it is a different kind of protectedness from that afforded by his humble estate. He has no sheltered space of ethical tranquillity, but only the paradoxical protection of a goddess who is savage toward her devotees. She hardly resembles the gods of the countryside to whom the farmer of 1.1 and 2.1 makes humble sacrifice and from whom he expects support in return. Acts of piety designed to secure the support of guardian deities were prominently displayed in 1.1.9–24, and the hopes of benign intervention of the gods fairly explicit: *agna cadet vobis, quam circum rustica pubes / clamet 'io, messes et bona vina date'* ('a lamb will be sacrificed to you, and around it the rural youth will cry, "ho, give a good harvest and

---

[155] Compare Lee-Stecum (1998), 83.

[156] On the distinctive Tibullan representation of love in old age, see Lyne (1998b), 265.

wines"', 23–4). By contrast, Venus' wantonly destructive tendency is shocking to the sensibility of the pious rural smallholder: why indeed does she burn her own harvest? The only way he can understand his sufferings at the hands of Venus is to assume that he has neglected the goddess or committed some sacrilege (1.2.79–86), but this looks like grasping at straws. In fact, there is no explanation, except that Love does not adhere to any intelligible logic of reciprocal benefit. It is becoming harder to reconcile the lover's and the farmer's respective worlds.

Tibullus' second book of elegies follows a similar path: he begins by marking out, and then proceeds to dismantle, the space of rural security. In 2.1, Tibullus orchestrates a literary simulation of the country festival of the Ambarvalia. Once again, the poet demarcates a realm of purity, security, piety, and bounty in an evocation of the Italian countryside.

> di patrii, purgamus agros, purgamus agrestes:
>   vos mala de nostris pellite limitibus,
> neu seges eludat messem fallacibus herbis,
>   neu timeat celeres tardior agna lupos.   (2.1.17–20)

Gods of our fathers, we purify the fields, we purify the labourers: drive away evils from our boundaries; let not the crop elude harvest with deceptive stalks, nor let the slow lamb fear the swift wolves.

In beginning his second book with an elegy composed out of a series of wishes, commands, and jussive subjunctives ordering an idealized vision of rural *pietas*, Tibullus invites comparison with 1.1. Demarcation of literary domain is here even more explicit: the festival of the Ambarvalia involves *lustratio*, or ritual perambulation of the fields' boundaries.[157] Love, however, at first appears to be absent from Tibullus' tranquil existence in this second book. Finally, the opening words of 2.3 announce a long-delayed return to the thematic of mistress and countryside: *rura meam, Cornute, tenent villaeque puellam* ('villas and the countryside, Cornutus, detain my girl'). Later in the same elegy, Tibullus' mistress' identity is revealed with alarming abruptness.

> heu heu divitibus video gaudere puellas;
>   iam veniant praedae, si Venus optat opes,
> ut mea luxuria Nemesis fluat utque per urbem
>   incedat donis conspicienda meis.   (2.3.49–52)

Alas, I see that girls delight in the rich. Then let Gain come, if Venus fancies wealth, so that my Nemesis may ooze luxury and parade through the city, a sight to see because of my gifts.

Up to this point, Tibullus has not named Nemesis, and for all we know, when he speaks of his *puella*, refers to Delia. Nemesis is named, significantly, at the moment when Tibullus overturns a major facet of his self-representation in Book 1. The juxtaposition of 'my' (*mea*, nom. sing.), 'luxury' (*luxuria*, abl. sing.), morally suspect fluidity (*fluat*) and 'Nemesis' announces a disturbing new self-representational theme. Throughout Book 1, emphatic uses of the first-person pronoun and possessive adjective align *paupertas* with the poet's core concept of

---

[157] Feeney (1998), 123; Fantham (2009), 25.

self: *me mea paupertas* (1.1.5).[158] Now, Tibullus reorients his *ego* and its attributes to cohere with the new system of *praeda* ('profit/plunder') and sexual bribery: *ut mea luxuria Nemesis fluat utque per urbem / incedat donis conspicienda meis* ('so that my Nemesis may ooze luxury and parade through the city, a sight to see because of my gifts'). From a humble, unostentatious rural existence, Tibullus has migrated to the opposite extreme: his mistress will become an index of the poet's luxurious wealth.

Scholars have variously interpreted the meaning of the name Nemesis, usually with reference to a presumed explanatory event or background, such as the poet's previous rejection of her and subsequent punishment. A more plausible and, I believe, more interesting explanation of the name arises out of Nemesis' status as a subversive force in Tibullan poetics. She punishes the self-representational smugness and presumptions of the poet's first book.[159] The *poetic* nature of Tibullus' punishment is suggested not least by the strongly poetic dimension in Apollo's paradigmatic humiliation during his servitude to Admetus as described earlier in same elegy (2.11–36): the god's aesthetic refinement encounters its nemesis in the intrusion of mooing cows (19–20). Tibullus' punishment also uniquely suits him; the traits of Nemesis are designed to overturn his central poetic tenets. Specifically, we may recall his programmatic adherence to a golden-age morality of non-violence and *paupertas* throughout the first book. As late as line 48 of the present elegy, Tibullus is still insisting on *paupertas* in the form of simple, clay tableware (47–8), and offering fairly standard criticism of the luxurious builder's transgression of natural boundaries (43–6). Abruptly, however, *paupertas* is routed, and *praeda* takes over (49–50). The presumption of anachronistic integrity on Tibullus' part must now encounter the corrosive power of Nemesis. She drags back him into the violent, money-obsessed world from which he had conspicuously withdrawn.

The process of dismantling we observed at work in Book 1 is thus pushed to a further degree in Book 2 with the introduction of Nemesis as the new driving principle of Tibullan elegy. In 2.3 and the following elegy, she systematically subverts the topoi of security built up by Tibullus throughout his first book. Whereas in Book 1 the field and its crops were the object of reverent cultivation, now the poet has come to resent the countryside that 'holds' (*tenent*) Nemesis at a distance from him. Nemesis' rural inaccessibility drives him to curse the field itself: *at tibi, dura seges, Nemesim quae abducis ab urbe, / persolvat nulla semina Terra fide* ('but to you, unfeeling field, who draw Nemesis away from the city, may Earth not reliably pay back its debt for the seeds [planted in it]', 61–2). This inversion of the farmer's prayers in 1.1 is calculated to shock: now the poet prays, not for the fields' continuing bounty, but that they will cheat the farmer of the expected reward. Next Tibullus vents his anger against Bacchus, and bids farewell to 'crops' (*fruges*, 67) altogether. Agricultural terms such as *seges* (field/crop) and *fruges* (fruits of the fields), which played a prominent part in the pious farmer's

---

[158] Compare 2.3.47, *at mihi laeta trahant Samiae convivia testae.*

[159] Similarly Bright (1978), 202, and Maltby (2002), 409: 'punishment for T.'s fond hopes of rural simplicity'.

prayers in 1.1, now attract his vehement curses (61–8).[160] It is for the closing section of the following elegy that the most devastating reversal of his previous poetic stance is reserved: Tibullus will be driven by the greedy Nemesis to sell his ancestral *Lares* (2.4.53–4). The emphatic site of his personal *securitas* in Book 1 will be converted into cash. The impiety of this wish and its subversion of the poet's previous ethical orientation could not be more explicit.[161]

As in Book 1, the peaceful rural idyll has been shattered by the destructive power of eros. The fields and crops the poet's voice sought to purify and protect in the book's opening elegy are now cursed under the baneful influence of Nemesis. We should not assume, however, that by subverting constructs of rural tranquillity Tibullus thereby necessarily destroys the only basis of his poetic autonomy. Rather the broader pattern of poetic self-subversion in both books of Tibullan elegy is consistent with a shift from one model of autonomy to another, from the autonomy of rural refuge to the autonomy of erotic subjection. Tibullus likes to keep both models in play, and to play them off each other, although in both books, the darker, less idealized scenario of love-slavery takes root after the initial fantasy of a beatific rural equilibrium passes away. The rural idyll is evoked and sustained by first-person speech-acts of wishing, prayer, and jussive exhortation. This idealized world does not seem to enjoy the same degree of intractable reality as Nemesis and her dark hold on the poet. Yet her power and solidity are also poetically useful. By making Nemesis the *sine qua non*[162] of his poetry, Tibullus incorporates her formidable independence and iron will. She is a law unto herself, and as she governs and constitutes his poetry, so will Tibullus' poetry draw upon her protection in maintaining its integrity of focus. Indeed, Nemesis affords Tibullus a new barrier between himself and any patron's putative demands for literary encomium: surely a patron could not expect the poet to be distracted from a mistress so obsessing and profoundly derailing that she undermines his very sense of self.[163]

Ultimately, however, it is difficult get a firm handle on what is supposed to be Tibullus' 'real' poetic self, and what is merely dream or fantasy.[164] Rural withdrawal appears as an unrealizable dream in Tibullus' literary text, a lost idyll to which the departing soldier or imprisoned lover can only hope one day to return. Yet does it not seem plausible, from the little we know of the author Tibullus, that he really did enjoy a life of material comfort and Epicurean autarky in the Italian countryside? Nemesis' dark reality governs Tibullus' poetic work, destroying his rural tranquillity. From an extra-textual perspective, on the other hand, the picture of a wealthy, country gentleman takes on a certain plausibility by contrast with his lurid literary portrait of the helpless victim of a *femme fatale*. The point,

---

[160] Compare 1.1.43 (*seges*); 1.1.9, 2.2.1 (*frux*).

[161] Maltby (2002), ad loc.: 'another example of how T.'s passion for Nemesis has turned his previous system of values [as defined in Book 1] on its head'.

[162] Literally: *usque cano Nemesim, sine qua versus mihi nullus / verba potest . . . reperire* (2.5.111–12). On the utility of the conception of the mistress' autonomy for the poet's, see McCarthy (1998).

[163] 2.5, in which Tibullus celebrates Messalinus' installation as one of the *quindecemviri sacris faciundis*, does offer poetic commemoration of a patron, paralleling the praises of Messalla in 1.7 (see below). Even in this case, however, the poet's intricate erudition is arguably at least as prominent as the patron's praises, and Nemesis makes a striking appearance near the elegy's close (see note 142 above). Compare White (1993), 182–6.

[164] Kennedy (1993), 13–15.

of course, is not to get to the hard, irreducible kernel of the 'real' Tibullus, but to recognize the sometimes underappreciated complexity of his strategies of poetic self-definition. One danger of committing, as Propertius does in his early books, to a relentless model of autonomist poetic identity is the possibility of being imprisoned by the constraints of one's own poetic fictions. Tibullus refuses to be confined even to one model of autonomist identity. By remaining detached, playful, and ironic in his manipulation of competing autonomist models of poetic self, he aims to project a sense of supreme detachment and self-determination as poet. We should resist the anachronistic impulse to ascribe the multiplicity of Tibullan self-fashioning to a postmodern fracturing of subjectivity, but instead appreciate how he crafts his poetic self around the conscious avoidance of any single set of identifying interests. Tibullus' elegant evasions, his cool dismantling of his own fictions, are designed to show him to be consummately in control, an autonomist *par excellence*.

TIBULLUS AND THE *PANEGYRICUS MESSALLAE*: THE RHETORIC OF HETERONOMY

Such constructs of self-determination are at risk of crumbling, however, in the face of the patron's power and prestige. This potential conflict between patronage and the poet's autarkic independence returns us to the central concerns of Horace's first book of satires. Tibullus, like Horace, strives to maintain an attitude of autarkic contentment despite the presence of a patron-figure, whose palpably immense status threatens to compromise his program of ethical and aesthetic self-limitation. Tibullus' powerful friend Messalla, whose 'circle' has been variously reconstructed in modern scholarship, was connected with several poets represented in the *Corpus Tibullianum*. It will not be my aim to recover the workings of the literary society centered around Messalla but to consider his discursive status within Tibullan elegy. Specifically, I will examine how Tibullus incorporates honorific mention of Messalla into his poetry, while simultaneously working to contain, distance, and circumscribe his sphere of influence. Even in honouring Messalla, Tibullus must shield his poetry from the gravitational force[165] of his patron's prestige. The effort of maintaining such distance is both intense and precarious. It is a continual rhetorical effort for the poet to establish his independence from a patron whom he nonetheless conspicuously honours, and from whose prestige his poetry inevitably draws support. There is a fine line between autonomy and heteronomy, a line that is continually redrawn by the poets themselves as they struggle to maintain a stance of integrity. The distinction is especially in danger of collapsing when we reflect that one probable function of the rhetoric of poetic autonomy is to confer greater legitimacy on praise.

    A very different approach to praise is essayed in an approximately contemporary poem composed by an unknown poet in Messalla's circle.[166] The *Panegyricus*

---

[165] Feeney (2002), 172, adapting a phrase from Freudenburg (2002b), 37.

[166] On Messalla's relation to Tibullus and other poems in the same circle, see Davies (1973), Gaisser (1971), Johnson (1990), Van Nortwick (1990), Miller (2004), 117–28. Much discussion of Tibullus and Messalla has been devoted to speculation as to Messalla's shifting political allegiance

Messallae employs what I might term a rhetoric of heteronomy: a set of rhetorical strategies emphasizing the poet's unflagging service and subservience to his patron's renown. The poet of the *Panegyricus*, as he writes the poem, probably does not belong to the circle of Messalla, but seeks to secure Messalla's patronage by praising his deeds. The date of the composition is traditionally assigned to 31 BC,[167] prior to the publication of Tibullus' first book of elegies. Some verbal similarities suggest an intertextual relation between the two poets. It is not necessary to argue, however, that Tibullus deliberately differentiates himself from the *Panegyricus* in order to appreciate that the composition represents a type of poetry he is intent on *not* writing. At the same time, there are limits to this strategy of differentiation. Tibullus is sometimes in danger, despite all his efforts, of resembling the client poet, of collapsing into his opposite or inverse image. The *Panegyric of Messalla* is thus helpful for exploring both the successes and the contradictions of Tibullus' autonomist rhetoric.

We have already observed how, in a brief, contrastive mention in the first elegy of his first book, Tibullus states that, while it may be fitting for Messalla to conduct wars, the bonds of love constrict the poet. The poet's address to Messalla provides an exemplary instance of the liberating power of confinement. Held immobile in Delia's chains, Tibullus cannot travel abroad in Messalla's cohort. Slavery to a woman shores up his self-determination in the male world of duty and obligation. And from a certain perspective, it is not the poet, but Messalla, who is truly hemmed in. First of all, he is enfolded within the dubious embrace of the poet's surrounding self-description, while mention of the elegiac *puella* brackets his solitary couplet on either side (*puella*, 52; *puellae*, 55). Moreover, Messalla, who doubtless prided himself on diverse achievements in public and private life, is accorded only the public glory of warfare.[168] The autonomist logic behind Tibullus' tight circumscription of Messalla in his opening elegy can be better appreciated by comparison with the praises accorded Messalla in the *Panegyricus*. If we recall the explicit, contrastive distinctions between *ego* and *alius* throughout Tibullus 1.1, and, in the lines addressed to Messalla, *ego* and *tu* (*te . . . decet . . . me retinent*, 'me . . . [the bonds of love] hold captive . . . you . . . it befits', 53–5), the unobstructed honour paid to Messalla's second-person pronoun in the poem's first word is striking.

> Te, Messalla, canam, quamquam tua cognita virtus
> terret: ut infirmae nequeant subsistere vires,

and the (political) significance of belonging to his literary circle: e.g. Davies (1973), 27; Syme (1939), e.g. 198, 206, 222, 237, 238, 368, 403, 411, 460, 483, 512. I do not tend to see Tibullus as belonging to an anti-Augustan splinter group: on his status as 'Augustan' poet, see Solmsen (1962); note also White (1993), 182ff.

[167] He celebrates Messalla's consulship (31 BC), but does not mention his triumph over the Aquitani in 27 BC. It has sometimes been assumed that the *Panegyricus* echoes Tibullus on the grounds that the lesser poet naturally apes the greater. The dating of the *Panegyricus*, however, suggests otherwise—on which, see White (1993), 311 n. 10; Momigliano (1950).

[168] On his considerable literary interests and accomplishments, see Gaisser (1971), 221–2; Davies (1973), 26–7. Of course, as Gaisser's article demonstrates, Tibullus *implicitly* flatters Messalla's literary erudition by packing the poetry addressed to him with references to Callimachus, Catullus, Ennius, and other poetic predecessors.

incipiam tamen, ac meritas si carmina laudes
deficiant, humilis tantis sim conditor actis,
nec tua praeter te chartis intexere quisquam
facta queat, dictis ut non maiora supersint,
est nobis voluisse satis. nec munera parva
respueris. etiam Phoebo gratissima dona
Cres tulit, et cunctis Baccho iucundior hospes
Icarus, ut puro testantur sidera caelo
Erigoneque Canisque, neget ne longior aetas.
quin etiam Alcides, deus ascensurus Olympum,
laeta Molorcheis posuit vestigia tectis,
parvaque caelestis placavit mica, nec illis
semper inaurato taurus cadit hostia cornu.
hic quoque sit gratus parvus labor, ut tibi possim
inde alios aliosque memor componere versus.   (*Panegyricus* 1–17)

You, Messalla, I shall sing, although the knowledge of your valour intimidates me. Though my feeble strength cannot stand up to the challenge, yet I shall begin, and if my songs fall short of the praises you deserve, if I am a lowly author for deeds so great, and if no one besides yourself is able to weave your actions onto the page, so that the deeds do not surpass the words, it is enough for me to have wished it. Do not reject the humble offering. Even to Phoebus did the Cretan bring most welcome gifts, and Icarus was a host more pleasing to Bacchus than all others, as the stars in the clear sky, Erigone and the Dog, attest, lest a later age deny it. Why even Alcides, destined to ascend Olympus as a god, gladly set foot in the dwelling of Molorcus, and a mere grain of salt has appeased the heaven-dwellers; nor it is always a bull with gilded horn that falls for them as victim. So also may this humble effort be welcome, that thereafter in gratitude I may compose more and more verses for you.

The panegyrist subsequently imagines a writing-competition in Messalla's honour (33–8). The various ingredients of these lines all but exactly fulfill Horace's recipe for bad poetry: the misguided identification of large volumes (*magna volumina*) with undying verse (*aeterno . . . versu*, 34), the instigation of a literary contest (*certamen* 37) apparently based on enthusiasm and quantity rather than skill. The submission of the unknown poet's *ego* to Messalla's *tu* throughout the poem is the rule rather than the exception, and is at times expressed with startling directness. The panegyrist openly puts his literary services at his patron's disposal, and makes it evident that a limitless poetic prolixity is available to be funnelled into the sole project of Messalla's renown: *alios aliosque . . . versus* ('more and more verses . . . '). Moreover, he does not offer poetry alone, but resembles Horace's boor in offering general services of clientage. At one point he declares that he is willing to brave stormy seas, face entire squadrons of enemies alone, and even leap into the depths of Mt Aetna.

nec solum tibi Pierii tribuentur honores:
pro te vel rapidas ausim maris ire per undas,
adversis hiberna licet tumeant freta ventis,
pro te vel densis solus subsistere turmis
vel parvum Aetnaeae corpus committere flammae.
sum quodcumque, tuum est.   (*Panegyricus* 193–7)

Nor will Pierian reverence alone be awarded to you. For you I would dare to go over the rushing waves of the sea, though the stormy waters were swollen with adverse winds; for you I would dare to take my stand against densely packed squadrons, or to commit my puny body to the flames of Aetna. All that I am is yours.

The sheer (and seemingly humourless) hyperbole of this offer is remarkable enough, but the most striking phrase is a simple and straightforward one: *sum quodcumque, tuum est* ('all that I am is yours'). It is hard to imagine a clearer expression of the panegyrist's heteronomist self-fashioning in the face of his powerful patron.

Especially notable in the light of Tibullus 1.1 is the panegyrist's assertion that no mere *titulus* (legend, or inscription) can contain the deeds of Messalla, which require immense volumes.

> at quodcumque meae poterunt audere camenae,
> seu tibi par poterunt seu, quod spes abnuit, ultra
> sive minus (certeque canent minus), omne vovemus
> hoc tibi, nec tanto careat mihi nomine charta.
> nam quamquam antiquae gentis superant tibi laudes,
> non tua maiorum contenta est gloria fama,
> nec quaeris quid quaque index sub imagine dicat,
> sed generis priscos contendis vincere honores,
> quam tibi maiores maius decus ipse futuris:
> at tua non titulus capiet sub nomine facta,
> aeterno sed erunt tibi magna volumina versu,
> convenientque tuas cupidi componere laudes
> undique quique canent vincto pede quique soluto.   (24–36)

But whatever my muses will be able to venture, whether poetry equal to you, or (which hope denies) beyond you, or inferior (and surely they will sing something inferior), all this I dedicate to you; nor let my page lack so great a name. For although you abound in the praises of your ancient family, your glory is not satisfied with your ancestors' renown, and you do not ask what the legend says beneath each mask. But you strive to surpass the old honours of your line, yourself a greater source of glory for posterity than your ancestors for you. No legend beneath your name will encompass your deeds, but you will have great rolls of immortal verse, and all who sing in verse or prose will gather from everywhere, eager to compose your praises.

Tibullus, however, attempts precisely such a feat of condensation, that is, to contain Messalla's praises within a couplet, his field of glory within a single arena (warfare). The author of the *Panegyricus* allows a broader range of excellence. Indeed, several lines, complete with epic simile, are devoted to denying that one sphere of Messalla's greatness outweighs the other (39ff.). Even when Tibullus gives greater scope to Messalla's praises in 1.7, he still only directly praises *military* accomplishment. By contrast, the nameless eulogist, hinting broadly at Messalla's literary abilities, effectively effaces any claims to an arena of achievement distinctly his own. Messalla is the only one capable of finding words adequate to his own great deeds (5–6).[169]

---

[169] As Gaisser (1971), 222, notes, both the *Panegyricus* and *Catalepton* 9 comment on his literary achievements. Compare *Catalepton* 9:

The end of the poem extends the promise of 'more and more verses' even
further. Whereas Ennius traced his poetic ancestry back to Homer in a Pythagor-
ean dream of transmigration of souls, the panegyrist devotes the future instantiations of his self to the continual praise of Messalla in a mega-panegyric that
transcends the scope of individual lifetimes.

> quod tibi si versus noster, totusve minusve,
> vel bene sit notus, summo vel inerret in ore,
> nulla mihi statuent finem te fata canendi.
> quin etiam mea tunc tumulus cum texerit ossa,
> seu matura dies celerem properat mihi mortem,
> longa manet seu vita, tamen, mutata figura
> seu me finget equum rigidos percurrere campos
> doctum seu tardi pecoris sim gloria taurus
> sive ego per liquidum volucris vehar aera pennis,
> quandocumque hominem me longa receperit aetas,
> inceptis de te subtexam carmina chartis.   (*Panegyricus* 201–11)

But if my verse, whether all of it or less than that, should either be well known to you, or
merely pass over the surface of your lips, no fates will set a limit to my singing of you. Nay,
even then when the grave covers my bones, whether an early day speeds on a swift death for
me, or whether a long life awaits me, whether a change of shape will make me a horse,
trained to run over the hard plains, or I am a bull, the pride of the slow-moving herd, or, a
bird, I am borne through the clear sky on wings—nonetheless, whenever the long lapse of
time receives me back as a human being, I shall append [more] verses to the writings about
you I had begun.

The more closely one examines the unapologetically heteronomist literary strategies of the *Panegyricus Messallae*, the more comprehensible the logic behind
Tibullus' careful alignment of the poet-patron relation becomes. Whereas the
anonymous panegyrist accords any and all virtues to Messalla, and sets no limits
to his own willingness to praise, Tibullus works largely on the principle of mutual
exclusion: war, public glory, and world-wide travel belong to Messalla; love,
immobility, privacy, non-violence, and poetry belong to Tibullus. In order to
appreciate this principle of exclusion at work, it will be helpful to consider a
passage in 2.1. Towards the end of the opening evocation of a country festival,
Tibullus' thoughts turn toward Messalla.

> victor adest, magni magnum decus ecce triumphi,
> victor, qua terrae quaque patent maria,
> horrida barbaricae portans insignia pugnae,
> magnus ut Oenides, utque superbus Eryx,
> nec minus idcirco vestros expromere cantus
> maximus, et sanctos dignus inire choros.
> hoc itaque insuetis iactor magis, optime, curis,
> quid de te possim scribere, quidve tibi.

(A conqueror has arrived—behold, the mighty glory of a mighty triumph—a conqueror, as far as lands
and seas extend, carrying the grim spoils of barbarian war, like the great son of Oeneus, and like proud
Eryx, and not less on that account the greatest at bringing forth your songs and worthy of entering your
holy choruses. Therefore, o best of men, I am tormented all the more by unaccustomed cares,
[uncertain] what I can write about you, or what to you.)

> sed 'bene Messallam' sua quisque ad pocula dicat,
>   nomen et absentis singula verba sonent.
> gentis Aquitanae celeber Messalla triumphis
>   et magna intonsis gloria victor avis,
> huc ades aspiraque mihi, dum carmine nostro
>   redditur agricolis gratia caelitibus.   (2.1.31–6)

But let each one as he drinks say 'health to Messalla', and let every word speak out the name of the absent one. Messalla, famed for your triumph over the Aquitaine people, and, as conqueror, a great source of glory for your unshorn ancestors, come here and inspire me, while in my song thanks is given to the gods of farming.

As usual, Messalla is significantly absent from the primary scene of Tibullan elegy: elegy is situated in the countryside at peace, whereas Messalla's arena of action is far-ranging war. Tibullus makes this distinction manifest by juxtaposing a couplet devoted to Messalla's victory over the Aquitani with a subsequent couplet on his own vocation of poetry. In toasting the absent Messalla, Tibullus excludes Messalla from his elegiac realm, and keeps his patron's arena of glory restricted by highly specific parameters.

In Book 1, Messalla makes an appearance in each odd-numbered elegy until 1.7. This variational scheme in itself speaks to Tibullus' interest in circumscribing and counterbalancing the patron's sway within his poetic domain. Even when mentioned, however, Messalla is most often notable for his absence. In the opening lines of 1.3, Messalla and his *cohors* are receding over the waves, as Tibullus lies on his sick bed in the mythical land of Phaeacia (often identified as Corcyra).[170]

> Ibitis Aegaeas sine me, Messalla, per undas,
>   o utinam memores ipse cohorsque mei!
> me tenet ignotis aegrum Phaeacia terris:
>   abstineas avidas Mors modo nigra manus.   (1.3.1–4)

You will go over Aegean waves without me, Messalla, not forgetting me, I hope, both you and your staff. Phaeacia holds me back, sick, in a strange land. Only keep away your greedy hands, black Death.

Nominally, Tibullus announces his own absence, not Messalla's: *sine me* ('without me'). In absenting himself from Messalla, however, Tibullus largely succeeds in keeping his patron out of the elegy, which is filled, instead, with Delia-dominated reveries. Many scholars have appreciated the rich layers of imagery and reminiscence in this complexly shifting poem, which seems to move in and out of the realm of dreams. The wandering path of Tibullus' sick-bed reverie provides a ready justification for his poetic wandering ever further from Messalla and the *cohors*, who, ironically enough, are asked to keep *him* in their minds (*memores*). By a seamless yet deceptively simple transition, the poet passes from the misery of facing death alone in a strange land to the misery of facing death apart from Delia, and thence to Delia's worries about his departure. From this point on, Delia and Love dominate the poem, and with one exception, Messalla makes no further appearance. The journeys Tibullus attempted to divert onto the scapegoat 'other' of 1.1 have now overtaken the poet himself, yet his poetically convenient sickness

---

[170] On this elegy, see Mills (1974), Bright (1978), 16–37, Ball (1983), 50–65, Kennedy (1993), 15–17, Lee-Stecum (1998), 101–31, and from the perspective of Ovidian allusion, Huskey (2005).

has managed to keep him absorbed in love all the same. Warfare in the service of Messalla is beginning to seem like a project indefinitely deferred.

Love is one kind of sickness, and a metaphorical reading of Tibullus' malady as the sickness of love is not unreasonable. On this reading, 1.3 reiterates the underlying theme of Tibullus' message to Messalla in 1.1: the chains of love prevent him from following his patron around the world and keep him absorbed in the composition of elegiac poetry. This larger strategy of displacing the patron and the poet's duty toward him is further reinforced by the elegy's Odyssean intertextuality.[171] In the scenario of heroic seafaring, Messalla should logically play the part of Odysseus, the captain of the expedition, but, by a subtle sleight of hand, Messalla has been packed off with the rest of the *cohors*, leaving Tibullus in the role of the poem's wandering hero. Seafaring, as always in ancient literature, can be a metaphor for poetry. Here Tibullus takes over the captain's chair, and appropriately for an elegist, submerges the poetic voyage in the murky waters of indeterminate delay (*mora*). Unlike Messalla and the *cohors*, Tibullus gets nowhere, but remains in his Phaeacian dreamland, turning the image of Delia over and over in his mind, converting a purposeful voyage into the elegant futility of elegiac repetition.[172] Instead of moving forward, the poet's meandering thoughts replay the sequence of events prior to his departure, looping back and forth between past and present. The displaced authority of the patron leaves the invalid Tibullus in control of this distinctively elegiac journey without destination.

In one notable instance, Tibullus appears to remove Messalla from his usual martial setting, and imagines what it would be like to integrate him within his own rural/amorous world. In 1.5, the elegist picks up on and extends the darker themes of 1.2: once again, the lover finds himself excluded outside Delia's door, and, even worse, his present ruinous condition has been brought about by the machinations of a procuress (*lena*) and the resources of a rich lover (*dives amator*). The tranquil existence outlined in 1.1 is beginning to seem like a dream now shattered by the dawning of a harsh new reality. Indeed, the core elements of 1.1—the countryside, Delia, Messalla—are introduced precisely in the form of an unfulfilled dream or fantasy.

> at mihi felicem vitam, si salva fuisses,
>   fingebam demens, et renuente deo.
> rura colam, frugumque aderit mea Delia custos,
>   area dum messes sole calente teret,
> aut mihi servabit plenis in lintribus uvas
>   pressaque veloci candida musta pede.
> consuescet numerare pecus; consuescet amantis
>   garrulus in dominae ludere verna sinu.
> illa deo sciet agricolae pro vitibus uvam,
>   pro segete spicas, pro grege ferre dapem.

---

[171] Several features reinforce the allusive link: the specification of Phaeacia as the poet's present location, the voyage to a literary underworld, the assimilation of Delia to Penelope in the closing description. Tibullus, like Odysseus, finds himself stranded in a faraway location, obstructed from returning home, and, perhaps most importantly, 'deprived of all companions'. See in particular Bright (1978), 16–37, Ball (1983), 50–65; for complications, Lee-Stecum (1998), 103–4.

[172] Ball (1983), 65: 'Tibullus ingeniously converts the epic hero into an elegiac anti-hero'.

> illa regat cunctos, illi sint omnia curae:
> at iuvet in tota me nihil esse domo.
> huc veniet Messalla meus, cui dulcia poma
> Delia selectis detrahat arboribus:
> et, tantum venerata virum, hunc sedula curet,
> huic paret atque epulas ipsa ministra gerat.
> haec mihi fingebam, quae nunc Eurusque Notusque
> iactat odoratos vota per Armenios.   (1.5.19–36)

Yet in my madness I used to dream that, if you were spared, I would lead a happy life—a god said no. 'I will farm, and my Delia will be there as guardian of the grain, while the threshing-floor winnows the harvest in the blazing heat, or she will watch over the grapes for me in the full vats and the treading of the white must with swift feet. She will become accustomed to counting the flock; the chattering house-born slave will become accustomed to playing in a loving mistress' lap. She will know how to make offerings to the farmer god—a grape-cluster for the vines, ears of corn for the field, an offering for the flock. Let her rule everyone, all things be her concern: but let it please me to be a cipher in all the household. My Messalla will come here; for him let Delia pull down sweet fruit from chosen trees; and, having shown veneration to so great a man, diligently tend to him, prepare and carry him his meal, herself his attendant'. These were my dreams, which now East and South winds toss around perfumed Armenia.

In Tibullus' fantasy-world,[173] Delia will cater to Messalla, perhaps more aptly and subserviently than Tibullus himself. She will act the farmer's wife. She will rule everything and absorb all mundane concerns. Rather than dominating him and exacerbating the awkward contradictions that plague and define his existence, she will perfect his autarky, and even take on even the role of offering choice (poetic[174]) fruit to Messalla.

The attractions of the fantasy are obvious. Delia willingly reconciles love and the countryside by becoming the perfect farmer's helpmate. At the same time, we must remain aware that Tibullus, who has carefully framed this scene of rural happiness with clear indications of its infeasibility, cannot want the fantasy to be fulfilled. The mistress, up until this point, has served as a figure of obstruction and detainment, keeping the poet within her orbit and preventing him from offering homage to anyone else, while the confines of his estate have kept him protected from the wider world. When Tibullus fantasizes that Messalla will come to his rural estate—*huc veniet Messalla meus*—and there encounter the meek subservience of Delia, who will supply him with the fruits of the estate of which she is steward, he is imagining, in effect, what it would be like if his elegiac poetry catered in subservient fashion to his powerful friend. Since it is impossible that elegy should do this unstintingly and yet remain elegy, the whole passage is framed contrafactually. Messalla, typically represented as absent from or marginal to the scene of Tibullan elegy, cannot have unimpeded access to the poet's world. It is therefore reassuring that his presence is, in fact, only a dream.

The lack of unimpeded access does not, however, mean that Messalla will gain no footing whatsoever in Tibullan elegy. The last in the sequence of odd-

---

[173] This imagined scene is variously discussed in Van Nortwick (1990), 16–17, Johnson (1990), 103–4, Lee-Stecum (1998), 163ff., Miller (2004), 127.

[174] Compare Catullus c.65.15–24.

numbered elegies that mention Messalla, 1.7, departs from the pattern of either representing him as absent from the elegist's world (1.1, 1.3, 2.1) or as an impossible presence within it (1.5). Messalla is now the elegy's prime focus, as Tibullus commemorates the occasion of his triumph over the Aquitani.

> Hunc cecinere diem Parcae fatalia nentes
>   stamina, non ulli dissolvenda deo:
> hunc fore, Aquitanas posset qui fundere gentes,
>   quem tremeret forti milite victus Atur.
> evenere: novos pubes Romana triumphos
>   vidit et evinctos bracchia capta duces:
> at te victrices lauros, Messalla, gerentem
>   portabat nitidis currus eburnus equis.
> non sine me est tibi partus honos: Tarbella Pyrene
>   testis et Oceani litora Santonici,
> testis Arar Rhodanusque celer magnusque Garunna,
>   Carnutis et flavi caerula lympha Liger.   (1.7.1–12)

The Fates sang of this day as they spun the threads of destiny that no god can unwind: they sang that this would be the day to rout the people of Aquitaine, the day to make the Adour, conquered by brave soldiers, tremble. These thing have come to pass. The Roman people have seen new triumphs and leaders with their captive hands bound, while you, Messalla, wearing the laurels of the victorious general, were being carried by the ivory chariot drawn by shining steeds. Not without me was your glory gained. The Tarbellian Pyrenees are witness, and the shores of the Santonic Ocean; the Saône is witness, the rapid Rhone, and great Garonne, and the Loire, blue stream of the blond Carnutes.

Tibullus has finally let Messalla occupy a central role in his elegy. The declaration of line 9, assuming it is the correct reading,[175] pointedly reverses the emphasis on absence in 1.3: it is *not* without Tibullus (*non sine me*) that Messalla has achieved glory. This statement has been interpreted to mean that Tibullus accompanied Messalla and participated in his victories. Surely it also contrasts the present act of poetic celebration with the poetic evasions of 1.3 (*sine me . . .*).

The form Tibullus' celebration takes has long provided fodder for scholarly inquiry and debate.[176] After the opening notice of Messalla's triumph, the list of far-flung locations that were 'witness' (*testis . . . testis*) to the accomplishments of Messalla and the poet's participation in them flows into a series of indirect questions further expanding on the world-wide scope of Messalla's operations and demonstrating the poet's geographical *doctrina* (13–24).[177] The focus then falls on Egypt, the mysterious origin and revered fertility of the Nile, and then, at greater length, Osiris' gifts to human civilization: agriculture, arboriculture, and viticulture (29–48). Tibullus includes within the Osiris passage an inset devoted to the praises of wine in which Osiris appears to be assimilated to Bacchus as the incarnation of wine (39–42). The elegist then calls upon Osiris/Bacchus to be present at the birthday celebrations of Messalla and to infuse his temples with wine. In the closing lines, Tibullus prays that Messalla's progeny will augment his deeds (55–6), and predicts that country-dwellers will praise the road built by

---

[175] Baehrens (1876) suggests the not very attractive emendation *non sine Marte ibi*. In line 4, I adopt Scaliger's *Atur* for *Atax*.

[176] See, for example, Gaisser (1971), Bright (1975), Konstan (1978), Moore (1989).

[177] Compare *Panegyricus* 107–10 and Gaisser (1971), 223 n. 24.

Messalla for enabling smooth passage from country to city (57–64). The series of metonymic links holding together the diverse parts of the elegy weave a dense poetic fabric that eludes easy interpretation. The breadth of the elegy's scope of geographical reference may help depict Messalla as a saviour figure on a global scale, and the encomium of Osiris/Bacchus as culture hero may play into Messalla's own contributions to civilization as road-builder.[178] On the other hand, much of the elegy only indirectly concerns Messalla, and there is no obvious way to harness its various erudite components to a uni-directional vehicle of praise.

The *Panegyricus Messallae* provides a helpful comparison. This poem comparably calls various geographical locations to 'witness' Messalla's achievement, but in this instance, the encomiastic intent is more transparent than in Tibullus' geographical excursus. Tibullus makes it difficult to understand where praise of Messalla ends and the display of erudition as a literary *tour de force* begins, and in what ways exactly Osiris is meant to correspond to Messalla. There is no such obliquity in the *Panegyricus*. The panegyrist devotes a major portion of his poem to heralding Messalla as a world-conqueror on a massive scale. Astonishingly, he proclaims that Messalla will conquer not only all the usual places in the known world—which include Gaul, Spain, Africa, Egypt, Parthia, India, and Scythia—but, apparently, the southern hemisphere as well.[179] Sheer overkill differentiates the *Panegyricus* from Tibullus.[180] Scholars have often drawn comparisons between the former and the latter to Tibullus' advantage, contrasting the inept or conventional *Panegyricus* with Tibullus' complex, original composition. I would add, however, that we must appreciate not only Tibullus' talent and originality, but the degree to which he *deliberately* mystifies the encomiastic import of his elegy's geographical and mythological references. Obliquity itself contributes to the rhetoric of autonomy.[181] We may well judge Tibullus to be a greater poet than Messalla's prolix eulogist, but we must also recognize that part of our eagerness to make this judgement derives at least in part from the fact that we, as moderns, respond more favorably to autonomist than heteronomist discourses of praise.

Appreciation of Tibullan obliquity and originality should not be taken so far as to suggest that Tibullus does not really praise Messalla, or that criticism somehow lurks within and secretly predominates over the ostensible praise. Moderns tend to want to rescue panegyric from its own appearances, and they do so not least because of their investment in poetic autonomy. In the modern view, poetry becomes merely a tool of propaganda and not a thing of intrinsic worth when it praises the ruler without the saving device of irony. The ancient perspective, however, is different. For Roman poets of the Augustan period, persuasive claims of literary autonomy are valuable for the reason that they enable worthwhile praise. This is not the only motivation for the rhetoric of autonomy, but it is an

---

[178] See, especially, Gaisser (1971) on the subtle ways in which Tibullus weaves connections between Osiris/Bacchus and Messalla, who appears to have been known for an interest in wine.

[179] White (1993), 161–2: 'Messalla's blitz of the two anti-worlds' (162).

[180] Again, White (1993), 163: 'Clearly our poet gets somewhat carried away'.

[181] Those who 'get' all the references to Callimachus, and appreciate Tibullus' syncretistic linking of deities and patron, will, of course, appreciate the multi-layered compliment to Messalla; but the point is that Tibullus is careful to weave Messalla's praises subtly into the fabric of an intricately erudite text whose overtly panegyrical declarations remain relatively muted.

important one. Messalla does get his due mead of praise, and making sure that praise is conferred within a framework of literary integrity is the work of the autonomist rhetoric we have seen in operation throughout the first book.[182] The rhetoric of autonomy provides the counterbalance that makes the exceptional instance of praise-poetry acceptable and not simply gratuitously offered flattery; it confers greater value on the praise by making it seem to arise out of a resistant, integral medium.

Let us consider one final aspect of poetic self-representation in both Tibullus and the *Panegyricus*. A major criterion distinguishing the Tibullan rhetoric of autonomy from the patron-centered discourse of the *Panegyricus Messallae* is the Tibullan insistence on self-sufficiency. This crucial difference becomes patent when the two poets discuss their respective attitudes toward wealth past and present. The poet of the *Panegyricus* explains that the vexations of adverse Fortune obstruct his devotion to poetry:

> non ego sum satis ad tantae praeconia laudis,
> ipse mihi non si praescribat carmina Phoebus.
> est tibi, qui possit magnis se accingere rebus,
> Valgius: aeterno propior non alter Homero.
> languida non noster peragit labor otia, quamvis
> Fortuna, ut mos est illi, me adversa fatiget.
> nam mihi, cum magnis opibus domus alta niteret,
> cui fuerant flavi ditantes ordine sulci
> horrea fecundas ad deficientia messis,
> cuique pecus denso pascebant agmine colles,
> et domino satis et nimium furique lupoque,
> nunc desiderium superest: nam cura novatur,
> cum memor ante actos semper dolor admonet annos.
> sed licet asperiora cadant spolierque relictis,
> non te deficient nostrae memorare camenae...
>
> . . . .
>
> nostri si parvula cura
> sit tibi, quanta libet, si sit modo, non mihi regna
> Lydia, non magni potior sit fama Gylippi,
> posse Meleteas nec mallem vincere chartas.   (177–91, 197–200)

My powers are not sufficient to spread abroad such glory, not if Phoebus himself were to dictate my songs. You have in Valgius the sort of poet who can gird himself for great achievements; there is no one else nearer to immortal Homer. It is not in indolent leisure that I pursue my [poetic] labour, although Fortune, as is her custom, opposes and wears me down. For I, though I once had a lofty house glittering with great wealth, and rows of yellow furrows enriching granaries insufficient for the rich harvest, and cattle that grazed on the hills in dense ranks, enough for the master and too much for thief and wolf, am now left with a sense of loss. For anguish is renewed, when long-remembering grief recalls years past. But even if harder times fall to my lot and I am stripped of what is left, my muses will not fail to commemorate you ... If you have a little bit of concern for me, however small, if

---

182 Compare Gaisser (1971), 223: 'unlike [the authors of the *Panegyricus* and the *Catalepton*, Tibullus] knew and preserved the distinction between compliment and flattery. We may expect his tribute to be subtle, witty, and artfully calculated to appeal to Messalla's intellect as well as his vanity'.

you but have it, neither the kingdom of Lydia nor the fame of great Gylippus would be preferable to me, nor would I rather be able to surpass the writings of Meles' son.

This autobiographical passage in the *Panegyricus* is superficially reminiscent of Tibullus 1.1: both poets confess that they enjoyed greater landed wealth in the days of old. In fact, however, the unknown eulogist precisely inverts the force of Tibullus' disclosure. Whereas Tibullus brought up the matter of his fallen fortunes in the context of demonstrating his *contentment* with his *present* degree of wealth, the eulogist unambiguously claims that he had 'enough' (*satis*) only in the *past*, and now lives in a condition of lack (*desiderium*)—the very opposite of autarky. The eulogist's introductory complaint that inadequate wealth mars his literary leisure, and prevents him from producing anything comparable to Valgius Rufus' compositions, brings him very close indeed to the bald appeals of Martial's begging-epigrams: *nostri si parvula cura / sit tibi...* ('If you should have a little bit of concern for me...'). The subsequent passage, where he declares his willingness to risk life and limb for Messalla, enforces the all too explicit message: he would be a worthy and profoundly grateful recipient of the patron's material support.

Tibullus, by contrast, insists that he does not need anything; his present store of wealth is perfect, and requires nothing to complete it. In general, he seems to require nothing from anyone—a self-representational motif echoed in modern analyses which observe that, as an *eques*, Tibullus is independent of the need for patronal support.[183] Of course, it is possible, despite such protestations, to read the eulogist's begging-strategy into Tibullus' more discrete confession of diminished means. His publicly advertised misfortune provides an obvious opening for a liberal patron, and if Tibullus suffered loss of property in the period of confiscations, the gift would be seen to compensate losses incurred during a regrettable episode in recent history. After all, there are degrees of wealth, and there is no reason to suppose that a modestly but not fabulously wealthy Tibullus did not receive and appreciate substantial gifts from Messalla, just as Horace and other poets reportedly benefited from the generosity of Maecenas and Augustus. Tibullus, in any case, is shrewder than the composer of the *Panegyricus*. He manages both to avow poverty and to disavow any desire for a gift to supplement his modest means.

By the intricate logic of ancient gift-exchange, the contented Tibullus' self-sufficiency may even qualify him as a more worthy recipient of material support. The patron's liberality is all the more conspicuously advertised, and deemed the more admirable, when it confers rewards on those who ask for nothing yet are recommended by their inherent worthiness. Like Horace in *Satires* 1, Tibullus advertises his connection with a powerful patron, all the while insisting on his self-sufficiency and utter lack of desire to benefit from his exalted connection. The evident success of both poets may be ascribed not least to the paradoxical efficacy of their gestures of independence. A patron ambitious for posthumous renown, as Horace admonishes in the 'Epistle to Augustus', must be prepared to fend off the eager versifier willing to spout his praises. This Horatian argument for the autonomy of literary standards, we might observe, is frankly based on a

---

[183] This is the general argument of White (1993), 5–14; on Tibullus, see 87–8, 182–6, 212, 252–4.

calculation of mutual benefit. This observation provokes a counter-intuitive insight: the rhetoric of autonomy may ultimately prove the more successful in promoting poetry's heteronomous utility for both poet and patron.

CONCLUSION

The construction of slender niches of poetic autonomy is a characteristic feature of the early Augustan period. Elegant books of ten frame carefully bounded literary worlds. As we move into the middle and later periods of the Augustan principate, the concepts of withdrawal, refuge, and autarky remain important, while the *libellus* of finely, crafted Callimachean poetry continues to provide the standard unit of literary value. In other ways, however, the definition of literary space begins to change. It is a well-worn topos of Roman literary history that the Augustan poets move toward greater seriousness, social commitment, and *Romanitas* in their later works. Virgil's marked rise up the scale of genres culminates in the *Aeneid*, which offers a new vision of Roman civilization informed by the historical perspective of the Augustan principate. Horace's third and fourth books of *Odes* move beyond the narrow confines of the symposion to embrace a public, vatic style of lyric. Propertius' third and fourth books refashion elegy to cohere with public themes, as he progressively abandons the narrowly confining model of *servitium* for historical, political, and aetiological subjects.

In each instance, the poet's autonomist niche is dismantled or significantly modified. In traditional narratives of Roman literary history, this process of expansion generally signifies the loss of autonomy. On the one side, we have Callimacheanism, Hellenism, exiguous scope, privacy; on the other, Augustus, Rome, grandeur, publicity. According to the standard narrative, the poets eventually give in to the pressures of the Augustan regime, abandoning the freedom of their private poetic realms. I will argue, however, that a modified autonomist model continues to inform poetic production. The commitment to an autonomist literary ideology is not abandoned, but adapted to a more public conception of the poetic role. In the following chapter, I will explore these shifts in autonomist rhetoric in the middle and later Augustan period.

3

The Expansion of Autonomy

Augustan poetry (ca. 25 BC–AD 17)

INTRODUCTION

The major works of poetry published in the years leading up to and immediately following the battle of Actium were produced amid considerable political turmoil and uncertainty. When, according to the conventional dating, Virgil's *Eclogues* appeared ca. 39/38 BC, the land confiscations, the siege of Perugia, and Julius Caesar's murder were still fresh in Italians' memories. Horace, in *Satires* 1 (ca. 35/34 BC), still vividly recalls serving under Brutus. At the later end of the spectrum, Propertius Book 1 (published ca. 29 BC) and Tibullus' first book of elegies (ca. 26 BC) must have been in large part composed in the years preceding or immediately after Actium, when Caesar's heir was not yet Augustus, and the duration and nature of his rule were far from certain. These works of Augustan poetry of the earlier period, when Octavian had not yet achieved unambiguous supremacy, define their autonomy in relation to the public realm and politics generally, and not so much in relation to any one specific political figure, regime, or ideological programme. The literary spaces of refuge and withdrawal examined in the previous chapter were constructed against the background of republican politics, civil unrest, socially competitive urban behaviour, and the accumulation of wealth. In each case, the poet presents an 'image of the world'[1] to varying degrees differentiated from conventionally valued pursuits and criteria of value. In subsequent decades, poets continue to define themselves and their poetry through the rhetoric of contrastive self-differentiation, but the terms and content of the contrast change significantly. These changes can be understood as responses to the emergence of the Augustan principate.

One key change involves the prominent role of Maecenas and Augustus himself as patrons of literature. While it is true that Maecenas was already the prime addressee of Horace *Satires* 1 and *Epodes*, and is known to have been a friend of several contemporary poets, he occupies an especially conspicuous place in the poetry of the 20s BC as the named patron of Virgil, Propertius, and Horace. The significance of Maecenas' role as literary patron, moreover, changes in scope and significance after Actium when his friendship inevitably comes to signify a connection, however loosely defined, between poets and the ruler of the

---

[1] Labate (1990).

Roman world. This chapter will not enter into the (probably unanswerable) question of whether or not Maecenas, as agent of Augustus, exerted pressure on poets to produce works on specified propagandistic topics.[2] More directly relevant to my arguments regarding autonomy are changes in the structure of autonomist rhetoric in poetry of the period. Whether or not Maecenas exerted explicit pressure, the poets chose to define themselves by setting up a tensional dialogue between 'Augustan' themes and their own independence, craft, and authority as writers. It should not be ruled out that Maecenas may have been complicit in and even encouraged such an opposition. The rhetoric of the *recusatio* ('refusal')—a Latin word employed by modern critics to describe the refusal to attempt epic or panegyric—arguably serves not only the poets themselves but also the interests of the Augustan regime, which, as Horace observed in his 'Epistle to Augustus', benefits from the cultural authority and aesthetic integrity of contemporary writers.

As poets engaged with and participated in the Augustan transformation of Roman society, the focus of autonomist rhetoric shifted from the task of carving out a private space of sequestration and withdrawal to defining the distinctive role and authority of poetry in the city of Rome, and ultimately, the world. A factor in this rhetorical shift is the newly prominent role designated for poetry under the Augustan principate. Already in the 30s BC, Maecenas' literary interests appear to have made poetry fashionable as an area of endeavour for social climbers such as Horace's unnamed persecutor in *Satires* 1.9. This aura of prestige could only have increased as the major Augustan poets rose to ever higher honours in the pursuit of their poetic 'careers'.[3] At the further end of this spectrum, we see Virgil's *Aeneid* becoming a classic and a school text shortly after his death, and Horace publicly honoured and commemorated in an inscription for his composition of the *Carmen saeculare* for the *ludi saeculares* of 17 BC. The most permanent and striking monument to the importance of literature in the nascent imperial city were the libraries integrated within the temple and portico complex of Palatine Apollo.[4] The public status and recognition (*honos*) conferred on poetry by this signal structure, which featured a statue of Apollo singing and playing the lyre, offered both challenges and new opportunities for autonomist self-representation. We see a shift from the delineation of spaces of withdrawal embodied in vivid images of private life to more explicit demarcation of the poet's honoured role within Roman society.

The Augustan principate did not present one continuous ideological aspect or constitutional form, but was an evolving experiment in quasi-monarchical power that changed emphases and procedures as time went on.[5] In the earlier years of the Augustan principate, the *princeps* was especially concerned to maintain (the

---

[2] Addressed by White (1993).   [3] Farrell (2002); Hardie and Moore (2010).

[4] The complex was dedicated in 28 BC, but it is possible that the portico and libraries were added later. See Suetonius 29.3 (*addidit . . .*) and Dix (1994), 291 n. 5. Certainly detailed poetic attention paid to the libraries in Propertius Book 2 and Horace *Epistles* 1 and 2 comes at a later date (see discussion below).

[5] An important discussion of the protean, multifaceted nature of Augustan ideology, as well as the epistemological difficulty involved in defining what 'Augustus' and 'Augustan ideology' were at any given moment, can be found in Feeney (1992), 1–3.

appearance of) the traditional forms of republican government, and at the same time, to placate a potentially hostile reception of his new regime among the senatorial class. His strategy in this period was to maintain control over political outcomes and military resources, while avoiding the appearance of a direct monopoly on power and decision-making. There were limits to such subtlety and show of restraint, of course, but this approach contributed to the task of stabilizing Augustus' rule in the early period.

In the literary domain, it is coherent with Augustus' broader strategy that he left much (but not all) of the interaction with poets to Maecenas, an *eques* nominally content to forgo public honours, who, in turn, appears to have tolerated, or possibly encouraged, the poets' independence to pursue their own projects. Maecenas' role as mediator between poets and emperor and his uniquely unconstraining style of patronage functioned well in this transitional period when the sight of a flock of court poets directly attached to Augustus himself might have offended the sensibilities of some aristocratic Romans. The poets' cultural authority, moreover, could be established all the more persuasively if they were given adequate space to define their public image in autonomist terms. It should be noted that I am not forwarding a 'puppet-master' theory of Augustus' control of literary production. The success of Augustan literature could not have been necessarily planned in advance or foreseen by the *princeps*; nor, in all likelihood, were all literary developments of the period wholly positive ones from his point of view. Yet it remains important to appreciate the ways in which the rhetoric of poetic autonomy, as purveyed by poets and supported by Maecenas' role as buffer-figure, was potentially in the interest both of poets and *princeps*.[6]

Much speculation has been applied to the question of Maecenas' eclipse as literary patron in the later years of Augustus reign. Peter White, in particular, has argued vigorously against the idea of Maecenas' waning influence.[7] My present argument, however, does not primarily concern fluctuations in Maecenas' personal efficacy, but rather the model of poetry's sheltered domain with which his friendship was associated. Especially in Horace's *Satires*, *Epodes*, and *Odes* 1–2, and in Propertius Book 2, Maecenas functions as a buffer-figure between poet and ruler, and his status as *eques* coincides with and offers support to the poet's choice of retiring *otium*. Even without positing any kind of fall from grace, it remains possible to trace the obsolescence of the autonomist shelter as literary construct and the emergence of a more public and unsheltered model of the poet's autonomy. In Horace's and the exiled Ovid's case, the emperor's status as direct addressee in their later works, and in Propertius' case, the turn towards more overtly 'Augustan' themes in *Elegies* 3 and 4, are suggestive of new modes of interaction between poet and *princeps* that anticipate aspects of early imperial literary culture.

It is often thought that having the emperor as direct addressee and patron must have threatened if not wholly undermined the Augustan poets' autonomy. Horace's fourth book of *Odes* and Propertius' fourth book of elegies are typically cited as instances of capitulation to the demands for encomium of the imperial

---

[6] The central work on the topic, focusing on Ovid's *Fasti*, is Barchiesi (1997).
[7] White (1991); for a different view, which White explicitly opposes, see Williams (1990).

family and truly 'Roman' themes. I would suggest, however, that this apparent patriotic turn in Roman poetry does not represent anything so dramatic as abandonment of the autonomist project. It is more useful to think in terms of a correlation between the rising arc of a Roman poet's reputation for literary integrity and his enhanced capacity to write encomium and take on more ambitious, public themes. It is no accident that Horace's sequence of ambitious 'Roman Odes' at the opening of his third book of *Odes* are accompanied by his strongest declarations yet of sacerdotal poetic identity and status as Callimachean *vates*. Subsequently, in *Odes* 4, Horace pushes to an even further degree both his encomium of princes and his insistence on poetry's unique status and power. Propertius finally assumes, in his explicit claims of literary inheritance and in his aetiological subject matter, the role of *Callimachus Romanus*, when, in his fourth book of elegies, he takes on public topics relating to the Roman city, legendary history, and Augustan propaganda. Callimachus became an emblematic figure for the Roman poets not just because of a fashionable 'cult of style', but because he represented an effective combination of exacting aesthetic standards and the panegyric of rulers.

The encounter between Callimachean integrity and public utility, while important, is imbued with a certain irony, given that Roman Callimacheanism had played an important role in establishing the validity and autonomy of poetry, and hence also poetry's availability as publicly valid currency, in the first place. The new poets consciously outperformed Ennius and other archaic practitioners in versification and *doctrina*,[8] and in doing so, placed emphasis on poetry's inherent formal excellence at the expense of traditionalist content. But these successes only renewed and increased the potential value of poetry as public medium. The public importance of poetry was thus not simply invented by Augustus and Maecenas; they capitalized on the emerging value and cultural authority of the new poetry, which combined specialized expertise with the social prestige of comparatively elite authors. Authors of the *eques* rank who, while they did not come from Rome, belonged in many cases to prominent Italian families, had a significant stake in the appearance of autonomy.[9] Their recalcitrance only added to their poetry's value as potential memorial of a great man's name.

Thus one tendency in the self-representation of Augustan poets works to preserve the aura of intrinsic worth by staging scenarios of resistance to the appropriation of the poet's expert production, even as the very premise of resistance confers prestige on the one thus resisted.[10] Strategies employed by Augustan poets include the rhetoric of the *recusatio* (the refusal to write panegyric) and the

---

[8] See, for example, Thomas (1982) on Catullus' 'polemical' engagement with predecessors.

[9] Wiseman (1982), 38–42, considers the status and independence of Catullus.

[10] The analysis of Badian (1985), 354, is especially apt: '... *recusatio* ... had its proper place in the new order. It demonstrated the poet's freedom.... The importance of this in the early years of the Principate, when the return to Republican *libertas* was a major part of the official image, is obvious. Freedom could demonstratively be granted where the whole of the educated class would be aware of it—and where it could do no political harm. Maecenas was personally much involved with this early period and its policies... Encouraged to proclaim their freedom of choice, for the benefit of the *optimus status*, poets naturally did so. As they no doubt realized, it was the complement of the praise of the regime which was both expected and provided, and which was enhanced by it'. The classic treatment of the Callimachean *recusatio* is Wimmel (1960).

various delineations of poetic topography (pure springs, sequestered groves, remote villas) that define the domain of poetry and the status of the poet in distinction from other spaces and roles. The rhetoric of autonomy that informs these strategies of disjunction, exclusion, and segregation has shaped the modern debate over the politics of Augustan poetry, and continues to polarize diverging interpretive tendencies. In the classic approach, scholars attempt to decide whether the intent of a given work is loyal or dissenting, Augustan or anti-Augustan. More recent scholarship has argued that it is not possible to assign a determinate label of loyalty or dissent, either because a given work's political stance is too complex and multi-layered, or because of the 'semantic indeterminacy' intrinsic to literary texts and the process whereby we assign meaning to texts. While this latter approach has some justification, there is a danger of classifying as somehow intrinsically 'indeterminate' a political position that is carefully crafted and designed to be received as such. An autonomist position is designed precisely to forestall the need to commit to an attitude of loyalty or dissent. In characterizing a given work's political content as resistant to simple classification, we risk reproducing, without consciously analysing, the autonomist rhetoric it enacts. The reason why it is hard to elicit unambiguous indication of either loyalty or dissent in major works of Augustan poetry, and why modern scholars can regularly make reasonably convincing cases for either possibility, is because Augustan poets were consciously fashioning an autonomist position. This is not the absence of a position or an 'indeterminate' one, but a carefully devised tactic of evasion.

This evasion of unambiguous political allegiance, moreover, can have important political uses. As I argued above, an autonomist rhetoric of self-representation may serve to confer greater authority on the poet's voice, which, in turn, all the more effectively legitimizes the Augustan regime. To take a concrete example: we may never produce a wholly convincing argument as to whether Propertius' attitude towards Augustus as evinced by his various references to the *princeps* and his deeds is somehow intrinsically politically subversive or supportive, but the very fact that Propertius continues to address Maecenas as a patron and write about Augustus in a manner that is not overtly hostile or dismissive attests, at the very least, to the acquiescence, if not the approval, of a proudly independent poet. Instead of trying to understand the poetry as the distillation of the poet's underlying attitude, we need to be attentive to what it *does* in rhetorical and tactical terms. When the same poet in 3.4 envisions himself viewing Augustus' future triumph procession while enfolded in his girlfriend's embrace, there is no unproblematic way to classify this gesture as inherently 'loyal' (on the grounds that he anticipates applauding Augustus' triumph) or wholly 'dissenting' (on the grounds that he values love over patriotic seriousness). Instead of searching for a non-existent kernel of belief in this ingeniously staged scene, we need to appreciate the structure of the poet's autonomist rhetoric. Propertius has fashioned a carefully poised speech-act that both suggests (at least token) acquiescence in and support of the regime, and at the same time insists on the poet's distinctive position and perspective as love elegist. If this tension seems irreducible, it is because it was designed to be.

I am not arguing that all political content in Augustan poetry is so perfectly and irreducibly poised between subversion and assent. When Horace, at the end of *Odes* 1.2, wishes to see Rome's military force redirected at foreign enemies like the

Parthians under Augustus' leadership (*te duce, Caesar*), there is no credible 'dissenting' interpretation of these particular lines, as far as I can see. Horace does make sure, however, to counterbalance this propagandistic declaration of Augustan militarism with the image of himself sequestered in his poet's grove in the closing lines of the previous ode (1.1), glorying in his triumph as lyric poet. He will praise Augustus, but on his own terms, from within the framework of his lyric symposion and simple Epicurean pleasures—a framework that is sometimes in tension with a more fulsome and militaristic patriotism.[11] The true beliefs of Horace, who had joined Brutus in the 40s and cannot be assumed to have undergone an unconstrained conversion to the Caesarian side, are no more self-evident than Propertius'.

Whereas I would characterize such tensions, both in Horace and in Propertius, as irreducibly built into their poetry's autonomist rhetoric, the fact that they so skilfully avoided tipping the scales in one direction or the other does not entail that the net political effect of their poetry was nil. On the whole, though not as an inflexible doctrine, I will argue that autonomist self-representation was a rhetorical structure that enabled (sometimes minimal or token) gestures of assent to the Augustan regime. I am accordingly sceptical of theories of literary resistance to Augustus.[12] This conclusion, however, does not derive from some identifiable kernel of 'loyalty' discernible in the political content of contemporary poetry—which, as I say, was designed so as to withhold unambiguous signs either of partisan support or hostility—but from an assessment of the historical conditions under which the poets wrote and of what would constitute meaningful 'resistance'. There is no question of the kind of resistance offered to Stalin by members of the Soviet-era intelligentsia, nor even of the political invective directed at Julius Caesar and Mamurra by Catullus.[13] If dissent is a matter of subtle ironies of juxtaposition, emphasis and allusion to be read between the lines of nominally apolitical verse, this is a form of resistance Augustus could comfortably tolerate, and, for reasons argued above, might even have encouraged with the help of Maecenas. He may have been ruthless towards adversaries especially during the civil wars, but the broader pattern of his principate includes a propensity to advertise tolerance of low-level expressions of resentment and criticism. Suetonius cites a declaration of precisely such strategic tolerance in one of Augustus' letters to Tiberius: *aetati tuae, mi Tiberi, noli in hac re indulgere et nimium indignari quemquam esse, qui de me male loquatur; satis est enim, si hoc habemus ne quis nobis male facere possit* ('my dear Tiberius, do not give free rein to your youthful impulse in this matter and take it personally that anyone should *speak* badly of me; it is sufficient, if we can be assured that no one *do* us any harm', *Div. Aug.* 51).[14] One potential outcome of Augustus' tolerance of 'free' speech is to

---

[11] See in particular Fowler (1995b).

[12] The picture of Tacitus that emerges in Sailor (2008) again offers an interesting comparison: the historian also sought to project an image of autonomy, even as he worked to limit the presence of serious dissent in his works. See, for example, Sailor's analysis of Cremutius Cordus' status in Tacitean history: 250–313.

[13] Syme (1939), 461. On the possibilities for expression of dissent in imperial Latin poetry, see the very different views of Ahl (1984a) and Dewar (1994); more generally on 'the art of safe criticism', see Ahl (1984b).

[14] On his tolerance of free speech, see in general Suet. *Div. Aug.* 51, 55–6.

undermine the potency of mere *verba*: by affecting to be relatively unconcerned, he effectively reduces the stakes of verbal dissent.

Correspondingly, the sometimes minimal and deliberately ambiguous gestures of assent made in Roman poetry of the period were more than acceptable for Augustus' purposes. The best-known case of ancient Roman literary 'censorship', Ovid's exile, inevitably comes to mind as a possible exception to Augustus' policy of tolerance. In this instance, however, we have to judge whether the *princeps*, in exiling Ovid, truly intended to make a statement about the moral qualities of a contemporary work of poetry. If the arguments I have made so far are valid, it makes more sense that Augustus relegated Ovid to the shores of the Black Sea primarily for the unspecified 'mistake' (*error*) and not so much for the 'poem' (*carmen*).[15] Augustus must have been chagrined not only at Ovid's lapse of judgment, but also at the distasteful necessity of compromising his strategic and thus far effective tolerance of poetic autonomy.

REDEFINING AUTONOMY IN PROPERTIUS BOOKS 2–4: THE SLAVE'S TRIUMPH

In his earlier elegy, Propertius self-consciously exemplifies and playfully defends worthlessness (*nequitia*).[16] He makes much of the dominating presence of the woman who has destroyed him. In this phase, autonomy means the totalizing love-absorption that excludes other ways of acting and being, a self-enclosing world seen from the inside. In the later books, the elegist's perspective becomes more external: he spends more time developing an explicit affiliation with Callimachus and Hellenistic poetics generally, with the groves, rivers, and mountains of poetic topography.[17] The tensions of the autonomist project have not been resolved so much as restructured. Poets under Augustus are still involved, as they were in the 30s, in a game of opposition and contrast, a paradoxical mode of self-definition whereby the poet's work is rife with references to and deeply informed by the discourses he nominally resists. Tensions between poetry and politics, quietist tranquility and public prominence continue to inform poetic self-representation, but the specific parameters of the autonomist project are altered. Now 'power' and 'politics' mean, effectively, the Augustan regime, its social and religious policies, foreign wars, and propaganda. The rhetoric of the *recusatio* and the elegiac opposition of *amor* and *arma* (love and war) belong to a broader effort to negotiate this altered ideological landscape, and to redefine autonomy at a time when poetry's restrictive spaces have taken on greater public significance.

Central to this redefinition of autonomist poetics are the efforts of poets to position themselves in relation to the great patrons of the age—Maecenas, Messalla, Pollio, Augustus. In older readings, the Augustan poet either declares his

---

[15] See, for example, Badian (1985), 348, and discussion below.

[16] See Keith (2008), 139–65.

[17] On Propertian Callimacheanism, see, for example, Hubbard (1974), 68–115; Ross (1975), 107–30; Debrohun (2003), 1–32; Sullivan (1976), 108–15; Boucher (1965), 161–226; Hollis (2006); Keith (2008), 45–87; Zetzel (1996).

allegiance to or fights off the pressures exerted by his powerful patron. I intend to examine the intricacies of poetic self-definition and the patron's role within this rhetorical web rather than attempt to gauge the exact degree of a poet's accommodation or resistance.[18] There is no such thing as autonomy without the potential for heteronomy, and thus the Augustan patron can be read as performing an important function within the poets' rhetorical economy of self-differentiation. The first elegy of Propertius' second book, in which he first mentions the name of Maecenas, presents a very different kind of beginning in comparison with the opening of his *Cynthia*. Whereas Book 1 introduces a lover subjugated by love and mistress, Book 2 steps back somewhat from the immediacy of the amatory fiction to acknowledge the publication of Propertius' elegiac poetry.

> Quaeritis, unde mihi totiens scribantur amores,
> unde meus veniat mollis in ora liber.

You ask what is the reason I write so often about love, how my tender book of love poetry comes to be on people's lips.

As in the closing elegy of Book 1, Propertius is answering an inquiry:[19] Tullus had asked about his friend's land of origin and lineage (*qualis et unde genus . . . quaeris*), and now an unnamed plurality[20] ask (*quaeritis*) about the origin (*unde . . .*), not of the poet, but of his poetry (*amores*). The shift in perspective is important. Instead of a personified, subjugating Amor ('Love'), and a named mistress dominating the book's incipit, now we have the writing (*scribantur*) of love poetry in generic terms (*amores*), as well as a book, generically identified as *mollis* ('soft', 'effeminate')[21] and circulated among readers (*veniat . . . in ora*). Perhaps most significant of all is the anonymous second person plural *quaeritis* ('you ask . . .'). Now a different type of questioning is taking place, not so much a personal question based on long-standing friendship (*pro nostra semper amicitia*) as a question notionally formed in the public arena of poetry and its Roman readership.[22]

As of yet, there is no mention of a socially prominent *amicus* comparable to Tullus in Book 1. All the talk so far in the new book's first elegy is of poetry, and the poet's (still unnamed) mistress.

> non haec Calliope, non haec mihi cantat Apollo:
>   ingenium nobis ipsa puella facit.
> sive illam Cois fulgentem incedere vidi,
>   totum de Coa veste volumen erit;
> seu vidi ad frontem sparsos errare capillos,
>   gaudet laudatis ire superba comis;
> sive lyrae carmen digitis percussit eburnis,
>   miramur, facilis ut premat arte manus;
> seu compescentis somnum declinat ocellos,

---

[18] Compare the arguments of Fowler on Horace (1995b).

[19] Compare Heyworth (2007a), 101.   [20] Heyworth (2007a), 113.

[21] But note also Fedeli (2005), 45, who sees *mollis* as referring to the musicality of the verse and as the opposite of *versus durus*.

[22] Fedeli (2005), 43, is right to point out 'la singolarità e la straordinaria novità' of this type of anonymous address. He further speaks of 'una vera e propria presentazione editoriale' comparable to what is found in Ovid and Martial (see discussions below).

> invenio causas mille poeta novas;
>   seu nuda erepto mecum luctatur amictu,
> tum vero longas condimus Iliadas:
>   seu quidquid fecit sivest quodcumque locuta,
> maxima de nihilo nascitur historia.   (3–16, text Goold 1990)

Calliope does not chant this poetry to me, nor does Apollo: the girl herself creates my talent. If I have seen her come forth shining in Coan silks, there will be an entire scroll *On Coan Clothing*. If I have seen scattered locks fall across her forehead, she then happily goes forth proud of the praises I have written of her hair. If she has plucked a song on the lyre with her ivory-white fingers, I am amazed how artfully she guides her nimble hands. If she flutters her eyes as they fight off sleep, as poet I discover a thousand new conceits. If she wrestles with me naked, her dress torn off, then truly I compose lengthy Iliads. Whatever she has done or said, the greatest history arises out of nothing.

Whereas the answer to Tullus' question regarding his personal origin at the end of Book 1 was 'Umbria, the site of civil violence', Propertius' answer to his readers' question regarding the origin of his poetry at the opening of Book 2 is 'the elegiac *puella*': she 'makes' his talent (*ingenium . . . facit*). Indeed, these lines are *explicitly* about poetry in a way that the opening elegy of his first book was not. Propertius pictures himself, as a poet (*poeta*), discovering thousands of fresh 'conceits' (*causas*) to celebrate his mistress' attractive features; he will compose 'long Iliads' on their erotic tussles. A 'volume about Coan garments' is fleetingly suggestive of Philetas of Cos. And the girl herself is imagined playing a 'song' (*carmen*) on the lyre (9–10).

This ingenious series of conceits relating amatory experience to literary composition (2.5–16) reinforces the absorption of Propertius' literary identity within strictly amatory confines. In each instance, the scope and importance of the elegist's subject matter (the sight of his mistress' hair scattered across her forehead, her eyes fluttering in the moment before sleep . . .) are in inverse proportion to his obsessive literary magnification of them; he will write 'long Iliads' on these transitory flashes of eros. Indeed, in a striking line, Propertius declares that the 'greatest history' will be generated out of nothing (*maxima de nihilo nascitur historia*).[23] There is more than a hint of humour in this image of a writer magniloquently absorbed in the microphenomenal fabric of his love affair, and yet behind the facetious manner, I would suggest, is a provocative declaration of literary ambition. Propertius, like Catullus, confounds traditional hierarchies of scale and genre in favour of his antinomian *modus vitae* and his slender aesthetic mode. The claim to write 'long Iliads' will be at least partially borne out by elegies in Book 2 that assimilate the lover to the mythic paradigms of epic heroism. At the same time, however, Propertius' opening claim that his elegiac *puella* controls and is the very premise of his literary talent circumscribes from the outset the arena of his literary ambitions. He will write powerful, ambitious poetry, while remaining within the confines of amatory elegy.

This opening formula for Propertian elegy is important in part because of the way in which it sets up what is to follow. In line 17, immediately following the culmination of the previous argument with the paradoxical notion of a vast

---

[23] These lines appear to be an allusion to the Gallan lines preserved in the papyrus from Qasr Ibrim: Miller (1981); note also Fedeli (2005) 57.

history generated out of nothing (*maxima de nihilo … historia*), Propertius reveals his new patron's name: *quod mihi si tantum, Maecenas, fata dedissent, / ut possem heroas ducere in arma manus …* ('But if, Maecenas, the fates had granted to me that I should be able to lead heroes' hands to arms …', 17–18). There is a striking similarity between what Propertius does here in order to pave the way for Maecenas' name, and what he does in the first elegy of Book 1 prior to addressing Tullus. In both cases, the elegist defines his literary project in the strongest possible terms so as to distance himself from the active life and disqualify himself from writing poetry about anything except love. By the time Tullus' name crops up in 1.1, Propertius has been irrevocably 'captured' and subjugated by a ruthless Amor. Here, he disqualifies himself from writing about Maecenas' and Augustus' deeds by demonstrating how his entire literary *ingenium* and output are funnelled into the representation of minute details of his love affair and his mistress' attractive traits. This literary devotion to love is not susceptible to rational choice and control—an important point, since it shores up Propertius' autonomist position. He is fundamentally incapable of writing panegyric; it is a matter of 'fate', as the contrafactual condition in which Maecenas' name is so artfully embedded implies (*si … fata dedissent*).

We can begin to observe the adaptation of Propertius' autonomist rhetoric to his new circumstances, among which two in particular stand out: his first book, 'Cynthia', has been published, and he has become a known author; he now has Maecenas as a patron. Propertius thus begins to define the bounded domain of elegy in more explicitly literary and generic terms than he had in his first book, which remained committed to the idea of utility-oriented courtship-poetry (*werbende Dichtung*[24]). At the same time, he sets this newly explicit literary domain in relation to Maecenas and the project of Augustan panegyric. To Maecenas the elegist offers the first clear instance in his work of *recusatio*.

> bellaque resque tui memorarem Caesaris, et tu
>   Caesare sub magno cura secunda fores.
> nam quotiens Mutinam aut civilia busta Philippos
>   aut canerem Siculae classica bella fugae,
> eversosque focos antiquae gentis Etruscae,
>   et Ptolemaeei litora capta Phari,
> aut canerem Aegyptum et Nilum, cum attractus in urbem
>   septem captivis debilis ibat aquis,
> aut regum auratis circumdata colla catenis,
>   Actiaque in Sacra currere rostra Via,
> te mea Musa illis semper contexeret armis,
>   et sumpta et posita pace fidele caput.   (2.1.25–36)

[If fate had granted me the capacity to do so,] I would commemorate the words and deeds of your Caesar, and you would be my second focus after great Caesar. For whenever I would sing of Mutina or the civil-war graves of Philippi or the naval battles of the Sicilian rout, the overturned hearths of the ancient Etruscan race, and the captive shores of Ptolemaic Pharos; or whenever I would sing of Egypt and the Nile, when, forcibly dragged into the city, it flowed feebly with its seven streams captive; or the necks of kings ringed round with golden chains; and the prows of Actium

---

[24] Stroh (1971).

conveyed along the Sacred Way; my Muse would always weave you into these battle stories—you, a reliable man in taking up as well as putting aside peace.

As in other Augustan *recusationes*, Propertius provides a memorable outline of the panegyrical content he will *not* write about, thereby balancing refusal with (compressed) praise. His refusal, moreover, takes the conventional and polite form of a refusal premised on lack of ability rather than lack of will. In other circumstances, he implies, he would be delighted to write Maecenas' and Augustus' praises. On the other hand, the list of potential laudatory subjects appears problematic: was not Augustus attempting to play down elements of civil war (*civilia busta*), *Roman* enemies, and, above all, divisive episodes such as the siege of Perugia, here described negatively as 'the overturning of the hearths of the ancient Etruscan race'?[25] The minimal form of the list, however, does not allow us to gauge exactly how Propertius envisioned Augustus' role in those conflicts, and just because Horace tows one propagandistic line in his *Odes*, does not mean Propertius is expressing dissent if he displays a different repertoire of topics.[26] There is no single, stable entity 'Augustan ideology' against which we can easily track Propertius' supposed divergence. Nor, however, can we wholly rule out a purposeful botching of the matter on Propertius' part. As in other instances, Propertius appears to have deliberately plotted a precarious path between flattery and dissent. Trying to extract the latent 'truth' of his attitude towards Augustus by reading between the lines of his *recusatio* misses the point.

But if Propertius' autonomist strategy allows him to evade both overt disaffection and unambiguous support for the regime, it also facilitates his connection with Maecenas. For reasons discussed above, 'poetic autonomy' could be a useful tool both from the poet's and patron's perspective; it allows Propertius to display his connection with Maecenas, while remaining within his elegiac realm. He is able to afford the regime a useful connection with his poetry's quasi-subversive glamour and growing cachet—a connection particularly useful in winning over the upper classes[27]—without undermining his elegiac 'brand'[28] by writing

---

[25] Richardson (1997), ad loc.: *focos* is 'a word charged with religious and emotional value'. More generally on this dubious list, see Cairns (2006), 263; Stahl (1985), 165–7.

[26] The comments of Cairns (2006) on the topic of patronage and 'dissent', for example at 265ff., are bracing. I largely agree with his views: Maecenas likely did not demand much in the way of epic poetry, and the poets were not 'implicitly ridiculing' their patrons. The importance of establishing 'artistic integrity' (266) seems a more likely motivation behind the *recusatio* and autonomist rhetoric generally.

[27] See Badian (1985), 354 (cited above).

[28] Cairns (2006), 320ff. But see the impressive counter-arguments of Heyworth (2007b). Note also the remarks of Wallace-Hadrill (1985), who sees the love elegists not as protesting individual laws, but as resisting the morality inherent in the Augustan social order. I agree with Heyworth that, first of all, the recent doctrine of 'indeterminacy' (i.e. there is no such thing as 'Augustan' or 'anti-Augustan' except insofar as we critics construct these categories for our own purposes) is ultimately an evasion of the critic's responsibility; and further, that it is not possible to explain away all instances of 'subversive' comments and positions in Propertian elegy as somehow neutralized by the elaborately paraded unseriousness of the elegiac persona (e.g. note in particular 2.7 on an early attempt at Augustan marriage legislation). I still hold, however, that this more 'subversive' style and tone can be accommodated within my model of autonomist rhetoric. Propertius was in the delicate position of pressing the subversive glamour of elegy as far as he could to maintain his ideological/generic position (the basis of his autonomy), without actually gravely offending Maecenas and Augustus.

panegyric. Autonomy is not freedom, but something more useful in tactical terms: self-determination within one's own sphere.

Propertius does not openly criticize Augustus, or even ignore him, but insists on the specific capacities and parameters of elegiac verse. It would require 'hard verse' (*duro . . . versu*, 41), Propertius protests, to help Augustus 'establish/found his name among his Trojan ancestors' (*Caesaris in Phrygios condere nomen avos*, 42)—an impressively dense encapsulation of the Augustan ideology of foundation that would come to be embodied in the Forum of Augustus and Virgil's *Aeneid*. The name of Caesar (*Caesaris . . . nomen*), is what enables the onomastic link (Ilium/Iulus/Iulius) underpinning the Augustan genealogy of rule. Propertius thus demonstrates, in epigrammatically compressed format, his acute understanding of key themes in the Augustan programme. There may be a hint here that the project of 'founding Caesar's name among his Trojan ancestors' or 'tracing his glory back to his Trojan ancestors'—the very project Virgil was pursuing in his *Aeneid* and which Propertius hails in the closing elegy of Book 2[29]—involves some willful rewriting of history. How does one 'establish/found' something in the past?[30] The difficulty of Propertius' idiom[31] mirrors the conceptual contortions of the project itself.

Yet this criticism remains inchoate—a subliminal impression difficult to confirm or dispel. The relevant point, Propertius insists, is that the development of such Augustan themes would be impossible in his *mollis liber* ('soft/effeminate book').

> nos contra angusto versamus proelia lecto:
>   qua pote quisque, in ea conterat arte diem.[32]   (Prop. 2.1.45–6)

I, on the other hand, conduct battles in the narrow bed; let each spend his time in the sphere of skill where he is competent.

Whereas Propertius previously contemplated the idea of writing the praises of Maecenas and Augustus, he now finally affirms his confinement to his own proper sphere: the Callimachean domain of the narrow bed, where he conducts the battles of love (*versamus proelia*), and writes elegiac verse (*vers-amus*). The syntactic neatness of the pentameter—*qua pote quisque, in ea conterat arte diem* ('let each spend his time in the sphere of skill where he is competent')—mimics the tightness of the fit between occupation and individual capacity, *ars* and the arena of its application.

The *recusatio* emphatically ends here, yet the elegy itself is still far from over. In the following lines, picking up on the question of how one 'spends one's time' (*conterat . . . diem*) in life, Propertius leaps forward to imagine an entire life spent devoted to his love for Cynthia, and the end of such a life: *laus in amore mori; laus*

---

[29] 2.34b.65–6: *cedite Romani scriptores, cedite Grai! / nescio quid maius nascitur Iliade.*

[30] So Auden, famously, in 'Secondary Epic': 'Not even the first of the Romans can learn / His Roman history in the future tense . . . Hindsight as foresight makes no sense' (lines 2–3, 4).

[31] For Richardson (1977), ad loc., the phrase has both present and historical/genealogical implications; for the diversity of possible senses of *condere*, see also Enk (1962), ad loc.

[32] The conjecture *versamus* is adopted in the recent text of Heyworth (2007c). The manuscripts' *versantes* (accus.) would have to be construed, somewhat awkwardly, to mean *sed ego contra narro de iis qui angusto lecto proelia versant* (so Richardson 1977, ad loc.).

altera, si datur uno / posse frui . . . ('It is glory to die in love; glory yet again, if one is allowed to enjoy a single love', 47–8). In the subsequent passage, Propertius further emphasizes his life-long passion for one woman (*una . . . femina*), how his funeral will set forth from her house (55–6). His love is utterly incurable (57–70), and when he dies, he will be reduced to a brief name on a marble slab. Maecenas, passing by on his British chariot, and seeing the lover's grave, is to proclaim: *huic misero fatum dura puella fuit* ('a hard-hearted girl was the fate of this wretched man!' 78).

This apparently abrupt transition to the theme of the poet's death contributes the closing sequence of a highly structured elegy: section I, programmatic introduction (16 lines); section II, *recusatio* (32 lines); section III, the poet-lover's death (32 lines).[33] The significance of this structure goes beyond the merely numerical and formal, however. After the programmatic opening sequence, in which Propertius vividly showcases his *puella*-driven talent, there follow two precisely balanced sections, one devoted to imagining (and finally declining) panegyric for Maecenas and Augustus, and another devoted to imagining the lover's faithful devotion until the end of his life. The prospective scene of the lover's death thus counterbalances the previous section's experiment in Augustan themes. Not only does Propertius' elegiac mistress control his *ingenium* ('literary talent'); he is destined to remain committed to her throughout his entire life, until one day his amatory fate will be summarized with inscriptional fixity.[34] This is another way of stating the permanence and inflexibility of his generic position and literary identity: he cannot bend to other topics and modes, such as panegyric of Augustus, because love is the permanent pattern of his life.[35]

The poet-lover's gravestone is the logical *telos* of a series of reflections on narrow spaces, exclusivity, and death. Maecenas is alive, vigorous, on the way to his next destination, although momentarily stopping to pay tribute to the dead poet. Propertius lies inert, fixed within a narrow compass, as he typically had, in fact, during his life.[36] The scenario of 1.7, wherein Propertius' inertia encounters Tullus' dynamism, recurs here with Maecenas, but now inertia takes the form of death's terminal stasis. Propertius' imagined 'death' thus effects a new and striking disjunction of poet and patron. Earlier in the poem, Propertius addressed Maecenas as the potential object of his encomium, a contemporary figure with whom he enjoyed a social and literary relationship. Now the two figures are ontologically separate: Maecenas is alive, and Propertius is (notionally) dead. Propertius can no longer change to adapt himself or his poetry to Maecenas; their contrasting modes of existence are final and irrevocable. The same circumstance applies to Propertius' poetry. He encourages us to picture him faithfully devoted to his elegiac genre and subject matter to the very end. Even while still

---

[33] Some scholars have sensed abruptness and incongruity in the sudden emergence of the death-theme, but see Heyworth (2007a), ad loc., for defense of the elegy's unity; note also Fedeli (2005), 40.

[34] On the evocation of epitaphic inscription and epigram in this passage, see Keith (2011a), 108–9; note also Ramsby (2007), 79.

[35] Heyworth (2007a), 103. Fedeli (2005), 105, makes the fine observation that the elegy's closing line recalls the notion of Propertius' total dependence on Cynthia articulated in the opening lines, and that line 78 is phonically reminiscent of verse 4 in particular (*ingenium nobis ipsa puella facit*).

[36] For the idea of death as narrowing and/or confining, compare Hor. *Carm.* 1.28.1–6.

alive and writing, the elegist manages to be 'entombed' within elegy's exiguous grave (or narrow bed), and his literary identity takes on the fixity of an inscription on stone.

This fixity is illusory, as Propertius doubtless knew,[37] but it effectively functions as a counterweight to the implied pressure to bend to the demands of Augustan panegyric in the present context. Again, the likely unanswerable question of whether or not Maecenas actually tried to commission panegyrical works from Propertius is not my central concern. Rather I am calling attention to how Propertius carefully balances the appearance of a demand for panegyric against the appearance of immoveable generic fixity. Also notable is the increased prominence of the death theme in 2.1 by comparison with the opening elegy of Book 1. Unfortunately, a precise comparison is impossible because of the obviously troubled textual transmission of the elegies that come down to us as Book 2. Several leading scholars have argued that these elegies in fact comprise two different books, 2a and 2b.[38] However this may be, the transition from Book 1 to Propertius' subsequent book(s) is accompanied by a notable expansion of the presence of death within the elegist's oeuvre in the form of complicated and impressive fantasies of burial, lamentation, and memorial. At the same time, the mythological component of elegy is amplified. The analogical presence of the dead yet deathless characters of myth reminds us that the two lovers are in the process of becoming literature, that they will survive after their death as paired *nomina* on a stone epitaph or in a papyrus text. Contemporary readers are encouraged to prospectively imagine the conversion of the living Propertius and Cynthia into a literary work received by posterity, while posthumous readers find their own perspective anticipated with an uncanny prescience.

Death is always potentially an occasion for publicity and the public advertisement of identity, accomplishment, and social status in Rome:[39] thus death-fantasies facilitate the transition to an increased public and monumental dimension in elegiac poetry. The crucial elegy for understanding this dynamic is 2.13,[40] where the rites of commemoration offered to the poet after his death converge with his

---

[37] A very different version of elegiac poetics might be seen embodied in the statue of Vertumnus, god of change, celebrated in 4.2.

[38] See in particular the arguments of Heyworth (1992), (1995) and (2007c), lxiii–lxiv; Butrica (1996); Lyne (1998a); and, with a very helpful summary and synthesis of the various positions taken, Fedeli (2005), 21–35. But note also the opposition offered by Keith (2008), 181 n. 138, and Tarrant (2006), 55–7. Fedeli, in any case, suggests that 2a and 2b may have been published around the same time: in that case, it would be valid to view them as belonging to roughly the same phase in Propertius' conception of elegy.

[39] See Flower (1996) and (2006) for exploration of both the Roman culture of commemoration and its complementary inversion—the *damnatio memoriae*.

[40] The unity of this poem has been defended by Enk (1956), Wilkinson (1966b), and Heyworth (1992), among others. If Heyworth (1992), 48, is correct, 2.13 merits special attention as the first poem of Propertius' third book (i.e. the putative Book 2b). Other scholars have put forward 2.10 or 2.12 as candidate for opening elegy of Book 2b. Fedeli (2005), 27–31, argues with some plausibility for 2.11 as the closing elegy of 2a and 2.12 as the opening elegy of 2b. Fedeli further argues against the unity of 2.13, reasoning that melancholy evocation of the poet's own death is unlikely to follow the rousing claim that, if Cynthia makes peace with him, he can stand up to even Jove's opposition. His argument does give pause, but I am inclined to think that Propertius (or his amatory persona) is often capable of such vacillation and rapid shifts in mood even within the same elegy (see comments below).

identity as elegiac lover and the books of poetry in which that identity was fashioned.

> quandocumque igitur nostros mors claudet ocellos
>   accipe quae serves funeris acta mei.
> nec mea tunc longa spatietur imagine pompa,
>   nec tuba sit fati vana querela mei;
> nec mihi tunc fulcro sternatur lectus eburno,
>   nec sit in Attalico mors mea nixa toro.
> desit odoriferis ordo mihi lancibus, adsint
>   plebei parvae funeris exsequiae.
> sat mea sat magna est, si tres sint pompa libelli,
>   quos ego Persephonae maxima dona feram.
> tu vero nudum pectus lacerata sequeris,
>   nec fueris nomen lassa vocare meum,
> osculaque in gelidis pones suprema labellis,
>   cum dabitur Syrio munere plenus onyx.
> deinde, ubi suppositus cinerem me fecerit ardor,
>   accipiat Manis parvula testa meos,
> et sit in exiguo laurus super addita busto,
>   quae tegat exstincti funeris umbra locum,
> et duo sint versus: 'qui nunc iacet horrida pulvis,
>   unius hic quondam servus amoris erat.'

Therefore listen to these rites to observe at my funeral whenever death shall close my eyes. On that day let my cortège not go forth with a long line of ancestral masks;[41] nor let a trumpet be the vain lament of my death; on that day let no bier be spread for me with ivory post, nor let my corpse be propped on a couch of Attalian gold cloth. Be absent a line of fragrant dishes; let the humble rites of a common funeral be present. Enough, grand enough is my procession, should it be three little books for me to give Persephone as the greatest gift I can offer. But you shall follow, your breast bare and torn, and not weary of calling out my name, and place last kisses on my chill lips when the onyx full of Syrian unguent is given. Then, when the fire beneath has made me ash, let a small urn receive my shade, and let a laurel be placed over the tiny tomb to cover the site of the burnt-out pyre with its shade, and let two verses be inscribed: 'Who now lies here, a handful of gruesome dust, was once the slave of one love' (2.13.17–36).

Death will close Propertius' eyes, the *ocelli* linked with erotic experience from the opening line of Book 1. Propertius stipulates that, when this happens, the same 'learned girlfriend' designated in line 11 as his ideal reader is to carry out the rites of his funeral. She is not to bury him in the grand style (19–22); instead, he is to have a common funeral (*plebei parvae funeris exsequiae*, 24). Appropriately enough, the rites conducted by Cynthia will feature only three little books in the funeral train. In other words, his memorial after death will consist in his books written in the Callimachean style. She is not to tire of calling out his name—a traditional element of the funeral rite, but one which neatly coincides with the perpetual endurance of the poet's *nomen* (name/fame) through his work. The following lines (31–6) enact a radical trajectory of reduction: fire will reduce the lover to ash; the ash will be confined in turn by a small jar; the burial site itself

---

[41] Richardson (1977), ad loc., suggests 'with lengthly show', but he also concedes that there is a glance at the *imagines*, or ancestral portrait-masks.

will be removed from prominence by a laurel's shade; and two verses will be inscribed to encapsulate the lover's entire life. The epitaph in its own way emphasizes the passage's effect of diminution. Its opening phrase—'Who now lies here as gruesome dust...' (*qui nunc iacet horrida pulvis...*)—leads the reader to expect an inversion at the close, that is, something along the lines of 'was once a great poet'. Instead, the epitaph boasts that the handful of dust here buried was once...a slave. Propertius' narrow, Callimachean genre produces a small funeral, which corresponds, in turn, to a circumscribed social status signified by plebeian rites, and finally, the epitaph of the loyal slave. This game of reduction is further emphasized by an implicit path of descending numerals: three books (*tres... libelli*), two verses (*duo... versus*), one love (*unius... amoris*).[42]

Death, Callimachean narrowness, and the lover's attenuated existence converge in the dense imagery of Propertian metapoetics. The transition made, both here and in 2.1, from Callimachean imagery to an imagined scene of death is not arbitrary. Propertian death is Callimachean, not only because he writes in a small genre, but also because it represents the ultimate reduction and encapsulation: the reduction of the poet to his books.[43] This account, however, glosses over an apparent paradox: Propertius' funeral-poem is not unproblematically Callimachean.[44] The elegy's opening at first seems poised to inject into elegy a new poetic grandeur. Love, armed with more arrows than Persia's capital city, has ordered him to scorn 'delicate Muses' (*gracilis... Musas*, 3). He will wield an Orphic power to astonish (*ut... stupefiat*, 7), however, not over trees or wild beasts, but over his Cynthia. In the funeral description, his three little books will nonetheless constitute a considerable gift (*maxima dona*) for Persephone. The fame of the lover, moreover, will rival that of Achilles: 'nor will the fame of our tomb be less widespread, than the blood-stained burial mound of the Phthian hero' (*nec minus haec nostri notescet fama sepulcri, / quam fuerant Pthii busta cruenta viri*, 37–8).[45] Finally, the description of the funeral (or rather, the richness of the description of what is *not* there) is at odds, as Papanghelis notes, with the ostensible message of simplicity.[46] The account of the common rites is packed with the polyphony, mélange of tastes and odors, and trappings of aristocratic glamour they ostensibly lack. This funerary pomposity is not necessarily inappropriate. Propertius has grand

---

[42] Another reason why perhaps too much has been made of the *tres libelli* as evidence that Book 2 represents two separate books; for other reasons, Richardson (1977), ad loc.; but see Heyworth (1992), 55; for Tarrant (2006), 56, it must remain a mystery. As noted by Heyworth (1992), 47, there is further play with reduction in the fact that 'the epitaph, which... wins his tomb more fame than the *Iliad* did for that of Achilles, is even shorter than the couplet allocated to it'.

[43] Perhaps here is the implicit connection between the opening sixteen lines of 2.13 and the rest that Fedeli (2005), 363, finds missing.

[44] Papanghelis (1987), 54.

[45] The choice of Achilles is significant: Achilles is the epic hero who was most absorbed in the project of his posthumous renown, and who arguably achieved the greatest *kleos* (Nagy 1979). For any Homeric hero, death is the privileged site of *kleos*: funeral rites, games, and the tomb are markers of the hero's fame, and the underworld a place to meditate on one's own and one's descendants' glory. This applies especially to Achilles, who chose to die early for the sake of his *kleos*, and who appears in the Odyssean underworld rejoicing in his son's deeds. Propertius' rivalry with the 'blood-stained burial mound' of Achilles is thus precisely targeted: he claims to outdo, in his own elegiac funeral and *nomen*, the very emblem of posthumous fame in the epic tradition.

[46] Papanghelis (1987), 55: a 'voluptuously lugubrious set piece'.

ambitions for his slight genre, and throughout Book 2 makes a point of elevating his ostensibly frivolous subject matter to the level of Homeric epic.

Other elegies belonging to our 'Book 2' show a similar interest in the manipulation of scale and the contradictions of elegiac grandiosity.[47] 2.14–15 in particular explore the intersections between elegiac 'triumph' and epic victory. There is continual alternation between self-aggrandizement and diminution, supreme self-confidence and morbid abjection. In 2.10, Propertius tries out some metapoetic themes inherited from Virgil's *Eclogues* and Gallan elegy along with the distinctive tropes and topography of Helicon: he exhorts his spirit to rise up and write a work of loftier ambition (11–12), and briefly runs through Augustan ambitions to humble Parthia, India, and Arabia (13–18). In the end, however, this panegyrical project turns out to be prospective rather than immediate: *haec ego castra sequar; vates tua castra canendo / magnus ero: servent hunc mihi fata diem* ('these camps I shall follow; by singing your camps I shall become a great bard: may destiny reserve for me this day', 19–20). For now, presumably, Propertius still 'follows the camps' of love, remaining at the foot of Helicon, whereas Virgil's Gallus had risen higher up the mountain (*Ecl.* 6.64–6): *nondum etiam Ascraeos norunt mea carmina fontes, / sed modo Permessi flumine lavit Amor* ('not yet do my songs know the springs of Ascra, but Love has now[48] washed them in the stream of the Permessus', 25–6). Propertius is pressing at the restrictive bounds of (without fully abandoning) amatory verse.[49] There are even signs that he is moving beyond Cynthia-driven elegy. The first four elegies of Book 2, for all that they speak of love and the *puella*, do not name Cynthia—a striking omission, given her emblematic position at the beginning of Book 1. Ovid usually gets the credit for irreverently dismantling the elegiac fiction by failing to name his mistress in the four opening elegies of his first book of *Amores*, but the opening sequence of Propertius 2(a) surely anticipates him.

The themes of death, epitaphic permanence, mythology, and epic grandeur together work to redefine elegiac autonomy in ways that press beyond the restrictive boundaries of the lover's personal perspective. Elegy is increasingly viewed as a substantial literary work that endures over time, maintains its generic identity among posthumous readers, and enjoys public prominence. We can discern the beginnings of a transition from the model of 'useful' courtship poetry to the enduring literary monument. A helpful place to begin considering Propertius' interest in literary monumentality is his elegiac appreciation of a major architectural monument, the temple and portico complex of Palatine Apollo dedicated by Octavian in 28 BC, followed by an elegy that includes ecphrastic description of Pompey's theatre and portico complex. 2.31–2 are not divided in the MSS,[50] but have sometimes been viewed as two separate, if complementary,

---

[47] Tarrant (2006), 57, points out that, if Book 2 as we have it represents a unitary book of more than 1350 lines, then the opening jokes in 2.1 about 'superabundant composition' are wittily 'literalized'.

[48] On the temporal sense of *modo*, see Fedeli (2005), 332.

[49] See Heyworth (1992), 52. Again, if Heyworth is correct in some of his hypotheses, 2.10 represents the final elegy of Book 2(a), and as such has special programmatic significance.

[50] One among several cases in Propertius where it is difficult to decide whether we are looking at one elegy or two. Williams (1980) 138–9, and Hubbard (1984) make arguments for unity. Heyworth (2007a), 246, accepts the continuity, but expresses scepticism that the entirety of the lines ascribed to 2.32 belong to this same elegy, especially after line 18. See also Welch (2005), 94. Fedeli (2005), ad loc., considers them separate elegies. As Fedeli points out, even those who defend a unitary elegy usually

elegies by modern scholars. Propertius begins 2.31 by excusing his lateness to his mistress on the grounds that he was visiting the recently opened 'golden portico of Phoebus' and admiring its works of art, including (apparently) two statues of Apollo (2.31.6,16).[51] The following elegy concerns the poet's anxieties regarding Cynthia: he cannot let her out in public because 'he who sees [her], sins' (*qui videt, is peccat* 2.32.1); he has heard nasty rumours about her (2.31.23–4); he is afraid to let her travel to such places as Aricia and the precinct of Diana Nemorensis (2.32.8–10). Midway through the elegy, however, Propertius turns to defending her: bad reputation has always been the penalty for beauty (2.32.26); small failings do not worry him (2.32.30); in Rome of the present day antique moral severity is not to be expected (2.32.47–8).

While 2.32 itself may seem meandering in its focus, a series of connected ideas, as often in Propertius, underlies the apparently disjointed series of conceits. He returns to issues of publicity, reputation in the city, visibility, exclusivity of possession. These are precisely the concerns (and recurrent ambivalence) associated with literary publication in ancient Rome.[52] Cynthia is the unofficial title of Propertius' first book, his prime *materia*, and reliably a stand-in for his poetic text.[53] It is thus not surprising that Propertius, in defending Cynthia's lack of perfect virtue, appeals to his predecessor's literary mistress (and text): *haec eadem ante illam iam impune et Lesbia fecit; / quae sequitur, certe est invidiosa minus* ('Lesbia has already done these same things before her with impunity; she who follows surely is less subject to opprobrium', 45–6). If 31–2 is a continuous elegy, the wish expressed by Propertius at 2.32.7–8 that Cynthia might spend some time in the newly dedicated Palatine complex (*hoc utinam spatiere loco, quodcumque vacabis, / Cynthia*)[54] would appear to be hinting at the potential presence of *Cynthia*, his first book of elegies, in the public libraries that formed part of the Danaid Portico. Her presence there would be all the more appropriate for the fact that her name derives, in the first place, from the cult title 'Cynthian' Apollo. But if, as I am inclined to think, 2.31 and 2.32 form a pendant-piece composed of two separate elegies, a similar set of concerns still applies. In both elegies, Propertius attests to his own (but *not* Cynthia's) presence in a key Augustan monument: in one case, a temple complex built by Augustus, and in another case, a theatre complex programmatically

need to suppose transpositions of verses (887); otherwise the transition would be excessively abrupt and confusing. He further argues that *hoc . . . loco* need not refer to the portico of the Temple of Apollo, but could simply mean *hic*, i.e. in Rome as opposed to other places. With some hesitation, I follow Fedeli in seeing two elegies here rather than one, and am intrigued by the suggestion of Kuttner (1999, 354ff.) that together they form an ecphrastic 'pendant-piece' devoted to the Palatine Apollo complex and Pompey's Portico respectively.

[51] Butler and Barber (1964) prefer only one statue and two poems. The more recent commentary of Richardson (1977), 301, champions the unity of this 'brilliant and difficult' elegy. See also Welch (2005), 89–96; Barchiesi (2005).

[52] The readings of Williams (1980) and Hubbard (1984) focus especially on sight and visibility. For a discussion of erotic possession as a figure for the 'anxieties of publication', see Fitzgerald (1995), 44–52; on publication as prostitution and as violation of exclusivity, see Horace *Epist.* 1.20, and Myers (1996), 16–17, 21.

[53] Wyke (1987a).

[54] Again, this would assume the transposition of the couplet 2.32.7–8 so that it follows immediately after 2.31.15: Richardson (1977), ad loc.; Heyworth (2007a), 246.

restored by him. Both monuments are associated with literary culture: the Palatine Apollo complex features libraries and an emphatically poetic Apollo, while Pompey's theatre complex, beyond its obvious association with drama, included statue groups of the Muses and female poets.[55]

Propertius goes out of his way in these paired elegies to make us think about the relation between books and monuments, poets and the Augustan city. But while the Temple of Palatine Apollo would seem to be a natural magnet for Augustan poets,[56] it is far from clear that Cynthia/*Cynthia* will 'spend time' either in Pompey's restored portico or in Augustus' splendid new Danaid Portico. To the poet's exasperation, she prefers to visit cult sites outside Rome, where he cannot keep her under surveillance. In the closing couplet of 2.32, he makes one of several punning links in Book 2 between the published book-scroll (*liber*) and the 'freedom' of promiscuous sexual behaviour (*lĭber*): *quod si tu Graias, si tu es imitata Latinas, / semper vive meo* <u>*libera*</u> *iudicio* ('but if you have imitated Greek and Roman women, then live forever <u>free</u> in my judgment', 2.32.61–2, text based on Heyworth 2007c). Two of the same elegy's exemplary mythic figures, Minos and Acrisius, failed to control their women. Propertius cannot control his lover, or, by extension, his literary work. This failure to control, however, is ultimately useful in autonomist terms. For all that Augustus' monuments, new and restored, extend his authority over cultural and literary matters, the poet's literary creation remains stubbornly independent, her integration within the new cultural order uncertain.[57]

If 2.31 and 2.32 hint at issues of publication, publicity, and Propertius' place in the new library and Augustan literary/social order, 2.34 focuses specifically on the elegist's place in the Greek and Roman tradition and contemporary literary scene. 2.34, the last poem in the book,[58] begins with a scenario reminiscent of 2.31. Propertius reproves his treacherous friend Lynceus for touching (*tangere*) his beloved (*meam . . . curam*, 9–10), a transgression whose literary dimensions are in no way concealed. As in comparable elegies in Book 1, the now erotically obsessed Lynceus (who may or may not be Propertius' contemporary Varius Rufus[59]), will have to take up love elegy, abandoning the poetry of natural science and tragedy (27–42). The paradoxical relation between exclusivity and wider exposure is at work here too. Other men's desire for Cynthia is a necessary corollary of her rare beauty and value. Similarly, Propertius' elegiac work

---

[55] See Kuttner (1999), 354 and *passim*; on statuary, note also Evans (2009).

[56] And possible setting for poetic recitations: Fantham (1996), 88–9; Hor. *Epist.* 2.2.92ff.

[57] It is illuminating to compare Ovid's persistent, and presumably politically significant, displacement of Apollo's aesthetic authority, e.g. at the beginning of the *Amores* and the *Ars amatoria*: R. Armstrong (2004). Cairns (2006), 341, characterizes 2.31 as 'an *ekphrasis* of the temple and its statuary which is pure eulogy of Augustus from start to finish'. This is a good corrective, but it is equally possible to interpret the elegy as an elaborately distracting excuse offered for Propertius' lateness and a cover for possible infidelities of his own (P. has 'turned the tables': Heyworth 2007a, 246). In 1.3, lateness has a similar implication, and the evidently close familiarity with Pompey's portico displayed in 2.32 should arouse suspicion (compare Catullus c. 55). Note also Heyworth (2007a), 246, on the 'cheeky' ambiguity of *falleris* at 2.32.17.

[58] Debates have arisen over this poem's unity as well: but see the comments of Fedeli (2005), 950ff., in favour of its unity.

[59] The identification was suggested in an article by Boucher (1958); but see Heyworth (2007a), 264–5, for discussion and further bibliography. Fedeli (2005), 951–2, is doubtful, but ultimately agnostic.

establishes itself as rare and exclusive in order to be admired by readers, who, in taking possession of the work, undermine its exclusivity.

The elegy goes on to give further precision to this emerging public value placed on Cynthia and elegy by setting Propertius' work in the context of Roman poetic genres and traditions. Elegiac verse, as Lynceus will come to appreciate, has its own distinctive power, and the elegiac poet enjoys a form of prestige independent of wealth and political achievement.

> aspice me, cui parva domi fortuna relicta est
>   nullus et antiquo Marte triumphus avi,
> ut regnem mixtas inter conviva puellas
>   hoc ego, quo tibi nunc elevor, ingenio!   (2.34.55–8)

Look at me (for whom there was left at home but a small fortune, and no triumph for an ancestor's age-old victory in war), see how I reign as banqueter among a crowd of girls on account of this literary talent for which you now make light of me!

Propertius remains committed to this amatory poetic realm, where he reigns supreme (*ut regnem*), yet, in the following passage, honours Virgil, who has written about Actium, Caesar, and Aeneas (61–4), and whose *Aeneid* even promises to surpass the *Iliad* (65–6). Propertius then goes on to honour Virgil's *Eclogues*, viewing his pastoral poetry from a distinctly amatory perspective (67–76), and finally, his *Georgics* (77–80). Despite this striking achievement, Propertius nevertheless insists that his amatory verse will please readers, and, employing Virgil's own simile (*Ecl.* 9.36), compares himself to the tuneful swan who, though his poetic output be slight, is superior to the inerudite yet loud goose. The book's closing lines install Propertius in the number of successful amatory poets alongside Varro of Atax, Catullus, Calvus, and Gallus: 'truly, Cynthia, praised in the poetry of Propertius, shall live, if Fame wishes to set me among these [poets]' (*Cynthia quin vivet*[60] *versu laudata Properti / hos inter si me ponere Fama volet*, 93–4).[61]

Propertius' use of the language of generic canonization and classification (*inter . . . ponere*) suggests the physical setting of the libraries in the temple of Apollo Palatinus celebrated earlier in the collection: his elegiac poetry will be classed with previous Roman love poets. 2.34 thus affords a fitting conclusion to a book that defines Propertian autonomy in terms of the space of literary genre and elegy's now more expansive scope and public prominence in the city.

---

[60] Reading [viv]et (instead of et[iam]) with Barber (1960) and Goold (1990).

[61] Compare Hor. *Carm.*1.1.35, *quod si me lyricis vatibus inseres*. Propertian elegy, the culmination of the Roman tradition of erotic poetry, presumably stands opposite Philetas and Callimachus in the new library: *tu satius memorem Musis imitere Philitan / et non inflati somnia Callimachi* ('better that you should imitate with your Muses the unforgetting Philetas and the Dream of unpretentious Callimachus', 2.34.31–2). This generic niche defines Propertius' elegiac poetry for the remainder of his career: at the opening of Book 3, Propertius asks the shades of Callimachus and Philetas to allow him to enter their grove (*nemus*); in 3.9, he will be satisfied if he has sung in Philetas' metre (*cecinisse modis, Coe poeta, tuis*, 44) and found favour 'among the books of Callimachus' (*inter Callimachi sat erit placuisse libellos*, 43); finally, in 4.1, Propertius asks Bacchus to give him leaves of ivy so that Umbria will swell with pride at his books, Umbria, the fatherland of Rome's Callimachus (*Umbria Romani patria Callimachi*, 64). On the language of classification and the new library, Horsfall (1993), 61. The mention of the now dead Gallus adds a further, interesting twist to Propertius' refusal to follow the encomiastic pattern of Virgil.

Whereas in his first book Propertius focused on his restrictive, love-obsessed life-path, he now delineates his arena of endeavour with explicit reference to aesthetic models (Callimachus, Philetas), generically defined content (*amor, puella*), and enduring posthumous reputation. His work has earned a place both in a literary tradition and in the public library on Augustus' newly transformed Palatine. By the end of the second book, elegy has become a publicly recognized field of literary accomplishment, and no longer relies, except in occasional nominal gestures, on the fiction of amatory utility. This fiction, of course, continues intermittently to be evoked as symbol of elegy's generic identity, but increasingly is displaced by concepts of the elegiac oeuvre as enduring monument and contribution to Augustan literary culture. Elegy's autonomist rhetoric has been adapted to suit a more public prominence for literary activity in Augustus' city.

Propertius' third book represents a further decisive stage in this development. The opening elegy of the book picks up where 2.34 left off.

> Callimachi Manes et Coi sacra Philitae,
>> in vestrum, quaeso, me sinite ire nemus.
> primus ego ingredior puro de fonte sacerdos
>> Itala per Graios orgia ferre choros.
> dicite, quo pariter carmen tenuastis in antro,
>> quove pede ingressi? quamve bibistis aquam? (3.1.1–6)

Shades of Callimachus and rites of Coan Philitas, allow me, I pray, to enter into your grove. I am the first priest to begin bearing, from the pure spring, Italian sacraments to the accompaniment of Greek music.[62] Tell, in what cave did you finely spin your song together? With what foot did you enter? What water did you drink?

Propertius heaps on the Callimachean imagery in this and subsequent elegies of Book 2: there will be no lack of groves, caves, grottoes, springs, rivers, sacerdotal trappings, Muses, dreams, Apollo. Still, even amid this 'cluttered' heap of 'poetic symbols', a few patterns clearly emerge.[63] First, Propertius now formally claims the classificatory niche of refined, Callimachean elegy intimated in the closing lines of Book 2: he wishes to be shelved among Roman elegiac love poets across from the Greek poets Callimachus and Philetas in the Palatine library.[64] Second, he now begins to articulate elegiac autonomy in terms of a sequestered poetic realm named as such: *in vestrum . . . me sinite ire nemus* ('allow me to enter into your grove'). Whereas in Book 1, the poet-lover occupied the confined world of his erotic obsession, now Propertius delineates his autonomist poetic domain through explicit spatial metaphors of grove (*nemus)*, cave (*antrum*), and circuit (*praescriptos . . . gyros*, 3.3.21). In other words, he redescribes his poetic domain from an external perspective as visibly demarcated space as opposed to illustrating his condition of erotic confinement from within the lover's tormented psyche. The role of elegiac poet accrues defined, public status in social and literary terms. In this and other respects, Propertius betrays the influence of Horace *Odes* 1–3 (published 23 BC), a collection that opens with the poet sequestered in his

---

[62] So Heyworth and Morwood (2011), ad loc.   [63] Hollis (2006), 112.

[64] Assuming that Horsfall (1993) is correct in picturing corresponding shelves and sections for the Greek and Roman libraries.

nemus surrounded by lyric instruments and Muses, and culminates with Horace's assumption of the role of *Musarum sacerdos* ('priest of the Muses', 3.1) and architect of a 'monument more enduring than bronze' (3.30.1).[65]

This more expansive poetic project is not easily compatible with the primacy of Cynthia and the chains of erotic *servitium*. The elegist now announces his literary 'triumph':

> ah valeat Phoebum quicumque moratur in armis!
>   exactus tenui pumice versus eat,
> quo me Fama levat terra sublimis, et a me
>   nata coronatis Musa triumphat equis,
> et mecum in curru parvi vectantur Amores,
>   scriptorumque meas turba secuta rotas (3.1.7–12).

Ah farewell to the one who detains Phoebus in warfare! Let the verse run smoothly, finished with fine pumice, the verse whereby lofty Fame raises me from the earth, and the Muse born of me triumphs with garlanded horses, and with me in the chariot little Loves are conveyed, and a crowd of writers follows after my wheels.

Propertius, accompanied by little 'Loves' and a crowd of writers, leads the triumphal procession. The power, authority, and autonomy of elegiac poetry are overtly on display, as amatory experience and its familiar humiliations fade to the background. At the same time, the public dimension of the poet's role and work are more explicitly figured. The triumph was traditionally the most coveted prestige-conferring ceremony of the Roman state.[66] Propertius still insists, of course, on the specific markers of elegy as opposed to epic or panegyric: he will not add praises to the annals of Rome (15–16), he has written a 'work to be read in a time of peace' (17), and demands elegiacally 'soft' (*mollia*) garlands for his poet's head (19–20). Yet he now appeals, not only to the parochial conventions of elegy, but more broadly to the distinctive power of literature, its capacity to withstand the passage of time and confer reputation and memorial (21–36).

Whereas mention of death in Books 1–2 typically confirmed the lover's perpetual *fides*, death now overtly signifies literary posterity. In an aesthetic system that privileges posthumous fame over immediate utility, the poet's death can only magnify his prestige.

> at mihi quod vivo detraxerit invida turba,
>   post obitum duplici faenore reddet Honos;
> omnia post obitum fingit maiora vetustas:
>   maius ab exsequiis nomen in ora venit.   (3.1.21–4)

But Esteem will pay back with double interest after my death what the envious mob takes from me while alive. The passage of time makes all things greater after death; after the funeral a name sounds greater on men's lips.

Orthodox Callimacheanism[67] is combined with a very Roman financial metaphor. Line 22 aligns aesthetic success with the afterlife: the poetic work is an investment

---

[65] See Nethercut (1970), for whom, however, Propertius does not simply reproduce the Horatian guise of *Musarum sacerdos*, instead taking on the role of 'ironic priest'; note also Solmsen (1948).

[66] Galinsky (1969). Significantly, the triumph ceremony was in the process being phased out in this period, with the exception of members of the imperial family.

[67] See Heyworth and Morwood (2011), ad loc., on the phrase *invida turba*.

that will be repaid with interest. The notion of profit ordinarily applies to immediate projects, whereas the paradox of posthumous gain distinguishes the anti-intuitive utility of the literary text.[68] Propertius' poetic logic constructs the elegiac work as a short-term liability for its living author precisely in order to isolate and maximize its posthumous value.

Just as posterity and the posthumous offer a different perspective on what is truly 'valuable',[69] literary immortality qualifies the splendor of physical monuments.

> quod non Taenariis domus est mihi fulta columnis,
>   nec camera auratas inter eburna trabes,
> nec mea Phaeacas aequant pomaria silvas,
>   non operosa rigat Marcius antra liquor;
> at Musae comites et carmina cara legenti,
>   nec defessa choris Calliopea meis.
> fortunata, meo si qua es celebrata libello!
>   carmina erunt formae tot monumenta tuae.
> nam neque pyramidum sumptus ad sidera ducti,
>   nec Iovis Elei caelum imitata domus,
> nec Mausolei dives fortuna sepulcris
>   mortis ab extrema condicione vacant.
> aut illis flamma aut imber subducet honores,
>   annorum aut tacito pondere victa ruent.
> at non ingenio quaesitum nomen ab aevo
>   excidet: ingenio stat sine morte decus.   (3.2.11–26, text based on Goold 1990)

If my house is not propped on columns of Taenarian marble, and my vaulted ceiling is not made of ivory alternating with gilded beams, and if I do not have fruit-orchards matching those of Phaeacia or artificial grottoes irrigated by the Marcian aqueduct; yet the Muses are my companions, my poems are dear to the reader, and Calliope is not weary of dancing to my songs. Fortunate woman, whoever has been praised in my book! My poems will be so many monuments to your beauty. For neither the costly structures of the pyramids built up to the stars, nor the temple of Jove at Elis that imitates the heavens, nor the rich splendor of the tomb of Mausolus are exempt from the final state of death. Either flame or rain will undermine their glory, or they will fall to ruin, overcome by the weight of silently passing years. But the renown won by literary talent shall not perish with time: talent enjoys a glory that does not die.

Propertius opposes materialistic and literary value on the plane of personal status (the poor poet vs the wealthy villa-owner) and monumental work (literary immortality vs physical structure). The luxurious structures described (or rather disavowed) in lines 11–14 are not without artifice: the expensive house is 'propped' on Taenarian marble columns, its beams are 'gilded', the fruit-trees emulate (*aequant*) the orchards of the Homeric Alcinous, and the grotto, fed by the Marcian aqueduct, is laboriously constructed (*operosa*).[70] Yet all these marvellously designed things, like the monuments described in 19–21, will perish.

---

[68] The fiction of utility has received close scholarly analysis: Stroh (1971); but see Wyke (1987a), 52, for problems with a straightforward understanding of elegy's utility.

[69] On this new interest, Fedeli's (1985) introductory remarks on Book 3.

[70] As Nethercut (1970), 387, observes, this adjective was recently used by Horace at a programmatic moment (*operosiores*, *Carm.* 3.1.48).

Only the poet's monuments to his mistress' beauty (*formae . . . monumenta*), the products of his literary talent (*ingenium*), will evade the mortal condition.

The programmatic concepts worked out in the book's opening sequence continue to inform elegies throughout Book 3. In 3.7, Propertius mourns the loss of his friend Paetus, who, drowned at sea in pursuit of riches, has only the sea as his tomb (9–12). The fate of Paetus describes the inverse of the elegiac poetics of immortality. Whereas the merchant in search of wealth wins short-term gain at the risk of an enduring loss, the poet lives an attenuated existence in order to expand his posthumous *nomen* (name/renown). In the closing couplet of the elegy, Propertius offers a snapshot of the lover's cautious inertia by contrast with the far-ranging Paetus: 'I must remain fixed before the doorway of my mistress' (*ante fores dominae condar oportet iners*, 72). The verb *condar*, which covers a range of possible meanings including burial,[71] alludes to Paetus' lack of burial. The lover will remain buried at the mistress' door indefinitely, frozen in his signature pose of inertia and exclusion, or in metapoetic terms, entombed in the enduring elegiac work. But so also will Paetus. The elegy, in which Paetus' name occurs seven times, constitutes the memorial Paetus would otherwise lack.

Even while intensifying his ethical investment in the poet's role and isolating the unique value of poetry, Propertius sharpens the contrast between *amor* and *arma*, elegiac poetry and martial panegyric. After dismissing martial themes in the book's opening elegy (3.1.7, 15–20), he nonetheless appears to be on the verge of composing an Ennian epic on early Roman legendary history, when Phoebus Apollo interrupts him and warns him to remain within the bounds of his talent (3.3.15–24). He then leads Propertius to the grotto of the Muses, where each of the nine maidens exercises her gifts within her allotted realm (*diversaeque novem sortitae iura puellae*, 3.3.33). Calliope then makes a speech in favour of Propertius' continuing commitment to his elegiac subject matter (3.3.39–50). As the poem ends, she moistens Propertius' lips with water from the spring from which Philetas once drank (51–2). The following two elegies, 3.4 and 3.5, develop and expand this theme, demarcating two contiguous yet opposing realms through their systematically contrasting opening words: *arma deus Caesar* (3.4.1, 'The god Caesar . . . arms'); *pacis Amor deus* (3.5.1, 'Love the god of peace . . .'). The realms of war and peace each have their own god, Caesar and Amor respectively. In 3.4, Propertius anticipates Augustus' prospective victories over India and Parthia, but will content himself with cheering from the sideline while leaning on his girlfriend's bosom (3.4.15).

Propertius is thus doubly removed, both temporally and spatially, from martial panegyric: the victories have not yet occurred, and should they take place, Propertius will remain in his *puella*-centred domain. In the following elegy, Propertius proclaims his poet's *paupertas* (3.5.3–6), hails death as the great leveler of wealth, power, and military supremacy (3.5.7–18), reaffirms the value of his poetic vocation (19–21), and anticipates that, in his old age, he may write poetry on themes of natural philosophy. In a somewhat different way, then, Propertius announces his life-long resistance to martial panegyric and epic. Even if, at some point, he should cease to write love poetry (which seems increasingly likely,

---

[71] Fedeli (1985) and Richardson (1977), ad loc.

given Propertius' persistent hinting at new poetic interests), he will still not write about war. The ending is sharply phrased almost to the point of sarcasm: *exitus hic vitae superest mihi: vos quibus arma / grata magis, Crassi signa referte domum* ('this is the end of life awaiting me; you, who take more pleasure in warfare, bring Crassus' standards back home', 47–8).[72]

Propertius' autonomist demarcation of his elegiac domain of *amor*, *pax*, and poetry has become highly explicit and insistent. Caesar is a god who inhabits his own separate realm, while Propertius exercises his talents in the love-domain ruled by the god Amor. In 3.9, the first and only elegy of the book addressed to Maecenas, Propertius at first seems simply to uphold this division of spheres. Employing the same metaphor as Apollo in 3.3, he asks Maecenas why he seeks to launch Propertius' little boat on a vast ocean of writing (*quid me scribendi tam vastum mittis in aequor?* 3.9.3). In making his argument, Propertius ingeniously refers to Maecenas' own choice to remain an *eques* rather than seek political office. If Maecenas is determined to 'remain within the bounds of his station' (3.9.2), to 'withdraw himself humbly into the tenuous shadows' (*tenuis . . . umbras*, 29), and to 'furl the full canvas of his sails' (30), then Propertius is surely justified in following his patron's example by remaining within the confines of his elegiac genre. Yet although he initially reiterates his refusal of epic or otherwise non-elegiac subject matter (35–46), Propertius goes on to suggest that, if Maecenas leads the way (*te duce*, 47), he *will* sing such themes as gigantomachy, Romulus and Remus, the humbling of the Parthians, and the suicide of Antony (47–56). He asks for his patron's encouragement, and gives Maecenas credit for his own glory as poet and for his affiliation with him: *hoc mihi, Maecenas, laudis concedis, et a te est / quod ferar in partis ipse fuisse tuas* ('so much glory, Maecenas, you grant me, and it is by your grace that I myself shall be said to have belonged to your party', 59–60).[73]

The elegy has puzzled some scholars. It is hard to square the new promise of panegyric in lines 47–56 with the disjunctive rhetoric of 3.3–5 and the *recusatio* Propertius has been constructing throughout this elegy. Yet ambiguity of this kind is not wholly unprecedented. He continues his familiar strategy of claiming that he will, at some unspecified time and unspecified way, write Augustan panegyric. It is true, however, that his promise in this instance seems stronger and the promised panegyric more imminent. Propertius seems more inclined to satisfy Maecenas' putative desire for panegyric of Augustus to the extent that he is no longer more than nominally committed to amatory elegy. The deeper point may be that the poet, for reasons of his own, is embarking on newly ambitious poetic subject matter, of which Maecenas is not the cause, but the pretext. We might observe in addition that Maecenas no longer occupies a prominent position at the head of the

---

[72] A sarcasm further intensified if, with Heyworth (2007a), 117, we see 'Crassi' as simultaneously suggesting 'the vocative plural *crassi*: "thickheads"'.

[73] Is there a touch of 'wry wit' in the claim that Maecenas shall be said to have won over 'even' Propertius (*ipse*) to his 'party'? (Richardson (1977), ad loc.). There are some points in support of this reading: *'ferar'* carefully distances the statement of partisanship by ascribing it to others; and *pars* (faction, party) is hard to take at face value as a term Maecenas would want applied to the circle of his *amici*. Propertius seems to be humorously congratulating Maecenas on an achievement both unlikely and dubious on its own terms: we might compare the crude view of 'partisanship' held by the 'boor' of Horace *Satires* 1.9, and recall Horace's response (see discussion above).

collection as he did in 2.1: he has been displaced by Propertius' triumph procession as victorious elegiac poet. Maecenas' name makes an appearance in the collection well after the Callimachean program of the book and its celebration of the poet's deathless *ingenium* have been established. Propertius, once again, has crafted an autonomist stance out of combined strategies of juxtaposition, evasion, and even (apparent) contradiction: he displaces Maecenas, then honors him; he refuses to write martial panegyric, then commits to write it anyway, although in an evasive future tense.

Behind this confusing series of moves, which appears both to satisfy and frustrate the expectation of encomium, there nonetheless exists, I would argue, a genuine interest in writing a different kind of elegy. What this new form of elegy consists in, and whether it will satisfy the stated demand for Augustan panegyric, however, remain open to question. Propertius may be looking forward to the aetiological elegy of Book 4 in much the same way that Virgil anticipates the *Aeneid* at the opening of *Georgics* 3. Then again, the present book contains some possibilities: 3.11 and 3.18, for example, might be taken as at least partially fulfilling the promise of a more ambitious style of poetry on Augustan topics. Neither elegy offers straightforward encomium, and what stands out in each case is the poet's insistence on controlling what kind of memorial he confers and how he confers it.

In 3.18, Propertius laments the death in 23 BC of M. Claudius Marcellus, the son of Octavia and presumed heir to Augustus. Propertius, of course, offers both praise and sadness for the dead Marcellus, yet also pursues some quirkier and more 'puzzling' themes: for example, a surprisingly dogged pursuit of etymological play on Marcellus' gentilician name.[74] Propertius also plays on the expectations of elegiac readers. The long opening sentence establishing the mythological pedigree of Baiae and its association with an unnamed *crimen* surely evokes the erotic notoriety of the place,[75] until, in line 9, Marcellus' name occurs, and we realize that Baiae is being recriminated as the location of his death. Most striking of all is the pointed, almost satiric tone of Propertius' remarks on death:

> i nunc, tolle animos et tecum finge triumphos,
>   stantiaque in plausum tota theatra iuvent;
> Attalicas supera vestes, atque ostra smaragdis
>   gemmea sint Indis: ignibus ista dabis.   (17–20, text based on Goold 1990)

Go ahead, raise your hopes and fantasize about triumphs; take pleasure in the thought of whole theatres rising to applaud you; surpass the garb of Attalus and stud your purple apparel with Indian emeralds: you will give all these things to the pyre.

We are to expect such gnomic statements about the inevitability of death in ancient epicedia. Yet the details of phrasing here betray a certain sharpness: the sarcasm of *i nunc* ('Go ahead . . .'), the cynicism of *finge triumphos* ('fantasize about triumphs'), the satirical exaggeration of *Attalicas* and, assuming Houseman's emendation is correct, *smaragdis . . . Indis* ('[the garb] of Attalus. . . . Indian emeralds'). At some level, these comments belong to the same ethical perspective as the elegy for Paetus: wealth and prestige will not help you in the face of death.

---

[74] Richardson (1977), 391: e.g. *clausus* (1), *claudit* (16), *inclusum* (26).
[75] Elsewhere this meaning is prominent in Propertian elegy (1.11).

As we know from the closing couplet of 3.3, the only force that stands a chance of withstanding death is poetic *ingenium*. Thus Marcellus and others are dependent on poets for something that, for all their wealth and power, they cannot provide themselves, but which Propertius provides in this very elegy: poetic commemoration that lives on after death destroys the mortal body.

In 3.11 Propertius provides another example of a new kind of elegy on public themes.[76] The poem begins with the poet's complaint that he cannot break the bonds of love (*rumpere vincla* 4), and goes on to document various cases of female power and domination: Medea, Penthesilea, Omphale, and Semiramis. Then the poem moves on to its central example, Cleopatra's domination of Antony (here unnamed), and attempted domination of Rome. The figure of Cleopatra integrates the two modes of domination, erotic and political, kept separate in the previous examples: 'she demanded as the price of her unholy marriage the walls of Rome and the Senate made over as bondsmen to her realm' (*coniugii obsceni pretium Romana poposcit, / moenia et addictos in sua regna Patres*, 31–2). Cleopatra threatened to take away the *libertas* wrested from the hands of Tarquinius Superbus (47–9), but in the end she herself is forced by Caesar to submit to Roman, or rather 'Romulean',[77] bonds (*Romula vincla* 52). As Michael Putnam notes, the momentum of the poem suggests a path of domination leading from Cynthia to Augustus, from elegiac *servitium* to imperial power: 'The liberator is at the same time the conqueror', and 'Augustus, on whose safety Rome depends, is the final secure example of power in the poem.'[78] After poisoning herself, Cleopatra devoted her dying words to Augustus: 'I was not to be feared, Rome, when you had so great a citizen as this' (*non hoc, Roma, fui tanto tibi cive verenda*, 55). Later, Propertius glibly implies Augustus' superiority to Jupiter (66). Augustus outperforms republican heroes as liberator and protector of Rome, but in the process, undermines the republican tradition of power-sharing and non-monopolistic apportioning of glory: *tantus civis* ('so great a citizen'), indeed.[79]

Yet however much 3.11 appears to allow (potentially subversive) reflection on power, servitude, and Augustus, the poem still offers at least 'surface' affirmation of Augustan ideals.[80] The elegist avoids explicit criticism, yet at the same time embeds praise within a dense nexus of controversial themes. In the end, Propertius seems less interested in damning or praising Augustus than in the mechanics of reputation and commemoration. What are the sources of glory, and how is public achievement converted into enduring cultural prestige? Augustus, Propertius reminds us, comes at the culmination of a long line of Roman heroes credited with 'saving' the state.

---

[76] Stahl (1985), 234–47, includes an extended, political reading of the elegy in terms of a strategy of 'aggressive self-preservation', whereby the poet at once offers 'surface' affirmation of Augustan ideals, and on another level, remains committed to a critical, independent outlook.

[77] *Romula* is poetic for *Romulea* (Richardson (1977), ad loc.); the term in the first instance means 'Roman', but also bears complicated, and not wholly positive, Augustan associations: see Hinds (1992).

[78] Putnam (1980), 101.

[79] For Heyworth (2007b), 117–19, 3.11 grimly and defiantly registers the realization that 'all that is possible now is the composition of Augustan panegyric'.

[80] Stahl (1985), 247.

> haec di condiderunt, haec di quoque moenia servant:
>   vix timeat salvo Caesare Roma Iovem.
> nunc ubi Scipiadae classes, ubi signa Camilli,
>   aut modo Pompeia, Bospore, capta manu?
> Hannibalis spolia et victi monumenta Syphacis,
>   et Pyrrhi ad nostros gloria fracta pedes?
> Curtius expletis statuit monumenta lacunis,
>   at Decius misso proelia rupit equo,
> Coclitis abscissos testatur semita pontes,
>   est cui cognomen corvus habere dedit.
> Leucadius versas acies memorabit Apollo:
>   tantum operis belli sustulit una dies.
> at tu, sive petes portus seu, navita, linques,
>   Caesaris in toto sis memor Ionio.   (65–8, 59–64, 69–72)[81]

These walls the gods founded, these walls the gods also preserve. While Caesar is secure, Rome would hardly fear Jove. Where now is Scipio's fleet, where Camillus' standards? Or those recently captured, Bosporus, by Pompey's hand? The spoils taken from Hannibal, the memorials of defeated Syphax, and Pyrrhus' glory shattered at our feet? Curtius established a monument by filling up a chasm; Decius gave full rein to his horse[82] and burst through the battle-line; the path of Cocles attests to the rending of the bridge; and there is one to whom the raven gave his *cognomen* to keep. Apollo of Leucas will preserve the memory of battle lines routed: a single day of war took away so much labour.[83] But you, sailor, whether you are approaching or leaving the harbour, remember Caesar throughout the entire Ionian sea.

Curtius 'established a monument' (*statuit monumenta*) in the act of filling up a chasm;[84] Decius 'burst through' battle lines on his horse; and Cocles' path is attested by bridges 'cut apart' (*abscissos . . . pontes*). Propertius offers a somewhat flippant summary of these hallowed historical *exempla*, stressing the peculiar and even fragmented nature of their 'monuments': chasms filled, broken battles, bridges cut apart, the honorary name of a 'crow' (M. Valerius Corvus). Assuming the troubled text of this passage is comprehensible, Propertius also openly casts doubt on the achievements of some other heroes of the republic: *nunc ubi Scipiadae classes, ubi signa Camilli . . .*? ('Where now the fleet of Scipio, the standards of Camillus . . . ?').[85] The implication seems to be that

---

[81] The text, and in particular the ordering of lines, is difficult in this passage: for defense of the ordering adopted here, see Heyworth and Morwood (2011), ad loc., and Heyworth (2007a), ad loc. Nonetheless considerable uncertainty remains, and I am sympathetic to the comments of Thomas (2011) on epigrammatic 'riffs' in Propertius and the tendency of modern editors to normalize his difficult, elliptical style by positing transpositions (although he does not address this passage, which is particularly difficult to understand in the order transmitted by the MSS).

[82] Many editors adopt Scaliger's emendation, which represents the 'normal expression' (Heyworth 2007a, ad loc.): *admisso Decius*.

[83] Following Heyworth (2007a), ad loc. Goold (1990), who adopts Housman's emendation (*tanti . . . bellum*), renders: 'one day put an end to a war of such vast array'.

[84] An evidently paradoxical phrase: Heyworth and Morwood (2011), ad loc.

[85] There is a certain cynicism regarding monuments and memory that pervades the poem. We might also recall Propertius' mention of the doubtful-sounding *victi monumenta Syphacis* ('monument of defeated Syphax') and Pyhrrus' 'shattered glory' (*gloria fracta*, 59–60). These conquered enemies are presumably to the credit of the Romans, yet the emphasis on 'shattering' and 'defeat' resonates with the broader theme of the fragility of monuments.

Augustus has eclipsed these earlier feats with his stunning Actian victory (69–70). Apollo of Leucas will 'commemorate' (*memorabit*) battle-lines turned back, and Propertius exhorts the sailor to 'remember' (*sis memor*) Caesar throughout the Ionian sea.

Caesar is the final name commemorated in the poem, yet equally prominent, as in the elegy on Marcellus, is the commemorative power of poetry itself. Poetry is the most reliable and enduring monument (3.2.17–26), and Propertius here demonstrates its capacity to shape the memory of a major historical figure. He is no longer merely content to shape monuments to his mistress' beauty, and to commemorate the vicissitudes of his love-affair. The broader direction of Propertius' third book is to disembed the poet's capacity for commemoration and the immortalizing power of poetic *ingenium* from the limiting confines of courtship poetry. Courtship of Cynthia is now viewed as a potentially limited and limiting poetic project: a woman's beauty cannot last for ever, and the pleasures of youth are ephemeral. At the same time, Propertius' newly august identity as elegiac author—a triumphing 'general', a priestly *vates* in the grove of Callimachus and Philetas—is no longer obviously compatible with the attitude of amatory servility. The latest accents in his evolving self-portrait as writer include a triumphal image of himself at the head of a 'crowd' (*turba* 3.1.12) of subordinate writers. Even the 'little Loves' (*parvi . . . Amores* 11), who should be busy subjugating and tormenting Propertius, are now tamely participating in his victory procession.

This shifting poetic orientation can be observed in the content of individual elegies throughout the book. First, there are relatively few Cynthia-centred poems. In the opening, programmatic elegies, Cynthia is not named, but is replaced by the generic *puella* signifying amatory elegy; indeed, surpassing the apparently calculated neglect of Book 2, Propertius now does not name her until 3.10. Even elegies written on amatory themes evince an interest in expanding the scope of elegy. 3.10, the elegy on Cynthia's birthday, is the exception that proves the rule. This poem constitutes a meta-reflection on the continuing textual existence of 'Cynthia' as topic of Propertian elegy. The occasion of the birthday allows the poet to view the affair from a detached vantage point, as a measurable temporal trajectory, and inscribe it as self-conscious literary ritual. This synoptic view of the affair as bounded, discrete entity rather than ongoing dynamic not accidentally occurs in a book devoted to its closure. Throughout the book, Propertius explores the connections between erotic experience and broader aspects of history, civilization and culture;[86] he presses beyond the confined mentality of the lover in order to view his own condition from an increasingly external and even analytical perspective.

Even as he reroutes and transforms his amatory poetics, Propertius includes within the collection elegies on a range of other topics that point towards closure of the affair and the initiation of a new form of elegy. Specifically, Propertius traces a trajectory from freedom to liberation. 3.6, a multi-layered poem on Propertius' communication with and persuasive manipulation of Cynthia's slave Lydgamus, plays overtly on themes of freedom and liberation, and at the same time, at an implicit level, displaces the condition of slavery onto an actual slave—a move that

---

[86] See especially Putnam (1980).

anticipates Ovid's *Amores* and *Ars amatoria*, where the *amator* ('lover') assumes a more cynically controlling and less servile persona, while manipulating, or attempting to manipulate, slaves both actual (e.g. *ancillae*) and metaphorical (writing tablets, see below). In 3.17, Propertius appeals to Bacchus in the hopes of becoming a true poet inspired by the god's power (20), and asks the god to free him from his erotic *servitium* (*tu modo servitio vacuum me siste superbo*, 41). Elegies on broadly amatory topics go out of their way to invert the classic motifs of erotic servitude. In 3.14, Propertius tries to imagine a society (in this case, Sparta), where the object of desire is not kept under lock and key, but is openly available, that is, where there is no *exclusus amator*, and the obstructions crucial to elegiac poetics are absent. In 3.20, Propertius seemingly turns away from the chronic vacillation (*mora*) of elegiac love in order to entertain a new possibility—love rendered stable and permanent by law, oaths, and a solemn pact (*foedus*). Propertius stipulates that whoever should violate this pact, will have as punishment... the precise conditions defining the life of the elegiac lover: 'may he ever love, ever lacking the enjoyment of love' (*semper amet, fructu semper amoris egens*, 30). He now describes, and ascribes to another person, the condition he embodied in Book 1.

Propertius is beginning to dismantle the paradoxical autonomist rhetoric of *servitium*, the confining space of elegiac independence that defined his earlier elegy. The four closing elegies of the book render this implicit process of dismantling overt. In 3.21, Propertius announces that he will travel to Athens so that the long voyage may free him of his 'oppressive love' (*ut me longa gravi solvat amore via*, 2). The lover who previously opposed all 'voyages' (*viae*) that might disrupt his Rome-centred love affair, now plans a trip himself on the theory of 'out of sight, out of mind' (*quantum oculis, animo tam procul ibi amor*, 10)—a telling motto for someone who was originally 'captured' by Cynthia's eyes. When he dies, moreover, he will not die a dishonorable death in the midst of a love affair (33–4), as he previously aspired to do (2.1.47). 3.22 welcomes home to Italy the same Tullus who was sent off to provincial administration in Book 1. We are coming full circle. The traditional man of action Tullus is no longer located at the margins of elegiac space, but honored on his return to Rome and his Roman marriage: *hic ampla nepotum / spes et venturae coniugis aptus amor* ('here is ample hope of offspring and fitting love of the bride to be', 42–3). Propertius now manifests admiration for a very different kind of love.

In 3.23, Propertius stages yet another encounter between the values of poverty and profit, poetic and financial interests, but now within the context of the book's valedictory closing sequence. In this elegy, we learn that the wax tablets containing the very communications between lover and beloved have been 'lost',[87] and that the lover is offering a cash reward for his 'learned' (*doctae*) tablets. He fears above all that these notebooks will end up in the possession of a miser and placed amidst his account-books (*ephemeridas*, 20), which, both in their use and etymology, are located in the realm of day-to-day transactions. As in 3.7, a contrast emerges

---

[87] On Propertius' lost tablets, see Baker (1973); Erbse (1979). The sophisticated studies of Ovid's version may be even more helpful in this context: McCarthy (1998), 182–4; Henderson (1991), 74–81; Fitzgerald (2000), 59–62.

between the poet, not concerned with money (as attested by his willingness to trade gold for wooden tablets, 21–2), and a figure focused on immediate profit. Yet there is a twist: reduced to a message-bearing instrument conveying the details of ephemeral assignations (10–18), the elegist's writing has become disturbingly similar to the miser's both in its utility (*usus*, 'use', 3; *effectus...bonos*, 'good outcomes', 10) and its orientation towards the day-to-day (*heri...hodie*, 'yester-day...today', 12,15).[88] These ironic inversions cannot but bring into play the enduring poetic monuments featured near the book's opening in 3.2. The lost tablets, immersed in mimetic immediacy and fictions of instrumentality, are now worn out and 'trite' (*detriverat usus*, 'use had worn them down', 3). They are to be replaced, presumably, by the elegist's emerging vatic identity and monumental poetics. In the elegy's final line, the author assumes the position of master (*dominus*), securely established on the Esquiline, removed from the sordid financial concerns of those who will take interest in his notice.[89]

One detail in 3.23 is particularly telling: the tablets, which presumably also conveyed their owner's messages, are here only specifically represented as bearing the words of the mistress. The employment of the woman's voice at this point is hardly accidental. As Propertius isolates and elevates the figure of the poet, extricating him from the confines of amatory speech, he singles out terms that refer to the poet's intrinsic capacity to confer memorial (*ingenium, monumentum*), while Cynthia's role as (ephemeral) *materia* becomes simultaneously more patent and more precarious.[90] She now only contributes to the story of the poet's overcoming of death; she does not define it. It is thus not entirely surprising when, in 3.24–25, Propertius renounces Cynthia, declaring that her confidence in her beauty was false (*falsa...fiducia formae*, 1). The poet, in ending his love affair with Cynthia, recalls its textual beginning in 1.1. He ascribes Cynthia's beauty to a flaw in his vision (*oculis* 2), a falsification of poetic language (3–8).[91] He bids farewell to the chief signifiers of elegy: the threshold (9), the door (11), the manipulative power of tears (5–7), shipwreck (12), captivity (14). He has returned to sanity, and dedicates himself to Mens Bona (19–20)—a pious intention all the more significant if we recall that the cult of this goddess was especially associated with freed slaves.

In the closing lines of the book, Propertius *un*writes his mistress' beauty:

> at te celatis aetas gravis urgeat annis,
>   et veniat formae ruga sinistra tuae!
> vellere tum cupias albos a stirpe capillos,
>   iam speculo rugas increpitante tibi,
> exclusa inque vicem fastus patiare superbos,
>   et quae fecisti facta quereris anus!

---

[88] Putnam (1980), 106; Putnam's discussion of this elegy's role in Book 3 (106–7) and the book's broader concern with temporality is fundamental.

[89] Putnam (1980). Note that the *servus amoris*, slave of a *domina*, now appears as *dominus* himself—further prefiguring of the end; on the phasing out of *servitium*, see Alvarez Hernández (1997), who traces the theme of *servitium* through Propertius' *oeuvre*; on Book 3 and its 'adiós definitivo al *servitium amoris*', see 197ff.; on 3.23, 257–61.

[90] On Cynthia as *materia*, Wyke (1987a), (1987b).

[91] The attempted cures of friends, witchcraft and cautery (10–11).

> has tibi fatalis cecinit mea pagina diras:
>   eventum formae disce timere tuae!   (3.25.11–18)

May the burdensome passage of time press you with the years you have dissembled, and may an unwelcome crease mar your beauty! Then may you desire to rip out your white hair from the roots as your mirror reproaches you with your wrinkles. Shut out of doors yourself, may you suffer another's arrogant disdain, and may you bewail, an old woman, the very things you did [when young]. These are the grim forebodings of doom my page has sung for you: learn to fear the outcome awaiting your beauty!

Whereas the *ingenium* lauded at the book's opening will evade death, Cynthia becomes a kind of living document of the effects of time on flesh.[92] The book's closing words perpetuate the image of her fading, as if, in order to enshrine the essence of his work as immortal, Propertius had to deflect temporality onto the merely mortal portion of his writing, the *materia* that would absorb time's destructive force. The book's opening elegies maintained the connection between poetry's power to memorialize and the mistress' beauty: *carmina erunt formae tot monumenta tuae* ('my songs will be so many memorials of your beauty', 3.2.18). Now feminine *forma* ('beauty') is repudiated, leaving the male poet's monumental song standing in magnificent isolation.

Cynthia's beauty turned out to be all too mortal: the poet, in the end, could not accompany her into old age as promised. Whereas Book 3 ends with the fading of an individual life, Book 4[93] opens by evoking the immeasurably longer life-span of a city and a civilization.

> Hoc quodcumque vides, hospes, qua maxima Roma est,
>   ante Phrygem Aenean collis et herba fuit;
> atque ubi Navali stant sacra Palatia Phoebo,
>   Evandri profugae procubuere boves.   (Prop. 4.1.1–4)

All that you see before you, stranger, where greatest Rome now stands, before the arrival of Phrygian Aeneas was grassy hillside; and where now stands the Palatine sacred to Phoebus of Naval Victory, the cattle of exiled Evander once lay down to rest.

Much of Propertius' fourth book concerns the contrast between present-day Rome and primitive Rome of the legendary period and the vast gulf of time and culture between the two. What is especially impressive over the *longue durée* is Rome's capacity for regeneration. Indeed, this ability to be 'reborn' is already present in the famous transfer of Aeneas' Trojan Penates to Rome: *arma resur-gentis portans victricia Troiae* ('bearing the victorious arms of Troy rising up again', 47); *Troia, cades et Troica Roma resurges* ('Troy, you will fall, and rise again as Trojan Rome', 87); *Ilia tellus / vivet* ('The land of Ilium shall live on', 53–4). At the same time, reference to contemporary monuments such as the Temple of Apollo Palatinus recalls the much more recent 'rebirth' of Rome from the ashes of civil war under Augustus, the latest founder of the City.

We move, quite pointedly, from the irreversible physical aging of Cynthia in 3.24/25 to *Roma aeterna* and the City's perpetual capacity to renew itself and expand the horizons of its power: in Virgil's words, *imperium sine fine* ('boundless

---

[92] Putnam (1980), 108. Note that Shackleton Bailey's *iam* has been adopted in line 14 in place of the manuscripts' *a*.

[93] A flood of recent scholarship investigates the distinctive aspects of Propertius' fourth book: Debrohun (2003); Janan (2001); Welch (2005); Hutchinson (2006).

empire', *Aeneid* 1.279). In the past, scholars have dwelled on the question of Propertius' supposed discovery of patriotism late in his oeuvre, a surprising reversal of programme in favour of 'Roman' and Augustan themes. It has not been adequately appreciated how Propertius' new subject matter in fact coheres with and is the culmination of a broader pattern in his oeuvre: the displacement of Cynthia and fictions of amatory utility with an increasing focus on literary monumentality and immortality. Propertius here specifically aligns himself with the Horatian project of linking the literary monument with the immortality of Rome. Horace, in *Odes* 3.30, predicted that his lyric oeuvre would endure as long as the religious rites symbolizing and ensuring Rome's *aeternitas*. In Propertius' case, confident declaration of the elegist's canonical status as 'Rome's Callimachus' (*Romani . . . Callimachi*, 4.1.64) coincides with the replacement of an aging Cynthia with the eternal City. We should not conclude, however, that a newly vatic Propertius is any less ironic and playful an elegist than in his earlier, *puella*-centred compositions. A disquietingly irreverent aetiologist, Propertius often insists on noting disjunctions and discontinuities rather than building up ideologically satisfying connections between virtuous early Rome and glorious Augustan Rome.[94] Before concluding that Propertius has capitulated to pressure from the regime, then, we should ask: which is the more subversive, focusing on Cynthia at the expense of Rome, or writing about Rome in an irreverently elegiac manner?

Propertius, moreover, does not limit himself to the role of interpreter and chronicler of the City; in the opening elegy of the book, he figures himself as its (literary) builder.

> moenia namque pio coner disponere versu:
>   ei mihi, quod nostro est parvus in ore sonus!
> sed tamen exiguo quodcumque e pectore rivi
>   fluxerit, hoc patriae serviet omne meae.
> Ennius hirsuta cingat sua dicta corona:
>   mi folia ex hedera porrige, Bacche, tua,
> ut nostris tumefacta superbiat Umbria libris,
>   Umbria Romani patria Callimachi!
> scandentis quisquis cernit de vallibus arces,
>   ingenio muros aestimet ille meo!
> Roma, fave, tibi surgit opus; date candida, cives,
>   omina, et inceptis dextera cantet avis!   (4.1.57–68)

For I would attempt to lay out [those] walls [founded by Romulus] in dutiful verse. Alas that only a small voice is on my lips! And yet, whatever sort of stream flows from my tiny breast, all of it will be in the service of my country. Let Ennius crown his words with a shaggy garland: furnish me with leaves from your ivy, Bacchus, so that Umbria may swell with pride in my books, Umbria, fatherland of the Roman Callimachus! Whoever sees the citadel rising up from the valley, let him appraise the value of those walls by my literary talent! Rome, show favour; my work rises for you; give good omens, citizens, and may a bird on the right chant success for my undertakings.

The poet expresses his wish to 'lay out the walls' of the city in 'dutiful verse' (*moenia . . . pio . . . disponere versu*, 57), and using the same language used of cities

---

[94] See Janan (2001), *passim*; Heyworth (2007b), 121ff.

under construction, speaks of his 'work' rising up (*surgit opus*). Then, as if he were presiding over the foundation of a city or building, Propertius asks citizens to give a fair omen and a bird to sing a favourable augury for his 'undertaking'. The book's first line works equally well if addressed to a stranger (*hospes*) visiting Rome, or to a reader opening Propertius' fourth book: *hoc quodcumque vides, hospes, qua maxima Roma est* ('All this that you see, stranger, where greatest Rome stands...', 4.1.1). The initial deictic pronoun *hoc* naturally points ahead to the 'Rome' that will unfold before our eyes in the following passage and subsequent elegies. This elegiac Rome constructed out of ink and papyrus will both comment on and potentially establish itself as independent of the city Augustus was busy remaking in marble.[95] Indeed, Propertius does not name Augustus or other contemporary builders in this opening elegy, although the poet's own name (1.71), country of origin, and biography are prominently recorded.

Whereas Propertius' earliest autonomist rhetoric functioned by sequestering the poet-lover in the narrow confines of amorous obsession, now Rome's Callimachus proudly unveils the literary monuments that make up his elegiac city. Yet even as Propertius strongly identifies the site of his poetry with the site of Rome, he reasserts his connection with his other *patria*, Umbria. His slender Callimachean books, he wryly notes, will make his native Umbria 'puff up with pride' (*tumefacta superbiat*). The theme of 'walls' performs a connective function: Rome's walls rose up from the milk of the she-wolf (56); he would like to lay out the 'walls' of Rome in verse; and whoever sees the citadel of Assisi will estimate the value of its walls by Propertius' literary talent (*ingenio muros aestimet*, 66).[96] This link between city walls and *ingenium* makes explicit Propertius' architectural and monumental poetics. At the same time, he sets up Umbria, the site of his fame and his country of origin, as counter-*patria* to Rome: *Umbria Romani patria Callimachi* ('Umbria, fatherland of Rome's Callimachus'). As at the end of his first book of elegies, so here, Propertius reminds us of his own walled city that lies outside the immediate circuit of the imperial capital.

All of these self-representational tactics shore up Propertius' autonomist rhetoric even as he devotes himself to prime Augustan subject matter. He will write about Rome and Rome's origins, but after his own fashion, in Callimachean style. He will not imitate the 'hirsute' style of Ennius (60); nor will he produce 'dutiful verse' (*pio...versu*) on the model of epic poetry such as Virgil's *Aeneid* (57). Propertius' new poetic interest in Roman origins, far from being evidence of a belated patriotic conversion, is the continuation of an already established pattern in his oeuvre: a progressive shift from amatory poetry enlivened by Callimachean leitmotifs to Callimachean poetry enlivened by amatory leitmotifs. Propertius' status as Callimachean poet now has priority over but does not erase his fame as lover of Cynthia. Whereas in the closing elegy of Book 2 the *iuncta nomina* of Cynthia and Propertius constituted the fundamental unit of the poet's fame, now it is his Callimachean poetry books (*nostris...libris*) that have won renown for himself and his native Assisi.

---

[95] On this phenomenon in general, see Edwards (1996).   [96] Compare 125–6.

Even as Propertius continues to counterbalance expansive Augustan subject matter with a slender, Callimachean style, he extends this counterbalancing tactic to the content of his entire book, starting with its introductory elegy. 4.1 is divided into two parts that, according to some editors, comprise separate elegies.[97] In the first portion (1–70), Propertius offers a tour of Rome past and present, outlines his new subject matter, and announces his fame as Callimachean poet. In the second section (71–150), the Babylonian astrologer Horos abruptly intervenes: *quo ruis imprudens?* ('where are you rushing off to in unthinking haste?', 71). He goes on to boast, in rambling fashion, of his own skill as astrologer, before he turns to Propertius, and, in a passage mirroring the elegist's earlier declaration of poetic fame (57–70), discusses the poet's land of origins, his literary renown, and the key events in his career (119–34). Finally, he insists that Propertius remain committed to amatory elegy: *at tu finge elegos, fallax opus (haec tua castra!), / scribat ut exemplo cetera turba tuo* ('but you fashion elegies, a deceptive mode of writing[98] (this is your camp!), so that the rest of the mob may write according to your example', 135–6).

There are strong hints throughout Horos' speech that he is a flawed speaker and not to be taken wholly seriously, yet in his remarks on Propertius' amatory calling, he echoes well established elegiac themes. The pattern of the first elegy, moreover, informs the rest of the book in its alternation between erotic and 'Roman' subject matter. Propertius thus applies to an entire book and its programmatic elegy the counterbalancing tactic we saw earlier in 2.1. In this latest version of autonomist rhetoric, ostensibly patriotic subject matter stands side by side with continuing testimony to Propertius' amatory identity, a tensional alternation that prevents his poetry from lapsing easily into any one category or ideological niche.

Even among the book's aetiological elegies, Propertius incorporates amatory themes familiar from his earlier books. Hercules, in Propertius' elegy on the Ara Maxima (4.9), assumes the typical pose of the pleading *exclusus amator* (locked out lover) at the *limen* (threshold), then shatters this paradigm when he brutally pushes aside the door to slake his thirst (61–2). In Propertius' version of the Tarpeia legend (4.4), she falls in love with the Sabine leader Tatius, thereby injecting an amatory element into the patriotic legend and complicating its otherwise fairly predictable moral slant.[99] It would not be difficult to demonstrate how Propertius' 'Roman' elegies are imbued *passim* with his signature amatory concerns so as to contribute a destabilizing factor to the high patriotic tone of their topics. An extended examination of Book 4, however, would exceed the bounds of the present argument, and numerous recent studies examine precisely such complicating factors in Propertius' poetic treatment of the Augustan city.[100] The elegy that is most difficult, on the surface at least, to accommodate to my view of

---

[97] See Heyworth (2007a), 424–5, for a summary of the arguments against unity; Richardson (1977) evidently sees 4.1a and b as a single poem; and Hutchinson (2006), 61, leans towards unity.

[98] Most modern editors follow the MSS rather than supplying Heinsius' *pellax*. Richardson (1977), ad loc., following Shackleton Bailey (1956), prefers to translate 'tricky, technically difficult'.

[99] On the Augustan importance of Tarpeia, and her representations on coins and in other media, see Welch (2005), 59–62.

[100] Welch (2005); Debrohun (2003); Janan (2001). Note also the comments on Propertius Book 4 in Rea (2007), 103–23.

Propertius' evolving autonomist rhetoric is 4.6, an aetiological treatment of the Temple of Palatine Apollo and the battle of Actium. It will be therefore helpful to examine this elegy written 'for the glory of Caesar' (*Caesaris in nomen*, 4.6.13) as a limit case for Propertius' autonomist poetics in Book 4.[101]

In 4.6, Propertius appears to make good on previous promises to write panegyric of Augustus' martial achievements. Since Apollo was the god hailed as responsible for Octavian's victory at Actium, the Temple of Palatine Apollo, dedicated a few years later in 28 BC, became associated with the victory over Antony and Cleopatra. The present elegy presents the victory at Actium as the *aetion* of the temple, and, more broadly, of Augustus' rule. Relatively few verses, however, are devoted to describing actual battle, and most of the poem is taken up with a description of the opposing battle lines (15–30), and an encouraging speech spoken by the god Apollo (37–54). The narrative compression and ellipsis at the moment of victory are remarkable: *vincit Roma fide Phoebi: dat femina poenas: / sceptra per Ionias fracta vehuntur aquas* ('Rome wins by the faithful support of Phoebus; the woman pays the penalty: her shattered scepter is carried over the waters of the Ionian sea', 57–8). It is thus somewhat surprising, and perhaps an ironic provocation, when the poet declares at the end of his non-narration: *bella satis cecini* ('I have sung enough of wars', 69). The song he did sing, moreover, gives pause. Most remarkably, Propertius renders the retrospective historical teleology that drives Virgil's *Aeneid*, and the Augustan view of imperial genealogy generally, awkwardly explicit in at least two passages. In one, Julius Caesar, looking on from his 'Idalian star', hails the Actian victory as proof of his divine bloodline: *sum deus; est nostri sanguinis ista fides* ('I am a god; this [victory] is proof of our bloodline', 60). The same backward/forward temporal logic is at issue when Apollo states that Romulus' augury of Rome's foundation will be retroactively discredited if the 'Augustan' side[102] fails to defeat Cleopatra (4.6.43–4).

These features, as well as some others, have been cited in interpretations of 4.6 that seek to establish its intrinsically critical or ironic stance. Such an approach, however, cannot help being tendentious and apologetic. We are asked to accept that subtle aspects of emphasis and treatment, which, depending on one's interpretive preference, *might* introduce a critical or not wholly reverential perspective, somehow undermine the panegyrical gesture as a whole. I would argue, instead, that everything in 4.6 points to Propertius' interest, not in subverting or 'resisting' the Augustan regime, but in controlling the nature of the praise he offers, in writing panegyric on his own terms. Indeed, the elegy is as much about poetics and the social role of poets as it is about Augustus' accomplishments at Actium. Poetological discussion frames the elegy: the opening section outlines a series of religious rites as an extended metaphor for Callimachean poetic composition (1–12), while the closing section describes a convivial gathering of poets trying

---

[101] 4.6 has been the object of study by many scholars, who come to varying conclusions regarding its status as (sincere) panegyric: for example, Johnson (1973); Baker (1983); Cairns (1984); Stahl (1985); 250–5; Gurval (1995), ch. 6; Janan (2001), 102–4; Debrohun (2003), ch. 5; Miller (2009), 80–92; Lowrie (2009), 188–95.

[102] Strikingly and anachronistically, Propertius identifies the 'Augustan side', employing *Augustus* as an adjective to indicate Augustus' *ratis* (23): Camps (1965), ad loc.

their hand at Augustan themes (71–86). The god Apollo himself, as Propertius makes explicit, is associated both with warfare and with poetry, and thus emblematizes the two poles around which the elegy pivots.[103]

Augustus shares space in Propertius' elegy with the self-representing poet and his metaliterary concerns. In Hutchinson's view, 'the poem flaunts its complication', and 'veers between imposing laudation and obsession with its own oddity and with genre':

> The tug between the metaliterary and the panegyrical does not produce so strong and destructive a conflict as ironic undermining or the clash of opinions . . . The oscillations and interaction between the poem's absorption in tradition and itself and its praise of god and princeps issue in an irresolvably double work. 'Postmodern' play and resounding praise coexist.[104]

Hutchinson rightly observes that the poem does not founder on fundamental contradictions, but remains carefully poised between metaliterary play and panegyric. Neither impulse wins out. Propertius toys with some potential contradictions of Augustan ideology, yet offers praise nonetheless, all the while balancing encomium of Augustus with advertisement of his own Callimachean aesthetics. In the end, Propertius writes his own kind of war poem, distinguished by intensive metaliterary reflection, an elliptical, erudite, and painterly[105] style of narrative, and a tendency to render explicit the difficult logic of Augustan narrative ideology.

Metaliterariness arises again in the scene of the poet's party at the elegy's close. Here an anonymous group of poets will compose poems on a range of Augustan themes, including the recovery of the Parthian standards (80–4). This closural 'group portrait' balances and complements the image of the isolated Callimachean poet-priest in the elegy's opening section.

> ingenium potis irritat Musa poetis:
>   Bacche, soles Phoebo fertilis esse tuo.
> ille paludosos memoret servire Sygambros,
>   Cepheam hic Meroen fuscaque regna canat,
> hic referat sero confessum foedere Parthum:
>   'reddat signa Remi, mox dabit ipse sua:
> sive aliquid pharetris Augustus parcet Eois,
>   differat in pueros ista tropaea suos.
> gaude, Crasse, nigras si quid sapis inter harenas:
>   ire per Euphraten ad tua busta licet.'
> sic noctem patera, sic ducam carmine, donec
>   iniciat radios in mea vina dies.   (75–86, text based on Goold 1990)

The Muse spurs the talent of poets in their cups; Bacchus, you are wont to be a source of fertile inspiration for your brother Phoebus. Let one commemorate how the marshy Sygambri are subjected, another sing Cephean Meroe and her swarthy realms, and yet

---

[103] Compare Hor. *Carm.* 2.10.18–20; the Palatine temple might be read as embodying a similar duality, encompassing both the god's triumphs over his enemies, including the Actian victory, and his role as patron of music and poetry. For Keith (2008), 165, 192 n. 82, 4.6 epitomizes the interconnectedness of elegiac leisure and Augustan imperialism.

[104] Hutchinson (2006), 154–5; on the programmatic elements of the poem's closing section, see Keith (2008), 84–5.

[105] On this pictorial dimension, see Lowrie (2009), 192.

another tell how the Parthian by a tardy pact owned up: 'Let him return the standards of Remus; soon he will give up his own. Or if Augustus spares the bowmen of the East in any way, let him put off those trophies for his own grandsons. Rejoice, Crassus, if you have any sentience amid the black sands: now we may go across the Euphrates to your tomb.'

Propertius sets himself amid a convivial party of patriotic Roman poets singing on bellicose topics. The elegist notionally joins them, although it would seem odd if, having introduced the section by declaring *bella satis cecini* ('I have sung enough of wars', 69), he immediately began singing about wars. His own war poem on Actium would be hard to characterize in terms of the straightforwardly panegyrical slant of his fellow convivialists' compositions. The broader structure of the elegy thus invites us to compare the communal project of Augustan praise (71–84) with Propertius' solitary status as exacting Callimachean elegist (1–10).[106] To what extent, and in what fashion, does he 'join the party'?

When we turn to the next elegy in the collection, we might imagine, for a moment, that he has picked up where the unnamed patriotic poet of 4.6.79–84 left off, answering the question of whether Crassus' sentience has survived his death.

> Sunt aliquid Manes: letum non omnia finit,
>   luridaque evictos effugit umbra rogos.   (4.7.1–2)

So ghosts exist: death is not the end of everything, and the pale shade overcomes and escapes the pyre.

The Homeric intertext (*Iliad* 23.103–4) refers, appropriately, to a dead warrior on the same side as the speaker. Will Propertius go on to sing about Crassus' lost standards? The first word of the following couplet dashes this possibility: *Cynthia namque meo visa est incumbere fulcro* ('For Cynthia appeared, leaning over my bed', 4.7.3). The transition from 4.6 to 4.7 is thus significant. Propertius has joined a festive group of poets singing on Augustan themes, when Cynthia, the embodiment of his amatory poetics, dramatically returns from the dead to claim him for her own: no dead Crassus, but the dead Cynthia, forms the focus of the elegy. This marvelous elegy, as well as its sequel 4.8, deserve their own separate discussion, and cannot be exhaustively appreciated here. Suffice it to point out that Cynthia makes good on Horos' prediction that 'one girl' will foil all the poet's efforts (4.1.139–46), and effectively counterbalances Propertius' praise of Augustus' Actian victory with her lurid and terrible apparition. Cynthia conveys all the greater impression of force and fixity in comparison with the brilliant yet evasive equivocations of 4.6. Whereas 4.6 ends with an intriguingly open-ended scene of an ongoing, late-night party and elliptically sketched out poetic content,[107] the closing epigram of Cynthia's speech in 4.7 testifies, in vividly physical terms, to her enduring power and ineluctable embrace: *nunc te possideant aliae: mox sola tenebo: / mecum eris, et mixtis ossibus ossa teram* ('for now let other women

---

[106] Propertius appears to be combining Callimachean/Apollonian elegy with the more exalted style of poetry associated with Bacchic inspiration and panegyric grandeur (compare Hor. *Carm.* 3.25 and Hutchinson (2006), 167–8. The closing image of the sun casting its rays onto Propertius' wine is suggestive of the combined presence of Bacchus and Apollo (Hutchinson ad loc.)

[107] By contrast, Lowrie (2009), 195, suggests that Propertius' closing assertion (*ducam*, 85) is most likely subjunctive rather than future indicative, 'a wish for poetic performance, for Augustan triumph, rather than the real thing'.

possess you; soon I shall hold you exclusively: you will be with me, and I shall press against your bones, intermingled with mine', 93–4).

Propertius' oeuvre has been widely seen in terms of a surprising evolution towards public, Roman themes and Augustan content. My argument in this section suggests a different characterization of this development: the autonomous space of poetry is at first viewed by Propertius from the inside, then increasingly from the outside. Book 2 expands the presence of death, myth, and posthumous reception in Propertian elegy as part of a transition towards greater publicity and canonical literary status. Books 3 and 4 rephrase autonomy as a dialect of integrity and inclusion, a confrontation between the poet's grove and the prestige of great men, but in a way that builds on and does not simply depart from the earlier project. It is thus not a transition from autonomy to accommodation, but from one style of autonomist rhetoric to another. Starting in the second book and definitively in the third, we hear less about servitude and more about the space and capacities of poetry; we are immersed less often in the lover's humiliated, confined subjectivity, and directed more often to admire the poet's distinctive domain. Both stances are premised on the autonomization of poetry: the poet's bounded grove redescribes, from a reverse perspective, the lover's prison.

We should not conclude, however, that the poet's autonomist rhetoric is free of ideological function within the Augustan social order. Elegy, both as notionally anti-conformist space of personal *libertas* and as integral aesthetic domain, arguably has all the greater political value for its rhetoric of independence and its subversive cachet. A Propertius who remains inexorably bound to Cynthia, and hence inexorably bound to his elegiac poetics, potentially offers more effective testimony to the tolerance of his powerful patrons and the integrity of his praise.

HORACE'S *ODES* AND *EPISTLES*: FROM LUDIC NICHE TO *UTILIS URBI*

Horace, like Propertius, wrote only first-person poetry, but unlike Propertius, he wrote in different first-person genres over the course of his career in accordance with his changing interests and poetic ambitions. After his second book of *Satires* (ca. 30 BC), Horace turned his attention to a new genre, lyric. This project resulted in the publication of a three-book lyric collection, *Odes* 1–3, in 23 BC. In metrical, thematic, and self-representational terms, Horace's *Odes* are the product of an ambitious synthesis. He draws upon diverse facets of the Greek tradition in inventing a Roman lyric genre and literary personality.[108] Just as Propertius shapes elegy in accordance with the literary personality he wishes to adopt, so Horace constructs a version of lyric that accentuates self-representational tendencies coherent with his broader literary aims. Horatian lyric eschews,

---

[108] On Horace and Greek lyric, see, for example, Fraenkel (1957), 154–213; Woodman (2002); Feeney (1993); Barchiesi (2000); G. Davis (2010b); Clay (2010); Race (2010).

as a conscious principle, the erotic monomania of elegy in favour of greater ethical variety, but components of a more or less consistent 'default' lyric personality are nevertheless discernible to any reader of the *Odes*: rural quietude; a devotion to the symposion and the pleasures of wine, women, and song; an orientation towards the here and now as opposed to memories of historical violence and the distracting cares of state. Once again we have the case of a Roman poet writing in a first-person genre who projects a literary personality carefully designed to cohere with his work's aesthetic aims. The reader is tacitly drawn to assume the synthesis of ethics and aesthetics by Horace's naturalizing self-representational rhetoric. Insofar as the first-person lyric speaker displays a retiring, autarkic character,[109] we are persuaded to align his poetic work with those same retiring, autonomist tendencies. The quiet niche or 'corner' (*angulus*) of retreat thus constitutes, at least initially, the basis for Horace's autonomist position in the *Odes*.

Quietist tranquillity and sympotic pleasures, however, do not represent the only side to Horatian lyric. The Alcaic model of lyric poetry equally allows the poet to speak on civic matters. By contrast with Horace's *Satires* and their ostensible mix of urban gossip, jokes, conversation, and ethical meditation, his *Odes* make more confident and authoritative claims on public attention.[110] In the *Satires*, Horace defines autonomy through the ethical qualities of a man who chooses to eschew the allures of ambition and wealth, remaining content 'in his own skin'. He 'just happens' to publish his private, self-improving ethical meditations in a book as an afterthought.[111] The speaker of the *Satires* specifically avoids claiming a public role and voice. In his lyric work, Horace continues to develop an autarkic ethical profile, but also begins to construct a more officially sanctioned and publicly visible poetic domain and identity. In the *Satires*, poetry is viewed as a bullying club, a mode of heteronomy. Now, as lyric poet, Horace looks to join the *poetarum . . . manus* ('band of poets', Sat.1.4.141), a move which, in turn, confers a more explicitly public value on his verse—no longer mere *sermo* ('chat, conversation'), but *carmen* ('song'). *Carmen*, and the *vates* (poet, bard) who produces it, have associations with religious solemnity and public authority in Roman culture,[112] and so the expectations are set provocatively high. Horace's 'autarkic privacy', in this context, assumes a public and political significance.

The image of the retiring ironist, devoted to moderate, Epicurean pleasures, characterized by a wry detachment, and humbly conscious of his minor foibles, has seemed so natural and convincing that modern readers have sometimes felt that they 'know' Horace. The author, of course, with his usual painstaking artifice, has constructed this self-portrait as objective correlative of his autonomist poetic domain. He thus naturalizes aesthetic ideology as the inevitable reflex of a singular personality. The notion of a sequestered rural existence, however, can only go so

---

[109] Compare Ancona (1994), 18, who argues that 'the poet/lover in the *Odes* seems driven by a desire for autonomy, which typically expresses itself through a distanced ironic stance'. Propertian erotic *servitium* is perhaps the other side of the self-representational coin, but both writers are, in different ways, invested in a set of autonomist concerns, at once ethical and aesthetic.

[110] Compare the difference in stance and attitude between the authorial personality of the *Odes* and *Epodes* as observed by Oliensis (1998), 102–5.

[111] *Sat.* 1.4.137–140.

[112] On the authority of Roman song, see Habinek (2005); for a contrasting perspective, Lowrie (2009).

far in shoring up his poetic autonomy. First of all, the credibility of this self-representational fiction comes to be limited by Horace's increasingly prominent, laureate status. Second, Horace, like other Roman poets, premises his autonomist self-portrait on a notionally antinomian existence (*otium, secessus, paupertas*), yet continues to insist on the division between ethics and aesthetics that remains fundamental to the autonomist conception of literary quality. In order to ground a strong conception of poetic autonomy, it is not enough to claim to be a certain kind of person living in a certain way (cut off from the crowd, detached, occupying a sequestered rural estate); one must also, as Catullus perceived, establish the poetic text as a different kind of realm where different criteria hold sway. Interpretive complications do not simply end here, though. Even this strong version of autonomy—the concept of the poetic work as a place where aesthetic criteria have priority over moral and utilitarian ones—is assimilable to the political interests of the Augustan regime. Aesthetic absorption is rendered both possible and justifiable by the *pax Augusta*, and thus accrues a new ideological valence absent from the Catullan insistence on literary quality.

The Sabine farm, as both emblem of Horace's retiring existence and metaphor for the separateness of literary space, is a crucial element in his autonomist rhetoric and the shifts it undergoes in the transition from satire to lyric.[113] In the opening ode of Horace's lyric collection, his rural location has undergone a significant transformation from its first appearance in the *Satires*. Now, the poet occupies a sanctified, god-filled realm, a grove (*nemus*), surrounded by the deities and instruments of lyric poetry.

> me doctarum hederae praemia frontium
> dis miscent superis, me gelidum nemus
> nympharumque leves cum Satyris chori
> secernunt populo, si neque tibias
> Euterpe cohibet nec Polyhymnia
> Lesboum refugit tendere barbiton.
> quodsi me lyricis vatibus inseres,
> sublimi feriam sidera vertice.   (*Carm.* 1.1.29–36)

Me ivy garlands, the reward of learned foreheads, set among the gods above, me the chill grove and light-footed choruses of Nymphs and Satyrs cut off from the populace, if neither Euterpe holds back the pipes nor Polyhymnia refuses to offer the Lesbian lyre. But if you include me in the canon of lyric poets, I shall strike the stars with my exalted head.

Horace's lyric retreat is more than merely a space of periodic respite from the obligations of the town; it is a site of poetic inspiration, the haunt of satyrs, nymphs, and muses. In *Satires* 2.6, Horace, Maecenas' close associate, and participant in the daily routines of civic life, rubs shoulders with his fellow Romans in his various capacities as purveyor of documents, street-corner conversationalist, and sponsor of bail. The satiric farm is not (yet) Horace's established poetic residence so much as tantalizing emblem of the rural autarky to which he aspires: *o rus, quando ego te aspiciam quandoque licebit / nunc veterum libris, nunc somno et inertibus horis / ducere sollicitae iucunda oblivia vitae* ('O country estate,

---

[113] On the representation of Horace's rural estate, see Schmidt (1997); Bowditch (2001), *passim*; on its possible identification with a villa at Licenza, Frischer et al. (2006).

when shall I lay eyes on you, and when will it be allowed, now amid the books of writers of old, now amid sleep and hours of inactivity, to pass my time in pleasing forgetfulness of the anxieties of life?', 60–2)? By contrast, in this opening scene of the *Odes*, the 'chill grove' of the Muses physically separates and morally differentiates Horace from his fellow citizens (*secernunt populo*).[114] Whereas *Satires* 2.6 shows Horace's time and self divided between two different locations and patterns of activity, *Odes* 1.1 effects an emphatic division between Horace, a *vates* (poet/bard) in his *nemus* (grove),[115] and everyone else absorbed in their diverse occupations.

The *Odes*, by comparison with the *Satires*, present a more firmly entrenched autonomist image of Horace's poetic vocation and literary space. The figure of the poet is here afforded a sharper separation from Rome and Romans than satire allowed; he is disembedded both from the physical site of the city and, in ethical terms, from the quotidian world of practical activities. At the same time, he takes on more ambitious, public subject matter. In the following ode, for example, Horace speaks of the anger of the gods against Rome for the *nefas* (crime/abomination) of civil war, and the emergence of a semi-divine figure (implicitly Augustus) who will expiate Rome's sins and redirect her martial energy towards external enemies. He writes, in other words, as a civic bard on the model of Alcaeus. What allows, anchors, and counterbalances this newly public orientation of Horatian poetry,[116] however, is precisely the sequestered grove of *Odes* 1.1. The civic voice and the autonomous space of the grove are two sides of the same coin. Horace speaks all the more persuasively to the extent that he speaks, or sings, from the independent space of his vatic authority, dignified by the hieratic status of *Musarum sacerdos* ('priest of the Muses', *Carm.* 3.1.3), protected by patron gods and Muses, and enrobed in the mantle of the Greek lyric tradition.[117]

Horatian freedom tends to be constructed in terms of sheltered spaces and a focus on the small pleasures of the here and now rather than the broad canvas of history and action. One of the principle rhetorical gestures of the *Odes* might be termed 'redirection of the addressee's attention'. Typically, Horace counsels a friend or other addressee to cease to worry about some larger state of affairs, over which, in any case, they are unlikely to have much control, and redirect their

---

[114] The contrasting and culminating effects of the priamel accentuate Horace's separateness, as does Horace's awareness of the different life-paths or *bioi* discussed in Greek philosophy (Nisbet and Hubbard (1970), 2–3). On the poetic life-path as articulated by Horace's contemporary Tibullus, see R. Perelli (1996). *Secernunt*, as noted by Nisbet and Hubbard, ad loc., refers both to the separation afforded by the countryside and the Callimachean 'rejection of popular tastes and values'. Compare Fraenkel (1957), 174–5, 231.

[115] For the association between literary composition and rural retreat along with parallels, see Nisbet and Hubbard (1970), ad loc.

[116] For Nisbet and Hubbard (1970), 19, Horace's 'eulogies of the princeps are astonishing'. Most scholarship on the ode has been concerned with the date of the *prodigia* and thus the notional compositional date of the poem (Nisbet and Hubbard (1970), 17–19), and the relation to Virgil's *Georgics* (e.g. Fraenkel (1957), 244–7). It is worth remarking that, despite the ode's notionally high patriotic tone, Horace is careful to '[anticipate] ridicule' by 'deflating' his own potential pomposity (West (1967), 89–91) with several playful details (e.g. 9–12; compare Lyne (1995), 49).

[117] But see the remarks of Nisbet and Hubbard (1970), 3, on the Greek/Roman tension in the phrase *lyricis vatibus*. Note also Lyne (1995), 71, who observes the 'sheer audacity . . . of even suggesting the possibility of canonization as one of the *lyrici*'.

attention to the immediate pleasures of the present: the small but exquisite details of life, love, the symposion, and ultimately, the very poem they are reading. In 1.11, for example, Horace advises Leucothoe, who apparently takes an interest in astrology and horoscopes, that there is no way to know the future: *tu ne quaesieris, scire nefas, quem mihi, quem tibi / finem di dederint* ('do not seek to find out—it is wrong to know—what end for me, what end for you, the gods have given') 1.11.1–2). We cannot know how many more years Jupiter has given us to live: . . . *seu pluris hiemes seu tribuit Iuppiter ultimam, / quae nunc oppositis debilitat pumicibus mare /* ('. . . whether Jupiter has bestowed more winters, or [only this] final one, which now grinds down the Tyrrhenian sea by setting it against the rocks', 4–6). The brilliantly surprising image of the rocky cliffs wearing out the sea rather than the other way around affords a brief glimpse of vast, forbidding landscapes and an inhuman scale of time and relentless repetition. The closing lines abruptly redirect our attention:

> . . . sapias, vina liques, et spatio brevi
>   spem longam reseces. dum loquimur, fugerit invida
>   aetas: carpe diem, quam minimum credula postero.   (*Carm.* 1.11.6–8).

Be sensible, strain the wine, and prune back long hope within a limited space. While we talk, envious time will have fled: harvest the day, having as little faith as possible in tomorrow.

The syntax becomes curt and direct, the phrasing denser and even more epigrammatic than usual for Horace. Space and time are condensed to the present place and moment.[118] *Aetas* ('time') falls with abrupt force and solitary emphasis at the beginning of the ode's final line. Who cares about, or in any case who can truly comprehend, the immensity of ocean, cliffs, and Jupiter's designs? Better simply to seize today's 'harvest' of pleasure (*carpe diem*).

Just as Propertius makes us understand, in plausible psychological terms, his abbreviated poetic focus on *amor* by devising the first-person fiction of his amorous obsession with Cynthia, so Horace naturalizes the restrictive domain of lyric poetry by appealing to the age-old wisdom of the brevity of life and the urgent need to enjoy the present moment. In *Odes* 1.9, Horace develops a similar set of ideas in even more ambitious terms.[119]

> Vides ut alta stet nive candidum
> Soracte, nec iam sustineant onus
>   silvae laborantes, geluque
>   flumina constiterint acuto.
> dissolve frigus ligna super foco
> large reponens atque benignius
>   deprome quadrimum Sabina,
>   O Thaliarche, merum diota:
> permitte divis cetera, qui simul
> stravere ventos aequore fervido
>   deproeliantis, nec cupressi

---

[118] Horace's treatment of the choriambic metre is inextricably part of the effect: see West (1995), 53.

[119] Commager (1962), 274, suggests that *Carm.* 1.11 might be seen as 'a more explicit redaction of the Soracte Ode'. On the ode's many, varying interpretations, see especially Edmunds (1992), *passim.*

> nec veteres agitantur orni.
> quid sit futurum cras fuge quaerere et
> quem Fors dierum cumque dabit lucro
>   appone, nec dulcis amores
>   sperne puer neque tu choreas,
> donec virenti canities abest
> morosa. nunc et Campus et areae
>   lenesque sub noctem susurri
>   composita repetantur hora,
> nunc et latentis proditor intimo
> gratus puellae risus ab angulo
>   pignusque dereptum lacertis
>   aut digito male pertinaci.   (*Carm.* 1.9.1–24)

Do you see how Mt Soracte stands there gleaming with deep-piled snow, how the labouring forests no longer sustain their burden, and the rivers have frozen solid with sharp ice? Melt the cold by generously putting logs on the fire, Thaliarchus, and more lavishly pour out the four-year-old wine from its Sabine jar. Leave the rest to the gods; once they have lulled the winds that do battle with the seething sea, neither the cypresses nor the aged ash trees are shaken. Don't seek to know what tomorrow will bring, and whatever sum of days Chance yields you, put it in the credit column, and don't disdain sweet love affairs and dancing, while you are still a lad and your bloom of youth is untouched by peevish, white-haired old age. Now let the Campus and public squares and gentle whisperings under cover of night be sought out at the agreed-on time; now is the time for lovely laughter that gives away a girl hiding in an intimate corner, now is the time for love-tokens stripped from arms or finger feigning resistance.

Horace begins with a formidable vision of a vast frozen landscape: Mount Soracte covered in snow; forests buried; rivers paralysed with ice. Inside, by contrast, everything is warm, generous, melting:[120] there is a fire blazing, and wine, made from an Italian grape and stored in a jar that is of Sabine manufacture yet of Greek lexical origin (*diota*), will be poured out for present enjoyment. Nothing in this absorbing, sensuous world is frozen like Mount Soracte and the forests and rivers described in the opening strophes.[121] By the time we reach the end of this brief ode, we can appreciate the powerfully vertiginous effect: a poem that begins with a vast, immobile landscape narrows its focus at the end to the image of a single, malleable finger . . . giving way (*male pertinaci*).

Horace once again persuades us to redirect our attention to what truly matters—a small realm of warmth, change, and ephemeral pleasure by contrast with the inhuman immensity of the wider world with its seas crashing against rocks and wintry ice. Horace, of course, is also redirecting our attention to the taut, vital intricacies of the lyric poem. The repeated 'now' of the closing strophes points to the text before us, the constantly re-enacted present moment of reading and enjoyment,[122] coinciding, spatially, with the intimate corner of hiding and erotic playfulness. In general, Horatian lyric aligns itself with sheltered, limited

---

[120] See Commager (1962), 271, on the 'antithesis between warmth, tossing waters, moving branches, and green youth against coldness, icy streams, stillness, and white old age'.

[121] Nisbet and Hubbard (1970), 117: 'the weather has changed marvelously since the beginning of the poem'.

[122] Lowrie (1997), 49–50, reflects on the *hic et nunc* of lyric.

spaces of sequestration and leisure.[123] There is an important ideological dimension to Horace's creation of a space of lyric shelter structured in accordance with a division between large and small, that which is beyond our control (the big picture) and the humble matters we can arrange according to our pleasure (choice of wine, more logs on the fire, choice of erotic partners, the rules of drinking). The motto of 1.9—'leave the rest to the gods'—naturalizes an attitude that fits comfortably with the private citizen's willingness to leave the running of the world to men like Augustus and Agrippa. At the same time, a focus on the present moment, in the context of an Italy still traumatized by civil war and land confiscations, nicely accommodates the Augustan impetus to forget the unpleasantness of recent history.

Horace's apolitical autonomy is thus politically significant, yet he naturalizes, and thereby partially works to conceal the political aspect of, his quietist lyric realm by evoking a psychologically and aesthetically satisfying devotion to small, manageable Epicurean pleasures. One consequence of Horace's emphasis on shelter, separation, and exclusivity is an intensified sense that the poet occupies a sequestered domain: the countryside, the *nemus* ('grove'), the grotto of the Muses. Neither the strolling conversationalist of the *Satires*, nor the iambic speaker of the *Epodes*, demarcates a separate poetic domain as clearly and emphatically as the lyric singer of the *Odes*. A similar pattern is discernible in the formation of the poet's literary personality. While Horace's satirist certainly manifests a distinctive set of ethical preoccupations, he tends to avoid being grouped in an exclusive, separate category as poet. The poet of Horace's *Odes* is emphatically not an ordinary person, and poetry is inextricably bound up with this difference. Horace typically advertises his poetic status at the very moment he announces his ethics of *paupertas*, his devotion to *otium*, and his distinction from the crowd. In 2.16, Horace praises the value of *otium*, or, as Rudd translates, the 'quiet life',[124] and ends with a reference to his favoured status with the Muses:: *mihi parva rura et / spiritum Graiae tenuem Camenae / Parca non mendax dedit et malignum / spernere vulgus* ('To me Fate gave—it was no false gift[125]—a humble estate, slender inspiration of the Greco-Roman Muse,[126] and the right to disdain the envious crowd', *Carm.* 2.16.37–41). A recurrent autobiographical motif suggests that Horace, as poet, is under divine protection, that he enjoys an almost sacrosanct status that shields him from the fortuitous risks of life.[127] In 2.13, we first hear of an incident that will become a staple of Horatian autobiography: a

---

[123] For the notion of limit, compare *modus agri non ita magnus* (*Sat.* 2.6.1). The discussion of lyric *fines* in Oliensis (1998), 107ff., is fundamental.

[124] Rudd (2004), 127. For a discussion of how 'Horace . . . points to the difference between his own valuation of *otium* and that voiced by Catullus', see Fraenkel (1957), 211–14, and Putnam (2006), 90–1, who suggests that 'by deliberately beginning where Catullus ends . . . Horace pointedly asks us to read the two poems as a sequence and therefore to watch the differences between himself and his predecessor' (90).

Note also Commager (1962), 334, for whom the closing 'reference to poetry is not an afterthought but an integral part of the poem's progress'.

[125] Or Rudd (2004), 129: 'The Thrifty One that does not belie her name'.

[126] Rudd (2004) for *Graiae . . . Camenae*.

[127] See Davis (1991), 78–144, on Horatian poetic autobiography and 'modes of authentication'.

falling branch from a tree on the poet's property nearly killed him. If he had died, he imagines, he would have gone down to the underworld, and there witnessed Sappho and Alcaeus singing lyric poetry to an audience of their fellow shades (21–40).[128] Horace does not explicitly state that he was saved from death by his poetic status, but the juxtaposition of salvation from one of life's fortuitous accidents (13–20) with the posthumous immortality of canonical lyric poets is telling. Sappho and Alcaeus have survived their own deaths, as Horace may also hope to do.[129]

A comparable juxtaposition of danger and poetry occurs in 1.22. Horace states that the man 'of irreproachable life and unstained by crime'[130] (*integer vitae scelerisque purus*, 1), has no need of weapons to defend himself, even if he travels to notoriously dangerous faraway lands. As proof, he cites an anecdote reminiscent of the nearly-deadly-branch story: straying beyond the bounds of his property, singing of his Lalage (*dum meam canto Lalagen*, 10), unarmed, he encountered a huge wolf, which, however, simply fled him. The boundaries of the farm notionally provide Horace with a protected precinct, yet when he strays beyond them, an aura of sacrosanctity still attends his person.[131] This protected status is connected with poetry. In the closing strophe, we catch a glimpse of a cheerfully insouciant Horace, in defiance of his forbidding surroundings, celebrating his love for Lalage, whose name refers to speech itself, and the description of whose attributes constitutes a lyric genealogy stretching back to Sappho via Catullus: *pone sub curru nimium propinqui / solis in terra domibus negata: / dulce ridentem Lalagen amabo, / dulce loquentem* ('place me where the sun's chariot is too close in a land prohibiting habitation: I shall love Lalage sweetly laughing, sweetly speaking', 21–4).

This intensely metaliterary (and meta-lyric) closure points towards an aspect of Horace's autonomist poetics that goes beyond the idea of the poet as a protected person leading an autarkic existence. The verb *amabo* ('I shall love'), within the conventions of Roman metapoetics, is virtually equivalent to the claim, 'I shall sing/write love poetry about'. The closing image of Horace singing love poetry about his Sapphic 'chatterer' (Lalage), then, constitutes a gesture towards the act of creating lyric poetry itself, and discloses a somewhat different mode of autonomy. Whether or not we are meant to believe that poets are truly a protected species, Horace builds into this gently facetious argument[132] another argument for the autonomy of the poetic text: beneath the figure of the poet miraculously sheltered from the dangers that surround him we may discern intimations of the text as a sequestered realm, a site of aesthetic absorption. Comparably, in *Odes* 1.9, the closing evocation of a twilight scene in a Roman piazza, sketched in exquisite pointillist manner through Horace's artfully disparate word-order, threatens to dissolve the ethical argument within its rich aesthetic texture. The lyric speaker's ethical injunctions to enjoy the 'here and now' can be read

---

[128] See again G. Davis (1991), 78–89.   [129] Nisbet and Hubbard (1978), ad loc.

[130] Tr. Rudd (2004).

[131] On Horace's play with boundaries here, see Oliensis (1998), 109–10.

[132] The question of the humour and/or seriousness of 1.22 is treated at length by Fraenkel (1957), 184–8; note also Nisbet and Hubbard (1970), 263.

simultaneously, as Lowrie has observed, as pointers towards the aesthetic *hic et nunc* of the lyric poem the reader is enjoying.[133]

Horace, then, with a touch of light humour, claims that poetry envelops him in a protective atmosphere that exempts him from the ordinary conditions and risks of humanity. The humour does not really detract from, but by disarming the reader's scepticism reinforces, the poet's project of fashioning a specialized poetic status for himself through an evolving autobiographical mythology. At the same time, these 'autobiographical narratives' double as delineations of the segregated realm of the lyric text, the boundaries of the poetic realm, which is thereby designated 'safe', 'sacrosanct', and autonomous. Horace does not openly proclaim a rift between ethics and aesthetics, verse and *vita*, as Catullus did, and, given the patriotic, Augustan themes that are treated in his work, it would be difficult to assert that he sharply divorces poetry from the notion of social benefit. At the same time, he incorporates into his poetry an awareness of the concept of intrinsic poetic quality. In the more explicitly metapoetic passages of his *Satires*, he writes of the hard work of revision and 'writing properly' (e.g. *Sat.* 1.4.6–13), and at the close of *Satires* 2.1, he ingeniously plays between aesthetic and legal meanings of the terms *bonus* and *malus* (80–6), between poetic and forensic judgements. In the rather different generic ambiance of the *Odes*, where voice notionally dominates over script and metapoetic argument remains implicit, there is a pervasive yet largely unspoken tension between ethics and poetics. Ethical tags or injunctions afford a notional anchor to many poems which contain aesthetically intricate imagery that does not always seamlessly reiterate the ethical message. An injunction to 'enjoy sympotic pleasures in the present and ignore foreign wars' might be read either as an ethical prescription for how to live one's life, or a deictic gesture towards the elegantly ordered sympotic realm of Horace's lyric text as site of aesthetic absorption and refuge. Horace simultaneously lends articulation to a notional *modus vitae* removed from the risks and dangers of existence, and gives shape to his autonomist aesthetics.

A series of thematically linked odes in Books 2 and 3 articulate the safe, autonomist space of lyric against the background of historical violence and contemporary dangers. Here too Horace vividly evokes the pleasures of the symposion, while implicitly constructing a textual symposion, a site of aesthetic absorption, discursively positioned in relation to politics and the world at large. *Odes* 2.7, in which Horace welcomes back his civil war comrade Pompeius from exile, recalls the battle of Philippi. Whereas Pompeius was drawn back into the seething tumult of war, Mercury, patron and protector of lyric poets, rescued Horace (2.7.13–17). Horace now will 'rage' (*furere*, 28), but within the safe confines of a wild drinking bout—hardly the kind of heated temperament he once displayed as partisan of Brutus. In the present time and place—which is ultimately all that matters according to lyric's stated policy—quondam *sodales* (comrades) return to each other's company as *amici* (friends) in the lyric symposion,[134] where very different kinds of power and control (*quem Venus arbitrum /*

---

[133] Lowrie (1997), 49–50.

[134] See Davis (1991), 89ff., for discussion of how this ode works to 'authenticate' Horace's status as lyric poet through its references to the Greek lyric tradition.

dicet bibendi, 'whom will a throw of Venus declare arbiter of drinking?', 25–6) are at stake. *Odes* 2.7 is suggestive of the extent to which Horace's secure, autarkic persona as lyric poet relies on the new world Augustus has created: he allows civil warriors to return to Italian soil as peaceful symposiasts, poets, and friends; he has banished civil war in the name of enduring peace. The response to the poem's opening question—*quis te redonavit Quiritem / dis patriis Italoque caelo ...?* ('who restored you as citizen to your ancestral gods and Italian sky?', 3–4)—can only be 'Augustus'.

Odes 2.7 is one of several odes articulating this set of ideas connecting the lyric symposion with the new social order. Whereas, in 2.7, a thick shower of party talk draws the mind of Pompeius away from the bellicose, political past to a private, convivial scene of leisure and oblivion (*oblivioso ... Massico*, 21), in 2.11, a similar sequence of brief, urgent questions and commands draws the war-minded addressee's thoughts away from present military concerns to convivial necessities. Life's needs, according, to Horace, are actually few and simple, and we ought not wear out our minds with excessively vast and complicated topics: *quid aeternis minorem / consiliis animum fatigas* ('why do you wear out your mind, which is not equal to the task, with boundless considerations?', 11–12)? By a well-established pattern, Horace bids us to redirect our attention from big questions of foreign invasions and 'plans that stretch to infinity'[135] to the immediate pleasures that are before us. Horace points to a specific *locus amoenus* (*sub alta vel platano vel hac / pinu*, 'beneath a tall plane tree or this pine'), and the specific concerns of the moment: perfume, wine, a prostitute. The 'discreet' or out-of-the-way prostitute Lyde draws the poem to a close, literally, with a knot:[136] *eburna dic age cum lyra / maturet incomptum Lacaenae / more comam religata nodum* ('Go tell her to hurry up and come with her ivory lyre, after tying her hair in an uncombed knot in Spartan style',[137] *Carm.* 2.11.13–24). Just as, in *Odes* 1.9, the focus shifts from a vast, wintry landscape to a single capitulating finger, so here, the geographically broad, wandering, and even 'infinite' concerns of the worry-prone addressee have been funnelled to a single, taut image of closure and restriction (*incomptum ... religata*). Horace's unspoken implication is that the satisfying neatness of the aesthetic gesture matches with and lends support to the poem's ethical injunctions. Part of the aesthetic effect, however, derives from the enlivening tensions between infinity and taut closure, vastness of scope and neat encapsulation. This aesthetic remainder does not seamlessly fold into the stated moral programme.

The third book features a comparable pairing of convivial odes. In 3.8, Horace bids Maecenas put aside cares of state (*mitte civilis super urbe curas*, 17), given that they now live in a world made safe by Augustan arms (18–24). He may assume an attitude of negligence in Horace's lyric space, live, for a moment anyway, like a private citizen, and put aside serious concerns (*linque severa*, 28). Whereas 2.7 and 2.11 trace a movement from past civil war to present frontier warfare, displacing both with absorption in convivial pleasures, the comparably convivial 3.8 and 3.14 reverse this movement, going from (now resolved) foreign conflicts to Horace's (emphatically past) partisan involvement. *Odes* 3.14, in fact, joins the two themes.

---

[135] Tr. Rudd (2004).   [136] Oliensis (1998), 123.
[137] The text is highly disputed: see Nisbet and Hubbard (1978), ad loc.

Horace begins by celebrating the return of Augustus from Spain in 24 BC: now that Caesar guards the world, we may all safely enjoy private festivity.

> hic dies vere mihi festus atras
> eximet curas; ego nec tumultum
> nec mori per vim metuam tenente
>   Caesare terras.
> i pete unguentum, puer, et coronas
> et cadum Marsi memorem duelli,
> Spartacum si qua potuit vagantem
>   fallere testa.   (*Carm.* 3.14.13–20)

This day, which is truly festal for me, will take away my dark anxieties; I shall not fear either instability or death by violent means while Caesar rules the lands. Go, slave boy, and get perfume, garlands, and a wine jar that remembers the Marsian War, if any jug managed to escape the notice of the roving Spartacus.

As always, the lyric gesture consists in drawing our attention away from the wider world, which has been adequately taken care of, to the immediacies of the symposion: perfume, garlands, a jar of wine. This particular wine, however, carries with it memories of violent history, and so breaking it open now for present consumption is all the more pointed a conversion of historical anxiety into oblivion-inducing pleasures of the moment. In the closing strophes, Horace's memory continues to wander beyond the bounds of the symposion he is so intent on enacting.

> dic et argutae properet Neaerae
> murreum nodo cohibere crinem;
> si per invisum mora ianitorem
>   fiet, abito.
> lenit albescens animos capillus
> litium et rixae cupidos protervae;
> non ego hoc ferrem calidus iuventa
>   consule Planco.   (*Carm.* 3.14.21–28)

Tell clear-voiced Neara to waste no time tying up her myrrh-anointed hair in a knot; if any delay arises on account of the hateful door-keeper, be off. Greying hair mellows the spirit once keen on conflicts and vehement quarrels; I would *not* have put up with this in my hot-headed youth, during Plancus' consulship.

As in 2.11, a courtesan's hair becomes a metaphor for aesthetic restraint and, perhaps, constraint of mental attention, neatly echoing the taut closure of the Sapphic adoneus. Still, restraining ourselves from remembering, from allowing the mind to wander over 'unbounded concerns' (*aeternis . . . consiliis*), might mean we have to call to mind what we are so intent on *not* thinking about. So it is with Horace and his own partisan past: he both recalls to mind, and carefully frames as a long-buried sentiment, his service under Brutus at Philippi in 42 BC.[138]

Many of Horace's recommendations of sympotic pleasures, as we have had occasion to note, culminate in a moment of conspicuous *aesthetic* intensity and absorption: for example, the resisting yet malleable finger at the close of 1.9, the

---

[138] Note especially the comments of Oliensis (1998), 148.

neat yet uncombed knot in Lyde's hair at the close of 2.11. The poet's response to
the external pressures of the world is not simply the symposion as pleasurable
diversion, but the aesthetic contours of the sympotic poem, on which the reader is
encouraged to focus a lingering and not wholly ethically purposeful attention.
Horace persuasively evokes an appealing, antinomian life-path (retirement,
symposion, *otium*), while simultaneously drawing our attention to his lyric
text's aesthetic realm. Even so, political resonance is hardly banished from lyric's
exquisite pleasure-world. Odes 2.7, 2.11, 3.8, and 3.14 outline the delimited frame
of Horatian lyric, yet in none of these cases is lyric hermetically sealed from
external elements: the definition of the sympotic *angulus* recalls to mind the very
realms of activity (warfare, politics) from which it notionally affords shelter.[139]
While critics have traditionally seen in Horace's *Odes* a divide between authentically lyric aesthetics and the expansive presence of Augustus, lyric autonomy and
the princeps' restoration of the Roman social fabric are, in fact, related ideas.
Augustus' 'refoundation' of Rome in the wake of civil war is at once the subject of
Horace's poetry, and its premise: the autonomization of the poetic calling relies at
least in part on Augustus' creation of a stable social framework in which poetry
can securely be pursued as a full-time occupation, and aesthetic absorption enjoys
a moral justification. Turning away from the public realm to symposion, poetry,
and aesthetic sophistication implies that the public realm is adequately cared for
and regulated by an authoritative and reliable power.

Horace defines his poetic autonomy both in relation to politics and history, and
on a personal level, in relation to his patron Maecenas. The figure of the patron, in
Roman poets such as Tibullus, is traditionally set in tensional relation to the poet's
autonomy. But in this instance, too, what is often initially viewed in terms of a
stable opposition (autonomy vs patronal demands) displays unsuspected elements of complicity. Maecenas offers Horace both the unparalleled prominence
that only a major patron can offer in Roman society (*dulce decus meum*, *Carm.*
1.1.2), and his protection and support (*praesidium* 2). In the closing description of the poet's grove in 1.1, Maecenas makes an appearance: *quodsi me
vatibus lyricis inseres, / sublimi feriam sidera vertice* ('but if you include me in
the canon of lyric bards, I shall strike the stars with my exalted head', 35–6).
Maecenas gave Horace the farm (here reworked as the sacral-idyllic *nemus* of
lyric inspiration), and, by protecting and sheltering him, underwrites his
tranquil existence as retiring *vates*. Maecenas, in this middle period of
Horace's career, at once serves as buffer-figure between poet and *princeps*,
and shelters Horace from the need to seek other sources of financial support
and social protection. His is a uniquely unconstraining style of patronage; he
does not require much in the way of explicit panegyric, and encourages his
poet friend to follow his own path and to lay claim to his own autonomous
domain, both in poetry and Italian real estate.[140]

---

[139] My use of this Horatian term (*angulus*, 'corner') derives from R. Ferri (1993), 12; a key
discussion of the two 'Horaces'—the one ironic, retiring, Callimachean, Epicurean, and the other
sublime, 'Bacchic', propagandistic—in Fowler (1995b), esp. 266.

[140] The bibliography on Maecenas is too vast to record here: but note the helpful synthesis of Lyne
(1995), 132–8 and *passim*, the trenchant observations of Syme (1939), 460, and the important
arguments of White (1993), 134–8.

In some respects, Maecenas actually facilitates Horace's autonomist stance by allowing the poet to define himself against him without forgoing the prestige and shelter his long-term patronage affords. In a short ode in the first book, Horace commemorates Maecenas' recovery from serious illness and his subsequent appearance in the theatre of Balbus.

> Vile potabis modicis Sabinum
> cantharis, Graeca quod ego ipse testa
> conditum levi, datus in theatro
>   cum tibi plausus,
> clare Maecenas eques, ut paterni
> fluminis ripae simul et iocosa
> redderet laudes tibi Vaticani
>   montis imago.
> Caecubum et prelo domitam Caleno
> tu bibes uvam: mea nec Falernae
> temperant vites neque Formiani
>   pocula colles.   (*Carm.* 1.20)

You shall drink cheap Sabine from modest cups, wine which I bottled and sealed in a Greek jar with my own hands on the occasion when, in the theatre, you received such applause, Maecenas, renowned knight, that the banks of your ancestral river and a playful echo from the Vatican Hill sounded back your praises. *You* can drink Caecuban and the grape tamed by the wine-press of Cales: *my* cups are not tempered either by Falernian vines or Formian hills.

Much has been written on this poem's layered metaliterary commentary on memory, publicity, genre, and mimesis.[141] Wine, as always in the *Odes*, is a potential metonym for lyric, and processes of storage, aging, and enjoyment figuratively evoke the creation of a commemorative text composed in Latin language, Greek metre, and on Italian soil (*Sabinum ... Graeca*), of humble generic pretensions but constructed with great personal care (*ego ipse ... levi*), a text that has undergone lengthy preparation in hopes of providing immediate pleasure at the moment of its reading/consumption. Horace will commemorate his distinguished friend Maecenas, but in a brief, intricately constructed poem remarkable more for precision of detail and artifice than for panegyrical grandeur. The premise of this ode is that Horace is allowed to write the kind of poetry he chooses to write; he enjoys the autonomy of his own values and domain, here figured by the wine served at Horace's house or villa by contrast with the wine Maecenas habitually drinks at home. Lexical nuance hints at an acerbic independence unmitigated (*temperant*) and untamed (*domitam*) by the smoother, richer vintages of the patron.[142]

Horace is preaching, of course, to the converted. Maecenas knows that Horace is giving him the best product he has to offer; he does not really feel a strong need to be served the richer vintages of epic and panegyric.[143] He has enough of that sort of thing, should he want it. Maecenas both confirms Horace's status as protected poet and, through friendly juxtaposition and contrast, reinforces

---

[141] e.g. Nisbet and Hubbard (1970), ad loc., Race (1978), Macleod (1979), Cairns (1992).
[142] West (1995), 97–8.
[143] White (1993), 22, on the 'publicity potential' of the minor genres.

lyric's slender aesthetic confines and ethics of humility. *Odes* 3.29, an ode near the end of the lyric collection, turns once more to Horace's friend and patron. The first line of this quasi-valedictory ode recalls the opening of 1.1: *Tyrrhena regum progenies* ('Etruscan descendant of kings'). Horace, not for the first time, calls his friend away from the weighty cares of state to the relaxation of the symposion. Yet in order to attend Horace's private party, he must tear himself away from his 'blasé surfeit' (*fastidiosam . . . copiam*, 9)[144] and towering residence, and cease to gaze in admiration at the 'smoke, wealth, and noise of prosperous Rome' (12).

There is more than a bit of teasing of Maecenas as a rich man obsessed with Rome and his luxurious properties,[145] but, as usual, we can assume a substratum of shared sensibility. Maecenas can easily appreciate Horace's independence, since he presumably encouraged him to stand apart from the crowd in the first place. The Sabine farm implied as much, and Maecenas' exclusive circle of writers was never meant for all and sundry. The closural portrait of the two friends weaves together the themes of Horace's previous poetry for Maecenas, distilling them in a singularly dense, unforgettable ode.

> . . . quod adest memento
> componere aequus; cetera fluminis
>   ritu feruntur, nunc medio alveo
>   cum pace delabentis Etruscum
>
>   in mare, nunc lapides adesos
> stirpesque raptas et pecus et domos
>   volventis una non sine montium
>   clamore vicinaeque silvae,
>
>   cum fera diluvies quietos
> irritat amnis. ille potens sui
>   laetusque deget, cui licet in diem
>   dixisse 'vixi': cras vel atra
>
>   nube polum Pater occupato
> vel sole puro: non tamen irritum,
>   quodcumque retro est, efficiet neque
>   diffinget infectumque reddet,
>
>   quod fugiens semel hora vexit.
> Fortuna saevo laeta negotio et
>   ludum insolentem ludere pertinax
>   transmutat incertos honores,
>
>   nunc mihi, nunc alii benigna.
> laudo manentem; si celeris quatit
>   pennas, resigno quae dedit et mea
>   virtute me involvo probamque
>
>   pauperiem sine dote quaero.
> non est meum, si mugiat Africis
>   malus procellis, ad miseras preces

---

[144] Tr. Rudd (2004).

[145] Lyne (1995), 111, detects a Horace who is more 'self-assertive', and who takes more liberties, than in previous poems to Maecenas. He also notes a more self-assured tone in Horace's advice to Maecenas to put aside his political responsibilities and his comments on his patron's wealth. On the 'teasing' tone, see Nisbet and Rudd (2004), 346.

> decurrere et votis pacisci
>   ne Cypriae Tyriaeque merces
> addant avaro divitias mari.
> tunc me biremis praesidio scaphae
>   tutum per Aegaeos tumultus
>   aura feret geminusque Pollux.   (*Carm.* 3.29.32–64)

. . . . remember to attend, level-headed, to what lies immediately at hand; all else flows away like a river, which one moment slides peacefully along the middle of its bed to the Etruscan sea, and the next whirls along wave-worn rocks, uprooted trunks, herd animals and houses, all together, to the accompanying roar of mountains and nearby woods, when savage deluge stirs up its tranquil waves. He will be master of himself and happy in his existence who can say at each day's end, 'I have lived': tomorrow let father Jove fill the skies with black clouds or unobstructed sun; but he will not annul whatever is past, nor will he render null and void what once the fleeing hour has carried away. Fortune, pleased with her brutal business, and persistent in her haughty game, shifts her fleeting honours, now generous to me, now to another. I praise her while she stays. If she shakes her swift wings in flight, I resign what she gave, wrap myself up in my own virtue, and seek to wed myself, without dowry, to honorable poverty. You won't catch me–if the mast should groan under blasts of the southwest wind–resorting to desperate prayers and haggling with vows to prevent merchandise of Cyprus and Tyre from increasing the riches of the greedy sea. Instead, in the protection of a two-oared life-raft, I will be wafted safely through the storms of the Aegean by the breeze and Pollux and Pollux' twin.

The main ideas are familiar from Hellenistic philosophy: the importance of being ethically self-sufficient, impervious to changes of fortune. Horace enjoys good fortune while it lasts, but if it flits away, he will 'resign what she gave' and wrap himself up in his own virtue (*mea / virtute me involvo*).[146] The reflexive language and syntax of this last phrase nicely embodies the intensely autarkic image of turning onto one's self and one's own intrinsic ethical resources and qualities. Horace clearly admires the immense power of chance as illustrated in the image of the river in flood wreaking its violence across the boundaries of lines and strophes, but, with a calm shrug, insists that, whatever happens in the wider world, one can only *cultiver son propre jardin*, or, as he puts it, 'calmly arrange what is at hand'. The man who appreciates this principle, and lives one day at a time, is, in another tellingly reflexive phrase, 'master of himself' (*potens sui*).

By the closing strophe, Horace's river imagery and philosophical diatribe have built up their own considerable momentum, and Maecenas remains only subliminally present in the reader's mind. The image of the autonomist poet, enfolded in the cloak of his own virtue, master of himself, has achieved a lonely dominance. In the closing strophe, we see Horace fearlessly facing a raging sea under the paradoxical protection (*praesidio*) of his two-oared life-raft. Once again, poetry itself, or the poet's attitude of autarkic integrity, surrounds him with an aura of security in a violent, unpredictable world. Maecenas, whom Horace conveniently

---

[146] Note the more explicit version at *Epistles* 1.7.34, where Horace, in the context of his relationship with Maecenas, states that, if confronted with the story of the vixen who is unable to escape from a bin of grain after gorging herself, he will give up/rescind/unseal/repay (*resigno*) everything (*cuncta*). This provocative statement is discussed by Oliensis (1998), 159–60; on *resigno*, Nisbet and Rudd (2004), ad loc.

omits amidst the torrent of strophes building up the portrait of his own splendidly defiant autonomy, is nonetheless intimately connected with Horace's security as poet. Horace is one of 'Mercury's men' (*Carm.* 2.17.29), but equally he might be counted one of 'Maecenas' men', and if Fortune has looked favourably on him, that is chiefly because Maecenas did.[147] Horace's sheltered poetic realm, his autonomy, though sometimes seen as intrinsically opposed to the figure of the patron, were arguably made possible by Maecenas in the first place. Maecenas had the shrewdness to perceive that his favoured poets would produce more convincing testimony to the changed character of the times if they were encouraged to do so in their own way, on their own terms. If the present ode finally loses sight of Maecenas, that is a measure of the extent to which Horace has internalized the principle of poetic autonomy fostered by his patron.

Ode 3.29 is the self-representational climax of the lyric collection. The rousing closing scene, in which Horace climbs into a tiny boat to face a wild storm at sea, is the dramatic culmination of a series of interconnected motifs of autarky, self-reliance, and Callimachean astringency built up over three books of lyric poetry. This ode is followed, appropriately, by the celebration of the poet's 'monument more enduring than bronze' in 3.30.

> Exegi monumentum aere perennius
> regalique situ pyramidum altius,
> quod non imber edax, non Aquilo impotens
> possit diruere aut innumerabilis
> annorum series et fuga temporum.
> non omnis moriar, multaque pars mei
> vitabit Libitinam: usque ego postera
> crescam laude recens, dum Capitolium
> scandet cum tacita virgine pontifex.   (*Carm.* 3.30.1–9)

I have built a monument more lasting than bronze and higher than the royal structure of the pyramids, which cannot be destroyed by corroding rain, uncontrolled Aquilo, and the numberless series of years and time's flight. I shall not wholly die, and a large part of me shall evade Libitina. I shall grow ever fresh with praise of posterity, as long as the pontifex ascends the Capitol with the silent virgin.

These two closural odes are more closely linked than has been adequately appreciated.[148] A series of implicit connections may be drawn between the poetic monument as described in 3.30 and the personality that is supposed to have created it. At the close of 3.29, Horace, in one final version of 'the poet's security in the face of danger', notionally entrusts himself to a tiny skiff in the midst of a vast raging ocean. In the next poem, his immaterial monument, more enduring than physically impressive structures, will accomplish the unlikely task of holding out against the corrosive forces of wind, rain, and time itself. The poet will live on in this monument (*non omnis moriar*), evading mortal danger one last time. The poetic work is an edifice that will endure as long as the fabric of Roman culture

---

[147] Discussion of Horace and Mercury in Fraenkel (1957), 163–6. As Oliensis (1998), 48, notes, in *Satires* 2.6, Mercury as donor of the Sabine farm alludes, through homophony, to the figure of Maecenas (*Maia nate*, 5; see also above).

[148] But see Commager (1962), 314–15.

itself (7–9). The kind of person capable of making such a monument, we are to understand, is no ordinary artisan answerable to quotidian interests and motives. Rather, he is someone very much like the figure who emerges in the previous ode, a figure who is not dependent on the gifts of fickle Fortune, but truly independent and autonomous. He and his immortal edifice are the perfect antidote to the devastating, chaotic whim of *Aquilo impotens* ('the out-of-control South Wind'): indeed, he is *potens sui* ('master of himself').

M. Lowrie acutely observes that the poetic 'monument' of 3.30, unlike broadly comparable metaphors in Pindar, is not nominally a monument *to* anyone—a patron, for example.[149] Rather, the autonomously valuable poetic work is a monument to itself and its author's talent. This observation has the further advantage of contributing to our understanding of why Maecenas recedes from view in the latter half of 3.29. Horace, at least to some degree, transcends the patronal dimension of his poetry, as he moves towards crowning himself with Apollonian laurels and imprinting his *monumentum* with a *sphragis* recalling the land of his origins (10–16).[150] The work, conceived as monument, is a fait accompli, as the perfect tense (*exegi*, 'I have built') indicates; it exists on its own terms as permanent item in the repertoire of Roman culture, rather than existing relationally, embedded within the communicative context of the asymmetrical friendship between Horace and his patron.[151] Implicitly, Horace's deathless poetic work enjoys the same autonomously valid, taken-for-granted existence as Capitolium, pontifex, and Vestal. Even as Horace hints at links between the autarkic figure of 3.29 and his poetic monument, he moves beyond the more restrictive autonomy of antinomian social posture or life-realm, and posits the independent value of his artisanally constructed work. The language of construction (*exegi*) and focus on the materiality of made objects stress this aspect. His monument is not immediately linked with moral utility, but will endure through its aesthetic excellence.

The first line of the first poem of *Odes* 1–3 showcases Maecenas, as does the opening line of 3.29, but in the closural 3.30, Maecenas makes way for Horace's splendidly isolated *monumentum aere perennius* ('monument more lasting than bronze') that manages to eclipse two wonders of the world in two lines, and, like Propertian *ingenium*, to overcome mortality itself. The absence of Maecenas in 3.30 is all the more striking for the fact that 1.1 and 3.30, the first and final odes of the collection, are the only two odes in first Asclepiadic metre in *Odes* 1–3. Maecenas, however, still lingers in the mind, if somewhat faintly, from the previous ode, while the metrical reminiscence of 1.1 might prompt us to recall that Horace's autonomy as poet owes much to Maecenas' protection and

---

[149] Lowrie (1997), 72–3.

[150] Lyne (1995), 111, on 3.29: 'the carefully displaced honour of penultimacy'; Nisbet and Rudd (2004), 345, compare the highly similar structure of *Epistles* 1, where initial and penultimate poems are addressed to Maecenas, and the final poem is a *sphragis*. Oliensis (1998), 180, observes, moreover, that both collections culminate in 'a meditation on poetic immortality that looks past Maecenas to a figure that embodies Horace's poetry—the Muse in *Odes* 3.3.30, the poetry book itself in *Epistles* 1.20'. Thus, the structure of the poetic book incorporates the autonomist strategy of displacing the patron with the isolated work (Zetzel 1982).

[151] Nisbet and Rudd (2004) note the shift from the cautious future tense at *Carm.* 1.1.29 (*quodsi me lyricis vatibus inseres*) to the confident perfect tense of 3.30.1.

tolerance. The *città eterna* against which Horace measures his poetry's eternity, moreover, is not just any Rome, but the Rome Augustus was *making* eternal as he went about transforming it from brick to gleaming marble. The specific metonyms employed here as symbols of Rome's *aeternitas*, the Capitolium and the Vestal Virgins, existed in their contemporary splendour by the grace of Augustus' assiduous efforts at restoring the physical and religious fabric of the City. Monument is hardly a casually chosen metaphor. Augustus was responsible for the monumental building in relation to which Horace defines his poetry's immortality and cultural importance. At the same time, these same symbols and monuments specified by Horace predate Augustus and will outlast him. They may evoke his interventions in the urban fabric, yet they equally suggest an eternal Rome (and Horatian poetic monument) that is independent of any given ruler.[152]

The conception of a monumental lyric oeuvre in 3.30 recaps and gives an explicit name to the evident ambitions of the so-called 'Roman Odes' at the start of *Odes* 3. The first six poems in Book 3 treat an interconnected series of themes relating to Augustan ideology and the moral restoration of Rome.[153] Throughout the sequence, intensified focus on the poet's sequestered status and authority accompanies a more elevated tone and overtly panegyrical intent.

> Odi profanum vulgus et arceo;
> favete linguis: carmina non prius
>   audita Musarum sacerdos
>   virginibus puerisque canto.
> regum timendorum in proprios greges,
> reges in ipsos imperium est Iovis,
>   clari Giganteo triumpho,
>   cuncta supercilio moventis.   (*Carm.* 3.1.1–8)

I abhor the profane mob and keep it far off. Observe silence. As priest of the Muses I chant to maidens and boys songs not heard before. Kings who inspire fear wield power over their own flocks; over kings themselves power is wielded by Jove, who, renowned for his triumph over the Giants, moves all things with his brow.

As in 1.1, Horace separates himself from the crowd, and occupies a specially designated poetry-space, where he receives inspiration from the Muses. As *Musarum sacerdos* ('priest of the Muses'), he occupies a hieratic status that further distinguishes him from the *profanum vulgus* ('profane crowd') and his fellow Romans generally. With no preamble, Horace then outlines a diagram of kingly authority, with the lines of power flowing from Jove to earthly kings. There is a certain abruptness in this opening juxtaposition of the poet's sacerdotal precinct, in which Horace's sole, authoritative voice enjoins silence, with the Olympian vision of cosmic *imperium*, in which a single Jovian 'eyebrow' (*supercilio*) controls the fate of everything (*cuncta*). Indeed, the two orienting compass points of the Roman Odes are, on the one hand, Horace's elevated vatic status,[154] and on the other, Augustus' Jovian authority.

---

[152] I owe this last point to an anonymous reviewer for Oxford University Press.

[153] See discussions of Oliensis (1998), 124–7, 131–3, and Lowrie (1997), 224–65; on the first Roman ode (*Carm.* 3.1), Woodman (1984).

[154] See Lyne (1995), 160, on the connotations of Horace's newly claimed status of 'poet-priest'.

Significantly, Maecenas has no place in this polarized scheme. Ode 3.4 is a perfect example of such polarization. The first half of the ode constitutes the most elaborate contribution so far to the mythologization of Horace's poetic status. The second half is taken up by a gigantomachy affording an extended symbolic parallel to the defeat of the impious, senseless violence of Cleopatra and Antony by the rationally controlled force of Augustus. Once again, poetic and political/military *imperium* are juxtaposed by carefully balanced structure. The 'pivot' between the two halves of the ode is a strophe in which the Muses entertain 'great Caesar' in the wake of his military exertions: *vos Caesarem altum, militia simul / fessas cohortis abdidit oppidis, / finire quaerentem labores / Pierio recreatis antro* ('you restore great Caesar in a Pierian grotto, as he seeks to bring an end to his toils, now that he has retired his war-weary cohorts in the towns', 37–41).

It is as if the inherent dignity and autonomy of poetry need to be increased proportionally to counterbalance the increased prominence and proximity, in these more overtly panegyrical odes, of Augustus' immense authority. Maecenas no longer affords a sheltering buffer for Horace. Poetry needs to generate its own protective aura, its own counterbalancing force-field of sacrosanctity. Horace still avoids direct contact with Augustus; he does not address Augustus, and it is the Muses, not Horace himself, who 'restore' Augustus in the Pierian grotto. E. Oliensis has persuasively argued that Horace works on a principle of mutual exclusion: odes that advertise Augustus' authority as *princeps* are not the same as those that advertise Horace's authority as *vates*.[155] I agree that Horace avoids contexts where these separate domains of authority might overlap or infringe on each other, but I would further suggest that he deliberately juxtaposes Augustus' sphere of power and his own space of autonomy in a way that is comparable to Propertius' juxtaposition of Love's and Caesar's respective domains. The strategy of juxtaposition (as opposed to sheer avoidance or exclusion) clarifies the boundaries of the political and poetic realms, emphasizing both their distinctness and their complementarity.[156] It also implicitly elevates and dignifies Horace's poetic realm.

This new pattern is broadly compatible with what we have seen thus far in the *Odes*. Poetic autonomy and Augustan power are not so much intrinsically opposed as tensionally related to and defined by each other. The Augustan peace provides the enabling conditions for the poet's *otium*, and the princeps' war-domain underwrites the poet's peaceful aesthetic absorption. The Roman Odes, however, represent some further developments. The Maecenas-paradigm of shelter and buffer-space between poet and princeps appears to be receding. At the same time, the poet starts to look more structurally similar to the *princeps*. Like Augustus, Horace associates himself with divinity, asserts control over his domain

---

[155] Oliensis (1998), 128.

[156] Note also Lowrie (1997), 264–5, on how Horace manages to give voice to imperial themes and 'policy', while maintaining his own authority and 'the rhetorical upper hand'. Moreover, 'the fact that Horace does not actually address Augustus contributes to his independence', for 'he speaks as *Musarum sacerdos* (*Carm.* 3.1.3), yes, a priesthood, but one that he has invented for himself and consequently outside the state' (265). Horace makes Augustus' decision look like his own recommendation, and creates a role 'outside the constraints of power' through the immunity granted by the Muses' protection (265).

of authority, and is the 'first and foremost' (*princeps*) in his chosen arena of endeavour. Given that poetic prestige and achievement were always based on conceptions of prestige in the public sphere, we should not underestimate the extent to which the emergence of the principate makes possible the Augustan conception of the poet. Augustan poets vaunt their quasi-military prestige and dominance over their rivals, their 'triumphal' honours, and their status as public purveyors of values and architects of enduring monuments.[157]

Comparison of Horace's with Propertius' third book produces some striking parallels. In both instances, an elevated, hieratic poet-figure advertises Dionysiac inspiration as the sign of more elevated panegyrical ambitions, and a monumental conception of the poetic work accompanies reduction of Maecenas' patronal role. Claims of poetic autonomy and authority are intensified in proportion as ruler panegyric becomes less cloaked and indirect. The image of poetry as an enduring, public monument, however, affords a conception of poetic autonomy very different from the motifs of sequestration and Callimachean restriction that define Horace's and Propertius' earlier poetry.[158] Those spaces of restriction were, from the outset, maintained through careful rhetorical strategies. The public, political dimension of the poet's sequestered role had to be carefully framed and controlled in relation to the notional sphere of Callimachean narrowness so as to avoid the appearance of incoherence. Both poets, moreover, play between different models of poetic identity and autonomy: on the one hand, the restrictive realm of axiological autonomy as embodied in the poet's ostensibly antinomian lifestyle, and on the other, the autonomy of the poetic work as defined by intrinsic criteria of value and quality. In this regard, the two Augustan poets follow Catullus, who insisted on a sharp division between the ethical and the aesthetic. In Propertius' and Horace's case, however, poetic autonomy takes on a new ideological significance in the context of Augustan *pax* and *otium* (leisure/political stability). Catullus' polemical aesthetic propositions have begun to be assimilated to the cultural ideology of the emerging imperial order.

Horace continued his efforts to develop the concept of literary autonomy in his later works, albeit in a changing social and political environment. His first and second book of *Epistles*, which were written approximately in the decade following the publication of *Odes* 1–3, are concerned with defining poetry's autonomy in the wake of developments that have decisively undermined the once helpful, but now increasingly outdated, fictions of poetic privacy and sequestration. The obsolescence of Maecenas' role as buffer-figure is accompanied by the emergence of a new paradigm of direct interaction between poets and princeps. Related to this new paradigm are shifts in political culture following the second 'constitutional settlement' in 23 BC. The princeps' role by this period has become better established, and the powers that now define him, *maius imperium* and *tribunicia potestas*, are both held for long periods, belong to Augustus and members of the imperial family, and, particularly in the case of *tribunicia potestas*, come to signify the emperor's period of rule. Both are more or less permanent powers that can be

---

[157] Feeney (2002).

[158] See Lyne (1995), 21–30 on Horace's shift to a more overtly public and political role as poet in the 20s.

handed on to a dynastic successor.[159] Even as he works to solidify dynastic stability, Augustus turns his attention more fully to the project of moral, civic, and religious renewal. From about 13 BC, Augustus focuses on a series of socially restorative and morally cleansing measures that would culminate in 17 BC with the *ludi saeculares* and the commencement of the New Age: these include restoration of Roman honour through the return of the Parthian standards (18 BC), the passage of the marriage and adultery laws (18 BC), and a census and purge of the senate. Poets, it was understood, were (unofficially) encouraged to contribute to this ambitious renovation of Roman values.[160]

Horace and Propertius' third and fourth books of poetry suggest that there was interest in a new kind of poetry on public themes to which the more sequestered style of poetic identity fostered by poets throughout most of the 20s was ill suited. Again, there are two potential reasons for this development. First, the poet's autarkic privacy becomes less persuasive an idea now that some Augustan poets have achieved lasting glory and enjoy association with the most prominent men in Rome. Second, the confinement of poetry to a sheltered niche, overseen by the sophisticated indulgence of Maecenas, belongs to the early, transitional period of Augustus' principate, when the fostering of patriotic renewal was not yet the full-time focus of the regime, and the *princeps* was laying a great deal of emphasis on republican traditions, the autonomy of traditional spheres of activity and modes of expression, and his own non-monarchical status. A cohort of publicly patronized court poets surrounding the emperor did not suit the image Augustus was hoping to foster at the time. Augustus probably saw himself as well served by the highly calculated impression of the poets' retiring status. Starting in the later 20s, the need for this transitional system of poetic sequestration and Maecenas' buffering role receded, and at the same time, poetry's public role came to the fore as the focus shifted to fostering and publicizing patriotic values and the renovation of *mores*.

The transition to a new pattern of literary patronage was not seamless; nor, as I hope to show, does autonomist rhetoric become any less prominent. The shift from Maecenas' patronage to a direct relation between poet and princeps, as well as some of the tensions in the new arrangement, are obliquely suggested by an anecdote in Suetonius. Augustus, seeking help during a period of ill health, invites Horace to assume the position of his secretary in charge of correspondence (*ab epistulis*); in doing so, Horace, as Augustus urbanely remarks, would be making a transition 'from [Maecenas'] parasite's table to this regal table'. Horace politely declines.[161] In subsequent years, Horace devotes himself to his new literary project, culminating in the publication of *Epistles* 1 in 20 BC. Horace, then, chooses to become the author of literary epistles, rather than Augustus' secretary *ab epistulis*,[162] and, in the process, subjects his position as writer in Roman society to a newly rigorous examination, unpacking the implications of the literary and political developments of the past decade.

---

[159] See the discussion of Gruen (2005).

[160] A few highlights: Syme (1939), 459–75; White (1993); Andrew Wallace-Hadrill (1997); the collections of Woodman and West (1984) and Woodman and Powell (1992).

[161] Suetonius *Vita Horati.*   [162] Freudenburg (2002b), 35–6.

Horace, in his *Epistles*, returns to the artfully colloquial hexameter line of his *Satires*, but with a more overtly writerly and philosophical bent. Horace comes off as more detached and less obliged to pursue the everyday *officia* of a friend of humble status than in the *Satires*, and there is no longer the cheerful background of the pleasure-apparatus and sympotic sociability of the *Odes*. Horace's ethical astringency and tendency to retire to the isolation of his farm, books, and writing are here all the more starkly apparent. The sense of autarkic isolation, however, is only one side of the picture. A duality informs the underlying dynamic of the *Epistles*: the letter is at once an established philosophical medium, and a medium employed for the practicalities of political position-taking and everyday communication.[163] Horace takes advantage of the position of letter-writer as a means of articulating the relation between himself and others, defining his own preferences and ethical commitment through dialogue and contrast (e.g. *Epist.* 1.11, 12). Letters, however, are also written at the behest of others, or to answer the concerns and demands of others. They are an eminently social medium, and partaking in epistolary correspondence implies at least a minimum level of commitment to the social world and social obligations. The Horatian letter-writer is thus at once isolated and socially engaged, autarkically detached and devoted to pushing his literary image out into the world—in some cases ostensibly to bring about real-world outcomes (1.9). Horace's letter-writer is a philosopher living and acting in Roman society.[164]

Horace's epistolary philosophy, moreover, is itself confessedly untethered in its affiliation. In *Epistles* 1.1, he announces that moral philosophy will now constitute his main concern as opposed to lyric *ludicra* (playthings), but insists that, in pursuing this new interest, he will not be 'bound to swear on the words of any one master', but instead will yield to the arguments of now one philosopher or school and now another. Ethical flexibility becomes a new strategy of Horatian autonomy.

> ac ne forte roges quo me duce, quo lare tuter,
> nullius addictus iurare in verba magistri,
> quo me cumque rapit tempestas, deferor hospes.
> nunc agilis fio et mersor civilibus undis,
> virtutis verae custos rigidusque satelles;
> nunc in Aristippi furtim praecepta relabor,
> et mihi res, non me rebus subiungere conor.   (*Epist.* 1.1.13–19)

And in case you should perchance ask under whose guidance, in what abode I take shelter: I am not bound to swear on the words of any master, and am carried as a sojourner wherever the storm takes me. One moment I become active and am submerged in the waves of civic life, a guardian and inflexible attendant of true virtue; the next moment, I stealthily slip back to the precepts of Aristippus, and strive to subordinate circumstances to myself, not myself to circumstances.

---

[163] Oliensis (1998), 154.

[164] Lyne (1995), 186–92, possibly goes too far in his emphasis on Horace's 'abandonment of the public role'. One might also argue that he was re-fashioning that role to suit different conditions. Oliensis' remark is apt: 'this portrait of studious retirement effectively keeps its author in the world's eye' (1998), 154.

The duality of the epistle, both as mode of social engagement and as sign of autonomy, is therefore nicely accommodated by the labile nature of Horace's philosophical position as defined at the outset of the collection. Significantly, a key question singled out as an example of this broader strategy of flexibility is whether one should, following Aristippus, 'bend circumstances to oneself', or, on the contrary, 'bend oneself to circumstances'. The very principle of self-determination or ethical autonomy appears to be up for negotiation depending on situation or plausibility of individual argument. Horace, whose literary production has been premised on withdrawal into a life of *otium*, now envisages the possibility of partaking in a life of active, civic participation (*nunc agilis fio et mersor civilibus undis*).[165]

The question is not merely theoretical, as ancient ethical philosophy was aimed towards the practical issue of how to live one's life. Two epistles, 1.17 and 1.18, offer advice on how to behave as friend of the powerful, a practical question highly relevant to Horace's own conduct as poet in Augustan Rome. In 1.17, Horace addresses his recommendations to the emblematically named 'Scaeva' ('Mr Gauche'), while in 1.18, he advises Lollius Maximus how to comport himself with socially superior friends. In 1.17, the flexible hedonist Aristippus helps uncover the path towards living with great men successfully. In this context, 'bending circumstances to oneself' means making the most of whatever circumstances one finds oneself in, as opposed to maintaining an inflexible concept of unwavering virtue that is non-context-dependent. Horace's Aristippus may have to perform services for others or 'play the *scurra*' in order to get what he wants, yet he insists that he does so (with a paradoxical hint of autarkic reflexivity) for himself alone (*scurror ego ipse mihi*, 19). A comparable line of thinking leads Horace to make some surprisingly heteronomist suggestions to Lollius in 1.18, at times coming perilously close to offering up the sort of *ars parasitica* the epistle's opening lines disavow (1.18.1–8).

For all that Horace appears to be provoking his readers with a deliberate travesty of the ethics of virile independence, his modest proposals to Scaeva and Lollius cannot be entirely dismissed as ironic. His own biography, appended to the book as a cleverly framed *sphragis*, documents among his successes his record of winning the approval of leading men.[166] Surely he did not succeed in doing so purely by following his own inclinations and insisting on his autonomy on *all* occasions. Nor was it an easy task: *dulcis inexpertis cultura potentis amici: / expertus metuit* ('Cultivation of a powerful friend is pleasant—for those who have not tried it: he who has, dreads it', *Epist.* 1.18.86–7).

The ending of the same epistle, finds the poet in his chilly, isolated retreat by the stream of Digentia, aspiring to 'live for himself' alone (*mihi vivam*, 107), subsisting on

---

165 Immersion metaphors, going back to *Odes* 2.7.15–16, often signify ethical autonomy vs heteronomy: being 'overcome' by an irresistible tide or current is opposed to self-regulation and successfully 'steering' a vessel (even a very small one: *Odes* 3.29.62) over the deep. 'Cool' vs seething is a leitmotif within this broader metaphor: 'cool' and 'shade' suggest a calm, detached, tranquil temperament and condition of retreat (e.g. the *gelidum nemus*); the *fretis . . . aestuosis* of *Odes* 2.7.16 are doubly opposed to the ethical state Horace aspires to maintain.

166 *Me primis urbis belli placuisse domique*, *Epist.* 1.20.23. The link between this autobiographical claim and the ethical 'philosophy' of 1.17 is explicit: *principibus placuisse viris non ultima laus est* (1.17.35).

his slender supply of books, food, and mental equanimity: *sed satis est orare Iovem qui ponit et aufert, / det vitam, det opes; aequum mi animum ipse parabo* ('but it is enough to pray to Jove, who gives and takes away, to give life, to give resources; I myself shall provide for myself a well-balanced mind', 1.18.111–12). Such reflexive constructions often tie a (deceptively) neat knot onto the end of Horace's epistles. The same Horace who advises adaptation to diverse circumstances, accommodating oneself to the grand tastes and interests of a patron, elsewhere admonishes his readers and addressee that 'each ought to willingly practise the trade (*ars*) that he knows' (*quam scit uterque libens... exerceat artem*, 1.14.44), and that 'each ought to be measured by his own rule and standard' (*metiri se quemque suo modulo ac pede*, 1.7.98). Autonomist reflexivity alternates with heteronomist flexibility to others' whims and demands.

Horace toys with the notion of incorporating such instability into his own persona. In 1.15, he describes the fascinating character of Maenius, a parasite with no fixed 'fold' (*scurra vagus, non qui certum praesepe teneret*, 28), who, Aristippus-like, managed to adapt with equal self-assurance to circumstances of poverty and wealth. 'Truly I am this man', Horace concludes, for when he is poor, he praises poverty and humility, and when he comes on better fortune, he praises property and landed wealth (42–6). Horace is daring us to convict him of hypocrisy, and deflating criticism in advance with ironic self-awareness. Yet the argument is not purely ironic and exculpatory. Like Maenius, the philosophical Horace 'has no fixed abode', and, as E. Oliensis observes, the slippery and adaptable parasite Maenius, who dwells everywhere and nowhere, enjoys a paradoxical autonomy. He depends on others' gifts as recompense for his wit, but lives with a kind of freedom more respectable men could never dream of.

The epistolary speaker's condition of living without fixed residence threatens the stability of a key component of Horace's autonomist self-representation: the farm's autarkic retreat. The farm, despite its association with simple living in *Satires* 2 and *Odes* 1–3, no longer affords a firm guarantee of Horatian *paupertas*. At times, it appears as a secluded space of shelter for the contemplation of philosophical questions, and at other moments, as *fundata pecunia* ('money invested' or 'landed wealth', *Epist.* 1.15.46), a property that 'feeds' and 'enriches' its owner (*Epist.* 1.16.2). There are strong hints throughout *Epistles* 1 that Horace's sickness is a more than merely physical malady, that it relates to an underlying disorder in the coherence of the values by which he lives.

> ... mente minus validus quam corpore toto
> nil audire velim nil discere, quod levet aegrum;
> fidis offendar medicis, irascar amicis,
> cur me funesto properent arcere veterno;
> quae nocuere sequar, fugiam quae profore credam;
> Romae Tibur amem ventosus, Tibure Romam.   (*Epist.* 1.8.7–12).

[If he asks, Muse, tell my friend Celsus that,] ... less healthy in my mind than my whole body, I wish to hear nothing, learn nothing, that could relieve my illness. I am vexed with my loyal doctors, irritated at my friends, for rushing to prevent me from falling into a fatal torpidity. I pursue what has harmed me, flee what I believe will help; changing with the wind, at Rome I love Tibur, at Tibur, Rome.

Horace is not even certain in his commitment to rural autarky, the organizing idea in his poetic self-representation since Satire 2.6. A sense of dislocation, or confusion about location, is one of the central concerns of the new work. A recurrent tendency in *Epistles* 1 questions the notion that there can be absolute value in a place. Against this background of uncertainty, change asserts itself as a thematic principle: *mutandus locus est* (*Epist.* 1.15.10). This insight accompanies a certain restlessness of spirit and intellect in a book that begins with uncertainty of philosophical residence (*quo lare tuter*) and continues through various stops on the way to an unknown final destination (1.20). Horace's sickness, it might be argued, has to do with a deeper uncertainty as to where he belongs, what is his proper 'place'.

Simply put, Horace's chief autobiographical fiction—the quiet, unambitious poet living simply on his modest farm—has become impossible to sustain without contradiction and irony. In the years following the publication of *Odes* 1–3 and leading up to the public performance of his *Carmen saeculare*, the latent tensions in Horace's self-representational profile have hardened and intensified into something more than mild rhetorical awkwardness—not outright hypocrisy, perhaps, but a substantive problem nonetheless.[167] Instead of simply falling prey to this problem of ethical compromise, Horace has chosen to incorporate it into his epistolary self-representation.

Horace's philosophical flexibility becomes a useful tactic in a situation where the core values of his poetic persona are in danger of losing their coherence. If flexibility is a defensible principle of an undogmatic approach to philosophical doctrine, then apparent self-contradiction becomes a virtue rather than a liability. Another major element in his established self-representational profile, the shelter afforded by Maecenas' patronage, also undergoes serious examination, and, it would appear, is all but dismantled. The paradigm shift is announced near the beginning of the collection's opening epistle.

> Prima dicte mihi, summa dicende Camena,
> spectatum satis et donatum iam rude quaeris,
> Maecenas, iterum antiquo me includere ludo.
> non eadem est aetas, non mens. Veianius armis
> Herculis ad postem fixis latet abditus agro,
> ne populum extrema totiens exoret harena.
>
> . . .
>
> Nunc itaque et versus et cetera ludicra pono;
> quid verum atque decens, curo et rogo et omnis in hoc sum;
> condo et compono quae mox depromere possim.   (*Epist.* 1.1.1–6; 10–12)

Maecenas, addressed by me in my earliest poetry, bound to be addressed in my last, you seek to enclose me—though I have been sufficiently exhibited now and awarded the wooden sword of retirement—once again within the old gladiatorial school. My age, my mind, are no longer what they were. Veianius, after affixing his arms to Hercules' door-post, disappears into rural seclusion so that he will not have to beseech the crowd again and again at the end of the match . . . Now therefore I put aside verses and other playthings; what is right and what is

---

[167] The tension between contentment and ambition is present from the very beginning, in the opening line of *Sat.* 1.1: see the comments of Gowers (2003), 65.

seemly, this is my focus and my inquiry; I am wholly absorbed in this. I am storing up and gathering resources so that I may afterward bring them forth [for my use].

Time has changed Horace, and while he still offers Maecenas the role of honour in his book of *Epistles*, he refuses to 'perform' the same role he has performed in the past. The metaphor of confinement in the gladiatorial *ludus*, if taken seriously, implies not only celebrity and antagonistic competition with other poets in a very public arena, but also constraint, loss of liberty, and even an element of degradation. The Latin word for gladiatorial school (*ludus*) also means 'play'—a point taken up and reinforced a few lines later when Horace renounces lyric poetry and other such *ludicra* (playthings).

'Play', a generically charged term in Horace's poetic lexicon, is inextricably linked with the lyric space of retreat. Now, however, Horace brilliantly picks apart and inverts his previous guiding metaphor.[168] The ludic space of the lyric grotto was by definition a site of tranquil withdrawal from weighty public concerns. Now, as it turns out, the site of play (*ludus*) was more like the confining prison of a gladiatorial barracks—a link underlined by an etymological conceit (*includere ludo*, 'confine in the *ludus*'). Playing at poetry, moreover, was a dangerous public performance (*spectatum satis*). Maecenas was the one who confined Horace there and drove him to such performances. The defining fictions of Horace's lyric persona—lack of patronal constraint and the privacy of withdrawal—are now revealed to be merely that, fictions. He might have wished, like the gladiator Veianius, to withdraw into rural concealment, but he was driven to continue performing for the populace. 'Apolitical play' and 'unconstraining friendship' were fictions cloaking their opposite.

The whole conceit might be interpreted as an urbane joke; for Horace is not really likening Maecenas to a *lanista* (gladiatorial trainer). Yet the joke has a serious side to it: it exposes anxieties surrounding the purchase, control, and display of literature by the Roman upper classes as a 'gift' for the populace. Whereas aediles of old bought scripts of Plautus and Terence for public entertainment, Maecenas 'bought' Horace; he can take credit for supporting a talented new Roman *vates*. This uncomfortable interpretation cannot be wholly dismissed, if only for the reason that Horace has hitherto fought so hard to suppress and refute it. In setting up epistolary philosophy to be his new medium of autarkic freedom, Horace redescribes lyric as heteronomous confinement, degrading showmanship, and literary performance-for-hire.

---

[168] See Freudenburg (2002a), 124–5, on this epistolary rewriting of the *Odes* and their public image. W. R. Johnson's (1993) monograph on *Epistles* 1 takes 'freedom' as its central theme, which includes the question of the poet's autonomy in regard to Maecenas (e.g. 68) and Augustus (e.g. 34). Macleod (1979) is fundamental on the nature and aims of Horatian moral philosophy in *Epistles* 1, and includes discussion of freedom and the poet's retiring *autarkeia* and its limits. On the philosophical dimension of the *Epistles*, note also Traina (1991), and Moles (2002). Moles, 151ff., deals specifically with the philosophical implications of Horace's relationship with Maecenas on the one hand, and the option of Epicurean retirement on the other. Traina, who sees Aristippus as central to Horace's epistolary philosophy, stresses in particular this philosopher's concern with moral freedom and the determination to be one's own master in all circumstances, even in dealings with the great and powerful. The relevance of such observations both to Horace's moral outlook and to the present discussion is evident.

Even after begging off further 'performances' on the public stage, Horace still has more to say to his old friend Maecenas. In *Epistles* 1.7, he will examine his friendship with Maecenas at great and awkward length.[169] In a series of near-allegorical fables and anecdotes, Horace questions whether Maecenas' enrichment of him has potentially compromised his core value of *paupertas*. If this should turn out to be the case, he will 'unseal' his 'pact' with his patron (*cuncta resigno*, 1.7.34). The wording resembles that of a key declaration in *Odes* 3.29: if forced to choose between poverty and wealth, he will give up (or pay back) everything Fortune gave him (*resigno quae dedit*, 3.29.54), and cloak himself in virtue alone. In that ode, too, Horace assumed a valedictory stance towards his patron. The founding and sustaining contradictions of Horace's relationship with Maecenas—autonomy and obligation, personal enrichment and autarkic *paupertas*, the gift of the farm and its burdens[170]—are now brought awkwardly and painstakingly to light. It is not clear that the fragile bundle of contradictions that make up Horace's autonomist construction of their unconstraining *amicitia* can survive this kind of public vivisection.

If Horace seems poised to abandon his old autonomist position premised on the concepts of shelter and retreat, he is not necessarily abandoning the autonomist project altogether, and may even be raising the stakes. Horace now insists on a conception of autonomy at once more rigorous and elusive. Horace dismantles any surviving vestiges of the lyric *angulus*, a comfortable niche where the poet can hide from the burdens of public existence. That convenient fiction no longer affords the poet easy immunity. Horace, in *Epistles* 1, is beginning to define what the poet's autonomy might mean as established *in* the public world rather than outside it. How can a poet address the powerful, and remain *sui iuris*?[171] Is it possible to write a versified letter of recommendation that is at once an adept social performance and aesthetically successful poem? Such questions animate Horace's book of private letters written for public admiration, a collection that comes into being in the rarified atmosphere of rural retreat, but will, inevitably, make its way into the city, and even into the hands of the emperor himself.[172]

Literature is beginning to have a more than nugatory importance for the Roman state.[173] For his part, Horace plays around the literature-politics divide with provocation and finesse. As he surveys his literary career in 1.19,[174] he ostentatiously bristles at the irritations afforded by both critics and the 'servile

---

[169] Oliensis (1998), 157–65, has acutely analysed the public renegotiation of their relationship in this letter; see also Freudenburg (2002a), 128–31; Mayer (1994), 174, who cites the remarks of Pseudo-Acro: *hac epistola asperius ac destrictius Maecenati praescribit libertatem se opibus non vendere.*

[170] Bowditch (2001), *passim*; on the *Epistles*, 161–246.

[171] Compare the interpretation of Freudenburg (2002a), 126ff., of *Epistles* 1 as an aggressive attempt on the part of Horace to establish his freedom in anticipation of his difficult and potentially compromising return to the lyric arena. For Oliensis (1995), 154–81, the first book of epistles is about publicly, and at times awkwardly, 'tearing up the contract' with Maecenas and writing it anew.

[172] It is in the more overtly 'public' *Odes*, however, that Horace prompts us to imagine travelling towards Augustus' hands (*Epist.* 1.13.17): see in particular Oliensis (1998), 185–9.

[173] *Epistles* 1.3 and 1.8 show Horace addressing the fashionable literary set accompanying Tiberius in urbanely avuncular mode. He is at once a laureate poet mildly lecturing junior practitioners, and a public figure connected with rising men.

[174] On this epistle, its negotiation of the poet's independence—in both literary and sociological terms—and its reflections on his lyric oeuvre, see Freudenburg (2002a), 133–40; Oliensis (1998), 133–4; note also Brink (1963), 179–83.

herd' of imitators. He is in the delicate position of being *princeps*, the first to establish his literary authority in his chosen fields of poetic endeavour. Horace's newly won authority in the wake of the publication of his *Epodes* and *Odes* has been both foolishly worshipped and keenly resented. In the following lines, Horace goes on to make this political reading of poetic careerism even more explicit:

> scire velis mea cur ingratus opuscula lector
> laudet ametque domi, premat extra limen iniquus:
> non ego ventosae plebis suffragia venor
> impensis cenarum et tritae munere vestis;
> non ego, nobilium scriptorum auditor et ultor,
> grammaticas ambire tribus et pulpita dignor.   (*Epist.* 1.19.35–40)

You might wish to know why the ingrate reader praises and adores my modest productions, but out of doors criticizes them unfairly. I am not one to hunt for the votes of the fickle plebs by paying for dinners and giving a tattered garment; I, who listen to noble writers and have my revenge on them,[175] do not stoop to canvass the tribes of grammarians and their lecterns.

Horace vehemently denies his 'political' ambitions as a poet, but there is no surer sign of a jaded politician than denial of political ambition. The problem is that any given justification of literary withdrawal—for example, *spissis indigna theatris / scripta pudet recitare et nugis addere pondus* ('I'm ashamed to recite unworthy works in a packed theatre, and add weight to trivialities', 41–2)—is bound to be interpreted by the critically inclined as thinly veiled ambition and self-regard: *rides . . . et Iovis auribus ista / servas: fidis enim manare poetica mella / te solum, tibi pulcher* ('you are having a laugh . . . and reserving these [works] for the ears of Jove: for, beautiful in your own eyes, you are confident that you alone drip with poetic honey', 43–5). Horace does not know how to stop this antagonistic dialogue with an unnamed adversary, since even a cool, detached response will only trigger further charges of high-minded arrogance (*ad haec ego naribus uti / formido . . . 45–6*). His only option is to call a truce to the game (*ludus*).[176]

> 'displicet iste locus' clamo et di*ludi*a posco.
> *ludus* enim genuit trepidum certamen et iram,
> ira truces inimicitias et funebre bellum.   (*Epist.* 1.19. 47–9).

'This place does not satisfy me,' I shout, and demand a truce. For play begets anxiety-producing competition and anger; anger begets fierce enmities and deadly war.

In the *Odes*, the principle of 'play' served to impose limits on the threat posed by serious, public themes to the poet's tranquil *secessus* ('withdrawal'). Now, in this open-ended ending that denies closure, playful lyric's sheltering niche has been replaced with the prospect of endless escalation. The closing anadiplosis (*ludus genuit . . . iram, / ira truces inimicitias . . .*) mimics the unfettered transition from play to competition, competition to rage, rage to the 'un-friendships' (*inimicitias*) and wars programmatically excluded by lyric. Without a secure sense of boundary and limit, exclusion of un-lyric violence is no longer possible.

---

[175] Or, 'who defend them' against criticism—so Mayer (1994), ad loc.
[176] See Freudenburg (2002a), 140.

Closure can be a key site for examining limit and/or the refusal of limits, which ultimately concerns the question of the boundedness of the literary domain. In 1.20,[177] the closural epistle of the collection, the author addresses his own book, which he represents as a slave eager to leave the rural residence of his owner in order to prostitute himself in the city.

> Vertumnum Ianumque, liber, spectare videris,
> scilicet ut prostes Sosiorum pumice mundus.
> odisti clavis et grata sigilla pudico;
> paucis ostendi gemis et communia laudas,
> non ita nutritus. fuge quo descendere gestis.   (*Epist.* 1.20.1–5).

Book, you appear to be gazing towards Vertumnus and Janus, doubtless with the aim of prostituting yourself, spruce with the pumice of the Sosii. You hate the locks and keys so dear to the chaste. You groan in exasperation at being shown to only a few, and you praise public places, though you were not brought up to be this way. Run off where you yearn to go . . .

The author chides the book/slave for his foolish eagerness to leave the protective space of his author's/master's home, and predicts an unhappy series of events that will befall the book/slave in the city: neglect; old age; provincial exile; and finally, a degrading job as elementary school teacher in the suburbs. Denigration, of course, conceals a proud boast: Horace's book will become well known in the city and circulated throughout the empire as a standard school text. At last, 'when a warmer sun brings a larger audience' (1.20.19), the book will tell the story of its author's life and character.[178]

Though the epistle's initial gesture is one of reluctance, Horace wrote these lines with full knowledge and acceptance of the inevitable outcome: his book's publication. 1.20 is not the first instance of an Horatian envoi to the book. *Satires* 1.10 offers a brief version, while *Odes* 2.29 and 3.30 predict the immortal fame of Horace's lyric oeuvre. Never before, however, has Horace gone so far out of his way to conspicuously set up, then brusquely dismantle, the Callimachean motif of the author's resistance to literary publicity.[179] Horace envisions his book becoming wholly dispersed throughout Roman society in the most public, unsheltered, and diffuse way possible, as merchandise in the bookshop and as text for schoolboys and provincial readers. The story the book will tell its future audience, moreover, concerns the poet's rising arc of prestige and social prominence in Rome. It will narrate how 'a freedman's son amid slender means spread his wings too wide for his nest . . . and found favour in both peace and war with the foremost men of the City' (1.20.20–3).

Poetry, in *Epistles* 1, has become a public endeavour, and the poet an all too familiar and recognizable figure in imperial Rome's emerging cultural landscape. A comparable pattern is discernible in *Epistles* 2. This collection, less structurally cohesive than *Epistles* 1 and possibly posthumously edited, consists of three longer

---

[177] On how the epistolary Horace reflects on and picks apart the grounding assumptions of lyric, see Harrison (1988); Freudenburg (2002a).

[178] On this epistle, see especially Oliensis (1995).

[179] See Oliensis (1998), 174ff., who notes in particular the ironic contrast with the 'elitism' (174) of 1.19.

epistles on broadly literary topics. Epistle 2.2, addressed to Julius Florus, examines the vocation of poet from the perspective of a writer who now views his own occupation with a certain satirical detachment. As in *Epistles* 1, Horace strives to come to grips with an arena of endeavour that has become problematic for him precisely to the extent that it has become more broadly accepted. Aware that everyone in the city has turned to scribbling verses—the very success of the great Augustan poets having spawned a generation of aspiring poets—Horace seemingly escapes from a game turned tedious: he has done his part, achieved immortality, and sees no more reason to be displayed before spectators with increasingly jaded tastes alongside a crowd of callow imitators.[180]

He is not wholly comfortable with what the new Roman poetry has become, how vulnerable it is to satire, and is therefore keen to be its first and fiercest satirist. Above all he wants to anticipate and control the debate arising from his own achievements. Was it not worth it to make an enduring contribution to Roman literature, to produce a canonical lyric monument? Perhaps, but the present, notably cagy Horace claims to be weary of the struggle. Turning again to the Palatine complex, Horace depicts the striving of the *vates* towards canonical status as a vainglorious competition into which he no longer wishes to enter:[181]

> fautor erat Romae consulti rhetor, ut alter
> alterius sermone meros audiret honores,
> Gracchus ut hic illi, foret huic ut Mucius ille.
> qui minus argutos vexat furor iste poetas?
> carmina compono, hic elegos. 'mirabile visu
> caelatumque novem Musis opus!' aspice primum,
> quanto cum fastu, quanto molimine circum-
> spectemus vacuam Romanis vatibus aedem.
> mox etiam, si forte vacas, sequere et procul audi,
> quid ferat et qua re sibi nectat uterque coronam.
> caedimur et totidem plagis consumimus hostem
> lento Samnites ad lumina prima duello.
> discedo Alcaeus puncto illius; ille meo quis?
> quis nisi Callimachus? si plus apposcere visus,
> fit Mimnermus et optivo cognomine crescit.
> multa fero, ut placem genus irritabile vatum,
> cum scribo et supplex populi suffragia capto;
> idem, finitis studiis et mente recepta,
> obturem patulas impune legentibus aures.   (*Epist.* 2.2.87–105)

A lawyer in Rome and his fan (a teacher of rhetoric) never conversed except in terms of mutual glorification. They even addressed one another as 'Gracchus' and 'Mucius'. Well now—doesn't the same delusion affect our warbling poets? I write lyrics, my friend elegiacs. 'A dazzling achievement; a work of the purest inspiration!' Note in the first place the lordly mien and portentous expression we wear as we gaze around the temple with its spaces ready for the bards of Rome. Then, if you've time, follow, and hear from a tactful distance what

----

[180] Brink (1963), 185, writes of a 'malaise of Roman poetry' and Horace's 'disenchantment'.
[181] On this scene and its relation to the Augustan building program and social/literary scene, see Freudenburg (2002), 49–51; on the 'Epistle to Florus', note also Oliensis (1998), 7–13; Brink (1982), 226ff.

each provides, and how he contrives to win his laurels. Like Samnites in the arena, giving and taking blows, we exhaust the foe in a weary duel that lasts till nightfall. I emerge as 'Alcaeus' on his verdict, and he as 'Callimachus', of course, on mine. If he seems unhappy with that, he at once becomes 'Mimnermus' and swells at the coveted title. When writing and humbly bidding for popular favour, I suffered a lot to placate the poets—that hypersensitive species. Now that my work is over and my mind restored to sanity I can safely block my spreading ears to our friends' recitations.[182]

This keenly observed comic scene depicts poets in a kind of mutual admiration society.[183] The opening anecdote shows an earlier version of such a society: an orator and a pleader bestow extravagant titles on one another, a 'Gracchus' and a 'Mucius' respectively. Among other things, this story of long ago serves to show how times have changed. Whereas orators and lawyers once strove in the forum, now poets crowd to compete on the Palatine, praising each other's work and approaching the new 'temple open for Roman bards' with a massive sense of self-importance. The mutual trade in compliments conceals self-destructive (*caedimur et totidem plagis consumimus hostem*, 'giving and taking blows, we exhaust the foe') and competitive aspects of poetic activity. Indeed, to judge by the shift from gladiatorial jargon to the language of elections and voting (*puncto*, 'vote', *supplex populi suffragia capto*, 'humbly bidding for popular favour'), poetry, as in Epistle 1.19, has become its own kind of *ambitio*, perhaps not so very unlike the forensic activities of the opening anecdote. As before, Horace finds the bullying solidarity of the band of poets (*genus irritabile vatum*) suffocating. Philosophy offers the only escape.[184]

Horace's latest work entertains the suspicion that the figure of the poet is becoming overexposed, too prestigious to remain humble and honest, and poetry too valuable a commodity to be wisely used. If the protected space of rustic withdrawal, the grove, the self-sufficient and exclusive world of the *angulus* figured poetry's autonomy, Horace's satiric perspective exposes poetry as yet another game played, or duel waged, in the world at large. Horace does not give up on the game of autonomy so easily, however; his corrosively critical perspective on the literary pretensions of the mid-Augustan period are suggestive of a struggle to avoid being subsumed into a literary identity that is becoming predictable and coercive. Horace preserves his independence by staging a 'disappearing act',[185]

---

[182] I here adopt the text and lively translation of Rudd (1979).

[183] The problems of faddish poetic activity and the low bar of mutual admiration are related to the stress Horace places elsewhere in the epistle on the difficult demands of poetic craft, the use of language, and the creation of a *legitimum . . . poema* (109), i.e. a proper poem or a 'poem according to the rules of art' (Rudd 1989, ad loc.): see Brink (1963), 186–90; on the figurative/associative dimension of *legitimum*, Freudenburg (2002), 40.

[184] This scene has sometimes been interpreted as reflecting personal hostility between Horace and Propertius. By my reading, Horace is commenting on the image of the *vates* delineated in both Propertius Book 3 and his own *Odes*, representing literary dialogue in vivid form as an actual dialogue between the two poets. Both Horace and Propertius carved out for themselves a space in the poetic *nemus*, becoming a Roman Alcaeus and Callimachus respectively; and both made reference to the new Palatine complex in ascending the heights of vatic glory. Horace may be satirizing Propertius but he is satirizing himself no less (see Putnam (1986), 28): together they were involved in a fierce competition for poetic status in which the Greek classics were used as pawns, a competition carried out on the very site of the Palatine *aedes*.

[185] Oliensis (1998), 153, describing not the *Epistles* but *Odes* 4.15.

fleeing the arena where his performances were burdened with the weight of too much anticipation.[186]

How honest is Horace's disgust? Is it not easier to disdain the competition for poetic prestige now that he is assured his own immortal *honos* as lyric poet? And has he really closed the door on lyric? The answer to the latter question, at least, must be 'no', as the *Carmen saeculare* and *Odes* 4 demonstrate by their existence. The *Carmen saeculare* was performed in 17 BC and *Odes* 4 published ca. 13 BC, both representing a return to lyric and the vatic persona in the poet's old age. In one of his latest epistolary works, 'The Epistle to Augustus' (*Epistles* 2.1), Horace addresses yet again the question of the poet's place in the city, this time with his participation in the *ludi saeculares*, and possibly his final panegyrical collection, specifically in mind. He continues to write about poetry from a position outside Poetry, and continues to seek to redefine poetic autonomy for the conditions of Augustus' later principate, but he does so with a less overtly satirical tone than in the 'Epistle to Florus' and a robust acceptance of poetry's place in the city and its distinctive cultural value.[187]

Horace, who has spent most of his literary career addressing only Maecenas or addressing Augustus in an oblique manner, now turns directly to the *princeps* to speak on matters of the greatest importance to himself and his career: namely, the role of the poet in Rome, the value and prestige of contemporary poetry, and the importance of rigorous criteria in judging the quality of literary works. Poetry is, indeed must be, a matter of serious public concern if Augustus would take time from his immense burdens of state (2.1.1–4) to read Horace's intricate lecture on the topic. Even more provocatively, Horace especially insists that *contemporary* poetry is worth attention. Romans value tradition, in poetry as in other things, but Horace here aims his pitiless aesthetic judgement and savage irony at the inherited canon of early Roman 'classics' and the fossilized epithets that grant them each their special domain and virtue.[188]

At some level, Horace is urging Augustus (along with his fellow Augustan Romans) to take literature more seriously, and to accept literary value on its own terms rather than subsume it under the pious category of 'tradition'. Plautus, in Horace's tendentious literary history, is little more than a meretricious hack, and the long discussion of drama (177–213) is an extended critique of the theatre as a space of heteronomy: the eye is captured, the ear flattered, and the poet himself subjugated by the alternately inflating and deflating whims of the crowd. The poet becomes a mere entertainer, or in Horace's sarcastic praise, a funambulist. Cicero's favourite poet, Ennius, is not so easy a target, and might even seem to satisfy Horace's emerging interest in public poetry, but the latter's stringent criteria of literary quality brings into question the value of all such poetry of venerable status and (from an Augustan viewpoint) modest technical sophistication.

---

[186] For both Oliensis (1998), 11, and Freudenburg (2002), Epistle 2.2, though addressed to Florus, is meant to be 'overread' by Augustus, and thus his *recusatio* has broader significance.

[187] On the 'Epistle to Augustus', see, among many others, Klingner (1950); Brink (1963), 191–209, and (1982); Rudd (1989); Lyne (1995); Oliensis (1998), 191–7; Barchiesi (2001), 79–103; Feeney (2002); Lowrie (2002).

[188] Brink (1963), 193–4.

Horace concedes that the 'craze' for writing poetry in the contemporary period does not necessarily produce verse of enduring value either: *scribimus indocti doctique poemata passim* ('we all write poetry without distinction, learned and unlearned alike', 117; see also 219–28). Horace's 'we', in these cases, however, is rhetorical. He includes himself in the despicable class of trendy poetasters, since, as lionized author of *Odes* 1–3, he can easily afford to do so.[189] As usual, Horace is building up a fairly complex and nuanced argument without laying out all its components in a transparent, expository manner. He is writing a letter, after all, and not a treatise.[190] He undermines the prestige of early Roman writers, implicitly builds up the prestige of contemporary literature, but at the same time, lets drop acerbic remarks about the recent fad for amateur versifying. Even as the reader begins to process Horace's complicated ideas about literary quality (modern is better, except when it isn't), he includes some further ideas regarding the civic function of poetry: not only is the poet himself a morally praiseworthy figure, he can, despite being a useless soldier, contribute to the city in other ways.

> militiae quamquam piger et malus, utilis urbi,
> si das hoc, parvis quoque rebus magna iuvari.   (*Epist.* 2.1.124–5)

> Although sluggish and inept at warfare, he is useful to the city,
> if you concede this: that great things may be aided by small.

As a subsequent list indicates, those 'small things' include forming children's budding Latinity, instilling salubrious moral examples, and bringing comfort to the sick and weak. As the composer of publicly performed poetry, such as the *Carmen saeculare*, the poet contributes to the even more august (and Augustan) labour of winning the favour of the gods for the Roman people: *castis cum pueris ignara puella mariti / disceret unde preces, vatem ni Musa dedisset?* ('whence would the girl who has not experienced a husband, along with chaste boys, learn prayers, if the Muse had not supplied a bard?', 132–3). In the passage introducing these instances of the poet's public utility, however, Horace also insists on the distinct and autonomous social character of the *vates*, who cares nothing about profit and loss, runaway slaves, fires, but only about his verses (119–20). He presents the poet as 'of no account in the activities which the *urbs* takes seriously—economic, political, military'—[191] so as to underline the autonomous status of his contribution.[192]

Horace is building an argument both for poetry's autonomous criteria of quality and for poetry's distinctive value to the citizenry and the state.[193] We are not to see poetry as a mere instrument, a medium that accommodates itself to the utilitarian requirements of a specific end, whatever that end may be and however disgracefully it might undermine aesthetic standards, but rather as a laboriously constructed work of intrinsic value. The aesthetic integrity of such a work makes poetry all the more powerful and effective in 'purifying the speech

---

[189] Compare Oliensis (1998), 194.   [190] Brink (1963), 3ff.   [191] Brink (1963), 200.

[192] Oliensis (1998), 193: 'by drawing the sharpest possible distinction between poetic disinterestedness and economic interest'.

[193] Compare Brink (1963, 193): 'Horace is debating whether Augustan Rome can create modern poetry which has a measure of the public status of archaic poetry and which can match the artistic standards of ancient Greece'.

of the tribe', educating youth, and purveying the core values of the *res publica*. Aesthetic value does not exist despite, or as a supplement to, the poetic work's utility, but rather the work's public value resides in and is inextricable from its aesthetic integrity. A similar concept can be seen at work in the figurative language employed in a passage of the 'Epistle to Florus'. Horace's description of the author as a 'censor' of words (2.2.110)—adding new words that are worthy of incorporation, rooting out old words that have become corrupt, and reviving previously obsolete words that remain valuable—melds social and aesthetic control in a single cohesive figure.[194]

This synthesis of aesthetic and social value, it must be emphasized, represents an aspirational ideal and is not necessarily to be found embodied in any specific work of poetry presently in existence. Horace himself does not claim to be able to produce such a work. Indeed, he recuses himself from writing panegyric of Augustus on the grounds of a lack of sufficient ability (*vires*, 259). Possibly Virgil and Varius have done better (247), but even here it is impossible to be certain. It remains difficult to reconcile exacting, Callimachean standards of literary style with large topics of public importance, to accommodate the refined, miniaturist impulses of the neoteric and post-neoteric aesthetics of the past several decades to the project of defining *virtus* for the Augustan age.

Horace's epistolary commentary continues to be written under the sign of irony perhaps for the very reason that no wholly credible synthesis of neoteric sophistication and civic *utilitas* has been found to exist, and thus Horace plays on the flaws and limitations of existing discourses rather than laying out an explicit programme in positive terms. His defense of poetry's utility comes off, at best, as dutiful, and at worst, sarcastic. Many have found his eloquence on this topic unconvincing, and ascribe the notion of useful, exemplary poetry to Augustus rather than Horace himself.[195] It is often impossible to gauge the exact valence of the descriptive terms Horace employs, the extent of his ironic distance. For example, in a highly compressed literary history, Horace states that in the wake of the Punic Wars, the Romans, no longer under direct military threat, began to contemplate their broader cultural horizons, asking themselves 'what use' an Aeschylus, Thales, or Sophocles might be (*quid . . . utile ferrent*, 163). At the other end of the connotative spectrum, Horace observes that Romans, like the Greeks before them, at a certain point in their history begin to be less exclusively devoted to traditional, practical concerns, and to develop a 'mania' for poetic composition (103–17) along with other self-consciously trivializing (*nugari*, 93) pursuits.[196]

These two descriptive frameworks—public utility and nugatory triviality—taken individually provide fairly meagre accounts of the nature and value of literary activity. They are each inadequate on their own terms, but Horace's ironic discourse only offers oblique criticism, and he leaves it to the reader to fill in the resulting gap. Catullan *nugae* and Ennian *virtus* define the opposing

---

[194] Freudenburg (2002), 47–9, connects this passage with Augustus' role as *censor* and his remaking of the Senate.

[195] See, for example, the discussion in Freudenburg (2002), 44–6, of the tension between the exemplary sort of poetry that Augustus appears to have favoured, and the prevalent themes and emphases of *Odes* 1–3.

[196] On these narratives, and their Aristotelian background, see Brink (1963), 197–8.

poles of literary ideology with no obvious term for what might exist between the two. In a certain sense, Horace's epistle is nudging us, and Augustus, to imagine what that middle term might be. In the closing section, Horace remarks on a telling discrepancy. Whereas Alexander the Great held to very exacting standards in his choice of visual artists entrusted to represent him, he allowed himself to be represented in poetry by the unworthy hack Choerilus, who received a fixed sum of coins per verse (*incultis qui versibus et male natis / rettulit acceptos, regale nomisma, Philippos*, 233–4). Horace prefers a more hieratic conception of the poet's role by contrast with Choerilus' debased mercantile model:

> sed tamen est operae pretium cognoscere, quales
> aedituos habeat belli spectata domique
> virtus, indigno non comittenda poetae.   (*Epist.* 2.1.229–31)

But it is nevertheless worth one's while to know what sort of temple-guardians belong to Valour, proven at home and abroad and not to be entrusted to an unworthy poet.

The phrase *sed tamen est operae pretium cognoscere* ('but it is nevertheless worth one's while to know') is an overt nod to Ennius,[197] but, we must presume, an ironic one, given Horace's earlier comment that the 'wise and valiant' Ennius, a 'second Homer', apparently did not take sufficient care to ensure the promised immortality of his own works. Horace has little patience for poetry that combines a lofty conception of *virtus* with technical incompetence.

Horace is thus promoting a conception of poetry that is Ennian in its devotion to immortalizing Roman *Virtus*,[198] yet (on Horace's view) un-Ennian in its insistence on rigorously high technical standards. Horace then goes on to demonstrate the rigour of his own standards by refusing to write the kind of panegyric that might succeed in flattering Augustus but would fall short of impressing posterity (250–9).[199] In the epistle's closing lines, Horace declares that *he* would not wish for his image to be preserved in a poem destined for the trash bin. Such preservation would be, in reality, a funeral, the burial of his reputation rather than its perpetuation.

> nil moror officium quod me gravat, ac neque ficto
> in peius voltu proponi cereus usquam
> nec prave factis decorari versibus opto,
> ne rubeam pingui donatus munere, et una
> cum scriptore meo, capsa porrectus operta,
> deferar in vicum vendentem tus et odores
> et piper et quidquid chartis amicitur ineptis.   (*Epist.* 2.1.264–70)

---

[197] Skutsch (1985), fragments 494–5: *audire est operae pretium procedere recte qui rem Romanam Latiumque augescere voltis.*

[198] On Virtus and the caretakers of the god's temple, see Rudd (1989), ad loc.: 'as if the poets were caretakers of the temple of *Virtus Augusti*'. Feeney (2002), 173, observes of Horace (*aedituus* of Virtue) and Augustus (builder of the Palatine temple and library complex): 'they each control the temple that will guarantee the other's immortality'.

[199] On this dilemma, see Oliensis (1998), 192: literary immortality 'may depend . . . as Augustus' question per *litteras* implies, on the success with which such poets avoid being absorbed into the contemporary center of power'.

I do not care for the sort of favour that oppresses me; nor do I elect to be exposed to view anywhere in wax, my face fashioned for the worse, nor to be glorified in disgracefully written verses, lest I blush at being given the crass gift, and along with my writer, stretched out in a closed box, I am carried away to the street that sells incense, aromatic herbs, pepper, and whatever else is wrapped in graceless papers.

Inept[200] verses doom the figure they represent to being subsumed within their own undignified 'funeral' in the market stalls of the Vicus Tuscus. Low literary quality, short span of existence, and subsumption to the utilitarian world of the market, where merchandise is purchased only to be used and discarded, are combined in this evocative visualization of degrading heteronomy. A passage that begins with a citation of Ennius ends with a Catullan condemnation of disposable poetry, leaving us to wonder how the criteria of public importance and literary polish can be simultaneously satisfied.[201]

Horace points towards the essential paradox of praise poetry and aesthetic quality: if a work devotes itself only to the instrumentality of praising a leader such as Alexander the Great, it will fail even in that effort. But if the work devotes itself to aesthetic quality and not, primarily, to panegyrical instrumentality, any praises embedded within it will live on and achieve their purpose. This paradoxical formulation, of course, may be interpreted as wishful thinking on Horace's part, a justification of his own practice and a blurring of the real potential for the compromise of aesthetic standards. Horace arguably underestimates (perhaps quite consciously) the intractability of the conflict between aesthetic and panegyrical interests. Indeed, the possibility of such conflict is no longer merely theoretical in Horace's supplementary fourth book of *Odes*, published in the same period as the 'Epistle to Augustus', and commissioned, in some accounts, by the emperor himself.[202] Augustus, who perhaps never felt an overpowering need for all of his poets to sing his praises in an extended way (and such encomium might have been especially undesirable in the anxious early years of his principate[203]), now, as he began to think more seriously about questions of succession, wanted publicity for the deeds of his stepsons Tiberius and Drusus in their campaigns against the Alpine tribes.[204]

Horace, then, was in the delicate position of writing poetry for the Alexander of his times. It remained important for him, however, not to allow these political

---

[200] On the word and its connotations, see Rudd (1989), ad loc.

[201] On this passage, see especially Oliensis (1998), 194–7.

[202] Horace's fourth book of odes has recently received significant scholarly attention in the monographs of Putnam (1986) and Johnson (2004). Note also Oliensis (1998), 150–3; Lyne (1995), 193–217.

[203] This tense, experimental situation is well brought out by Horace's comparison of Augustus as potential subject of poetic praise to a horse who will kick if touched by an inexpert hand: *Sat.* 2.1.17–20.

[204] Suetonius *Vita Horati*. On the question of imperial pressure and Horace's motives for returning to lyric, see Lyne (1995), 194–5; note also Putnam (1986), 21. Oliensis (1998), 152, suggests that, 'whereas the poet gains autonomous poetic authority in the course of the earlier collection . . . he seems to forfeit this authority in the course of *Odes* 4'. ('Forfeits'? Or merely spends the aesthetic capital he built up in *Odes* 1–3?) Lyne (1995), 202, largely sees Horace in *Odes* 4 as 'performing the task of a court poet'; but he also notes signs that a possibly resentful Horace was deliberately 'sapping' or 'undermining' aspects of his panegyric (207–14).

factors to assume the overt status of underlying *raison-d'être* of the collection. The fundamental pattern of the book resembles the studied alternation in Propertius 4 between subject matter giving at least token representation to the 'default' concepts of the genre (love, Cynthia) and a new kind of elegy exploring the layered meanings of the Augustan city. Comparably, Horace alternates poems of a more or less traditional 'lyric' character on love (4.1, 10, 11, 13), the symposion (4.12) and the passage of time (4.7, 10–13) with odes devoted to praises of Augustus (4.5), Tiberius and Drusus (4.14) and the principate (4.15). Yet another layer incorporates a sequence of odes celebrating the power of poetry and Horace's status as Augustan poet laureate (4.3, 8, 9). Wary of the dangers of becoming for Augustus what Choerilus was to Alexander, Horace embarks on his new panegyrical project with an acute awareness of maintaining his poetry's prestige and reputation for enduring quality.[205]

Horace, in the prefatory 4.1, maintains his 'default' identity as lyric poet by justifying his return to the genre as an involuntary return to the helpless iterations of desire in all its uncontrollable flux—as if this supplementary work were motivated by the core concerns of lyric poetry, and not devised in the first place to advance certain panegyrical interests at Augustus' behest. Horace's autonomist rhetoric, for all the immensely skilled lyrical finesse of 4.1, appears calculating and manipulative. Part of his strategy in maintaining a credible lyric stance is to adapt his repertoire of erotic and sympotic themes to the context of his later years. The book has a nostalgic flavour, and several odes reflect on the passage of time, the 'end of love', and the final chapter in Horace's lyric career. At the same time, he reflects on his own achievements. In 4.3, Horace runs through a veritable summary of his poetological repertoire, including Tibur, poetic *nemora*, his insertion among the 'choir of lyric *vates*' (4.3.15), comparison of poetry with athletic victory, and the poet's defeat of Envy. Significantly, it is not his patron Maecenas who now 'inserts' him among the canon of lyric authors, but the collective youth of Rome, 'foremost among cities' (*principis urbium*, 13).

This latest self-representational turn is a far cry from the quiet corner of retreat espoused in earlier odes. Now the Roman public, the city itself, confirms Horace's status as lyric poet: his poetic identity, disembedded from the context of private *amicitia* and the secluded symposion, has been installed in Roman culture at large. In 4.7, which ends with the inscriptional phrase *vatis Horati* ('the poet Horace', 44) neatly framed in the adonic verse, he identifies himself with the role of public teacher of lyric poetry to his fellow Romans at the *ludi saeculares*. In 4.8, poetry is a gift (*munus*) of surpassing value; statues and public inscriptions are inferior to poetry in commemorating great men. Ode 4.9 follows up on these ideas by applying them to the case of Lollius, who evidently craves poetic commemoration: without poetry, none of the deeds of heroes would be known, and many unsung deeds have been lost in the oblivion of time.

> vixere fortes ante Agamemnona
> multi; sed omnes illacrimabiles
> 　　urgentur ignotique longa
> 　　　nocte, carent quia vate sacro.　　(*Carm.* 4.9. 25–9)

---

[205] Questions of panegyric, 'sincerity' and 'intention' are discussed by Johnson (2004), e.g. xvi–xix.

Many brave heroes lived before Agamemnon; but all of them are oppressed by the long night, unlamented and unknown, because they lack a holy bard.

In Horace's formulation, the power of poetry consists in nothing less than conferring, or by its silence denying, existence on the people and actions of the past.[206]

Poetry, in *Odes* 4, approaches the status of autonomously powerful agent in the city. It now needs no patron to elevate and protect it, but through its intrinsic capacities instructs the citizenry and does battle against the corrosive power of time. This fortified version of the autonomist position surprisingly, or, if one accepts the arguments forwarded in this chapter, understandably, accompanies the most blatantly panegyrical compositions of Horace's oeuvre. Poetry can be put to ostensibly heteronomist uses precisely to the degree that its autonomy is pre-established as the condition of poetic speech. This formulation might seem paradoxical, but the autonomy/heteronomy tension was always part of Horace's autonomist rhetoric from the very start. Putting poetry to a contemporary use only becomes plausible and effective when brilliant strategies of literary self-fashioning have divorced the poet from vulgar, quotidian interests and oriented his gaze towards future *saecula*. Praising Augustus is allowable when the poet has already established that he *chooses* to confer praise, and does so on his own terms.[207] *Odes* 4 represents a newly marmoreal and laureate extension of this ongoing project.

PERMANENT EXTREMITY: OVID'S AUTONOMIST POETICS

Ovid's self-representational works afford an appropriate coda to this chapter's examination of the shifting paradigm of poetic autonomy in the middle and later Augustan period. Ovid immediately comes to mind as a key figure in any discussion of Roman poetic autonomy. His poetry has been at the centre of discussions in recent scholarship of the relation between poetry and imperial power. Ovid's later works, the *Fasti* and *Metamorphoses*, portions of which appear to have been revised during the poet's exile, have been subjected to especially close scrutiny.[208] It will be helpful to view Ovid within the context of a broader discussion of poetic

---

[206] See Lyne (1995), 213–14, on how these lines possibly come into conflict with the idea of Virtus previously articulated in *Odes* 3.2 as 'independent' and 'transcendent'. Numerous scholars have struggled with the problematic background of M. Lollius' defeat by the Sygambri in 16 BC in Gallia Comata and its potential implications for this poem: Fraenkel (1957), 425; Putnam (1986), 168–9; Johnson (2004), 82–4; Lyne (1995), 205–6.

[207] The concern with time, *saecula*, and endings apply not only to the poet and his love affairs, but perhaps implicitly to Augustus as well: an anonymous reviewer for Oxford University Press observes that in *Odes* Book 4 Horace praises Augustus in a context in which the princeps' personal *saeculum* might already be seen to be fading, as he looks towards his successors. Poetry's power to preserve the past thus assumes an even more marked importance.

[208] On politics and Augustus in the *Fasti*: McKeown (1984); Wallace-Hadrill (1987); Hinds (1992); Feeney (1992); Herbert-Brown (1994); Newlands (1995). On the changed perspective of exile, see Hinds (1985).

autonomy at Rome, since his exile has sometimes misleadingly served to isolate him as an exceptional instance of the encounter between free poetic speech and the *princeps*. In fact, Ovid participates in an established autonomist tradition whose core concepts and motifs he manipulates, develops, and maintains. At the same time, Ovidian poetry does not represent simply a continuation of the poetics of autonomy as established by the earlier generation of Augustan writers. He pushes autonomist rhetoric to a new degree of intensity, and effectively tests the limits of the system. Like Horace and Propertius, Ovid abandons the concept of the exclusive 'niche' of literary *otium*, while developing autonomist thought in different directions.

As we have seen, the concept of the autonomist shelter that governs early Augustan poetic production comes to be undermined and eventually abandoned under the later years of Augustus' principate. By the time Ovid was embarking on his literary career, Horace and Propertius were moving away from the confining spaces that defined their earlier metapoetics. The restrictive literary realms of the 30s and 20s were beginning to seem *passé*, and a new kind of poetry was coming to light. In the late 20s and in the following decade BC, Horace's 'Roman Odes' and *Odes* 4, Propertius Books 3 and 4, and Virgil's *Aeneid* were published and Horace's *Carmen saeculare* publicly performed. A few key Augustan poets were now celebrities, and in some cases, their obituaries were being written.[209]

In this context, rural withdrawal no longer holds the same importance in poetic self-representation. Poetry cannot claim to be removed from the spotlight of urban culture with the same degree of credibility, and there is no strong incentive to insist on its autarkic privacy. At the same time, improved networks of distribution, and the rising profile of literature as prestigious medium for conveying imperial values, begin to establish the celebrity of Roman writers in the provinces. It is Ovid who first fully exploits the literary implications of world-wide empire and imperial circulation of books. Elements of Ovid's approach can be discerned in his earliest collection, the *Amores*. Whereas previous love elegists design their literary love-domains to conform with Callimachean narrowness of scope and contrast the lover's private world with the public world of war and politics, Ovidian love is from the start quite explicitly a virtuoso performance for a broad audience of urban readers.

Like his predecessors in love elegy, Ovid builds his literary system around the lover's distinctive psychology. In other ways, however, Ovid pushes the elegiac genre in new and provocative directions.[210] An aspect of Ovidian innovation especially relevant to the present discussion is his conspicuous lack of interest in developing the concept of a small, restrictive literary domain. He banishes, for example, even the

---

[209] e.g. Tibullus: Ovid *Amores* 3.19.

[210] Scholars have frequently cited his aggressive exposure of the core fictions of elegy, his assumption of an explicitly cynical and manipulative persona, his acute deconstruction of the driving motifs of elegiac love-psychology, and his introduction of disconcerting elements that serve to disclose the founding exclusions of the genre (pregnancy, abortion, impotence). Of course, some of these tendencies have been exaggerated, or allowed to lapse into exegetical cliché, and more recent scholars, in some cases, have been critical of the notion of Ovid as simply a parodist or deconstructionist: fundamental on this question is Hinds (1987b). See, for example, Otis (1938); Luck (1969), 141–57; Sullivan (1961); Curran (1966); J. T. Davis (1989); Kennedy (1993), 58–63; Keith (1994); Buchan (1995); Stapleton (1996), 1–37; Boyd (1997), especially the helpful survey of approaches, 1–18; Miller (2004), 64–83; Ramsby (2007), 89–112.

nominal and dubious exclusivity of Propertius' *una . . . puella* ('one and only girlfriend', 1.11.29).[211] Ovid's entire tone and approach bespeak his rejection of the early
Augustan prizing of the rare, the exclusive, the non-promiscuous, the simple, the
unadorned, the retiring, and the sequestered on the ethical and aesthetic plane.[212]
Ovid appears as a supremely confident player in the field of Roman poetry, who does
not feel the need to fence round his literary domain as a defensive tactic. Nor does he
make an effort to ground his poetic activity in familiar fictions of sociability and
literary exchange. At the opening of the *Amores*, Ovid's first published collection,
there is no overarching patron figure. The poet simply begins speaking, and as he
does, the generic character of his composition begins to take shape.

> Arma gravi numero violentaque bella parabam
>   edere, materia conveniente modis.
> par erat inferior versus—risisse Cupido
>   dicitur atque unum surripuisse pedem.   (*Am.* 1.1.1–4)

I was preparing to bring forth arms in weighty measure and violent wars, the metre
matching the subject matter. The lower verse was equal—it is said that Cupid laughed,
and stole away one foot.

The absences in this opening metapoetic scene are striking. Not only is there no
patron: there is no immediately discernible love-object. Ovid reverses the notional
priority of lived experience over generic convention. Whereas Propertius put
Cynthia and her 'eyes' at the originary opening of his text, Ovid premises his
elegiac production on the metrical manipulations of Cupid.[213]

   This is not the place to demonstrate at length Ovid's dismantling and rewriting
of previous elegy. Still, it will be helpful to run through a few main points. There is,
in Ovidian elegy, a 'deconstructive' bent that explicitly unpacks some of the
unspoken, or softly spoken, premises of the elegiac fiction: the exchange of sex
for money and gifts, men's and women's *interests* in the relation; the barrier as
erotic instigator; the importance of self-deception and delusional belief in maintaining the condition of *amor*; the lover's darker side, and tendency to manipulate
(multiple) women into sex through his rhetorical skills; the anomalous and
impermissible status of pregnancy in elegy's fictive world. It is evident that
Propertius, Tibullus, and Gallus were self-conscious and sophisticated practitioners, whereas Ovid can hardly be reduced to the image of mercilessly shallow
ironist promoted by some earlier readings.[214] Still, it would be hard to deny that
Ovid makes the self-conscious, 'deconstructive' streak in elegy a main attraction of

---

[211] Already in the third elegy of the first collection, the Ovidian lover appears to profess (behind a
patently dubious pose of *fides)* Jovian promiscuity. On this elegy, see Curran (1966); Olstein (1975);
Davidson (1980); Cairns (1993); Kennedy (1993), 58–63.

[212] I do not mean to suggest, of course, that Ovid no longer reflects Callimachean concerns in his
elegy (see in particular Keith (1994); Lateiner (1978); Hinds (1987b)); but only that acute consciousness
of Callimachean aesthetics is accompanied by a tendency to dismantle some of its central clichés
(exclusivity, constrictive spaces, moral/aesthetic simplicity).

[213] Of course Ovid reminds us that Propertius also was subjected to Amor's 'feet' in his first book's
opening scene (1.1.4). See Hinds (1987b), who makes a fundamental point: the difference between Ovid
1.1 and Propertius 1.1 is not the difference between 'literature' and 'life', but between 'overt' and 'covert'
literary programme (11–12). On 1.1, see also Moles (1991), Boyd (1997), 147–9; Buchan (1995), 54–6.

[214] Note the comments of Boyd (1997), 91–12.

his *Amores*. For Ovid, there is very little initial respect for the mimetic premise of falling in love with an extra-textual *puella*.[215] This brutal insouciance matters for our assessment of his elegy.

Ovid's provocatively 'deconstructive' flair also means that he is fairly flippant on the topic of literature's usefulness and embeddedness in a plausible social context. Some of the *frisson* generated by his *Amores* derives from the impression they give of a new degree of autonomy from real-world grounding in any actual relationship or quotidian urgency of expression. The *Amores* overtly convey their status as literary enterprise in a very technical sense from the opening lines of the first book, and at the end of the same book, proudly advance claims of immortality other authors reserve for the crowning poem of a multiple-book collection. Ovid's literary project is born fully armed, as it were, from the quiver of Cupid. Provocatively independent of grounding context or extra-literary object, Ovidian elegy flaunts its status as self-sustaining and even patently self-creating literary opus. In Propertian elegy, by contrast, Cynthia determines the poet-lover's indifference to material wealth and conventional prestige, while friends and patrons such as Tullus and Maecenas serve as anchoring foil-figures, who both connect his elegiac fiction with Roman social reality and define his sphere of activity through contrastive juxtaposition. All of these strategies serve at some level to situate and contextualize Propertius' poetic activity.

Ovid does not play by the same rules. At the beginning of his elegiac text, he is *already writing* (albeit in the wrong genre). He dispenses with what might be called the rhetoric of the anchoring pretext. The presumption is that Roman poetry, and within that larger category, the different genres of poetry, have been securely established, and can now be taken for granted as autonomous domains of culture. To what extent Ovid owes this sense of entitlement to the hard work of his predecessors in defining and establishing poetry within the existing grid of cultural categories, and to what extent we may see his intervention as an aggressive push in the direction of a more radically autonomist metaliterary rhetoric, is open to debate. Certainly Ovid plays up elegy's unanchoredness as autonomously valid literary practice, and does so with conscious reference to the more situationally embedded fictions of his predecessors. For Ovid, no protective, ludic niche of dogmatic Callimacheanism is required, since poetry now constitutes an intrinsically valid realm of endeavour. In the retrospective autobiography of *Tristia* 4.10, Ovid represents his youthful poetic enthusiasm as belonging to the natural, indeed irrepressible, impulses of his character.

> at mihi iam puero caelestia sacra placebant,
>   inque suum furtim Musa trahebat opus.
> saepe pater dixit, 'studium quid inutile temptas?
>   Maeonides nullas ipse reliquit opes.'
> motus eram dictis, totoque Helicone relicto
>   scribere temptabam verba soluta modis.
> sponte sua carmen numeros veniebat ad aptos,
>   et quod temptabam scribere versus erat.   (*Tr.* 4.10.19–24)

---

[215] See in particular Wyke (1989); Keith (1994); Buchan (1995).

But already as a boy I was attracted to the celestial rites, and the Muse was stealthily drawing me to her work. Often my father said, 'Why are you attempting a pointless endeavour? Homer himself left behind no wealth'. I was persuaded by his words, and, abandoning Helicon entirely, tried to write in prose. Song would come unbidden in the proper measures, and whatever I would try to write . . . was verse!

The pragmatic Roman father's words echo in Ovid's ears, but no matter how hard he tries to write prose, verses come flowing from his stylus. Ovid no doubt simplifies this narrative of his youthful turn towards poetry, or possibly fictionalizes it altogether, but even in this latter case, the implications of the autobiographical fiction remain important. Ovid represents poetry as a natural and, for him, inevitable pursuit. The father voices a conventional complaint, but his worry fades in importance as Ovid's predilections gather an irresistible momentum. Ovid, by his own account, does not begin writing poetry because he fell in love (and thus needed the aid of elegy), or out of poverty (Horace's account of his own beginnings, *Epist.* 2.2.51), but simply because it suits him, because he excels at it.

Callimacheanism, the rhetoric of *recusatio*, and Maecenas' sheltering patronage were all components of a coherent paradigm of autonomist poetics in the early to mid-Augustan period: the paradigm of the sheltered, Callimachean niche. Part of the sheltering aspect of the early Augustan Maecenas-paradigm was the limitation on audience. The Callimachean poet does not write for all and sundry. The elect few, such as Maecenas and other sophisticated readers, can appreciate the poet's refined, erudite verse. The vulgar mob finds its pleasures elsewhere. Ovid, however, once again seems to go out of his way to subvert the expected literary protocol. Even before the beginning of the *Amores* cited above, there is another, paratextual beginning that comments on the very edition we are reading and the history of its publication.

> Qui modo Nasonis fueramus quinque libelli,
>   tres sumus; hoc illi praetulit auctor opus.
> ut iam nulla tibi nos sit legisse voluptas,
>   at levior demptis poena duobus erit.   (Epigram, *Am.* 1)

We, who were once the five books of Naso, are three; the author preferred this recent version over that earlier one. Even if now there is no pleasure for you in having read us, yet, with two books removed, the punishment will be lighter.

Some have seen this epigram's value as merely informational. More recent readings view it as participating in Ovidian play with authorial role and metaliterary self-positioning. Accepting the informational value of Ovid's explanation of his second, abridged edition of the *Amores* need not exclude, of course, the latter line of analysis. M. Citroni in particular has commented acutely on the significance of Ovid's construction of a general, anonymous readership.[216] When compared with the framing fictions of other first-person, Augustan collections, the Ovidian epigram is striking for its bluff dismissal of the anchoring pretext of literary exchange among *amici*. The book, which is not represented as an integral conveyor of voice, but as an explicitly constructed object that the author configures and reconfigures at will, encounters its readers directly and unapologetically

---

[216] Citroni (1995), 431ff.

in the public sphere of literary culture. This introductory epigram, for all its disarming jocularity, constitutes a powerful dismantling of the early Augustan concept of the sheltering niche of literary exchange.

A further aspect of Ovid's re-positioning of elegy concerns the settings and milieu of erotic activity. In the first place, the lover's 'narrow bed' is no longer as concealed and private as in previous elegy. There is very little in terms of extended description of the act of love in Propertius and Tibullus.[217] The classic elegiac lover is defined by his failure to achieve erotic satisfaction except on rare occasions of triumph. The bed and the mistress' physical charms, when evoked, are metonymic pointers towards erotic experiences not explicitly narrated. Ovid, after making us doubt the extra-textual reality of his mistress in *Amores* 1.1–4, in 1.5 overturns the tradition of non-explicitness in elegy with cool insouciance, presenting a scene of seduction and love-making.[218]

> deripui tunicam—nec multum rara nocebat;
>   pugnabat tunica sed tamen illa tegi.
> quae cum ita pugnaret, tamquam quae vincere nollet,
>   victa est non aegre proditione sua.
> ut stetit ante oculos posito velamine nostros,
>   in toto nusquam corpore menda fuit.
> quos umeros, quales vidi tetigique lacertos!
>   forma papillarum quam fuit apta premi!
> quam castigato planus sub pectore venter!
>   quantum et quale latus! quam iuvenale femur!
> singula quid referam? nil non laudabile vidi
>   et nudam pressi corpus ad usque meum.　(*Am.* 1.5.13–24)

I pulled off her tunic (nor was the flimsy garment much of an obstacle) yet she still fought to be covered by the tunic. She was fighting as if she did not want to win, and so was easily conquered through betrayal of her own cause. As she stood before my eyes, her clothing put aside, there was no flaw anywhere on her entire body. What shoulders, what arms I saw and touched! How fit for squeezing was the shape of her breasts! How sleek the belly beneath her slender chest! What a long beautiful flank! How youthful her thigh! But why detail the individual features? I saw nothing unworthy of praise, and pressed her naked body right up against mine.

Ovid is, of course, playing the familiar game of disclosure/non-disclosure in literary representation. Ovid's readers, consequently, may not 'see' as much as they think in this artfully constructed twilight vignette. Indeed, the scene described above is prefaced by an elaborate instance of playfully indirect, chiaroscuro scene-setting.[219]

> Aestus erat, mediamque dies exegerat horam;
>   adposui medio membra levanda toro.
> pars adaperta fuit, pars altera clausa fenestrae;
>   quale fere silvae lumen habere solent,
> qualia sublucent fugiente crepuscula Phoebo,
>   aut ubi nox abiit, nec tamen orta dies.

---

[217] See McKeown (1989), 103, who compares Propertius 2.15; Connolly (2000).

[218] See the discussion of Buchan (1995), 67ff.; Keith (1994), 29–33; Hinds (1987b), 4ff.

[219] Buchan (1995), 68ff., on the theme of vision and eyes.

> illa verecundis lux est praebenda puellis,
>   qua timidus latebras speret habere pudor.
> ecce, Corinna venit, tunica velata recincta,
>   candida dividua colla tegente coma—
> qualiter in thalamos fomosa Semiramis isse
>   dicitur, et multis Lais amata viris.   (*Am.* 1.5.1–12)

It was hot, and the day had driven out the middle hour. I laid my limbs in the middle of the bed to ease them. The window was partly open, and partly closed. There was almost the kind of light forests typically have, the kind of light that gleams in twilight as Phoebus flees, or when night has departed, but day has not yet risen. This is the sort of light that must be offered to bashful girls: in this light their timid modesty may hope to find a hiding place. Look, Corinna comes, wrapped in a belted tunic, her parted hair covering her fair neck, just as beautiful Semiramis is said to have entered her marriage chamber, and Lais loved by many men.

Everything is at a midpoint between extremes, a point of transition or division between different states of being—between night and day, exposure and concealment, modesty and sexual union (*mediam . . . medio . . . pars . . . pars*). Ovid's description of Corinna's hair seems to emphasize this point with an unusual adjective marking its divided shape: *dividua . . . coma*. Ovid's deceptively straightforward elegy is as much about division, concealment, and obscurity as it is about mimetic transparency and physical union.[220]

Still, the bedroom is not quite the snug, exclusive niche, kept out of the direct sight of readers, that we find in earlier elegy. Ovidian love partakes of a literary theatricality: the lovers play roles in order to deceive each other; there is a recurrent cast of characters (bawd, *ancilla*, husband); and the act of love requires its own elaborate mise-en-scène.[221] Rather than being immersed in the retrospective, subjective response of the lover to his recent failure or success in an ongoing soliloquy, we are encouraged to take the role of spectator of miniature dramas of seduction, deception, and manipulation that play out over the course of one or more elegies.[222] Here, love-making is presented to the reader as a kind of spectacle (*ecce Corinna . . . qualiter . . . Semiras . . . et . . . Lais*, 'behold—Corinna . . . just as Semiras . . . and Lais'), a scene of storied, virtuoso eroticism ending in a catalogue of physical wonders first presented to the reader and then teasingly cut off: *singula quid referam* ('why enumerate individual features?')?

The theatricality of Ovidian elegy[223] becomes an explicit metaliterary theme in cases where the actual setting of seduction is the physical edifice of the theatre or other venue of mass entertainment and spectatorship. Whereas Propertius works slowly up to this theme, for Ovid, Love and the propaganda of martial victory are intertwined from the beginning, and the settings of amatory elegy coincide with

---

[220] On Ovid's interest in 'midpoints' in this elegy, Hinds (1987b), 9–10.

[221] On the more salient narrative dimension of *Amores* 1.5 by comparison with Propertius 2.15, see McKeown (1989), 104.

[222] See J. T. Davis (1977).

[223] Hinds (1987b), justifiably critical of the old idea of Ovid as an 'over-explicit' poet, nonetheless notes how the 'staged arrival' of Corinna recalls, through subtle wordplay, the epiphany of Catullus' *candida diva* at c. 68.70–1. Conte (1994a) discusses how Ovid's *Amores* assume a more 'external' vantage point, attempting to 'look at elegy instead of looking with the eyes of elegy', enlarging the scope of vision; the speaker, moreover, 'impersonates' the role of elegiac lover in a quasi-theatrical manner (46).

spaces of public display and political theatre. In 1.2, Ovid presents himself as part of the triumph-procession of Love. In 2.2, Ovid's *puella* is observed by the overzealous custodian Bagoas in the Danaid portico, the temple complex of Isis in the Campus Martius, and at an unspecified theatre.[224] In 3.2, Ovid gives advice on how to conduct oneself successfully as a lover while attending chariot races at the Circus. The furious pursuit of the *puella* constitutes an implicit parallel to the competitive manoeuvres of the racers themselves.[225] The theatre affords similar opportunities for meta-elegiac subtext.[226] Love is presented as a public mode of behaviour in Ovid, embedded in the life, structures, and culture of the imperial city, and incorporating aspects of the theatricality of the settings in which it is represented as taking place. Even the more 'secretive' aspects of love affairs involve private communications and seductions played out in a public or semi-public setting.[227] Love is a world-conqueror like Rome itself (2.9a), and the lover prides himself on being 'ambitious' to extend his seductive endeavours to an entire populace of elegiac *puellae*.[228]

Ovid pursues many of the same themes as previous love elegists, while expanding the stage of action to include the broader urban fabric of Rome, and, in the larger perspective, Rome's empire. In Propertius, the lover preferred to remain within a circumscribed orbit near his mistress' doorway by contrast with the soldier or imperial administrator, who ranged further abroad. This dichotomy has been abandoned by Ovid, who works to assimilate the most important venues for imperial benefaction and mass spectatorship to his elegiac project. Ovid's aim is not to seclude elegy, but to define elegy's distinctive vision on the very terrain of public life and mass spectacle. The lover attends the triumph-procession, the Circus, and the theatre, but as he does so, defines his different manner of experiencing these public venues through his specifically amatory focus.[229] Like the late Horace, Ovid works to define poetry's distinct perspective and value *within* the arena of public culture and discourse, and as in Horace, the poet/teacher assumes a role in some aspects paralleling that of the *princeps*. The totalizing ideology of the *amator* mirrors, even as it inverts, the systematically pervasive nature of the princeps' large-scale intervention in the moral fabric of the city. The lover, too, sees his favoured life-principles infusing patterns of urban behaviour and civic attitudes within the context of an elegantly enhanced physical environment.

Ovid's most ambitious attempt to rewrite the Augustan city to conform with his literary interests comes in an ambitious follow-up to his early elegiac output, the

---

[224] Such places, in Ovidian elegy, tend to signify an involvement in love affairs, but they also represent important elements in the Augustan programme of public building: Boyle (2003), ad loc.

[225] Compare *Ars am.* 1.165–70: *et pars spectati muneris ipse fuit* (170).

[226] *Ars am.* 1.89–134.   [227] e.g. in 2.5.17ff., the dinner party.

[228] *Amores* 2.4.48: *noster in has omnes ambitiosus amor*. Keith (1994), 35, notes that this statement 'undercuts the poet-lover's repeated assurances that Corinna is the sole inspiration of his verse', but otherwise connects it with Ovid's commitment to elegiac values within a broadly Callimachean framework. I would also stress the tension with the core doctrines of Roman Callimacheanism, the pointed appropriation of an ethical category (*ambitio*) nominally excluded from elegiac discourse.

[229] It is not that there is no precedent for such a procedure: love's triumph and *militia* are recurrent themes in Propertius. Ovid's *Amores*, however, represent the intensification, systematization, and culmination of tendencies already present in earlier elegy.

Ars amatoria (2 BC). While the *Ars* is a work of didactic poetry and thus not primarily self-representational, its themes and underlying concepts are so closely tied to first-person love elegy that it is worthy of brief consideration in light of our present concerns. The *Ars* further intensifies the concept of the poet's public status. Ovid addresses entire portions of the populace—sexually eligible men and women of Rome—and, at least notionally, excludes others (*Ars am.* 1.31–4). What he enjoins, moreover, applies generally to masses of people, and is largely presented as a mode of collective behaviour, often in mass settings (theatre, circus). Rather than excluding the *profanum vulgus*, Ovid offers generalized erotics applicable to the crowd.[230]

> Siquis in hoc artem populo non novit amandi,
> > hoc legat et lecto carmine doctus amet.   (*Ars am.* 1.1–2)

If anyone in this populace does not know the art of love, let them read this, and after reading the poem, knowledgeably conduct their love affairs.

Both Ovid's poetic 'art', and his technical treatise on love (*Ars amatoria*), are overtly oriented towards the populace.[231] Within the frame of this markedly public orientation, the combination of the terms *carmen* ('song'), *ars* ('art'), *populus* ('the populace'), and *doctus* ('erudite') is a telling one. Doctitude, of course, defines the *carmina docta* (learned poetry) of Ovid's elegiac predecessors and other Augustan poets writing in a Callimachean vein. Now, however, members of the broader Roman *populus* will be taught, and thus become erudite, in the technicalities of seduction. The doctitude of the crowd is a near-paradox by the traditional standards of Roman metapoetics. A new kind of knowledge is on display—not the abstruse erudition of the Muses, Phoebus, and Hesiodic initi-ation, but knowledge of how to gain tactical advantage in love affairs. For this type of *doctrina*, as Ovid enjoins with another knowing subversion of contemporary vocabulary, readers need to consult an 'experienced bard' (*vati parete perito*, 1.29).[232]

As we read on, nearly every didactic utterance consciously travesties the premise of the Callimachean values of earlier love elegy:

> dum licet, et loris passim potes ire solutis,
> > elige cui dicas 'tu mihi sola places.'
> haec tibi non tenues veniet delapsa per auras:
> > quarenda est oculis apta puella tuis.   (*Ars am.* 1.41–4)

While you still can, and are able to roam everywhere with free rein, choose someone to whom you may say, 'Only you are attractive to me.' Such a one will not come to you by falling through the empty air. A suitable girl must be sought out with your eyes.

---

[230] It is tempting to think of Ovid's interest in declamation, as attested by Seneca the Elder (*Controv.* 2.2.8–12), along with the remarks of White (2002), 8: 'Ovid never dissembled his desire to appeal to a broad audience or his pride in being able to'.

[231] As Hollis (1977) notes, ad loc., Ovid departs from didactic tradition in not addressing a single individual (Memmius, Perses), but an entire segment of a population.

[232] i.e., a bard who derives knowledge from practical experience rather than from the inspiration of Apollo and the Muses. As Hollis (1977) observes, ad loc., Ovid, in disavowing inspiration of Apollo, has Callimachus as his 'main target'.

Ovid has already been explicit about his elegiac girlfriend's status as literary *materia*: *principio quod amare velis, reperire labora* ('first of all, work hard to find an object you would like to love', 1.35). Now he replaces the elegiac lover's mythic surrender to the sudden power of love, 'love-at-first-sight' that inexplicably 'descends from the skies' (*delapsa per auras*), with studied, laboured intentionality: *reperire labora . . . quarenda est* ('work hard to find . . . must be sought').[233] Propertian uniqueness has been supplanted by a wilful simulation of a unique relation, as the final subjunctive *dicas* makes explicit: *cui dicas 'tu mihi sola places'* ('. . . [choose] someone to whom to say, "You alone are attractive to me"').[234] The production of a sense of Callimachean exclusiveness has itself become a systematic strategy of *ars*, employed by an urban mob of would-be *amatores*—an interesting comment on the now presumably diffuse fashion of elegiac love. In the meanwhile, tenuousness, the refined quality of Callimachean poetry, has become, in Ovid's use of the familiar term, mere insubstantiality, the emptiness of an indulgent, romantic dream (*tenues . . . auras*, 43).

The 'advice' Ovid gives to lovers corresponds to the literary conventions of elegy, now deflatingly rewritten as the demythologized instructions of a technical handbook. His work's title might with some justice be translated *The Art of Writing Love Elegy*.[235] Manipulative intention replaces passive surrender, and replicable strategy replaces unique experience. Singularity becomes a trope employed by multitudes, while multiplicity emerges as an overt theme of Ovidian didactic.

> tot tibi tamque dabit formosas Roma puellas,
>   'haec habet' ut dicas 'quicquid in orbe fuit.'
>
> .   .   .   .
>
> sive cupis iuvenem, iuvenes tibi mille placebunt:
>   cogeris voti nescius esse tui:
> seu te forte iuvat sera et sapientior aetas,
>   hoc quoque, crede mihi, plenius agmen erit.   (*Ars am.* 1.55–6, 63–6)

Rome will give you so many and so beautiful girls that you will say, 'This city possesses whatever there is in the world' . . . If you prefer a young woman in her prime, a thousand such women will be attractive to you: you will be forced to be ignorant of your own desire. If perchance a mature and wiser age pleases you, there will be—believe me—a dense squadron of this sort as well.

Although the would-be lover previously was enjoined to choose an appropriate love-object, the vast number of eligible Roman girls undermines even the capacity for this generic choice. Never mind *una puella*: Ovid's trademark image becomes the eroticized *agmen* ('squadron'). The following passage further develops this impression. Running through various settings amenable to the pursuit of girls, Ovid describes well-known monuments of the Augustan city: the theatre and

---

[233] He even seems slyly to suggest a new etymology for 'elegy' in this act of intentional choice: *elige cui dicas 'tu mihi sola places'*: see Hollis (1977), ad loc.

[234] Compare Hollis (1977), ad loc.: 'a delightful combination of the two concepts of love', i.e. 'cool rational choice' and involuntary passion. For *tu mihi sola places*, compare Propertius 2.7.19 and [Tibullus] 3.19.3 (as noted by Hollis).

[235] McCarthy (1998), 176: 'the didactic narrator's advice describes the textual practice of the poets of elegy'.

portico of Pompey, the portico of Livia, the Danaid portico, the temple of Venus, the temple of Isis, and Rome's theatres. The latter venue provides the pretext for an epic simile comparing the multitude of female spectators with an *agmen* ('swarm') of ants or bees. Finally, Ovid moves from the topic of love in theatres to the book's first fully developed *exemplum*: the rape of the Sabine women at a festive theatrical gathering.[236] The mass rape of the Sabines represents a case of sexual behaviour on the scale of the entire Roman populace. Throughout the *Ars amatoria*, Ovid crafts a tightly woven fabric consisting of love's urban setting, his ideal audience (would-be *amatores*), his actual audience (a broad urban readership), and the objects of love (myriad *puellae*). On every level, elegiac love is expanded, multiplied beyond the restrictive bounds of previous elegy.

A further strategy of the *Ars* is to generalize and systematize elegiac tropes that were at least partially premised on the notion of the lover's irreducibly unique passion for a specific love-object. By systematizing and reducing to a teachable predictability love's figures and themes, Ovid suggests that they belong, precisely, to the iterative dynamic of a literary system (or 'genre'). Ovid's 'technical treatise' (*ars*) on *amor* thus has implications for the configuration of poetic autonomy. *Ars* indicates a sphere of endeavour susceptible of treatment in a technical treatise; it belongs to a specialized class of practitioners, and needs to be taught as a discrete discipline. *Amor* and the poetry of *amor* now display the inward-looking tendencies of an autonomous sphere of expertise. T. Habinek has argued that the technical discourse on love in the *Ars amatoria* is a sign of the autonomization of sex in Augustan Rome.[237] My metapoetic reading of the same phenomenon suggests that, whatever degree of sociological truth Ovid's vision of an amatory City may contain, his organization of erotic discourse intensifies the autonomist self-presentation of elegiac poetry. We get the sense that love is played like a game, for its own sake, without even the urgent drive of an all-consuming passion motivating it. Elegiac poetry on the model of *ars*, then, is not grounded in some specific, concrete scenario of sociability, utility, or need, but is instead viewed as an autonomously valid, autotelic practice, its rules and techniques transferrable and replicable as a self-contained system.[238]

In making this argument, I have not even touched on what is perhaps the most salient aspect of Ovidian autonomy: his aggressive assertion of elegiac cultural values. Here too Ovid furthers an argument already substantially developed in previous elegy. Gallus, Tibullus, and Propertius saw the world through the lover's eyes, valued the love of their mistresses over military plunder and prestige, and contrasted themselves with patrons and foil-figures such as Tullus, Maecenas, and Messalla. There is one truly important contrastive figure for Ovid: Augustus himself. Augustus is too grand and distant, however, to function as *amicus* within

---

[236] *Ars Am.* 1.111–34. In this passage, plurality and unity constitute an explicit theme: *turba* (117) . . . *nam timor unus erat, facies non una timoris* (121).

[237] Habinek (1997).

[238] The absence of named patron-figures in all of Ovid's poetry prior to the *Epistulae ex Ponto* is often noted and discussed: e.g. White (2002), 8–9. I would suggest as a possible explanation for this absence the strong autonomizing tendency of Ovidian poetics: the constraints of situationally embedded speech tend to be replaced by fictions of generalized, didactic utterance and engagement with a broad, anonymous urban audience: Citroni (1995), 431–74.

a scenario of literary exchange or as conventional foil-figure. Rather, Augustus represents a dominant ideology in Roman society; he is a figure at the centre of a nexus of moral, religious, and political discourses. It is here that most scholars have concentrated their efforts in assessing the question of Ovid's so-called 'dissent'. Against the background of a public discourse that increasingly celebrated the value of marriage and the production of Roman offspring among the upper classes, Ovidian love poetry, with its equivocal hints of adulterous intrigue, has been seen as subversive.[239] I would argue, however, that 'autonomy' is both a more accurate and more usefully flexible term than subversion or resistance. The point is not opposition to state policy, as if Ovid were heading a protest movement, but definition of the poet's axiological domain.

Once again, there is a difference in intensity and approach. Ovid expands, intensifies, and systematizes the elegiac strategy of axiological contrast. Ovid's ambulatory urban lover is an especially effective instrument for mapping *amor*, both as activity and as system of values, onto the city's monuments and the broader Augustan enterprise. This newly expanded amatory mode allows the elegiac poet to re-envision important aspects of the Augustan city in an elegiac key: Augustan genealogy, military ideology, occasions of imperial benefaction and mass spectatorship, the connection between *urbs* and *orbis*, the sanctity of the past, and so forth. The scope of the opening book of the *Ars amatoria* is startlingly broad in this respect. Ovid's didactic canvas encompasses the Roman populace as pupils, his *praecepta* notionally address any and all amatory encounters in the city, and lovers suffer their torments and apply their stratagems in the magnificent *aurea Roma* of theatres, sprawling porticoes, and gleaming marble temples of the later Augustan period. Augustus' *naumachia* of 2 BC in the Trastevere region becomes the site of cosmopolitan eros, as young men and *puellae* from across the Roman world fill the city: *quis non invenit, turba quod amaret in illa* ('who did not find something to love in that crowd', 175)? Propertius' Callimachean exclusivity is obsolete; now the urban *turba* becomes enabler and multiplier of passion on a world-wide scale.

Ovid at once continues and pushes to a new scope of immensity the elegiac tradition of converting military victory into erotic glory[240] and the imperial triumph-procession into an occasion for displaying and reinforcing amatory values.[241] In the passage that follows Ovid's comments on the *naumachia*, he imagines a future triumph-procession for Augustus' putative victories in the East, at which, however, a troupe of amorously inclined young men and women take the opportunity to engage in flirtatious conversation.

> spectabunt laeti iuvenes mixtaeque puellae,
>   diffundetque animos omnibus ista dies,
> atque aliqua ex illis cum regum nomina quaeret,

---

[239] On Ovid and the Augustan *leges Iuliae*, see Barchiesi (2006). Debate over the 'anti-Augustan' status of Ovid's poetry, and the *Ars amatoria* in particular, continues: see, e.g. P. J. Davis (1999) and (2006), who argues that we *can* discern the political intent behind Ovid poetry, despite the arguments of Kennedy (1992); an especially nuanced discussion in Labate (1984); note also Sharrock (1994); Barchiesi (1997); Volk (2006); Casali (2006); Gibson (2006).

[240] On the *militia amoris* in Ovid, see Cahoon (1988).

[241] Compare Propertius 3.4 and Hollis (1977), 81–2.

> quae loca, qui montes, quaeve ferantur aquae,
> omnia responde, nec tantum siqua rogabit . . .
>
>   . . .
>
> ille vel ille, duces, et erunt quae nomina dicas,
>   si poteris, vere, si minus, apta tamen.   (*Ars am.* 1.217–21, 227–8)

Happy young men mingling with young women will watch the show, and that day will exhilarate everyone's spirits. And when one of the girls asks the names of the kings, and asks what places, mountains, and bodies of water are being conveyed past [in the triumphal procession], respond to all her questions, and not only if she asks . . . That fellow and the other one—they're commanders; and you will find names to give them, their actual names if you are able, but if you can't, ones that are fitting in any case.

The triumph is an occasion for representing Rome's conquests, power, and empire, as well as her leaders' superior *virtus*, to the populace as a whole. This troupe of *amatores*, however, plays fast and loose with language, employing their own mode of representation, their own manipulation of *nomina*, to achieve distinctly amatory ends. Propertius proclaimed his own personal 'triumph' as elegiac poet in 3.1, and proposed to watch a future triumph of Augustus from his girlfriend's arms in 3.4. Ovid broadens the canvas: his significantly pluralized crowd of lovers assimilates to their own interests the culminating spectacle of political and military power.

While I have argued that it is not accurate to characterize this type of autonomist literary strategy as 'subversive',[242] it would be equally misleading to suggest that Ovidian love is wholly innocuous from an Augustan perspective. There is not sufficient space for exhaustive discussion, but a few salient points can be mentioned. Ovid's lover is more overtly calculating, manipulative, and promiscuous than his literary predecessors, and, more importantly, he is not someone who has been unlucky and miserable enough to fall victim, against his own will, to Love. Ovid's lover, unlike Propertius', consciously *chooses* love as a provocative, counter-cultural lifestyle, and tries to press his advantage and maximize his erotic success amidst the incalculably vast number of opportunities afforded by a city of one million inhabitants.[243] Ovid presents himself explicitly as a 'poet of wickedness', and elsewhere as an 'acrobat' or 'trickrider' of love; he turns elegiac identity into an intrinsic moral provocation. Propertius and Tibullus tended to present themselves as being prone to the particular weaknesses of a lover's disposition—an inveterate *desidia* (indolence) and *mollitia* (effeminacy). Unfortunate but ultimately excusable traits of individual character afforded a non-polemical pretext for the amatory project. In Ovid's case, elegiac love is paraded as an intentional, practised, consciously avowed, and systematically applied *ars*. He intensifies the provocation and confrontation with traditional values by refusing to allow eccentricities of

---

[242] Syme (1978), 199: 'of authentic opposition to the new order, no sign or prospect . . . While the brave and bold had perished, the *nobiles* now renascent through support and subsidy from Caesar were arrogant and pretentious—and also subservient'. But note Hinds' (1987b) arguments against the idea that Ovidian panegyric was merely 'passive' adulation offered as a kind of escapism (23–9).

[243] Compare Syme (1978), 190: 'malicious frivolity or even muted defiance'.

individual character to limit and mitigate the ideological challenge of elegiac *Amor* to Augustan *Roma*.[244]

Here too Ovid tests the capacities of the autonomist paradigm: how far can a poet go in aligning himself with counter-traditional values in order to define the discursive independence of his poetic domain? Earlier elegists, for all their anti-nomian posturing, maintained an implicit connection with core Augustan moral values. The Tibullan and Propertian lovers defined themselves as simple in lifestyle, peace-loving, artifice-despising, respectful of antiquity, loyal, and indifferent to the lures of wealth. The lyric Horace, for all that he devotes himself to symposiastic pleasures of wine and *hetairai*, largely adopts the persona of a loyal imperial citizen, hewing to the party line in religious, moral, and political attitudes. Even his explicitly stated preference for prostitutes and freedwomen (*Sat.* 1.2) is far more acceptable in 'Augustan' terms than the provocative indeterminacy of the elegists. In Ovid, however, the link between *amor* and the civic virtues of the Pax Augusta has been severed. Ovid celebrates sophistication, artifice, modernity, promiscuity, and the refinements of sensual pleasure. Special pleading is required, moreover, to bring the many concrete scenarios of amatory deception in the *Ars amatoria* in line with the poet's profession of adultery-free erotic instruction.[245] Yet whereas the break with official Augustan values has been further radicalized in line with Ovid's consistent testing of the limits of the autonomist paradigm, we should not necessarily see Ovid as a subversive poet in the strong sense of the term, or even as anything so determinate as a 'critic of the regime'. On my reading, Ovid still happily works *within* the system of autonomy, even as he presses at its boundaries.

If anything, Ovid took the autonomist paradigm too much for granted, unlike his predecessors of the early Augustan period, whose autonomist rhetoric is counterbalanced by gestures of deference and affirmation.[246] Certainly Augustus did not rejoice in Ovid's manipulation of sexual morality to shore up his aggressively autonomist posture. There must have been some basis for his choice of the *Ars amatoria* as the nominal justification for Ovid's relegation in AD 8. Augustus, if we judge by Horace's epistle to him, favoured the poet's role as teacher of civic morality, but the Ovidian *praeceptor* is the purveyor of precisely the opposite lesson to the one he had in mind. He cleverly mimics the form of the Augustan didactic *vates*-figure, yet employs it to purvey the wrong content. That said, it still seems unlikely to me that Augustus relegated Ovid to Tomis primarily, or even partially, for the *Ars*. Doubtless the mystery of Ovid's exile has been over-examined proportional to its capacity for being solved, but it will be helpful briefly

---

[244] Compare the analysis of Armstrong (2004), who traces Ovid's persistent displacement and subversion of Apollo's authority throughout his work (*Amores* 1.1., the opening of the *Ars*, Apollo and Daphne in *Metamorphoses*, etc.). Armstrong argues that Ovid displaces Apollo in the name of greater 'independence' (528, 549) both in regard to the doctrinaire version of Callimachean poetic tradition, and in regard to the authority of Augustus, who closely linked himself with Apollo as god of the Actian victory and of poetry and song.

[245] Syme (1978), 192: 'Ovid's writings portrayed the normal habits of high society in everything that was distasteful to Caesar Augustus'; the *Ars*, moreover, was inconveniently published in the wake of the scandal of Julia's 'adulteries' (191).

[246] On the 'two generations' theory, see Syme (1978), 188–9; but he notes that literary genre and tradition also furnish an explanation for diverging literary attitudes (189).

to reconsider the controversy in the light of the present argument, since it has implications for the understanding of the rhetoric of poetic autonomy and its limits under the principate.[247] We must first of all recognize Augustus' long-established pattern of strategic tolerance of free speech. He may have assumed a more direct style of involvement in literary matters in the later years of his principate, and there is some limited evidence for the emergence of a harder stance towards published writings directly critical of the Caesars, but none of this makes it likely that Augustus would have wished to deal with a popular poet in a heavy-handed way when no seriously treasonous intent was in question. Even more decisive is the great span of time between the publication of the *Ars amatoria* (2 BC) and the pronouncement of Ovid's sentence of relegation (AD 8), a discrepancy pointed out by Ovid himself.[248] Indeed, as Ovid also observes, he continued to be pronounced worthy of his knighthood by Augustus as censor despite his morally frivolous poetry.[249]

If the timing of Ovid's *relegatio* fails to accord with the publication date of the *Ars*, it fits much better the exile of Agrippa Postumus and the scandal of Julia the Younger. The exile of both Julias were justified on ground of moral misconduct, although in each case, there are strong reasons to think that a near-treasonous dispute over succession within the imperial family motivated their exile.[250] The presumption of scholars has been that Ovid 'witnessed' or knew something about these goings on and did not disclose them to Augustus. Augustus, then, would be pursuing the same strategy with Ovid's indiscretion as with the Julias. Rather than openly discuss an awkward conflict within his own family over succession, he pronounces the punishment on grounds of sexual morality, pinning the blame on the exiled individual instead of undermining his own position as paterfamilias and princeps. Arguments similar to the one advanced here have been made by previous scholars, but it has been necessary to recall the basic parameters of the question in order to appreciate the likelihood that Augustus' relegation of the poet Ovid was not primarily motivated by the moral failings of his poetry. Both Augustus and Ovid were still working on the loose assumption of autonomy as the defining protocol of poetic activity. Augustus was driven to contravene this protocol, at least ostensibly, by the need to present an acceptable reason for the poet's relegation.

Even if Augustus exiled Ovid for the *Ars amatoria* only in appearance, this very appearance nearly instantaneously takes on the status of crucial, paradigm-shifting fact in the emerging field of early imperial poetry. Ovid himself draws literary consequences from his exile, and partly because he has no choice, since he cannot speak of the politically sensitive 'mistake' (2.208–11), and partly because it suits him, makes literature into the key exhibit of his case for recall from exile, or, in any case, ameliorative relocation. Here is a court in which Ovid, who declined to pursue a career as an advocate, might be expected to advance a persuasive case, and indeed, in *Tristia* 2, Ovid launches a lengthy defense of poetry's moral

---

[247] There are numerous scholarly hypotheses on the subject: e.g. Wilkinson (1955), 294–8; Thibault (1964); Norwood (1963); Syme (1978), 215–29; Green (1982); Goold (1983); White (1993), 152–4; Gibson (2003), 36–7; Raaflaub and Samons (1990), 445ff.; Watson (2002), 154–7.

[248] *Tr.* 2.539–546. [249] *Tr.* 2.89–90, 541–2. [250] Syme (1978), 194–5, 209–10.

autonomy.[251] *Tristia* 2, which, instead of being broken up into individual elegies, is composed of one long elegy, resembles, in disconcerting ways, Horace's 'Epistle to Augustus'—another long, epistolary poem, which is addressed to the emperor on the subject of past and contemporary poetry, and which begins by doubting the princeps' ability to spend extended periods of time reading poetry, given his tremendous duties of state.[252] The arguments of the two poetic epistles approach a similar set of issues from opposite directions. The result is a surprising complementarity. Horace argues for the public utility and moral exemplarity of poetry, yet insists on exacting technical standards. Ovid argues that the questionable moral content of a literary work neither entails damage to public morals, nor carries negative implications about its author's morals. Thus whereas Horace insists that socially beneficial content does not merit praise in the absence of aesthetic rigour, Ovid argues that disreputable content does not undermine the validity and social esteem of a literary work. The emphasis is assuredly different, but both authors, the laureate and the exile, effectively set up barriers between literary value and socially useful content.[253]

The difference, of course, is that Horace is defending a literary career deemed successful by the princeps, Ovid a career condemned by the princeps. Ovid, in any case, turns out to be a fluent and even prolix advocate for his case. He cites an exhaustive list of authors and genres whose content, though disreputable, caused their authors no disgrace, but even won them esteem and immortality (*Tr.* 2.363–496). As he approaches the Augustan period, his remarks become yet more pointed: Gallus' downfall was due to injured friendship, not poetry (445–6); Tibullus and Propertius, Ovid's predecessors, wrote of love without suffering for it (447–70)—Tibullus in a vein that anticipates, as Ovid's lengthy citations demonstrate, the didactic cynicism of his own *Ars* (447–64). Finally, the temples and sculptural programme of Augustus' city, the pre-eminently popular Dido episode in Augustus' 'own' *Aeneid* (*tuae . . . Aeneidos*, 533), and the theatrical shows Augustus himself funded and watched without concern (*vidisti lentus*, 514), are rife with themes of erotic enticement. Ovid, acting as his own lawyer, tilts the evidence in favour of his autonomist case, while picking apart some of the contradictions of Augustus' charge against him. Did Augustus not tolerate other poetic works of dubious moral content? Did the princeps himself not adhere, in broad terms, to an autonomist model of literary activity?

The truth is, he *did*—and the past tense matters. Ovid picks apart an apparent contradiction, but also (deliberately) ignores the emperor's more recent advances towards direct involvement in literary production, including censorial actions. Ovid also declines to mention how he himself pressed at the limits of the 'gentleman's agreement' that enabled the autonomist model to persist. That the disreputable associations of gambling (*Tr.* 2.471–84) and love affairs do not always trigger the condemnation of literary works in which they feature is credible; but that Ovid's provocative 'teaching' of extramarital love to the

---

[251] A summary of Ovid's arguments on behalf of poetic autonomy in Stabryla (1994).

[252] See, for example, Ingleheart (2010), 8–10.

[253] We might also observe that both the epistolary Horace and the epistolary Ovid focused substantial and prominent attention on the circulating book, liberated from its author's control, and so also, presumably, from imperial control: on the Ovidian book in exile, see especially Hinds (1985).

populace should be published without some serious moral disapproval in Augustan Rome, in the years following the passage of the princeps' highly controversial marriage and adultery legislation, is less obvious. Now that Augustus has purview over the public libraries he constructed on the Palatine and in the portico of Livia, and in the library of the Atrium Libertatis built earlier by Asinius Pollio, literature is, in some sense, a matter of state, a 'public' matter associated with the emperor. This new state of affairs was not enough to motivate the condemnation of Ovid when the *Ars amatoria* was first published in 2 BC, but becomes powerfully evident when, following Ovid's relegation, his works were banned from the public libraries. The autonomist paradigm has not ceased to operate altogether, but it no longer operates in quite the same way, and it is not enough simply to insist on literature's moral autonomy in the face of overt imperial disapproval. Again, we may note some unexpected parallels between the condemned Ovid and the late Horace: the latter's *Epistles* comparably confront the now 'public' status of works held in the Palatine library and the implications of such public status for the poet's autonomy.

Horace was favoured, Ovid quite the opposite, but both feel the need to set up rhetorical bulwarks to defend poetic autonomy under shifting cultural conditions. In Ovid, but not solely in Ovid, we discern the more threatening aspect of the imperial involvement in literature and of the imperial libraries for which Propertius and Horace initially expressed such enthusiasm. Horace, as we have noted, came to view the matter in a more ambivalent light. Neither Horace nor Ovid simply gave up on the autonomist model of poetic activity in the face of increased imperial scrutiny. They did, however, adapt their rhetorical strategies to new circumstances. Augustus, for his part, did not initially wish to send a heavy-handed announcement of direct imperial control over poets and their books, but nonetheless ended up resorting to a poet's relegation and the banning of his works. This quasi-accidental act of literary censorship, however, had immediate and enduring consequences. Already in Ovid's *Tristia*, the emperor is viewed as having direct, punitive purview over the poet and the books. A wrathful Jupiter, armed with thunderbolts, pervades the *Tristia* like a malevolent patron god.

Ovid's place of exile was chosen with a cruel precision, as he himself observed.[254] Augustus possibly wanted to teach the *praeceptor amoris* what the stakes of empire and *pax* are. The ideological cohesion of the empire, he seems to suggest, is not just a banality to be toyed with by clever poets. Living out the rest of his life in a barren outpost, Ovid will come to appreciate the stakes of civility and stability, how a modicum of respect for the slogans that prop it up are a small price to pay for the kind of life that Ovid used to enjoy as a privileged city-dweller. Ovid, for his part, hopes that Augustus will allow him to come back, if he can show, through his poetry, that he has learned the lesson. Augustus, however, was content with leaving Ovid in the humiliating role of eager pupil for the rest of his life. It is a bitter irony that Ovid, who of all Augustan poets took for granted the condition of peaceful leisure (*otium*) in which he pursued his craft, who felt no urgent need to defend his poetic vocation or fence off a sequestered literary realm, is deprived of precisely such *otium*, precisely such tranquillity of surroundings.

---

[254] On *regio* as part of the punishment: *Tr.* 2.194.

On the other hand, Ovid manages to make the most of the figurative and self-representational potential of his exilic extremity. Dispatched on a sea voyage to what he views as the ends of the earth, Ovid works to intensify the sense of extreme vulnerability, displacement, and unshelteredness that this barbarian realm would have evoked in the minds of his early readers. Augustan poets such as Tibullus and Horace played with concepts of security and danger, shelter and lack of shelter, in constructing their cosy literary domains and *loci amoeni*. Such games are now over. From Ovid's perspective on the Black Sea, the sheltering niche of autonomist 'play' is definitively obsolete. It is hard to take seriously again the idea of poetry's protected grotto or grove when the poet, soaked with spray and tossed violently on the high seas, is being driven from his homeland to the distant land of the barbarous Tomitians. The sea affords a powerful and recurrent imagery-set throughout *Tristia* 1, and in 1.2, Ovid writes as if in the midst of a mighty and terrible storm: *me miserum, quanti montes volvuntur aquarum* ('wretched me—what huge mountains of water are heaving [all around]!' 1.2.19). The sea's power over the helpless individual is a forcefully concrete figuration of heteronomy, and as the poet contemplates his dire situation, 'being at the mercy of the waves' is both a vivid description of his journey into exile and an insistent metaphor for the loss of self-determination he is experiencing in his life.

In the opening poem of the collection, Ovid already signals his interest in exploring how his new situation works to dismantle clichés of the poet's tranquillity and sequestered retirement.

> carmina secessum scribentis et otia quaerunt;
>   me mare, me venti, me fera iactat hiems.
> carminibus metus omnis obest; ego perditus ensem
>   haesurum iugulo iam puto iamque meo.
> haec quoque quod facio, iudex mirabitur aequus,
>   scriptaque cum venia qualiacumque leget.
> da mihi Maeoniden et tot circumice casus,
>   ingenium tantis excidet omne malis.   (*Tr.* 1.1.41–8)

Poetry demands the seclusion and leisure of the writer. I am tossed about by the sea, the winds, the savage winter storm. Any fear is an impediment to poetry. In my ruined condition, I think that the sword is about to be hanging above my neck at any moment. An impartial judge will be amazed that I even manage to produce these verses, and will read my writings with indulgence, whatever their quality may be. Take Homer and surround him with so many misfortunes–all his poetic ability will vanish amid such great troubles.

Writing in exile will require a new kind of writing, a new conception of the poet's identity and autonomy under radically changed conditions. For Ovid's predecessor Propertius, we recall, the writer's *ingenium* constituted his distinguishing quality and served to protect him and his works from the ravages of time: *ingenio stat sine morte decus* ('talent enjoys a glory that does not die', 3.2.26). His deathless talent allows the poet to transcend mere ephemeral concerns, ephemeral modes of communication. In Ovid, the lines of power and control have been reversed. The poet's *ingenium*, which in the first place played a regrettable role in bringing about his exile, now has become subject to the contingencies of fortune, as Ovid remarks hypothetically of Homer: *ingenium tantis excidet omne malis* (all of [Homer's] talent will fall away amid such great misfortunes', *Tr.* 1.1.48). At the opening of

Tristia 2, Ovid complains that his *ingenium* has brought about his punishment, and yet he still turns to poetry to ameliorate his situation: he is like Telephus, cured by the very object that wounded him. The reversal of the autonomy of poetic *ingenium* is thus not total: though harmed by his song, he can still sing.

A vivid enactment of this dialectic of autonomy and heteronomy—the poet's submersion in the overwhelming forces of the storm and waves on the one hand, and his capacity to continue writing and controlling his own image through poetry on the other—can be found in the culminating elegy of *Tristia* 1. Here Ovid announces that the verses that constitute the present book were not written on a couch or in the garden, as previously (1.11.37–8), but on the storm-tossed deep, and the very paper is splashed by the waves.

> littera quaecumque est toto tibi lecta libello,
>   est mihi sollicito tempore facta viae.
> sed haec me, gelido tremerem cum mense Decembri,
>   scribentem mediis Hadria vidit aquis;
> aut, postquam bimarem cursu superavimus Isthmon,
>   alteraque est nostrae sumpta carina fugae,
> quod facerem versus inter fera murmura ponti,
>   Cycladas Aegaeas obstipuisse puto.
> ipse ego nunc miror tantis animique marisque
>   fluctibus ingenium non cecidisse meum...
> saepe maris pars intus erat; tamen ipse trementi
>   carmina ducebam qualiacumque manu.   (*Tr.* 1.11. 1–10, 17–18)

Every letter you have read in this entire book was composed by me during the anxious time of my journey. The Adriatic saw me writing these words in the middle of the sea as I shivered in the chill month of December; or, after I sailed past the Isthmos that lies between two seas, and boarded the second ship of my exile, the Aegean Cyclades were astonished, I think, that I was fashioning verses amid the savage roaring of the sea. I myself am amazed even now that amid such turbulent waves of mind and ocean my poetic talent did not fail... Often part of the sea was inside the ship, and yet I myself with trembling hand went on composing poetry, whatever quality it may be.

Now would be the moment to cite the usual parallels for the idea of the poem as a journey at sea, and yet while Ovid clearly builds on such a tradition, the point he is making is sharper: the waves, both of sea and his spirit, threaten to overwhelm him; he writes in the midst of overwhelming circumstances, yet his hand continues producing *carmina*, he continues to control his stylus instead of allowing these enormous forces to control him.[255] Whereas previously Ovid stated that even Homer's *ingenium* would fail in such circumstances, he now reveals that his own poetic talent did *not* fail; indeed, it produced the book we have just finished reading.

Since Catullus in c. 11, Roman poets have been imagining themselves transported to the margins of the empire. The premise of the topos of far-flung travel, however, is that the poet actually remains in or near the city, focused on a woman and his poetry. Horace barely strays beyond the boundaries of his farm, but

---

[255] Or is it poetry itself that, in some sense, continues on autonomously despite the fact that the poet himself is overwhelmed? An anonymous reviewer for Oxford University Press poses this question, and it is worth considering: the hand that continues to write is potentially a figure for the text that endures and continues to be read despite the author's fall.

reassures himself and his readers that his 'integrity' is such that he would remain serenely, autarkically secure and self-sufficient even if transported to barren wastes at the edge of the earth.

> pone me pigris ubi nulla campis
> arbor aestiva recreatur aura,
> quod latus mundi nebulae malusque
>   Iuppiter urget;
> pone sub curru nimium propinqui
> solis in terra domibus negata:
> dulce ridentem Lalagen amabo,
>   dulce loquentem.   (*Carm.* 1.22.17–24)

Put me in barren fields where no tree is refreshed by a summer breeze, the part of the world that is oppressed by clouds and gloomy Jupiter; place me in a land prohibiting habitation where the sun's chariot is too close, and I will love Lalage sweetly laughing, sweetly speaking.

Song, encoded both in Lalage's name ('chatterer'), and in the Sapphic allusion of the poem's closing lines, mysteriously keeps Horace safe; it guarantees his autarkic *securitas* amid forbidding environs. The tone is light and ironic, but, as argued above, the deeper point is not meant to be taken entirely lightly. Horace enjoys the security of his Sabine estate, *otium* guaranteed by powerful patrons, an Italy pacified and protected by Augustan arms, but realizes that poetic autonomy dependent on a specific location and friendship with the great is only a partial, contingent autonomy, and both here and elsewhere experiments with the idea of a sacrosanctity intrinsic to his status as divinely protected *vates*, a more profoundly self-sufficient mode of autonomy.

Ovid, in the meanwhile, really has been deprived of the temperate Italian climate and the *otium* of a charmed elite existence in the capital. Whereas previously Ovid guiltlessly 'played' (*lusi*) in verse, and his Muse was 'merrier than his life' (*magis vita Musa iocata mea est*, 3.2.5–6), now he dwells on the shores of frost-scorched Pontus.[256]

> quique fugax rerum securaque in otia natus,
>   mollis et inpatiens ante laboris eram,
> ultima nunc patior, nec me mare portubus orbum
>   perdere, diversae nec potuere viae;
> suffecitque malis animus; nam corpus ab illo
>   accepit vires vixque ferenda tulit.   (*Tr.* 3.2.9–14)

I who formerly was averse to the fray, born to carefree leisure, delicate and intolerant of toil, now endure extremity; neither distant journeys nor harbourless sea have been able to destroy me. My spirit was strong enough for my misfortunes; for my body took strength from it, and endured things barely endurable.

Otium ('leisure'), *lusus* ('play'), *ioci* ('jesting'), tranquil retirement—the key themes of Augustan poetic self-representation—have been abolished by exile, and Ovid must rely on a tougher capacity for endurance. The resilience *in extremis* about which Horace safely fantasized can now be claimed by Ovid in the present

---

[256] See Williams (1994), 25ff., on Ovid's 'Pontic ethnography' and description of the climate and conditions of his land of exile.

indicative (*ultima nunc patior*, 'I now endure extremity') as a real quality tested in genuinely harsh conditions. Even if the poet embellishes his sufferings, he does not falsify the underlying experience of exile as a harsh and relentless one.[257] Ovid, by a peculiar turn of fate, finds himself in a position to make good on the fantasies of far-flung travel crafted by his predecessors, and to test his own capacity to create a new, less contingent basis for poetic autonomy in the forcible absence of the sheltered niche of Italian *otium*.

Especially in the later books of the *Tristia*, Ovid offers a more defiant posture, and insists that his poetic *ingenium*, though it did him harm, is resurgent, and provides him with a source of fame and pleasure that is not contingent on his place of habitation, his fortune, or the will of the princeps. In the letter to Perilla (3.7), he admonishes her to continue writing poetry, as she had in the past, since everything else—beauty, fortune—can be taken away:

> singula ne referam, nil non mortale tenemus
>   pectoris exceptis ingeniique bonis.
> en ego, cum caream patria vobisque domoque,
>   raptaque sint, adimi quae potuere mihi,
> ingenio tamen ipse meo comitorque fruorque:
>   Caesar in hoc potuit iuris habere nihil.
> quilibet hanc saevo vitam mihi finiat ense,
>   me tamen extincto fama superstes erit,
> dumque suis victrix omnem de montibus orbem
>   prospiciet domitum Martia Roma, legar.   (*Tr.* 3.7.43–52)

I won't enumerate all the instances—we have nothing exempt from death except the resources of our spirit and talent. Look at me: though I lack you two, my fatherland, and home, and everything that could be taken from me has been taken, nevertheless I have my literary talent as companion and have recourse to my talent: Caesar could not have any jurisdiction over this. Let anyone end this life of mine with cruel sword: still, when I am dead, my fame will live on, and as long as Mars' city, Rome, shall gaze, victorious, upon the entire subjugated world from her hills, I shall be read.

Ovid's vision of poetry's scope and power to survive is expansive. The circulation of his book is spatially and temporally coterminous, and figuratively comparable, with Rome's imperial hegemony over the 'conquered world'. Caesar, as ruler of that world, has immense power, but it is ultimately finite. Poetry, by contrast, presents the prospect of a nearly limitless dominion through space and time. A similar point is made in Ovid's autobiographical *sphragis*-elegy, 4.10. Here the elegist recalls the major events of his life and literary career, as well as offering a brief, personalized literary history of Augustan poetry. Once again, he makes a point of rising above his misfortune, displaying an autarkic fortitude that limits fortune's (and Augustus') power over him, and counterbalances the catastrophe of his life with the immortality of his verse.

> indignata malis mens est succumbere seque
>   praestitit invictam viribus usa suis;

---

[257] On the question of the 'reality' of Ovid's exile, see Williams (1994), 3ff., who sensibly concludes that Ovid's evident manipulation of persona and rhetorical topoi of exile do not somehow cancel the fact of exile itself.

> oblitusque mei ductaeque per otia vitae
>   insolita cepi temporis arma manu
>
> .   .   .   .
>
>   hic ego, finitimis quamvis circumsoner armis,
>   tristia, quo possum, carmine fata levo.   (*Tr.* 4.10.103–6, 111–12)

My mind thought it unworthy to succumb to misfortune, and showed itself unvanquished, relying on its own resources. Forgetting myself and my life of leisure, I took up with unaccustomed hand the arms of the occasion...Here, though the sound of weapons surrounds me at very close range, I ease my sorrowful fate with what poetry I can.

It is a commonplace sentiment in Roman philosophical discourse, including Horace's *Epistles*, to celebrate the philosopher's ability to rely on 'virtue alone' in times of misfortune or persecution by a tyrant. In the present case, however, the topos becomes something like reality. Ovid really has been separated from the sources of his protection and happiness, and must 'rely on his own resources'. Following these defiant lines, in a passage reminiscent of Horace's expression of gratitude to Melpomene in *Odes* Book 4, Ovid thanks his Muse for his continuing will to live: *ergo quod vivo durisque laboribus obsto, / nec me sollicitae taedia lucis habent, / gratia, Musa, tibi* ('and so, the fact that I live and face up to my hard labours, and am not grown weary of my anxiety-ridden life, is thanks, my Muse, to you', 4.10.115–17).[258] The Horatian reminiscence is pointed: Horace represents himself as a famous, prominent figure in Rome thanks to his poetry; Ovid enjoys world-wide fame, though no longer able to remain in Rome. From a certain perspective, Ovid's poetry is even more powerful, displays greater resources of autonomy, than Horace's; it overcomes greater obstacles and provides a more desperately needed recompense. Ovid, through his immortal fame, his Muse, and the favour of readers throughout the empire (not just Rome), is able to evade the corporeal and legal constraints of his relegation, and to go on living amid exile's living death.

The above quoted passage, with a reference to the work's title, advertises a programmatic link between 'sad' subject matter and the power of song to relieve the poet's sadness (*tristia*...*carmine*). This dyad recurs throughout the collection with varying emphasis. At times, Ovid's 'sad' *materia* appears to absorb his poetic art, his *ingenium* subordinated to his misfortune; at other times, his *ingenium*, along with the *carmen* it produces, overcomes and provides solace for his sufferings. The work's title participates in this duality: *tristia* are at once the subject matter of Ovid's poetry, the sad circumstances of his life in exile, and the poetry itself, 'sad songs' sung by the exiled poet. At times his sufferings appear to overwhelm him and engulf his song, and at other times, song seems to transcend the poet's immediate surroundings, to provide him with a connection with the wider world and future generations.

Like Daedalus, Ovid uses *ars* to escape the tyrant's prison (compare *Ars am.* 2.17–98). The problem is, only the artwork escapes, not the artisan. A comparable mythic exemplum makes an appearance in *Tristia* 3.11. Addressing an unnamed

---

[258] Compare Hor. *Carm.* 4.3.21–4: *totum muneris hoc tui est / quod monstror digito praetereuntium / Romanae fidicen lyrae; / quod spiro et placeo, si placeo, tuum est* ('it is entirely by your gift that I am pointed out by the finger of passers-by as minstrel of the Roman lyre; the fact that I have inspiration and that I please, if I do please, is your gift').

enemy, Ovid compares his cruelty to that of the artisan Perillus, who created a
bronze bull in which Phalaris, tyrant of Agrigentum, could roast his enemies alive.
He could then listen to their groans come out of the mouth of the bull artfully
transformed into bellowing. Phalaris, in return, makes the artisan Perillus into the
bull's first victim: *'poenae mirande repertor, / ipse tuum praesens imbue'* dixit
'opus' ('Marvellous inventor of punishment,' he said, 'dedicate in person your own
work', 51–2). The implications are disturbing, if, as seems inevitable,[259] we
imagine Ovid as the artisan. The artist's creation (*opus*) becomes a mouthpiece
for his own agony, which the ruler enjoys hearing as evidence simultaneously of
the artisan's skill and the painful effects of the punishment he himself sadistically
inflicted on the artist through the agency of the artist's own work. Can we read the
myth as emblematic of a work of poetry called *Tristia*? Of course, Ovid does not
openly label Augustus a sadistic reader who enjoys perusing the poet's expression
of the desolation he himself caused, but the story of Perillus and Phalaris hardly
affords an encouraging paradigm for the relation between artisan and ruler. It is
difficult to pin Ovid down to a single, coherent attitude. At times, he seems to
court Augustus' good opinion and interest in his panegyrical powers. At other
times, he seems defiant, as if he has nothing to lose and might as well shore up his
reputation for posterity.

Stahl, who believes that Ovid's *Tristia* might have been selectively presented in
snippets to the emperor, characterizes the poet as 'playing it both ways' in the
expectation that the appropriate passages would be forwarded to the emperor,
while less panegyrical passages could be appreciated by private readers. Whether
or not Stahl's hypothesis of selective imperial reception is accepted, I concur with
his broader characterization of Ovid's dual attitude. He at once pleads before the
emperor in submissive fashion, and defiantly insists on the autonomy of his poetic
art. Ovid's exile poetry, perhaps because he did not wish to 'put all his eggs in one
basket' and depend exclusively on the favourable reception of either posterity or
the princeps, reveals a systematic bifurcation of tendencies. On the one hand, the
poet's exile furnishes the ultimate example of literary heteronomy, the loss of
power over his books and life, and of the emperor's role as 'judge' and 'censor' of
literature. Ovid, as a result of this exercise of imperial power, must make his
poetry conform with his intention of persuading Augustus to rescind his edict—a
starkly heteronomist poetic orientation. On the other hand, in other moods and
other moments (whether from the perspective of author or reader), Ovid appears
to conclude that that he has nothing to lose, and that, as an enemy of the emperor,
he speaks *ipso facto* as a marginalized, un-Augustan voice, and might as well make
the most of his adversarial position.

Ovid represents the more contentious side of the bifurcation that emerges in
the later Horace. Horace, no longer buffered by Maecenas, addresses Augustus
directly. In doing so, he demonstrates the newly unsheltered status of literary
discourse, the extent to which the writer is now *answerable* to the princeps—
quite literally, since the 'Epistle to Augustus' constitutes a versified answer to

---

[259] Compare *Amores* 1.1 and Cupid's syntactically similar, metapoetic dictum: *'quod'que 'canas,
vates, accipe' dixit 'opus!'* (1.1.24). Ovid, in alluding to this earlier line, calls attention to his structurally
comparable, but clearly very different, programme statement for the present work. Augustus/Phalaris
takes the role of Cupid as sadistic *auctor* of the work's content.

Augustus' intentionally provoking letter. At the same time, however, Horace insists all the more sharply on the aesthetic rigour of poetry and its autonomy vis-à-vis utilitarian aims. Both Horace and Ovid must debate literature and literature's special qualities with the emperor, and both also begin to look beyond the bounds of Rome to Roman literature's reception in the provinces. The power that literature wields is now even more impressive given its newly ecumenical reach under the empire. But unlike most other significant, public exertions of power within the Roman imperial system, literature wields a power that is at least potentially independent of the emperor's oversight and *maius imperium*. One leitmotif of the *Tristia* is the limited reach of imperial power in the face of uncontrolled circulation of books and literature in an empire hungry for Roman culture. Presumably Ovid's *Tristia*, not to mention his banned *Ars amatoria*, were furiously copied and circulated in the wake of his relegation.

CONCLUSION

Ovid's exile poetry and the late works of Horace signal a redefinition of poetic autonomy and a newly overt recognition of the public status of poetry.[260] The restrictive *angulus* (corner, niche) of the poet's retiring *otium* is now irrevocably changed; it persists as a cliché, a reminiscence, and point of reference, but rarely if ever resumes its status as a core theme of self-representation. Ovid, in *Tristia* 5.1, renounces poetic *lusus* ('play') and *ioci* ('jesting'), the kind of writing that did him harm, and characterizes the new kind of poetry he is writing in exile as *publica carmina* (public poetry).[261] Ovid's exilic works are indeed 'public'. They respond to a public decree of relegation, a matter of public record; they carry out in public an argument with the emperor over literature, and they mount a defence of the poet's actions in the court of public opinion. Horace, comparably, addresses Augustus, and lectures him on the value of contemporary literature and the poet's value to society. Poetry's 'publicity' now extends beyond the bounds of the city to the provinces, which, not accidentally, will furnish Rome with future generations of poets.

---

[260] On the transition to early imperial culture, see Citroni (1992), 383–90; and on the early imperial figure of the poet, and Horace's prescience in that regard, Labate (1995), 156ff.

[261] *Tristia* 5.1.23—a debated line that has attracted the attention of textual critics: so, for instance, Hall (1995), in his Teubner edition, suggests *pudibunda* to provide an appropriate contrast to the (now chastened) *lusor amoris* of the previous line. For Evans (1983), 108, the phrase somehow distinguishes the particular content of Book 5 both from amatory elegy and from the previous four books of exile poetry.

4

Materialities of Use and Subordination

The challenge of the autonomist legacy

INTRODUCTION

The early Augustan rhetoric of autonomy was premised in large part on concepts of privacy and withdrawal. These claims, however, became falsifiable when several poets in the circle of Maecenas achieved remarkable celebrity and won signal marks of imperial favour. In the previous chapter, we examined Horace's late works and the emergence of literary strategies to confront precisely the problem of literary celebrity and overexposure. Could Horace sustain the image of retiring, self-limiting poet, after he became known in the city as the author of the *Carmen saeculare* and enjoyed the role of *vates* laureate? The claim of literary *secessus* no longer has the appearance of distinterestedness. Yet the notion of the poet cloistered in his grove, while evidently compromised, does not simply disappear, insofar as it has become attached to the very idea of the poet's vocation, glamorized by its association with the Augustan classics. Post-Augustan writers therefore must come to terms both with the continuing power and appeal of the autonomist model, and with the problematization of its central tenets. The buffering factors that gave the Augustan poets their unique space to manoeuvre—Maecenas' mediating role and Augustus' strategic tolerance of free speech—are notably lacking under the Julio-Claudians and Domitian, and it is debatable how robust a model of literary *libertas* revives under Nerva, Trajan, and Hadrian.[1] Indeed, one could argue that the *libertas*-paradigm was already breaking down in the later Augustan period.

The Augustan ideology of autonomy worked to keep poetry at least nominally and partially shielded from public ambitions and encomiastic interests, to preserve (the appearance of) poetic independence even as poetry assumed a newly public prominence in the city. That ideology becomes a problematic legacy when the fictions of privacy, exclusivity, and the boundedness of the poet's sphere are confronted with spectacular examples of poetic renown and imperial benefaction, and equally striking examples of the emperor's power to control and chastise literary freedom. There is no need to ascribe the problematization of the autonomist model to crueller emperors or the withering of literary culture. The

---

[1] This question informs the collection of papers published in the *American Journal of Ancient History* (15.1): *The Year 96: Did it make a difference?* (1996).

compromised status of poetic autonomy can already be discerned in the late works of Horace, where Maecenas plays a more marginal role, and in Ovid's exile poetry, which hardly conceals the emperor's power over the poet and his books.

In this chapter, I will explore the varied and often brilliant responses to the problematic legacy of Augustan autonomy in the self-representational poetry of Persius, Statius, Martial, and Juvenal. First, however, I will briefly consider two prose works that bring to the fore the question of the poet's role and identity in post-Augustan culture. In each case, the figure of the poet is generalized and genericized to certain degree, and represents a life-path or a social identity more than a specific individual. In Tacitus, a specific individual (Maternus) turns to poetry in specific circumstances, but the larger tendency of the dialogue is to compare poetry as a way of life with oratory. In Petronius, the poet is viewed from a scathingly satiric perspective, yet represents, again, a social type. It will be helpful to be aware of these broader perspectives on the poet's role in Roman society before considering specific self-representational strategies adopted by the poets themselves.

Tacitus is a keen student of poetry, and the Augustan classics are rarely far from his mind. In Tacitus' *Dialogus de oratoribus*, the speakers represent diverse views after the Ciceronian pattern. Aper does not speak wholly against poetry as a vocation, but ranks it below oratory in pleasure, prestige, and utility, deeming it worthy of being adopted only by those who lack forensic ability. Maternus passionately defends poetry both as a sublimely pleasing occupation in itself and as a preferable arena of ambition to the now reduced yet still dangerous field of public eloquence. A central preoccupation of Tacitus' dialogue-participants is the degree of fame accruing to different pursuits, and examples of poetic fame include not only the poets of classical Greece, but also distinguished Augustans: Pollio, Messalla, Ovid, Varius, and above all, Virgil (*Dial.* 12.5; 13.1–2). Yet Tacitus' speakers calculate the prestige garnered by poetic achievement and measure the social ambitions of poetry with a frankness and practicality the Augustan writers generally avoided. The Augustan poets in the first-person genres were skilled at maintaining a delicate balancing act. Avowing a life of tranquil self-sufficiency, they nonetheless invested considerable hopes for lasting renown in their retiring studies. They do not shrink from trumpeting their glory at times, but lay emphasis more on the posthumous endurance of their literary monument than on the glamorous figure they cut among contemporaries.

In Tacitus' dialogue, this carefully poised ambiguity hardens into a familiar profile. On the one hand, both Aper and Maternus allude to the well-known retreat of the poet away from the city's pleasures (or burdens) into the solitude of woods, groves, and streams.[2] While differing in their assessment of its desirability, both accept the poet's solitude as an essential aspect of his vocation. On the other hand, both also refer to the ambitious, reputation-building elements in poetic activity. According to Aper, the poet who wishes to make himself known is obliged to run about and canvass (*ambire*) the support of audience members for

---

[2] Note in particular: *in nemora et lucos, id est solitudinem, secedendum est* (9.6); *nemora vero et luci et secretum* (12.1); *me vero dulces, ut Virgilius ait, Musae, remotum a sollicitudinibus et curis et necessitate cotidie aliquid contra animum faciendi, in illa sacra illosque fontes ferant* (13.5).

an upcoming recitation; he must also get the loan of a house, fit out a recitation hall, rent chairs, and distribute programmes (9.3). He does not deny that one can get oneself included in the poetic canon (*nomen inserere...famae*, 10.3), but argues that the fame deriving from poetry is often short-lived, and generally empty and fruitless (*laudem inanem et infructuosam*, 9.1) in comparison with the orator's. Maternus counters Aper's arguments by frankly narrating the making of his own reputation: he started on the path of fame by 'breaking the power of Vatinius', profaner of the sanctity of letters under Nero (11.2),[3] but derives his current renown more from poetry than speeches (11.2–3). The striking combination of retreat from the city and prominence in the city in both Aper's and Maternus' characterization of poetry reveals how profoundly Augustan precedent has determined the pattern for early imperial literary culture. Tacitus inherits among other things the distinctive inward/outward orientation of the Augustan poet's life so aptly described by Maternus in the case of Virgil: *malo securum et quietum Virgilii secessum, in quo tamen neque apud divum Augustum gratia caruit neque apud populum Romanum notitia* ('I prefer the safe, tranquil withdrawal of Virgil, in which, however, neither the favour of the divine Augustus nor reputation among the Roman people was lacking', 13.1). Yet for Tacitus' men of letters, the poet's contemporary celebrity is no longer even notionally the innocent byproduct of poetic achievement. Now the profession of poetry is unapologetically viewed as a way of making one's way in society.

In the meantime, the possibilities for true *secessus* have been undermined in crucial respects. For Maternus, poetry *seems* to offer the possibility of autonomy, a space apart from forensic uproar, urban obligations, and the dangers of public eloquence. *Delatio* ('denunciation') provides a vivid instance of such dangers. The informers Crispus and Marcellus are prey to fear and inspire it in others; bound (*adligati*) by their all-encompassing drive to adulation, they oscillate between excessive *libertas* towards their victims and excessive servility towards the rulers (13.4). The world of the *delatores* ('informers'), where licentious freedom and servility co-exist in complementary extremity, lies at the opposite pole from Maternus' secluded grove. His memory will be honoured not by a motion in the senate or petition to the emperor, but by a simple graveside effigy of the poet garlanded and serenely smiling (13.6). But of course, as Aper keenly observes, Maternus' chosen path is not as tranquil, apolitical, and safe as he makes it out to be. The atmosphere of scandal surrounding the recitation of his *Cato* frames the dialogue. Maternus appeals to Virgil as his ideal, but we may also note the distance between Virgil and himself. Maternus' tranquillity seems to require special pleading and a determinedly serene smile amidst the risks he undergoes.[4] For the early imperial poet the compatibility of poetic freedom with the emperor's good will can hardly be taken for granted.

The poet's autonomy, as Maternus' eloquent speech attests, continues to be invoked as an inherited ideal, but the tensions, limits, and even failure of autonomy as viable cultural model mark poetic practice. There is no Maecenas to keep

---

[3] This passage is plagued by some difficulties of interpretation; see Mayer (2001), ad loc.; Stroux (1931).

[4] On the fate of Maternus, and the various possibilities for identifying him with an historical figure, see Bartsch (1994), 105.

poetry nominally separate from politics, sheltered within the realm of sophisticated exchange among *equites*. Post-Augustan writers thus take for granted the
public import of poetry, both as prestige-garnering occupation and as potential
vehicle of panegyric or dissent. One more figure will serve to demonstrate the
prescience of Horace's image of the poet as all-too-familiar social type, displaying
his distinctive ethos with a self-promoting audacity that renders ironic the
notionally retiring solitude on which that ethos is premised. As the fundamental
article of Mario Labate eloquently argues, the poet Eumolpus makes his appearance in Petronius' satiric novel bearing all the trappings of the poet's status as
'marginalized intellectual' (*l'intellettuale emarginato*)[5] situated at a principled
remove from the values of the community:

> 'Ego' inquit 'poeta sum et ut spero, non humillimi spiritus, si modo coronis aliquid
> credendum est, quas etiam ad imperitos deferre gratia solet. "Quaere ergo" inquis "tam
> male vestitus es?" Propter hoc ipsum. Amor ingenii neminem unquam divitem fecit.'
>
> (*Sat.* 83)
>
> 'I am a poet' he said, 'and one, I hope, of no mean ability, at least if one may lend any
> credence to victory garlands, which influence so often confers even on the incompe-
> tent. "Why", you ask "are you so badly dressed then?" For this very reason: devotion to
> intellect never made anyone rich'.[6]

Labate has commented in detail on how the extreme poverty of *cultus* displayed by
Eumolpus marks out his marginality, his rejection of communal standards. As the
narrative goes on, however, he turns out to be motivated by the same interests and
desires as everyone else. He too, despite his superficial claim to sterner ethical
standards, will be found in pursuit of ordinary things—the very triad of sex, food,
and money which drives virtually every character in the novel.[7] Petronius' depiction of Eumolpus plays around this essential pattern of hypocrisy. He affects to be
opposed to riches *qua* poet, and blames the decline of the arts on the corrupting
influence of wealth, but elsewhere displays a persistent interest in money. Eumolpus later takes up a dishonest scheme of *captatio* with an alacrity that
surprises the narrator, and in a significant reversal, doffs his impoverished guise
for another equally self-interested one: that of terminally ill millionaire deprived
of his only heir (116). The *pinacotheca* ('painting gallery') was an appropriate
backdrop for his 'impoverished poet' complete with artfully tattered rags. Now, as
the group approaches Croton where 'no literary pretensions are honoured' and
'eloquence has no standing', it is more expedient to adopt a different costume: 'I
wish we had more elaborate stage-properties, more civilized costumes, and a more
splendid set-up to give plausibility to the imposture'.[8]

Petronius' satiric outlook on Eumolpus' poverty is so corrosive that we may
come to suspect the authenticity of *any* claim to the poet's distinctive ethos. As
Mario Labate observes, the very figure who lays claim to the exclusive status of
the poet attests by his example to the dispersion and banality of poetic activity.
He recites everywhere, on any occasion, in a variety of modes, a figure familiar
enough to be despised by his fellow citizens, habitually driven from recitation by a
hail of stones:

---

[5] Labate (1995), drawing upon the work of La Penna (1990).
[6] Tr. Sullivan (1965).   [7] Conte (1996), 104–39.   [8] Tr. Sullivan (1965).

Petronius' poet is a figure who is capable of producing verses with fluidity and spontaneity, verses suited to every thematic occasion, verses of appreciable 'professional' craftsmanship. But the *Satyricon* also shows us a form of poetry which, while it has become 'pervasive', while it is capable of making room for itself in every moment and every place, has at the same time lost its own exclusive space, no longer lays claim to an autonomous role, but is, as it were, resigned to a condition of ubiquitous marginality—the ironic paradox of a period in which poetry was making a spectacular conquest of official status and was even rising as high as the emperor's throne.[9]

Labate's 'ubiquitous marginality' nicely captures the dilemma of early imperial poetry. Poetry has become well established in Rome, even taken for granted as a feature of the urban landscape. The cultural tendency that brings poetry more prominently into the public domain, disembedding it from the informal sociability of the aristocratic villa, re-embeds it within the fabric of everyday urban life. What I have called the autonomization of poetic activity—the process whereby poetry achieves its own sphere of prestige, its own distinctive trappings of identity, its own space and *honos*—leads to the dispersion and (in the eyes of some) banalization of poetry. Now everyone wants to appear marginal, to display the signs of heroic devotion to *ingenium*. Autonomy has been installed among the standard clichés of ambitious self-fashioning.

This compromising diffusion of autonomist literary rhetoric does not, however, obstruct the creation of richly and vividly realized poetic personae. As is now widely accepted, post-Augustan literary culture did not wither but continued to flourish in new and surprising ways. Early imperial poets work out the tense ambiguities of their own status by consciously inverting and dismantling autonomist concepts. The degraded 'client poets' Martial and Juvenal are thus the ironic inheritors of the Augustan self-representational tradition. In their version, the poet is poor, but not self-sufficient and autarkic; lazy and inclined to leisure, he nonetheless lacks continual enjoyment of a sheltered *otium*. Statius does not take up a satiric stance along these lines, but in his *Silvae* adopts a poetic role similar to Martial's in its lack of a permanent sheltered domain: he too has no major patron-protector on the scale of Maecenas, but must shift between the emperor and a multitude of lesser patrons;[10] and his poetry comparably affects to be ephemeral, rapidly composed, and radically occasion-oriented. Neither Statius nor Martial consistently inhabits an autarkic literary dwelling-place. More typically, they visit as admiring guests the marvellously sophisticated villas of their patrons. As I will argue, however, these conscious departures from the path of Augustan self-representation evidence the continuation of autonomist themes albeit in altered form.

---

[9] Labate (1995), 172: 'Il poeta petroniano è uno capace di produrre versi con fluidità e naturalezza, versi adatti a ogni occasione tematica, versi di apprezzabile fattura "professionistica". Ma il *Satyricon* ci mostra anche una poesia che, se è diventata "pervasiva", se è capace di presentarsi e farsi largo in ogni momento e in ogni luogo, ha perso al tempo stesso il proprio spazio exclusivo, non rivendica più un ruolo autonomo, ma è come rassegnata a una condizione di ubiqua marginalità: ironico paradosso di un'epoca in cui la poesia conquistava clamorosamente la ribalta dell'ufficialità e addirittura assurgeva al soglio dell'imperatore'.

[10] On Statius' need for patrons and the difference between his position and Horace's, Newlands (2002), 29ff.; on the status, and position vis-à-vis patrons, of Statius and Martial, see Myers (2000), 128ff.

In exploring the post-autonomist poetics of the early empire, I will focus on the relation between poetry and materiality/materialism.[11] A central feature of Roman poetic self-representation is the effort to distinguish poetic value from the value of ordinary objects, and the poet himself from other social roles. Horace, when he represents himself as 'cut off' from the populace in his poet's *nemus* ('grove') at the opening of his *Odes*, only renders explicit a broader impulse in poetic self-representation that is expressed in various ways and with varying degrees of intensity. The hieratic status of the *Musarum sacerdos* ('priest of the Muses') would seem to represent one extreme version of the poet's special status within society, but it is worth recalling that the very different self-representational style of the elegists incorporates a similar aspect of sequestration. The lover is a different kind of person, inassimilable to the quotidian concerns and interests of his fellow citizens.

Thus, one major premise of the Augustan poetics of autonomy is the very status of poetry as segregating and differentiating activity. In modern sociological terms, the status of poet (*poeta/vates*) confers social distinction.[12] The different social status of the poet is further expressed through his distance from ordinary motives, qualities, criteria of value. Specifically, the poet and his activity are not tarnished by materialist motives to the degree that his product transcends mere economic and utilitarian value. The poet espouses a life of *paupertas* ('simplicity') precisely in order to establish the unworldliness of his motives: poetry does not make a person rich; thus the life devoted to poetry must have some higher non-material aim. Poetry, moreover, affirms its trans-quotidian value by its authorizing references to the immaterialities of fame and Muses. Poetry, the argument implies, is not reducible to any single material instantiation of itself, but exists as immortal text above and beyond its individual copies; otherwise it would perish along with the materials of its transmission. Materiality and what we moderns term 'materialism' are thus tightly linked concepts. Poetry seeks to define forms of value that are independent of the value accruing to physical objects and monuments. The poem, moreover, is presented as autonomous of its own physical container. In a recurrent motif, it is only *bad* poetry that ends up being reduced to the expendable utility of a physical object.

Of course, to state that Augustan poetry eschews materialism/materiality *is* a generalization, however useful. This generalization is especially problematic for the later Augustan period, when Horace and Ovid manifest a newly intricate absorption in images of the book and the materiality of literary circulation. In Horace's case, this new materialist perspective combines with a frank, satiric vision of literary activity. But while the exemplary status of Ovid and the later Horace for the poetics of literary materiality in the early empire is incontestable, it is worth appreciating how much further the so-called client poets of the early empire go towards dissolving the barrier between poetry and materiality/materialism. Martial relentlessly represents literary activity in materialist terms and his own book as a commodity for sale. Juvenal's satiric perspective and persona hinge on the poetic speaker's essentially degraded, materialist view of human society. In

---

[11] Newlands (2002), *passim* (e.g. 130ff.), examines the provocative praise of luxury in Statius' *Silvae*.
[12] This is the topic of Zeiner (2005).

Satire 7, he unveils a money-driven view of the paucity of literary rewards expressed in vividly material terms. The querulous theme pervading Martial and Juvenal—that a devotion to the liberal arts does not make a person wealthy—implies the desire to benefit materially from literary activity, and thus neatly subverts the ideological emphasis of the Augustan rhetoric of *paupertas*. Martial's and Statius' urbane appreciation of luxuriously appointed villas and their owners' elegant uses of wealth contrasts markedly with the Horatian *rejection* of the status-conferring power of expensive materials (ivory, marble, gold, citron wood).

Horace's distinctive pose as *Musarum sacerdos* sequestered in his rural *nemus* proves impossible to repeat in a convincing way. It is striking to find the early imperial period dominated by writers of prose (Tacitus, Pliny Minor and Maior, Quintilian), poets who critique/subvert/problematize the poetic vocation (Persius, Lucan, Martial, Juvenal) and prosimetric satirists (Petronius' *Satyricon*, Seneca's *Apocolocyntosis*). Satire supplies the dominant tonality of the age, and satire traditionally inhabits the margins of the poetic grove. A small but telling indication of the compromised integrity of poetry's bounded domain can be discerned in the novel phenomenon of prose prefaces in books of poetry in informal genres (Martial *Epigrams*; Statius *Silvae*).[13] This prefatory technique introduces a prosaic element into what are notionally poetic collections, and contributes to deflating fictions of Muse-inspired *carmen* and a wholly poetic modality. It is not entirely surprising that the question of whether or not to write poetry informs Tacitus' *Dialogus*.

Flavian epic occupies a more traditional poetic terrain, though even here one might remark the extent to which the epic poets frame their poetic identity in very close association with the figure of Virgil. They inherit a poetic mantle rather than inventing a radically new one, and however much they subvert, rewrite, and innovate within the Virgilian tradition (as an avalanche of recent scholarship insists), they still work within the framework of Virgil's poetic project as his 'epic successors'.[14] This exercise in creative recycling might suggest, among other things, that richer possibilities existed for subverting and satirizing the poetic identity than for inventing a wholly new, august poet-figure in the post-Augustan age. Poetry, in the grand sense, became problematic for the Julio-Claudians and Flavians, as it already had for the late Horace,[15] and those who choose to write it without overt self-ironization work within the consecrated boundaries established by the now canonical *vates* of the Roman empire.

The poet, as we can already discern in Horace's *Ars poetica*, has become an object of satire. He is now too deeply implicated in the Roman economy of status to make the strong claims of autonomy that characterize the early Augustan period. Is the poet really secluded in a holy *nemus*, or simply marked off from others by the intensity of his manias and hypocrisies? With Horace's late works, we reach the limits of a model and the emergence of a new paradigm that culminates in the blatant contradictions of Eumolpus, who shamelessly cashes in on poetry's associations with austere *secessus*, while energetically pursuing all the material and corporeal pleasures of an ordinary life.

---

[13] On prose prefaces in Martial and Statius, see Johannsen (2006).
[14] Hardie (1993).　　　[15] Feeney (2002), 187.

PERSIUS' *SATIRES*: AUTONOMY AND ISOLATION

The Neronian satirist Persius occupies an interesting point in the trajectory from Horace to Eumolpus.[16] Under Augustus, as Andrew Wallace-Hadrill has shown, the public language of power in Rome was profoundly remodelled and, in the process, underwent a new degree of Hellenization.[17] In this context, it is important to note the role played by poetry in the ceremonies of the Roman state as manifested most notably by Horace's authorship of the *Carmen saeculare*. This trend towards the public patronage[18] of literary culture on the Hellenistic model reached its culmination (although hardly its end) in the reign of the last Julio-Claudian emperor. Nero provocatively surpassed traditional aristocratic dilettantism in the field of literature and enthusiastically assumed the roles of author, critic, reciter, and public performer.[19] We read in Suetonius that he declaimed in public and read his own poetry both at home and in the theatre; a thanksgiving was subsequently voted for this recital, and the recited portion inscribed in gold letters and dedicated to Jupiter Capitolinus (Suet. *Ner.* 10). New forms of literary patronage and new cultural institutions accompanied Nero's personal espousal of poetic activity: he established the Neronia, a quinquennial festival on the Greek model that included competitions in oratory and poetry (Suet. *Ner.* 12). Lucan is said to have premiered as a poet at this festival with his *Praises of Nero* (*Neronis laudibus*, Suet. *Vita Luc.*). In this context, it is not hard to imagine an intense fad for literary recitation and poetry among the Roman elite, just as, in a later period, Hadrian's beard would inspire his contemporaries to adopt a similarly 'philosophical' appearance.[20]

Nero's defining literary proclivities—Hellenophilia, performance-mania, poetastry, elaborate self-display—are precisely those that Persius makes a point of viciously excoriating in his first satire. This correspondence does not mean that Persius is necessarily engaging in a specific, clandestine attack on Nero, as one exegetical tradition would have it.[21] Even if Nero's taste for literary performance may have kindled his contemporaries' enthusiasm, his personal tendencies, as I began to suggest above, are themselves informed by the long, cumulative processes of the Hellenization of the Roman elite and the increasing cachet of literary status. The factors that vindicate for literature its own autonomous *honos* in Roman society simultaneously make it vulnerable to appropriation by the prestige-hungry. (Indeed, if we believe a quarter of the biographical tradition on Nero, he would have to be counted a 'prestige-glutton'). Persius' first satire pitilessly satirizes the prestige-hungry poetic reciter in grotesquely corporeal terms.

> scribimus inclusi, numeros ille, hic pede liber,
> grande aliquid, quod pulmo animae praelargus anhelet.
> scilicet haec populo pexusque togaque recenti

---

[16] See again the study of Labate (1995).   [17] Wallace-Hadrill (1990).

[18] Rawson (1985), 100–16, discusses the beginnings of the trend in the late republican period; note also the discussion of the restructuring of traditional disciplines and forms of knowledge under the principate in Wallace-Hadrill (1997).

[19] On the Neronian 'theatrical paradigm', see Bartsch (1994), 1–62.

[20] Zanker (1995), 198–266.

[21] For a recent spin on this idea, see, for example, Freudenburg (2001), 129–30.

> et natalicia tandem cum sardonyche albus
> sede leges celsa, liquido cum plasmate guttur
> mobile conlueris, patranti fractus ocello.
> tunc neque more probo videas nec voce serena
> ingentis trepidare Titos, cum carmina lumbum
> intrant et tremulo scalpuntur ubi intima versu.   (1.13–21)

We shut ourselves in and write—one in verse, the other in prose—some masterwork for a truly enormous lung-full of breath to pant forth. No doubt you will read out this work to the populace some day, hair combed, wearing a fresh toga, gleaming white, birthday sardonyx on the finger, in an elevated seat, first having rinsed your supple throat with a liquid trill,[22] effeminate with lascivious eye.[23] Then you'll see the great sons of Rome palpitate indecently, losing control of their voices, as the poetry penetrates their loins and their innards are scratched with the quivering verse.

The Horatian scenario of dubious, compromising recitation is pushed to a new extreme. While Horace satirized recitation in passing, Persius makes us watch an actual scene of recitation in graphic detail. The poet, on Persius' intentionally twisted reading, sexually pleasures his audience, an undistinguished crowd of 'Tituses'.[24] Already we know something is wrong when we read the words *haec populo* ('these . . . to the populace')—the verses composed in pretentious isolation are now brought forth to titillate the populace. The scene itself, moreover, is further banalized by its generic nature: the generalizing second-person verbs, and denigrating, generic plural *Titos*, suggest a tediously recurrent scenario is being played out *yet again*. One of the ironies is that this trite, repeated prostitution of poetry to the populace involves exactly the kind of hyper-refined, erudite Hellenistic verse that was originally associated with a sophisticated, exclusive audience, and that boasted recherché subject matter—that is, *not* for the populace, *not* banal and expected. Now everyone writes faux-erudite mythological tripe. It has become an all too familiar emblem of bourgeois status—the equivalent of a reproduction of a Monet painting in the living room. We are a long way from the quiet excitement of Catullus' *lepidum novum libellum* ('elegant new little book').

Persius' anatomy of recitation effects a systematic reduction of poetry to its corporeal and material dimensions. As we mentally scan the scene, we pass from the lung, mouth, and eye of the reciter to the loins and innards (*intima*) of the audience. We observe the reciter vividly installed on an elevated platform sporting a newly brushed toga and wearing a sardonyx birthday ring. The poet's mouth is prepared with a light gargle, described by Persius with an accumulation of slippery-sounding terms of liquidity and flow: *liquido cum plasmate guttur / mobile*

---

[22] *Liquidus* plays on two sense of the word, 'clear-sounding', but also 'liquid' with *conlueris*: Harvey (1981), ad loc.; Conington and Nettleship (1872), ad loc., give 'after gargling your supple throat by a liquid process of tuning'.

[23] *Patranti* is notoriously difficult, but seems to refer to sexual stimulation, or simply sex, if the scholiast is correct: if Persius were implying 'the stimulation of the audience towards orgasm' with his eyes (Harvey (1981), ad loc.), it would fit with the general idea of the passage; compare Lee and Barr (1987) 'with orgasmic eye'. Bramble (1974), 76–7, aptly notes the paradoxical combination: a 'broken' reprobate, worn out by pleasure, with a perversely active, sexually penetrating 'eye'.

[24] Cowherd (1986), ad loc.: 'Generically and ironically for all upper-class Romans'; compare Harvey (1981), ad loc., 'an ironically heroic designation'.

conlueris ('first having rinsed your supple throat with a liquid trill . . .').[25] The poet's words, in turn, resonate through the bodies of those who hear them: they tremble (*trepidare*), are penetrated sexually (*lumbum / intrant*), scratched (*scalpuntur*) in their inmost parts. The verbal juxtapositions *carmina lumbum* ('songs . . . groin') and *intima versu* ('inner guts . . . with verse') make Persius' point emphatically.

As in the case of Eumolpus, an austere, self-sequestering impulse is only the thinnest and briefest pretext for the pursuit of literary celebrity and recitative éclat. The writer begins by 'shutting himself in' (*inclusi*)[26] to produce his magnum opus (*grande aliquid*), but it is not long at all before this inwardness is converted into exteriority: what is inside the chest is 'puffed' out towards its audience.[27]

> tun, uetule, auriculis alienis colligis escas,
> articulis quibus et dicas cute perditus 'ohe'?
> 'quo didicisse, nisi hoc fermentum et quae semel intus
> innata est rupto iecore exierit caprificus?'
> en pallor seniumque! o mores, usque adeone
> scire tuum nihil est nisi te scire hoc sciat alter?   (1.22–7)

Satirist: Do you compose tidbits, old man, for others' ears, tidbits to which you, ruined in your joints and skin, would say 'whoa there, enough!'[28] *Interlocutor:* What's the point of having studied hard, unless this yeast, unless this wild fig-tree, once it has taken root within, come forth and break through the liver? Look, my pale and time-worn appearance! *Satirist:* Oh corrupt age! Is your knowledge so utterly null and void, unless someone else knows you have it?

Persius' imagery recurrently traces a path from inside (*intus / innata*) to outside (*exierit*).[29] The satirist's ostentatiously fictitious interlocutor worries that the writer's hard work, if not disseminated through recitation, will fail to find an outlet in the world. Specifically, he employs the metaphors of yeast (*fermentum*) and the fig-tree, which was celebrated for the capacity to force its way through stone (24–5). The poet's phrasing even suggests that the passage from interiority

---

[25] *Mobile* ('supple', 'moveable') is difficult, a 'bizarre collocation' (Harvey 1981, ad loc.), and so both Harvey and Nikitinski (2002), ad loc., take it as predicative; 'i.e. guttur collueris ut mobile sit' (Nikitinski, 60). Perhaps the grotesque mobility and suppleness of the throat, however, simply contribute to the scene's horrors of liquidity: nothing is able to remain rigid or integral.

[26] Harvey (1981), ad loc., aptly cites Hor. *Epist.* 2.1.117 (*scribimus indocti doctique poemata passim*). Persius picks up on Horace's theme of fashionable poetastry as a generalized social practice, but renders it more extreme both in the element of 'literary' sequestration and the subsequent desire for fame and approval.

[27] See Bramble (1974), 81, on the leitmotif of turgidity and swelling in this passage.

[28] Most scholars prefer the emendation *articulis* to the manuscript reading *auriculis*; there is still substantial uncertainty and dissent, however, and plausible arguments in favour of the manuscript reading have been made: Rudd's idea, for example, that the reciter's skin in destructively 'puffed up' by the admiring ears of his audience is attractive (Rudd 1970, 283f.); compare Bramble (1974), 80, citing Hor. *Sat.* 2.5.96. Note also Reckford (1962), 476–83 and now (2009), 190, n.52; Freudenburg (2001), 172; Harvey (1981), ad loc.; Lee and Barr (1987), ad loc.; Hooley (1997), 38; Dessen (1968), 35–6.

[29] Compare the tensional formulation at 5.19–29, where he claims to speak 'in private' to Cornutus, to be offering up his 'heart' (*praecordia*); he appropriates the epic figure of a 'hundred voices' to suggest how he will draw forth 'in pure speech' how much he has Cornutus fixed in the folds of his breast (*sinuoso in pectore fixi*), 'unsealing' what is hidden and inexpressible inside him. See Hooley (1997), 76–8.

to performance involves a certain destructive violence (*rupto iecore*) and rage (*fermentum*).[30]

The work goes out into the world via a burst liver (*rupto iecore*);[31] the skin of the reciter, worn out by repeated pleasures and indulgences, has been 'destroyed' (*cute perditus*); he is broken (*fractus*). The prototype of these images of stretching, bursting, and breaking may be Horace's frog that puffs itself up to the point of harming itself through misplaced social emulation (*Sat.* 2.3.314–20), or the flatterer who 'puffs up' the 'swelling bladder' of his *laudandus* with 'turgid' utterances, until, like Persius' reciter, he cries '*ohe iam!*' (*Sat.* 2.5.96–8). Penetration and impotence, hardness and flaccidity, energy and exhaustion, are confused and intertwined in Persius' corporeal metaphors so as to create a monstrous sense of miscegenation and destruction of boundaries.[32] Degrading images of the bodily grotesque[33] accompany the perversion of social mores. Poets and audience become unbeautiful and even deformed bodies, defined by their appetites rather than their aesthetic propensities. As Persius states in his Prologue, the stomach (*venter*, 11) is the source of poetry, not the Muses and other fictitious entities. Contemporary poets, like Hesiod's shepherds, are 'mere bellies', their desire to create poetry motivated by nothing more than bestial appetite. Similarly, in the passage cited above, the reciter's verses are edible 'tidbits' or 'bait' (*escas*). Persius appears to concede that publication may be appropriate for some truly worthy works, but the reciter's corporeal display and vanity put the cart before the horse. Prestige, not quality, is the aim. What is the use of Callimachean *ponos* if no one knows how hard you worked? The writer, with hypocrisy reminiscent of Petronius' Eumolpus, cultivates the serious appearance of a literary recluse only to make a display of it to others: *en pallor seniumque!* ('Look! My pale and aged appearance!').[34]

Broadly speaking, Persius' attention to materiality and the body are inherited features of the satiric tradition. Yet some aspects are new. For one thing, Persius

[30] Lewis and Short, s.v. *fermentum*, II.

[31] For Bramble (1974), 90–3, the burst liver implies 'the release of pent-up sexual impulses' (91), and the sexual double-entendre continues through *pallor* and the image of the *caprificus*. The associations of the *caprificus* are especially complex: in Pliny the Elder, the *caprificus* is sterile in itself, but enables the pollination of the cultivated fig (*HN* 15.211.79). Dessen (1968), 37, suggests an interpretation: the fig symbolizes 'poetry which, arising from a barren source (the homosexual poet), arouses the productive sexual urges of its audience'. In any case, the associations of the *caprificus*, as in the case of the reciter himself, include both sexual generation and impotence, penetration and infertility—a set of tensional associations that correspond nicely to Persius' paradoxical notion of contemporary's poetry's sterile efficacy, its combination of electrifying effect and exhaustion.

[32] See in particular Bramble (1974), 93: the reciter is 'an impotent *paedicator*, who nonetheless desires satisfaction'. On sexual metaphors and puns, see also Bramble (1974), 95, on, e.g. *auri-culis*; compare Freudenburg (2001), 172.

[33] See, e.g. Miller (1988). On corporeal and alimentary metaphors for literary style in Persius and others, see Dessen (1968), 23ff.

[34] I have given these lines to the interlocutor (see Harvey (1981), ad loc.), although many commentators assign them to Persius himself, speaking with characteristically brutal sarcasm: 'here is the reward for your pale and age-worn appearance!'. Of course, as Reckford (2009), 41, suggests, Persius is in dialogue with an aspect of himself, and for that reason, it is difficult to determine whether he is ironically showing his contempt for the pretentious toil in search of literary fame, or putting such pretensions (again with ironic effect) into the mouth of the foil/adversary. On the interlocutor (or absence of one), see also Hendrickson (1928), 102–7; Dessen (1968), 29–32.

pushes his vision of literary society to new extremes of degradation and materialist reduction. A good example is the scene described at the opening of Satire 3, in which a student wakes up, is berated by a comrade for lying late in bed with a hangover, and demands pen and papyrus for writing (3.1–14). The scene is based on Davus' excoriation of an indolent Horace at the opening of *Satires* 2.3, but Persius' attention to the clogged mechanics of writing, the runny ink, etc. intensifies both the materiality of writing and its connection with the writer's physical body: he snores, explodes with bile, suffers discomfort as narrow slits of light penetrate the blinds.[35] His Stoic interlocutor employs a tellingly corporeal turn of speech to castigate him: *ego te intus et in cute novi* ('I know you inside out—inside your skin', 30).

An important new element in Persius' representation of contemporary literature is the expansion of the space devoted to heteronomist literary practices. Much of Persius' literary self-definition in his first satire is negative; the literary practices he despises take and hold centre stage. Persius inhabits a heteronomist literary world in which his own voice—angry, harsh, erratic, marginal—cannot be expected to make much of an impact. The isolation of the satirist's voice is the first satire's dominant theme. Indeed, an emptiness—literally a 'void' (*inane*)— hovers over the opening lines.

> 'O curas hominum, o quantum est in rebus inane!'
> 'quis leget haec?' 'min tu istud ais? nemo hercule.' 'nemo?'
> 'vel duo vel nemo.' 'turpe et miserabile!' 'quaere?
> ne mihi Polydamas et Troiades Labeonem
> praetulerint? nugae. non, si quid turbida Roma
> elevet, accedas examenque improbum in illa
> castiges trutina, nec te quaesiveris extra' (1.1–7).

Satirist: O the idle cares of humanity! O what emptiness there is in things! *Interlocutor*: Who will read this? *Satirist*: What? This question is meant for me? No one, to be sure. *Interlocutor*: No one? *Satirist*: One or two—or no one. *Interlocutor*: Disgraceful, pathetic! *Satirist*: Why? Afraid that Polydamas and the Trojan ladies might prefer Labeo to me? Nonsense. If muddle-headed Rome makes light of anything, don't you come and correct the inaccurate tongue on that balance of theirs; do not look outside yourself.

The grand-sounding, Lucretian[36] tones of the opening line are interrupted by an immediate complaint. To the interlocutor, poetry such as this, deprived of any likely audience, is shameful and pathetic (*turpe et miserabile!*). Yet according to the satirist, true triviality (*nugae*) resides in the airs of seriousness people give themselves, as they wag sage heads about Culture and Wisdom. Persius cannot suppress a laugh, yet his braying laughter (*cachinno*, 12) is perhaps less truly childish than these 'uncles' who have put aside childish pursuits (*nucibus ... relictis*, 10).

---

[35] Bramble (1974), 1: 'the vocabulary of philosophical enlightenment ... is interwoven with more mundane detail concerning windows and chinks in the shutters'.

[36] The scholiast indicates a borrowing from Lucilius: see in particular Freudenburg (2001), 151–2, for possibilities. Others suspect that the scholiast has confused Lucilius with Lucretius, e.g. *DRN* 2.14: see Harvey (1981), ad loc., and Lee and Barr (1987), ad loc.

But what about the pretensions of his own opening line? The opening line suggests a conventional starting point for earnest satire in a quasi-declamatory vein. The poem emerges only as a footnote to this vapid opener—the extended footnote, comprising the rest of the satire, in which Persius and his interlocutor debate issues of poetic audience and fame.

Persian satire proper never gets written,[37] only the anxious commentary on the question of its futility. Yet after some 43 lines of back and forth, Persius deconstructs the rhetorical device of the interlocutor in a quick aside: *quisquis es, o modo quem ex adverso dicere feci* . . . ('whoever you are, whom I have just made to speak as an adversary . . .', 44). Now that Persius' original *duo vel nemo* ('two or no one') has been effectively reduced to *unus vel nemo* ('one or no one'), the isolation of satiric voice is maximized: so much for *sermo* ('chat, conversation') in the robust Horatian or Lucilian sense. We have been drawn into overhearing a non-dialogue, addressed to no one. Again, it is the first line that tells the story in advance: *o quantum est in rebus inane* ('O how much emptiness there is in things')!

It is not accidental that editors have struggled to assign lines definitively to either Persius or his interlocutor, and that the putatively conventional interlocutor's words are sometimes laced with a corrosive sarcasm reminiscent of the satirist himself. Persius' satiric dialogue constantly threatens to collapse into monologue. Horace could be scathing on the use of poetry as an extension of the technologies of aristocratic reputation and the preening ambitions of some of his contemporaries, yet Horace's Epicurean sympathies mean, among other things, that he values friendship.[38] Even Horatian autarky is not austere, but is premised on a delicate balancing act. The satiric Horace struggles, with a subtle mix of evasion, diplomacy, and outright avoidance, to maintain his detached tranquillity in the midst of the Roman *turba* (crowd) and his own conspicuous social connections. Can we imagine Persius politely humouring 'the boor' of Horace *Satires* 1.9 long enough for a substantial anecdote to emerge from the encounter? Horace is no admirer of mere solitude. While Horace had little time for those who employed literature as a means of crass self-inflation, he equally cast a mocking glance at extreme and pointless reclusivity. We might recall the Stoic philosopher reduced to comic degradation as children flock around and torment him (*Sat.* 1.3.133–6), or the long-term literary recluse who emerges pale and shrunken after years of study, a mute statue, ridiculed by his fellow citizens (*Epist.* 2.2.81–4).

Horace, at the end of *Satires* 1, gathers round him an entourage of literary friends, whose eminence and *dignitas* will ennoble and protect his own satiric project (*Sat.* 1.10.81–90). Persius' friendships are considerably sparser—the best example being his Stoic teacher Cornutus. It is telling that Cornutus, as the poet's freedman guardian, takes the place simultaneously of Horace's 'freedman father' and of his patron, Maecenas. Compared with Horace's relation to Maecenas, Persius' friendship with Cornutus reverses the status-distinction: the freedman Cornutus acts as friend and guardian to the wealthy, well-born poet. The debt of gratitude he owes to Cornutus is philosophical and didactic, not material.

---

[37] Bramble (1974), 67: 'Persius begins with a false start'.
[38] See in particular Kilpatrick (1986).

Cornutus taught him how to live, and kept him clear of self-destructive behaviour (5.30–51). From this perspective, Persius' personal autonomy is arguably more radical than Horace's, his segregation from the world more emphatic, his poetry even less crowd-pleasing, and his social position more independent. At the same time, Persius' model of autonomy is consciously self-undermining. The absolute corruption of literary values Persius describes threatens to engulf him, while his isolation and ferocity come to seem a desperate remedy, a last-ditch defence against the overpowering force of corruption in contemporary culture.

The dinner affords another example. Recitation of poetry at a dinner party was a common practice among the Roman elite, and a poet of modest status such as Horace might have been expected to entertain the company at his patron's dinner with a recitation of his poems. Horace's *Satires*, however, largely avoid representing him as a *scurra* or client at Maecenas' table, and the one dinner described at length—besides the wistful evocation of the simple dinners at his own Sabine farm—is the dinner of Nasidienus in Satire 2.8, which Horace emphatically did *not* attend.[39] Horace's avoidance of the compromising dinner-scenario, however, is discrete, and does not extend to unsociable anger or disdain. Persius is predictably less restrained.

> ecce inter pocula quaerunt
> Romulidae saturi quid dia poemata narrent.
> hic aliquis, cui circum umeros hyacinthina laena est,
> rancidulum quiddam balba de nare locutus
> Phyllidas, Hypsipylas, uatum et plorabile siquid,
> eliquat ac tenero subplantat uerba palato.
> adsensere uiri: nunc non cinis ille poetae
> felix? non leuior cippus nunc inprimit ossa?
> laudant conuiuae: nunc non e manibus illis,
> nunc non e tumulo fortunataque fauilla
> nascentur uiolae?   (Pers. 1.30–9)

Behold, the descendants of Romulus, after they've dined, inquire amid their cups what divine poesy[40] has to say. And here's one with hyacinthine cloak around his shoulders who mutters something rancid from his sniveling nose, burbles forth 'Phyllises', 'Hypsipyles'—any tear-jerking poetic theme you like—and trips out words on ladylike palate. The worthies have bestowed applause! Now the poet's ash is happy, is it not? Does not the stone now press more gently on his bones? The [humbler] guests applaud in turn: now, from his shade, now from his tomb and fortunate ash, shall not violets spring?

Again the satirist savagely anatomizes poetic performance, as the pitiably bad verses emerge from the nose (*de nare*) and palate (*palato*) of the poet in his 'hyacinthine' mantle. The description, moreover, incorporates unpalatable hints of food—the mildly 'rancid' fare offered by the effete poet, 'sieved out' in unappetizing dribbles. In the light of such eminently ephemeral literary fare, the sarcasm

---

[39] Oliensis (1998), 60.
[40] *Dia* is an archaism, contributing to the sarcastically faux-heroic tone: Harvey (1981), ad loc.

of Persius' subsequent evocation of conventional motifs of poetic immortality is all the more cruel. Horatian irony was less extreme, and significantly, it is Persius' interlocutor who voices Horatian sentiments regarding the desirability of literary fame: *at pulchrum est digito monstrari* ... ('but it is a fine thing to be pointed out by others' fingers', 28).[41] Horace hardly disdains fame; he disdains vulgar forms of self-promotion. He is in no position to reject outright his patron or patronage as an institution. Persius, by contrast, sneers at the literary delusions of the patron class designated in generic terms: *proceres* ('lords', 52), *patricius sanguis* ('patrician blood', 61). Persius' Roman aristocrats bribe and coerce their dependants into flattering their own pretensions (*verum ... amo, verum mihi dicite de me*, 'I love the truth, tell me the truth about me', 55). The dependants, in turn, mock them behind their backs (1.55–62). There is no common ground.

There is a connection between Persius' interest in the autonomy of radical isolation and his diagnosis of the ills of contemporary literary taste.[42] There is a further connection between these two items and the difficulty of his language. Finally, all these phenomena are bound up with Persius' circumspect attitude towards poetry itself. Poetry, Persius' insists, has become a hopelessly corrupt medium. Satire lies at the boundaries of poetry, and thus offers at least a partial refuge for those who see poetry's integrity as compromised and the role of Poet as potentially compromising. Persius insists in his prologue on his merely partial membership in the *pagus* of the bards (*semipaganus*, 6).[43]

In Catullus' day, the Alexandrian style was new and esoteric; it represented a kind of poetry that was not appreciated by the mob, and so was notionally resistant to appropriation for banalizing, quotidian uses, for example the crass display of Culture. The cretins of Persius' day have absorbed aesthetic esotericism itself into their daily routines and entertainments: *his mane edictum, post prandia Callirhoen do* ('for these I recommend the play-bill in the morning, Callirhoe after lunch', 134). This advance in the cultural absorption of poetry leaves very little space—the merest margin—for the autonomist poet to occupy. Hence derives the infamous difficulty of Persius, his departure from customary patterns of expression. Given the now pervasive dispersion of a popularized idiom of literary sophistication at Rome, the poet who craves integrity and independence may be driven to develop a designedly acerbic, rebarbative, and even opaque poetic style: *aliquid decoctius* ('something more concentrated', literally 'boiled down', 1.125).[44]

---

[41] *Carm.* 4.3.22: *quod monstror digito praetereuntium* ...

[42] On the sense of isolation and 'rejection of society' in Persius, see Anderson (1982), 169–93 (originally published 1966).

[43] So Conington in Conington and Nettleship (1872), ad loc.; Lee and Barr (1987), ad loc.; Harvey (1981), ad loc. Another line of interpretation, beginning with the scholiast, glosses *semipaganus* as 'half a rustic': e.g. Nikitinski (2002), ad loc. Yet for Persius to use *semipaganus* simply as a synonym for *subrusticus* at this crucial moment of literary self-definition seems feeble and pointless—a mild quip rather than a clever reformulation of satire's tensional relation with the traditions of ancient poetry. Hooley (1997), 234ff., and Freudenburg (2001), 147ff., prefer to emphasize the indeterminacy of the word's meaning.

[44] See discussion of Gowers (1993b), 180: Persian satiric language is 'a tightly knotted, unparaphraseable riddle, which we must work to decipher', and, as Gowers points out, Persius follows the recipe books by 'reducing' or 'boiling down' his satiric output to one third of Horace's *oeuvre* of eighteen satires.

Poetry has been so profoundly compromised as an integral pursuit that it is unclear how an autonomous domain can be sustained—except perhaps by the most rigorous form of secession imaginable, which Persius arguably achieves by his isolationist self-representation, philosophical severity, and esoteric use of language.

Persius' first satire thus affords a good example of the challenges facing practitioners of autonomist literary rhetoric in the early imperial period. As argued above, the new celebrity and social prominence of poetry undermine any easy notion of the poet's reclusive domain. At the same time, the conditions of imperial culture place obvious limits on the exercise of poetic aggression on the Lucilian model of satiric *libertas*.[45] At the end of Satire 1, Persius anticipates the infuriated impotence of the early Juvenalian persona. He cannot attack named contemporaries in his verse in the way Lucilius did, nor even, he claims, play on his audience's conscience with sly ironic wit in the manner of Horace.

> 'sed quid opus teneras mordaci radere uero
> auriculas? uide sis ne maiorum tibi forte
> limina frigescant: sonat hic de nare canina
> littera.' per me equidem sint omnia protinus alba;
> nil moror. euge omnes, omnes bene, mirae eritis res.
> hoc iuuat? 'hic' inquis 'ueto quisquam faxit oletum.'
> pinge duos anguis: 'pueri, sacer est locus, extra
> meiite.' discedo. secuit Lucilius urbem,
> te Lupe, te Muci, et genuinum fregit in illis.
> omne uafer uitium ridenti Flaccus amico
> tangit et admissus circum praecordia ludit,
> callidus excusso populum suspendere naso.
> me muttire nefas? nec clam? nec cum scrobe? nusquam?
> hic tamen infodiam. uidi, uidi ipse, libelle:
> auriculas asini quis non habet?   (1.107–121)

Interlocutor: But what need is there to scrape tender ears with the biting rasp of truth? Do take care that the thresholds of your betters don't freeze you out some day. Methinks I hear the snarling letter of the dog... *Satirist*: Well then, as far I am concerned let everything be whitewashed from this moment forward. I won't get in the way. Bravo! All of you, each one of you, will be utter marvels. Is that better? 'In this place', you are saying, 'I formally forbid anyone to crap'. Draw two snakes: this is holy ground, boys—go piss elsewhere! I'm off. Lucilius savaged the city—*you*, Lupus, and *you*, Mucius—and broke his molar on them. The sly Horace touches on his friend's every vice while making him laugh, and, once admitted, plays on his friend's innermost thoughts. He is deft at turning up his nose and then catching the populace on it. Is it a crime for *me* to mutter a word? Not even secretly, whispering to a ditch? Nowhere? Here, in any case, I will dig a hole and bury it. I have seen it, seen it with my own eyes, my dear book: *Who is there that does not have an ass's ears?*

[45] Perhaps too much has been made of the possibility that Nero's monstrously tyrannical ways 'determined' Persius' inward philosophical turn: Freudenburg (2001), 125ff. On the other hand, I am not quite convinced that Persius and his fellow Neronian writers simply 'construct' (127) the contemporary cultural milieu as oppressive and threatening. Freudenburg is nevertheless surely correct in arguing that Persius plays up the suppression and isolation of his own satiric voice (130).

The interlocutor again offers sensible advice and warning: don't attack the wealthy and powerful; you may regret it. Persius offers a magnificently sarcastic reply, and then, recurring to the secret he refused to tell at the opening of the satire (1.8), takes on the role of Midas' barber, forbidden to tell the world the secret of the Roman people's collective ass's ears. Like Midas' barber, Persius will bury the secret. Yet just as Midas' secret was subsequently spread abroad by the rustling words of the reeds that grew from the spot of ground where the secret had been buried, so Persius' secret has been buried in the dubious hiding place of a published book: *vidi, vidi ipse, libelle* ('I have seen it, seen it with my own eyes, my dear book'). Persius literalizes and concretizes the implied model of text and circulation in Ovid's version of the story in his *Metamorphoses* (11.85–193), while adding his distinctive motif of a phantom or non-existent readership. If, as he implied at the outset, no one will read his poetry, then indeed he has effectively 'buried' the secret. If, on the other hand, as the satirist has hinted, he is not wholly averse to the publication of worthy writing, then the apparently obscure hiding-place of his book will end up whispering the secret abroad. The satire's broader concerns with fame, audience, isolation, and suppression/release of speech find their culmination in this closing image of the 'hole' that publishes Persius' satiric insight against his putative wishes.

Still, this generalized comment—'who in Rome does not have ass's ears?'—which Persius claims is more valuable to him than the *Iliad*, may seem anticlimactically bland. No one is singled out, hence no one can be harmed. Persius is not capable of Lucilian freedom of expression, nor can he remain content with offering a poetic product purely decorative. This puts him in the awkward position of dramatizing the evolution of his satiric stance, from suppression to release. This arc of satiric liberation is not, however, filled out with any concrete or dangerous content. The Midas-allusion at the end has Persius resorting to the very Greek mythology which he has criticized mercilessly as a cheap replacement for grainier, Roman subject matter. What remains for Persius to produce is philosophically informed moral self-castigation in the style of Horace's *Satires* or *Epistles*. The savagery of satire has been redirected in various ways: diffused outward, towards social convention in general, and turned inward, towards the flaws in our own thoughts, desires, and motives. As in Horatian satire, the poet is still presumed a dangerous figure—but to whom?

STATIUS: PANEGYRIC, HETERONOMY, AND THE FIRST-PERSON TRADITION

Persius, in a rare example of self-representational poetry from the Julio-Claudian period, presents a case of almost total secession from the public realm. For Persius, the writer's autonomy is possible, and not too dangerous, in part because it is an autonomy premised on the removal of the writer to the margins of society, and on the development of a nearly opaque style of poetic speech comprehensible only to a very few. It is hard to imagine a Neronian Horace publicly lecturing the emperor in an 'Epistle to Nero'. While Persius' extremity has the advantage of distinguishing him from his mellifluous contemporaries, in other ways his approach represents a dead end: he pushes the isolationist strand in the first-person tradition to its furthest plausible extreme. In the next major period of literary activity under the Flavian emperors, a different set of self-representational tendencies emerges. Unlike the self-sequestering Persius, Martial and Statius court a broad popular audience, embrace scenes of public festivity, advertise the emperor's social legislation, and insert their poetry into occasions of imperial pageantry and display. The addressees of Martial's *Epigrams* and Statius' *Silvae* are the important, approved men of the age: magistrates, imperial freedmen, provincial commanders.

There is a connection between the new modes of poetry and the social climate of Flavian Rome. The Flavian emperors, in the wake of the fire of AD 64 and the civil discord of 69, set considerable importance on rebuilding the city, stabilizing the social order, and promoting communal values. Vespasian and his sons made great show of trimming back Neronian excesses, renewing the Augustan pattern of public benefaction and private austerity, and refocusing military energy on external foes. In the literary domain, this ideologically freighted project of societal reconstruction brought back into fashion the Augustan concept of the public-mindedness and moral responsibility of the *vates*, but with a new emphasis on the panegyric of patrons, imperial and otherwise. The new poetry is socially deferent, ideologically correct, and pliant to the demands of diverse social occasions.[46]

Statius, in his *Silvae*, capitalizes on precisely the cultural tendencies that appall and exasperate Persius. Persius carves out an isolationist space of counter-poetic, satiric difficulty—everything that the smooth, polished, euphonious aesthetic currently popular is *not*. Statius, by contrast, aligns his position as poet with his patrons' literary and cultural ideals. Statius' poetry is studded with learned mythological exempla, and he frequently prefaces his performance with invocation of the Muses, the geography of Helicon, and other forms of poetological erudition. Immersed in the Greek tradition of writing poetry for performance at festival competitions,[47] Statius does not distance himself from the conventional markers of Poetry. His *Silvae* display much of the self-assured fluidity Persius despises, and he does not scruple to use poetry as a means of generating prestige among well-heeled Romans.[48]

Statius is in no position to insist, as Persius does, on a distinction between the serious writer and the wealthy dilettante routinely flattered (and secretly mocked) by clients. Statius speaks with particular authority as a publicly established poet, shown favour by the emperor, and as author of the *Thebaid*, yet he does not mark himself out as singular in his literary pursuits. He lives a life of 'learned leisure' (*docta . . . otia*, 1.3.108–9) and poetry, but then so do many of his patrons. They too seek glory in the aesthetic realm, and elicit Statius' poetic advertisement of their literary 'deeds'. They write poetry and exhibit connoisseurship of art objects;

---

[46] As I hope to show, social deference is not the whole story, but it does represent a central aspect of Flavian poetry: on Martial, Statius, and patronage, see in particular White (1974) and (1975).

[47] See Hardie (1983), 15–30.   [48] Zeiner (2005), *passim*.

their pet architectural projects embody their qualities of refinement. Statius is the socially inferior colleague of many of these figures, not the possessor of a categorically different type of prestige.

None of this means, however, that the Flavian poets simply cease to care about poetic autonomy. Autonomist self-representation remains a significant concern not least because emperors and other patrons still desire credible praise from authoritative writers. This continuing demand for dignified praise from poets of demonstrated integrity, however, placed writers in a nearly impossible bind: they needed to project a sense of their own integrity and dignity without overemphasizing their autonomy in ways that might come into conflict with the emperor's increasingly authoritarian role. In the Flavian period, the maintenance of the poet's autonomy belongs to a more slender margin of the poet's work, but it does not cease to exist for all that.[49]

The poet is not a proud, recalcitrant, and isolated a figure in Statius; to find signs of independence sometimes requires a subtle reading of inexplicit juxtapositions and unspoken declarations. The poet pays court to his grand addressees, assuming a markedly deferent role, and thus signs of independence must be sought in literary allusions and understated autonomist elements embedded within more conspicuous discourses of praise and poetic humility. In order to carry out this difficult balancing act, poets of the period needed to invent a new public identity. The Flavian poet—often termed 'client poet' in modern scholarship—is careful to present himself as overtly deferent towards superiors, but in other moments, parades his *libertas* and *licentia*. The client poet, depending on context, occasion, and addressee, can be flattering, sardonic, sly, evasive, aloof, and satirically scathing. Flexibility becomes his ultimate asset.

The invention of the client-poet persona signals a new set of impulses in Roman poetry; it is a not a straightforward question of choosing heteronomy over autonomy. In crafting a poetics of supple sociability, ephemerality, impromptu ease of composition, and materialism, the Flavians subvert, but also display their continuing awareness of, the rhetoric of poetic autonomy as established by the Augustans. Modern scholarship has largely missed the point. Previous scholars condemned the servility and cynicism of the Flavian court poets, as if the poets themselves were not aware of the autonomist ideals from which they were straying, and had simply been overpowered by the temptations of aesthetic depravity. More recent revisionist scholarship prefers to pretend that nothing has changed, that the Flavians manifest just as much ideological independence and poetic originality as the Augustans if we scrutinize them closely and cleverly enough.[50] The truth is probably less tidy and encouraging, but more interesting: the Flavians continued to be constrained by the prestige of the autonomist model that had become encoded in the Roman literary tradition at its canonical moment, even though they were no longer in a position to adhere to the strong version of

---

[49] Newlands (2002) in particular sees elements of autonomy and dissent embedded within the panegyrical texture of the *Silvae;* for a different perspective, see D. C. Feeney's review in *TLS* (15 November 2002).

[50] For example, it is now difficult to find any scholars who read Statius' famous declaration of adherence to his Virgilian model at the close of the *Thebaid* as the statement of deference it might appear to be in the eyes of unsophisticated readers.

this model. The solutions they devised to this dilemma were in many cases brilliant and compelling.

The Augustan poets, of course, no less eagerly pressed poetry into encomiastic service under cover of their protestations of independence. We may assume that Horace, Propertius, and Virgil did not win the patronage of Maecenas and Augustus, nor Tibullus that of Messalla Corvinus, by remaining continually in autarkic, rural seclusion. The issue, however, is not whether the poets occupied an intrinsically autonomous position, but whether the rhetorical construction of such a position was plausible. Statius and Martial begin from the point at which the Augustan rhetoric of autonomy, in its strong version, is recognized to be irrecuperable. No poet now can simply claim to occupy a secluded grove, or refuse the demand for panegyric on grounds of high literary principle. The ambitions inherent in the poetic calling, the potential benefits and dangers of writing poetry in the early empire, are now far too apparent to sustain any unproblematic conception of the poet's secluded realm.

The challenges posed by this situation are evident, but they are more than adequately met by Statius' considerable capacity for self-representational finesse. Statius, like Martial, is a master of double-edged self-denigration, and opens his first collection of *Silvae* with a portrait of the poetic artist composing impromptu poems of mediocre quality at high speed in response to demands from his patrons on specific occasions (*subito calore...festinandi voluptas*; 'in the heat of the moment...the pleasure of haste', Book 1 *praef.*). He characterizes his *Silvae* as sub-serious diversion along the lines of the *Culex* and *Batrachomyomachia*, then goes on to produce credible witnesses to the rapidity of composition of each poem in his first collection.

> nullum enim ex illis biduo longius tractum, quaedam et in singulis diebus effusa. quam timeo ne verum istuc versus quoque ipse de se probent!
>
> primus libellus sacrosanctum habet testem, sumendum enim erat 'a Iove principium'. centum hos versus, quos in ecum maximum feci, indulgentissimo imperatori postero die quam dedicaverat opus tradere ausus sum. 'potuisti illud' dicet aliquis 'et ante vidisse'. respondebis illi tu, Stella carissime, qui epithalamium tuum quod mihi iniunxeras scis biduo scriptum (audacter mehercules, sed ter centum tamen hexametros habet). at fortasse tu pro collega mentieris. Manilius certe Vopiscus, vir eruditissimus et qui praecipue vindicat a situ litteras iam paene fugientes, solet ultro quoque nomine meo gloriari villam Tiburtinam suam descriptam a nobis uno die.
>
> (*Silv.* 1, praef.)

None of these took longer than two days to compose, and some were dashed off in a single day. How I fear lest the verses testify on their own behalf to the truth of it!

The first book has a sacrosanct witness; for I had to 'make a beginning from Jove'. These hundred verses, which I wrote on the Greatest Horse, I dared to offer to the most indulgent emperor on the day after he had dedicated the work. Someone will say, 'You could have seen it beforehand'. To him you will have a response, dearest Stella; for you know that the epithalamium you had enjoined on me was written in two days—a bold statement indeed, but it has three hundred hexameters all the same, and perhaps you will lie for a colleague. Manilius Vopiscus, to be sure, a highly erudite man who plays the starring role in saving from neglect our now almost extinct literature, is accustomed to boast on my behalf, without being prompted, that I composed the description of his villa at Tivoli in a single day.

Statius' protestations are not utterly insincere. Occasional verse had its own decorum, and Statius was trained in a discipline of competitive poetic display that valued compositional facility.[51] Nevertheless elements in Statius' self-denigration must be conventional and strategic, as when he suggests that the low quality of his poetry is itself proof of rapid composition, and that his verses' only recommendation is their celerity.[52] If nothing else, Statius' formidable mastery of the hexameter line tells against the claims he makes in his prose preface.

Statius is surely aware that the Roman poetic tradition sharply differentiates high-quality poetry from ephemeral performance-piece, and identifies literary value with painstaking composition. An enduring work of poetry is crafted for eternity, not rapidly dashed off to serve the purposes of a fleeting occasion. Statius, however, exalts occasion-driven utility with full awareness of the implications of doing so.[53] He introduces his occasional verse-form and panegyrical focus, while directing a knowing wink at his learned readers. In the end, insistence on rapidity of composition becomes an elegant, mildly facetious performance in its own right, one that Statius manages with a masterful deadpan countenance. The overt programme is heteronomist in emphasis—occasional, utility-driven, patron-oriented—but the poet's stage-managing of his poetry's *entrée* into the world is all about his ability to control the terms of his reception, to display his subversion of the rules of a tradition in which he is so clearly immersed.

THE POET'S PRESTIGE

Statius accommodates poetic self-representation to the demands of his encomiastic mode, while keeping the autonomist model of his predecessors in view. Statius aims to confer on his patrons special attributes of character that mark them out as extraordinary. There is nothing unusual about such a strategy, of course. Since Pindar, poets have endeavoured to supply patrons with unmatchable publicity and imbue their achievements with the aura of heroic glory. Notable in Statius, however, is the fact that he shares his own arena of *literary* glory with the patrons he is praising. Statius thereby contravenes an informal tendency among Roman poets to apportion public prominence and praiseworthy deeds to the patron, while ascribing literary renown, reclusivity, and idleness to the poet himself. In the preface to Book 1, Statius praises Arruntius Stella in the opening sentence for his distinction in their shared domain of literary studies (*in studiis nostris eminentissime*), and later in the same passage, the erudite Manilius Vopiscus for 'rescuing our now almost vanishing literature from neglect'.[54] Statius, rather

---

[51] See the discussion of improvisation and occasion in Hardie (1983), 76–85; note also Bright (1980), 29–31; Newmeyer (1979), 5–6.

[52] So Newlands (2002), 33: 'He adopts here a rhetoric of self-depreciation … We should know better than to take such declaimers at face value'.

[53] As Newlands (2002), 33, observes, prefatory self-depreciation is a tradition going back at least as far as Catullus. I would still maintain, however, that the extent and nature of Statian self-denigration are in some respects new: Catullus, for example, was not writing panegyric, overtly valued painstaking composition, and ironically subverted the occasion-driven aspect of his poetry as much as he advertised it.

[54] Tr. Shackleton Bailey (2003).

than defining himself as a poet amidst men of power and casting a spotlight on himself, positions himself within a broader social network of men who take an interest in literary *studia* ('studies, pursuits') across their various sub-categories. In this regard, he anticipates and exerts an underappreciated influence on the letters of Pliny the Younger, for whom *studia*, far from being the specialized interest of only a few, form an essential and even furiously advertised component of the life of the senatorial elite.[55]

The patron in some cases even inspires or guides the poet's activities. In the preface to *Silvae* 3, Statius addresses one of his major patrons, Pollius Felix.

> Tibi certe, Polli dulcissime et hac cui tam fideliter inhaeres quiete dignissime, non habeo diu probandam libellorum istorum temeritatem, cum scias multos ex illis in sinu tuo subito natos et hanc audaciam stili nostri frequenter expaveris, quotiens in illius facundiae tuae penetrale seductus altius litteras intro et in omnes a te studiorum sinus ducor. (*Silv.* 3, praef.)

> To you in any case, dearest Pollius, most worthy of this life of tranquillity to which you so faithfully adhere, I do not have to spend a long time defending the audacity of these little works, since you know that many of them came into being suddenly on our lap, and you have often been taken aback by this boldness of my stylus, whenever you draw me aside into the inner sanctum of your eloquence, and I enter on a deeper study of literature, guided by you into all the recesses of erudition.

After praising Pollius' life of tranquillity (*quies*), Statius goes on to describe him as an exemplary instructor of literary studies: he guides and enlightens Statius, leading him into every recess and intimate corner of literature (*in illius facundiae tuae penetrale seductus . . . in omnes a te studiorum sinus ducor*). At the preface's close, Statius proclaims that, in settling on Naples as his place of retirement, he is retiring not so much to his land of origin as to Pollius himself (*non tam in patriam quam ad te secedere*). *Secessus* (retirement/withdrawal) conventionally denotes the poet's retreat into his own space of independence and tranquillity, away from the demands of the city, and in particular, cliental obligations. Statius, however, withdraws to his patron Pollius. The patron, far from being excluded from the poet's autarkic retreat, actually bestows access to the hidden, reclusive domains of literature (*penetrale . . . sinus*).

Comparably, in *Silvae* 1.4, Statius calls on Rutilius Gallicus, who was City Prefect during Domitian's Dacian campaign, to come in person (*ipse veni*, 1.4. 22) and to provide inspiration in place of Apollo, the Muses, Mercury, and Bacchus.

> ast ego nec Phoebum, quamquam mihi surda sine illo
> plectra, nec Aeonias decima cum Pallade divas
> aut mitem Tegeae Dircesve hortabor alumnum:
> ipse veni viresque novas animumque ministra
> qui caneris; docto nec enim sine numine tantus
> Ausoniae decora ampla togae centumque dedisti
> iudicium mentemque viris. licet enthea vatis
> excludat Piplea sitim nec conscia detur

---

[55] See the discussion of Woolf (2003), 215–18.

> Pirene, largos potius mihi gurges in haustus
> qui rapitur de fonte tuo, seu plana solutis
> cum struis orsa modis seu cum tibi dulcis in artem
> frangitur et nostras curat facundia leges.
> quare age, si Cereri sua dona merumque Lyaeo
> reddimus, et dives praedae tamen accipit omni
> exuvias Diana tholo captivaque tela
> Bellipotens, nec tu (quando tibi, Gallice, maius
> eloquium fandique opibus sublimis abundas)
> sperne coli tenuiore lyra. vaga cingitur astris
> luna et in oceanum rivi cecidere minores.   (1.4.19–37)

But I shall not call upon Phoebus, although without him my lyre is voiceless, nor shall I call upon the nine Aeonian goddesses, with Pallas as the tenth, nor the gentle nursling of Tegea or of Dirce; come in person, and you who are the subject of my song, supply fresh strength and spirit; for not without erudite inspiration did you obtain plentiful honours of the Ausonian toga and give the benefit of your judgement and intelligence to the Hundred Men. Though inspired Pimplea exclude the thirsty poet and Pirene's complicity be refused, the flood drawn from the spring of your inspiration is better for my deep drinking, whether you compose works of plain prose unbound by metre, or your sweet eloquence is broken to conform with rules of art and respects our laws. Lead on, then! For if we give back to Ceres her own gifts, and to Lyaeus, wine; and if Diana, who is rich in the spoils of the hunt, nonetheless receives spoils in every domed shrine; and if the Warlord receives captured weapons—so you, Gallicus, mustn't scorn the honour of a more exiguous lyre because your eloquence is grander and you magnificently abound in wealth of speaking. The wandering moon is encircled by stars and lesser streams flow to the Ocean.

The man of action, who is the object of Statius' encomium, is so fecund a writer himself that a drink of water from the fountain of his inspiring talent will suffice for Statius in the absence of his usual sources of inspiration.[56] The poet not only shares his arena of glory with the City Prefect Gallicus; he is dependent on him for his very capacity to write. Statius goes on to compare Gallicus with Ceres, Diana, and Mars. Just as these divinities receive gifts deriving from their own domains, so the divinely talented Gallicus may receive the homage of Statian verse.

Even in subordinating himself to Gallicus, however, Statius identifies his own poetry with approved images in the Callimachean tradition. He will cultivate Gallicus with a *tenuis lyra* ('slender lyre'). Statius' river of praise, moreover, while overtly inferior to Gallicus' Ocean, is very respectable and even preferable within the context of Roman Callimacheanism. Lines 36–7 recall a specific passage in Horace's *Odes*.

> crescit occulto velut arbor aevo
> fama Marcelli; micat inter omnis
> Iulium <u>sidus</u> velut inter <u>ignis</u>
> <u>luna minores</u>.   (*Carm.* 1.12.45–8)

The fame of Marcellus grows like a tree with the imperceptible passage of time;[57] among all the rest the Julian star shines out like the moon amid lesser lights.

---

[56] Bright (1980), 57: 'a fulsome compliment'.
[57] See Nisbet and Hubbard (1970) ad loc.

The intertext affords a very precise and telling context for the present poem. *Odes* 1.12 is an example of an encomiastic poem in an explicitly Pindaric style that at the same time displays impeccable aesthetic credentials in the neo-Callimachean tradition. The Sapphic strophe, with its adonic conclusion, is Horace's metre of choice when he wishes to demonstrate his capacity to impose lyric narrowness on Pindar's rhetorical sublimity and panegyrical mode. Statius thus defers to Gallicus' greater literary powers, all the while packing his gesture of deference with references to key terms and passages of Roman Callimacheanism, which, if they do not subvert, certainly work to qualify, our sense of Statius' humility and self-subordination. What Statius yields on points of scale and vastness, he recoups in craftsmanship, and while he affects to be dependent on Gallicus, he demonstrates an independent capacity to define his place in the Roman literary tradition.[58]

An important means by which the autonomist writer exerts control over his self-representational domain is a rigorously contrastive definition of self and the self's domain of concern. A key example is the closing passage of Horace *Odes* 1.1. The poet runs through a series of conventional occupations (athlete, politician, merchant, hunter, soldier, hedonist) before drawing a portrait of himself sequestered in his poetic realm: *me doctarum hederae praemia frontium / dis miscent superis; me gelidum nemus / nympharumque leves cum Satyris chori / secernunt populo*... ('*Me* ivy, the prize of literary foreheads, mingles with the gods above; *me* the cool grove and the nimble choruses of Nymphs and Satyrs cut off from the populace...', 1.1.29–32). This syntactic arrangement, with the first-person pronoun placed first, followed by subject and verb, used disjunctively to contrast the speaker's own concerns from what has preceded, emphasizes the poet's distinctive *modus vitae* and contributes to Horace's autonomist construction of his literary realm. Such a personal projection of autonomy should notionally have no place in the encomiastic scheme of the *Silvae*, which is largely, by definition, *other*-directed poetry. As we have seen, however, the rhetoric of deference in Statius is not without complication and nuance.

In 3.2, the propempticon to Maecius Celer, Statius imagines a future occasion on which the emperor will send Maecius on his provincial command.

> ergo erit illa dies qua te maiora daturus
> Caesar ab emerito iubeat discedere bello.
> at nos hoc iterum stantes in litore vastos
> cernemus fluctus aliasque rogabimus auras.
> o tum quantus ego aut quanta votiva movebo
> plectra lyra, cum me magna cervice ligatum
> attolles umeris atque in mea pectora primum
> incumbes e puppe novus servataque reddes
> colloquia inque vicem medios narrabimus annos!
> tu rapidum Euphraten et regia Bactra sacrasque
> antiquae Babylonis opes et Zeugma...
>
> .   .   .   .
>
> ast ego devictis dederim quae busta Pelasgis
> quaeve laboratas claudat mihi pagina Thebas.   (3.2.127–37, 142–3)

---

[58] This is not to deny that Statius' Augustan allusion works to magnify and flatter Gallicus: see Newlands (2002), 224, who cites Henderson (1998a), 56, 'an Apollo and Augustus rolled-into-one'. Nonetheless, as Newlands also notes, 'the final image... shifts between deference and self-assertion on the part of the poet'. Note also the telling allusion at *Silv.* 1.4.25–7 to Horace *Carm.* 1.1.32–6, where divine sources of inspiration are not displaced but complemented by the patron.

Therefore the day will come when Caesar, to bestow on you still greater honours, commands you to depart from the war you have completed. As for me, I shall be standing once again on this shore, and, seeing the vast waves, shall pray for different winds. O then with what great pride, and with how mighty a lyre, I shall pluck the votive strings, when you, fresh off the ship, fall into my embrace first of all, and, my arms around your great neck, raise me onto your shoulders and proffer all the conversation you have been saving for me, and, taking turns, we tell the stories of the intervening years! *You* shall tell of the swift-flowing Euphrates, royal Bactra, the sacred treasures of ancient Babylon, and Zeugma... whereas *I* shall tell of the tombs I have given the defeated Pelasgi, and of the page that brings to a close my laboured-over Thebes.

The passage as a whole responds to the ending of the *Georgics*, when Virgil contrasts 'great Caesar thundering in war by the deep Euphrates' (*Caesar dum magnus ad altum / fulminat Euphraten bello*, 4.560–1) with himself engaged in literary pursuits in Naples (*studiis florentem ignobilis oti*, 4.564). In the closing lines, Virgil recalls his previous work, the *Eclogues*, through a citation of its opening line (4.566). Statius evokes the Virgilian passage in several details: the juxtaposition of Caesar, 'war', and the poet (*Caesar... bello... at nos*), the mention of the Euphrates (*rapidum Euphraten*), and the closing reference to the poet's previous work.[59]

Statius here follows a strategy pursued by Virgil, Horace, and Propertius, all of whom are at pains to sharpen the difference between the idle man of letters and the participant in public life. Specifically, Statius is drawing on two well-known scenarios in Roman love elegy. One scenario is the prospective triumph, in which the elegiac love poet effectively puts off the task of panegyric by stating vaguely that one day he *will* be present at or offer words of praise for the celebration of some future victory: *ergo erit illa dies...* ('and so that day will come...').[60] In Statius, however, instead of the expected triumph celebration, we find both the warrior and the poet prospectively set on an equal footing as narrators[61] of their deeds (*inque vicem medios narrabimus annos! / tu... ast ego...* 'taking turns, we shall tell the stories of the intervening years; you... whereas I...'). Statius' poem significantly ends with reference to Statius' literary accomplishments (which are real and completed), rather than his patron's deeds in the East (still prospective).

A second elegiac scenario replayed by Statius is exemplified by Propertius, who envisions his addressee Tullus engaged in imperial administration in the soft, effeminate East, while, as lover, Propertius undergoes harsh sufferings and toils (*Elegies* 1.5). Statius develops a similar contrast: whereas Maecius will travel in the

---

[59] Statius, of course, makes us notice differences and changes as well: for example, whereas Virgil famously moves up the scale of genres, from bucolic to didactic to epic, Statius has moved in the opposite direction, from epic to *Silvae*. Note also Statius' advertisement of his Neapolitan/Virgilian retirement in the closing poem of the same collection (3.6).

[60] e.g. Propertius 2.10.19–20, 3.5.11–22; Ovid *Ars am.* 1.205–28.

[61] Compare Ovid's reduction of conquered rivers and nations to mere *nomina*, to be changed or substituted at the whim of the lover (*Ars. am.* 1.219–28). As the anonymous reviewer for Oxford University Press has pointed out to me, Statius also seems to have in mind Catullus 9. But whereas Catullus anticipates hearing only his friend Veranius' stories of his travels abroad, Statius insists that he will tell also of his own literary labours.

luxurious lands of the East amidst various sensual delights, Statius has laboured hard (*laboratas*) over his *Thebaid*, which treats the grim mythology of the Seven Against Thebes. Statius even surpasses Propertius in heaping up a great mass of words connoting luxury (*opes . . . dulce nemus florentis . . . pretiosa . . . rubeat . . . purpura . . . sudent opobalsama . . .*, *Silv.* 3.2.137–41). By the poem's end, a series of familiar dichotomies—word and deed, insubstantial scribbling and solid accomplishment, effeminate *otium* and hard labour—has been playfully subverted. The insertion of this kind of passage within the fabric of a highly deferent, panegyrical poem speaks to the complexity of Statius' self-positioning as poet.

THE VILLA AS SITE OF AUTONOMY

By far the most conspicuous image of autonomy projected by Statius' *Silvae* is the secluded realm of the luxury villa.[62] The villa culture of the early empire might be seen as the culmination of a process begun in the middle republic, whereby the Roman elite began to construct a sophisticated realm of private life infused with Greek culture and literary and philosophical ideals.[63] An important development occurred in the Augustan period, when poets contrasted the poet's rural retreat with the urban *negotia* of the mercantile and political classes. The Flavian period, however, sees a new fusion and blurring of boundaries. Now poets and patrons not infrequently occupy the same space of *otium*, and devote themselves to the same ideals of literary study. In the broad historical perspective of the *longue durée*, there is nothing exceptional about the fact that poets and politicians alike enjoy the villa as space of relaxation and literary diversion. What is significant in the present context of literary self-definition is the fact that the villa-as-the-site-of-writing has been wrested from the hands of poets and redistributed more widely among Rome's elite.

Early imperial poets, for their own reasons, may not have wished to intensify the impression of their autarky. In the cultural milieu of Flavian Rome, it was harder, for various reasons, to set oneself up as an autonomous author in the grand old style. The poet's *nemus* is a weakened cliché which no one can claim any longer with a straight face, and in any case, an autarkic stronghold is no place for an obliging client-poet. Finally, the villa as site of authorial autonomy is now, quite simply, outdated, the guiding literary trope of a past generation—suitable for grand men annexing literary laurels to their already considerable prestige, but not for socially marginal but ferociously ambitious poets like Martial and Statius. Martial and Statius, both of whom owned rural estates, do not lavish set-piece descriptions on them, or present them as sites of the poet's life of autarkic

---

[62] On the significance of the villa as space of *otium* in Statius and other imperial writers, see especially Myers (2000); Newlands (2002), especially 119–98.

[63] See, e.g. Zanker (1988), 31.

tranquillity.[64] Conversely, both poets offer laudatory descriptions of their wealthy patrons' villas in precisely such terms.

Silvae 1.3 praises the sophistication of Manilius Vopiscus' villa spanning the banks of the river Anio.

> scilicet hic illi meditantur pondera mores,
> hic premitur fecunda quies virtusque serena
> fronte gravis sanusque nitor luxuque carentes
> deliciae, quas ipse suis digressus Athenis
> mallet deserto senior Gargettius horto.
>
> .   .   .   .
>
> hic tua Tiburtes Faunos chelys et iuvat ipsum
> Alciden dictumque lyra maiore Catillum,
> seu tibi Pindaricis animus contendere plectris
> sive chelyn tollas heroa ad robora sive
> liventem saturam nigra rubigine turbes
> seu tua non alia splendescat epistula cura.   (1.3.90–4, 99–104)

Here, to be sure, your tranquil way of life is devoted to contemplating weighty matters, here fertile repose lies hidden, here lies virtue, serious yet with serene countenance, sensible elegance, and pleasure *sans* luxury. Such a place the old man of Gargettus would have preferred; he would have left Athens and abandoned his garden … Here your lyre gives enjoyment to the Fauns of Tibur, Alcides himself, and Catillus, celebrated by a greater lyre, whether you are inclined to emulate Pindar's plectrum, or raise up your lyre to the heights of heroes' deeds, or stir up satire, livid with black salt, or apply a similar degree of polish to your sparkling Epistles.

Statius' Vopiscus out-Horaces Horace, reproducing not only the Augustan poet's Epicurean retreat, but also most of his literary genres (lyric, satire, epistles). The connection is significant. As Newlands has demonstrated, Statius' praises of Vopiscus' Tiburtine villa allude to Horatian descriptions of Tibur, while replacing Horace's programmatic *paupertas* with the distinctly Flavian themes of artifice, luxury, and elegantly deployed wealth.[65] Tiburtine literary/philosophical retreat has hardened into a cliché to which it is now possible to add luxurious amenities beyond anything Horace would have avowed. In the poem's closing words, Statius adroitly mediates the tension between Epicurean philosophical meditation and immense wealth, playing on two senses of *bona*, both material and spiritual:[66] *digne Midae Croesique bonis et Perside gaza, / macte bonis animi* ('You who are worthy of the wealth of Midas and Croesus and the riches of Persia, hail to your wealth of spirit!', 105–6).

---

[64] Compare Juvenal *Sat.* 3.318–22 (discussed below). The closest Martial comes to such a description of his Nomentan farm is a nostalgic reminiscence on the point of his departure for Spain, when he must commend his property to another's care (10.92). Some of the larger issues concerning patronage in the Flavian age, and the distinct position of Flavian poets vis-à-vis the Augustans, are discussed by Newlands (2002), 29–30: whereas Augustan poets such as Horace were in a position, for various reasons, to maintain some distance from the emperor, and even to limit the patronal dimension of their poetry, 'Statius needed patrons' (30) as being neither a member of the elite nor from a Roman background. On Statius' recurrent status as guest at others' villas, see Newlands (2002), 120.

[65] See in particular Newlands (2002), 127–38.   [66] Newlands (2002), 137.

In 2.2, Statius describes Pollius Felix' villa sheltered in a reclusive nook designed by Nature. The villa imitates its owner's own temperate outlook (*dominique imitantia mores*).

> placido lunata recessu
> hinc atque hinc curvas perrumpunt aequora rupes.
> dat natura locum montique intervenit unum
> litus et in terras scopulis pendentibus exit
>
> .   .   .   .
>
> mira quies pelagi. ponunt hic lassa furorem
> aequora et insani spirant clementius austri.
> hic praeceps minus audet hiems, nulloque tumultu
> stagna modesta iacent dominique imitantia mores.   (2.2.13–16, 26–9)

Crescent-shaped waters break through cliffs curving inward on either side, forming a calm space of retreat.[67] Nature furnishes a place: an uninterrupted beach is set amid the cliffs,[68] and passes inland between the overhanging rocks … Amazing is the sea's quiet. Here weary waves lay aside their frenzy and the wild south winds blow more gently. Here the headlong storm becomes less precipitous, and the pool lies still, temperate, with no uproar, imitating its owner's character.

The cliffs on either side form a kind of shield, creating a natural space (*dat natura locum*) sheltered from the sea. The result is the villa's site of tranquil retreat: *placido … recessu*. Pollius, like Vopiscus, displays an Epicurean bent:[69] he spurns magistracies, armies, laws. He keeps clear of the 'whirlwind of events' (*non in turbine rerum*, 127), and instead, in supremely Lucretian style, 'from the high citadel of [his] mind, gaze[s] down on those wandering below and laugh[s] at human joys' (*celsa tu mentis ab arce / despicis errantes humanaque gaudia rides*, 131–2).[70] Furthermore, Pollius writes poetry here (*hic ubi Pierias exercet Pollius artes*, 112): philosophical poetry of an Epicurean bent, epic, elegy, and iambic poetry (113–15). Again, it is the patron who assumes the role of villa-owning poet, and who occupies the autarkic citadel of philosophy.[71]

Elsewhere Statius does not altogether omit mention of his own property. In 3.1, a poem dedicated to Pollius Felix's villa at Surrentum, Statius makes a point of referring both to his Alban villa and the emperor's gift of running water.

> ast ego, Dardaniae quamvis sub collibus Albae
> rus proprium magnique ducis mihi munere currens
> unda domi curas mulcere aestusque levare
> sufficerent, notasque Sirenum nomine rupes
> … facundique larem Polli non hospes habebum.   (3.1.61–5)

As for me, although my own rural property beneath Dardan Alba's hills, with its residential supply of running water bestowed on me by the gift of the great Leader, sufficed

---

[67] On the syntax and meaning here, see Van Dam (1984), ad loc.

[68] For defence of the manuscripts' *unum*, see Van Dam (1984), ad loc.

[69] See Nisbet and Hubbard (1978); also discussed by Newlands (2002), *passim*: see in particular 137–8, 141–2, 170–3.

[70] Compare *DRN* 2.7–10: *sed nil dulcius est bene quam munita tenere / edita doctrina sapientum templa serena / despicere unde queas alios passimque videre / errare, atque viam palantis quaerere vitae* … See Nisbet and Hubbard (1978), 2.

[71] At *Sat.* 2.6.16, Horace occupies the 'citadel' (*arx*).

to soothe my cares and relieve the heat, I was staying by the cliffs known by the Sirens' name at the home of eloquent Pollius, not as a stranger . . .

Statius has his own villa (*rus proprium*), which he describes as a place of amenity and sufficiency (*curas mulcere aestusque levare/sufficerent*), although he does not align this setting with his position as poetic speaker, as Horace does with the Sabine farm. In this poem, Statius speaks as a guest of Pollius' villa, yet insists that he is *not* a visiting stranger or guest (*non hospes*): he is 'at home' at Pollius' villa. Statius, while avoiding explicit assumption of the Horatian role of poet-as-villa-owner, displays an effortless fluency in the Augustan idiom of rural autarky. More than that, he takes possession of Pollius' villa on the literary plane, aligning it with his poetry's core themes of literature and leisure (*docta otia*).[72]

POETRY, EPHEMERALITY, MATERIALISM

As C. Newlands has observed, luxurious building materials and physical opulence tend to be disfavoured in the literary ideology of the Augustans.[73] One potential reason for this bias is well known. The princeps set the tone for a new emphasis on humility and simplicity of private life (*paupertas*) by contrast with the conspicuous consumption of the morally tainted late republican aristocracy. The Augustan poets, however, go beyond castigating private luxury. They proclaim that their poetry will prove more enduring than public monuments, and advertise the immortality of the poetic text. Following Catullus' lead, they denigrate the ephemerality utility of mere objects as the antitype of literature's enduring, non-use-specific value. This emphasis on the transcendence of material utility contributes to the autonomist presumption of poetry's distinctive value.

The Flavians develop a sophisticated aesthetic of materialism, and in the process, distance themselves from the Augustan ethos of *paupertas*. Elegant buildings and art objects—temples, villas, baths, statuary—stand alongside poems as artifacts imbued with aesthetic sophistication. Martial's 'aesthetic of objects' informs his epigrammatic oeuvre, and his poetry engages with the sordid materialities of urban existence.[74] Statius avoids the epigrammatist's sordidity and radical posture of self-denigration, yet, in his own way, is no less closely attuned to the material dimension of life and the poetic resonance of objects. Statius articulates an enhanced, exalted materialism that idealizes the capacity of the Roman ruling class to control, shape, and ultimately improve on Nature through ingenious artifice, immense resources, and a rich variety of imported materials. In the

---

[72] Note also the closing poem of *Silvae* 3, in which, as Newlands has argued, Naples emerges as a kind of counter-Rome. In enumerating the many attractions of Naples in this epistle to his wife, Statius is laying claim to his own separate place that is worthy of admiration and, crucially, beyond the immediate orbit of the imperial city. See Newlands (2002), e.g. 257: 'the alternative culture of Naples'.

[73] Newlands (2002), 3–7.   [74] See Salemme (1976), and below.

Silvae, immense material wealth and rarified literary value co-exist. Statius' villa-owners are praised both for the lavish construction of their rural abodes, and for the sophistication of their literary pursuits. A neat complementarity is at work: villas are aestheticized to emphasize their owners' refinement of taste, while literary pursuits are reified to emphasize the social prestige they generate.[75]

Memories of the *paupertas*-tradition nonetheless persist. For example, Statius adeptly cites poetic *paupertas* near the end of 1.4, although in a context that ultimately qualifies its force.

> tu Troica dignus
> saecula et Euboici transcendere pulveris annos
> Nestoreique situs. qua nunc tibi pauper acerra
> digna litem? nec si vacuet Mevania valles
> aut praestent niveos Clitumna novalia tauros,
> sufficiam. sed saepe deis hos inter honores
> caespes et exiguo placuerunt farra salino.   (1.4.125–31)

You are worthy of surpassing Trojan centuries, the years of Euboean dust, and Nestor's decay. With what incense-box am I, a poor man, to make sufficiently worthy offerings on your behalf? Not if Mevania should empty her vales or the fields of Clitumnus furnish their snowy bulls, would I have enough. But often among such offerings as these, sod and spelt with tiny saltcellar have pleased the gods.

The scene of the humble sacrifice belongs to the repertory of Roman Callimacheanism. We might recall, for example, Horace's contrast between the more expansive Pindaric poetry of Antonius Iullus and his own carefully crafted, small-scale productions: *ego apis Matinae / more modoque . . . operosa parvus / carmina fingo* ('In the manner and style of a Matine bee . . . I fashion on a small scale poetry with painstaking care', *Carm.* 4.2.27–32). While Iullus will sacrifice ten bulls and ten cows in celebration of Augustus' return from his campaign in Gaul and Spain, Horace will offer a single calf, carefully chosen and exquisitely described (53–60). Statius' humble sacrifice, however, comes at the end of a fulsome encomium of Gallicus in hexameter verse. He appends a brief closural advertisement of poetic *paupertas* to the sort of panegyrical composition that Horace attempted to foist onto his addressee and foil-figure, Antonius Iullus (*concines maiore poeta plectro / Caesarem,* 4.2.33–4).[76]

In the Augustan poets, who advertise their nostalgia for the Golden Age and the verdant simplicity of early Rome, the mastery of nature through human artifice is rarely the object of warm appreciation. Statius, by contrast, praises patrons who subdue, control, and surpass nature in their building projects.

> hic primus labor incohare sulcos
> et rescindere limites et alto
> egestu penitus cavare terras;
> mox haustas aliter replere fossas
> et summo gremium parare dorso,
> ne nutent sola, ne maligna sedes
> det pressis dubium cubile saxis;

> tunc umbonibus hinc et hinc coactis
> et crebris iter alligare gomfis.
> o quantae pariter manus laborant!
> hi caedunt nemus exuuntque montes,
> hi ferro scolopas trabesque levant,
> hi saxa ligant opusque texunt
> cocto pulvere sordidoque tofo,
> hi siccant bibulas manu lacunas
> et longe fluvios agunt minores.
> hae possent et Athon cavare dextrae
> et maestum pelagus gementis Helles
> intercludere ponte non natanti;
> his parens, nisi di viam vetarent,
> Inous freta miscuisset Isthmos.   (*Silv.* 4.3.40–60)

The first task here was to begin the furrows and cut back the edges and dig out the earth far down with deep excavation. Next, to fill up the excavated ditches with other material and prepare a bed for the uppermost ridge, lest the ground underneath wobble and a niggardly base afford an unstable bed for the stones stacked above. Then, to bind the road together with slabs forced in place on either side and with many pegs. O how many hands toil together! Some cut down a grove and strip mountains, some smooth stakes and beams with iron; others bind rocks together, weaving the work with baked sand and dirty tufa; and others still dry out thirsty pools by hand and draw lesser streams aside. These hands could even hollow out Athos and close off the sorrowful sea of lamenting Helle with a bridge that *didn't* float. Ino's Isthmus, if the gods didn't forbid a pathway through,[77] might have obeyed these hands and mingled the waters.

Hendecasyllables made famous by the light playfulness of Catullan *facetiae* have been adapted to the task of recording for posterity the layers of earth, stone, and concrete that went into making the Via Domitiana. Nothing quite like this passage may be found in Catullus or the Augustan poets. The poetic interest in enduring monuments of empire, however, is well established. Horace, in *Odes* 3.30, magnificently declared that his poetic monument would outlast the pyramids, and, we might infer, contemporary structures such as the Mausoleum of Augustus. The deeper point is that the poetic text outperforms mere material objects in its capacity to endure over time and preserve reputation. Statius, by contrast, bends his poetic medium to confer immortality on that most quotidian, utilitarian, and essential of Roman constructions—a road.[78] The priority of immortal poetic medium over the materiality of contemporary building projects has been reversed.[79]

Statius, while subverting the concept of poetry's superior temporal endurance, explicitly alludes to his predecessors' articulations of that very motif. Describing

---

[77] Reading *di viam* for the impossible *deviae* of the manuscripts: Coleman (1988), ad loc., sees this as the least offensive solution. I also adopt in line 51 *scolopas* (Coleman at the suggestion of Nisbet). In line 51, I follow Shackleton Bailey (2003) in adopting Postgate's *parens* in place of *parvus*.

[78] Compare Coleman (1988), 116: Domitian's road-gangs are 'miracle-workers'.

[79] Statius' praise, however, is not unambiguous: Newlands (2002), 292–3, notes in particular the motif of the violated grove and the negative *exempla* associated with Domitian's road (Hannibal, Nero, Xerxes). Further, the highway is *ipso facto* 'an anti-Callimachean project', 299. So all this manual labour is inevitably also seen as the *wrong* kind of composition, the inverse of the poet's singular, exquisite toil.

the great equestrian statue of Domitian in 1.1, Statius concludes with prediction of its eternity.

> non hoc imbriferas hiemes opus aut Iovis ignem
> tergeminum, Aeolii non agmina carceris horret
> annorumve moras: stabit, dum terra polusque,
> dum Romana dies.   (1.1.91–4)

This work does not shudder at stormy winters, the triple fire of Jove, the squadrons confined in Aeolus' prison or the slow passage of years: it will endure, as long as the earth and the firmament, as long as Roman daylight.

Domitian's statue will somehow resist and overcome the destructive natural forces that Horace, in *Odes* 3.30, singled out as the ones that eventually consign all statues and monumental structures to physical decay.[80] The correspondences with Horace are precise and deliberate.[81] The meaning, however, is inverted. The physical structure, and not the immaterial edifice of the poet, is described as resistant to time's destructive force.

One might argue that such conceits belie the poet's true ambitions, and that while Statius' poetry survives, Domitian's statue does not.[82] Even so, there remains a crucial difference in rhetorical emphasis. At the end of his poem on Domitian's gifts to the populace on the Saturnalia (1.6), Statius proclaims the eternity of the day of celebration.

> quos ibit procul hic dies per annos?
> quam nullo sacer exolescet aevo,
> dum montes Latii paterque Thybris,
> dum stabit tua Roma dumque terris
> quod reddis Capitolium manebit.   (1.6.98–102)

Through how many years will this day travel? Sacred, it shall not pass away in any age, so long as the Latian hills and father Tiber, so long as *your* Rome and the Capitolium you restore to the world, shall remain.

Embedding Horatian syntax (*dum … stabit*) in Catullan metre,[83] Statius fuses the former's concerns with monumentality and eternity of empire with the latter's

---

[80] On this passage, see Geyssen (1996), 117–33.

[81] Compare, for example, *imbriferas hiemes* ('rainy winters', *Silv.* 1.1.91) with *imber edax* ('corroding rain', *Carm.* 3.30.3); *Aeolii … agmina* ('the squadrons of Aeolus', *Silv.* 1.1.92) with *Aquilo impotens* ('the uncontrolled north wind', *Carm.* 3.30.3); *annorumve moras* ('the slow passage of years', *Silv.* 1.1.93) with *innumerabilis / annorum series* ('the innumerable sequence of years', *Carm.* 3.30.5); and *dum terra polusque / dum Romana dies* ('as long as the earth and firmament, as long as Roman daylight', *Silv.* 1.1.93–4) with *dum Capitolium / scandet … pontifex* ('as long as the priest shall climb the Capitol', *Carm.* 3.30.8–9).

[82] So Geyssen (1996), 121: 'It is not only the statue that will be immune to the forces of time and nature, but also Statius' poem commemorating the statue'. He therefore sees *hoc … opus* (1.1.91) as having 'a double referent'. All this is no doubt true, but then again, Statius still reverses Horace by tacitly and prudently incorporating his own poetic immortality into the explicitly advertised immortality of Domitian's monument. The Flavian poet's tactful rhetoric of self-subordination is a far cry from *Odes* 3.30.

[83] On possible associations of the hendecasyllabic metre, see Damon (1992), 304; Newlands (2002), 228; Morgan (2000), 115–16.

themes of ephemerality, pleasure, and license.[84] Like Catullus, Statius immortalizes a fleeting day in verse (*dies*, cf. Catullus c. 14.15, *optimo dierum*), but unlike Catullus, he equates that day's immortality with the eternity of Rome's buildings, cults, and lands. It is possible to infer, from Statius' declaration of the day's perpetual memory, that the medium of Statian poetry will achieve this perpetuation. Significantly, however, Statius does not make any such explicit claim. What matters is the perpetuation of the ephemeral occasion of imperial benefaction, not the intrinsic monumentality of Statius' oeuvre.

The Flavian poets cannot claim to *confer* immortality on their most important patron, the emperor Domitian, since he is already presumed to be a god. At the close of 3.4, the imperial eunuch Earinus expresses the wish that Domitian will live an unspecified number of lifetimes, and will grow old along with his own *lares* and the 'Tarpeian temple' (3.4.100–5). Domitian's life will be coterminous with his own signature building projects: his Palace, and the restored Capitoline temple.[85] Yet even as Statius develops and extends elements of the Roman poetic tradition, he brings that tradition to a strange new place by placing the declaration of *aeternitas* in the mouth of the court eunuch and imperial Ganymede, Earinus.[86] It is worth contemplating for a moment how Horace might have viewed this latest evolution of his *monumentum aere perennius*. Perhaps the most striking instance of the emperor's monopoly on eternity occurs at the end of 4.3 in the predictions of a markedly encomiastic Sibyl.

> et laudum cumulo beatus omni
> scandes belliger abnuesque currus,
> donec Troicus ignis et renatae
> Tarpeius pater intonabit aulae,
> haec donec via te regente terras
> annosa magis Appia senescat   (4.3.158–63).

'Blessed with every surplus of glory, you shall mount chariots as warlord and decline triumphal chariots, so long as Trojan fire burns and the Tarpeian father thunders in palace reborn, until, under your rule on earth, this road grows older than the ancient Appian Way'.

The god-emperor Domitian will continue to be voted and to refuse triumphs as long as Rome's core rites and institutions (the flame of Vesta, the Temple of Capitoline Jupiter), and as long as the newly built Via Domitiana, endure. Just as Statius appropriates the power of Horace's *monumentum* to declare Domitianic eternity, he also specifically draws on the poetic authority of Virgil. The *sanctior vates* of line 120 before whom Statius deferentially recedes, while overtly the Sibyl,

---

[84] For different interpretations of the significance of Saturnalian *libertas* in 1.6, see Damon (1992), Newlands (2002), 227–59.

[85] Domitian's interest in the Capitoline conveniently converges with its traditional 'use as an image of permanence': e.g., in addition to Hor. *Carm.* 3.30, Verg. *Aen.* 9.446ff. See the remarks of Coleman (1988), 134 on *Silvae* 4.3.160–1.

[86] For an exploration of how Statius treats the sometimes troubling and problematic figure of the eunuch in 3.4, see the discussion of Newlands (2002), 105–18, and for both Martial and Statius, see the recent discussion in Vout (2007), 267ff.; note also Henriksen (1997); Garthwaite (1984) and Garthwaite (1992).

may be read as implicitly suggesting the Mantuan bard.[87] This entire closing section is saturated in Virgilian reminiscence,[88] and in some sense, the prophetic speech of Virgil's Sibyl has been refashioned by Statius to suit the new encomiastic circumstances of Flavian Rome.[89]

These closural declarations of the eternity of a structure, statue, occasion of benefaction, or extraordinary person take the place of the closural declaration of the immortality of the poetic work. Horace's lyric *Schlussgedichten* often make overt declarations of literary immortality (*Carm.* 2.20, 3.30; *Epist.* 1.20). In Ovid's *Metamorphoses*, the last metamorphosis is the poet's own transformation into an immortal text: *vivam* ('I shall live', 15.879). In an autonomist paradigm, the closing focus significantly falls on the poetic work's distinctive value and capacity to withstand the passage of time, not a patron's or ruler's achievements. Statius' repeated practice of allusively citing such closural passages, while replacing the immortal poem with an immortal building or patron, calls attention to itself as a strategy of heteronomist poetics. The autonomist model is at once subverted and recalled.

SILVAE 4

Thus far I have argued that Statius presents a broadly heteronomist stance as poetic speaker in his *Silvae*. At the same time, however, Statius alludes to aspects of autonomist self-representation even as he adapts them to the panegyric of patrons. This pattern, broadly and loosely understood, applies to *Silvae* 1–3. Statius' fourth book, however, represents a noticeable shift in authorial self-presentation and literary manner, and as such, merits further examination. A good starting point is provided by a recent treatment of *Silvae* 4 by Ruurd Nauta.[90] Nauta argues that autobiographical elements are scarce in *Silvae* 1–3. Statius assumes the role of praise poet, and the first-person singular and plural statements he makes are designed to enhance his authority as poetic encomiast. *Silvae* 4 is exceptional in that, while it contains much familiar content, it also manifests a greater engagement with the tradition of autobiographical poetry, especially Catullus and Horace. Statius accordingly incorporates a greater dimension of self-reference and also more frequent references to writing and books. Whereas the general tendency of his *Silvae* is to suppress references to writing in favour of a poetics of presence, Book 4 aligns more closely with the Roman tradition of authorial autobiography. In addition to writing in Catullan and

---

[87] Coleman (1988), ad loc., notes that 'Virgilian associations govern the use of *vates* here, the sole instance in the *Silvae*'—surely a significant point.

[88] See the various comments of Coleman (1988), ad loc.: to cite only example out of many, *magnus . . . ordo saeculorum* (147), a phrase which in Virgil is one of 'cosmic relevance', 'becomes hyperbolic flattery of the emperor'.

[89] See in particular Newlands (2002), 309–23, for a discussion of the figure of the Sybil and her 'multivalent speech' (323).

[90] Nauta (2008), 173: 'the non-imperial poems in Book 4 are closer to the Roman tradition of autobiographical poetry than those in Books 1–3 and again in Book 5, in which the poet stages himself as the less individualized praise poet of the Greek tradition, even though combining this, as necessary, with the requirements of the role of a Roman *amicus*'.

Horatian metres, Statius employs key scenarios and strategies of the Roman first-person tradition.

The letter to Vitorius Marcellus (4.4) is a good example. As in the meta-epistolary poetry of Catullus, Horace, and Ovid, Statius addresses his own epistolary text. Statius begins by imagining the letter's trajectory through space: the letter will run from Naples to Rome along the Via Domitiana lauded in 4.3, the previous poem in the collection. He then engages in a highly traditional metatextual game by exhorting his *epistula* to commit to memory a verse-epistle, which, in turn, is to be conveyed to Marcellus. Sophisticated layering of multiple frames is at work here: epistolary poem framing personified epistle framing verse-epistle. Statius here focuses on words and literary medium to a greater degree than in previous books of the *Silvae*, and so also on his own role as poet and producer of literary texts. Appropriately, the core of Statius' letter to Marcellus, who was praetor in 95, curator of the Via Latina in 96, and a celebrated orator and advocate, is a brief essay on *otium* and the life of action.

> sed tu, dum nimio possessa Hyperione flagrat
> torva Cleonaei iuba sideris, exue curis
> pectus et assiduo temet furare labori.
> et sontes operit pharetras arcumque retendit
> Parthus et Eleis auriga laboribus actos
> Alpheo permulcet equos et nostra fatiscit
> laxaturque chelys. vires instigat alitque
> tempestiva quies; maior post otia virtus.
> talis cantata Briseide venit Achilles
> acrior et positis erupit in Hectora plectris.
> te quoque flammabit tacite repetita parumper
> desidia et solitos novus exsultabis in actus.   (4.4.27–38)

But as for you—as long as the savage mane of Cleone's star blazes under the control of too potent Hyperion, strip off your heart's cares and steal yourself away from continual toil. The Parthian covers his guilty quiver and unstrings his bow, the charioteer soothes his horses, driven hard in the labours of Elis, in the Alpheus river, and my lyre grows weak and slack. Timely relaxation spurs and nourishes the exercise of strength. Manly action is greater after leisure. So Achilles, after singing of Briseis, came forth more fiercely, and, after putting his lyre aside, launched himself at Hector. Idleness, sought again in silence for a little while, shall rekindle you as well, and, refreshed, you will throw yourself back into your habitual endeavours.

In broad terms, the relation between action and *otium* here articulated is a traditional one. *Otium* is subordinate to action, providing respite and recreation for the weary warrior, orator, or politician: *maior post otia virtus* ('manly action is greater after leisure'). As the poem goes on, however, Statius further manipulates the distinction between literary leisure and the life of action, reviving the contrastive rhetoric of Augustan polemic.

> felix curarum, cui non Heliconia cordi
> serta nec imbelles Parnasi e vertice laurus,
> sed viget ingenium et magnos accinctus in usus
> fert animus quascumque vices. nos otia vitae
> solamur cantu ventosaque gaudia famae
> quaerimus. en egomet somnum et geniale secutus

> litus ubi Ausonio se condidit hospita portu
> Parthenope tenues ignavo pollice chordas
> pulso, Maroneique sedens in margine templi
> sumo animum et magni tumulis accanto magistri.   (*Silv.* 4.4.46–55)

Happy is he amidst his responsibilities, who delights neither in Helicon's garlands nor in unwarlike laurels from Parnassus' peak; whose intellect flourishes with vigour and whose spirit, girded for great employments, endures whatever may come. *I* find in song solace for my life of leisure, and seek fame's delights that are fickle as the wind. See, here I am, pursuing slumber and the genial shore where stranger Parthenope hid herself in an Ausonian harbour; I strike the slender strings with idle thumb, and, sitting within the precinct of Maro's shrine, take heart and sing by the great master's tomb.

Statius combines here two syntactic motifs reminiscent of his Augustan predecessors: the *felix qui* pattern ('happy he, who…'), employed, in Virgil's *Georgics* for example, to politely disavow a literary approach or *modus vitae* belonging to someone else;[91] and the syntactic pattern of the sentence-initial first-person pronoun (*me/nos*…'me…it pleases…') employed to designate the poetic speaker's particular realm of accomplishment or concern.

Statius here incorporates a more robust element of contrastive poetic self-definition than anywhere in *Silvae* 1–3. The poem in particular revolves around the crucial act of self-differentiation. Whereas Marcellus will go on to achieve notable feats in war, Statius will write about the deeds of others: *nos facta aliena canendo / vergimus in senium: propriis tu pulcher in armis / ipse canenda geres…* ('I am declining into old age, singing the deeds of others; you, resplendent in your own arms, shall yourself perform deeds worth singing of', 69–71). The sentiments are expressive of the long-established Roman prioritization of deeds over words, action over narration. The deferent tone fits with the self-denigrating lexicon of literary idleness employed throughout (*ventosaque gaudia famae…ignavo pollice*; 'fame's delights, fickle as the wind…with idle thumb'). Vigour, heat, action, manliness are all on the side of Marcellus; on Statius' side are sleep, idleness, old age, passivity. At this point in the tradition of Roman poetic self-representation, however, we have come to be wary of self-denigrating claims on the part of accomplished poets, who urbanely insist on their own inutility and indolence. This is another way of claiming a special status, coolly disavowing traditional *virtus* in a manner that only someone assured of their own counter-traditional achievement in the literary realm could pull off.

Statius, moreover, boasts his own 'labours' in the completion of the *Thebaid* (*Sidonios…labores*, 88), and, in meditating the fearsome task of writing about Domitian's military campaigns, he himself, in a certain sense, is embarking on a dangerous expedition (95–100). The entire closing section of the poem (78–105) is devoted, not to some final panegyrical flourishes in praise of Marcellus, but to a portrait of the author in Naples. Statius describes his past, present, and future projects, his pride in his accomplishments and anxieties regarding tasks to come. Even the complimentary reference in the closing lines to Marcellus' fidelity as a friend doubles as an advertisement for Statius' already published *Thebaid* (featuring a heroic Theseus in its closing episode) and his forthcoming *Achilleid*: *cedet*

---

[91] *Georgics* 2.490–4: *felix qui potuit rerum cognoscere causas…*

tibi gloria fidi / Theseos, et lacerum qui circa moenia Troiae / Priamiden caeso solacia traxit amico ('Loyal Theseus' glory shall yield to you, and he too shall yield who dragged the body of the son of Priam around the walls of Troy to be mutilated as consolation for the slaying of his friend', 103–5).

Thus, along with the increased autobiographical dimension observed by Nauta, *Silvae* 4 brings an increased focus on the contrastive definition of self and privileging of the poet's role that were central to the Augustan rhetoric of autonomy. The self-representational nexus of *paupertas*, rural autarky, and Callimachean restriction now also comes to the fore, especially in Statius' imitations of Horace. *Silvae* 4.5, the lyric ode to Septimius Severus, replays the Horatian scenario of the *contentus / beatus parvo* (compare especially *Carm.* 2.16.33–41), while in 4.7, attempting to 'thin out [his] song for Maximus' (*Maximo carmen tenuare tempto*, 9), Statius plays the instantly recognizable Horatian game of juxtaposing an expansive Pindaric model with the diminishing contour and finesse of the Sapphic strophe. What is especially striking here is not Callimacheanism itself—an unremarkable commitment at this point in Roman literary history—but the explicit assumption of the role of Callimachean *vates* (poet/bard) on the Horatian model. Statius defines himself as the kind of poet who not only offers versified praise, but also negotiates and 'authenticates'[92] his poetic status in relation to such figures as Horace and Pindar.

A similar set of concerns informs the domain of visual art in 4.6 on Novius Vindex's Hercules statuette. This strikingly original poem begins in the Saepta Julia, where Statius, strolling at sunset, receives a dinner invitation from Vindex. At dinner, he has occasion to view a masterpiece of miniature artistry, a statuette of Hercules small in actual size yet giving an impression of strength and massiveness. The poem's opening lines recall Horace *Satires* 1.9, the satire on the 'boor':

> Forte remittentem curas Phoeboque levatum
> pectora, cum patulis tererem vagus otia Saeptis
> iam moriente die, rapuit me cena benigni
> Vindicis. haec imos animi perlapsa recessus
> inconsumpta manet....   (*Silv.* 4.6.1–5)

My cares put aside and my mind relieved of Phoebus, I was spending my free time wandering the expansive Saepta at sunset, when, as it happened, a dinner invitation from kindly Vindex snatched me up. The dinner slipped into the deepest recesses of my mind, and remains there, unconsumed...

Statius, like Horace, is wandering through the city, when he meets someone by chance. The dinner party that ensues ends up transcending its status as mere food (it 'remains unconsumed', *inconsumpta manet*), and living on as poem and cultural document in Statius' *Silvae*. Similarly, Horace's urban stroll and simultaneous conversation turn out to be more than the chance encounter of a day; they take on an emblematic significance in the poet's *Sermones* ('Conversations'). There is an important difference between Statius and Horace, however: Horace resents the intrusion of the unnamed acquaintance, and resists being drawn in by the boor's attempts at sociability. He wishes to maintain his solitary state of urban

---

[92] G. Davis (1991), 78–144.

wandering and meditation, and there is no mention of a dinner date with Maecenas or anyone else. Statius' eminently sociable, patron-oriented poetry affords a different scenario: he praises the hospitality he receives from Vindex and compliments his friend's artistic taste and erudition.

The main focus of the poem is a Hercules statuette made by Lysippus that supposedly passed through the hands of various famous owners, including Alexander, Hannibal, and Sulla, before coming to adorn Vindex's table. In aesthetic terms, the statuette represents a paradoxical achievement in Statius' description, encompassing at once miniaturist refinement and colossal scale all at once: *tantus honos operi finesque inclusa per artos / maiestas . . . quanta experientia docti / artificis, curis pariter gestamina mensae / fingere et ingentes animo versare colossos* ('such great dignity the work has, such grandeur confined within narrow boundaries . . . what expertise in the cunning artist, at once to fashion by his pains a table ornament and to envision gigantic statues in his mind', 35–6, 44–6). The statue's peculiar status speaks to the situation of a wealthy connoisseur like Vindex living under the early empire. Vindex could not possibly hope to rival the heroic *virtus* of great warriors past like Alexander, Hannibal, and Sulla, yet all three are presented as ambitious, violent men who did not ideally suit the genial, refined character of the Hercules statuette. Vindex himself, whose 'lyre and garlands and song-loving laurel' are much more pleasing to the statue, represents the apparent paradox of expansive virile prestige confined within a small space. Vindex and other early imperial Roman elites, like the miniature Hercules, express their *virtus* within the more restricted field of aesthetic refinement. They too are able to cut an impressive figure without leaving the convivial domain of the dining room.

Statius' table-top Hercules represents a new and striking contribution to the now cliché-ridden repertory of Roman Callimacheanism. Statius begins by revisiting Horace's satiric self-representation, and then goes on to explore concepts of art, refinement, and manly character in Flavian Rome. In this and other poems of *Silvae* 4, Statius develops a more robust autobiographical presence than in *Silvae* 1–3, recalling the self-representational strategies of his Augustan models; yet he does so without abandoning his predominantly encomiastic mode. Even as Statius lends a contrastive, Horatian emphasis to his self-representation as poet, he still happily shares the poetic arena with patrons and addressees. *Silvae* 4 hardly represents a complete overturning of Statius' hitherto panegyrical style. It does, however, bring into further relief the continuing presence of elements of the first-person, autonomist tradition within Statian panegyric.

What is the reason for the increased prominence of autobiographical content, Augustan intertextuality, and autonomist self-definition in Statius' fourth book of *Silvae*? One possible answer might be simply that Statius has gained greater confidence and sense of accomplishment as the author of occasional poems, and accordingly feels emboldened to incorporate more notable markers of authorial presence and status. While this answer might be sufficient, I believe a further explanation can be derived from Statius' own words, which, although the text is marred by lacunae, are easily understood in their general sense. In the second sentence of the preface, he states: *reor equidem aliter quam invocato numine maximi imperatoris nullum opusculum meum coepisse; sed hic liber tres habet . . .* ('Indeed I do not think that any little work of mine has begun otherwise than by invoking the divinity of the greatest emperor; but this book has three [such invocations]'). While all his books of *Silvae* offer pride of place to poems honouring the emperor, the fourth book honours Domitian to a special degree, dedicating the first three poems to his praise. This statement provides another angle for interpreting Statius' newly authoritative and Augustan poetic persona. Like the Augustans themselves, he elevates and dignifies his status as poet in concert with and as a support for newly ambitious panegyrical aims. In order to offer praise of the highest possible value, the poet must himself appear to be a figure of integrity, exacting standards, and independence. Thus while a strong autonomist position, as I have argued, was no longer tenable in the Flavian period, it might remain desirable for a poet to augment, in certain circumstances and in small but noticeable ways, his own authority and thereby the weight and value of his words.

Statius' *Silvae* arguably present some of the most lucid and powerful images of literary autonomy in the Roman poetic tradition. He delineates a realm of aesthetic connoisseurship, refinement, wealthy, luxury, and literary activity that is marvelously self-contained and independent. Statius' contemporaries design hyper-elegant villas, build temples in the latest style, collect art works, and write poetry and prose all at the same time. On the one hand, these refined leisure pursuits provide the poet with an ideal milieu in which to create and circulate his works. He may even find a limited form of autonomy in the world of *docta otia*, an escape from or counterpoint to the demands of imperial panegyric. On the other hand, the Flavian poet qualifies and undermines a crucial item in the lexicon of autonomist self-definition, the contrastive articulation of the poet's values and world. He shares his world with men of wealth and power. Even as the social distinction conferred by literary activity has gained increased prominence and acceptance, the poet himself has lost an element of his own distinction. This apparent paradox lies at the heart of Statius' work.

At the same time, the poet must adapt his poetry's tone and content to a new type of patron, an authoritarian ruler who is at once urgently important to the poet and immensely remote, a weighty presence and a distant divinity. Poetry inevitably loses some of its power and prestige in praising a figure who is himself a god, and who putatively transcends the need for praise. The emperor *must* be praised, yet how puny and ineffectual any mere poet's words are in comparison with their intrinsically immortal subject. Such, at any rate, is the guiding presumption behind the more radically self-effacing rhetoric of the Flavian poets. At the same time, the poet remains implicitly an important figure for the circulation and preservation of the emperor's reputation. This implicit yet still valued role creates a loophole for the client-poet's dignity and authority, and a motive for maintaining, albeit discretely, elements of the autonomist self-representational model. A poet who maintains a degree of independence and devotion to the integrity of his craft offers the most effective form of commemoration, even in a period when the authoritarian character of imperial rule threatens to undermine autonomy of any kind.

MARTIAL'S *EPIGRAMS*: THE HETERONOMOUS BOOK

Martial, Statius' contemporary and competitor, writes poetry that similarly addresses a multiplicity of patrons and emphasizes its own occasionality. He too fluctuates between flattery of the emperor and courtly dialogue with lesser figures, and prefaces his verse collections with prose epistles characterized by minutely calibrated tactics of social self-positioning. Martial lives in the same social world as Statius, and even cuts a superficially similar figure as client-poet. Finally, Martial, like the author of the *Silvae*, plays a broadly comparable metapoetic game. He displaces the Augustan rhetorical emphasis on transcendent literary value and the immaterial virtues of *paupertas* with a persistent materialist focus on the fascinating, multi-textured object-cache that makes up the early imperial Roman world. In Martial's epigrammatic vision, however, materiality takes on a darker and more sordid aspect. The immense physical untidiness and uproar of the City press relentlessly on the epigrammatist, while his own poetry repeatedly disintegrates into mere *materia*, fragments into individual, use-specific *libelli*, and flaunts its own quotidian ephemerality. Whereas Statius fashions an elegant, heightened materiality of artifice and splendour to suit his patrons' distinctive tastes, Martial delves into the material side of existence both as an acute inquiry into human degradation, and as a new polemical *riposte* to the Augustan conception of literature's transcendent value.[93]

A leitmotif of this study has been the representation of the material book. In Martial's *Epigrams*, this theme comes into its own, and bears directly on the question of the autonomy or heteronomy of literary activity. The majority of this chapter will be devoted to unpacking Martial's representations of the material book and the radically heteronomist conception of literary activity he develops in and through such images. First, however, it is necessary to address the relation between Martial's literary personality and his epigrammatic genre. The image of the writer projected in the *Epigrams* frames and informs our conception of his poetry's underlying nature.

The tradition of scholarship on Martial offers two diverging accounts of his existence as a writer. According to a literalist reading, Martial is an impoverished writer who lives under degrading social conditions: clients grovel in order to obtain gifts and dinners, and patrons, no longer concerned with the traditional ideals of *amicitia*, are stingy and illiberal in their attitude towards social inferiors.[94] This social dynamic has consequences for the conception of literary endeavour. The integrity of the literary work is undermined by its author's need to ingratiate himself. There are, however, notable problems with this account. First, poetic avowals of poverty do not necessarily correspond to reality,[95] and second, there are other poems and themes in Martial's *oeuvre* that indicate a more positive ideology of *amicitia*. For these reasons, a counter-image of Martial has been constructed in recent scholarship. Martial's representation of the patron-client relation as degraded, and literature as tainted by this subservience, is interpreted as part of epigram's fictive world. By contrast, in poems directed to actual friends and patrons of the poet, rather than to fictitious straw men, we are able to discern

---

[93] Some recent approaches to Martial's epigrammatic poetics include Rimell (2008); Fitzgerald (2007); Hinds (2007).

[94] A good example of this line of interpretation can be found in Marache (1961). Note, for instance: 'les relations humaines de jadis ont fait place à un automatisme impitoyable', 45; 'sous l'ironie et les plaisanteries éclatent le désespoir et la révolte', 57.

[95] White (1993).

the traditional ideals of *amicitia* as an unquantifiable exchange; the value-system of literary autarky grounded in the detachment afforded by a rustic estate; and a role for the poet which is more dignified than that of the lowly, urban *salutator* ('morning caller').[96] In the epigrams addressed to real patrons, the revisionist reading suggests, Martial allows us to see the distinguished author behind the mask of the cynical jester.[97]

Yet there are problems with this view also. First of all, there is no way to draw a hard and fast line between the world of the degraded, satiric persona and that of the distinguished author and his friends. Moreover, even if we were to accept this schematic division, we would have to admit that the dignified, authorial figure, who conforms closely to Roman ideals of *amicitia*, does not represent a more authentic voice by contrast with the degraded epigrammatic *persona*, but is himself simply another *persona*, and an equally suspect *persona*, insofar as Martial would be apt to present his 'real' thoughts about patronage and literature in a positive light in order to indulge the patron's pretensions of liberality. The nature of Martial's *persona*, and in particular, that aspect of his *persona* relating to patronage, is important in the larger context of my argument because it has implications for our understanding of the nature of Martial's literary activity.[98] How we view the exchange between writer and patron affects how we view the nature of the writer's gift, that is, his work. While the ancient Roman ideology of gift-exchange does require that friends remunerate each other with alternating acts of generosity,[99] the issue of literary remuneration is more complicated. The literary work, if it hews to the pattern of ordinary gift-exchange, risks becoming associated with ephemeral social motivations and rewards. Thus if we take a more cynical perspective, we will see the exchange between writer and patron as a *quid pro quo*, and the writer's work as designed to elicit gifts or money from the patron, rather than rigorously constructed according to criteria of literary value.[100]

At stake is the autonomy of literary ends. The central criterion of literary autonomy is the work's orientation towards posterity, by contrast with an orientation towards immediate social uses in the present *saeculum*. The work's enduring relevance for future readers is understood as being proportional to its dissociation from immediate social and financial motivations in the author's own lifetime. The writer's devotion to posthumous glory contains a simultaneous

---

[96] Spisak (1998) observes that, since even motifs of *amicitia* can be read cynically in terms of the idea of 'gifts as hooks', some external standard is required; Spisak chooses the sociological model of gift-exchange as a means of resolving the dilemma (248). Yet this seems to beg the question, and further, does not address the distinct nature of the writer's *munus*. See Walter (1998), esp. 225, on the rhetorical nature of Martial's motifs of social degradation.

[97] Damon (1997) establishes a distinction between poems with real addressees and those with anonymous, satirical targets (see also Saggese (1994) on this distinction). The more positive indications of the former set of poems reveal the limitations of the literalist reading of Martial as parasite. My reading seeks only to add the qualification that poems with named contemporaries do not necessarily represent Martial's authentic opinions any more than poems directed at fictitious targets.

[98] White (1975) and (1978), and Saller (1983) are the important works on this topic in Martial's case. Note also Sullivan (1991).

[99] Spisak (1998), 248ff.

[100] Oliensis (1998), 48ff. provides an insightful analysis of Horace's evasion of open gratitude to Maecenas for his gift of the farm; see also 161–2, 164–5. Many of these issues arise in relation to Pliny's famous letter about Martial (3.21): see Henderson (2001).

implication of the autonomy of literary ends, because it is difficult to construe the work's posthumous celebrity as 'profiting' its author in any ordinary sense. Martial's position in regard to poetic immortality and the autonomy of literary ends is complex. On the one hand, Martial echoes the language of earlier poets, such as Catullus, Propertius, Ovid, and Horace, in his claims to poetic immortality. On the other hand, he also engages in a more equivocal mode of self-representation in poems that express a preference for literary fame during one's own lifetime, as distinguished from posthumous reputation, which comes too late to be enjoyed: *si post fata venit gloria, non propero* ('if glory comes after death, I'm in no hurry', 5.10.12).[101] This motif does not rule out posthumous glory, and often a hint of such glory is incorporated into the claim to contemporary reputation, but Martial's emphasis subverts the traditional link between the autonomy of literary ends and the work's posthumous, literary orientation.[102] There is no inherent reason why a writer could not court celebrity in his own times, and also attain literary immortality, or why a writer could not receive gifts from patrons, and still achieve success with future readers. Yet rhetorical emphasis on one as opposed to another constitutes a significant declaration within the aesthetic code of Roman poetry: contemporary motives, and in particular financial motives, are understood to undermine the work's literary integrity.

Martial's un-Callimachean recommendation of contemporary celebrity is jocular and appropriate to the fluent, occasional mode of composition associated with epigram,[103] but at the same time, forms part of the deeper tension in Martial's work regarding literary autonomy. Martial establishes epigram as the site of conflicting literary tendencies, as both the subversion, and paradoxical continuation, of the aesthetic criteria informing the tradition of first-person poetry from Catullus to Ovid. A reading that divides Martial's self-representation neatly into fiction and reality renders this pervasive ambiguity hermeneutically inert. Both the image of the degraded poet-journeyman, whose parasitical existence undermines his work's integrity, and that of the dignified author, who enjoys the friendship of literary patrons in a spirit of polite urbanity, derive from irreducible aspects of Martial's complex self-representation.

A further weakness in the attempt to establish a clear division between serious and fictive, authentic and playful, in Martial's self-representation is the implicit suggestion that motifs of literary self-denigration can simply be discarded on the grounds that they are conceits or jokes. Most statements made in epigram fall within the category of joking to some degree, but this does not mean that these jokes cannot also have serious content.[104] Take, for instance, the motif of the book's erasure in water: 1.5, 4.10, 3.100, and 9.58 all revolve around the notion of

---

[101] Note also 1.1.4–6; 8.69.

[102] A similar reversal of traditional aesthetic priorities occurs in the motif of immediate publication, by contrast with the long period of compositional *labor limae* recommended by Horace and Catullus: e.g. *Epigrams* 1.25.

[103] Fowler (1995a), 199–200.

[104] Macleod (1977), 359–76, demonstrates the importance of not simply aligning the jocular with whimsical irrelevance: 'we should beware of making "serious" mean the same as "factual", or "funny" the same as "imaginary": for on that criterion Attic tragedy would be far funnier than Attic comedy. And a poem represents a unitary world: to distinguish real from invented elements within it is to sift what the poet has deliberately blended', 360.

erasure by water as an appropriate fate for Martial's writings, presumably with the expectation that the book can be recycled. This motif is itself obviously a joke, given that Martial probably does not really expect recipients of his *libellus* to scrub it clean with a sponge or otherwise allow it to be erased in water. Yet the conceit nonetheless presents structural similarities to the Catullan and Horatian *topos* of the recycling of the literary work of low quality in the form of wrapping for incense or fish, a conceit ostensibly facetious, but also serious insofar as it distinguishes the immortal work, defined by its transcendence of a limited, physical existence, from the ephemeral work, that ends its short life devoted to a sordid, and purely material, function.[105] The rhetoric of playful joking in Martial presents the reader with scenarios that cannot be taken literally, but cannot be disregarded either. Another good example of this is the degrading notion of 'writing for money'. *Epigrams* 1.117, 4.72, 9.73, and 11.108 present scenarios in which the author seeks payment from the reader, avoids sending a copy *gratis* by directing the potential reader to the bookseller, or regrets that the occupation of poetry is not sufficiently profitable. This is clearly, on some level, a joke, but the joke of 'poetry for hire' is one that Martial makes throughout his *Epigrams* in many different forms, with the effect that it imprints itself onto the pattern of his self-representation as a writer.

Yet even if we choose to take such jokes seriously, and confer on them a metaliterary significance beyond that of a transparently disingenuous conceit, we face a deeper problem: the lexicon of literary concepts on which such jokes or conceits are based derive from the standards set by classical literary aesthetics. In the case of 'writing for money', the joke very precisely subverts the aesthetic criterion of the literary work's inexhaustibility as an object of the reader's interest, that is, its distinctness from other commodities that are 'used up' in their ephemeral function and thus can be assigned a finite, monetary value.[106] The criteria of literary quality and the writer's integrity as established by Catullus and the Augustan poets—the immortality of the work, the writer's ethical autarky, eschewal of motives of financial enrichment, avoidance of the appearance of dependence on the patron, and disdain for recitation—are precisely those which post-Augustan writers, such as Juvenal and Martial, often consciously invert in the construction of their own literary *personae*. Thus Juvenal presents himself as a reciter, obsessed with the material success of others, undermined ethically by his *ira*, who, far from achieving rustic autarky, writes his satires under direct pressure from the sordid, urban reality of contemporary Rome. Martial, in the meanwhile, produces a self-avowedly ephemeral work that is ideal for recitation at dinner parties, typically located within the sphere of urban sociability, and compromised by the author's ingratiating attitude towards patrons. These subtle inversions of the Augustan rhetoric of autonomy, however, do not define literary activity on a totally new basis: rather, the terms of denigration themselves function as an implicit continuation of the aesthetic standards they appear to undermine. Martial disavows the autonomy of the work, depicting instead a mode of writing

---

[105] Catullus c. 95.8; Hor. *Epist.* 2.1.269–70.

[106] Oliensis (1998), 197, observes the presence of this criterion in Horace's evocation of 'exchanges that are finished when they are transacted, exchanges that leave no saving remainder' at the close of *Epistles* 2.1.

subordinated to social uses, yet his disavowal so precisely traces out the contours of the Augustan aesthetic as to invoke it by negative image. Thus Martial's claim that his epigrams are sub-literary, use-directed, and bounded by specific material modes—that is, not autonomous, not Augustan—must be seen as a rhetorical move made *from within* the assumptions of literary autonomy, not as a means of departure from them.

My characterization of Martial's tensional metaliterary attitude towards classical standards depends on the assumption that he participates in a broader debate regarding the nature of literary activity with his predecessors in first-person poetry such as Catullus and Horace, rather than simply playing out inherent reflexes of the epigrammatic genre. It is in the lower genres with a realist orientation that one usually sees reference made to writing and books in explicit, material terms, as opposed to metaphorical expressions, and even more specifically, epigram's focus on simple or everyday objects constitutes one of the most established aspects of its theory and tradition.[107] If these generic features are seen as determining Martial's poetics of the book, then it becomes harder to argue that Martial's images of literary materiality afford a particularly striking conception of literature, and further, that they can be read as part of a post-classical literary aesthetics. Yet the argument from genre cuts both ways. According to another reading of the same set of facts, Martial's choice to write epigram in the first place, and continue to write it, stems from his interest in creating a form of literature that is based on the notion of ephemeral usefulness, and vividly advertises the concrete aspects of its production, circulation, reception, and use. We thus need to appreciate both the extent to which Martial's work is informed by generic conventions, and also how, by controlling the selection of generic traits to be foregrounded, expanded, modified, or marginalized, Martial reinvents epigram in order to construct a particular conception of literature.

Martial's most salient image relating to the physical book takes the form of a Catullan commendation of the *libellus* to a patron.[108] The patron, like Catullus' Nepos who can vouch that his poems *esse aliquid* ('are something', c.1.4), plays the role of *vindex* ('protector'), both in socially supporting, disseminating, and vouching for the quality of the book, and in guaranteeing its quality through emendation. These poems are Catullan not only in the way they depict a *libellus* of nugatory *versiculi* commended to a patron in a vividly imagined moment of social exchange, but in many cases, recall details of Catullan phrasing.[109] Catullus' tentative and somewhat deprecatory attitude towards his 'little book', the impression of a playful social gesture, and the work's link with the patron all become part of Martial's literary self-representation.

There are important differences, however. Martial does not usually choose to express his expectation of immortality in these particular poems, and if not simply self-disparaging, tends to focus on the patron's confirmation of the work's value and its contemporary circulation, as opposed to its inherent value and posthumous glory. Another important difference, so obvious that it may escape notice,

---

[107] See Salemme (1976), and La Penna (1992), 7–44.
[108] Citroni (1986) and (1988); White (1974).
[109] For examples, see Paukstadt (1876), 10–11.

lies in the very fact that Martial dedicates his *libellus* frequently throughout his *oeuvre*, often many times within a given book, and to many different patrons. Martial, by comparison with Catullus, both intensifies the emphasis on his book's social function, and defines that function as iterable, applicable to diverse situations and patrons. The reader is given the impression of a work that, rather than having one, discrete moment of dedication placed liminally at its opening, is continually and everywhere permeable to such uses and social applications. In 4.10, Martial goes as far as to literalize this permeability, inverting Catullus' *arida modo pumice expolitum* ('[my little book] just now polished with dry pumice' c. 1.2) with the image of a book *novus*, but not yet trimmed and still damp (*nec adhuc rasa mihi fronte libellus, / pagina dum tangi non bene sicca timet*, '[while] my little book's edges are not yet trimmed, while its page, not properly dry, is afraid to be touched . . .', 1–2), to be sent to his patron Faustinus. The Catullan tonality, which includes the term *nugae* and the book being sent as a *munus* ('gift'), is unmistakable, but so is Martial's ingenious subversion of Catullus' neat, trimmed, and integral Callimachean *libellus*. The book, already damp, is, of course, ready for erasure with a sponge (5–6). In general, Martial accepts Catullus' neoteric programme only selectively,[110] and where Catullus achieves a delicate balance between the rhetoric of occasionality and the work's orientation towards posterity, in Martial the emphasis on ephemeral usefulness has become so insistent and pervasive as to convert this balance into paradox and polarity.

In general, Martial develops Augustan motifs of Callimachean humility, but in such a way as to undermine the implicit criterion of aesthetic rigor which typically accompanies such motifs. I mentioned above the rhetorical structure known as the *recusatio*, whereby the poet disavows expansive, poetic ambitions, sometimes on the grounds of a lack of poetic capacity, in order to claim for himself instead the 'slender' (*tenuis*) domain of Callimachean rigour. This *topos*, ostensibly self-deprecating, but only barely concealing a claim to superior aesthetic control within a narrowed domain, is crucial to the poetics of Horace, Virgil of the *Eclogues*, and the elegists. Catullus, while he does not follow the Callimachean blueprint in its particular details, nonetheless balances an intense consciousness of the triviality of his work with a commitment to aesthetic rigor. Martial, then, in his own disavowal of grand ambitions for the micro-domain of epigram, can be seen as the inheritor of an element of Catullan and Augustan literary rhetoric. Yet there are differences of tone and emphasis in Martial's epigrammatic *recusationes*, and in his corresponding avowal of the values proper to Callimachean aesthetics. Take, for instance, the Callimachean criterion of the poet's association with poverty: Martial applies this ethical trait to his own *persona*, but instead of an idealized, Epicurean poverty, we have, in Martial's case, harsh, urban poverty, which, according to a recurring joke in the *Epigrams*, does not signify the writer's autarky, so much as render him dependent on patrons for the basic comforts of life. Another example can be found in Martial's translation of Callimachus' *mega biblion mega kakon* ('big book, big nuisance') into epigram: the concern with *brevitas* becomes associated, not with the work's aesthetic density, but with the need to fend off the reader's boredom, and

---

[110] For Martial's resistance to certain elements of the neoteric programme and Callimachean aesthetics, see Citroni (1968), 280ff.; and Preston (1920), 342.

the financial constraints of book-production.[111] Finally, the *otium* ('leisure') of Catullus and the Augustans becomes, in Martial's epigrammatic translation, *pigritia* ('laziness'). In each case, a motif of rigour and integrity in the small genres is literalized, pushed to extremes, and in the process, undermined in its basic premise.

Martial's references to literary materiality display an understanding of the intricate code and protocols that belong to this tradition, even as they activate a potential already present within the epigrammatic genre. For Martial, epigram does not much determine, as allow, his striking materialist vision of literature, affording him a unique position from which he can carve out a niche for himself within the Roman literary landscape. His poetics of the book reflects on, develops, and ultimately caps the already significant tradition of metaliterary interest in the physical book from Catullus to Ovid. Martial positions himself at the culmination of such metaliterary interest, not only by combining elements of the literary programme of Catullus, Horace, and Ovid in his own distinct formulation, but in the sheer relentlessness of his materialist vision.[112] All of the various details regarding writing and book-format occur in other writers than Martial, but in Martial we find them all together, consistently repeated, so as to create a fully articulated poetics of the physical book. Martial chooses not only to represent a world composed of physical reality and sordid objects, but chooses to situate his own activity as a writer, and his books' existence, within the same potentially degrading framework. Martial's perspective, which retrieves the elegant Catullan *libellus* only to refigure it as the product of the arbitrary errors of copyists, the merchandise of a bookseller, and the object of financial calculation, applies epigram's predilection for realistic description to the continual scrutiny and inversion of classical literary standards.

Like Horace of the *Satires*, Martial feels free to represent the materiality of his text because of his low-style genre, but there is a relentlessness in his representation of the material conditions of book production absent even from Horace's hexametric compositions. One of the main models of Horatian *sermo* ('speech'), after all, is that of refined conversation among elite *amici* ('friends'): the publication of his book is viewed with reluctance and concern[113] rather than—as in Martial—an incontestable fact providing opportunity for endless ironic manipulation.

> Qui tecum cupis esse meos ubicumque libellos
>   et comites longae quaeris habere viae,
> hos eme, quos artat brevibus membrana tabellis:
>   scrinia da magnis, me manus una capit.
> ne tamen ignores ubi sim venalis et erres
>   urbe vagus tota, me duce certus eris:

---

[111] *Ep.* 2.1, 1.118. Citroni (1975), xxxviii, on 1.118: 'una brillante e orginale versione epigrammatica del principio callimacheo'.

[112] Fowler (1995a), 199.

[113] This reluctance is explicit in *Epistles* 1.20, but seems already to be implied in *Satires* 1.10, in which the speaker offers up his polished *libellus*: he is *contentus paucis lectoribus* ('content with few readers' 74), including Maecenas, Virgil, Pollio, etc., but must envisage the possibility of wider circulation (*villibus in ludis*, 'in common schools', 75). On this epistle and Horace's treatment of the topic of publication, see Oliensis (1995).

libertum docti Lucensis quaere Secundum
limina post Pacis Palladiumque forum.   (1.2)

You who want to have my little books with you wherever you go, and seek to have them as companions for a long trip, buy these, which parchment compresses in compact tablets. Give book boxes to the great,[114] one hand takes hold of me. So that you may know where I am for sale, and not stray wandering over the whole city, you will be sure of your way under my guidance: seek Secundus, freedman of learned Lucensis, behind the entrance of the Temple of Peace and Pallas' forum.

Horace, in *Epistles* 1.20, manifested concern that his book, like a slave who leaves his master's farm to go to the city, would end up prostituting itself. No such worries here: the second poem of Martial's first book—in sharp contrast to Horace's melancholy epilogue—immediately proclaims itself for sale (*venalis*). Thus the notion of the work as a physical object of specifiable monetary value, sold at a specific location within the city like any other commodity, is brought to the fore in this introductory poem, whereas in Horace, the book's self-prostitution is presented as the regrettable after-effect of writing, not its opening guise. The other metaphor implicit in Horace's epistle, besides prostitution, is that of manumission: the freedman, like the book, is liberated from the hand of his *dominus* ('master') and sent out into the world to make his fortune. Horace, by contrast with Martial, seems almost ponderously metaphorical in his meditation on the 'liberation' of his manuscript. The epigrammatist does not appear to concern himself with such metaphors of liberation, but does mention an actual *libertus* ('freedman')—the one in charge of selling his book.

By presenting his book as an object for sale, and even going so far as to mention the precise address at which it might be bought, Martial effectively discourages the notion of his poetry as transcendent and autonomous of its material conditions of production. At the same time, the status of this gesture as a joke, and the joke's dependence, in turn, on the classical notion of the work's transcendence of mere physicality, render Martial's literary position here complex. Martial displays his awareness of, and concern with, this criterion even as he subverts it. Moreover, the main piece of 'information' communicated by the epigram—that Martial's book can be obtained in codex form—is not without programmatic meaning. The advertisement of the codex format first of all gives an impression of portability and hence mobility. A book which can accompany its owner on a journey more resembles a practical instrument of casual entertainment—a way to beguile the long hours of travel with easy reading—than a serious text designed to engage the reader's deepest powers of concentration. The lightness and portability of the text, according to this reading, corresponds to the triviality of its content. The text does not demand the consecration of the reader to its depths of meaning, but is easily adapted to whatever the reader is doing.

This idea of the book as completely adapted to the various circumstances of its use and social circulation can be seen as a failure in regard to autonomy. This impression of the book's lack of independence recurs in the final lines, where we

---

[114] Howell (1980), ad loc., suggests as a meaning for *magnis*, 'great authors', which is tempting, as it would fit Martial's interest, as manifested in his *Apophoreta*, in the harmony, or dissonance, between the 'size' of a genre and the size of a book; on which, see below.

see it for sale in the shadow of one of Domitian's building projects.[115] Yet at the same time, another possibility remains implicit in the language of the book's description: *hos eme, quos artat brevibus membrana tabellis … me manus una capit* ('buy these, which parchment compresses in compact tablets … one hand grasps me', 3–4). The language describing the book's portability also hints at its physical self-containment (*me manus una capit*, 'one hand encompasses me') and restricted domain (*artat*, 'compresses'). The delimited sphere of Martial's *Gedichtsbuch* recalls the confined spaces of Augustus literary discourse: the Horatian *angulus* ('corner, nook'), the *angustus lectus* ('narrow bed') of elegy.[116] Even this brief description of the physical book, then, carries larger literary meanings: it points simultaneously towards the outward movement of the book in circulation (*longae … viae*, 'long journey') and the inwardness and self-limitation of poetic discourse (*brevibus … tabellis*, 'compact tablets').

With these reflections, we arrive at a central paradox: Martial's representation of his poetry in terms of utility, discardability, transparency of meaning, and proximity to the sub-literary is itself a carefully devised strategy of literary self-definition. I have been suggesting that this materialist viewpoint on literary activity is itself part of Martial's strategy of self-denigration and identification with an ephemeral mode of writing dedicated to immediate social uses. The book is merely an object, and as such, can be used and discarded. Yet the relentlessness of Martial's presentation of the book as a material object for sale at the bookshop may also have the effect, paradoxically, of bringing the book's literary qualities more insistently to the fore. The reader, if s/he has access to 1.2, already owns Martial's book, and needs no directions to the bookshop.[117] For such a reader, these (belated) details regarding the book's availability for sale and physical attributes only serve to focus attention on the fictional nature of the representation. The relentlessness of Martial's materialist fiction thus creates the basis for a striking polarization of hermeneutic options: the reader must either accept the problematic fiction afforded by the text's literal account of itself, or assume a literariness the text persistently disavows.

My reading of literary materiality in Martial has so far suggested that his metaliterary attitude is characterized by a simultaneous affirmation and negation of his work's literary status and importance. In order to gauge the extent to which this polarity informs Martial's *oeuvre*, it will be helpful to focus on a major self-representational motif in the *Epigrams*: the motif of Saturnalian entertainment. The idea of Saturnalian entertainment defines two of Martial's earliest collections of verse, the *Xenia* and *Apophoreta*. Martial's representation of epigrammatic activity in Saturnalian terms, however, persists throughout his *oeuvre*, as does the denigratory conception of epigram as light entertainment. Examination of the early, explicitly Saturnalian collections will allow us to see in a particularly clear

---

[115] As Sullivan (1991), 149, remarks, Martial's description of the *forum transitorium* as the *forum Palladium* is 'a specific compliment to Domitian', since the emperor was building a Temple of Pallas there. Coleman (1998), 31ff., examines Martial's relation to the Flavian amphitheatre.

[116] Propertius 1.8.33; on Horace and the *angulus*, see Ferri (1993).

[117] See Fowler (1995a), 202ff., for a discussion of such ironies, and in particular, the question of codex vs book-roll.

form the implications of this model, and specifically, how they envision a link between poetry and occasion.[118]

A book devoted exclusively to a single occasion is by definition ephemeral, and corresponds, as a single, concrete object, to the individual occasion on which it is used, in this case, the exchange of gifts on the Saturnalia. This one-time deployment of the individual book in an act of gift-exchange undermines the more expansive notion of the literary work that does not reside in any single copy or performance, and outlives the occasions with which it is associated. The basic dimensions of this idea can be found already in Catullus c. 14, which was discussed in Chapter 2 above, but which merits reconsideration in light of present concerns. Here, as in c. 1, we have a *libellus*, but this time a bad one (*horribilem et sacrum libellum*, 'a dreadful and execrable little book', 12), which Catullus' friend Calvus, in sending it to him on the Saturnalia, maliciously identifies with the ephemeral chapbooks traditionally enjoyed as a holiday diversion and discarded. The poets who make up this book are significantly described, in the final line, as *saecli incommoda* (23), that is, as burdens on *their own* age, rather than poets who produce a legacy for future ages. In the meanwhile, the occasional and ostensibly situation-specific nature of Catullus' own poem enters into the equation. On the one hand, Catullus presents a poem narrowly focused on an ephemeral act of joking between friends, which occurs, moreover, within a tightly circumscribed occasional time-frame: the day, and immediate aftermath, of the Saturnalia, *optimo dierum* ('best of days', 15). On the other hand, Catullus' choice to preserve this otherwise ephemeral joking in his poetry book makes available a set of implicit aesthetic criteria for the contemplation of future readers.

Martial inherits this set of issues regarding occasion, ephemerality, and the *libellus*, but, rather than looking on the Saturnalian *libellus* as a foil to his own *libellus*, the epigrammatist chooses to associate his own work with a Saturnalian model and inhabit a fully elaborated literary world based on this model. Just as Martial exceeds Catullan self-denigration in inhabiting, rather than rejecting, the Saturnalian *libellus*, he applies, in an epigram that appears at the opening of the *Xenia*,[119] the Catullan image of the recycled work not to a foil-figure such as Catullus' Volusius, but to himself.

<blockquote>
Ne toga cordylis et paenula desit olivis
    aut inopem metuat sordida blatta famem,
perdite Niliacas, Musae, mea damna, papyros:
    postulat ecce novos ebria bruma sales.
non mea magnanimo depugnat tessera talo,
    senio nec nostrum cum cane quassat ebur:
haec mihi charta nuces, haec est mihi charta fritillus:
    alea nec damnum nec facit ista lucrum.   (13.1)
</blockquote>

That tuna may not lack a toga, olives a coat, nor the filthy bookworm fear poverty and hunger, waste some papyrus of the Nile, Muses—the loss is mine. See, the drunken winter season demands new jokes. My dice do not contend with great-hearted knucklebones, nor

---

[118] For a treatment of poetic aspects of the *Xenia* and *Apophoreta*, see Stroup (2006).

[119] It has been suspected that 13.1–2 do not belong to Martial's original collection, but have been imported from elsewhere: see Leary (2001), 37.

does my ivory rattle with six and ace. This page is my nuts, this page my dice box: such gambling does not bring loss or gain.

The tone of self-disparagement here is particularly strong: Martial enlists the help of his nugatory Muse for the purpose of wasting paper, and describes his writing as 'his own loss' (*mea damna*)—presumably a monetary loss incurred by the purchase of paper—, thereby subjecting his verse to a degrading financial calculation. Moreover, it is not his poetic vocation which leads Martial to write poetry, but his poetry follows as the effect, as it were, of the holiday season itself: *postulat ecce novos ebria bruma sales* ('See, the drunken winter season demands new jokes'). This line, along with the reference to his poetry as a form of Saturnalian gambling, establishes a close link between book and ephemeral occasion.

Even as Martial identifies his own work with the ephemeral, Saturnalian chapbook, he engages in dialogue with the classic, immortal works of Greek and Roman literature by absorbing them among his hospitality gifts. The works are described more in terms of their physical format than their literary qualities, but there are nonetheless, embedded in these descriptions, elegant metaliterary observations, often revolving around issues of the large and the small, the trivial and the ambitious. Thus in 14.183–6, four poems on works by Homer and Virgil form a neat, interlocking structure: nugatory Homer (*Batrachomyomachia*); serious Homer (*Iliad* and *Odyssey*); nugatory Virgil (*Culex*); serious Virgil (complete works). In the second distich of each pair, the vastness of the work, both in length and literary ambition, is contrasted with its compact codex format.[120] Thus on Homer: *Ilias et Priami regnis inimicus Ulixes / multiplici pariter condita pelle latent* ('The *Iliad* and Ulysses, enemy of Priam's realm, both lie hidden in multiple folds of skin', 14.184). And on Virgil: *Quam brevis immensum cepit membrana Maronem! / ipsius vultus prima tabella gerit* ('How small the parchment which has encompassed vast Maro! The first page has his portrait on it', 14.186). Not only, then, does Martial choose light works of literature for his gift list, he reduces great works by the same authors to a compact format—he epigrammatically compresses them (*artat*, 14.190). Virgil and Homer do indeed form part of Martial's text, but the complex texture of meaning of these classic works has been reduced to the compass of a gift tag, set alongside distichs about monkeys and lapdogs. Further, the presence of Virgil in Martial's text does not consist in the incorporation of Virgilian themes, language, and motifs into the fabric of the poetry, but in a two-line description of Virgil's text as a physical object. 'Virgil', in Martial's epigrammatic materialism, becomes a gathering of animal skins, not a repertory of figures and poetic structures.

It is not only the codex format that sustains metaliterary scrutiny, but the very fact that Martial evokes the classics of Latin literature as concretely imagined copies, rather than as materially indeterminate works enjoying an existence larger than any single copy. One of the defining fictions of the *Apophoreta* is the

---

120 This alternation of light and serious is interestingly juxtaposed with the collection's central motif of alternation between poor and rich gifts (*divitis alternas et pauperis . . . sortes*, 14.1.5). Literary weight and seriousness may be reduced to the scope of a modest codex, while a relatively trivial work may be granted the honour of a deluxe edition. On the question of the worth of books in Martial's *Apophoreta*, see Birt (1882), 71ff.

exchange of holiday joke-books: Martial's book, according to this fiction, takes the form of an individual copy handed from one person to another, like the *libellus* given to Catullus by Calvus. The general reader, however, does not encounter Martial's *Apophoreta* as a gift-book donated by Martial on some, determinate occasion, but as a literary work available in any number of copies or material formats. The tension, then, between the occasional deployment of a specific, material copy, and the work's existence in a broader, less materially circumscribed mode, informs not only the series of epigrams devoted to classics in codex format, but Martial's Saturnalian poetry as a whole. The work as general entity exists above and beyond particular, social contexts in which it might be used, whereas in Martial's fiction of the concrete gift-book, that general entity is fragmented into individual copies and use-contexts. Martial's Saturnalian *libellus*, if we take this fiction literally, is itself just one more concrete gift-item like those represented in his poetry; conversely, if we view this fiction sceptically (as, to a certain degree, we must), Martial's 'book' becomes the materially indeterminate, mimetic space within which such gift-items are playfully evoked.

Within this larger fiction of the work's fragmentation into gift-copies, there is yet another fiction at work, namely the internal scenario whereby Martial's distichs function as tags for various gifts (including books): these objects are to be 'carried away' (*apophoreta*) by the various guests. Within the book itself, then, the notion that each individual distich, or object, can be sundered from the collection and put to separate use, suggests an internal fragmentation of subject matter comparable to the fracturing of the work into individual copies.

> Quo vis cumque loco potes hunc finire libellum:
> versibus explicitum est omne duobus opus.
> lemmata si quaeris cur sint adscripta, docebo:
> ut, si malueris, lemmata sola legas.   (14.2)

You can finish this little book wherever you like. Each piece is completed in two lines. If you want to know why headings are added, I will tell you: so that, if you prefer, you may read only the headings.

Not only is the reader excused from the obligation of confronting Martial's poetic discourse as a coherent totality, he may even limit his experience of it to the bare denotative lemmata themselves: *lemmata sola legas*.[121] The reader of epigram, then, hardly need enter its discursive world at all, since it is possible to experience it in terms of pure denotation, pure referentiality. This is an unsparing refusal of literary meaning, and should give some sense of how Martial's *poetica degli oggetti* and the issues of occasion and literariness are closely interconnected. At the furthest horizon of literary materialism, the work is no longer a fabric of

---

[121] There is a strikingly similar motif of the non-integrity of the book in the Elder Pliny. In the preface to his *Naturalis historia*, he introduces his work with the vocabulary of nugatory triviality so common in Martial, and in *HN praef.*33 points out to Titus how the table of contents allows his reader to read certain parts of his work and skip others. On this correspondence, see Citroni (1988), 10. The same idea may be implied by Pliny the Younger's claim that he put together his collection of epistles *ut quaeque in manus venerat* ('as each one came to hand', 1.1.1); i.e. there is no integral structure.

interconnected motifs available to the synthetic understanding of a general reader, but a collection of disparate items, each applied to their own, occasional use.

Of course, it is impossible to take this fiction literally. Indeed, as Fowler notes, the fact that 'these objects have no existence outside Martial's poetry' undermines the notion of anyone physically carrying them off.[122] It goes almost without saying, moreover, that only the most literal-minded reader will actually follow the instructions given by Martial in 14.2, and pay no attention to the structuring of his poetic discourse. It does not take long before the reader begins to think about the relations among the various objects, the meanings which emerge in the course of the collection as a result of accumulating impressions and motifs.[123] By countering the reader's expectation of a literary work defined as an object of sustained, hermeneutic scrutiny and integral discourse, Martial obliges the reader to read constantly against the grain of the work's own directives.

The idea of the book as a collection of detachable, individual units rather than an autonomous discourse to be encountered as a totality, far from being limited to the *Apophoreta*, recurs throughout Martial's later work. In 10.1, Martial advises the reader to whom his book seems long to 'make' it short by choosing to read only a few poems: *fac tibi me quam cupis ipse brevem* ('make me as short for yourself as you like', 4). Such a motif, although clearly facetious, is based on the premise that the *Epigrams* provide a repertory of entertainment pieces, not an integral fabric of poetic meaning. One of the most important ways in which Martial's book gives the appearance of fragmentation, and dispersal over various social occasions, is the fiction of its performance of social duties. In 3.5, the book departs to perambulate the city on its own in an Ovidian manner, *sine me cursurus in urbem* ('off to the city without me', 1), but the author, fearing for his book, confers on it a social procedure which will secure it hospitality at the house of Julius Martialis and his wife: *hos tu seu pariter sive hunc illamve priorem / videris, hoc dices: 'Marcus havere iubet'* ('whether you see them together or him or her first, you will say this: "Marcus sends his greetings"', 9–10). Other poems similarly emphasize the book's need of a *vindex* ('champion').[124] These epigrams, as discussed above, fragment the work into multiple, social applications, with each patron allotted his own dedicatory poem. Other poems depict how the book, after making its entry into society as the *protégé* of a literary patron, ranges freely among the various dinner parties, colonnades and crossroads of the city, or is otherwise recited in an urban setting.[125] In yet others, the book as surrogate client performs *officia* on Martial's behalf.[126]

Thus the way in which Martial stages the fragmentation of his book into various social situations—its performance of the duty of *salutatio* ('morning greeting'), its use as repertory of entertaining *nugae* ('trifles') in a convivial context, its quotability in casual conversation—suggests that his book is always disintegrating into multiple use-functions. The insistent quality of this fiction, however, is matched by discrete, but nonetheless important, expressions of Martial's concern with the

---

[122] Fowler (1995a), 223.

[123] Leary (1998), 41–2, discusses the artistic principles of selection, and skill in arrangement, which lie behind the ostensible form of the miscellany.

[124] *Ep.* 3.2, 4.86, 7.26, 7.97, 8.72. [125] *Ep.* 5.16, 7.97, 7.51.

[126] *Ep.* 1.107, 1.108, 3.5, 10.58.

book's existence as an integral entity: thus in 7.85, he writes: *facile est epigram-mata belle / scribere, sed librum scribere difficile est* ('it is easy to write epigrams prettily, but it is hard to write a book'). This epigram, with analytic precision, brings out the difference between epigrams produced singly, and a book that is somehow more than the sum of its contents.[127] The same distinction is expressed from a more jocular and negative perspective in 1.16, in which Martial admits that his book has its share of good, mediocre, and bad poems, but that this is in the nature of the thing: *aliter non fit, Avite, liber* ('in no other way, Avitus, does a book get made'). In other words, the emphasis must fall on the book's success as a whole, not on the success or failure of individual pieces.[128] This insistence counters, and is meant as response to, the conventional idea of epigram as the quintessential one-off piece. There was something provocative and novel in the project of creating a monumental *oeuvre* of epigrams endowed with continuity by a sustained authorial persona. Martial was aware of the challenge to convention this presented, and was careful to answer potential criticism that might arise from it. The fact, then, that Martial not only structured his *oeuvre* around the book as a unit of organization, and paid careful attention to the internal structuring of individual books, but also dedicated programmatic epigrams to this particular topic, reveals the depth of his concern with the book as an integral entity.

We have once again arrived at a hermeneutic dilemma created by diverging tendencies of self-representation in Martial's work. The overt fiction of fragmentation, dispersal, and discardability at work in the Saturnalian poetry conflicts with the work's potential to be understood in a traditionally literary manner, as a coherent, mimetic domain, to be read and reread for its literary interest, rather than discarded as a holiday diversion linked to a specific occasion. It is not, however, simply a matter of disregarding such fictions and re-instating the reality, because such fictions, even if not taken literally, nonetheless do relate in some, broader way to Martial's definition of his poetics. This latter point applies not to Martial alone, but to many works in the tradition of Roman poetry. Particular to Martial is the manner in which the fictional premises governing his work's self-representation are constructed so as to disavow, not only the grand, but literary status and importance per se. In order to be considered literary, a work must possess a relevance broader than that of an ephemeral occasion, transcend mere usefulness, and have the potential to endure over time, and yet Martial's epigrammatic fictions continually emphasize the occasional, the useful, and the ephemeral. At the furthest point of its development, Martial's disavowal of the autonomous, integral work thus approaches the category of the subliterary.

Augustan poets spent a great deal of effort steering their works away from the appearance of direct insertion into contexts of ephemeral, social utility. If their work was allowed to present some element of 'utility', it was the more dignified,

---

[127] This epigram, and Martial's conception of the *liber*, are discussed by Citroni (1968), 272ff.; Fowler (1995a), *passim*. Note also the important discussion in Fitzgerald (2007), 139–66 of 'the society of the book'. For the debate over pre-publication *libelli*, see Fowler (1995a) and White (1996).

[128] Note also 7.81: *'triginta toto mala sunt epigrammata libro.' / si totidem bona sunt, Lause, bonus liber est* ('"There are thirty bad epigrams in the whole book." If there are as many good ones, Lausus, it is a good book').

generalized moral utility of the *monumentum*, an integral contribution to Roman culture and values. Martial, as I have shown, reverses this self-representational emphasis, and makes of point of directing his epigrams towards ephemeral, quotidian ends. The most explicit staging of the work's insertion into the social realm is the frequent gesture of the commendation of the book to the patron. The commendation poem follows a recognizable syntax, which may include any of the following: the characterization of the book as timid and waiting for the appropriate moment to disturb the patron; the description of the book's itinerary through Rome towards the patron's house; the playful disparagement of its quality; an expression of admiration for the patron's learning and literary taste; the association of the book with late-night drinking and/or Saturnalian festivity; and an appreciation of the patron's ability to emend, protect, and circulate the *libellus*.[129] There is much in this poetic 'grammar' of commendation that might inspire a reading of Martial's epigrams as primarily oriented towards pleasing individual patrons. Specifically, motifs of deference, marginality, and timidity before the patron reverse the expectations built into the aesthetic code of first-person poetry. According to this code, the work, if it is to attain independent validity in the eyes of future readers, must maintain its own, literary values in its confrontation with the patron; otherwise it risks adapting itself to the patron's wishes and thereby undermining its integrity and universal literary relevance.

Martial's reversal of such strictures is too systematic to be accidental. In 3.2, Martial commends the book to the protection of his patron, Faustinus:

> Cuius vis fieri, libelle, munus?
> festina tibi vindicem parare,
> ne nigram cito raptus in culinam
> cordylas madida tegas papyro
> vel turis piperisve sis cucullus.
> Faustini fugis in sinum? sapisti.
> cedro nunc licet ambules perunctus
> et frontis gemino decens honore
> pictis luxurieris umbilicis,
> et te purpura delicata velet
> et cocco rubeat superbus index.
> illo vindice nec Probum timeto.

Whose gift do you wish to be, little book? Quickly find yourself a protector, lest you are rushed off to a sooty kitchen and wrap tuna with your damp papyrus, or become a hood for incense or pepper. You flee to Faustinus' embrace? You are wise. Now you may walk about anointed with cedar, handsomely adorned on both brows, and luxuriating in your painted bosses, you may clothe yourself in delicate purple, and your proud title may blush with scarlet. With his protection, have no fear even of Probus.

The epigram's opening phrase recalls Catullus' similarly rhetorical question: *cui dono lepidum novum libellum...?* ('To whom do I give this new, charming little book...?') More interesting, however, is the reference to the closing lines of

---

[129] *Ep.* 1.52, 1.70, 3.2, 3.5, 4.10, 4.82, 4.86, 5.5, 5.6, 5.80, 7.26, 7.97, 7.99, 8.72, 9.99, 10.20, 10.93, 12.1, 12.2, 121.11.

Horace *Epistles* 2.1: *deferar in vicum vendentem tus et odores / et piper et quidquid chartis amicitur ineptis* ('. . . [lest] I am carried into the quarter where incense and perfumes are for sale, and pepper, and whatever is wrapped in graceless sheet of paper', 269–70). Horace's evocation of the failed work, in which, he says, he would not wish to find himself entombed because of the inept praise of an inferior poet, occurs within the context of a larger argument, which itself has the function of *recusatio*. In this particular section of the argument (250ff.), Horace is suggesting that a patron should not wish for inept praise, because it will not serve him well, and so, in Horace's case, Augustus should allow him remain within the lowly domain of his *sermones* ('conversations'), rather than oblige him to sing the emperor's *res gestae* ('deeds'). Implicitly, of course, Horace is also concerned that, if the integrity of his small, Callimachean domain were compromised, his own work would not last beyond its ephemeral use as praise-poetry. Thus the image of the failed work recycled as wrapping for incense, in the larger context of Horace's epistle, acts as a warning against the danger presented by forced praise of the patron. Martial, in adapting this image, reverses the emphasis: rather than evoking the spectre of the failed work in order to pry the work free from obligation to the patron, he suggests that the work's immortality depends directly on the patron's protection. Martial, then, not only flatters the patron, he alerts the reader, through an unmistakable literary allusion, to the way in which this flattery reverses the aesthetic principle implicit in an Augustan *recusatio*.

Martial similarly displays consciousness of the aesthetic code informing the relation between patron and poet in his treatment of the theme of the *cena*. Horace, in *Odes* 1.20, renders the literary implications of the *cena* explicit in his insistence that if his patron Maecenas visits him, it will be on the poet's terms: Maecenas will drink inexpensive wine (*vile potabis modicis Sabinum / cantharis*, 'you will drink cheap Sabine in ordinary tankards', 1–2). Martial, in 10.45, shows himself acutely aware of the metaliterary significance of Horace's discourse on vintages, even as he reverses its priorities. Addressing an *adversarius* who finds Martial's poetry too 'rich' (*pingue*) in flattery and panegyric (*si quid lene mei dicunt et dulce libelli, / si quid honorificum pagina blanda sonat*, 'If my little books say anything smooth and pleasing, if my flattering page rings out with anything complimentary'), he advises him: *Vaticana bibas, si delectaris aceto* ('drink Vatican, if you delight in vinegar').[130] Martial, then, builds into representations of his relation with patrons an implicit comparison with his literary predecessors. In other poems, Martial goes beyond implicit comparison, and directly addresses the issue of broader historical changes in the structure of literary patronage. In 1.107, Martial offers a *recusatio* to his friend Julius Martialis, but whereas Augustan poets disavowed the grand in favour of their own slender style, Martial disavows the grandeur of the Augustans themselves:[131]

---

[130] Citroni (1968), 266, discusses this poem in terms of Martial's avoidance of personal attack; this may be implied in the contrast between *aceto* ('vinegar') and *lene . . . et dulce* ('smooth and pleasing'), but *honorificum* ('complimentary') and *blanda* ('flattering') suggest that more is at stake than an absence of defamatory content.

[131] On this form of *recusatio* in Martial, see Citroni (1968), 287ff.

> Saepe mihi dicis, Luci carissime Iuli,
>   'scribe aliquid magnum: desidiosus homo es.'
> otia da nobis, sed qualia fecerat olim
>   Maecenas Flacco Vergilioque suo:
> condere victuras temptem per saecula curas
>   et nomen flammis eripuisse meum.
> in steriles nolunt campos iuga ferre iuvenci:
>   pingue solum lassat, sed iuvat ipse labor.

Often you say to me, dearest Lucius Julius: 'Write something big. You are a lazy man'. Give me leisure of the sort that Maecenas once made for his Flaccus and his Virgil. I would try to fashion works that would live through the ages and snatch my name from the flames. Oxen are not willing to bear the yoke into barren fields. A rich soil is tiring, but the very labour is enjoyable.

According to this poem, Martial might be capable of producing a more ambitious work, destined for immortality, if he enjoyed patronage of the sort provided by Maecenas to Horace and Virgil. The putative motive for producing *aliquid magnum* ('something big') is represented, at least in part, as financial. The great patron would provide the poet with a level of remuneration that would in turn inspire a higher level of work, insofar as the poet, thus honoured, would not feel that he was ploughing a 'sterile' field (*steriles . . . campos*). Yet the issue here is not exclusively financial. A *Maecenas redivivus* would also, by some means not specified, alter the quality of the poet's literary *otium* (*otia . . . qualia*), freeing him to devote himself to a deeper, more exhausting, and ultimately more rewarding poetic labour, reminiscent, as the agricultural metaphor implies, of the poetic *labor* of Virgil's own *Georgics*.

We need not take this idea literally, any more than we take Augustan *recusationes* literally.[132] The motif remains significant, however, for the manner in which it connects Martial's nugatory genre of epigram (defined as <u>not</u> *aliquid magnum*) with a representation of contemporary patronage as somehow inferior to Maecenas' patronage of the Augustan poets. In 5.19 Martial develops this scenario with even greater specificity. The poet complains that Domitian's age is marred by one flaw alone, the fact that patronage has been degraded (*colit ingratas pauper amicitias*, 'the poor man cultivates thankless friendships', 8); therefore he suggests that Domitian himself assume the role of *amicus*.[133] If we combine the picture presented by this epigram with 1.107 and 7.55, and with other poems in which Martial represents himself as being forced to beg various patrons for small-scale gifts and in general suffer their ingratitude,[134] a broader picture begins to emerge: the writer, because he lacks the shelter provided by a long-term patron such as Maecenas provided for Augustan poets, becomes a sort of journeyman

---

[132] D'Elia (1981), 652, argues, on the basis of such indications in Martial, that patronage went into decline because *arrivistes* from the provinces did not know how to patronize in the grand old style: 'In un mondo "borgesizzato" il distacco fra "letteratura aristocratica" e "subletteratura popolare" si è attenuato in nome della "massificazione della cultura"'. But as White (1978), 77, points outs: 'We should not assume that, a century before Martial, the roles and rules of literary and social life were so differently arranged that the rewards of poets were generally more abundant'.

[133] The ideological dimension of this poem is discussed in Walter (1998), 225–6; see also Sullivan (1991), 119ff.

[134] On Martial's treatment of the *ingratus*, see Sullivan (1991), 118.

who must peddle his poetic compositions to various, minor patrons. He would be able to dedicate himself to the continuous labour involved in producing a literary masterpiece, instead of fragmenting his work into disparate, occasion-bound epigrams, if he were no longer required to serve the needs of multiple patrons. We have, then, in 1.107 an explicit connection made by Martial between patronage, epigram, and the decline from classical standards of literary depth and autonomy. The depth and integrity of the Augustan work are aligned with the issue of autonomy: if the poet were afforded the shelter of a grand patron, that is, if he enjoyed a measure of independence by virtue of high-level generosity, he would be able to focus on an ambitious, integral work, rather than continuously pursuing many smaller gifts.

It is significant that, after the assassination of Domitian and the accession of Nerva, Martial's position on the question of patronage (at least superficially) changes. With the tolerance and *cauta potestas* ('cautious exercise of power', 12.6.3) of Nerva, figured as a civilized ruler on the model of Numa, comes a new model of liberality. In 11.3, Martial pursues a familiar jocular argument, namely that he would write great works if he derived substantial, financial benefit, but here expresses the wish that a new Maecenas might follow on Nerva's restoration of the Augustan age (*cum pia reddiderint Augustum numina terris / et Maecenatem si tibi, Roma, darent!*, 9–10). In 12.6, developing this idea further, Martial effects a pointed contrast with Domitian in his praise of Nerva's tolerance of generosity: *largiri, praestare, breves extendere census / et dare quae faciles vix tribuere dei / nunc licet et fas est* ('to be generous, to provide, to broaden narrow means and to give what agreeable gods have scarcely bestowed is now allowed and lawful', 9–11).

In 12.4, Martial reverses his own 'there is no Maecenas' motif, claiming instead, in one of his most emphatic allusions to Horace, that his friend Terentius Priscus has been playing precisely that role for him all along:

> Quod Flacco Varioque fuit summoque Maroni
> Maecenas, atavis regibus ortus eques,
> gentibus et populis hoc te mihi, Prisce Terenti,
> fama fuisse loquax chartaque dicet anus.
> tu facis ingenium, tu, si quid posse videmur;
> tu das ingenuae ius mihi pigritiae.

What Maecenas, knight descended from ancient kings, was to Flaccus, Varius, and greatest Virgil, this, Priscus Terentius, talkative fame and my page in its old age will say to peoples and nations that you were to me. You make my talent, you make it, if I seem to have any ability; you give me the right to liberal idleness.

This epigram is dense with allusions to Martial's predecessors. Besides the citation of Horace *Odes* 1.1 in line 2, there is the allusion to Catullus' expression of gratitude to a friend in line 4, a glance at Propertius in his *tu facis ingenium* ('you make my talent'), and Catullus again, this time c. 1, is evoked in *si quid posse videmur* ('if we seem to have any ability').[135] The strong foregrounding of the poetic tradition is significant here, because Martial is stating that Priscus Terentius was a patron to him according to the ideals posited by that tradition, someone who gives the poet the right to a life of leisure dedicated to liberal studies

---

[135] Catullus c. 58.6; 1.3–4, 8–9; Propertius 2.1.4.

(*ingenuae . . . pigritiae*, 'liberal idleness'). One of the implications of this belated declaration, especially given its proximity to the *nunc licet et fas est* of 12.6 ('*now* it is allowed and lawful'), is that Martial would not have been able to make such a declaration under Domitian. Martial takes the opportunity provided by a new, more tolerant regime to record for posterity his gratitude to his long-time patron. The unstated understanding is that anyone who set themselves up, and were advertised in Martial's poetry as a major patron on the scale of Maecenas would have attracted the emperor's *invidia*. Closely connected, then, to Martial's persistent complaints regarding the absence of a Maecenas, and his suggestion that the emperor himself absorb this role, is Domitian's probable desire to dominate a field without any notable competitors.

There is more at work here, however, than Domitian's vanity alone, but a deeper structural feature of the relation between literature and power in the early empire. The figure of Maecenas, who stands at the centre of Martial's reflections on the historical changes in the patronage relation, was notable not only for the substantial gifts he was capable of offering poets, but because he constituted an intermediary figure between the writer and the emperor.[136] Maecenas at once relieved the writer of the need to court many, minor patrons by granting permanent *otium*, or to cite Martial's phrase, *ingenua pigritia*, and at the same time, shielded him from the potentially compromising situation of having to address the emperor directly as patron. This does not mean that poets were somehow essentially more independent under Augustus than under later emperors, but rather that the intermediary status of Maecenas, who was defined in his own way by a stance of humility and retreat as an *eques* ('knight'), allowed poets a loophole whereby they could construct a rhetoric of independence in their poetry. The rhetorical shelter provided by Maecenas allowed a writer such as Horace to balance his poetry's undeniable ideological and social commitments with motifs of ethical autonomy appropriate to the circumscribed, Callimachean domain of a small genre: poverty, rustic autarky, *otium*, and a focus on the quality of private life rather than political affairs and the outward symbols of social status.[137]

The organizing idea behind these various strategies of rhetorical retreat, shelter, and mediation is that of autonomy. Maecenas' high-level, long-term patronage, represented as freeing the poet from social obligations and allowing him to dedicate himself full-time to the production of a timeless masterpiece, forms part of this larger ideology of autonomy. The idea of literary *otium* as a space of permanent withdrawal, the writer's autarky, and the role of Maecenas are thus combined within a larger model, which in its own way serves an immediate, social use in guaranteeing, not only the quality of the work, but the authenticity of the poet's praise of the new order. Augustus' successors, however, had different conceptions of what constituted appropriate poetic encomium that did not always accommodate an autonomist position. In Martial's case, we have seen how his epigrammatic self-representation continues Augustan concerns with poverty, autarky, and *otium*, but in each case subverts the dominant emphasis, establishing in place of the expected

---

[136] On Maecenas' role as mediator and the consequences of the later obsolescence of this role, see Citroni, (1992), 385.

[137] La Penna (1963) and Fowler (1995b) examine the tensional relation between imperial ideology and Horace's small, Callimachean domain of lyric.

elements a sordid, urban poverty, a rhetoric of dependence on the patron, and an *otium* fragmented into multiple social occasions. The epigrammatist's materialist vision of literature contributes a crucial aspect to this post-classical aesthetics: Martial represents his work's individual, concretely imagined copies fragmented into disparate contexts of social use. Autonomy remains an important concern, but must occupy a less prominent and overtly advertised margin of the work.

The existence of polarized and irreconcilable aesthetic tendencies in Martial's work relates to his place in a tradition defined by standards of autonomy which he cannot fully and explicitly avow. Martial found it ideologically advantageous to create a conception of literature dedicated to immediate uses and affirmed by contemporary celebrity, rather than grounded in a rhetoric of autonomy. The claim of autonomy implies, among other things, that the work is not ultimately to be held answerable to the contemporary social order, an implication not tolerable under the early imperial organization of literary culture. Yet Martial could not simply re-invent the standards of evaluation built into Roman literary culture. Even as he attempted to redefine literary success in terms of contemporary celebrity, popularity, and the immediate pleasure afforded by his *oeuvre conviviale*,[138] he was unable to do so without an ironic consciousness of the impossibility of replacing the very standards his emphasis subverts. This difficulty applies not only to Martial's own conceptualization of his work, but also to its social and ideological value. The patrons and emperors who may hope to benefit from Martial's mention of their virtues and achievements similarly rely on his work's integrity and enduring importance. These simultaneous pressures place the poet in a double bind: if he wishes to maintain the idea of his work's inherent value, both for literary and social reasons, he must do so within the constraints of a post-Augustan model defined by the absence of a sheltered space for the rhetorical construction of autonomy.

JUVENAL: *QUIS LOCUS INGENIO?*

It seems perfectly plausible that Juvenal led a tranquil life of equestrian *otium* like most other major Roman authors of the late republic and early empire. Only scant evidence exists, however, in the major works of Juvenal's first-person poetic oeuvre that would allow us to do more than imagine or theorize such a life, since, like his predecessor Martial, he assumes in his poetry the role of weary client of indifferent or sadistic grandees. Arguably our best window onto Juvenal's life and work is afforded by a late epigram of Martial that envisions Juvenal retracing the epigrammatist's poetic itineraries through the neighbourhood of the Subura.[139]

> Dum tu forsitan inquietus erras
> clamosa, Iuvenalis, in Subura
> aut collem dominae teris Dianae;
> dum per limina te potentiorum
> sudatrix toga ventilat vagumque

---

[138] Laurens (1989), 219ff. elegantly characterizes Martial's poetic of sociability.

[139] Compare 7.24, 7.91. On 12.18, see the comments of Watson and Watson (2003), 143–50; Rimell (2008), 193–7; Highet (1954), 18: 'a vivid little poem, but not wholly likeable'.

> maior Caelius et minor fatigant:
> me multos repetita post Decembres
> accepit mea rusticumque fecit
> auro Bilbilis et superba ferro.   (12.18.1–9)

While *you* perchance wander without rest in noisy Subura, Juvenal, or tread the hill of mistress Diana; while the sweat-producing toga fans you amid the thresholds of the powerful, and the greater and lesser Caelian exhaust you in your wanderings; *I* have been received and made into a rustic by my Bilbilis, sought out again after many Decembers, proud of its gold and iron.

The 'Juvenal' of the poem, whom most scholars assume (not with total certainty) to be the poet Juvenal, finds himself climbing hills early in the morning, enduring urban sordidity, and sweating in pursuit of patrons and *salutationes* very much like the 'Martial' represented throughout most of the epigrammatist's oeuvre. Martial is, in some sense, addressing a previous version of himself, a young poet taking up the cliental persona and associated urban topography which he himself is now leaving behind for Spanish retirement. The 'thresholds of the powerful', and the *tu/ego* contrast, culminating in a statement of tranquil quietude with verse-initial *me*, bring to mind the rhetoric of personal autarky in Horace's *Odes*. The reversal is pointed: Martial, who for so long inhabited the heteronomist role of urban client, deprived of Horatian *otium* and the patronage of a Maecenas, subjected to the relentless pressure of the city for lack of a true 'citadel' of rural autarky, now takes up the mantle of retiring autarkist ensconced in rustic serenity.[140] He accordingly displaces onto Juvenal, his *semblable* and *frère*, the persona of urban heteronomy he inhabited successfully for three decades.

It is impossible to know whether Juvenal's evident expert knowledge of the burdens and humiliations of clientship derives from direct experience or not; it could as easily have been garnered from general knowledge of Roman society, or even, in circular fashion, from Martial's *Epigrams*.[141] Martial, in turn, describes Juvenal's cliental 'itineraries' in such a way as to make it impossible to decide whether he is referring to the activities of Juvenal the man, or Juvenal the literary personality. Certainly the latter option is tempting: Martial is 'being made a rustic' (*me ... rusticumque fecit*) both in his life and his epigrammatic text, while Juvenal produces the literary image of a man wandering amid the clamorous streets of the Subura, ascending the Aventine, being worn out by the two peaks of the Caelian, and sweating in his client's toga. The urban itinerary was a major metonym for literary textuality in the *Epigrams*; now Juvenal is 'following the same path'. Particularly interesting in this picture of diverging paths is the complementarity of the two associated ethical attitudes: urban clientship and rustic retirement, heteronomy and autarky. As throughout Martial's work, the act of proclaiming, in explicit terms, 'I am heteronomous' implies *de facto* participation in autonomist discourse; it is a claim to occupy autonomy's inverse image.

---

[140] But see Rimell (2008), 195–6, with Watson and Watson (2003) ad loc., on how Martial inevitably 'imports' urban vocabulary and attitudes into this ostensibly rural scene.

[141] There is a long history of studies of the relation between Juvenal and Martial and the influence of the latter on the former: e.g., Wilson (1898), Boissier (1899), Highet (1951), Anderson (1970), Townend (1973), Malnati (1987), Colton (1991).

Of course, Juvenal ends up doing more than simply reprising Martial's literary clientage, but it is in Martial's interest in that particular poem to represent him as the image of his earlier poetic self;[142] he conveniently absorbs what Martial now affects to leave behind and transcend. The underlying concept, however, of a writer exposed to and engulfed by an infinitely sordid city fits Juvenal's literary project fairly well, and the satirist's literary debt to Martial is large. For Juvenal, as for Martial, literary activity is tightly embedded in concrete urban settings and the materialities of writing and reception. Juvenal opens his oeuvre with an evocation of a particular place in the city associated with literary recitation.

> Semper ego auditor tantum? numquamne reponam
> vexatus totiens rauci Theseide Cordi?
> impune ergo mihi recitaverit ille togatas,
> hic elegos? impune diem consumpserit ingens
> Telephus aut summi plena iam margine libri
> scriptus et in tergo necdum finitus Orestes?
> nota magis nulli domus est sua quam mihi lucus
> Martis et Aeoliis vicinum rupibus antrum
> Vulcani. quid agant venti, quas torqueat umbras
> Aeacus, unde alius furtivae devehat aurum
> pelliculae, quantas iaculetur Monychus ornos,
> Frontonis platani convolsaque marmora clamant
> semper et adsiduo ruptae lectore columnae:
> expectes eadem a summo minimoque poeta.
> et nos ergo manum ferulae subduximus, et nos
> consilium dedimus Sullae privatus ut altum
> dormiret; stulta est clementia, cum tot ubique
> vatibus occurras, periturae parcere chartae.
> cur tamen hoc potius libeat decurrere campo
> per quem magnus equos Auruncae flexit alumnus,
> si vacat ac placidi rationem admittitis, edam.   (1.1–21)

Will I always be a mere listener? Harassed so many times by the *Theseid* of hoarse Cordus, shall I not make a response? Will this one recite elegies, that one comedies in Roman dress, and get away with it? Will immense *Telephus* devour the day and get away with it? What about *Orestes*, written over the entire margin, to the very end of the scroll, onto the back, and still not finished? No one knows his own house better than I know Mars' grove and the cave of Vulcan, neighbour to the cliffs of Aeolus. What the winds are up to, what dead souls Aeacus tortures, whence somebody else drags off the gold of a stolen pelt, how vast are the ash-trees Monychus hurls like a javelin—these themes are perpetually cried aloud by the plane trees and shattered marble of Fronto, the columns burst apart by unrelenting recitation. You can expect the same from the greatest and the most negligible poet. I too have flinched before the rod, I too have advised Sulla to take a deep nap as private citizen. When one runs into so many Inspired Bards everywhere, it's misplaced mercy to spare paper that will perish anyway. But why I prefer to traverse this plain over which Aurunca's great son directed his horses, I shall tell—if you have time to receive the reason I shall calmly offer.

---

[142] Rimell (2008), 195, notes a possible allusion in 12.18 to Juvenal 3, where a satiric speaker also departs from the city and offers many of the same complaints; thus Martial would be putting Juvenal into the same role that Juvenal himself occupied in relation to Umbricius.

Juvenal begins by staging the scene of his own inception into literary agency:[143] *semper ego auditor*? ('Will I always be a listener?'). His starting-point is very different from Horace's notionally personal chat with Maecenas. Not only does he not wholly disdain recitation, as Horace does; he is driven to recite himself by resentment and stifled rage.[144] He more closely resembles Persius in beginning with literature as satiric topic, but diverges in placing himself within a social, crowded, saturated scene of literary activity, peopled with numerous practitioners in diverse genres, by contrast with Persius' emphatic isolation. Horace's premise was always that his poetry stood outside the defiling *turba* (crowd) of his satiric targets; satiric *sermo* took place in some more intimate setting—a private conversation, the secluded space of the poet's self-improving meditations. Persius, who struggles to maintain any kind of conversation, still insists on Horatian autarky and detachment, though to an extreme degree. Juvenal, in the meanwhile, stands alongside (albeit resentfully, impatiently) the 'well-combed' effeminate reciters Horace, and, yet more fiercely, Persius, despised.

Beginning the text of Satire 1 with a first-person claim to being a reciter is a striking and pointed reversal of satire's autarkic, anti-performance bias built up over decades. Even Lucilius affected the playful *sermo* of an upper-class Roman man speaking to his contemporaries and equals: he was sharply critical of the more public genres of tragedy and epic. As Juvenal unveils the basic structure of his literary project, we become aware of his ambitious intention to produce a post-Augustan, counter-autonomist cliental oeuvre on the model of Martial, yet on the very ground of satire's hallowed *libertas*, and with the more sweeping 'epic' drive of the hexameter line. Like Martial, Juvenal is acutely aware of the fatiguing banality of imperial literary activity and the fossilized system of genres: *ille togatas, / hic elegos* ('that one writes comedies in Roman dress, this one elegies'). Everything in this grim metaliterary vignette bespeaks saturation and plurality.[145] Both the written medium and spoken word are pushed to the point of exhaustion (*totiens . . . rauci . . . consumpserit . . . summi plena iam margine libri*).

Where is the poet's place of refuge and contact with poetic deities? With sharp irony, the *lucus* ('grove') and *antrum* ('grotto') frequently identified as sites of poetic autonomy and inspiration are absorbed here into the tedium of trite mythological doctrine: *nota magis nulli domus est sua quam mihi <u>lucus</u> / Martis et Aeoliis vicinum rupibus <u>antrum</u> / Vulcani* ('No one knows his own house better than I know Mars' grove and the cave of Vulcan, neighbour to the cliffs of Aeolus'). As the scene reveals itself, we find that the speaker is not in a grove, but nonetheless occupies a space designated for literary activity: the portico of 'the house of Fronto', where the marble is wrenched apart, the columns are shattered, and the plane trees assaulted by the continual reverberation of reciting voices. Juvenal here inherits a well-known bucolic trope, the responsive 'echo' of poetry in the surrounding natural environment, but adapts it to a scene of city sociability: a wealthy residence known as a popular locale for reciting poets. In such a setting,

---

143 On this meta-recitational gesture, see Jones (2007), 139–40.

144 Highet (1954), 48: 'an odd way to begin one's career as a poet'.

145 Henderson (1999), 249–73, attempts to uncover the possible sources behind Juvenal's allegations of triteness; note also Freudenburg (2001), 209ff.

the poet's words come already scripted on many levels. The originary moment of creation and assertion of voice (*semper ego auditor...*?) turns out to be re-performance, a *re*citation. The moment he speaks, moreover, his declamatory rhetorical questions are proven untrue, an unreal conceit in a tired literary environment. For now he *is* no longer merely a listener. The passive author turns hypocrite, and we, his readers, become victims in turn.[146]

The satirist thus locates himself in a crowded, artificial, urban, un-natural anti-*nemus* (grove).[147] There are some minimal natural elements, yet even the sculpted plane trees tend to be associated with porticoes and other places where nature is framed and controlled by human technology. This particular portico, moreover, is pervaded by a sense of violence (*convolsaque*) and destruction (*ruptae*) rather than tranquil creativity. From a Callimachean perspective, there is nothing rare or exclusive about Juvenal's site of poetic activity; instead, it is wretchedly overpopulated, worn away and degraded by the assiduity of what takes places there (*adsiduo... lectore*). No solitary *vates* occupies a secluded grove; rather a crowd of poets writing in all known genres crank out undifferentiated tripe. The very phrase *tot ubique / vatibus occurras* ('[when] you run into so many "bards" everywhere') is oxymoronic: the term *vates* occurs in the plural, stripped of the exclusive aura that notionally defines it. The poet's speech, in this setting, is profoundly determined by the Roman system of education and its fixed canon of approved genres. This entire web of social conditioning is indicated metonym-ically by the reflexive response of a schoolboy's training: 'I too have flinched before the rod'. The poet has no more control over his literary preconceptions than a schoolboy has over his hand's 'flinch' response. The result is all too predictable: a mind saturated with declamatory conceits.[148]

The satirist, then, purports to be just another cog in the imperial literary machine. But if, in the reverberating sameness of Fronto's colonnade, works in all genres are hackneyed and predetermined, why this particular terrain, why *this* territory? Juvenal offers an answer early on in the first satire.

> cum tener uxorem ducat spado, Mevia Tuscum
> figat aprum et nuda teneat venabula mamma,
> patricios omnis opibus cum provocet unus
> quo tondente gravis iuveni mihi barba sonabat,
> cum pars Niliacae plebis, cum verna Canopi
> Crispinus Tyrias umero revocante lacernas
> ventilet aestivum digitis sudantibus aurum,
> nec sufferre queat maioris pondera gemmae,
> difficile est saturam non scribere.   (1.22–9)

When a tender eunuch takes a wife; when Mevia pierces a Tuscan boar and, with breast bared, holds hunting-spears; when a fellow, under whose shears my thick beard would grate when I was a young man, single-handedly challenges the entire patriciate with his

---

[146] Compare Freudenburg (2001), 240–1.

[147] The general outline of these ideas emerged in a conversation with Cedric Littlewood.

[148] For Freudenburg (2005), 77–85, the polemical point being made is not simply that the satiric speaker criticizes contemporary mythological poetry, but that he is maniacally obsessed with the prevalence of specifically *Greek* material as opposed to the equally ghastly, but also real, figures to be encountered on Roman streets.

wealth; when a representative of the Nilotic underclass, when Crispinus, a home-bred slave of Canopus, hitching onto his shoulder a Tyrian cloak, flashes summer's gold on sweating fingers, unable to endure the weight of a greater gem—it is difficult *not* to write satire.

Juvenal produces a series of urban satiric portraits, and then turns around and claims that the figures represented in those portraits originate his satiric genre.[149] Questions of circularity aside, the underlying trope is that urban social reality controls and determines his poetry. This is a strikingly different premise from the self-definitional attitudes of previous satire. Horace and Persius in part based their self-representation on the idea of distance from the *volgus* ('mob'). Their brittle autonomist stance was constantly maintained through distance from and deferral of contact with the urban onslaught to which they stood in close proximity.[150] Lucilius' social position was such that there was no question of humiliating subjection to a sordid procession of perverts and criminals. According to an established pun, surfeit drives satire, and the writer has no choice but to succumb to the density of his material. Crispinus' outrageous display is too much, it is insufferable (*nec sufferre queat*), too great a weight (*pondera*). This overpowering sense of 'too much' produces . . . *satura*, a mode of writing that, in Juvenal's hands, depicts a world stuffed with vice and excess, and does so in an overheated, declamatory, exaggerated style. Juvenal pushes the heteronomist response to Augustan poetics to a new level. The *nemus* is gone, reduced to the memory of an obsolete idyll, and now the city takes on horrific immensity and determinative power. His satiric language, in this context, reflects comparable reversals of power and agency, passivity and penetration: the 'tender' (*tener*) eunuch takes (*ducat*) a wife, when it is a wife who ought to be 'tender', and a eunuch pathic; Mevia, a woman, 'transfixes' (*figat*) a wild boar. The spectator of such abnormality finds himself unable to restrain his rage (*teneat se*) as the city forces him to 'suffer' its moral perversity (*iniquae / . . . patiens urbis*), as the moral dregs of humanity, in their wealth and pride, 'push him aside' (*te summoveant*) from their path. The satiric writer/onlooker has passively *suffered* endless recitations; he *suffers* the horrors of the sordid urban scene. Yet the inevitable turn from passive suffering to active anger and revenge still leaves him the product of his environment: *facit indignatio versum* ('indignation makes my verse', 79).

Juvenal's satiric speaker never attains true autonomy, but alternates between a degrading passivity and an indignant rage[151] that determines (*facit*) his poetry's content and tone. Like the exiled Ovid, he is immersed in a hostile environment and presents himself as nearly overwhelmed amidst the topics of his indignation: *nonne libet medio ceras implere capaces / quadrivio, cum . . . ?* ('Does one not wish to fill wax tablets to the brim in the middle of the cross-road, when . . . ?', 63–4). Juvenal's 'streetcorner' writing in wax could hardly be further from the quiet,

---

[149] Of course, these satiric figures are not wholly invented, but are in some cases based on Domitianic figures (e.g. Crispinus): see Freudenburg (2001), 213–14.

[150] Highet (1954), 50: 'Juvenal does not make us watch it from a distance. He places us in the crowded thoroughfare . . . and the thick closely packed sentences, filled with drastic and shocking words, themselves carry us along as though we were being pushed and buffeted by the crowds of Rome'.

[151] Highet (1954), 47 on Satire 1: 'an uninterrupted shout of fury from the beginning until almost the end'.

meditative spaces of Horatian lyric and satire.[152] It is true that in the *Satires*, Horace finds himself subjected to the currents of city life in ways he did not anticipate and cannot wholly control. But part of the point in such experiments (e.g. *Sat.* 1.9) is to show that, even when moderately provoked, he does not allow himself to be prodded out of his autarkist's shell into an undignified anger.

Most of the first satire works to intensify the sense of the speaker's pent-up rage, which, we assume, will spill forth in the form of thrilling invective power. At the close, however, the speaker reveals that the apparently contemporary street-corner scene of immediate observation and impromptu composition was more than a bit misleading.

> 'securus licet Aenean Rutulumque ferocem
> committas, nulli gravis est percussus Achilles
> aut multum quaesitus Hylas urnamque secutus:
> ense velut stricto quotiens Lucilius ardens
> infremuit, rubet auditor cui frigida mens est
> criminibus, tacita sudant praecordia culpa.
> inde ira et lacrimae. tecum prius ergo voluta
> haec animo ante tubas: galeatum sero duelli
> paenitet.' experiar quid concedatur in illos,
> quorum Flaminia tegitur cinis atque Latina.   (1.162–71)

'Without worry you may pit Aeneas and the fierce Rutulian against each other in battle. How Achilles was wounded, or how Hylas, who followed his water-jug, was much searched for, is an offensive topic to no one. Whenever Lucilius, seething, roars, as if with sword unsheathed, the hearer, whose mind is chilled with crime, grows red, his heart sweats with secret guilt. Hence anger and tears. Therefore turn the matter over in your mind before the trumpet sounds; it is too late to have second thoughts about war when your helmet is on.' I'll see try what may be allowed against those whose ashes are covered by the Flaminian and Latin roads.

There are good reasons for Juvenal to associate himself with satire's well-known harshness and rebarbative tone (what Lucilius likened to the canine 'growl' of the letter 'r'). Juvenal wants to avoid the silken courtly fluency of his Flavian predecessors, Martial and Statius, and satire helps him do that. Whereas epigram and occasional verse have a history of accommodating encomiastic, courtly compositions, Roman satire claims a tradition of *libertas*.[153] Yet Juvenal cannot claim to exemplify true *libertas* in his satiric criticism of individuals; nor has the underlying structure of imperial power changed significantly since the time of Martial and Statius. He claims *libertas* in a minor key. He uses satire's (admittedly conventional) savagery of manner and outlook to rip into literary conventionality, though he cannot project a truly independent poetic voice himself. He is at once liberated by rage and confined by circumstance, simultaneously savage and servile.[154]

---

[152] Compare Freudenburg (2001), 246.

[153] He may have Valerius Flaccus in mind as well in the satire's opening section: Freudenburg (2001), 210–11, who notes on the present passage that 'the only ones who get hurt in epic are the heroes of the story' (211).

[154] Freudenburg (2001), 234ff., reads the above cited passage in light of the post-Domitianic mania for trying to present oneself as having been heroically hostile to Domitian through retroactive condemnations and rewriting of history. The phrase 'a savage servility slides by on grease', which

Juvenal's Rome destroys poetic autonomy because poetry, as the opening vignette illustrates, has become a self-promoting game in a world premised on unscrupulous self-promotion. Literature mimics the violence, competition, saturation, and tedium of all the city's innumerable quotidian routines, from *sportula* to *cena*. Trying to escape such tedium with satire's vaunted *libertas* seems like a reasonable tactic, but true *libertas* is out of the question in the imperial city. None of this would have shocked or even mildly surprised Martial, although he might have admired how Juvenal adapts *his* epigrammatic city to the larger canvas of satire. Also comparable to Martial is the recurrent problem of the satiric speaker's identity. In order to be able to satirize urban unpleasantness at close range, the satiric poet takes on the role of someone who suffers outrageous treatment in the city, who knows what it means to be poor, cultured, and honest in Rome. But can a writer, who almost certainly belongs to the wealthy, educated elite, be as subject to urban sordidity as his satiric fictions suggest? Does not the satiric stance, even in Juvenal's new heteronomist framing of it, still imply a critical, if not a physical, distance from the practices and persons he converts into literary portraits of degradation?

In Satire 3, which occupies the middle-point of Juvenal's first book, the possibility of distance from the city emerges as a distinct question. Juvenal's friend Umbricius has finally had enough of life in Rome, and has resolved to move to Cumae.

> Quamvis digressu veteris confusus amici
> laudo tamen, vacuis quod sedem figere Cumis
> destinet atque unum civem donare Sibyllae.
> ianua Baiarum est et gratum litus amoeni
> secessus. ego vel Prochytam praepono Suburae;
> nam quid tam miserum, tam solum vidimus, ut non
> deterius credas horrere incendia, lapsus
> tectorum adsiduos ac mille pericula saevae
> urbis et Augusto recitantes mense poetas?   (3.1–9)

Although troubled by the departure of my old friend, I nonetheless praise him for deciding to fix his dwelling-place in empty Cumae and award a single citizen to the Sibyl. Cumae—the 'gateway to Baiae', a charming seaside locale with delightful seclusion! I rate even Prochyta above the Subura. For what place have we seen so wretched, so isolated, that you would not judge it worse to live in fear of fires, continual collapse of buildings, and the thousand dangers of the cruel city, not to mention poets reciting in the month of August?

Umbricius, whose name refers to 'shade'—either *a* shade, a dead soul, or *the* shade (leisure, relaxation)[155]—appears to be embarking on the very sort of retreat from which Juvenal's satiric self is intrinsically barred. Juvenal occupies the city, which in turn preoccupies and obsesses him—all of which means that true release, autonomy, and tranquillity are impossible for him. Juvenal speaks with Umbricius

would seem to apply very well to Juvenal, comes from Robert Lowell, 'For the Union Dead' (In *For the Union Dead*, New York, Farrar, Straus & Giroux, 1964).

[155] So some scholars, e.g. Braund (1989), 29: the implication is that Umbricius' departure for Cumae is likened parodically to a departure to the underworld. But note also Freudenburg (2001), 267, who suggests that Umbricius is being marked as someone who tags along at a dinner (*umbra*), or as a true, native Italian (from Umbria).

at the margins of the city, near the Porta Capena. The satire's discursive frame situates itself at the border between city and not-city, between the urban conditions that plague both Juvenal and Umbricius (fires, falling houses, beggars, poets) and putative rural tranquillity. At another level, this scene replays the setting and concerns of the opening scene of Satire 1. Not only do the city's disadvantages include 'poets reciting through the month of August', but the specific landmark grounding the dialogue is the grove of Egeria, here set up by Juvenal as another anti-*nemus* along the lines of Fronto's colonnade.

> hic, ubi nocturnae Numa constituebat amicae,
> nunc sacri fontis nemus et delubra locantur
> Iudaeis, quorum cophinus fenumque supellex
> (omnis enim populo mercedem pendere iussa est
> arbor et eiectis mendicat silva Camenis).
> in vallem Egeriae descendimus et speluncas
> dissimiles veris. quanto praesentius esset
> numen aquis, viridi si margine cluderet undas
> herba, nec ingenuum violarent marmora tofum. (3.12–20)

Here, where Numa held rendezvous with his mistress at night, now the grove with its sacred spring and the shrine are rented out to Jews, whose only furniture is a hay-lined chest. (For every tree is required to pay rent to the people, the Camenae have been kicked out, and the wood goes begging.) We descend into the vale of Egeria and into caves quite unlike real ones. How much more present the spring's spirit would be, if grass enclosed the waters with green border, and marble did not violate the native tufa!

Here is a true sacred grove (*sacri fontis nemus*) with resident Camenae,[156] a place where a poet might credibly receive inspiration and detach himself from the vulgar mob. Yet, as it turns out, the grove has been degraded into a makeshift camping ground for mendicant Jews, while the Camenae have been evicted.[157] All the traditional terms of poetic topography are present (*fons, nemus, silva, valles, spelunca*), but each one of them has been stained with financial motives (*locantur, mendicat silva*) and artificiality (*dissimiles veris, marmora*). The violation (*violarent*) of the natural setting of the precinct recalls the reverberating marble 'grove' with its sculpted plane trees at the opening of Satire 1.The intellectual genealogy of Juvenal's ideas goes back to Persius, who, in the prologue to his satires, disavowed Parnassus, Helicon, Pirene, and ivy (prol. 1–6), asserted the materialist underpinnings of art (prol. 12), derived poetry from the needs of the 'gut' (*venter*), and presented himself as 'semi-clansman' (*semipaganus*, 6) of the community of bards. Juvenal, too, is neither wholly absorbed into nor wholly excluded from poetic spaces; he inhabits a tainted grove at the margins of the countryside, where city motives still tarnish the natural and the divine. *Sermo* occurs at the problematic transition point. Juvenal's awareness of the interconnection between poetry

---

[156] See Courtney (1980), ad loc.; Fantham (2009), 82–3; Highet (1954), 69. The association of the grove with the Camenae makes it something along the lines of a Roman Mount Helicon, and thus its violation is all the more significant.

[157] Larmour (2007), 191ff. offers numerous observations on the liminal region of the Porta Capena as well as this grove and its background in Livy. In particular, he notes how Juvenal transforms the grove into an instance of the moral and religious corruption Numa originally sought to avoid by his activities there.

and Roman space draws on Virgil's first eclogue, another poem that negotiates metapoetics through space, dialogue, and figures marked by their diverging trajectories. One figure departs from, and the other remains committed to, the territory which defines the poet's genre—the idyllic countryside for Vergil, the corrupted *urbs* for Juvenal. Umbricius, whose complaints about Rome's degradation into a *Graeca Urbs* take up most of the satire, is a surrogate author-figure, whose perspective, like that of both the Virgilian Tityrus and Meliboeus, distils central tensions of the literary work in which he appears.[158]

The opposition between remaining in and departing from the city lies at the heart of Juvenalian satire, and significantly dominates the long poem at the centre of the satirist's first book. It is worth recalling that in Martial *Epigrams* 12.18, Martial has left Rome, while Juvenal remains trapped there—a situation closely parallel to that of Satire 3. Location is a central theme of Umbricius' speech: his opening salvo is that there is no place (*locus*) for respectable occupations or arts (*artibus . . . honestis*, 21–2) in Rome. Neither a client, nor a practitioner of the poetic art, can practice his craft with integrity and satisfaction in a city overwhelmed with foreign flatterers. The point is not simply, as Umbricius' resentful discourse sometimes suggests, one of financial remuneration; autonomy is simultaneously at stake. To live successfully in Rome, you ultimately need to form yourself into the shape that others expect. If you insist on integrity and autonomy, you will starve for attention—or simply starve.

We know what Umbricius' position is: having found himself incapable of matching his competitors in clientage, he departs from Rome. What about Juvenal? Umbricius' departure at least to some extent serves to define Juvenal as the figure who *remains*, like Virgil's Tityrus, within a generically determining space. He is condemned to the condition of urban heteronomy that defines satire. On the other hand, like Horace in *Satires* 2, Juvenal uses the framed speech of another to distance himself from a more simplistic moral discourse than his own. It becomes evident, as his speech proceeds, that Umbricius' heated indignation at others' unscrupulous behaviour is premised on his jealousy of their greater material success. 'Tranquil retirement' turns out to be the last resort of failure. Umbricius, then, corresponds to one layer of the Juvenalian satirist's literary personality, a figure who undergoes feelings of *indignatio* when others are preferred to him in the competition for urban patronage. Juvenal courted such an impression in Satire 1, when, standing on the street-corner, he indignantly watched criminals glory in the splendour of their ill-gotten wealth.

By the logic of framed citation, however, Juvenal, who cites Umbricius' speech, is a more expansive and more complex figure than Umbricius himself. He cannot be wholly reduced to the alternative between urban heteronomy and rural escape, the threadbare dynamic of *indignatio*. Juvenal, as satirist, does indeed remain in the city, but now, in the act of citing Umbricius, analyses what it means to be imprisoned in the city from a certain distance. Umbricius, the weary client, who, in despair, flees to the Bay of Naples, becomes a case study of *indignatio* and urban heteronomy, rather than *the* confining framework for Juvenal's literary identity.

---

[158] Could *this* be one of the allusions couched in Umbricius' 'shadowy' name: *maioresque cadunt altis de montibus umbrae* (*Ecl.* 1.83)?

His exhaustive, valedictory speech can even be read as giving definitive expression to, and to a certain degree exorcizing, the element of cliental *indignatio* in Juvenalian satire. The indignant client par excellence, he departs from the city, and at the same time, from Juvenal's satiric text. It is perhaps significant that subsequent books begin to display progressively less anger (*ira*) as the speaker's defining trait, and even in the remaining satires of the first book, the satirist seems more indignant on others' behalf than on his own.

The poem's closing lines add a further dimension to the question of satire's location and the possibility of detachment from the city.

> '... ergo vale nostri memor, et quotiens te
> Roma tuo refici properantem reddet Aquino,
> me quoque ad Helvinam Cererem vestramque Dianam
> converte a Cumis. saturarum ego, ni pudet illas,
> auditor gelidos veniam caligatus in agros'.   (3.318–22)

'And so farewell, keep me in mind, and whenever Rome returns you to your native Aquinum, where you eagerly go to be restored, summon me also from Cumae to your Helvine Ceres and Diana. I will come to your chilly fields wearing heavy boots to hear your satires, if they are not embarrassed by me.'

Umbricius asks Juvenal to 'keep him in mind' or memory (*nostri memor*), which, indeed, he does, by preserving his words in a satire. He then goes on to hint at settings for literary activity that exist outside the limiting framework of satire's relentlessly urban metafictional locale; for Umbricius lets drop, in faintly but significantly Horatian phrasing, that the satirist occasionally goes to Aquinum to 'be restored' (*refici*).[159] Juvenal turns out not to be as wholly imprisoned by the city as we might have thought, and not only that, he recites, and possibly composes, his satires at some distance from Rome. The phrase *saturarum ego ... auditor* ('I ... hearer of your satires') closely echoes the opening phrase of the entire work, *semper ego auditor ...?* ('I ... always a listener?'), but affords an alternative scenario of satiric recitation.[160] In this latter option, Juvenal recites, not at another man's city mansion, amid reverberating marble and a crowd of poets, but at his own country property in the chill remoteness of Aquinum.

No sooner does Juvenal produce the 'angry' persona of urban heteronomy in his opening satire than he begins to undermine key aspects of it. Traces of the autonomist model co-exist with the ostensibly dominant model of the humiliated client poet. A persistent question behind these alternations is whether or not the poet still has access to the sheltered realm of poetic autonomy in imperial Rome. In Satire 7, Juvenal addresses, explicitly and at length, the state of contemporary literature and the prospects of the imperial writer.[161] The satire's organizing idea occupies the first line: *et spes et ratio studiorum in Caesare tantum* ('the hopes and *raison-d'être* for literary studies reside in Caesar alone').[162] The picture Juvenal

---

[159] Compare Horace *Epist.* 1.18.104 (*reficit gelidus Digentia rivus*) and Courtney (1980), ad loc.

[160] Ferguson (1979), ad loc.: 'the wheel has come full circle from 1.1'.

[161] On this satire, see Hardie (1990); note also Highet (1954), 106–12; Helmbold and O'Neil (1959); Rudd (1976), 84–118; Wiesen (1973); Braund (1988), 24–68; Bartsch (1994), 125–47.

[162] Much ink has been spilled on the question of which Caesar Juvenal has in mind: Highet (1954), 111, for example, sees this opening poem of the book as 'virtually a dedication to the emperor' Hadrian,

paints of literary culture in second century AD Rome is bleak indeed: there are no great, non-imperial patrons anymore, and writers must look towards the emperor for support, which is a little like pinning all one's hopes for financial security on winning the lottery. The explicit point of comparison is, chiefly, the Augustan period, when patrons such as Maecenas supported Horace, Virgil, Ovid, and others (94–5): *tum par ingenio pretium, tunc utile multis / pallere et vinum toto nescire Decembri* ('back then intellect had its just reward, then it benefited many to grow pale and stay off wine for the whole of December', 96–7). Juvenal's turn of phrase has a very sharp edge here: back then, a selfless devotion to literature was 'useful'; it 'paid'. The satirist appears to go out of his way to praise the Augustans for succeeding in attaining a goal they themselves repeatedly disavowed. For the Augustans, *ingenium* was more precious than material wealth, and serious devotion to literature implied a life divorced from quotidian ends. In Juvenal's version, however, *ingenium* actually produces wealth, and absorption in literature serves a utilitarian purpose. He praises in order to deconstruct.

The spaces of poetry, according to an established tradition, are pure, sacrosanct, cut off from the spaces of buying, selling, and everyday business. In Juvenal's world, however, there is no 'space apart' for poetry, no shelter from the mercantile, the profit-driven, and the urban. It is thus no surprise when Juvenal, in the opening passage of the satire, gets down to the familiar business of contaminating poetic locales with finance and sordidity.

> solus enim tristes hac tempestate Camenas
> respexit, cum iam celebres notique poetae
> balneolum Gabiis, Romae conducere furnos
> temptarent, nec foedum alii nec turpe putarent
> praecones fieri, cum desertis Aganippes
> vallibus esuriens migraret in atria Clio;
> nam si Pieria quadrans tibi nullus in umbra
> ostendatur, ames nomen victumque Machaerae
> et vendas potius commissa quod auctio vendit
> stantibus, oenophorum tripedes armaria cistas,
> Alcithoen Pacci, Thebas et Terea Fausti.   (7.2–12)

For he alone has shown regard for the sorrowful Camenae in this age of ours, in which celebrated, well-known poets were considering renting baths at Gabii, or bakeries in Rome, while others deemed it neither disgraceful nor shameful to become public heralds, and when a starving Clio, abandoning the vale of Aganippe, was moving her operations into the auction rooms. For if a farthing doesn't come your way in the Pierian shade, you'd better get to love Machaera's name and means of earning a living, and sell to bystanders various items on the auction's field of battle—wine jugs, three-footed tables, book-boxes, trunks, Paccius' *Alcithoë*, Faustus' *Thebes* and *Tereus*.

Juvenal uses line-breaks to brutal effect here as elsewhere. The *celebres notique poetae* ('celebrated, well-known poets') are rapidly deflated by the revelation in the following line that they were 'considering renting baths at Gabii, bakeries in Rome'. The role of public herald (*praecones*, 6) involves a rather different use of voice and eloquence, as does auctioneering. The poets of Juvenal's age reverse the

---

who would have been seen as reinvigorating literature. Another possibility is a sarcastic address to the (now dead) emperor Domitian: see Rudd (1976), 85.

trajectory of Horace, who, faced with the option of following in his father's footsteps as auctioneer, chose the less mercantile and ultimately more prestigious career of poet. With degradation of the poet's voice comes degradation of locale: the 'vale of Aganippe' is deserted in favour of auction rooms (*atria*), bathhouses, bakeries. At those auctions, alongside the usual objects for sale may be found tragedies 'on remainder'. Juvenal's materialist vision of literature reaches a brilliant climax here: poets are reduced to working at auction houses, where poetry itself has been reduced to the status of a second-hand commodity.[163]

The theme of spatial degradations continues. Poets desert the temples of the Muses and Apollo (*Musarum et Apollinis aede relicta*, 37) in order to take up with a patron, who, in turn, supplies them with a far worse 'temple'—a dilapidated, rented house at the margins of the city, filled with hired auditors and rented furniture (36–47). Juvenal relentlessly presses the point that the poets of his time have no integral space of their own. Never mind that the house itself is rented: even the chairs supplied for their recitations will have to be returned when the performance is over (*reportandis...cathedris*, 47). The recurrent tactic is to deprive poetry of what makes it distinctive, what differentiates it from quotidian interests and practices in spatial, material, and axiological terms. Like Martial, he reduces literature to its material basis—papyrus that can be bored by bookworms (26), burned (25), or simply heaped up in useless, doomed superfluity: *nullo quippe modo millensima pagina surgit / omnibus et crescit multa damnosa papyro* ('regardless of limit, every one of you [writers of history] goes on to the thousandth column, and the page-count continues to grow, ruinously expensive in quantity of papyrus', 100–1). A recurrent image in Juvenal is the uncontrolled accumulation of writing and wasted paper, literary frenzy disproportionate to the ability to say anything original or enduring. Poetry, as in Ovid's exilic oeuvre, is its own worst enemy, but in this case, the poetic medium does not so much harm its author through subversive speech, as condemn itself to vacuity through lack of any meaningful place in the Roman world.

Juvenal does not rule out the possibility of a deeply inspired poet of the traditional cast. But what he has to say about such a poet is not particularly encouraging.

> Sed vatem egregium, cui non sit publica vena,
> qui nil expositum soleat deducere nec qui
> communi feriat carmen triviale moneta,
> hunc, qualem nequeo monstrare et sentio tantum,
> anxietate carens animus facit, omnis acerbi
> inpatiens, cupidus silvarum aptusque bibendis
> fontibus Aonidum. neque enim cantare sub antro
> Pierio thyrsumque potest contingere maesta
> paupertas atque aeris inops, quo nocte dieque
> corpus eget: satur est cum dicit Horatius 'euhoe!'
> quis locus ingenio, nisi cum se carmine solo
> vexant et dominis Cirrhae Nysaeque feruntur
> pectora vestra duas non admittentia curas?

---

[163] Note the comments of Rudd (1976), 90: 'a particularly dense effect is obtained when lofty tragedies with noble old titles are included in a pile of secondhand junk'; compare Braund (1988), 30.

> magnae mentis opus, nec de lodice paranda
> attonitae, currus et equos faciesque deorum
> aspicere et qualis Rutulum confundat Erinys.
> nam si Vergilio puer et tolerabile desset
> hospitium, caderent omnes a crinibus hydri,
> surda nihil gemeret grave bucina: poscimus ut sit
> non minor antiquo Rubrenus Lappa cothurno,
> cuius et alveolos et laenam pignerat Atreus?   (7.53–73)

But the exceptional poet, the sort of poet who has no common vein of talent, who neither is in the habit of 'spinning out' anything trite, nor strikes an ordinary poem from a common mint, the sort of poet I am not able to point out but only conceive of—this sort of poet is the product of a mind free of anxiety, not obliged to endure anything bitter, eager to be in the woods and well-suited to drinking from the springs of the Muses. For Poverty, miserable and short on cash, whereof the body has need day and night, cannot chant poetry 'beneath Pierian grotto' or seize the thyrsus. Horace's stomach is full when he says 'Euhoe!' What place is there for literary talent, except when one's heart is agitated by poetry alone, and swept along by the lords of Cirrha and Nysa, incapable of having more than one concern? There is need of a great mind (not one mesmerized by the question of how to get a blanket) to have visions of chariots, horses, and the faces of the gods, to see the appearance of the Fury that dismayed the Rutulian. For if Virgil didn't have a slave-boy and a decent dwelling, all the snakes would fall from the Fury's hair, the trumpet would fall mute and would not sound its deep note. Do we require Rubrenus Lappa to be equal to the tragic buskin of old—Lappa, who pawned his *Atreus* for dishes and a cloak?

Juvenal's 'extraordinary poet' (*vatem egregium*), is evidently original, Callimachean, and formed in the autonomist mold. He is wholly absorbed in poetry, with no concern for anything else. Yet as in other instances, however, Juvenal undercuts the very ideal he evokes. In his description of the poet's vatic originality, he includes language evoking valuable metal (*vena*) and coinage (*communi . . . moneta*). Then, as if this weren't enough, he specifically identifies Horace's and Virgil's material wealth as the basis for the secure state of mind underpinning their poetic achievement.[164] In the subsequent age, as Rubrenus Lappa's pawned *Atreus* illustrates, poetry is converted back into negligibly small sums of money. Throughout the satire Juvenal presses his devastating point: in the past, material wealth underpinned the motivating illusion of poetry's autonomy; now, lack of wealth strips away this illusion, and reduces the writer to the role of a street-merchant or low-level tradesman, enjoying neither material comfort nor immaterial prestige.

The discussion of the *vates egregius* ('exceptional poet') ultimately points to contradictions inherent in the autonomist ideal. Even a poet like Horace, who affected to lack worldly anxiety, needed food and money to back up his antinomian pose. Now, in the present age, there is no Maecenas to prop up even the *illusion* of the poet's autonomy. The emperor alone is capable of providing such support. So far, so good—but what is Juvenal getting at by lecturing us on the

---

[164] The reference to a Dionysiac *euhoi* is perhaps an allusion to Horace *Odes* 2.19.5, 7; Rudd (1976), 97: 'Juvenal cleverly chooses two of the most "mantic" passages of Horace'. Note also, earlier, *sub antro / Pierio* (Juv. 7.59–60); compare Hor. *Carm.* 3.4.40, 2.1.39 and Courtney (1980), ad loc. Note also Rudd's comments on Virgilian reminiscence in this passage (97–8).

futility of literature in the absence of imperial patronage? Should we conclude that Juvenal is, or aspires to be, a court poet? If we find this aspiration unlikely, ought we to assume that, lacking such patronage, he irrelevantly fills up doomed papyrus like everyone else? Juvenal's statement that 'the emperor alone' can now supply the role of a proper patron alludes to Martial's nearly identical declaration.[165] Martial, however, certainly did aspire to be recipient of Domitian's patronage. Is Juvenal repeating Martial's message in the realization that, however distasteful his flattery, the epigrammatist's analysis of social conditions is inescapably accurate? Or, as Shadi Bartsch has argued,[166] is he offering an ironic travesty of the courtly conceit?

There is a danger of giving Juvenal more credit than he gives himself. It is true that Juvenal reserves special savagery for Statius' prostitution of his own poetry, and we may assume that Martial's flattery of Domitian was no more admirable in his eyes. Juvenal is unlikely, however, to be simply excoriating his target with a sense of justified outrage. In Satire 1, he worked himself into a white-hot rage of indignation over social injustice only to retreat from the Lucilian stance and limit himself to satirizing the famous dead. A similar impossibility defines his position here: righteous indignation over the capitulation of the Domitianic court poets is obstructed by the stubbornly persistent realities of early imperial literary patronage that motivated them to capitulate in the first place. Juvenal may be casting an ironic glance at Martial's courtly conceit, but he satirizes himself no less. The fact that he too lives under authoritarian emperors, who monopolize patronal authority and prestige, limits his options.[167]

So what is Juvenal left with? On the one hand, imperial patronage purchased by imperial panegyric, and on the other, the tattered remnants of the autonomist ideal. No passage more vividly reifies the latter condition than the schoolroom scene in which the beleaguered *grammaticus* finds himself in a squalid location teaching students who sullenly grip grimy copies of 'Flaccus and Maro'. Addressing the celebrated grammarian Q. Remmius Palaemon, Juvenal sarcastically taunts him with the suggestion that his humiliating wage is accompanied by degrading working conditions:

> ... cede Palaemon,
> et patere inde aliquid decrescere, non aliter quam
> institor hibernae tegetis niveique cadurci,
> dummodo non pereat mediae quod noctis ab hora
> sedisti, qua nemo faber, qua nemo sederet
> qui docet obliquo lanam deducere ferro;
> dummodo non pereat totidem olfecisse lucernas
> quot stabant pueri, cum totus decolor esset
> Flaccus et haereret nigro fuligo Maroni.   (7.219–27)

Cave in, Palaemon, and suffer that [your wage] decrease somewhat further, just like the street-vendor of mats and white Cadurcian coverlets for the winter, so long it is not a *total* loss that you have sat from before dawn in a place where no blacksmith, no one who teaches how to draw out wool with slanting iron comb, would sit; so long as it is not a *total* loss that

---

[165] *Epigrams* 5.19, 8.56.   [166] Bartsch (1994), 139.
[167] See note 1 for discussion of whether the year 96 'made a difference'.

you have inhaled the smoke from as many lamps as the students in your class thumbing a completely discolored Flaccus and a Maro grimy with clinging soot.

The materialist reduction of Horace and Virgil to soiled, tattered school texts is worthy of Martial's brilliant reflections on literary decline.[168] Literature cannot truly be produced in a spiritually elevated vacuum, supported by *ingenium* alone. Objects, settings, material conditions, and places matter. Juvenal in particular puts special emphasis on the degradation of *place*, the absence of dignified spaces for literary activity and the impact such a lack has on the very nature of the enterprise. Indeed, the question of place lies at the heart of the satire: *quis locus ingenio* ('what place is there for literary talent')?

If literature does not have an integral, dignified space of its own, then writers cannot continue to produce lasting and valuable works worthy of the interest of posterity, or such is the implication of Juvenal's corrosive comments on literary decline in Satire 7. From the jaded perspective of the second century AD, poetry's sense of autonomy was a kind of happy illusion, based on the assumption that the most successful Augustan poets were able to take for granted a certain level of material support. They were 'free' because they were well fed (*satur*, 7.62). In any case, satire (*satura*) favours such an interpretation.[169] Still, the deconstructive and nihilistic bent in Juvenalian satire can only go so far. Criticizing vice implies *some* concept of the good, located somewhere, in some imaginable place or time period.

This problem comes more fully to the fore when, in his later satires, Juvenal comes to abandon the 'angry' persona of his first book.[170] Now that angry condemnation of vice no longer dominates, Juvenal adopts an ostensibly more tranquil, philosophical role, yet without fully abandoning the devastating flashes of irony that work to undermine the possibility of a fully coherent moral position. Some scholars have even noted, especially in Satires 11 and 12, a more 'Horatian' style of self-representation. The poet forgoes excessive expenditure, rich dinners, and sumptuous sacrifices in favour of the simple, the unadorned, and the moderate.[171] This new Juvenal speaks in a performative first-person voice from the space of his own *domus*, insisting on his axiological standards for dinner invitation or sacrificial ceremony. He makes such declarations, however, in poems that do not themselves exemplify a pared down aesthetic of autarkic stringency, but rather the opposite. These are long, brilliant, eccentric, baroque compositions that go out of their way to flout the tidy aesthetic/moral principles they seem to espouse (and, one should add, they do so to an even greater extent than is 'normal' in Roman Callimacheanism).[172] Juvenal knowledgeably and effortlessly manipulates the autonomist self-representational lexicon—self-sufficiency, sequestration,

---

[168] Braund (1988), 66, observes that the effect is even sharper if we recall the supposedly sublime Horace and Virgil (now irreverently called Flaccus and Maro) from earlier in the satire: 'the move from being inspired poets at the height of success to being grubby and grimy set books in the mundane lowly school-room shows what fate has in store for the very best'.

[169] Compare Persius, prologue.

[170] This shift is the subject of Braund (1988); note also Anderson (1982), 277–92.

[171] Highet (1954), 130–3, sees a conversion to Epicureanism, and a positive change in material circumstances, as the reason for the shift in tone from the first book: 'Then he was a parasite. Now he is independent' (132). On the idea of a 'Horatian' persona, see Littlewood (2007), 390, with bibliography.

[172] See in general Littlewood (2007), esp. 413ff.

insistence on one's own values vs those of the world at large—but there are too many dissonant notes here to accommodate a coherent impulse. He is playing at the edges of autonomy, rather than attempting a full-scale revival of autonomist rhetoric.

Satire 12, to take one example, starts with the motif of the 'simple sacrifice' in celebration of his friend Catullus' survival of a shipwreck. This starting-point precedes a rambling, virtuoso detour consisting in a quasi-epic and/or declamatory 'description of a storm', which includes, for example, its own inset discussion of the self-castrating habits of beavers. He eventually gets back to the framing theme of the humble sacrifice, but instead of ending neatly here, turns aside in the closing passage to encompass a discussion of elephant herds in Italy (102–10) and the perversity of legacy hunters in (putatively) choosing human sacrificial victims (111ff.). Simple sacrifice and monstrous satirical excess stand side by side; the satirist is contented with modest wealth, and yet, unable to contain himself, quilts this 'message' out of a patchwork of outrageous detours and exorbitant tirades.[173]

A similar pattern of artfully contrived inconcinnity characterizes Satire 11. This satire begins with some fairly typical sermonizing on the topic of wealth enlivened by extremity of detail and example: everyone needs to 'take their own measure' and spend according to their capacities, so that they do not end up becoming ridiculous, forced to sign themselves over to the gladiatorial trainer. Then the satirist declares that the time has come for him to make good his high-sounding maxims with a demonstration of his own deeds and manner of existence: *experiere hodie numquid pulcherrima dictu, / Persice, non praestem vitae tibi moribus et re* ('Today, Persicus, you will find out whether, for you, I live up, in manner of life and in deed, to my maxims most fair', 56–7). In effect, Juvenal is signalling that he will now no longer simply castigate vices but will also produce a self-representational image of himself as author that is morally consistent with the terms whereby he excoriates others. Juvenal's respectably Callimachean theme of invitation to a modest banquet, however, leads him onto a meandering, declamatory romp on a diversity of satirical topics, including the attractions of nearly nude cupbearers of rural extraction, the lewd wiggling of Spanish dancers, the exotic materials of present-day dining tables, and, most provocative of all, the adulterous exertions of the invitee's own wife. How is this worrying disclosure supposed to help the satirist's honoured guest 'put aside his cares' (*dilatis . . . curis* 183)? Surely Juvenal is affectionately toying with the addressee, and with his reader's expectations.

Again, Juvenal plays at the edges of autonomist rhetoric, and while not wholly discarding such aspirations, lays claims to a realm of autarkic sequestration writ small, as in the engagingly quotidian autonomist self-portrait at the satire's close.

> Interea Megalesiacae spectacula mappae
> Idaeum sollemne colunt, similisque triumpho
> praeda caballorum praetor sedet, ac mihi pace
> immensae nimiaeque licet si dicere plebis,

---

[173] Some readers are unimpressed, e. g. Courtney (1980), 518: 'this is not only his shortest complete poem, but also his weakest'.

> totam hodie Romam circus capit, et fragor aurem
> percutit, eventum viridis quo colligo panni.
> nam si deficeret, maestam attonitamque videres
> hanc urbem veluti Cannarum in pulvere victis
> consulibus. spectent iuvenes, quos clamor et audax
> sponsio, quos cultae decet assedisse puellae:
> nostra bibat vernum contracta cuticula solem
> effugiatque togam. iam nunc in balnea salva
> fronte licet vadas, quamquam solida hora supersit
> ad sextam. facere hoc non possis quinque diebus
> continuis, quia sunt talis quoque taedia vitae
> magna: voluptates commendat rarior usus.   (Juv. 11.193–208)

In the meanwhile, the spectacles of the Megalesian napkin celebrate the Idaean rite, and the praetor sits as if in triumph, the plunder of nags, and (if I may say so with the permission of the immense, exceedingly numerous plebs) the circus today holds the entirety of Rome, and the roar strikes my ear, whereby I gather that the Green has won. For if it should lose, you would see this city sorrowful and stricken as when the consuls lay defeated in the dust of Cannae. Let young men enjoy the spectacle, young men for whom shouting, bold wagering, and sitting near one's elegant girlfriend are suitable. Let my shrivelled old skin drink in the vernal sun, and escape the toga. Already now you could go to the baths with unembarrassed brow, although it is a full hour before the sixth. You could not do this five days in a row, since one gets truly tired of even such a life. Rarity of enjoyment lends pleasure its grace.

Juvenal creates a vivid and intense sense of sequestration with this division between himself (who only hears the distant roar of the crowd from the private space of his sunbathing) and 'all Rome' celebrating the Megalesian games. For others, spectatorship (*spectent . . .*), noise, hubbub, the fury of the crowd; for Juvenal, a sub-symposiastic sort of 'drinking' (*bibat . . . solem*), and flight from the formalities of public appearance (*effugiatque togam*). The satirist wryly notes that the crowd of spectators would take the loss of the Greens in the chariot racing as seriously as the defeat of the Roman armies at Cannae. All of this bespeaks a cool detachment from popular enthusiasms, as does the casual philosophizing in the closing line, which could easily be the closing line of a Horatian epistle: *voluptates commendat rarior usus* ('Rarity of enjoyment lends pleasure its grace').

Juvenal stops short of claiming his sequestered existence as a superior *modus vitae* on its own terms. He appeals, instead, to the principle of decorum: it is all very well for young men to flirt with young women in the circus; at his advanced age, it is better to stay at home in informal ease. The details are homely and veristic: his 'wrinkled skin' (*contracta cuticula*) 'drinks in' the sun (*bibat . . . solem*), and he is grateful for the easy informality of everyday clothing (*effugiatque togam*). If the scene affords a glimpse of Juvenal's autonomy, it is autonomy written with a lower-case 'a'. Still, this closural vignette suffices to suggest that there is less distance than has been sometimes thought between the vatic dignity of the Augustan poets and the degraded cliental personae of the early imperial period. The solitary poet hearing the distant cries of the urban crowd furnishes a pointed contrast with the vividly degrading street-scene opening Satire 1, where an angry satirist is physically jostled by notorious criminals and perverts.

In Juvenal's case, a tension between urban heteronomy and sequestered detachment, indignant rage and tranquil reflection informs his poetic career and its aesthetic alternations. He never wholly embraces one side or the other of the dialectic, but the same terms remain in play. Those terms, in turn, derive from the autonomist self-representational tradition he at once dismantles and, through his impassioned critique, sustains.

Conclusion

Poetry and other 'games'

> Hesterno, Licini, die otiosi
> multum lusimus in meis tabellis,
> ut convenerat esse delicatos:
> scribens versiculos uterque nostrum
> ludebat numero modo hoc modo illoc,
> reddens mutua per iocum atque vinum.   (Catullus c.50.1–6)

> Yesterday at leisure, Licinius, we played around a great deal on my writing tablets, since we had determined to indulge ourselves. Each of us took turns writing verses and playing now in one meter, now in another, answering back and forth amidst joking and wine.

We have had occasion to observe throughout this study how the question of Roman poetic autonomy is closely connected with questions of permanence and continuity. An activity that is fragmented, dispersed amidst numerous small occasions of utility and diversion, necessarily lacks the cohesion and self-sufficiency of its own autonomous domain. In other words, poetry can never even pretend to be intrinsically and autotelically valid, a context-independent mode of endeavour containing its own inherent justification, if it is always only contextually allowed, an indulgence appropriate to certain moments and certain occasions on which it depends for its momentary instantiation. Of course, there is no such thing as a truly autonomous and 'context-independent' activity; yet the manner of *presenting* an activity still crucially matters. Does poetry require specific contextual justification, or is it presumed to be inherently valid as an occupation and presented as such?

Catullus, who pioneered key aspects of autonomist rhetoric in Latin verse, was keenly aware of the vulnerability of poetry to criticism as a nonessential pursuit, and of its conventional confinement to ephemeral occasions of 'play' (*lusus*). He was also aware that he himself was pressing at the conventional limits assigned to leisure-time activities such as poetic composition. In the elusive closing stanza of his free translation of Sappho (c. 51), Catullus reflects more broadly on his life of literary *otium*.

> otium, Catulle, tibi molestum est:
> otio exsultas nimiumque gestis:
> otium et reges prius et beatas
> perdidit urbes.

> Leisure, Catullus, is your bane; in leisure you exult and revel too much; in the past leisure has destroyed both kings and flourishing cities.

In what appears to be a *sphragis*, sealing off the end of his *libellus* with a self-referential gesture, Catullus identifies an excessive—and triply repeated—*otium* as his own bane and the cause of destruction of kings and cities. Perhaps he is mischievously repeating, with implicit mockery, a gnomic statement of the sort often intoned by traditionalist elders (*pete nobiles amicos!*), yet given the sometimes 'tragic' tonality of his affair with Lesbia, his frequent and fertile play between the categories of serious and ludic, and the darker implications of some of his mythological ruminations in the *carmina maiora* (Ariadne, the corruption of heroic *virtus*, Attis' loss of virile identity), it is impossible to rule out a streak of seriousness in this closural self-condemnation. Catullus at once seems to concede the permanence of his own commitment to literary pursuits, and to frame it as destructive, as impossible to avow without self-denigration and a consciousness of going against the grain of the dominant ideology. One is reminded of the adulterous love-affair of Anna and Vronsky in Tolstoy's *Anna Karenina*: occasional, non-serious indulgence of such activity is perfectly acceptable in good society, but passionate, long-term devotion is not, and is bound to be profoundly destructive to those involved.

Reliability of recurrence and iteration are thus established by Catullus as key elements in the organization of literary leisure. His underlying ideas continue to inform later structurings of metaliterary time. The Augustan poets maintain an interest in the poetics and erotics of repetition, yet, in both elegy and Horace, iteration often assumes a more palpable and positive aspect in the articulation of literary modality. For the elegists, the iterative condition of desire/writing is hardly precarious or brief. Erotic *servitium* is the poet-lover's permanently inscribed destiny. Horace also occupies a continual leisure-state, although he avoids the degrading connotations of elegiac *servitium*. Moreover, he pointedly rewrites the axiological emphasis of Catullus' *otium*-strophe. At *Odes* 2.16.1–8, he too underlines the permanence of *otium* through a triple repetition, yet in order to praise the life of leisure rather than regret or criticize it.

> Otium divos rogat in patenti
> prensus Aegaeo, simul atra nubes
> condidit lunam neque certa fulgent
>   sidera nautis;
> otium bello furiosa Thrace,
> otium Medi pharetra decori,
> Grosphe, non gemmis neque purpura ve-
>   nale neque auro.

A quiet life is what a man prays the gods to grant him when caught in the open Aegean, and a dark cloud has blotted out the moon, and the sailors no longer have the bright stars to guide them. A quiet life is the prayer of Thrace when madness leads to war. A quiet life is the prayer of the Medes when fighting with painted quivers: a commodity, Grosphus, that cannot be bought by jewels or purple or gold.[1]

Horatian leisure is a condition intrinsically opposed to *cura* and aligned with the tightly regulated value-system of retirement and *paupertas*, a central facet in the

---

[1] I adopt here the translation of Rudd (2004).

ethos of the Muses' priest.[2] Of course, we may not 'believe' Horace any more than we 'believe' Catullus' artfully contrived letter to Calvus. Was Maecenas' client truly so deeply opposed to ambition? Yet even if we refuse to ascribe an objective, sociological reality to Horace's declaration, we can nonetheless appreciate how the contours of the fiction have significantly shifted.

Evidently such claims of deep, existential *otium* made an impression on the broader literate Roman world. The Spanish-born epigrammatist Martial, writing a century later, still pines for the mythical literary leisure of the Augustan age.

> otia da nobis, sed qualia fecerat olim
>   Maecenas Flacco Vergilioque suo:
> condere victuras temptem per saecula curas
>   et nomen flammis eripuisse meum.　　(1.107.3–6)

Give me leisure of the sort that Maecenas once made for his Flaccus and his Virgil. I would try to fashion works that would live through the ages and snatch my name from the flames.

Martial's epigrammatic leisure hardly presents the tranquil, unruffled aspect of an otherworldly bard's rural withdrawal. The menace, surprise, and jolting sounds of the city disrupt his thoughts and his peace at almost every moment. True leisure belongs to another time, and another social world. Yet even as Martial cunningly and not wholly ingenuously disavows Augustan literary seriousness, he attempts to revive some of the distinctive flavour of Catullan *otium* in an imperial age. Both Martial and his contemporary Statius subtly recast Catullus' hendecasyllabic wit, ludic poetics, and Saturnalian atmosphere to suit altered times. Perhaps it was seen as no longer plausible, not to mention potentially naive and humourless, to claim the lofty untroubled *otium* of a grand Augustan *vates*; or perhaps such leisured independence implied a degree of autarky unacceptable in the more authoritarian environment of Flavian Rome. Regardless of the precise causality, it is striking to see this explicit return to the fragmentation and ephemerality of literary leisure immortalized in Catullus' polymetric *nugae*.

These three self-representational poets writing in three different periods and in different poetic modes afford an opportunity for reflecting on the significance of shifting representations of literary *otium* that are informed, in turn, by shifting rhetorical attitudes toward the issue of poetry's autonomy within Roman society. For none of these poets is the 'autonomy' of literary leisure simply a set of institutionally embedded attitudes that can be taken for granted. In the perspective of the *longue durée*, Horace's proud claims of autonomist *otium* appear as the exception rather than the rule. Literary composition was never a wholly straightforward activity to defend, and poetry never wholly lost its early associations with time-wasting indulgence and clientage. Perhaps for this very reason, strategies of self-representation mattered a great deal, and poets applied their often considerable powers of rhetorical artifice to devising images of literary activity and styles of literary personality that enabled them to position themselves with both precision and playfulness in relation to established discourses and traditional forms of prestige.

---

[2] See Fraenkel (1957), 211–14.

Changes in self-representational strategy, then, need not correspond reliably with (although it would be reductive to deny that they bear no relation to) actual shifts in the social conditions of literary creation. The potential discontinuity between poetically generated image and social reality has understandably been the cause of major differences of interpretation for modern scholars. James Zetzel and others have hailed the newly autonomist self-representational rhetoric of poets in the first century BC as a sign that poetry was coming to be regarded as a 'way of life itself',[3] a valid and self-sufficient pursuit for upper-class Romans. For such scholars, Horace's praises of *otium* correspond to a veritable shift in values. Ernst Badian, however, responded in a 1985 review article with a trenchant critique. He argues that the notion of a profound 'inversion' of social values is exaggerated, and that finer gradations of social status and position need to be taken into account.[4] Finally, while poetry won some degree of acceptance in Roman society, it never truly challenged public life for supremacy.

> The writing of poetry had long been an accepted form of cultured *otium* in which, as early as around 100 B. C., even aristocrats like Q. Catulus or C. Caesar Strabo could indulge. That generation was already remote, in respect of both pursuits, from the days when (as the elder Cato reminded his contemporaries) their ancestors had called those who indulged in banquets or in poetry vagabonds (*grassatores*). The shift from that attitude, through client status, to the minor legitimacy shared with other cultural pursuits, is an important phenomenon, and so is the emergence of one or two men of equestrian standing who made poetry their sole pursuit. But the limitations of the phenomenon are as important as its occurrence. Whatever the games poets played on themes like equating love and war, no one seriously thought that it was the duty of the political aristocracy to devote itself to love to the exclusion of war and government.[5]

Badian's arguments are powerful enough to make one think twice about taking statements about the value of love and poetry in Catullus, Propertius, and Ovid as signs of a deeper social shift away from the *mos maiorum* and toward a new valuation of literary leisure among the Roman elite. On the other hand, Badian, no less than others, needs to read interpretively, and at times tendentiously, between the lines of literature and history in order to arrive at his own conclusions.[6] Did Augustan *recusationes* merely serve to mitigate, and thereby make possible, the encomiastic aims of the Augustan poets, as Badian argues? Or does the motif of the *recusatio* reflect some degree of autonomy sought by these writers of independent means? Similarly, does the elegiac *militia amoris* suggest an actual shift in attitudes toward new forms of cultural behavior among the Roman elite? Or was

---

[3] Zetzel (1982), 92; discussed by Badian (1985), 344.

[4] E.g., there are important differences between the aristocratic Calvus, the municipal *eques* Catullus, the freedman's son Horace, and the socially independent historian Livy: Badian (1985), 344.

[5] Badian (1985), 344–5.

[6] Were there really only 'one or two men of equestrian standing who made poetry their sole pursuit'? The truth of this statement depends on how one sets the criteria: for a very different assessment, see White (1993). Badian places Horace and Virgil in a 'Hogarthian' world of clientage, and sets their social status (at the beginnings of their careers) fairly low. Only later, on his reading, did they rise to equestrian status. Yet he must also know that much of this reconstruction must depend upon our interpretation of these poets' representations of their own backgrounds and careers.

this merely a literary 'game' played by the poets, quite separate from their more sober realizations?

Catullus c. 50 affords a vivid reminder both of the precariousness of literary activity in ancient Rome, and the elusiveness of its sociological realities. Poetry, for the neoteric poet, is a seductive, pleasurable, and wholly absorbing 'game' which he does not wish to cease playing, but which he cannot reliably hope to share with others. The poem frames itself as parodic exaggeration and self-mocking extremity, but only an unusually literal reader would fail to detect in Catullus' ludic 'trifle' (*nugae*) the presence of ideas about poetry and its practice in republican Rome. The precariousness and vulnerability to scorn to which Catullus c. 50 calls attention are distinctive features of Roman literary culture, but these are also the very features which give autonomist rhetoric in Roman poetry its explicit edge and sharpness. Traditional Roman disdain for literary pursuits and the vigorous rhetorical battle for their legitimacy and autonomy are two sides of the same coin. Even Badian concedes the shift from an attitude of scorn to an acceptance of literature's 'minor legitimacy' in Roman society. I would add that the autonomist rhetoric employed by Roman poets played an important role in fostering this hard-won cultural legitimacy. Even patently exaggerated and playfully humorous claims of axiological self-sufficiency (e.g. the *militia amoris*) contribute, in a complicated way, to the autonomist project.

I hope to have justified the interest and value of studying the rhetoric of Roman poetic autonomy in its changing forms. It should be clear by this point that the aim has never been to prove the emergence of 'literary autonomy' in ancient Rome, but rather to show how an interest in autonomy informs key aspects of Roman poetic self-representation. By contrast with modern Western societies, ancient Roman society did not have an established set of ideas, practices, and institutions based upon a culturally pervasive presumption of aesthetic autonomy. Poetic activity in particular was both precarious and in need of constant efforts of self-justification. Many of these efforts were focused on linking poetic identity with qualities of self-sufficiency, autarky, and self-determination—in other words, with working to establish poetry's autonomy as a cultural pursuit.

This study began by confronting the problem of potential anachronism in the study of ancient poetic autonomy. The concept of autonomy is so dominant in modern aesthetics that it threatens to derail modern perceptions of earlier literature and art. Obsessive avoidance of anachronism, on the other hand, risks rendering research into earlier societies overly cautious and anemic. We inevitably view past societies through the lens of our own concepts and social categories. The point is to do so in such a way as to produce insight into earlier modes of thought and behavior, not to dispense altogether with the corrupting overlay of modern thought (which would be impossible in any case).[7] From this perspective, we may begin to see how our modern preoccupation with aesthetic autonomy might actually be a positive and helpful factor in our study of ancient Roman poetry rather than a source of confusion. Roman poets, like modern ones, display a highly developed interest in the nature of their own medium and in the differences

---

[7] See in particular the arguments of Feeney (2006).

between poetry and other modes of communication. We are especially well-positioned to appreciate both the metaliterary dimension of ancient texts and their autonomist rhetoric. Our own values and assumptions, based upon the distinctive cultural configuration of modern society, afford the beginning-point from which to commence the extended exercise in comparison between present and past, self and other that constitutes the necessary foundation for study of the literary ideas of ancient Rome.

Bibliography

Classical works not listed below are cited according to the abbreviations provided in *Oxford Classical Dictionary*, 3rd edn, ed. Simon Hornblower and Antony Spawforth. Oxford: Oxford University Press.

Adorno, Theodor. 1991. 'Lyric Poetry and Society'. In *Notes to Literature*, tr. by Shierry Weber Nicholsen, i. New York: Columbia University Press, 30–7.

——. 1997. *Aesthetic Theory*. Tr. and ed. Robert Hullot-Kentor. Minneapolis: University of Minnesota Press.

Ahl, Frederick. 1984a. 'The Rider and the Horse: Politics and Power in Roman Poetry from Horace to Statius'. *ANRW* ii. 32.1, 78–85. Berlin: W. de Gruyter.

——. 1984b. 'The Art of Safe Criticism in Greece and Rome'. *AJP* 105.2: 174–8.

Allen, A. W. 1950. 'Elegy and the Classical Attitude toward Love: Propertius I, I'. *YCS* 11: 255–77.

Alpers, Paul J. 1979. *The Singer of the Eclogues: A Study of Virgilian Pastoral, with a new translation of the Eclogues*. Berkeley: University of California Press.

——. 1996. *What Is Pastoral?* Chicago: University of Chicago Press.

Alvarez Hernández, Arturo. 1997. *La poética de Propercio: autobiografía artística del Calímaco romano*. Assisi: Accademia properziana del Subasio.

Ancona, Ronnie. 1994. *Time and the Erotic in Horace's Odes*. Durham, NC, and London: Duke University Press.

Ancona, Ronnie and Judith P. Hallett. 2007. 'Catullus in the Secondary School Curriculum'. In Skinner (ed.) (2007), 481–502.

Anderson, W. S. 1963. 'The Roman Socrates: Horace and his *Satires*'. In J. P. Sullivan (ed.), *Critical Essays on Roman Literature: Satire*. London: Routledge and Kegan Paul, 1–37.

——. 1970. '*Lascivia* vs. *ira*: Martial and Juvenal'. *California Studies in Classical Antiquity* 3: 1–34.

——. 1982. *Essays on Roman Satire*. Princeton, NJ: Princeton University Press.

André, Jean. 1966. *L'otium dans la vie morale et intellectuelle romaine, des origines à l'époque augustéenne*. Paris: Presses Universitaires.

Armstrong, David. 1986. '*Horatius eques et scriba*: Satires 1.6 and 2.7'. *Transactions of the American Philological Association* 116: 255–88.

——. 2004. *Virgil, Philodemus, and the Augustans*. Austin: University of Texas Press.

Armstrong, Rebecca. 2004. 'Retiring Apollo: Ovid on the Politics and Poetics of Self-Sufficiency'. *Classical Quarterly*, ns 54: 528–50.

Asmis, Elizabeth. 1995. 'Philodemus on Censorship, Moral Utility, and Formalism in Poetry'. In Obbink (1995), 148–77.

Atkins, Margaret and M. T. Griffin (eds). 1991. *Cicero: On Duties*. Cambridge: Cambridge University Press.

Badian, Ernst. 1985. '*Nobiles amici*: Art and Literature in an Aristocratic Society'. Review of B. K. Gold (1982). *Classical Philology* 80.4: 341–57.

Baehrens, Emil. 1876. *Tibullische Blätter*. Jena: H. Dufft.

Baker, R. J. 1970. '*Laus in amore mori*. Love and Death in Propertius'. *Latomus* 29: 670–98.

——. 1973. '*Duplices tabellae*: Propertius 3.23 and Ovid *Amores* 1.12'. *Classical Philology* 68: 109–13.

——. 1983. '*Caesaris in nomen* (Propertius IV.vi)'. *Rheinisches Museum für Philologie* 126: 153–74.

Ball, Robert J. 1983. *Tibullus the Elegist: A Critical Survey*. Göttingen: Vandenhoeck & Ruprecht.

Balsdon, J. P. V. D. 1960. '*Auctoritas, Dignitas, Otium*'. *Classical Quarterly* 10: 43–50.

Balsdon, J. P. V. D. 1969. *Life and Leisure in Ancient Rome*. New York: McGraw-Hill.

Barber, E. A. (ed.). 1960. *Sexti Properti carmina*. Oxford: Clarendon Press.

Barchiesi, Alessandro. 1997. *The Poet and the Prince: Ovid and Augustan Discourse*. Berkeley: University of California Press.

——. 2000. 'Rituals in Ink: Horace and the Greek Lyric Tradition'. In Mary Depew and Dirk Obbink (eds), *Matrices of Genre: Authors, Canons, and Society*. Cambridge, MA: Harvard University Press, 167–82.

——. 2001. *Speaking Volumes: Narrative and Intertext in Ovid and Other Latin Poets*. Ed. and tr. Matt Fox and Simone Marchesi. London: Duckworth.

——. 2005. 'Learned Eyes: Poets, Viewers, Image Makers'. In Galinsky (ed.) (2005), 281–36.

——. 2006. 'Women on Top: Livia and Andromache'. In Gibson, Green, and Sharrock (eds) (2006), 96–120.

Bartsch, Shadie. 1994. *Actors in the Audience: Theatricality and Doublespeak from Nero to Hadrian*. Cambridge, MA: Harvard University Press.

——. 1997. *Ideology in Cold Blood: A Reading of Lucan's Civil War*. Cambridge, MA: Harvard University Press.

Batstone, William Wendell. 1992. '*Amor improbus*, *Felix qui*, and *Tardus Apollo*: The *Monobiblos* and the *Georgics*'. *Classical Philology* 87.4: 287–302.

——. 1998. 'Dry Pumice and the Programmatic Language of Catullus 1'. *Classical Philology* 93.2: 125–35.

——. 2007. 'Catullus and the Programmatic Poem: The Origins, Scope, and Utility of a Concept'. In Skinner (ed.) (2007), 235–53.

Batstone, William Wendell and Cynthia Damon. 2006. *Caesar's Civil War*. Oxford: Oxford University Press.

Birt, Theodor. 1882. *Das antike Buchwesen in seinem Verhältniss zur Litteratur*. Berlin: W. Hertz.

Block E. 1984. 'Carmen 65 and the Arrangement of Catullus' Poetry'. *Ramus* 13: 48–59.

Bloomer, Martin. 1997. 'A Preface to the History of Declamation: Whose Speech? Whose History?' In Habinek and Schiesaro (eds) (1997), 199–215.

Boes, Jean. 1990. *La Philosophie et l'action dans la correspondance de Cicéron*. Nancy: Presses Universitaires de Nancy.

Boissier, G. 1899. 'Relations de Juvenal et de Martial'. *Revue des Cours et Conférences* 7.2: 433–51.

Bonner, Stanley Fredrick. 1949. *Roman Declamation in the Late Republic and Early Empire*. Liverpool: Liverpool University Press.

Booth, Joan. 2001. 'Problems and Programmatics in Propertius 1.1'. *Hermes* 129.1: 63–74.

Boucher, Jean-Paul. 1958. 'L'Oeuvre de L. Varius Rufus d'après Properce II, 34'. *Revue des Études Anciennes* 60: 307–22.

——. 1965. *Études sur Properce, problèmes d'inspiration et d'art*. Paris: E. de Boccard.

Bourdieu, Pierre. 1984. *Distinction: A Social Critique of the Judgement of Taste*. Cambridge, MA: Harvard University Press.

——. 1993. *The Rules of Art: Genesis and Structure of the Literary Field*. Translated by Susan Emanuel. Stanford: Stanford University Press.

Bowditch, Phebe Lowell. 2001. *Horace and the Gift Economy of Patronage*. Berkeley: University of California Press.

Bowersock, Glen W. 1971. 'A Date in the Eighth Eclogue'. *Harvard Studies in Classical Philology* 75: 73–8.

Boyance, Pierre. 1941. 'Cum dignitate otium'. *Revue des études anciennes* 43: 172–91.

Boyd, Barbara Weiden. 1984. '"Parva seges satis est": The Landscape of Tibullan Elegy in 1.1 and 1.10'. *Transactions of the American Philological Association* 114: 273–80.

——. 1997. *Ovid's Literary Loves: Influence and Innovation in the Amores*. Ann Arbor: University of Michigan Press.

—— (ed.). 2002. *Brill's Companion to Ovid*. Leiden: Brill.

Boyle, A. J. 2003. *Ovid and the Monuments: A Poet's Rome*. Bendigo: Aureal Publications.

Bramble, J. C. 1974. *Persius and the Programmatic Satire: A Study in Form and Imagery*. Cambridge: Cambridge University Press.

Braund, David. 1996. 'The Politics of Catullus 10: Memmius, Caesar and the Bithynians'. *Hermathena* 160: 45–67.

Braund, Susanna H. 1988. *Beyond Anger: A Study of Juvenal's Third Book of Satires*. Cambridge: Cambridge University Press.

——. 1989. 'City and Country in Roman Satire'. In S. H. Braund (ed.), *Satire and Society in Ancient Rome*. Exeter: University of Exeter Press, 23–48.

Bright, David F. 1975. 'The Art and Structure of Tibullus 1.7'. *Grazer Beiträge* 3: 31–46.

——. 1978. *Haec mihi fingebam: Tibullus in his World*. Leiden: Brill.

——. 1980. *Elaborate Disarray: The Nature of Statius' Silvae*. Meisenheim am Glan: Hain.

Brink, C. O. 1963. *Horace on Poetry: Prolegomena to the Literary Epistles*. Cambridge: Cambridge University Press.

——. 1982. *Horace on Poetry: Epistles Book II, the Letters to Augustus and Florus*. Cambridge: Cambridge University Press.

Brown, Michael P. (ed. and tr.). 1993. *Horace: Satires I*. Warminster: Aris & Phillips.

Buchan, Mark. 1995. 'Ovidius imperamator: Beginnings and Endings of Love Poems and Empire in the *Amores*'. *Arethusa* 28: 53–85.

Buchheit, Vinzenz. 1959. 'Catulls Dichterkritik in c.36'. *Hermes* 87: 309–27.

——. 1975. 'Catulls Literarkritik und Kallimachos'. *Grazer Beiträge* 4: 21–50.

——. 1976. 'Catulls c.50 als Programm und Bekenntnis'. *Rheinisches Museum* 119: 162–80.

Bürger, Peter. 1984. *Theory of the Avant-garde*. Minneapolis: University of Minnesota Press.

——. 1998. 'Critique of Autonomy'. In Michael Kelley (ed.), *Encyclopedia of Aesthetics*, i, 175–8.

Butler, H. E. and Barber, E. A. (eds). 1964. *The Elegies of Propertius*. Hildesheim: Georg Olms.

Butrica, James L. 1996. 'The *Amores* of Propertius: Unity and Structure of Books 2–4'. *Illinois Classical Studies* 21: 87–158.

Cahoon, Leslie. 1988. 'The Bed as Battlefield: Erotic Conquest and Military Metaphor in Ovid's *Amores*'. *Transactions of the American Philological Association* 118: 293–307.

Cairns, Francis. 1974a. *Generic Composition in Greek and Latin Poetry*. Edinburgh: Edinburgh University Press.

——. 1974b. 'Some Observations on Propertius 1.1'. *Classical Quarterly* 24: 94–110.

——. 1979. *Tibullus: A Hellenistic Poet at Rome*. Cambridge: Cambridge University Press.

——. 1984. 'Propertius and the Battle of Actium (4.6)'. In Woodman and West (eds) (1984), 129–68.

——. 1992. 'The Power of Implication: Horace's Invitation to Maecenas (Odes 1.20)'. In Woodman and Powell (eds) (1992), 84–109.

——. 1993. 'Imitation and Originality in Ovid *Amores* 1.3'. *Papers of the Leeds International Latin Seminar* 7: 101–22.

——. 2006. *Sextus Propertius: The Augustan Elegist*. Cambridge: Cambridge University Press.

Camps, W. A. (ed.). 1965. *Elegies. Book 4*. Cambridge: Cambridge University Press.

Casali, Sergio. 2006. 'The Art of Making Oneself Hated: Rethinking (Anti-) Augustanism in Ovid's *Ars amatoria*'. In Gibson, Green, and Sharrock (eds) (2006), 216–35.

Citroni, Mario. 1968. 'Motivi di polemica letteraria negli epigrammi di Marziale'. *DiArch* 2: 259–301.

——. (ed.). 1975. *M. Valerii Martialis Epigrammaton Liber Primus*.

Citroni, Mario. 1986. 'Le raccomandazioni del poeta: apostrofe al libro e contatto col destinatario'. *Maia* 40, 111–46.

——. 1988. 'Pubblicazione e dediche dei libri in Marziale'. *Maia* 40: 3–39.

——. 1989. 'Marziale e la letteratura per i Saturnali (poetica dell'intrattenimento e cronologia della pubblicazione dei libri)'. *Illinois Classical Studies* 14: 201–26.

——. 1992. 'Produzione letteraria e forme del potere. Gli scrittori latini del I secolo dell'impero'. In A. Schiavone and A. Momigliano (eds), *Storia di Roma*, ii: *L'impero mediterraneo. 3: Una cultura e l'impero*. Torino: Einaudi, 383–490.

——. 1995. *Poesia e lettori in Roma antica*. Bari: Laterza.

Claridge, Amanda. 1998. *Rome: An Oxford Archaeological Guide*. Oxford: Oxford University Press.

Clausen, Wendell Vernon (ed.). 1959. *Persi Flacci et D. Iuni Iuvenalis Saturae*. Oxford: Clarendon Press.

——. 1964. 'Callimachus and Latin Poetry'. *Greek, Roman and Byzantine Studies* 5: 181–96.

——. 1976. 'Catulli Veronensis liber'. *Classical Philology* 71: 37–43.

——. 1986. 'Cicero and the New Poetry'. *Harvard Studies in Classical Philology* 90: 159–70.

—— (ed.). 1994. *A commentary on Virgil, Eclogues*. Oxford: Oxford University Press.

Clay, Jenny Strauss. 2010. 'Horace and Lesbian Lyric'. In G. Davis (ed.) (2010), 128–46.

Coffey, Michael. 1976. *Roman Satire*. London: Methuen.

Coleman, K. M. (ed.). 1988. *Statius: Silvae IV*. Oxford: Oxford University Press.

——. 1998. '*The liber spectaculorum*: Perpetuating the Ephemeral'. In Grewing (1998), 15–36.

Coleman, Robert (ed.). 1977. *Vergil: Eclogues*. Cambridge: Cambridge University Press.

Colton, Robert E. 1991. *Juvenal Use of Martial's Epigrams: A Study of Literary Influence*. Amsterdam: A. M. Hakkert.

Commager, Steele. 1962. *The Odes of Horace: A Critical study*. Bloomington: Indiana University Press.

——. 1974. *A Prolegomenon to Propertius*. Norman: University of Oklahoma Press.

Conington, John (tr. and comm.) and Henry Nettleship (ed.). 1872. *The Satires of A. Persius Flaccus*. Oxford: Clarendon Press.

Connolly, Joy. 2000. 'Asymptotes of pleasure'. *Arethusa* 33: 71–98.

Connors, Catherine. 2000. 'Imperial Space and Time: The Literature of Leisure'. In O. Taplin (ed.), *Literature in the Greek and Roman Worlds*, Oxford: Oxford University Press, 492–518.

Conte, G. B. 1986. *The Rhetoric of Imitation: Genre and Poetic Memory in Virgil and Other Latin Poets*. Tr. Charles Segal. Ithaca, NY: Cornell University Press.

——. 1994a. *Genres and Readers: Lucretius, Love Elegy, Pliny's Encyclopedia*. Baltimore, MD: Johns Hopkins University Press.

——. 1994b. *Latin Literature: A History*. Baltimore, MD: Johns Hopkins University Press.

——. 1996. *The Hidden Author: An Interpretation of Petronius' Satyricon*. Berkeley: University of California Press.

Copley, Frank O. 1947. '*Servitium Amoris* in the Roman Elegists'. *Transactions of the American Philological Association* 78: 285–300.

——. 1953. 'Catullus 35'. *AJP* 74: 149–60.

——. 1956. *Exclusus amator: A Study in Latin Love Poetry*. Madison, WI: American Philological Association.

——. 1958. 'Catullus c.4: The World of the Poem'. *Transactions of the American Philological Association* 89: 9–13.

Corti, Rosella. 1991. 'La tematica dell'*otium* nelle *Silvae* di Stazio'. In M. Pani (ed.), *Continuità e trasformazioni fra repubblica e principato: Istituzioni, politica, società*, Bari: Edipuglia, 189–224.

Courtney, Edward. 1968. 'The Structure of Propertius Book 1 and Some Textual Consequences'. *Phoenix* 22.3: 250–58.

——. 1980. *A Commentary on the Satires of Juvenal*. London: Athlone Press.

——(ed.). 1990. *P. Papini Stati Silvae*. Oxford: Clarendon Press.

——(ed.). 1993. *The Fragmentary Latin Poets*. Oxford: Oxford University Press.

——. 1994. 'Horace and the Pest'. *Classical Journal* 90.1: 1–8.

Cowherd, Carrie. 1986. *Persius: Saturae*. Bryn Mawr, PA: Thomas Library, Bryn Mawr College.

Crowther, N. B. 1970. 'ΟΙ ΝΕΩΤΕΡΟΙ, Poetae Novi, and Cantores Euphorionis'. *Classical Quarterly*, ns 20: 322–7.

Cucchiarelli, Andrea. 2001. *La satira e il poeta: Orazio tra Epodi e Sermones*. Pisa: Giardini.

Curran, Leo C. 1966. '*Desultores Amoris*: Ovid *Amores* 1.3'. *Classical Philology* 61.1: 47–9.

D'Elia, S. 1981. 'Appunti su Marziale e la civiltà letteraria dell'età flavia'. In *Letterature Comparate: Problemi e Metodo: Studi in onore di Ettore Paratore*, ii, 647–66.

Damon, Cynthia. 1992. 'Statius *Silvae* 4.9: *Libertas Decembris*?'. *Illinois Classical Studies* 17.2: 301–8.

——. 1997. *The Mask of the Parasite: A Pathology of Roman Patronage*. Ann Arbor: University of Michigan Press.

Davidson, J. F. 1980. 'Some Thoughts on Ovid *Amores* 1.3'. In C. Deroux (ed.), *Studies in Latin Literature and Roman History* 2, Brussels: Latomus, 278–85.

Davies, Ceri. 1973. 'Poetry in the "Circle" of Messalla'. *Greece and Rome*, 2nd ser., 20: 25–35.

Davis, Gregson. 1991. *Polyhymnia: The Rhetoric of Horatian Lyric Discourse*. Berkeley: University of California Press.

——(ed.). 2010a. *A Companion to Horace*. Chichester, Blackwell.

——. 2010b. 'Defining a Lyric Ethos: Archilochus lyricus and Horatian melos'. In Gregson Davis (ed.) (2010a), 105–27.

——. 2002. '*Ait phaselus*: The Caricature of Stylistic Genre (*genus dicendi*) in Catullus *Carm.* 4'. *Materiali e discussioni per l'analisi dei testi classici* 48: 111–43.

Davis, John. T. 1977. *Dramatic Pairings in the Elegies of Propertius and Ovid*. Bern: Paul Haupt.

——. 1989. *Fictus adulter: Poet as Actor in the Amores*. Amsterdam: Gieben.

Davis, P. J. 1999. 'Ovid's *Amores*: A Political Reading'. *Classical Philology* 94: 431–49.

——. 2006. *Ovid and Augustus: A Political Reading of Ovid's Erotic Poems*. London: Duckworth.

Debrohun, Jeri Blair. 2003. *Roman Propertius and the Reinvention of Elegy*. Ann Arbor: University of Michigan Press.

Dessen, Cynthia S. 1968. *Iunctura callidus acri: A Study of Persius' Satires*. Urbana: University of Illinois Press.

Deuling, Judy K. 1999. 'Catullus and Mamurra'. *Mnemosyne* 52.2: 188–94.

Dewar, Michael. 1994. 'Laying it on with a Trowel: The Proem to Lucan and Related Texts'. *Classical Quarterly* 44(i): 199–211.

Dix, T. Keith. 1994. '"Public Libraries" in Ancient Rome: Ideology and Reality'. *Libraries & Culture* 29.3: 282–96.

Dougherty, Carol and Kurke, Leslie. 1998. *Cultural Poetics in Ancient Greece: Cult, Performance, Politics*. New York: Oxford University Press.

Du Quesnay, I. M. Le M. 1981. 'Vergil's First Eclogue'. *Proceedings of the Liverpool Latin Seminar* 3: 29–182.

Duclos, G. S. 1976. 'Catullus 11: Atque in perpetuum Lesbia, ave atque vale'. *Arethusa* 9: 77–89.

Dupont, Florence. 1997. '*Recitatio* and the Reorganization of the Space of Public Discourse'. In Habinek and Schiesaro (eds) (1997), 44–59.

——. 1999. *The Invention of Literature: From Greek Intoxication to the Latin Book.* Baltimore, MD: Johns Hopkins University Press.

——. 1984. 'Horace and Maecenas: The Propaganda Value of Sermones I'. In Woodman and West (eds) (1984), 19–58.

——. 1992. '*In memoriam Galli*: Propertius 1.21'. In Woodman and Powell (eds) (1992), 52–83.

Earl, D. C. 1961. *The Political Thought of Sallust.* Cambridge: Cambridge University Press.

Eckert, V. 1985. *Untersuchungen zur Einheit von Properz I.* Heidelberg: C. Winter.

Eco, Umberto. 2004. *History of Beauty.* New York: Rizzoli.

Edmunds, Lowell. 1992. *From a Sabine Jar: Reading Horace, Odes 1.9.* Chapel Hill: University of North Carolina Press.

Edwards, Catharine. 1996. *Writing Rome: Textual Approaches to the City.* Cambridge: Cambridge University Press.

——. 2002. *The Politics of Immorality in Ancient Rome.* Cambridge: Cambridge University Press.

Elder, J. P. 1967. 'Catullus I, His Poetic Creed, and Nepos'. *Harvard Studies in Classical Philology* 71: 143–9.

Enk, P. J. 1956. 'The Unity of Some Elegies of Propertius'. *Latomus* 15: 181–5.

—— (ed.). 1962. *Sex. Propertii Elegiarum Liber Secundus.* 2 vols. Leiden: A. W. Sijthoff.

Erbse, Hartmut. 1979. 'Properz III 23 und Ovid Am. I 11–12'. In *Ausgewählte Schriften zur Klassischen Philologie*, 529–46. Berlin: Walter de Gruyter.

Evans, Harry B. 1983. *Publica carmina: Ovid's Books from Exile.* Lincoln: University of Nebraska Press.

Evans, Jane DeRose. 2009. 'Prostitutes in the Portico of Pompey?: A Reconsideration'. *Transactions of the American Philological Association* 139.1: 123–45.

Fantham, Elaine. 1996. *Roman Literary Culture: From Cicero to Apuleius.* Baltimore, MD: Johns Hopkins University Press.

——. 2009. *Latin Poets and Italian Gods.* Toronto: University of Toronto Press.

Farrell, Joseph. 1991. 'Asinius Pollio in Virgil Eclogue 8'. *Classical Philology* 86.3: 204–11.

——. 2002. 'Greek Lives and Roman Careers in the Classical *vita* Tradition'. In Patrick Cheney and Frederick A. de Armas (eds), *European Literary Careers: The Author from Antiquity to the Renaissance.* Toronto: University of Toronto Press, 24–46.

——. 2005. 'The Augustan Period: 40 BC–AD 14'. In Harrison (ed.) (2005), 44–57.

——. 2009. 'The Impermanent Text in Catullus and Other Roman Poets'. In W. A. Johnson and H. N. Parker (eds), *Ancient Literacies.* New York: Oxford University Press, 164–85.

Fear, Trevor. 2000. 'The Poet as Pimp: Elegiac Seduction in the Time of Augustus'. *Arethusa* 33: 217–40.

Fedeli, Paolo (ed.). 1980. *Sesto Properzio: il primo libro delle Elegie.* Firenze: Olschki.

—— (ed.). 1985. *Properzio: il libro terzo delle Elegie.* Bari: Adriatica.

——. 1986. 'Properzio e l'amore elegiaco'. In *Bimillenario della morte di Properzio*, Atti del convegno internazionale di studi Properziani, Rome-Assisi (Accad. Properziana del Subasio), 277–301.

——. (ed). 2005. *Properzio: Elegie, Libro II. Introduzione, testo e commento. ARCA Classical Texts, Papers, and Monographs 45.* Cambridge: Francis Cairns.

Feeney, Denis. 1991. *The Gods in Epic: Poets and Critics of the Classical Tradition.* Oxford: Oxford University Press.

——. 1992. 'Si licet et fas est: Ovid's *Fasti* and the Problem of Free Speech under the Principate'. In Anton Powell (ed.) (1992), 1–25.

——. 1993. 'Horace and the Greek Lyric Poets'. In N. Rudd (ed.), *Horace 2000: A Celebration, Essays for the Bimillennium*, 41–63.

——. 1998. *Literature and Religion at Rome: cultures, contexts, and beliefs*. Cambridge: Cambridge University Press.

——. 2002. '*Una cum scriptore meo*: Poetry, Principate and the Traditions of Literary History in the Epistle to Augustus'. In Woodman and Feeney (eds) (2002), 172–87.

——. 2006. 'Classics and Modern Criticism'. In Andrew Laird (ed.), *Oxford Readings in Ancient Literary Criticism*. Oxford: Oxford University Press, 440–54.

Ferguson, John (ed.). 1979. *Juvenal: The Satires: With an introduction and commentary*. New York: St Martin's.

Ferri, Rolando. 1993. *I dispiaceri di un epicureo: uno studio sulla poetica oraziane delle Epistole (con un capitolo su Persio)*. Pisa: Giardini.

Finnamore, John F. 1984. 'Catullus 50 and 51: Friendship, Love, and *otium*'. *Classical World* 78.1: 11–19.

Fisher, J. M. 1971. 'Catullus 35'. *Classical Philology* 66: 1–5.

Fitzgerald, William. 1989. 'Horace, Pleasure, and the Text'. *Arethusa* 22: 81–104.

——. 1995. *Catullan Provocations: Lyric Poetry and the Drama of Position*. Berkeley: University of California Press.

——. 1996. 'Labor and Laborer in Latin Poetry: The Case of the *Moretum*'. *Arethusa* 29.3: 389–418.

——. 2000. *Slavery and the Roman Literary Imagination*. Cambridge: Cambridge University Press.

——. 2007. *Martial: The World of the Epigram*. Chicago: University of Chicago Press.

Flower, Harriet. 1996. *Ancestor Masks and Aristocratic Power in Roman Culture*. Oxford: Oxford University Press.

——. 2006. *The Art of Forgetting: Disgrace and Oblivion in Roman Political Culture*. Chapel Hill: University of Carolina Press.

Ford, Andrew. 1992. *Homer: The Poetry of the Past*. Ithaca, NY: Cornell University Press.

——. 2002. *The Origins of Criticism: Literary Culture and Poetic Theory in Classical Greece*. Princeton, NJ: Princeton University Press.

Fordyce, C. J. (ed.). 1961. *Catullus: A Commentary*. Oxford: Oxford University Press.

Forsythe, Phyllis Young. 1991. 'The Thematic Unity of Catullus 11'. *Classical World* 84.6: 457–64.

Fotiou, A. S. 1975. 'Catullus 11: A New Approach'. *Grazer Beiträge* 3: 151–8.

Foucault, Michel. 1986. *The History of Sexuality*, iii: *The Care of the Self*. New York: Pantheon.

Fowler, Don P. 1995a. 'Martial and the Book'. In A. J. Boyle (ed.), *Roman Literature and Ideology: Ramus Essays for J. P. Sullivan*. Bendigo, Australia: Aureal Publications, 199–226.

——. 1995b. 'Horace and the Aesthetics of Politics'. In Harrison (ed.) (1995), 248–66.

Fraenkel, Eduard. 1957. *Horace*. Oxford: Clarendon Press.

Fredrick, David. 1999. 'Haptic Poetics'. *Arethusa* 32.1: 49–83.

Fredricksmeyer, E. A. 1973. 'Catullus 49, Cicero, and Caesar'. *Classical Philology* 68.4: 268–78.

——. 1985. 'Catullus to Caecilius on Good Poetry'. *American Journal of Philology* 106: 213–21.

——. 1993. 'Method and Interpretation: Catullus 11'. *Helios* 20: 89–105.

Freudenburg, Kirk. 1993. *The Walking Muse: Horace on the Theory of Satire*. Princeton, NJ: Princeton University Press.

——. 2001. *Satires of Rome: Threatening Poses from Lucilius to Juvenal*. Cambridge: Cambridge University Press.

Freudenburg, Kirk 2002a. '*Solus sapiens liber est*: Recommissioning Lyric in *Epistles* 1'. In Woodman and Feeney (eds) (2002), 124–40.

——. 2002b. 'Writing to/through Florus: Criticism and the Addressee in Horace *Epistles* 2.2'. *Memoirs of the American Academy in Rome* 47: 33–55.

——. 2005. 'Making Epic Silver: The Alchemy of Imperial Satire'. In M. Paschalis, (ed.), *Roman and Greek Imperial Epic*. Heracleion: Crete University Press, 91–115.

Frier, Bruce W. 1985. *The Rise of the Roman Jurists: Studies in Cicero's Pro Caecina*. Princeton, NJ: Princeton University Press.

Frischer, Bernard and Iain Gordon Brown (eds). 2001. *Allan Ramsay and the Search for Horace's Villa*. Burlington, VT: Ashgate Publishing.

Frischer, Bernard, Jane W. Crawford and Monica de Simone. 2006. *The Horace's Villa Project, 1997–2003: Report on New Fieldwork and Research*. Oxford: Archaeopress.

Fuhrmann, M. 1960. 'Cum dignitate otium: Politisches Programm und Staatstheorie bei Cicero'. *Gymnasium* 67: 481–500.

Gaisser, Julia H. 1971. 'Tibullus 1.7: A Tribute to Messalla'. *Classical Philology* 66.4: 221–9.

Galinsky, Karl. 1969. 'The Triumph Theme in the Augustan Elegy'. *Wiener Studien*, NS 3: 75–107.

——. 1988. 'The Anger of Aeneas'. *American Journal of Philology* 109.3: 321–48.

——. 1994. 'How to be Philosophical about the End of the *Aeneid*'. *Illinois Classical Studies* 19: 191–201.

——. 1996. *Augustan Culture: An Interpretive Introduction*. Princeton, NJ: Princeton University Press.

——(ed.). 2005. *The Cambridge Companion to the Age of Augustus*. Cambridge: Cambridge University Press.

Gamberale, Leopoldo. 1982. 'Libri e letteratura nel carme 22 di Catullo'. *Materiali e discussioni per l'analisi dei testi classici* 8: 143–69.

Garrod, W. H. and E. C. Wickham (eds). 1901. *Q. Horati Flacci opera*. Oxford: Clarendon Press.

Garthwaite, John. 1984. 'Statius, *Silvae* 3.4: On the Fate of Earinus'. *Aufstieg und Niedergang der römischen Welt*. Berlin: W. de Gruyter, ii, 32.1: 111–24.

——. 1992. 'The Panegyrics of Domitian in Martial Book 9'. *Ramus* 22: 79–102.

Geyssen, John W. 1996. *Imperial Panegyric in Statius: A Literary Commentary on Silvae 1.1*. New York: P. Lang.

Gibson, Roy K. (ed.). 2003. *Ovid: Ars amatoria. Book 3*. Cambridge: Cambridge University Press.

——. 2006. 'Ovid, Augustus, and the Politics of Moderation in *Ars amatoria* 3'. In Gibson, Green, and Sharrock (eds) (2006), 121–42.

Gibson, Roy K., Steven J. Green, and Alison Sharrock (eds). 2006. *The Art of Love: Bimillennial Essays on Ovid's Ars amatoria and Remedia amoris*. Oxford: Oxford University Press.

Gigante, Marcello. 1995. *Philodemus in Italy: The Books from Herculaneum*. Tr. Dirk Obbink. Ann Arbor: University of Michigan Press.

Gold, Barbara K. (ed.). 1982. *Literary and Artistic Patronage in Ancient Rome*. Austin: University of Texas Press.

Goldberg, Sander. 1995. *Epic in Republican Rome*. New York: Oxford University Press.

——. 2005. 'The Early Republic: The Beginnings to 90 BC'. In Harrison (ed.) (2005), 15–30.

Goldhill, Simon. 1991. *The Poet's Voice: Essays on Poetics and Greek Literature*. Cambridge, New York: Cambridge University Press.

Goold, George P. 1983. 'The Cause of Ovid's Exile'. *Illinois Classical Studies* 8: 94–107.

——(ed. and tr.). 1990. *Elegies: Propertius*. Cambridge, MA: Harvard University Press.

Gowers, Emily. 1993a. 'Horace, *Satires* 1.5: An Inconsequential Journey'. *Proceedings of the Cambridge Philological Society* 13: 48–66.

——. 1993b. *The Loaded Table: Representations of Food in Roman Literature*. Oxford: Oxford University Press.

——. 2003. 'Fragments of Autobiography in Horace *Satires* I'. *Classical Antiquity* 22: 55–91.

——(ed.). 2012. *Horace: Satires Book I*. Cambridge: Cambridge University Press.

Gransden, K. W. 1970. 'The Pastoral Alternative'. *Arethusa* 3: 103–21.

Gratwick, A. S. 1991. 'Catullus 1.10 and the Title of his *Libellus*'. *Greece and Rome*, 2nd ser., 38: 199–202.

Green, Peter. 1982. 'Carmen et error: *Prophasis* and *aitia* in the Matter of Ovid's Exile'. *Classical Antiquity* 1.2: 202–20.

Greene, Ellen. 1998. *The Erotics of Domination: Male Desire and the Mistress in Latin Love Poetry*. Baltimore, MD: Johns Hopkins University Press.

Grewing, Farouk (ed.). 1998. *Toto notus in orbe: Perspektiven der Martial-Interpretation*. Stuttgart: Steiner.

Griffin, Jasper. 1984. 'Augustus and the Poets: Caesar qui cogere posset'. In Fergus Millar and Charles Segal (eds), *Caesar Augustus: Seven Aspects*. Oxford: Oxford University Press, 189–218.

Griffin, Miriam. 1976. *Seneca: A Philosopher in Politics*. Oxford: Clarendon Press.

Griffin, Miriam and Barnes, Jonathan (eds). 1989. *Philosophia togata*, i: *Essays on Philosophy and Roman Society*. Oxford: Oxford University Press.

Griffith, J. G. 1983. 'Catullus Poem 4: A Neglected Interpretation Revived'. *Phoenix* 37: 123–8.

Grube, Georges Maximilien Antoine. 1965. *The Greek and Roman Critics*. London: Methuen.

Gruen, Erich. 1992. *Culture and National Identity in Republican Rome*. Ithaca, NY: Cornell University Press.

——. 1996. *Studies in Greek Culture and Roman Policy*. Leiden: Brill.

——. 2005. 'Augustus and the Making of the Principate'. In Galinsky (ed.) (2005), 33–52.

Guillemin, Anne Marie. 1929. *Pline et la vie littéraire de son temps*. Paris: Les Belles Lettres.

Günther, Hans-Christian (ed.). 2006. *Brill's Companion to Propertius*. Leiden: Brill.

Gurval, Robert Alan. 1995. *Actium and Augustus: The Politics and Emotions of Civil War*. Ann Arbor: University of Michigan Press.

Habermas, Jürgen. 1997. 'Modernity: An Unfinished Project'. In Maurizio Passerin d'Entrèves and Seyla Benhabib (eds), *Habermas and the Unfinished Project of Modernity: Critical Essays on 'The Philosophical Discourse of Modernity'*. Cambridge: MIT Press, 38–58.

Habinek, Thomas. 1994. 'Ideology for an Empire in the Prefaces to Cicero's Dialogues'. *Ramus* 23: 56–67.

——. 1997. 'The Invention of Sexuality in the World-City of Rome'. In Habinek and Schiesaro (eds) (1997), 23–43.

——. 1998. *The Politics of Latin Literature: Writing, Identity, and Empire in Ancient Rome*. Princeton, NJ: Princeton University Press.

——. 2005. *The World of Roman Song: From Ritualized Speech to Social Order*. Baltimore, MD: Johns Hopkins University Press.

Habinek, Thomas and Alessandro Schiesaro (eds). 1997. *The Roman Cultural Revolution*. Cambridge: Cambridge University Press.

Hall, John Barrie (ed.). 1995. *P. Ovidi Nasonis Tristia*. Stuttgart: Teubner.

Hallett, Judith. 1988. 'Catullus on Composition. Response'. *Classical Weekly* 81: 395–401.

Halliwell, F. S. 1984. 'Plato and Aristotle on the Denial of Tragedy'. *Proceedings of the Cambridge Philological Society* 210: 49–71.

——. 1986. *Aristotle's Poetics*. London: Duckworth.

——. 2002. *The Aesthetics of Mimesis: Ancient Texts and Modern Problems*. Princeton, NJ: Princeton University Press.

Halliwell, F. S. 2003. 'Aesthetics'. In S. Hornblower and A. Spawforth (eds), *The Oxford Classical Dictionary*, 3rd edn. Oxford: Oxford University Press, 29–30.

——. 2011. *Between Ecstasy and Truth: Interpretations of Greek Poetics from Homer to Longinus*. Oxford: Oxford University Press.

Halperin, David M. 1983. *Before Pastoral: Theocritus and the Ancient Tradition of Bucolic Poetry*. New Haven, CT: Yale University Press.

Hansen, Mogens Herman. 1995. 'The "Autonomous City-State": Ancient Fact or Modern Fiction?' In M. Hansen and K. Raaflaub (eds), *Studies in the Ancient Greek Polis*. Stuttgart: Steiner, 21–44.

Hansen, Wells S. 2007. 'Caecilius' Response to the Invitation in Catullus 35'. *Classical Journal* 102.3: 213–20.

Hardie, Alex. 1983. *Statius and the Silvae: Poets, Patrons, and epideixis in the Graeco-Roman World*. Liverpool: F. Cairns.

——. 1990. 'Juvenal and the Condition of Letters: The Seventh Satire'. *Papers of the Leeds International Latin Seminar* 6: 145–209.

Hardie, Philip. 1993. *The Epic Successors of Virgil: A Study in the Dynamics of a Tradition*. Cambridge: Cambridge University Press.

Hardie, Philip and Helen Moore (eds). 2010. *Classical Literary Careers and their Reception*. Cambridge: Cambridge University Press.

Harding, James M. 1992. 'Historical Dialectics and the Autonomy of Art in Adorno's *Ästhetische Theorie*'. *Journal of Aesthetics and Art Criticism* 50.3: 183–95.

Harrison, S. J. 1988. 'Deflating the *Odes*: Horace, *Epistles* 1.20'. *Classical Quarterly*, NS 38: 473–6.

——. (ed.). 1995. *Homage to Horace: A Bimillenary Celebration*. Oxford: Clarendon Press.

——(ed.). 2005. *A Companion to Latin Literature*. Oxford: Blackwell.

Harvey, R. A. 1981. *A Commentary on Persius*. Leiden: Brill.

Haskins, Casey. 1989. 'Kant and the Autonomy of Art'. *Journal of Aesthetics and Art Criticism* 47.1: 43–54.

——. 1990. 'Kant, Autonomy, and Art for Art's Sake'. *Journal of Aesthetics and Art Criticism* 48.3: 235–7.

——. 1998. 'Autonomy: Historical Overview'. In Michael Kelley (ed.), *Encyclopedia of Aesthetics*, i, 170–5.

——. 2000. 'Paradoxes of Autonomy; or, Why won't the Problem of Artistic Justification Go Away?' *Journal of Aesthetics and Art Criticism* 58.1: 1–22.

Haß, Karin. 2007. *Lucilius und der Beginn der Persönlichkeitsdichtung in Rom*. Stuttgart: Steiner.

Heath, J. R. 1989. 'Catullus 11. Along for the Ride'. In C. Deroux (ed.), *Studies in Latin Literature and Roman History* 5, Brussels: Latomus, 98–116.

Heine, Rolf. 1975. 'Zu Catull c. 35'. In R. Heine (ed.), *Catull*. Darmstadt: Wissenschaftliche Buchgesellschaft, 62–84.

Helmbold, W. C. and E. N. O'Neil. 1959. 'The Form and Purpose of Juvenal's Seventh Satire'. *Classical Philology* 54.2: 100–8.

Henderson, A. A. R. 1987. 'Tibullus 1.2.1'. *Liverpool Classical Monthly* 12.2: 21.

Henderson, John. 1987. 'Lucan/The Word at War'. *Ramus* 16: 122–64.

——. 1991. 'Statius' *Thebaid*/Form Premade'. *Proceedings of the Cambridge Philological Society* 37: 30–79.

——. 1991–2. 'Wrapping up the Case: Reading Ovid *Amores* 2.7 (+ 8)'. Part I: *Materiali e discussioni per l'analisi dei testi classici* 27: 38–88; Part 2: *Materiali e discussioni per l'analisi dei testi classici* 28: 27–83.

——. 1993. 'Be Alert (Your Country Needs Lerts): Horace, Satires 1.9'. *Proceedings of the Cambridge Philological Society* 39: 67–93.

——. 1998a. *A Roman Life: Rutilius Gallicus on Paper & in Stone*. Exeter: University of Exeter Press.

——. 1998b. 'Virgil, Eclogue 9: Valleydiction'. *Proceedings of the Virgilian Society* 23: 149–76.

——. 1999. *Writing Down Rome: Satire, Comedy, and Other Offences in Latin Poetry*. Oxford: Oxford University Press.

——. 2001. 'On Pliny on Martial on Anon . . . (*Epistles* 3.21/*Epigrams* 10.19)'. *Ramus* 30: 56–83.

Hendrickson, G. L. 1911. 'Satura—The Genesis of a Literary Form'. *Classical Philology* 6.2: 129–43.

——. 1928. 'The First Satire of Persius'. *Classical Philology* 23.2: 97–112.

Henriksén, C. 1997. 'Earinus: An Imperial Eunuch in the Light of the Poems of Martial and Statius'. *Mnemosyne* 50.3: 281–94.

Herbert-Brown, Geraldine. 1994. *Ovid and the Fasti: A Historical Study*. Oxford: Oxford University Press.

Hess, Jonathan M. 1999. *Reconstituting the Body Politic: Enlightenment, Public Culture, and the Invention of Aesthetic Autonomy*. Detroit: Wayne State University Press.

Heyworth, Stephen. 1992. 'Propertius 2.13'. *Mnemosyne* 45.1: 45–59.

——. 1995. 'Propertius: Division, Transmission, and the Editor's Task'. In *Papers of the Leeds International Latin Seminar*, viii: *Roman Comedy, Augustan Poetry, Historiography*, ed. R. Brock and A. J. Woodman. Leeds: F. Cairns, 165–85.

——. 2007a. *Cynthia: A Companion to the Text of Propertius*. Oxford: Oxford University Press.

——. 2007b. 'Propertius, Patronage, and Politics'. *Bulletin of the Institute of Classical Studies* 50.1: 93–128.

—— (ed.). 2007c. *Sexti Properti Elegos*. Oxford: Clarendon Press.

——. 2010. 'An Elegist's Career: From Cynthia to Cornelia'. In Hardie and Moore (eds) (2010), 89–104.

Heyworth, Stephen J. and James Morwood. 2011. *A Commentary on Propertius. Book 3*. Oxford: Oxford University Press.

Highet, Gilbert. 1951. 'Juvenal's Bookcase'. *American Journal of Philology* 72.4: 369–94.

——. 1954. *Juvenal the Satirist: A Study*. Oxford: Clarendon Press.

Hinds, Stephen. 1985. 'Booking the Return Trip: Ovid and *Tristia* I'. *Proceedings of the Cambridge Philological Society* 31: 13–32.

——. 1987a. *The Metamorphosis of Persephone: Ovid and the Self-conscious Muse*. Cambridge: Cambridge University Press.

——. 1987b. 'Generalizing about Ovid'. *Ramus* 16: 4–31.

——. 1992. 'Arma in Ovid's *Fasti*. Part 1: Genre and Mannerism. Part 2: Genre, Romulean Rome and Augustan Ideology'. *Arethusa* 25: 81–153.

——. 1998. *Allusion and Intertext: Dynamics of Appropriation in Roman Poetry*. New York: Cambridge University Press.

——. 2001. 'Cinna, Statius and "Immanent Literary History" in the Cultural Economy'. In *L'Histoire littéraire immanente dans la poésie Latine*. Entretiens sur l'antiquité classique 47. Genève: Fondation Hardt, 221–65.

——. 2007. 'Martial's Ovid / Ovid's Martial'. *Journal of Roman Studies* 97: 113–54.

Hollis, Adrian (ed.). 1977. *Ovid: Ars amatoria, Book 1*. Oxford: Oxford University Press.

——. 2006. 'Propertius and Hellenistic Poetry'. In Günther (ed.) (2006), 97–125.

—— (ed.). 2007. *Fragments of Roman Poetry, c.60 BC–AD 20*. Oxford: Oxford University Press.

Hooley, Daniel M. 1997. *The Knotted Thong: Structures of Mimesis in Persius*. Ann Arbor: University of Michigan Press.

——. 2007. *Roman Satire*. Malden, MA: Blackwell.

Hooper, Richard W. 1985. 'In Defence of Catullus' Dirty Sparrow'. *Greece & Rome*, 2nd ser., 32: 162–78.

Hopkins, Keith. 1978. *Conquerors and Slaves*. Cambridge: Cambridge University Press.

——. 1983. *Death and Renewal*. Sociological Studies in Roman History 2. Cambridge: Cambridge University Press.

Hornsby, Roger A. 1963. 'The Craft of Catullus (Carm. 4)'. *American Journal of Philology* 84: 256–65.

Horsfall, Nicholas. 1976. 'The Collegium Poetarum'. *Bulletin of the Institute of Classical Studies* 23.1: 79–95.

——. 1981. 'Some Problems of Titulature in Roman Literary History'. *Bulletin of the Institute of Classical Studies* 28.1: 103–14.

——. 1993. 'Empty Shelves on the Palatine'. *Greece and Rome* 40, no. 1: 58–67.

Höschele, Regina. 2011. 'Inscribing Epigrammatists' Names: Meleager in Propertius and Philodemus in Horace'. In Keith (ed.) (2011), *Latin Elegy and Hellenistic Epigram*, 19–32.

Howell, Peter. 1980. *A Commentary on Book One of the Epigrams of Martial*. London: Athlone Press.

Hubbard, Margaret. 1974. *Propertius*. London: Duckworth.

Hubbard, Thomas K. 1983. 'The Catullan Libellus'. *Philologus* 127: 218–37.

——. 1984. 'Art and vision in Propertius 2.31/32'. *Transactions of the American Philological Association* 114: 281–97.

——. 1995. 'Allusive Artistry and Virgil's Revisionary Program: *Eclogues* 1–3'. *Materiali e discussioni per l'analisi dei testi classici* 34: 37–67.

Huskey, Samuel J. 2005. 'In Memory of Tibullus: Ovid's Remembrance of Tibullus 1.3 in *Amores* 3.9 and *Tristia* 3.3'. *Arethusa* 38.3: 367–86.

Hutchinson, G. O. 1984. 'Propertius and the Unity of the Book'. *Journal of Roman Studies* 74: 99–106.

—— (ed.). 2006. *Propertius: Elegies Book IV*. Cambridge: Cambridge University Press.

Ingersoll, J. W. D. 1912. 'Roman Satire: Its Early Name?' *Classical Philology* 7.1: 59–65.

Ingleheart, Jennifer (ed.). 2010. *A Commentary on Ovid, Tristia, Book 2*. Oxford: Oxford University Press.

Janan, Micaela. 1994. *'When the Lamp is Shattered': Desire and Narrative in Catullus*. Carbondale: Southern Illinois University Press.

——. 2001. *The Politics of Desire: Propertius IV*. Berkeley: University of California Press.

Janko, Richard (ed.). 2000. *Philodemus: On Poems Book 1*. New York: Oxford University Press.

—— (ed. and tr.). 2010. *Philodemus, On Poems Books 3–4; with the fragments of Aristotle On Poets*. Oxford: Oxford University Press.

Jocelyn, H. D. 1999. 'The Arrangement and the Language of Catullus' so-called *polymetra* with Special Reference to the Sequence 10–11–12'. *Proceedings of the British Academy* 93: 335–75.

Johannsen, Nina. 2006. *Dichter über ihre Gedichte: Die Prosavorreden in den Epigrammaton libri Martials und in den Silvae des Statius*. Hypomnemata, 166. Göttingen: Vandenhoeck & Ruprecht.

Johnson, Timothy S. 2004. *A Symposion of Praise: Horace Returns to Lyric in Odes IV*. Madison: University of Wisconsin Press.

Johnson, W. R. 1973. 'The Emotions of Patriotism: Propertius 4.6'. *California Studies in Classical Antiquity* 6: 151–80.

——. 1983. *The Idea of Lyric: Lyric Modes in Ancient and Modern Poetry*. Berkeley: University of California Press.

——. 1990. 'Messalla's Birthday: The Politics of Pastoral'. *Arethusa* 23.1: 95–113.

——. 1993. *Horace and the Dialectic of Freedom: Readings in Epistles 1*. Ithaca, NY: Cornell University Press.

Jones, Frederick. 2007. *Juvenal and the Satiric Genre*. London: Duckworth.

Jusdanis, Gregory. 2005. 'Two Cheers for Aesthetic Autonomy'. *Cultural Critique* 61: 22–54.

Kant, Immanuel. 1951. *Critique of Judgment*. Tr. J. H. Bernard. New York: Hafner.

Keith, Alison M. 1994. '*Corpus Eroticum*: Elegiac Poetics and Elegiac *Puellae* in Ovid's *Amores*'. *Classical World* 88.1: 27–40.

——. 2008. *Propertius: Poet of Love and Leisure*. London: Duckworth.

——. 2011a. 'Latin Elegiac Collections and Hellenistic Epigram Books'. In Keith (ed.) (2011b), 99–116.

——(ed.). 2011b. *Latin Elegy and Hellenistic Epigram*. Newcastle upon Tyne: Cambridge Scholars Publishing.

Kennedy, Duncan. 1992. '"Augustan" and "Anti-Augustan": Reflections on Terms of Reference'. In Anton Powell (ed.) (1992), 26–58.

——. 1993. *The Arts of Love: Five Studies in the Discourse of Roman Love Elegy*. Cambridge: Cambridge University Press.

Kenney, E. J. (ed.). 1994. *P. Ovidi Nasonis Amores; Medicamina faciei femineae; Ars amatoria; Remedia amoris*. Oxford: Clarendon Press.

Kidd, D. A. 1964. 'Imitation in the Tenth Eclogue'. *Bulletin of the Institute of Classical Studies* 11.1: 54–64.

Kilpatrick, Ross S. 1986. *The Poetry of Friendship: Horace Epistles I*. Edmonton: University of Alberta Press.

King, Joy K. 1975. 'Propertius' Programmatic Poetry and the Unity of the *Monobiblos*'. *Classical Journal* 71: 108–24.

Klingner, Friedrich. 1950. *Horazens Brief an Augustus*. München: Verlag der Bayerischen Akademie der Wissenschaften.

Knoche, Ulrich. 1975. *Roman Satire*. Bloomington: Indiana University Press.

Knox, Peter E. 2011. 'Cicero as a Hellenistic Poet'. *Classical Quarterly*, NS 61: 192–204.

Konstan, David. 1977. *Catullus' Indictment of Rome: The Meaning of Catullus 64*. Amsterdam: Hakkert.

——. 1978. 'The Politics of Tibullus 1.7'. *Rivista di Studi Classici* 26: 173–85.

——. 1995. 'Patrons and Friends'. *Classical Philology* 90: 328–42.

——. 2005. 'Friendship and Patronage'. In Harrison (ed.) (2005), 345–59.

——. 2007. 'The Contemporary Political Context'. In Skinner (ed.) (2007), 72–91.

Krenkel, Werner (ed.). 1970. *Lucilius, Satiren*. Leiden: Brill.

Kristeller, Paul Oskar. 1951. 'The Modern System of the Arts'. *Journal of the History of Ideas* 12: 496–527.

Krostenko, Brian. 2001. *Cicero, Catullus and the Language of Social Performance*. Chicago and London: University of Chicago Press.

Kuttner, Ann L. 1999. 'Culture and History at Pompey's Museum'. *Transactions of the American Philological Association* 129: 343–73.

Kutzko, David. 2006. 'Lesbia in Catullus 35'. *Classical Philology* 101.4: 405–410.

La Penna, Antonio. 1963. *Orazio e l'ideologia del principato*. Torino: G. Einaudi.

——. 1977. *L'integrazione difficile: un profilo di Properzio*. Torino: G. Einaudi.

——. 1990. 'L'intellettuale emarginato nell' antichità'. *Maia* 42: 3–20.

——. 1992. 'L'oggetto come moltiplicatore delle immagini'. *Maia* 44: 7–44.

Labate, Mario. 1984. *L'arte di farsi amare: modelli culturali e progetto didascalico nell'elegia ovidiana*. Pisa: Giardini.

——. 1990. 'Forme della letteratura, immagini del mondo: da Catullo a Ovidio'. In Arnaldo Momigliano and Aldo Schiavone (eds), *Storia di Roma*, ii: *L'impero mediterraneo*. 1: *la repubblica imperiale*. Torino: Einaudi, 923–65.

——. 1995. 'Eumolpo e gli altri, ovvero lo spazio della poesia'. *Materiali e discussioni per l'analisi dei testi classici* 34: 153–75.

Labate, Mario and Emanuele Narducci. 1981. 'Mobilità dei modelli etici e relativismo dei valori: il "personaggio" di Attico'. In A. Giardina and A. Schiavone (eds), *Società romana e produzione schiavistica*, iii: *Modelli etici, diritto e trasformazioni sociali*. Rome: Laterza.

Laidlaw, W. A. 1968. '*Otium*'. *Greece & Rome* 15: 43–52.

Larmour, David H. J. 2007. 'Holes in the Body: Sites of Abjection in Juvenal's Rome'. In David H. J. Larmour and Diana Spencer (eds), *The Sites of Rome: Time, Space, Memory*. Oxford: Oxford University Press, 168–210.

Lateiner, Donald. 1978. 'Ovid's Homage to Callimachus and Alexandrian Poetic Theory (*Am.* 2, 19)'. *Hermes* 106.1: 188–96.

Laughton, E. 1970. 'Dissertissime Romuli Nepotum'. *Classical Philology* 65: 1–7.

Laurens, Pierre. 1989. *L'Abeille dans l'ambre : célébration de l'épigramme de l'époque alexandrine à la fin de la Renaissance*. Paris: Belles Lettres.

Leach, Eleanor Winsor. 1971. 'Horace's *Pater Optimus* and Terence's Demea: Autobiographical Fiction and Comedy in *Sermo*, I, 4'. *American Journal of Philology* 92.4: 616–32.

——. 1978. 'Vergil, Horace, Tibullus: Three Collections of Ten'. *Ramus* 7: 79–105.

——. 1980. 'Poetics and Poetic Design in Tibullus' First Elegiac Book'. *Arethusa* 13: 79–96.

Leary, T. J. (ed). 1996. *Martial Book XIV: The Apophoreta*. London: Duckworth.

——. 1998. 'Martial's Early Saturnalian Verse'. In Grewing (ed.) (1998), 37–47.

—— (ed). 2001. *Martial Book XIII: The Xenia*. London: Duckworth.

Lee, Guy (tr.). 1982. *Tibullus: Elegies*. Liverpool: F. Cairns.

Lee, Guy (tr.) and William Barr (intr. and comm.). 1987. *The Satires of Persius: the Latin text with a verse translation*. Liverpool: F. Cairns.

Lee-Stecum, Parshia. 1998. *Powerplay in Tibullus: Reading Elegies Book One*. Cambridge: Cambridge University Press.

Leigh, Matthew. 1997. *Lucan: Spectacle and Engagement*. Oxford: Oxford University Press.

Littlewood, C. A. J. 2007. 'Poetry and Friendship in Juvenal's Twelfth Satire'. *American Journal of Philology* 128.3: 389–418.

Littlewood, R. J. 1970. 'The Symbolic Structure of Tibullus Book 1'. *Latomus* 29: 661–9.

Lindsay, Wallace Martin (ed.). 1929. *M. Val. Martialis Epigrammata*. Oxford: Clarendon Press.

Lowrie, Michèle. 1997. *Horace's Narrative Odes*. Oxford: Oxford University Press.

——. 2002. 'Horace, Cicero and Augustus, or the Poet Statesman at *Epistles* 2.1.256'. In Woodman and Feeney (eds) (2002), 158–71.

——. 2009. *Writing, Performance, and Authority in Augustan Rome*. Oxford: Oxford University Press.

Luck, Georg. 1969. *The Latin Love Elegy*. London: Methuen.

Lyne, R. O. A. M. 1979. '*Servitium Amoris*'. *Classical Quarterly*, ns 29.1: 117–30.

——. 1995. *Horace: Behind the Public Poetry*. New Haven, CT: Yale University Press.

——. 1998a. 'Introductory Poems in Propertius: 1.1 and 2.12'. In R. O. A. M. Lyne, *Collected Papers on Latin Poetry* (2007). Oxford: Oxford University Press, 184–210.

——. 1998b. 'Propertius and Tibullus: Early Exchanges'. *Classical Quarterly*, ns 48: 519–44.

Macleod, Colin. 1973. 'Parody and Personalities in Catullus (Catullus 50, 55, 58b, 24, 15, 21, 23, 16, 11, 89)'. *Classical Quarterly*, ns 23: 294–303.

——. 1977. 'The Poet, the Critic, and the Moralist: Horace *Epistles* 1.19'. *Classical Quarterly*, ns 27: 359–76.

——. 1979. 'Ethics and Poetry in Horace's *Odes*'. *Greece and Rome*, 2nd ser., 26.1: 21–31.

Malnati, T. P. 1987. 'Juvenal and Martial on Social Mobility'. *Classical Journal* 83.2: 133–41.

Maltby, Robert (ed.). 2002. *Tibullus: Elegies: text, introduction and commentary*. Cambridge: Francis Cairns.

Mankin, David. 1988. 'The Addressee of Virgil's Eighth Eclogue: A Reconsideration'. *Hermes* 116.1: 63–76.

Manuwald, Gesine. 2006. 'The First Book'. In Günther (ed.) (2006), 219–43.

Marache, René. 1961. 'La Révendication sociale chez Martial et Juvénal'. *Rivista di Cultura Classica e Medioevale* 3: 30–67.

Martin, Stewart. 2000. 'Autonomy and Anti-Art: Adorno's Concept of Avant-Garde Art'. *Constellations* 7.2: 197–207.

Martindale, Charles (ed.). 1997. *The Cambridge Companion to Virgil*. Cambridge: Cambridge University Press.

——. 2005. *Latin Poetry and the Judgement of Taste: An Essay in Aesthetics*. Oxford: Oxford University Press.

Marx, Friedrich (ed.). 1904. *C. Lucilii Carminum Reliquiae*. Leipzig: Teubner.

Masters, Jamie. 1992. *Poetry and Civil War in Lucan's Bellum Civile*. Cambridge: Cambridge University Press.

Mayer, Roland. 1994 (ed.). *Horace Epistles Book 1*. Cambridge: Cambridge University Press.

——(ed.). 2001. *Tacitus: Dialogus de oratoribus*. Cambridge: Cambridge University Press.

McCarthy, Kathleen. 1998. '*Servitium amoris: Amor servitii*'. In S. Murnaghan and S. Joshel (eds), *Women and Slaves in Greco-Roman Culture: Differential Equations*, London: Routledge, 174–92.

——2010. 'First-Person Poetry'. In Alessandro Barchiesi and Walter Scheidel (eds), *The Oxford Handbook of Roman Studies*. Oxford: Oxford University Press, 435–49.

McKeown, J. C. 1984. '*Fabula proposito nulla tegenda meo*: Ovid's *Fasti* and Augustan Politics'. In Woodman and West (eds) (1984), 169–88.

——(ed.). 1989. *Ovid: Amores: Text, Prolegomena, and Commentary*, i–iv. Leeds: F. Cairns.

McNelis, Charles. 2007. *Statius' Thebaid and the Poetics of Civil War*. Cambridge: Cambridge University Press.

Millar, Fergus. 1988. 'Cornelius Nepos, "Atticus" and the Roman Revolution'. *Greece & Rome*, 2nd ser., 35.1: 40–55.

Miller, John F. 1981. 'Propertius 2.1 and the New Gallus Papyrus'. *Zeitschrift für Papyrologie und Epigraphik* 44: 173–6.

——. 2009. *Apollo, Augustus, and the Poets*. Cambridge: Cambridge University Press.

Miller, Paul Allen. 1988. 'The Bodily Grotesque in Roman Satire: Images of Sterility'. *Arethusa* 31.3: 257–83.

——. 1994. *Lyric Texts and Lyric Consciousness: The Birth of a Genre from Archaic Greece to Augustan Rome*. London: Routledge.

——. 2004. *Subjecting Verses: Latin Love Elegy and the Emergence of the Real*. Princeton, NJ: Princeton University Press.

Mills, Donald H. 1974. 'Tibullus and Phaiacia: A Reinterpretation of 1.3'. *Classical Journal* 69.3: 226–33.

Moatti, Claudia. 1997. *La Raison de Rome: naissance de l'esprit critique à la fin de la République*. Paris: Éditions de Seuil.

Moles, John. 1991. 'The Dramatic Coherence of Ovid, *Amores* 1.1 and 1.2'. *Classical Quarterly*, NS 41.2: 551–4.

——. 2002. 'Poetry, Philosophy, Politics and Play: *Epistles* I'. In Woodman and Feeney (eds) (2002), 141–57.

Momigliano, Arnaldo. 1950. '*Panegyricus Messallae* and "Panegyricus Vespasiani": Two References to Britain'. *Journal of Roman Studies* 40: 39–42.

Moore, Charles W. 1960. 'Hadrian's Villa'. *Perspecta* 6: 16–27.

Moore, Timothy J. 1989. 'Tibullus 1.7: Reconciliation through Conflict'. *Classical World* 82.6: 423–30.

Morgan, Llewelyn. 2000. 'Metre Matters: Some Higher-Level Metrical Play in Latin Poetry'. *Proceedings of the Cambridge Philological Society* 46: 99–120.

Morgan, Llewelyn 2005. 'Satire'. In Harrison (ed.) (2005), 174–88.

Most, Glenn W. 1981. 'On the Arrangement of Catullus' *Carmina maiora*'. *Philologus* 125: 109–25

Mulroy, David. 1977–8. 'An Interpretation of Catullus 11'. *Classical World* 71: 237–47.

Murgatroyd, Paul (ed.). 1980. *Tibullus: A Commentary on the First Book of Elegies of Albius Tibullus*. Pietermaritzburg: University of Natal Press.

Myers, K. Sara. 1996. 'The Poet and the Procuress: The *lena* in Latin Love Elegy'. *Journal of Roman Studies* 86: 1–21.

——. 2000. '*Miranda fides*: Poet and Patrons in Paradoxographical Landscapes in Statius' *Silvae*'. *Materiali e discussioni per l'analisi dei testi classici* 44: 103–38.

Mynors, R. A. B. (ed.). 1958. *C. Valerii Catulli Carmina*. Oxford: Clarendon Press.

—— (ed.). 1969. *P. Vergili Maronis Opera*. Oxford: Clarendon Press.

Nagy, Gregory. 1979. *The Best of the Achaeans: Concepts of the Hero in Archaic Greek Poetry*. Baltimore, MD: Johns Hopkins University Press.

——. 1990. *Greek Mythology and Poetics*. Ithaca, NY: Cornell University Press.

——. 1996. *Poetry as Performance: Homer and Beyond*. Cambridge: Cambridge University Press.

Nappa, Christopher. 2001. *Aspects of Catullus' Social Fiction*. Frankfurt am Main: P. Lang.

Narducci, Emanuele. 1989. 'Le risonanze del potere'. In G. Cavallo, P. Fedeli, and A. Giardina (eds), *Lo spazio letterario di Roman antica*, ii: *La circolazione del testo*, 533–77.

——. 1997. *Cicerone e l'eloquenza romana: retorica e progetto culturale*. Roma: Laterza.

Nauta, Ruurd R. 2008. 'Statius in the *Silvae*'. In Johannes Jacobus Louis Smolenaars, Harm-Jan van Dam, and Ruurd R. Nauta (eds), *The Poetry of Statius*. Leiden: Brill, 143–74.

Németh Béla. 1974–5. 'Catullan Twin-Poems (c. 50–c. 14)'. *Acta classica Universitatis Scientiarum Debreceniensis* 10–11: 45–53.

Nethercut, William R. 1970. 'The Ironic Priest'. *American Journal of Philology* 91.4: 385–407.

Newlands, Carole. 1995. *Playing with Time: Ovid and the Fasti*. Ithaca, NY: Cornell University Press.

——. 2002. *Statius' Silvae and the Poetics of Empire*. Cambridge: Cambridge University Press.

Newman, J. K. 1967. *The Concept of vates in Augustan Poetry*. Brussels: Latomus.

Newmeyer, Stephen Thomas. 1979. *The Silvae of Statius: Structure and Theme*. Leiden: Brill.

Nicholson, Nigel. 1998–99. 'Bodies without Names, Names without Bodies'. *Classical Journal* 94: 143–61.

Nikitinski, Oleg (ed.). 2002. *A. Persius Flaccus Saturae: accedunt varia de Persio iudicia saec. XIV–XX*. München: Saur.

Nisbet, R. G. M. 1984. 'Horace's *Epodes* and History'. In Woodman and West (eds) (1984), 1–18.

Nisbet, R. G. M. and Margaret Hubbard. 1970. *A Commentary on Horace: Odes, Book I*. Oxford: Oxford University Press.

——. 1978. *A Commentary on Horace: Odes, Book II*. Oxford: Oxford University Press.

Nisbet, R. G. M. and Niall Rudd. 2004. *A Commentary on Horace: Odes, Book III*. Oxford: Oxford University Press.

Noonan, J. D. 1986. 'Myth, Humor and the Sequence of Thought in Catullus 95'. *Classical Journal* 81: 299–304.

Norwood, Frances. 1963. 'The Riddle of Ovid's *Relegatio*'. *Classical Philology* 58.3: 150–63.

Obbink, Dirk (ed.). 1995. *Philodemus and Poetry: Poetic Theory and Practice in Lucretius, Philodemus, and Horace*. Oxford: Oxford University Press.

Oliensis, Ellen. 1995. 'Life after Publication: Horace, *Epistles* 1.20'. *Arethusa* 28: 209–24.

——. 1997a. 'The Erotics of *amicitia*: Readings in Tibullus, Propertius, and Horace'. In J. P. Hallett and M. P. Skinner (eds), *Roman Sexualities*. Princeton, NJ: Princeton University Press, 151–71.

——. 1997b. '*Ut arte emendaturus fortunam*: Horace, Nasidienus, and the Art of Satire'. In Habinek and Schiesaro (eds), 90–104.

——. 1998. *Horace and the Rhetoric of Authority*. Cambridge: Cambridge University Press.

Olstein, Katherine. 1975. '*Amores* 1.3 and Duplicity as a Way of Love'. *Transactions of the American Philological Association* 105: 241–57.

Oost, Irwin. 1976. Review of A. U. Stylow, *Libertas und Liberalitas: Untersuchungen zur innenpolitischen Propaganda der Römer* (1972). *Classical Philology* 71.2: 196.

Osborne, Peter. 1989. 'Aesthetic Autonomy and the Crisis of Theory: Greenberg, Adorno and the Problem of Postmodernism in the Visual Arts'. *New Formations* 9: 31–50.

Østerud, Svein. 1978. 'Sacrifice and Bookburning in Catullus' Poem 36'. *Hermes* 106: 138–55.

Otis, Brooks. 1938. 'Ovid and the Augustans'. *Transactions and Proceedings of the American Philological Association* 69: 188–229.

——. 1965. 'Propertius' Single Book'. *Harvard Studies in Classical Philology* 70: 1–44.

Owen, S. G. (ed.). 1915. *P. Ovidi Nasonis: Tristium libri quinque; Ibis; Ex ponto libri quattuor; Halieutica; Fragmenta*. Oxford: Clarendon Press.

Papanghelis, Theodore. 1987. *Propertius: A Hellenistic Poet on Love and Death*. Cambridge: Cambridge University Press.

Patterson, Annabel. 1987. *Pastoral and Ideology: Virgil to Valéry*. Berkeley: University of California Press.

Paukstadt, Rudolf. 1876. *De Martiale Catulli imitatore*. Diss. Halle.

Pedrick, Victoria. 1986. 'Qui potis est, inquis ? Audience Roles in Catullus'. *Arethusa* 19: 187–209.

Perelli, Raffaele. 1996. *Il tema della scelta di vita nelle elegie di Tibullo*. Soveria Mannelli: Rubbettino.

Perkell, Christine. 1996. 'The "Dying Gallus" and the Design of Eclogue 10'. *Classical Philology* 91.2: 128–40.

——. 2001. 'Vergil Reading his Twentieth Century Readings: A Study of Eclogue 9'. *Vergilius* 47: 64–88.

Petersmann, Gerhard. 1980. *Themenführung und Motiventfaltung in der Monobiblos des Properz*. Horn, Austria: Berger & Söhne.

Petrain, David. 2001. 'Hylas and *Silva*: Etymological Wordplay in Propertius 1.20'. *Harvard Studies in Classical Philology* 100: 409–21.

Pichon, René. 1902. *De sermone amatorio apud latinos elegiarum scriptores*. Paris: Hachette.

Pincus, Matthew. 2004. 'Propertius's Gallus and the Erotics of Influence'. *Arethusa* 37.2: 165–96.

Platter, Charles. 1995. '*Officium* in Catullus and Propertius: A Foucauldian Reading'. *Classical Philology* 90: 211–44.

Porter, James. 2010. *The Origins of Aesthetic Thought in Ancient Greece: Matter, Sensation, and Experience*. Cambridge: Cambridge University Press.

Postgate, J. P. (ed.). 1905. *Tibulli aliorumque carminum libri tres*. Oxford: Clarendon Press.

Powell, Anton (ed.). 1992. *Roman Poetry and Propaganda in the Age of Augustus*. London: Bristol Classical Press.

Powell, Barry B. 1974. 'The Ordering of Tibullus Book 1'. *Classical Philology* 69.2: 107–12.

Preston, Keith. 1920. 'Martial and Formal Literary Criticism'. *CP* 15: 340–51.

Pucci, Pietro. 1961. 'Il carme 50 di Catullo'. *Maia* 13: 249–56.

Putnam, Michael. 1962. 'Catullus' Journey'. *Classical Philology* 57: 10–19.

Putnam, Michael. 1970. *Virgil's Pastoral Art: Studies in the Eclogues*. Princeton, NJ: Princeton University Press.

——. 1973. *Tibullus: A Commentary*. Norman: University of Oklahoma Press.

——. 1974. 'Catullus 11. The Ironies of Integrity'. *Ramus* 3: 70–86.

——. 1980. 'Propertius' Third Book: Patterns of Cohesion'. *Arethusa* 13: 97–113.

——. 1986. *Artifices of Eternity: Horace's Fourth Book of Odes*. Ithaca, NY: Cornell University Press.

——. 1990. 'Anger, Blindness and Insight in Virgil's *Aeneid*'. *Apeiron* 23.4: 7–40.

——. 2006. *Poetic Interplay: Catullus and Horace*. Princeton, NJ: Princeton University Press.

Quinn, Kenneth (ed.). 1972. *Approaches to Catullus*. Cambridge: Heffer.

——. 1973. *Catullus: An Interpretation*. New York: Barnes and Noble.

Quint, David. 1993. *Epic and Empire: Politics and Generic Form from Virgil to Milton*. Princeton, NJ: Princeton University Press.

Raaflaub, Kurt and L. J. Samons. 1990. 'Opposition to Augustus'. In Kurt Raaflaub and Mark Toher (eds), *Between Republic and Empire: Interpretations of Augustus and his Principate*. Berkeley: University of California Press, 417–54.

Race, William H. 1978. '*Odes* 1.20: An Horatian *recusatio*'. *California Studies in Classical Antiquity* 11: 179–96.

——. 2010. 'Horace's Debt to Pindar'. In G. Davis (ed.) (2010), 147–74.

Ramsby, Teresa R. 2007. *Textual Permanence: Roman Elegists and the Epigraphic Tradition*. London: Duckworth.

Raschke, Wendy J. 1987. '*Arma pro amico*: Lucilian Satire at the Crisis of the Roman Republic'. *Hermes* 115.3: 299–318.

Rawson, Elisabeth. 1985. *Intellectual Life in the Late Roman Republic*. Baltimore, MD: Johns Hopkins University Press.

Rea, Jennifer A. 2007. *Legendary Rome: Myth, Monuments, and Memory on the Palatine and Capitoline*. London: Duckworth.

Reckford, Kenneth J. 1962. 'Studies in Persius'. *Hermes* 90.4: 476–504.

——. 2009. *Recognizing Persius*. Princeton, NJ: Princeton University Press.

Reed, Brian W. 2006. *Pastoral Inscriptions: Reading and Writing Virgil's Eclogues*. London: Duckworth.

Richardson, Lawrence (ed.). 1977. *Propertius Elegies I–IV*. Norman: University of Oklahoma Press.

Richlin, Amy. 1992. *The Garden of Priapus: Sexuality and Aggression in Roman Humor*, rev. edn. Oxford: Oxford University Press.

Riggsby, Andrew. 1998. 'Self and Community in the Younger Pliny'. *Arethusa* 31: 75–97.

Rimell, Victoria. 2008. *Martial's Rome: Empire and the Ideology of Epigram*. Cambridge: Cambridge University Press.

Roberts, John. 2000. 'After Adorno: Art, Autonomy, and Critique'. *Historical Materialism* 7.1: 221–39.

Roller, Matthew. 1998. 'Pliny's Catullus: The Politics of Literary Appropriation'. *Transactions of the American Philological Association* 128: 265–304.

——. 2001. *Constructing Autocracy: Aristocrats and Emperors in Julio-Claudian Rome*. Princeton, NJ: Princeton University Press.

Rosen, Ralph M. and Joseph Farrell. 1986. 'Acontius, Milanion, and Gallus: Virgil, *Ecl.* 10.52–61'. *Transactions of the American Philological Association* 116: 241–54.

Rosenmeyer, Thomas G. 1969. *The Green Cabinet: Theocritus and the European Pastoral Lyric*. Berkeley: University of California Press.

Ross, D. O. 1969. *Style and Tradition in Catullus*. Cambridge, MA: Harvard University Press.

——. 1975. *Backgrounds to Augustan Poetry: Gallus, Elegy, and Rome*. Cambridge: Cambridge University Press.

——. 1986. 'Tibullus and the Country'. In *Atti del convegno Internazionale di studi su Albio Tibullo* (Rome-Palestrina 10–13 May 1984). Rome: Centro di studi ciceroniani, 251–65.

Rudd, Niall. 1966. *The Satires of Horace: A Study*. Cambridge: Cambridge University Press.

——. 1970. 'Persiana'. *Classical Review* 20.3: 282–8.

——. 1976. *Lines of Enquiry: Studies in Latin Poetry*. Cambridge: Cambridge University Press.

—— (tr.). 1979. *Horace: Satires and Epistles*. New York and London: Penguin.

—— (ed.). 1989. *Horace: Epistles Book II and Epistle to the Pisones*. Cambridge: Cambridge University Press.

—— (ed. and tr.). 2004. *Horace: Odes and Epodes*. Cambridge, MA: Harvard University Press.

Ruffle, I. A. 2003. 'Beyond Satire: Horace, Popular Invective, and the Segregation of Literature'. *Journal of Roman Studies* 93: 35–65.

Saggese, Paolo. 1994. 'Lo scurra in Marziale'. *Maia* 46: 53–9.

Sailor, Dylan. 2008. *Writing and Empire in Tacitus*. Cambridge: Cambridge University Press.

Salemme, Carmelo. 1976. *Marziale e la 'poetica' degli oggetti: Struttura dell'epigramma di Marziale*. Naples: Studi e testi dell'antichità 6.

Saller, Richard. 1982. *Personal Patronage under the Early Empire*. Cambridge: Cambridge University Press.

——. 1983. 'Martial on Patronage and Literature'. *Classical Quarterly* 33: 246–57.

Scarry, Elaine. 2006. *On Beauty and Being Just*. Princeton, NJ: Princeton University Press.

Schlegel, Catherine. 2000. 'Horace and his Fathers: Satires 1.4 and 1.6'. *American Journal of Philology* 121.1: 93–119.

——. 2005. *Satire and the Threat of Speech: Horace's Satires, Book 1*. Madison: University of Wisconsin Press.

Schmidt, Ernst. 1997. *Sabinum: Horaz und sein Landgut im Licenzatal*. Heidelberg: C. Winter.

Schwabe, Ludwig. 1862. *Quaestionum Catullianarum Liber 1*. Giessen: I. Ricker.

Scodel, Ruth. 1987. 'Horace, Lucilius, and Callimachean Polemic'. *Harvard Studies in Classical Philology* 91: 199–215.

Scott, R. T. 1983. 'On Catullus 11'. *Classical Philology* 78.1: 39–42.

Scott, William C. 1971. 'Catullus and Caesar (C.29)'. *Classical Philology* 66.1: 17–25.

Sear, Frank. 1992. *Roman Architecture*. Ithaca, NY: Cornell University Press.

Segal Charles. 1970. 'Catulllan *otiosi*: The Lover and the Poet'. *Greece and Rome* 17: 25–31.

Selden, Daniel. 1992. '*Ceveat lector*: Catullus and the Rhetoric of Performance'. In D. Selden and R. Hexter (eds), *Innovations of Antiquity*. New York: Routledge, 461–512.

Shackleton Bailey, D. R. 1956. *Propertiana*. Cambridge: Cambridge University Press.

—— (tr.). 1999. *Cicero: Letters to Atticus*. 4 vols. Cambridge, MA: Harvard University Press.

—— (tr.). 2003. *Statius: Silvae*. Cambridge, MA: Harvard University Press.

Sharrock, Alison. 1994. *Seduction and Repetition in Ovid's Ars amatoria 2*. Oxford: Oxford University Press.

——. 2000. 'Constructing Characters in Propertius'. *Arethusa* 33: 263–84.

Sider, David. 1997. *The Epigrams of Philodemus: introduction, text, and commentary*. Oxford: Oxford University Press.

Skinner, Marilyn. 1981. *Catullus' passer: The Arrangement of the Book of Polymetric Poems*. New York: Arno.

——. 1989. '*Ut decuit cinaediorem*: Power, Gender and Urbanity in Catullus 10'. *Helios* 16: 7–23.

——. 1993. '*Ego mulier*: The Construction of Male Sexuality in Catullus'. *Helios* 20: 107–30.

——. 2001. 'Among Those Present'. *Helios* 28: 57–73.

Skinner, Marilyn 2003. *Catullus in Verona: A Reading of the Elegiac libellus, Poems 65–116.* Columbus: Ohio University Press.

—— (ed.) 2007. *A Companion to Catullus.* Malden, MA: Blackwell.

Sklenar, Robert J. 1998. '*La République des signes*: Caesar, Cato, and the Language of Sallustian Morality'. *Transactions of the American Philological Association* 128: 205–20.

Skutsch, Otto. 1963. 'The Structure of the Propertian *Monobiblos*'. *Classical Philology* 58: 238–9.

—— (ed.). 1985. *The Annals of Q. Ennius.* Oxford: Clarendon Press.

Solmsen, Friedrich. 1948. 'Propertius and Horace'. *Classical Philology* 43: 105–9.

——. 1962. 'Tibullus as an Augustan Poet'. *Hermes* 90.3: 295–325.

——. 1970. 'On Propertius 1.7'. *American Journal of Philology* 91: 77–84.

Solodow, Joseph. 1989. 'Forms of Literary Criticism in Catullus: Polymetric vs. Epigram'. *Classical Philology* 84: 312–19.

Spaeth, John W. 1931. 'Cicero the Poet'. *Classical Journal* 26.7: 500–12.

Spisak. Art L. 1998. 'Gift-Giving in Martial'. In Grewing (ed.) (1998), 243–55.

Stabryla, Stanislaw. 1994. 'In Defence of the Autonomy of the Poetic World (Some Remarks on Ovid's *Tristia* II)'. *Hermes* 122.4: 469–78.

Stahl, Hans-Peter. 1985. *Propertius: 'Love' and 'War': Individual and State under Augustus.* Berkeley: University of California Press.

Stapleton, Michael L. 1996. *Harmful Eloquence: Ovid's Amores from Antiquity to Shakespeare.* Ann Arbor: University of Michigan Press.

Stroh, Wilfried. 1971. *Die römische Liebeselegie als werbende Dichtung.* Amsterdam: Hakkert.

Stroup, Sarah C. 2006. 'Invaluable Collections: The Illusion of Poetic Presence in Martial's *Xenia* and *Apophoreta*'. In R. R. Nauta, H.-J. Van Dam and J. J. L. Smolenaars (eds), *Flavian Poetry.* Leiden: Brill, 299–313.

——. 2010. *Catullus, Cicero, and a Society of Patrons: The Generation of the Text.* Cambridge: Cambridge University Press.

Stroux, J. 1931. 'Vier Zeugnisse der römischen Literaturgeschichte der Kaiserzeit'. *Philologus* 86: 338–68.

Stylow, Armin U. 1972. *Libertas und Liberalitas: Untersuchungen zur innenpolitischen Propaganda der Römer.* Diss., Munich.

Sullivan, J. P. 1961. 'Two Problems in Roman Love Elegy'. *Transactions and Proceedings of the American Philological Association* 92: 522–36.

—— (tr.). 1965. *The Satyricon and the Fragments.* Harmondsworth: Penguin.

——. 1976. *Propertius: A Critical Introduction.* Cambridge: Cambridge University Press.

——. 1991. *Martial: The Unexpected Classic. A Literary and Historical Study.* Cambridge: Cambridge University Press.

Svavarsson, Svavar Hrafn. 1999. 'On Catullus 49'. *Classical Journal* 95.2: 131–8.

Svennung, Josef. 1945. *Catulls Bildersprache: vergleichende Stilstudien.* Uppsala: Lundequistska.

Sweet, D. R. 1987. 'Catullus: A Study in Perspective'. *Latomus* 46: 510–26.

Syme, Ronald. 1939. *The Roman Revolution.* Oxford: Oxford University Press.

——. 1978. *History in Ovid.* Oxford: Oxford University Press.

Syndikus, Hans Peter. 1986. 'Catull und die Politik'. *Gymnasium* 93: 34–47.

Tanner, Jeremy. 2006. *The Invention of Art History in Ancient Greece: Religion, Society and Artistic Rationalisation.* Cambridge: Cambridge University Press.

Tarrant, Richard. 1978. 'The Addressee of Virgil's Eighth Eclogue'. *Harvard Studies in Classical Philology* 82: 197–9.

——. 1997. 'Poetry and Power: Virgil's Poetry in Contemporary Context'. In Martindale (ed.) (1997), 169–87.

——. 2006. 'Propertian Textual Criticism and Editing'. In Günther (ed.) (2006), 45–65.

Tatum, W. Jeffrey. 1988. 'Catullus' Criticism of Cicero in Poem 49'. *Transactions of the American Philological Association* 118: 179–84.

——. 1997. 'Friendship, Politics, and Literature in Catullus: Poems 1, 65 and 66, 116'. *Classical Quarterly*, NS 47.2: 482–500.

——. 2007. 'Social Commentary and Political Invective'. In Skinner (ed.) (2007), 333–54.

Theodorakopoulos, Elena. 1997. 'Closure: the Book of Virgil'. In Martindale (ed.) (1997), 155–66.

Thibault, J. C. 1964. *The Mystery of Ovid's Exile*. Berkeley: University of California Press.

Thibodeau, Philip. 2011. *Playing the Farmer: Representations of Rural Life in Vergil's Georgics*. Berkeley: University of California Press.

Thomas, Richard F. 1982. 'Catullus and the Polemics of Poetic Reference (64.1–18)'. *American Journal of Philology* 103: 144–64.

——. 1988. *Virgil, Georgics*, 2 vols. Cambridge: Cambridge University Press.

——. 2011. 'Propertius and Propertian Elegy's Epigram Riffs: Radical Poet/Radical Critics'. In Keith (ed.) (2011), *Latin Elegy and Hellenistic Epigram*, 67–86.

Thomson, D. F. S. (ed.). 1997. *Catullus, edited with a textual and interpretative commentary*. Phoenix, Supplementary volume 34. Toronto: University of Toronto Press.

Toner, J. P. 1995. *Leisure and Ancient Rome*. Cambridge: Polity Press.

Townend, G. B. 1973. 'The Literary Substrata to Juvenal's *Satires*'. *Journal of Roman Studies* 63: 148–60.

Traina, Alfonso. 1991. 'Le *Epistole* e l'arte di convivere'. *Rivista di Filologia e di Istruzione Classica* 119: 285–305.

Troxler-Keller, Irene. 1964. *Die Dichterlandschaft des Horaz*. Heidelberg: C. Winter.

Tyrrell, R. Y. 1895. *Latin Poetry*. Boston: Houghton and Mifflin.

Van Dam, Harm-Jan (ed.). 1984. *P. Papinius Statius, Silvae Book II: a commentary*. Leiden: Brill.

Van Nortwick, Thomas. 1990. '*Huc veniet Messalla meus*: Commentary on Johnson'. *Arethusa* 21: 115–23.

Van Sickle, John. 1981. 'Poetics of Opening and Closure in Meleager, Catullus, and Gallus'. *Classical World*: 75: 65–75.

Volk, Katerina. 2006. '*Ars amatoria romana*: Ovid on Love as a Cultural Construct'. In Gibson, Green, and Sharrock (eds) (2006), 235–51.

Vout, Caroline. 2007. *Power and Eroticism in Imperial Rome*. Cambridge: Cambridge University Press.

Vretska, Karl. 1955. 'Tibulls Paraclausithyron'. *Wiener Studieren* 68: 20–46.

Wagenvoort, Hendrik. 1956. 'Ludus poeticus'. In *Studies in Roman Literature, Culture and Religion*. Leiden: Brill, 30–42.

Wallace-Hadrill, Andrew. 1985. 'Propaganda and Dissent? Augustan Moral Legislation and the Love-Poets'. *Klio* 67: 180–4.

——. 1987. 'Time for Augustus: Ovid, Augustus, and the Fasti'. In Michael Whitby, Philip Hardie, and Mary Whitby (eds), *Homo viator: Classical Essays for John Bramble*. Bristol: Bristol Classical Press, 221–30.

——(ed.). 1989. *Patronage in Ancient Society*. London: Routledge.

——. 1990. 'Roman Arches and Greek Honours: The Language of Power at Rome'. *Proceedings of the Cambridge Philological Society* 36: 143–81.

——. 1997. '*Mutatio morum*: The Idea of a Cultural Revolution'. In Habinek and Schiesaro (eds) (1997), 3–22.

Walter, Uwe. 1998. 'Soziale Normen in den Epigrammen Martials'. In Grewing (ed.) (1998), 221–41.

Watson, Lindsay and Patricia Watson. 2003. *Martial: Select Epigrams*. Cambridge: Cambridge University Press.

Watson, Patricia. 2002. '*Praecepta amoris*: Ovid's Didactic Elegy'. In Boyd (ed.) (2002), 141–65.

Welch, Tara S. 2005. *The Elegiac Cityscape: Propertius and the Meaning of Roman Monuments*. Columbus: Ohio State University Press.

West, David A. 1967. *Reading Horace*. Edinburgh: Edinburgh University Press.

—— (ed. and tr.). 1995. *Horace Odes 1: carpe diem*. Oxford: Clarendon Press.

Wheeler, Arthur Leslie. 1912. 'Satura as a Generic Term'. *Classical Philology* 7.4: 457–77.

——. 1934. *Catullus and the Traditions of Ancient Poetry*. Berkeley: University of California Press.

White, Peter. 1974. 'The Presentation and Dedication of the *Silvae* and the *Epigrams*'. *Journal of Roman Studies* 64: 40–61.

——. 1975. 'The Friends of Martial, Statius and Pliny, and the Dispersal of Patronage'. *Harvard Studies in Classical Philology* 79: 265–300.

——. 1978. '*Amicitia* and the Profession of Poetry in Early Imperial Rome'. *Journal of Roman Studies* 68: 74–92.

——. 1982. 'Positions for Poets in Early Imperial Rome'. In Gold (ed.) (1982), 50–66.

——. 1993. *Promised Verse: Poets in the Society of Augustan Rome*. Cambridge, MA: Harvard University Press.

——. 1991. 'Maecenas' Retirement'. *Classical Philology* 86.2: 130–38.

——. 1996. 'Martial and Pre-Publication Texts'. *Échos du monde classique* 40: 397–412.

——. 2002. 'Ovid and the Augustan Milieu'. In Boyd (ed.) (2002), 1–25.

Wiesen, David S. 1973. 'Juvenal and the Intellectuals'. *Hermes* 101.4: 464–83.

Wilkinson, L. P. 1955. *Ovid Recalled*. Cambridge: Cambridge University Press.

——. 1966a. 'Virgil and the Evictions'. *Hermes* 94.3: 320–4.

——. 1966b. 'The Continuity of Propertius II, 13'. *Classical Review* (New Series) 16: 141–4.

Williams, Gareth D. 1994. *Banished Voices: Readings in Ovid's Exile Poetry*. Cambridge: Cambridge University Press.

Williams, Gordon. 1980. *Figures of Thought in Roman Poetry*. New Haven, CT: Yale University Press.

——. 1990. 'Did Maecenas Fall from Favor? Augustan Literary Patronage'. In Kurt Raaflaub and Mark Toher (eds), *Between Republic and Empire: Interpretations of Augustus and his Principate*. Berkeley: University of California Press, 258–75.

——. 1995. '*Libertino Patre Natus*: True or False?'. In Harrison (ed.) (1995), 296–313.

Wilson, Harry Langford. 1898. 'The Literary Influence of Martial upon Juvenal'. *American Journal of Philology* 19.2: 193–209.

Wimmel, Walter. 1960. *Kallimachos in Rom: die Nachfolge seines apologetischen Dichtens in der Augusteerzeit*. Wiesbaden: Steiner.

Winterbottom, Michael. 1976. 'Virgil and the Confiscations'. *Greece & Rome*, 2nd ser., 23: 55–9.

Wirszubski, Chaim. 1954. 'Cicero's *Cum Dignitate Otium*: A Reconsideration'. *Journal of Roman Studies* 44: 1–13.

Wiseman, T. Peter. 1969. *Catullan Questions*. Leicester: Leicester University Press.

——. 1979. *Clio's Cosmetics: Three Studies in Greco-Roman Literature*. Leicester: Leicester University Press.

——. 1982. '*Pete nobiles amicos*: Poets and Patrons in Late Republican Rome'. In Gold (ed.) (1982), 28–49.

——. 1985. *Catullus and His World: A Reappraisal*. Cambridge: Cambridge University Press.

——. 1987. *Roman Studies: Literary and Historical*. Liverpool: F. Cairns.

Woodman, Tony. 1984. 'Horace's First Roman Ode'. In Woodman and West (eds) (1984), 83–94.

——. 2002. '*Biformis Vatis*: The *Odes*, Catullus, and Greek Lyric'. In Woodman and Feeney (eds) (2002), 53–79.

Woodman, Tony and Denis Feeney (eds). 2002. *Traditions and Contexts in the Poetry of Horace*. Cambridge: Cambridge University Press.

Woodman, Tony and Jonathan Powell (eds). 1992. *Author and Audience in Latin Literature*. Cambridge: Cambridge University Press.

Woodman, Tony and David West (eds). 1984. *Poetry and Politics in the Age of Augustus*. Cambridge: Cambridge University Press.

Woodmansee, Martha. 1984. 'The Interests in Disinterestedness: Karl Philipp Moritz and the Emergence of the Theory of Aesthetic Autonomy in Eighteenth-century Germany'. *Modern Language Quarterly* 45: 22–47.

Woolf, Greg. 2003. 'City of Letters'. In Catharine Edwards and Greg Woolf (eds), *Rome the Cosmopolis*. Cambridge: Cambridge University Press, 203–21.

Wray, David. 2001. *Catullus and the Poetics of Roman Manhood*. Cambridge: Cambridge University Press.

Wright, J. R. G. 1983. 'Virgil's Pastoral Programme: Theocritus, Callimachus, and Eclogue 1'. *Proceedings of the Cambridge Philological Society* 29: 107–60.

Wyke, Maria. 1987a. 'Written Women: Propertius' *scripta puella*'. *Journal of Roman Studies* 77: 47–61.

——. 1987b. 'The Elegiac Woman at Rome'. *Proceedings of the Cambridge Philological Society*, NS 33: 153–78.

——. 1989. 'Mistress and Metaphor in Augustan Elegy'. *Helios* 16: 25–47.

——. 2007. *The Roman Mistress: Ancient and Modern Representations*. Oxford: Oxford University Press.

Yardley, J. C. 1981. 'Carmen 11: The End of a Friendship'. *Symbolae Osloenses* 56: 63–9.

Young, Elisabeth M. 2011. 'Catullus's *Phaselus* (C.4): Mastering a New Wave of Poetic Speech'. *Arethusa* 44.1: 69–88.

Zanker, Paul. 1988. *The Power of Images in the Age of Augustus*. Ann Arbor: University of Michigan Press.

——. 1995. *The Mask of Socrates: The Image of the Intellectual in Antiquity*. Trans. A. Shapiro. Berkeley: University of California Press.

Zeiner, Noelle K. 2005. *Nothing Ordinary Here: Statius as Creator of Distinction in the Silvae*. London and New York: Routledge.

Zetzel, James. 1972. 'Cicero and the Scipionic Circle'. *Harvard Studies in Classical Philology* 76: 173–9.

——. 1980. 'Horace's *Liber Sermonum*: The Structure of Ambiguity'. *Arethusa* 13: 59–78.

——. 1982. 'The Poetics of Patronage in the Late First Century BC'. In Gold (ed.) (1982), 87–102.

——. 1983. 'Recreating the Canon: Augustan Poetry and the Alexandrian Past'. *Critical Inquiry* 10: 83–105.

——. 1984. 'Servius and Triumviral History in the *Eclogues*'. *Classical Philology* 79.2: 139–42.

——. 1992. 'Roman Romanticism and Other Fables'. In K. Galinsky (ed.), *The Interpretation of Roman Poetry: Empiricism or Hermeneutics?* Frankfurt/Main: Lang, 41–57.

——. 1996. 'Poetic Baldness and its Cure'. *Materiali e discussioni per l'analisi dei testi classici* 36: 73–100.

——. 2002. 'Dreaming about Quirinus: Horace's Satires and the Development of Augustan Poetry'. In Woodman and Feeney (eds) (2002), 38–52.

Zuidervaart, Lambert. 1990. 'The Social Significance of Autonomous Art: Adorno and Bürger'. *Journal of Aesthetics and Art Criticism* 48.1: 61–77.

Index of Passages

General Index